Here is what the critics say about Merriam-Webster:

"It is the closest we can get, in America, to the Voice of Authority."—*The New York Times*
WEBSTER'S THIRD NEW INTERNATIONAL DICTIONARY, UNABRIDGED

"It is the most up-to-the-minute dictionary in America today, one that keeps up with the headlines."—John Barkham
WEBSTER'S NINTH NEW COLLEGIATE DICTIONARY

"It is so ample and easy to use that for many it will largely supersede Roget ..."—*The Wall Street Journal*
WEBSTER'S COLLEGIATE THESAURUS

"... one of the great books on language in this generation ..."
—William Safire, *The New York Times*
WEBSTER'S DICTIONARY OF ENGLISH USAGE

"A must for every writer's library."—*The Boston Globe*
WEBSTER'S NEW DICTIONARY OF SYNONYMS

The Merriam-Webster New Book of Word Histories

A Merriam-Webster®

Merriam-Webster Inc., Publishers
Springfield, Massachusetts

A GENUINE MERRIAM-WEBSTER

The name *Webster* alone is no guarantee of excellence. It is used by a number of publishers and may serve mainly to mislead an unwary buyer.

A *Merriam-Webster*® is the registered trademark you should look for when you consider the purchases of dictionaries and other fine reference books. It carries the reputation of a company that has been doing business since 1831 and is your assurance of quality and authority.

Preface

Etymology—it's not exactly a household word. A lot of people would probably guess that it has something to do with insects. In any case, it must be one of those dusty, academic disciplines, empty of any interest for ordinary people. Prompted by a distant memory of classroom instruction years ago, some people may associate it with dictionaries: it's the part of the entry that is full of abbreviations and symbols, the part that is often stuck at the end because, really, who cares. After all, everybody knows that the dictionary is for getting quick answers to immediate questions about things like meaning and spelling.

But even if *etymology* may strike us as a discouraging word that should never be heard, the information that etymologists gather for us can often be not just interesting, but downright delightful. Turned into brief word histories, which is just what this book attempts to do, etymological information has a special kind of appeal to anyone who reads and uses words, which is, of course, anyone at all. And you don't have to be a learned scholar to enjoy word histories. Your interest can easily be piqued by realizing that one word goes back to a myth of the ancient Greeks (see **volcano** in this book and **money** and **hypnosis**), while another can be traced to twentieth-century American social reality (see **yuppie**), and still another was just made up out of nothing by an ordinary person like us (see **boondoggle**). Once that happens, it is only too easy to become addicted to the lure of etymology—to turn into a sort of "etymaholic," you might say (see **workaholic**).

One of the aims of The Merriam-Webster New Book of Word Histories is to foster the reader's interest in etymology in the hope that it will deepen into fascination. Although the articles in this book have been arranged alphabetically for ease of reference, they invite browsers to move about in the book as their fancy takes them. Abundant cross-references assist this movement. Thousands of English words have histories of great interest, but only a small sampling could find space here. Still, the more than six hundred articles which form the heart of the book, many of them discussing several related words, offer material to catch the eye of all readers, no matter what their interests may be.

English as a language is rather like the magpie of folklore. It picks up bits of whatever draws its interest, and it is interested in nearly everything everywhere. So you will find the stories not only of words from Greek and Latin and French but also of words from languages as little known to most of us as Natick (see **mugwump**) and Old Norse (see **window**). English also likes to turn the names of people and places, famous or obscure in their own right, into everyday words (see **silhouette** and **denim**). And it delights in creating new words by transforming old ones (see **umpire** and **penthouse**).

Many of the histories in this book also reflect the fact that the meanings of English words never seem to be at rest, because we who speak and write the language simply won't let them rest. We keep applying old words to new things and new situations, and we have done so as long as there has been an

English language. Sometimes a simple extension of meaning takes place (see **handicap**), but sometimes the development of meaning takes so long and involves so many steps that the original meaning drops away and the word is almost stood on its head (see **silly**). The word histories of English have something close to unlimited variety, and readers are invited to discover that variety for themselves in this book. Here you can catch glimpses of the social, cultural, and religious history of the English-speaking peoples and of the peoples we have borrowed from as well.

Beyond the biographies of interesting words, this book offers something else that etymology fans will appreciate but that people distrustful of the scholarly side of etymology may skip, if they like. Nearly every entry, whether it includes an article or merely refers to an article elsewhere in the book, is accompanied by an etymology presented in the style of Webster's Third New International Dictionary. The cross-references (which are likely to be more frustrating than revealing outside of the dictionary) have been omitted, though. The table of abbreviations used in these etymologies, which begins on page xvi, will give readers a lot of help with the compressed presentation of information in an etymology. The pronunciation symbols used in several articles are explained on page xv. Finally, an interesting introduction follows this preface and briefly discusses topics like the history of English and its relation to its language family, the sources of the words we've borrowed, and the development of new meanings. The closing paragraphs clarify some points about the formal dictionary etymologies so that the reader may know just what they say—and what they don't say.

The material in this book is taken from Webster's Word Histories. The articles were drafted by seven members of the editorial team of Merriam-Webster, working under the direction of Dr. David B. Justice, editor of etymology: Dr. Justice himself, E. Ward Gilman, James G. Lowe, Julie A. Collier, Stephen J. Perrault, Michael G. Belanger, and Kelly L. Tierney. Robert D. Copeland served as copy editor for the project. Eileeen M. Haraty was responsible for cross-reference. Proofs were read by many of the editors already named, and also by Kathleen M. Doherty, Daniel J. Hopkins, Peter D. Haraty, Paul F. Cappellano, and Karin M. Henry. The difficult job of typing the manuscript was ably accomplished by Georgette B. Boucher, Barbara A. Winkler, and Florence A. Fowler of the editorial department's clerical and typing staff, as well as by Helene Gingold, department secretary.

Frederick C. Mish
Editor

Introduction

A look at the origins of the words that make up our language involves also a look at the origins of our language itself. With the abundance of words derived from Latin and from Greek by way of Latin, the casual observer might guess that English would be, like French, Spanish, and Italian, a Romance language derivative of the Latin spoken by the ancient Romans. But although the Romans made a few visits to Britain in the first century A.D., long before the English were there—before there was even an England—English is not a Romance language. In terms of its genetic stock, English is a member of the Germanic group, and thus a sister of such extinct tongues as Old Norse and Gothic and such modern ones as Swedish, Dutch, and German.

The history of English is intimately tied to the history of the British Isles over the last 1500 years or so. We may speak of English as having its beginnings with the conquest and settlement of a large part of the island of Britain by Germanic tribes from the European continent in the fifth century, although the earliest written documents of the language belong to the seventh century. Of course these Germanic peoples did not, upon their arrival in England, suddenly begin to speak a new language. They spoke the closely related Germanic tongues of their continental homelands. From these developed the English language. In fact, the words *English* and *England* are derived from the name of one of these early Germanic peoples, the Angles. From its beginnings English has been gradually changing and evolving, as language tends to do, until the earliest written records have become all but incomprehensible to the speaker of Modern English without specialized training.

By virtue of being a member of the Germanic group, English belongs to a still larger family of languages called Indo-European. The languages of this family, which includes most of the modern European languages as well as such important languages of antiquity as Latin, Greek and Sanskrit, all resemble each other in a number of ways, particularly in vocabulary. One needs no training in the fine points of philology to see that the similarities between forms like English *father*, German *vater*, Latin *pater*, Greek *patēr*, and Sanskrit *pitṛ*, all of which have the same meaning, are not likely to be the result of accident. We account for resemblances like these by the assumption that all of these languages are descended from a common ancestor. We have no written remnants of this assumed ancestral language, which was spoken thousands of years ago, perhaps in central Europe—even the location is not certain. But we can learn something about it by comparing its descendants, and it has been given a name—Proto-Indo-European. Words in the various Indo-European languages which are ultimately derived from a common ancestral word assumed to have existed in Proto-Indo-European are called cognates. The words mentioned above with *father* are all cognates. The variations between the initial *p* of some of the words and the *f* of others is accounted for by philologists with reference to regular patterns of sound changes over long periods of time.

The oldest form of English, known as Anglo-Saxon or Old English and dating from the beginning of the language to about A.D. 1100, retained the basic grammatical properties of the Germanic branch of the Indo-European family. For example, some verbs (called "weak") formed their past tense and past participle by adding an ending with -*d* or -*t* while others (called "strong") did this by changing a vowel. Nouns belonged to one of three genders (masculine, feminine, or neuter) and appeared in one of two numbers (singular or plural) and one of five possible cases according to their function within the clause (nominative, accusative, genitive, dative, or instrumental). Adjectives not only took inflectional endings for gender, case, and number but also had different sets of endings depending on whether a word like *that* or *your* preceded them or they stood alone. To get a sense of how far evolution has taken us from the early tongue, we need only glance at a sample of Old English. Here is the beginning of the Lord's Prayer:

> Fæder ūre, þu þe eart on heofonum: si þin nama gehālgod. Tōbecume þin rīce. Geweorþe þin willa on eorþan swāswā on heofonum.

The difference between this language and today's is more radical than just a difference in spelling, since several of the letters signify sounds different from what the same letters signify today. Much of this came about during the Great Vowel Shift in the fifteenth, sixteenth, and seventeenth centuries. That is the name given to a set of changes most readily recognizable in the changing values of long vowels. From the older values that resembled those of vowels in the modern continental languages (*ā* \ä\, *ē* \ā\, *ī* \ē\, *ō* \ō\, *ū* \ü\) came our Modern English pronunciations (*a* \ā\, *e* \ē\, *i* \ī\, *oo* \ü\ or \u̇\ or \'ə\, *ou* \au̇\). Thus, for example, the Old English ancestor of *five* would have been pronounced \'fēf\, the ancestor of *clean* would have been pronounced something like \'klān-e\, and the ancestor of *root* would have been pronounced \'rōt\. In looking back at the Old English Lord's Prayer, we see the ninth word *þin* 'thine' characterized by two distinctive differences from modern *thine:* the first is the unusual letter þ, called thorn (which had a \th\ sound); the second is the long *i* which had a sound closer to the vowel sound of the modern word *mean*. The next word, *nama* 'name', was pronounced something like \'näm-ä\.

Between the vocabularies of Old English and Modern English, there is a certain continuity at the core, since something over half of the thousand most common words of the Old English poetic vocabulary have survived into Modern English more or less intact, apart from normal sound change. And of the thousand most common Modern English words, four-fifths are of Old English origin. But away from this ancestral core of words like *be, water,* and *strong,* the picture is one of radical change. Perhaps five-sixths of the Old English words of which we have a record left no descendants in Modern English. And a majority of the words used in English today are of foreign origin. Of the foreign languages affecting the Old English vocabulary, the most influential was Latin. Ecclesiastical terms especially, like *priest, vicar,* and *mass,* were borrowed from Latin, the language of the Church. But words belonging to aspects of life other than the strictly religious, like *cap, inch, kiln, school,* and *noon,* also entered Old English from Latin. The Scandinavians, too, influenced the language of England during the Old English period. From the eighth century on, Scandinavians raided and eventually settled in England, especially in the north and the east. This prolonged, if frequently unfriendly, contact had a considerable and varied influence on the English vocabulary. In a few instances the influence of a Scandinavian cognate gave an English word a new meaning. Thus our *dream,* which meant 'joy' in Old English, probably took on the now familiar sense 'a series of thoughts, images, or emotions occurring during sleep' because its Scandinavian cognate *draumr* had that meaning. A considerable number of common words, like *cross, fellow, ball,* and *raise,* also became naturalized as a result of the Viking incursions over the years. The initial consonants *sk-* often reveal the Scandinavian ancestry of words like *sky, skin,* and *skirt,* the last of which has persisted side by side with its native English cognate *shirt.* (See the discussion at SKIRT.)

The Middle English period, from about 1100 to 1500, was marked by a great extension of foreign influence on English, principally as a result of the Norman Conquest of 1066, which brought England under the rule of French speakers. The English language, though it did not die, was for a long time of only secondary importance in political, social, and cultural matters. French became the language of the upper classes in England. The variety of French spoken then is now called Anglo-Norman or Anglo-French. The lower classes continued to speak English, but many French words were borrowed into English. To this circumstance we owe, for example, a number of distinctions between the words used for animals in the pasture and the words for those animals prepared to be eaten. Living animals were under the care of English-speaking peasants; cooked, the animals were served to the French-speaking nobility. *Swine* in the sty became *pork* the table, *cow* and *calf* became *beef* and *veal.* (See the discussion at PORK.) Anglo-French also had an influence on the words used in the courts, such as *indict, jury, oyez,* and *verdict.* (See the discussion at JUDGE.) English eventually reestablished itself as the major language of England, but the language did not lose its habit of borrowing, and many foreign words became naturalized in Middle English, especially loanwords taken from Old French and Middle French (such as *date, escape, infant,* and *money*) or directly from Latin (such as *alibi, library,* and *pacify*).

Modern English, from about 1500 to the present, has been a period of even wider borrowing. English still derives much of its learned vocabulary from Latin and Greek. And we have also borrowed words from nearly all of the languages in Europe, though only a few examples can be given here. From Modern French we have words like *bikini, cliche,* and *discotheque,* from Dutch, *easel, gin,* and *yacht,* from German, *delicatessen, pretzel,* and *swindler,* and from Swedish, *ombudsman* and *smorgasbord.* From Italian we have taken *carnival, fiasco,* and *pizza,* as well as many terms from music (including *piano*). Portuguese has given us *cobra* and *molasses,* and the Spanish of Spain has yielded *sherry* and *mosquito,* while the Spanish of the New World has given us *ranch* and *machismo*. From Russian, Czech, and Yiddish we have taken *czar, robot* and *kibitz*.

And in the modern period the linguistic acquisitiveness of English has found opportunities even farther afield. From the period of the Renaissance voyages of discovery through the days when the sun never set upon the British Empire and up to the present, a steady stream of new words has flowed into the language to match the new objects and experiences English speakers have encountered all over the globe. English has drawn words from India (*bandanna*), China (*gung ho*), and Japan (*tycoon*), as well as a number of smaller areas in the Pacific (*amok* and *orangutan* from the Malay language and *ukulele* from Hawaiian). Arabic has been a prolific source of words over the centuries, giving us *hazard, lute, magazine,* and a host of words beginning with the letter *a*, from *algebra* to *azimuth*.

English has also added words to the vocabulary in a variety of ways apart from borrowing. Many new words are compounds of existing words (like *humble pie*) or coinages without reference to any word element in English or other languages (like *googol* and *quark*). Many words derive from literary characters (like *ignoramus* and *quixotic*), figures from mythology (like *hypnosis* and *panic*), the names of places (like *donnybrook* and *tuxedo*), or the names of people (like *boycott* and *silhouette*). The Roman emperor Julius Caesar has lent his name to a number of English words, including *cesarean, czar, July,* and *kaiser*. Still other words have come to us through the processes discussed at FOLK ETYMOLOGY, CALQUE, BACK-FORMATION, BLENDS, CLIPPING, and similar entries.

Whether borrowed or created, a word generally begins its life in English with one meaning. Yet no living language is static, and in time words develop new meanings and lose old ones. There are several directions in which semantic development frequently moves. Two common tendencies of language are generalization and specialization. A word used in a specific sense may be extended, or generalized, to cover a host of similar senses. Our *virtue* is derived from the Latin *virtus*, which originally meant 'manliness'. But we apply the term to any excellent quality possessed by man, woman, or beast; even inanimate objects have their *virtues*. In Latin, *decimare* meant 'to select and kill a tenth part of' and described the Roman way of dealing with mutinous troops. Its English descendant, *decimate*, now simply means 'to destroy a large part of'. Perhaps more frequent in its operation than generalization is the phenomenon of specialization, or narrowing, in which a word of general application becomes limited to a small part of its former wide range. *Tailleur,* the Old French ancestor of our *tailor,* first meant simply 'one who cuts', whether the cutting was of stone, wood, or cloth. Gradually the meaning was restricted to cloth, and the word came into English with that sense. *Deer* once meant 'animal'. Now only the members of a single family of mammals are called *deer*.

In addition to what could be thought of as a horizontal dimension of change—the extension or contraction of meaning—words also may rise and fall along a vertical scale of value. Perfectly unobjectionable words are sometimes used disparagingly or sarcastically. If we say, "You're a fine one to talk," we are using *fine* in a sense quite different from its usual meaning.

If a word is used often enough in negative contexts, the negative coloring may eventually become an integral part of the meaning of the word. A *villain* was once a peasant. His social standing was not high, perhaps, but he was certainly not necessarily a scoundrel. *Scavenger* originally designated the collector of a particular kind of tax in late medieval England. *Puny* first meant no more than 'younger' when it passed from French into English and its spelling was transformed. Only later did it acquire the derogatory meaning more familiar to us now. Euphemism too, though very well-intentioned, has caused many a word to take on a pejorative meaning. People are often reluctant, from a sense of decency or prudery or even simple kindness, to use a word whose denotation is unpleasant. Eventually, however, the good new word may become as unloved as the bad old one, and a new euphemism must be found. *Cretin* originally meant 'Christian' and was used charitably for a kind of mentally deficient person. The Modern English word retains no trace of its etymological meaning.

The opposite process seems to take place somewhat less frequently, but amelioration of meaning does occasionally occur. In the fourteenth century *nice*, for example, meant 'foolish'. Its present meaning, of course, is quite different, and the attitude it conveys seems to have undergone a complete reversal from contempt to approval. *Pioneer* now has overwhelmingly favorable connotations. A pioneer leads ordinary people along the way to new territory or new realms of knowledge. When the word first appeared in English, however, a pioneer was only a common foot soldier who performed such unexalted tasks as digging trenches. Another word that has followed the course of amelioration is *urbane*. In its earliest recorded occurrences in English, its meaning was the same as that of its etymological twin *urban*. Yet within a hundred years *urbane* had taken on the honorific sense of 'smoothly courteous or polite' in which we know it today.

We must not suppose, however, that these processes of semantic development are mutually exclusive or that a word must move neatly and consistently along a single path. The history of a word like *yen*, which began as 'a craving for opium or other narcotic' and later developed the sense 'a strong desire or propensity', clearly shows the forces of generalization at work but could also be considered to exemplify amelioration and a general lessening of intensity as well. *Sad* is a word whose semantic history is rather complex and not easily classifiable. Its earliest sense is 'sated'. The development of the sense 'firmly established or settled' does not clearly exemplify any of the processes just discussed; yet, that sense was current for more than three centuries, only to yield finally to several meanings still in use, such as 'mournful' and 'deplorable'. Whatever the history of their meanings, words are finally as individual—even sometimes eccentric—in their development as people.

The words discussed in this book reflect the diverse origins of the English vocabulary. They also indicate some of the ways in which words change in meaning. Each article traces the history of a word as far back as we have been able to follow it. The evolution of English words from their earliest use in English into modern times is given in great detail, with a wealth of quotations, in the Oxford English Dictionary. We have, of necessity, made use of this monumental work in the preparation of the articles. Frequently we quote instances of a word's use in English. Many of these quotations are drawn from the Oxford English Dictionary; others, especially the more modern ones, come from our own files. Occasionally, in the discussion of a word's history, we say that a word entered the language in some specified century. By this we mean only that the earliest attested use of the word occurred during that century. For only a few words, especially coinages like *jabberwocky* and *googol,* can we be certain of the actual date of first use. Other words may well be years, perhaps even centuries, older than their first citations.

Etymology is not an exact science. Many times we are unable to discover the origin of a word. Unproved but often ingenious etymological theories are put forward frequently, some plausible and very attractive, some wildly improbable. For *posh* and *ofay,* two words of obscure origin, explanations are regularly offered, but Merriam-Webster etymologists have compelling reasons for rejecting these suggestions. Sometimes, even when a word's origin is fairly certainly known, an unlikely story catches the popular imagination. For the expression *tinker's damn,* we offer an explanation of why a rather mundane theory of origin is to be preferred to a more popular story. (See discussion at TINKER.)

Recall always that we, like all other etymologists and most other human beings, are imperfect. The articles in this book are to the best of our present knowledge, accurate. But approach them with caution. Any day, new information may come to light that could prove us wrong. Consider the word *OK.* Time and again, etymologists have felt that they had reached the final answer, only to find themselves faced with new evidence and so forced to revise their explanations.

At the end of each article in this book, and at each cross-referenced entry, there is a bracketed etymology, which is a compact statement of the history of the entry word. An article that treats two or more homographs—words with the same spelling—is followed by a bracketed etymology for each. The style in which these etymologies are written is based upon that used for the etymologies in Webster's Third New International Dictionary. The etyma of the word are printed in italics, preceded by appropriate language labels. An italicized word is followed by its meaning, printed in roman type:

hoosegow . . . [Sp *juzgado* panel of judges, tribunal, courtroom . . .]

If no meaning, form, or language label is given for a word cited in an etymology, then the meaning, form, or language of the word is identical with that of its immediate descendant, the word that precedes it in the etymology:

panache . . . [earlier *pennache,* fr. MF, fr. OIt *pennacchio,* fr. LL *pinnaculum* small wing]

The earlier *pennache* cited is a Modern English word, like its descendant *panache,* and has the same meaning. The Middle French word is identical in form and meaning with English *pennache.* Old Italian *pennacchio* means, like its Middle French and Modern English descendants, 'panache'. Its Late Latin ancestor, however, had a different meaning. The word *literally,* abbreviated "lit.," indicates that the word that precedes it has the same meaning as its immediate descendant but also has the more literal meaning that follows:

canapé . . . [F, lit., sofa . . .]

The French word *canapé* is used in the same sense as its English borrowing, but its literal meaning is 'sofa'.

Often several different spellings, separated only by commas, follow a single language label. These are not distinct words, descended the one from the other, but simply variant spellings of a single word. Earlier writers of English and other languages did not insist, as we do today, on uniformity of spelling:

ferret . . . [ME *feret, ferret, furet,* fr. MF *furet, fuiret* . . .]

Some of the languages from which English words are derived are not commonly written, like English, in the Roman alphabet. Words belonging to such languages as Greek, Arabic, Hebrew, Chinese, and others are cited in standard Roman transliterations of their own alphabets or other writing system. In tone languages, variations in tone distinguish words of different meaning that would otherwise sound alike. For words cited from such languages, a small superscript number indicates the tone of the word it follows:

tycoon . . . [. . . Chin (Pek) *ta*[4] great + *chün*[1] ruler]

Common English prefixes and suffixes occasionally appear in the bracketed etymologies. An English affix may be cited as a component of the etymologized English word:

stentorian . . . [*stentor* + *-ian*]

English affixes are also used to translate affixes in other languages:

animal . . . [L, . . . fr. *anima* breath, soul + *-alis* -al]

The articles tell the stories of the words in greater detail than the short space allotted to the bracketed etymologies permits. But the bracketed etymologies often add some information which is not included in the text. In particular, the brackets often include lists of cognates, following the phrase "akin to":

sad . . . [akin to OHG *sat* sated, ON *sathr, saddr,* Goth *sads,* L *satur* sated, *satis* enough, Gk *hadēn* to satiety, enough, Skt *asinva* insatiable]

A few words used in the etymologies may require some explanation. An *augmentative* indicates large size, as a *diminutive* indicates small. The *frequentative* of a verb indicates repetition of an action or recurrence of a state. The *inchoative* of a verb indicates the beginning of an action, state, or occurrence. *Denominative* means 'derived from a noun or adjective'. Other possible sources of confusion in a bracketed etymology should be clarified by the text of the article.

Pronunciation Symbols

ə ....abut, collect, suppose

ˈə, ͵ə ....humdrum

ə ....(in ᵊl, ᵊn) batt**le**, cott**on;** (in lᵊ, mᵊ, rᵊ) French tab**le,** pris**me,** tit**re**

ər ....op**er**ation, furth**er**

a ....m**a**p, p**a**tch

ā ....d**ay**, f**a**te

ä ....b**o**ther, c**o**t, f**a**ther

a ....a sound between \a\ and \ä\, as in an Eastern New England pronunciation of **au**nt, **a**sk

au̇ ....n**ow**, **ou**t

b ....**b**a**b**y, ri**b**

ch ....**ch**in, ca**tch**

d ....**d**i**d**, a**dd**er

e ....s**e**t, r**e**d

ē ....b**ea**t, **ea**sy

f ....**f**i**f**ty, cu**ff**

g ....**g**o, bi**g**

h ....**h**at, a**h**ead

hw ......**wh**ale

i ....t**i**p, ban**i**sh

ī ....s**i**te, b**uy**

j ....**j**ob, e**dg**e

k ....**k**in, coo**k**

ḵ ....German Ba**ch**, Scots lo**ch**

l ....**l**i**l**y, coo**l**

m ....**m**ur**m**ur, di**m**

n ....**n**i**n**e, ow**n**

ⁿ ....indicates that a preceding vowel is pronounced through both nose and mouth, as in French bon \bôⁿ\

ŋ ....si**ng**, si**ng**er, fi**ng**er, i**ŋ**k

ō ....b**o**ne, holl**ow**

ȯ ....s**aw**

œ ....French b**œu**f, German H**ö**lle

œ̄ ....French f**eu**, German H**ö**hle

ȯi ....t**oy**

p ....**p**e**pp**er, li**p**

r ....**r**a**r**ity

s ....**s**our**ce**, le**ss**

sh ....**sh**y, mi**ss**ion

t ....**t**ie, a**tt**ack

th ....**th**in, e**th**er

t̲h̲ ....**th**en, ei**th**er

ü ....b**oo**t, few \ˈfyü\

u̇ ....p**u**t, pure \ˈpyu̇r\

ᴜe ....German f**ü**llen

ᴜ̄e ....French r**ue,** German f**ü**hlen

v ....**v**i**v**id, gi**v**e

w ....**w**e, a**w**ay

y ....**y**ard, cue \ˈkyü\

ʸ ....indicates that a preceding \l\, \n\, or \w\ is modified by having the tongue approximate the position for \y\, as in French di**gn**e \dēnʸ\

z ....**z**one, rai**s**e

zh ....vi**s**ion, plea**s**ure

\ ....slant line used in pairs to mark the beginning and end of a transcription: \ˈpen\

ˈ ....mark at the beginning of a syllable that has primary (strongest) stress: \ˈshəf-əl-͵bȯrd\

͵ ....mark at the beginning of a syllable that has secondary (next-strongest) stress: \ˈshəf-əl-͵bȯrd\

- ....mark of syllable division in pronunciations (the mark of end-of-line division in boldface entries is a centered dot •)

( ) ....indicate that what is symbolized between sometimes occurs and sometimes does not occur in the pronunciation of the word: **fac•tory** \ˈfak-t(ə-)rē\ = \ˈfak-tə-rē, ˈfak-trē\

Abbreviations

ab	about	*Fr*	French
abbr	abbreviation	*freq*	frequentative
abl	ablative	*Fris*	Frisian
accus	accusative	*G*	German
act	active	*Gael*	Gaelic
A.D.	anno Domini	*gen*	genitive
adj	adjective	*Ger*	German
adv	adverb	*Gk*	Greek (to A.D. 200)
AF	Anglo-French	*Gmc*	Germanic
Alb	Albanian	*Goth*	Gothic
alter	alteration	*Heb*	Hebrew
Am	American	*Hitt*	Hittite
AmerSp	American Spanish	*IE*	Indo-European
Ar	Arabic	*imit*	imitative
Arm	Armenian	*imper*	imperative
art	article	*incho*	inchoative
aug	augmentative	*indic*	indicative
Av	Avestan	*interj*	interjection
AV	Authorized Version	*Ir*	Irish
b	born	*IrGael*	Irish Gaelic
B.C.	before Christ	*irreg*	irregular
Bret	Breton	*ISV*	International Scientific
Brit	British		Vocabulary
c, ca	circa	*It*	Italian
CanF	Canadian French	*Jn*	John
Cant	Cantonese	*Jp*	Japanese
Catal	Catalan	*L*	Latin (to A.D. 200)
Celt	Celtic	*Lev*	Leviticus
cent	century	*LG*	Low German
Chin	Chinese	*LGk*	Late Greek (A.D. 200-600)
comb	combining	*lit*	literally
compar	comparative	*Lith*	Lithuanian
contr	contraction	*Lk*	Luke
Corn	Cornish	*LL*	Late Latin (A.D. 200-600)
D	Dutch	*masc*	masculine
Dan	Danish	*MBret*	Middle Breton
dat	dative	*MD*	Middle Dutch
def	definite	*ME*	Middle English (A.D. 1100-1500)
dial	dialect		
dim	diminutive	*MexSp*	Mexican Spanish
E	English (since A.D. 1500)	*MF*	Middle French (A.D. 1300-1600)
Egypt	Egyptian		
Eng	English	*MGk*	Middle Greek (A.D. 600-1500)
esp	especially		
F	French (since A.D. 1600)	*MHG*	Middle High German
fem	feminine	*MIr*	Middle Irish
ff	and the following ones	*ML*	Medieval Latin (A.D. 600-1500)
fl	flourished		
Flem	Flemish	*MLG*	Middle Low German
fr	from		

modif ....modification
mt ....mountain
Mt ....Matthew
n ....noun
neut ....neuter
NGk ....New Greek (since A.D. 1500)
NGmc ....North Germanic
NL ....New Latin (since A.D. 1500)
nom ....nominative
Norw ....Norwegian
obs ....obsolete
OBulg ....Old Bulgarian
OE ....Old English (to A.D. 1100)
OF ....Old French (to A.D. 1300)
OFris ....Old Frisian
OHG ....Old High German
OIr ....Old Irish
OIt ....Old Italian
OL ....Old Latin
ON ....Old Norse
ONF ....Old North French
OProv ....Old Provençal
OPruss ....Old Prussian
orig ....originally
ORuss ....Old Russian
OS ....Old Saxon
OSlav ....Old Slavic
OSp ....Old Spanish
PaG ....Pennsylvania German
part ....participle
Pek ....Pekingese
Per ....Persian

perh ....perhaps
pers ....person
Pg ....Portuguese
pl ....plural
PM ....post meridiem
pres ....present
prob ....probably
pron ....pronoun, pronunciation
Prov ....Provençal
Ps ....Psalms
RSV ....Revised Standard Version
Russ ....Russian
Sc ....Scots
Scand ....Scandinavian
ScGael ....Scottish Gaelic
Scot ....Scottish
Sem ....Semitic
Serb ....Serbian
sing ....singular
Skt ....Sanskrit
Slav ....Slavic
Sp ....Spanish
St ....Saint
subj ....subjunctive
suff ....suffix
superl ....superlative
Sw, Swed ...Swedish
trans ....translation
US ....United States
v ....verb
var ....variant
VL ....Vulgar Latin
W ....Welsh
WGmc ....West Germanic

+ ....plus sign joins words or word elements
† ....dagger precedes a death date
* ....asterisk precedes a hypothetical reconstructed form

A

abigail See LOTHARIO.
[after *Abigail*, serving woman in the play *The Scornful Lady*, by Francis Beaumont †1616 and John Fletcher †1625 Eng. dramatists]

abound See ABUNDANCE.
[ME *abounden*, fr. MF *abonder*, fr. L *abundare* to abound, overflow, fr. ab- ¹ab- + *undare* to rise in waves, fr. *unda* wave]

abundance Images of flowing water are at the origin of several of our Latin-derived terms for abundance. *Abundance* itself goes back to Latin *abundantia*, whose most basic meaning is 'overflow'. It is a derivative of *unda* 'wave', which, focusing on a different property of waves, is also at the root of our word *undulate*. The related verb *abundare* 'to overflow, be plentiful' is the ultimate source of our word *abound*.

Affluence meant 'plentiful flowing' or abundance in general before it came to mean specifically 'wealth'. Its Latin source *affluentia* is derived from the prefix *ad-* 'towards' and *fluere* 'to flow' (this last, despite appearances, bears no relation to English *flow*, which is rather related to Latin *pluere* 'to rain'). The original sense is thus close to another Latin-derived term whose root is *fluere*, namely *influx*.

Profusion, finally, is ultimately derived from Latin *profundere* 'to pour forth'. *Fundere* 'pour' also had a more literal English offspring, namely the verb *found*, in the foundry sense, 'to melt (metal) and pour into a mold'.

[ME *abundaunce, habundaunce*, fr. MF *abundance*, fr. L *abundantia*, fr. *abundant-, abundans* + *-ia*]

academy When Helen was only twelve years old (long before she ran away with Paris to become the cause of the Trojan War), she was abducted by Theseus, who hoped eventually to marry her. But her brothers, Castor and Pollux, went in search of her. It was a man named *Akadēmos* who revealed to them the place where Helen was hidden and won for himself a place in Greek mythology.

The *Akadēmeia*, a park and gymnasium located near Athens, was named in honor of the legendary hero Akademos. It was there that Plato established his school, which is, in name at least, the grandfather of all modern academies. English *academy* was first used in the fifteenth century simply to refer to Plato's school. But in Italian, and later in French, the descendants of Greek *Akadēmeia* were losing their status as no more than proper nouns and developing more general senses. A French *académie* may be any school above the elementary level, or it may be a learned society (the most famous being *l'Académie française* 'the French Academy', which has, since it was established in 1634, been trying heroically to preserve the French language from corruption). These later senses of *academy* entered English from French.

See also STOIC.

[L *academia*, the school of philosophy founded by Plato, fr. Gk *Akadēmeia*, *Akadēmia*, fr. the name of the gymnasium near Athens where Plato taught, fr. *Akadēmos* Attic mythological hero + Gk *-eia* or *-ia* *-y*]

accident   See CHANCE.
[ME, fr. MF, fr. L *accident-*, *accidens* nonessential quality or circumstance, accident, chance, fr. pres. part. of *accidere* to happen, fr. *ad-* + *-cidere* (fr. *cadere* to fall)]

acquire   See QUESTION.
[alter. (influenced by L *acquirere*) of earlier *acquere*, fr. ME *aqueren*, fr. MF *aquerre*, fr. L *acquirere*, fr. *ad-* + *-quirere* (fr. *quaerere* to seek, gain, obtain, ask)]

acronymic etymologies   An acronym is a word formed from the initial letters of a phrase. We may distinguish three stages of integration of the result into the general non-acronymic vocabulary:

(1) At one extreme, the result still clearly shows its alphabetic origin, like *FBI* from "Federal Bureau of Investigation." Such forms are the principal ingredient of today's "alphabet soup" of government agencies and technological innovations. In many cases the acronym is more familiar than the source phrase, so that there are people who know, say, that TNT and PCBs are hazardous, without being able to tell you what the letters stand for.

(2) The next step of integration into the lexicon involves pronouncing the form like a regular word instead of a succession of letter-names: thus *NASA* and *NATO* are pronounced as two-syllable words. If the form is written lowercase, there is no longer any formal clue that the word began life as an acronym: thus *radar* ('radio detecting and ranging'). Sometimes a form wavers between the two treatments: *CAT scan* pronounced either like *cat* or like *C-A-T*.

(3) The furthest state of blending in with the non-acronymic vocabulary is achieved by words whose acronymic letters have been transformed or suffixed with non-acronymic material. Thus we have *vipoma*, from "vasoactive intestinal polypeptide" plus the suffix *-oma*, which looks no more acronymic than *viremia*, or *Seabee*, an appropriately naval-looking alteration of the initials of "construction battalion," a group in the U.S. Navy.

No origin is more pleasing to the general reader than an acronymic one. Reading that a word comes down to us via a seemingly endless cascade of meaningless little sound changes from the remote and ultimately unknowable Indo-European, many readers find their lids have turned to lead. But opening up a word into a comprehensible English phrase is like opening a present, like sticking in your thumb and pulling out a plum. Accordingly, fanciful acronymic etymologies are perennially popular. You will from time to time find it stated as fact that *news* comes from "north, east, west, south," which is certainly more colorful than its actual derivation from *new* (possibly on the model of French *nouvelles* 'news', from *nouvelle* 'new'). Such purported origins are especially tenacious when the word in question is in fact of obscure or disputed or unknown etymology. Thus we have *spud* 'potato' falsely explained as being from "Society for the Prevention of an Unhealthy Diet"; *tip,* as from "to improve performance"; *wop,* from "without passport"; and *gorp* (trail-munch), from "good old raisins & peanuts." (See also COP, POSH.) Such expansions amount to a parlor game and are pursued even when the non-acronymic origin is known to everyone. Thus when the Ford cars first came out, everyone knew they were named for Henry Ford, but it was still more fun to etymologize the word as being from "found on road dead" or "fix or repair daily."

A special class of acronyms consists of words for which the alleged phrasal origin is indeed connected with the word but is essentially post hoc: an appropriate word or other form was targeted and a phrase was invented to fit. This is quite common in the case of names for organizations: *PUSH* ("People United to Save Humanity"), *CORE* ("Congress Of Racial Equality"), *MADD* ("Mothers Against Drunk Driving"), and *TNT* ("Tactical Narcotics Team").

adamant   See DIAMOND.
[ME, a fabulous mineral, diamond, lodestone, fr. OF, fr. L *adamant-, adamas* hardest iron or steel, diamond, fr. Gk]

adder   See APRON.
[ME *addre,* alter. (resulting from incorrect division of *a naddre*) of *naddre,* fr. OE *nǣdre* adder, snake; akin to OHG *nātara* adder, ON *nathr,* Goth *nadrs,* L *natrix* water snake]

adjudicate   See JUDGE.
[L *adjudicatus,* past part. of *adjudicare,* fr. *ad- + judicare* to judge]

adolescent   The English adjectives *adolescent, adult,* and *old,* which designate stages of life, share a common Indo-European ancestor, whose meaning was 'to nourish' or 'to grow'. *Alere,* 'to nourish', and its derivative *alescere,* 'to grow', are Latin descendants of this Indo-European root. Latin *adolescere,* 'to grow up', is formed by the addition of the common Latin prefix *ad-,* meaning 'to' or 'at', to the verb *alescere.* The present participle of *adolescere* is *adolescens,* which gives us English *adolescent;* an *adolescent* person, then, is one who is growing up. A person who is *adult* has grown up: Latin *adultus* is the past participle of *adolescere.*

Old is not of Latin origin but is a native English word. Old English *ald* or *eald* like Latin *adultus* is ultimately a past participle form, not formed in Old English itself but descended from the past participle of an earlier Germanic verb cognate with Latin *alere*.

Other native English words formed from the same root as *old* are *elder* and *alderman*.

[F, fr. L *adolescent-, adolescens,* pres. part. of *adolescere* to grow up]

adroit   See RIGHT.

[F, fr. *à droit* properly, fr. *à* to, at (fr. L *ad*) + *droit* right, fr. L *directus* straight, direct]

adult   See ADOLESCENT.

[L *adultus,* past part. of *adolescere* to grow up, fr. *ad-* to, at + *-olescere* (fr. *alescere* to grow, incho. of *alere* to nourish)]

adulterate   See ADULTERY.

[L *adulteratus,* past part. of *adulterare* to pollute, defile, commit adultery, fr. *ad-* to, at + *-ulterare* (fr. *alter* different, other)]

adultery   The resemblance between *adult* and *adultery* is great enough to give anyone pause. Indeed, one young lady is reported to have answered, in an apparent slip, when asked about her job, that she worked for a household of several children, "one adult, and one adultress." Yet the words are unrelated. (For the origin of *adult* see ADOLESCENT.) *Adultery* comes to us, through the French, from Latin *adulterium,* derived from the verb *adulterare,* 'to pollute, defile, or commit adultery'. Later influence of the original Latin source word has meant that we spell *adultery* more like its distant Latin than its immediate French ancestor, *avoutrie. Adulterare* itself is a compound of the prefix *ad-,* 'to, at', and the adjective *alter,* which means 'different' or 'other'.

Etymologically, then, *adulterare* would simply have meant 'to alter', but a sense development from 'to change' to 'to change injuriously' is a fairly common one. Within English, *alter* itself underwent such a change, in the nineteenth century developing the meaning 'to castrate'.

Another English derivative is *adulterate,* which means 'to corrupt or make impure by the addition of a foreign substance'. But the English word once had another sense as well; it meant 'to commit adultery'. In Shakespeare's *King John* (ca. 1596), Constance speaks to her son Arthur of fortune's inconstancy: "But Fortune, O,/ She is corrupted, chang'd, and won from thee!/ Sh' adulterates hourly with thine uncle John."

[ME *adulterie,* alter. (influenced by L *adulterium*) of *advoutrie, avoutrie,* fr. MF *avoutrie,* alter. of OF *avoutire,* fr. L *adulterium,* fr. *adulter* adulterer, back-formation fr. *adulterare* to pollute, defile, commit adultery]

advent   See CATHOLIC.

[ME, fr. ML *adventus,* fr. L, arrival, fr. *adventus,* past part. of *advenire* to come to]

aegis Today when we speak of something as being "under the aegis of
. . ." (as the word *aegis* is almost invariably used nowadays), we generally
mean that it is under the authority, sponsorship, or control of another. In
a way, then, the thing that is in the subordinate position is being "protected" by the other; hence, an aegis is something that protects or shields. In
ancient Greece the word *aigis* was used literally of something that offered
physical protection. In Greek mythology the aegis in one sense was a thundercloud, housing the thunderbolts that Zeus wielded as his signature
weapon. In another sense (probably the original) it was a cloak or mantle
made of goatskin taken from the she-goat who had suckled Zeus as a babe
(in Greek, *aigis* literally means 'goatskin'). In this incarnation it was part
of Zeus's protective armor in his war against the Titans. In another tradition the aegis became an impregnable, shield-like weapon that was fash-
ioned by the metalworking god Hephaestus to resemble a thundercloud
and fringed with tassels suggestive of thunderbolts.

Zeus occasionally entrusted the aegis to other gods and especially to
Athena, of whom the aegis later became an attribute. In the myths centering on Athena, the aegis became a goatskin mantle bearing the likeness
of the Gorgon Medusa and fringed with serpents, actual or illustrated. In
artistic representations Athena is shown wearing the aegis as a sort of protective buffcoat over her chest, or she is shown draping the leather cloak
over her arm and using it as a conventional shield to ward off blows. The
aegis became an attribute of the goddess's divine protection and power.

The aegis became a familiar classical reference in English literature. It
appears, for example, in the poetry of Thomas Gray and Lord Byron. Zeus,
especially in poetical contexts, is identified by his Homeric epithets "aegis-
bearer" and "aegis-bearing." By the eighteenth century the word *aegis*
was being used figuratively for any kind of seemingly impregnable shield.
While *aegis* is still used as a synonym of *protection*, the sense of the word
equivalent to *auspices* has become dominant.

[L, fr. Gk *aigis* goatskin, shield of Zeus, perh. fr. *aig-*, *aix* goat; akin to
Arm *aic* goat, Av *izaēna* leathern]

affluence See ABUNDANCE.
[ME, fr. MF, fr. L *affluentia*, fr. *affluent-*, *affluens* + *-ia*]

aggregate See EGREGIOUS.
[ME *aggregat*, fr. L *aggregatus*, past part. of *aggregare* to add to, fr. *ad-*
to, at + *greg-*, *grex* flock]

agnostic An *agnostic* is one who holds the view that any ultimate reality, such as God, is unknown and probably unknowable. The word was
coined in 1869 by Thomas Henry Huxley, the noted English biologist.
Though the date of coinage is known, the specific etymology that Huxley
had in mind has been a matter of debate for some years. The following portion of a letter dated 13 March 1881 (which has since disappeared) from
R. H. Hutton was printed by the editors of the Oxford English Dictionary
at the entry for *agnostic:* "Suggested by Prof. Huxley at a party held previ-

ous to the formation of the now defunct Metaphysical Society, at Mr. James Knowles's house on Clapham Common, one evening in 1869, in my hearing. He took it from St. Paul's mention of the altar to 'the Unknown God.'" The Greek form of the altar inscription given in Acts 17:23 is *agnōstō theō*.

The Metaphysical Society held an organizational meeting on 21 April 1869, and the first appearance of *agnostic* in print is in the *Spectator* for 29 May of that year in an article probably written by the same R. H. Hutton, who was the magazine's literary editor at the time: "All these considerations, and the great controversies which suggest them, are in the highest degree cultivating, and will be admitted to be so even by those Agnostics who think them profitless of any result." In 1889 Huxley himself said that he "invented what I conceived to be the appropriate title of 'agnostic.' It came into my head as suggestively antithetic to the 'gnostic' of church history, who professed to know so much about the very things of which I was ignorant; and I took the earliest opportunity of parading it at our Society." The most reasonable statement that can be made reconciling these differing opinions of Hutton and Huxley is that both are correct to a degree and each point of view is influenced by the other.

Agnostic is formed from the Greek *agnōstos*, meaning 'unknown' or 'unknowable'. The ending *-ic* of *agnostic* is clearly influenced by English *Gnostic*, from Greek *gnōstikos*, since in Greek the termination *-ikos* does not occur in words, like *agnōstos*, containing the prefix *a-*. This same prefix is found in *atheist*, 'one who does not believe in the existence of a deity'. *Atheist* is borrowed from Middle French *athéiste*, from *athée*, which in turn comes from Greek *atheos*, 'godless, not believing in the existence of gods'.

[modif. (influenced by E *Gnostic*) of Gk *agnōstos* unknown, unknowable, not knowing, fr. *a-* not, without + *gnōstos* known, fr. *gignōskein* to know]

agony   The ancient Greeks were fond of celebrations that included games and athletic contests. From their verb *agein* 'to lead, celebrate', the Greeks derived the noun *agōn* to denote a public gathering for such celebrations. The struggle to win the prize in the athletic contests then came to be called *agōnia*. This word also took on the general sense of 'any difficult struggle'. From this sense *agōnia* additionally came to refer to the pain, whether physical or mental, that was involved in such a struggle. The Romans, as was their custom, borrowed the Greek words *agōn* and *agōnia* with essentially the same meanings.

Agōnia became *agonie* in Middle French and in fourteenth-century Middle English, when Chaucer used it for 'mental anguish or distress'. During the seventeenth century, *agony* acquired the sense of 'intense pain of body' and then took on the additional sense of 'a violent struggle, conflict, or contest', harking back to its Greek origins.

An entirely new sense of *agony* developed in the eighteenth century: 'a strong sudden and often uncontrollable display (as of joy or delight)'. Thus we see the shift from intense pain to intense pleasure. This is exemplified by Henry Fielding in *Tom Jones* (1749): "The first agonies of joy which were felt on both sides are indeed beyond my power to describe," and more recently by Edith Wharton in *New Year's Day* (1924): "My cousin Kate . . . was pinching my arm in an agony of mirth." Nevertheless, the distressful senses of *agony* still predominate, even though the word originally came from a verb meaning 'to celebrate'.

The Greek *agōn* also forms the root of such English words as *antagonism, antagonize, antagonist,* and *protagonist.*

[ME *agonie,* fr. MF & LL; MF *agonie,* fr. LL *agonia,* fr. Gk *agōnia* contest, struggle, anguish, fr. *agōn* gathering, assembly at games, contest for a prize, fr. *agein* to lead, celebrate]

ain't   Even though everybody knows *ain't,* almost nobody has any idea of where it came from. How is this strange-looking word related to the verb *be?* The connections are not obvious.

They begin back in the seventeenth century. During the Restoration period—after 1660—we begin to find the first printed evidence of several negative contractions that had come into spoken use during the century. (We actually don't know when spoken use started; a good guess by historians of the language is about 1600.) Several of these contractions look unfamiliar now: *ben't, an't, en't, han't*—these have either been replaced by other, newer contractions or have simply gone out of use. But several others are quite familiar: *can't, shan't, don't, won't.*

The one we are interested in is *an't* (sometimes given an extra apostrophe to make *a'n't*). Our first printed evidence for it comes from a Restoration comedy; it means 'am not':

> *Miss Prue.* You need not sit so near one, if you have any thing to say, I can hear you farther off, I an't deaf.
> *Ben.* Why that's true as you say, nor I an't dumb, I can be heard as far as another —William Congreve, *Love for Love,* 1695

Hard on the heels of the 'am not' use comes one for 'are not'. This too is from a Restoration comedy:

> *Lord Foppington.* Hark thee, shoemaker, these shoes *a'n't* ugly, but they don't fit me —Sir John Vanbrugh, *The Relapse,* 1696

How *an't* came to be used for *am not* is fairly easy to figure out. *Am not* was contracted to *amn't* (a contraction that is still used in Irish and Scottish English), and then the sounds of *m* and *n* were combined. The conversion of *aren't* to *an't* is easier to understand if we remember that in the principal British dialects the *r* would not have been pronounced. The spelling *an't* should also warn us that the *a* of *are* was not then pronounced as it is today; it must have been close enough in sound to the *a* of *am* that writers were satisfied to use the same spelling for both meanings. The evidence of rhymes has been cited, too. For instance John Donne in some of his poems rhymed *are* with *bare, starre,* and *warre,* which do not rhyme among themselves in present-day English. But they must have all been close enough to make passable rhymes in Donne's time (Donne died in

1631). Presumably the development of the pronunciation of *are* in Donne's time would lead in some dialects to a pronunciation spelling, when -*n't* was attached and *r* not pronounced, of *an't*.

An't came to be used for 'is not' too. Jonathan Swift used "an't he" as early as 1710 in his *Journal to Stella*. How this use developed is not clear. A development through a series of sound-variations has been postulated, but it leads more comfortably to the spelling *ain't* than to *an't*, which is earlier. One historian supposes that *an't* was simply extended to the third person singular since it already served all the other forms of present-tense *be*.

So *an't* was established in the meanings 'am not', 'are not', and 'is not' by early in the eighteenth century. Remember that *an't* is a speech form. We don't have a lot of printed evidence for it, and what we have comes from fictional dialogue and from letters.

> ". . . I am sure I shan't go if Lucy an't there." —Jane Austen, *Sense and Sensibility*, 1811

> A'nt you sorry for her —Emily Dickinson, letter, 24 Dec. 1851

You can see from the quotations that *an't* continued to be used well into the nineteenth century, but by then it was competing with another spelling, *ain't*. *Ain't* is first attested in print in Fanny Burney's *Evelina*, a novel published in 1778. It represented the way a countryman said the word. This spelling probably represents one of the main directions in the development of the vowel sound of *are*, mentioned earlier. Just how this pronunciation became extended to the uses of *an't* meaning 'am not' and 'is not' is not known. But *ain't* was popularly associated with Cockney speech in the nineteenth century—in some of Dickens's novels, for instance. (The other main branch in the development of the vowel of *are* would bring it in the direction of *aunt*—a plausible pronunciation for *an't*—and would by the end of the nineteenth century result in the spelling—remember southern British English omits the *r*—*aren't*. The spelling *aren't I?* looked very strange to Americans when it was first noticed in British novels around the turn of the century.)

Ain't is also used in the meanings 'have not' and 'has not'. The connection here is a little plainer. We have evidence of a seventeenth-century contraction *ha'nt* used for both 'have not' and 'has not'. (Have you noticed how the middle consonant always seems to disappear from these old contractions?) The long *a* needed for *ain't* came from a variant pronunciation of *have* (we still pronounce it that way in *behave*). And the *h* is not aspirated in some dialects of British English. All of these forces combined to produce the 'have not' and 'has not' meanings of *ain't*.

The development of *ain't* in the United States has not been traced. Both *an't* and *ain't* are attested in the late eighteenth century, and presumably both appeared here because they were brought by early settlers. Some of the same influences on pronunciation were present here, too; for instance, nineteenth-century dialect humorists use the spelling *air* for *are*.

Ain't began to displace *an't*, for reasons we do not understand, during the nineteenth century. We have one hint, perhaps, in the fact that Johnson J. Hooper in a book published in 1845 has a story about his rascally hero Simon Suggs in which young Simon regularly says *ain't* but his father says *a'n't.* Hooper's tale is set in the South; in New England we find Emily Dickinson using *an't* in 1851 and the elder Oliver Wendell Holmes hearing it from his fellow boarders in 1860. The evidence is slim, but perhaps the change worked its way from south to north. At any rate, *an't* is hard to find after the 1870s, and even New England writers like Harriet Beecher Stowe and Mary E. Wilkins Freeman spell it *ain't.* In some parts of the U.S. *hain't* is interchangeable with *ain't.*

That's about all we know about *ain't.* You can see that there are some murky areas that could do with further investigation, but currently *ain't* is far more often reprehended than researched.

[prob. contr. of *are not, is not, am not* & *have not*]

aisle See DEBT.
[alter. (influenced by F *aile* wing, aisle) of earlier *isle,* alter. (influenced by *isle* "island") of ME *ile,* alter. (influenced by *ile* isle, island) of *ele, eile,* fr. MF *ele, aile* wing, wing of a building, fr. L *ala* wing, armpit; akin to OE *eaxl* shoulder, ON *öxl,* OHG *ahsala,* L *axilla* armpit]

alack See LACKADAISICAL.
[ME *alacke,* prob. fr. *a* ah! + *lack* fault, loss, fr. MD *lac*]

alas See LACKADAISICAL.
[ME, fr. OF, fr. *a* ah! + *las* weary, wretched, fr. L *lassus* weary]

alchemy See LUTE.
[ME *alkamie, alquemie,* fr. MF or ML; MF *alquemie,* fr. ML *alchymia, alchimia,* fr. Ar *al-kīmiyā'* the philosopher's stone, the alchemy, fr. *al* the + *kīmiyā',* fr. LGk *chēmeia,* prob. alter. of *chymeia,* prob. fr. Gk *chyma* fluid, fr. *chein* to pour]

alcohol See LUTE.
[NL & ML; NL, liquid produced by distillation, fr. ML, finely pulverized antimony used by women to darken the eyelids, fr. OSp, fr. Ar *al-kuḥul, al-kuḥl* the powdered antimony]

alcoholic See WORKAHOLIC.
[*alcohol* + *-ic*]

alderman See ADOLESCENT.
[ME, fr. OE *aldorman, ealdorman,* fr. *aldor, ealdor* parent, head of a family (fr. *ald, eald* old) + *man*]

alfalfa See LUTE.
[Sp, modif. of Ar dial. (Spain) *al-faṣfaṣah* the alfalfa, alter. of *al-fiṣfiṣah*]

algebra   See LUTE.
[ML, *algebra*, bonesetting, fracture (whence ME, bonesetting, fracture), fr. Ar *al-jabr* the algebra, the bonesetting, lit., the reduction]

alibi   In Latin, *alibi* was used only as an adverb meaning 'elsewhere'. This word was formed by the contraction of the words *alius* 'other' and *ubi* 'where'. When *alibi* was first brought into English in the early eighteenth century, it was still used as an adverb. In his satirical pamphlet "The History of John Bull," written in 1727, the Scottish writer John Arbuthnot illustrates this usage: "The prisoner had little to say in his defence; he endeavoured to prove himself Alibi."

By the last quarter of the eighteenth century, however, *alibi* also began to be used as a noun in legal contexts for 'the plea of having been at the time of the commission of an act elsewhere than at the place of commission'. It was then also applied to 'the fact or state of having been elsewhere at the time'. These legal senses were included in Noah Webster's Dictionary in 1828.

By 1912, *alibi* had also acquired in American English the generalized sense of 'an excuse, especially for failure or negligence'. An early example of this appeared in the dialogue of a baseball player in Ring Lardner's 1915 story "Alibi Ike":

> "He's got the world beat," says Carey to Jack and I. "I've knew lots o' guys that had an alibi for every mistake they made. . . . But this baby can't even go to bed without apologizin'. . . ."

This sense of 'excuse' gained footholds in other contexts too, especially politics. Newspaper and magazine writers were quick to pick up this useful sense, but usage writers, both American and British, were also quick to voice their disapproval. The Second Edition of Webster's New International Dictionary (1934) labeled this sense *Colloq*[uial]. British disapproval appeared in Eric Partridge's book *Usage and Abusage* in 1942. More recently, some usage commentators have accepted and have even defended this sense of *alibi*, but the controversy continues, more so in British English than in American English.

[L]

aliment   See ALIMONY.
[ME, fr. L *alimentum,* fr. *alere* to nourish + *-mentum* -ment]

alimentary   See ALIMONY.
[L *alimentarius,* fr. *alimentum* + *-arius* -ary]

alimony   *Alimony* is simply an Englishing of the Latin *alimonia* 'sustenance', which is derived from *alere* 'to nourish'. In English *alimony* has meant not only 'an allowance given to a spouse' but also 'a means of living, maintenance'. Both meanings appeared at almost the same time in the middle of the seventeenth century. *Alimony* is related to such words as *alimentary* and *aliment; aliment* is the Scottish legal term for 'an allowance given to a spouse'. (For more terms related to Latin *alere* see ADOLES-CENT.)

Palimony is a recent addition to the language that grew out of the suing of an actor for support by his former mistress. It is a blend of *pal* and *alimony* and looks very much like it was intended as a witty coinage at first. When the mistress won the suit, it was taken very seriously indeed. See also BLENDS.

[L *alimonia* sustenance, fr. *alere* to nourish]

almanac   See LUTE.

[ME *almenak,* fr. ML *almanach,* prob. fr. Ar *al-manākh* the almanac, calendar]

ambidextrous   See RIGHT.

[LL & ML *ambidexter* (ML, double-dealing, fr. LL, dexterous with both hands, fr. L *ambi-* both + *dexter* on the right, skillful) + E *-ous*]

ambrosia   The Greek and Roman gods were in many ways like mortal men, but they had the major distinction of immortality, which came as a result of their eating-habits. Ambrosia, the food of the gods, and nectar, their drink, had the property of preventing death. Greek *ambrosia,* literally 'immortality', is a derivative of *ambrotos,* 'immortal'. The prefix *a-* (sometimes known as the *alpha privative*) indicates negation, as does the related Latin *in-* or *im-*. And *-mbrotos* is close kin to Latin *mortalis.*

Nectar comes from Greek *nektar,* which may have a similar etymological meaning of 'overcoming death', if it is derived from the Greek root *nek-* 'death'. This root is reflected in several English words of classical derivation, such as *necrosis* and *necrophilia.* But the origin of the Greek term is uncertain.

The name *ambrosia* has been given to many things whose taste or smell is especially pleasing. The ancient Greeks and the ancient Romans called several aromatic-leaved plants *ambrosia,* but modern botanic use of the name is less appropriate. *Ambrosia* is the scientific name of a genus of plants, the ragweeds, which have neither flavor nor fragrance, nor even beauty, to recommend them.

[L, fr. Gk, lit., immortality, fr. *ambrotos* immortal (fr. *a-* not + — assumed — Gk *mbrotos* mortal — whence Gk *brotos* mortal) + *-ia;* akin to OE *morth* death, murder, OHG *mord,* L *mort-, mors* death, *mori* to die, Gk *mortos* mortal, Skt *mrta* death]

amethyst   Ancient peoples made innovative use of gemstones. They found precious stones to be not only ornamental but therapeutic as well, a fact that influenced the naming of the *amethyst.* The Greeks believed that this violet-colored variety of quartz could protect its owner from harm and from drunkenness. The Greeks called this stone *amethyst,* which comes from the Greek word *amethystos,* meaning 'not intoxicating'. A story told by Aristotle is that Amethyst was a beautiful nymph who invoked the aid of the goddess Artemis to protect her from Dionysus. Arte-

mis did this by turning her into a precious gem, and Dionysus, in honor
of his love for the nymph, gave the stone its color and quality of preserving
its wearers from the influence of wine. (For another word associated with
Dionysus see BACCHANALIA.)

The color of the amethyst varies in intensity, but is always clear purple
or bluish violet. Throughout the Middle Ages, the stone was greatly admired for its beauty. Eventually it found its way into poetry, becoming a
standard by which earthly beauty was measured. In his "Endymion: A Poetic Romance" (1818) John Keats writes:

> Although, before the crystal heavens darken,
> I watch and dote upon the silver lakes
> Pictur'd in western cloudiness, that takes
> The semblance of gold rocks . . .
> And towers of amethyst,—would I so teaze
> My pleasant days, because I could not mount
> Into these regions?

Another gemstone whose name is rooted in ancient folklore is the sapphire. The name *sapphire* comes from the Sanskrit term *śanipriya*, which
means 'dear to the planet Saturn'. The exact nature of this association of
the sapphire with Saturn is obscure. It may have to do with the star-like
sparkle exhibited by certain sapphires. Or it may have its foundations in
ancient astrology; in modern Western astrology, however, the sapphire is
associated with Venus rather than Saturn.

Over the years, sapphires have served a variety of purposes, many of
them mystical. Like jade the sapphire was believed to cure illness, particularly of the eye. The bright blue stone was associated with calmness and
tranquility of mind and body. Supposedly the person who wore the stone
would be granted peace and happiness, so long as that person led a moral
life. Today the sapphire and the amethyst are valued as ornamental rather
than medicinal gems. See also JADE.

[ME *amatist, ametist,* fr. OF & L; OF *amatiste, ametiste,* fr. L *amethys-*
tus, fr. Gk *amethystos* remedy against drunkenness, amethyst (so considered), fr. *amethystos* not drunk, not intoxicating, fr. a- ²a- + -*methystos*
drunk (fr. *methyskein* to make drunk, fr. *methyein* to be drunk, fr.
methy wine)]

Amish   See CATHOLIC.
[prob. fr. G *amisch,* fr. Jacob *Amman* or *Amen* fl1693 Swiss Mennonite
bishop, the founder of the sect + G -*isch* -ish]

ammonia   The modern names of many chemical elements and compounds have their origins in the obscure lore of the ancient world. In
Egyptian mythology Amen was a god variously represented as a ram with
great horns, as a creature with a ram's head and a human body, or as simply a man—either enthroned or standing. To the Greeks, Amen became
known as Ammon. His chief temple and oracle were at an oasis in the Libyan desert near Memphis. It is said that near this temple a cesspool was lo-

cated, where the urine of camels was collected. For centuries in Egypt camel's urine, soot, and sea salt were heated together to form sal ammoniac, which in its Latin form literally means "salt of Ammon." To designate the gas produced when sal ammoniac is heated with an alkali, the Swedish chemist Torbern Olof Bergman in 1782 coined the New Latin term *ammonia*. In less than two decades *ammonia* entered English.

In Greek mythology Cadmus was the reputed founder of the Greek city of Thebes. His most celebrated exploit was his battle with a man-eating dragon. After slaying the monster, he removed its teeth and sowed some of them in the ground. From these sown teeth sprang up a company of armed men. Cadmus reacted by surreptitiously striking them with stones; the men, suspecting one another, began a mutual slaughter until only five remained. With these five men Cadmus founded his new city of Thebes. The ancient citadel of Thebes was named Cadmea in his honor. It was in this Greek city that the ancients first discovered the substance known to us as zinc oxide. For zinc oxide, or for any ore abounding in zinc, the ancients used the Latin word *cadmia*, after Thebes's legendary founder. It was not until centuries later, in 1817, that the German chemist Friedrich Stromeyer discovered the presence of another metal in a zinc compound, which in his case happened to be zinc carbonate. Stromeyer called this new discovery *cadmium*, the old name for any zinc-rich ore.

Niobe was the daughter of the Lydian king Tantalus in Greek mythology. She is most famous as the proud mother of twelve children who insulted the goddess Leto. For her affront, all of her children were killed. She grieved bitterly, and even after she was turned into a block of marble, a stream of tears continued to flow. Her father, Tantalus, was the subject of an even more famous myth. For his offenses against the gods, he was condemned to perpetual thirst in Hades, even though he was standing chin-deep in water. Whenever he attempted to drink the water, the prize receded just out of reach. Appropriately, the metallic element *tantalum* was named after him because its inability to absorb acid suggested the king's inability to drink. *Tantalite* is a rare mineral of which tantalum is a basic component. When *niobium* was first identified, it was discovered in tantalite, so it was only fitting that the metallic element be named after the daughter of the parched king. See also TANTALIZE.

For other articles on words derived from ancient mythology and legend see VOLCANO.

[NL, fr. L *(sal) ammoniacus* sal ammoniac, lit., salt of Ammon, fr. *ammoniacus* of Ammon, fr. Gk *ammōniakos*, fr. *Ammōn*, an Egyptian deity identified by the Greeks with Zeus, fr. Egypt *Amōn;* fr. its having been prepared near a temple of Ammon in Egypt]

amok   See BERSERK.

[Malay *amok*, fr. *amok*, n., furious attack, charge (as in *mĕngamok* he runs amok, *pĕngamok* one that runs amok)]

ampersand   In the late Middle Ages, spelling, though less rigidly standardized than it is today, was already a subject studied in schools. The usual practice was to spell by syllables rather than taking on the whole word at once. So in the *Promptorium Parvulorum* ("Storeroom for Young Scholars"), an English-Latin dictionary compiled in 1440, English *Spellyng* is rendered by Latin *Sillabicacio* (syllabication). When a single letter formed a word (like *I*) or a syllable (like the first *i*- in *iris*), it was spelled *I per se, I* or in other words *I by itself, I*. The *per se* spellings were used especially for the letters that were themselves words. Because the alphabet was augmented by the sign &, which followed *z*, there were four of these: *A per se, A; I per se, I; O per se, O;* and & *per se, and. A,* as the first letter, had a special position, and *A per se, A* became a figurative expression for a most excellent or distinguished person or thing. Robert Henryson's *Testament of Cresseide* (ca.1475) describes Cresseide as "the floure and A per se of Troie and Grece." *I*'s uniqueness is in its meaning as a word rather than its place in the alphabet. In 1622 James Mabbe wrote: "I only was compleat; I was I per se I; I was like a Rule, without exception." *And per se, and* was not liable to such figurative use, but it did become, in slightly altered and contracted form, the standard name for the character &. Jacob Storey, in George Eliot's *Adam Bede* (1859), who was trying to acquire a rather belated education, expressed his poor opinion of the letter *z:* "It had only been put there to finish off th' alphabet, like, though ampusand would ha' done as well, for what he could see."

The character & is derived from *&*, the ligature of Latin *et* 'and'.

[alter. of *and (&) per se and,* lit., (the character) & by itself (is the word) *and*]

amuse   A couple of our words show a curious sense development from 'delude' to 'entertain'. One of these is *amuse,* which originally meant 'cheat, mislead', a meaning it retained down through the eighteenth century. *Beguile* began life with the same meaning, which remains in its base *guile,* but it has added the sense 'charm, entertain', a meaning which now predominates exclusively in the adjective *beguiling. Divert,* which in its adjectival form likewise means only 'amusing, entertaining', originally had only meanings like 'avert, deflect, deviate'. While never meaning precisely 'cheat', it could still have a rather negative implication in context, as when someone was diverted from his true aim. The Latin etymon, *divertere,* etymologically 'to turn away', typically meant 'to divorce'. In all three instances, the evolution of the new sense 'entertain' arose from the image of leading someone away from his or her cares.

Delude, or rather its Latin source *deludere,* almost illustrates the opposite evolution, since it means 'deceive, dupe' yet is etymologically a derivative of *ludere* 'to play', via the prefix *de-* 'away from'. Here the deciding implication was evidently that of leading someone away from his or her best interests, rather than cares.

[MF *amuser* to cause to waste time, amuse, bemuse, deceive, fr. OF, fr. *a-* (fr. L *ad-*) + *muser* to muse]

anacreontic   See LYRIC.

[L *Anacreonticus,* adj., fr. *Anacreont-, Anacreon* †*ab*488 B.C. Greek poet noted for his gay songs of love and drinking (fr. Gk *Anakreont-*, *Anakreōn*) + L *-icus* -ic]

anarchy   See HIERARCHY.
[ML *anarchia*, fr. Gk, fr. *anarchos* rulerless (fr. *an-* not + *archos* ruler) + *-ia* -y]

anathema   The word *anathema* is of Greek origin, deriving from the verb *anatithenai* 'to set up, dedicate'. *Anathema* was used in the Old Testament originally to mean 'something offered (that is, placed on high in the temples) to God', and in the early use it could have referred to a revered object or an object representing a destruction brought about in the name of the Lord. Such was the use in this passage from Judith (16:22–23, Douay): "And it came to pass after these things, that all the people, after the victory, came to Jerusalem to adore the Lord: and as soon as they were purified, they all offered holocausts, and vows, and their promises. And Judith offered for an anathema of oblivion all the arms of Holofernes, which the people gave her, and the canopy that she had taken away out of his chamber." Here we see that what was offered up as an anathema were the spoils of war, representing the destruction of the enemy Holofernes; *anathema* ultimately came to represent something odious or accursed.

This development is not surprising since *anathema* translates the Hebrew word *herem*, which comes from a verb *haram*, 'to cut off; separate, curse'. The following passage from Deuteronomy (7:26, Douay) exemplifies this use: "Neither shalt thou bring anything of the idol into thy house, lest thou become an anathema, like it. Thou shalt detest it as dung, and shalt utterly abhor it as uncleanness and filth, because it is an anathema."

In the New Testament, St. Paul uses the term in the sense of a curse and the forced exclusion of one from the community of Christians. In the early Church *anathema* was used interchangeably with *excommunication* and was pronounced chiefly against unrepentant heretics. In the sixth century, *anathema* came to mean the severest form of excommunication, in which the person is judged to be "condemned to eternal fire with Satan and his angels and all the reprobate, so long as he will not burst the fetters of the demon, do penance, and satisfy the Church" (Roman Pontifical). All of the church councils since the Council of Nicaea have worded their dogmatic canons to include the sentence "If anyone says . . . let him be anathema."

Among the more famous anathemas were those of 1054, the year of the schism between the Eastern and Western Churches. The pope's legate to Constantinople, Cardinal Humbert, issued an anathema against Patriarch Michael Cerularios, who in retaliation issued a similar one against the cardinal. These mutual anathemas have often been considered the final consummation of the schism. Although this schism has never been healed, in 1965 Pope Paul VI and the ecumenical patriarch Athenagoras I nullified the mutual anathemas of 1054.

In English, the word *anathema* has been and continues to be used in its ecclesiastical sense. By the eighteenth century, however, its use in a weakened sense for 'the denunciation of anything as accursed' is attested. That secular use continues to be common. Joseph W. Scott provided an example in a 1969 magazine article: "Anathema to the university, with its long-standing tradition of humanism, are all the trappings of the military life" (*Trans-Action,* September 1969).

[LL, fr. Gk, anything devoted, anything devoted to evil, curse, fr. *anatithenai* to set up, dedicate, fr. *ana-* up, upward + *tithenai* to place, set]

ancestor   Sound changes that took place when French grew out of Latin have obscured the etymology of *ancestor* for present-day English speakers. From Old French, Middle English borrowed *ancestre,* which in turn is derived from the Late Latin *antecessor,* having much the same meaning as its English descendant. In earlier Latin *antecessor* meant literally 'one who goes before or in front', from *ante-,* 'before', familiar to us in many Modern English words like *antechamber,* plus *cedere,* 'to go'. Thus our ancestors are those who went before us.

Much the same metaphor lies at the root of the English formation *forebear,* literally 'one who was before'. Here the *-bear* is an agent noun formed from the verb *be,* though again the spelling obscures this relation.

[ME *ancestre,* fr. OF, fr. LL *antecessor* predecessor, fr. L, one that goes before, fr. *antecessus* (past part. of *antecedere* to go before, fr. *ante-* ante- + *cedere* to go) + *-or*]

anecdote   Procopius, who died in A.D. 562, was an official and historian at the court of the eastern Roman emperor Justinian at Constantinople. Procopius, who wrote in Greek, left three historical works, one dealing mostly with wars against the Vandals in North Africa and the Ostrogoths in Italy, and a second dealing with the many buildings (including the church of Hagia Sophia) built by Justinian's order. The third work was titled *Anekdota,* meaning 'unpublished things'. *Anekdota* was ultimately derived from Greek *an-* 'not' and *ekdotos* 'published', from *ekdidonai* 'to publish, give out', from *ek-* 'out' and *didonai* 'to give'.

Procopius's unpublished things were published after his death and are often referred to as *Historia Arcana* or *Secret History.* These *anecdota* could not have been published in Procopius's lifetime or it would have been shorter than it was, for the work contains bitter attacks on the emperor Justinian and his wife, Theodora, as well as on many other noted officials in Constantinople. Some of these attacks are in the form of juicy bits of scandalous gossip. From Procopius, for instance, we learn that the Empress Theodora was the daughter of a bearkeeper in the Constantinople circus and had been an actress and a courtesan before she attracted the attention of Justinian. It is easy to understand why Procopius dared not publish it in his lifetime and just as easy to understand why his title became a familiar word after the work was published.

English did not borrow the word until the second half of the seventeenth century, first as the Medieval Latin form of Procopius's title, *anecdota,* and then as *anecdotes* from the French. The first meaning in English was 'unpublished secret history'—straight from Procopius.

By the eighteenth century a singular use had developed that is our familiar one today: 'a short account of some amusing or biographical incident'. Boswell tells us that Samuel Johnson did not approve this meaning, considering it an affectation imported from French. Johnson did, however, show the sense in his dictionary (1755). It appears that the meaning actually developed earlier in English than it did in French.

[F & Gk; F, fr. Gk *anekdotos* unpublished, fr. *an-* + *ekdotos* given out, fr. *ekdidonai* to give out, publish, fr. *ek-* out, out of + *didonai* to give]

animal Latin *anima* means 'breath' or 'soul' and the derived adjectival form *animalis* means 'having breath or soul'. Though plants may be said to breathe insofar as they take in certain gases from the atmosphere and release others, this is not a process detectable to the naked eye. Thus the noun *animal*, derived from *animalis*, is used to designate those living beings that breathe perceptibly. The English adjective *animate*, 'alive, possessing life', is derived from the Latin verb *animare*, 'to quicken, endow with breath or soul'. Another distinguishing characteristic of animals is the capacity for spontaneous movement. When cartoons are filmed in such a way that lifelike movement is produced we say that they are *animated*, though they are brought to life only metaphorically. The ability of animals to move about also accounts for the senses of *quick* relating to motion. The original sense of *quick* is 'alive', familiar today in the phrase "the quick and the dead." Derived from Old English *cwicu*, *quick* is related to Latin *vivus*, 'alive', and Greek *zōē*, 'life'.

[L, fr. *animale*, neut. of *animalis* animate, fr. *anima* breath, soul + *-alis* -al]

animate See ANIMAL.
[ME *animat*, fr. L *animatus*, past part. of *animare* to quicken, enliven, endow with breath or soul, fr. *anima* breath, soul; akin to OE *ōthian*, *ēthian* to breathe, OFris *omma* breath, ON *önd*, gen. *andar* breath, life, soul, Goth *uzanan* to breathe one's last, expire, L *animus* soul, mind, Gk *anemos* breath, wind, Skt *aniti* he breathes]

antagonism See AGONY.
[F *antagonisme*, fr. LGk *antagōnisma*, fr. Gk *antagōnizesthai* to contend with, fr. *anti-* ¹anti- + *agōnizesthai* to struggle, fr. *agōn* contest]

antagonist See AGONY.
[LL *antagonista*, fr. Gk *antagōnistēs*, fr. *antagōnizesthai* to contend with, fr. *anti-* ¹anti- + *agōnizesthai* to struggle, fr. *agōn* contest]

antagonize See AGONY.
[Gk *antagōnizesthai*, fr. *anti-* ¹anti- + *agōnizesthai* to struggle, fr. *agōn* contest]

antenna *Antenna* can be traced back to Latin, where the word meant 'sail yard', a sail yard being a long spar tapered toward the ends to support and spread the head of a sail on a sailing vessel. The Greek word for a sail yard was *keraia*, but 'sail yard' was only the secondary meaning of this word; the primary meaning was 'horn'. Aristotle, in his *History of Animals*, used *keraiai* for the "horns" or feelers of insects, probably because of their resemblance to the horns of some larger animals. In a Latin translation of Aristotle's work made during the Renaissance, the word *antennae* appears for the Greek *keraiai*.

Entomologists continued using the word *antennae* for those feelers, and in the nineteenth century Charles Darwin borrowed the term to refer to the long slender parts of the male flower of certain orchids. By the twentieth century nonbiological senses had appeared, as when Ezra Pound writes, "My soul's antennae are prey to such perturbations." With the invention of radio, radar, and television, new kinds of antennas were devised, many of which do not even remotely resemble the sail yards of ancient vessels or the antennae of insects. These popular uses of *antenna* have also led to the application of the usual English plural noun suffix *-s* as an alternative to the traditional Latin ending *-ae*.

[ML, fr. L *antemna, antenna* sail yard]

anthem   The Old English *antefn* was derived from the Late Latin *antiphona*, which in turn was derived ultimately from the Greek *antiphōnos*. Compounded from *anti*, 'over' or 'against', and *phōnē*, 'sound' or 'voice', *antiphōnos* meant 'responsive'. *Antefn* evolved by stages into our modern word *anthem*. The original sense of the word, current from the beginning through the fourteenth century, was the same as the current sense of *antiphon:* 'a line or verse sung as a response during a religious service'. The English word *antiphon* is actually a doublet of *anthem*. *Antiphon* was derived from the Greek *antiphōnos*, of course, but independently of *anthem* and not until about five hundred years later. Today *antiphon* is the usual term for the sung liturgical response, while *anthem* has developed other meanings.

The early anthems were unaccompanied choral compositions. The fifteenth century witnessed the development of the verse anthem, a composition in which verses for soloists and instrumental accompaniment (normally the organ) alternated with passages for a full choir. Both the "full anthem" and the verse anthem incorporated antiphony, that is, the use of two groups (as two separated choirs) echoing or singing against each other. During the sixteenth century, when English replaced Latin as the principal language of the Anglican Church, an English text became integral to an anthem. By the seventeenth century, the established meaning of *anthem* was a musical composition designed to be sung by a choir, generally for liturgical performance, and having an English text taken from the Bible, a prayer book, or a work of religious or moral character. Anthems were most often used as optional conclusions to the service of matins or evensong.

In the early nineteenth century *anthem* became the term of choice for a composition that serves as the musical symbol of a nation. Taking the form of anything from a hymn to a march or fanfare, an anthem is the musical equivalent of a nation's flag or motto. The oldest national anthem is Great Britain's "God Save the King," which is actually a hymn. (In fact, in most languages the term used to refer to an official patriotic song is the word most closely corresponding to *hymn* in English.) Although "God Save the King" is known to have been performed as early as 1745, it is not known to have been referred to as the "National Anthem" or "Royal Anthem" until the following century. The stately rhythms of "God Save the King" served as a model for many other national anthems, some countries doing no more than adding their own lyrics to the hymn's music. It may be that hymnlike patriotic songs became known as anthems because they were in typical circumstances sung chorally and at the conclusion of solemn occasions. Today an anthem is any inspirational musical composition that serves to symbolize or identify a nation, a group, an individual, or a cause.

[alter. of ME *antem, antefn,* fr. OE *antefn,* fr. LL *antiphona, antefana,* fr. LGk *antiphōna,* pl. of *antiphōnon,* fr. Gk, neut. of *antiphōnos* concordant, responsive, fr. *anti-* ¹anti- + *-phōnos* (fr. *phōnē* sound, voice)]

antic Grotesques, the fantastic mural paintings found in the ruins of ancient Roman buildings, were, by reason of their age, *antichi,* 'ancient things', to the Italian descendants of the Romans. A painting of the kind that Italians called a *grottesca* was usually an *antike* or *anticke* (from Italian *antico*) in English. Edward Hall's *Chronicle* (1548) describes "a fountayne, ingrayled with anticke woorkes." Sir Henry Wotton, in *The Elements of Architecture* (1624), discussed "*Grotesca* (as the Italians) or Antique worke (as we call it)." Very early any bizarre gesture or strange behavior reminiscent of the ancient Roman paintings became in English an *antic.* In fact, the earliest attested English antic was not a fantastic work of art. Simon Fish, in his pamphlet "Supplication for the Beggars" (1529), wrote of Sir Thomas More: "In sothe it maketh me to laugh to see yᵉ mery Antiques of M. More." See also GROTESQUE.

[It *antico* ancient thing or person, fr. *antico,* adj., fr. L *antiquus,* fr. *ante* before]

antiphon See ANTHEM.
[LL *antiphona*]

anxiety See STRAITEN.
[L *anxietas,* fr. *anxius* (fr. *angere* to strangle, distress) + *-tas* -ty]

Apache See INDIAN.
[Sp, prob. fr. Zuñi *Apachu,* lit., enemy]

apatosaurus See BRONTOSAURUS.
[NL, fr. *apato-* (fr. Gk *apatē*) + *-saurus*]

aphaeresis *Aphaeresis* (\ə-ˈfer-ə-səs\; also spelled *apheresis*) refers to the shortening of a word by dropping an initial sound or sounds, especially an unstressed syllable, as when *lone* was formed from earlier *alone,* or *fence* from *defence. Aphaeresis* itself is formed from Greek roots meaning literally 'take away' (the same root meaning 'take' appears in the makeup of our word *heresy*). Terminology in this area is not uniform, but useful distinctions include the use of the term *aphesis* (\'af-ə-səs\) for the variety of aphaeresis in which the omitted segment is a single vowel, as for *lone,* or *cute* (from *acute*), and the use of *fore-clipping* to cover all cases in which something is omitted from the front of a word, including particular cases in which an accented syllable is dropped. Thus *coon* (from *raccoon*) would show *aphaeresis,* while *gater* (from *alligator*) would show *fore-clipping,* since here two syllables have been omitted, one of which bore the main stress.

Aphaeresis has given us a number of new words, like *drawing-room* (from *withdrawing-room*), *fend* (from *defend;* whence *fender*), *sport* (from *disport*), and *stain* (from *distain*). A number are aphetic in the narrow sense: *pert* (from now obsolete *apert,* going back ultimately to Latin *apertus* 'open'), *peal* (from *appeal*), *mend* (from *amend*), *fray* (from *affray*), the verb *ply* (from *apply*), the adjective *live* (from *alive*), *spy* (from *espy*), and *tend* (from both *attend* and *intend*). In the above cases, significant semantic development followed the aphaeresis, so that one does not normally connect in one's mind the shortened and the original longer forms. Occasionally an aphetic and a non-aphetic form live on side by side with little semantic differentiation, as for instance *special* and *especial.*

[LL, fr. Gk *aphairesis,* lit., taking off, fr. *aphairein* to take away (fr. *apo-* + *hairein* to take) + *-sis*]

aphesis   See APHAERESIS.

aphrodisiac   See VOLCANO.
[Gk *aphrodisiakos* sexual, fr. *aphrodisia,* pl., sexual pleasures, fr. neut. pl. of *aphrodisios* of Aphrodite, fr. *Aphroditē* Aphrodite, Greek goddess of love]

apocope   See SHORTENED FORMS.
[LL, fr. Gk *apokopē,* lit., cutting off, fr. *apokoptein* to cut off, fr. *apo-* + *koptein* to strike, cut off]

apocrypha   Etymologically, *apocrypha* is the neuter plural form of the Late Latin adjective *apocryphus,* meaning 'secret' and 'uncanonical'. Latin took the word from the Greek *apokryphos,* meaning 'hidden', which was a derivative of the verb *apokryptein* 'to hide away'. The root verb *kryptein* 'to hide' is also the source of the English words *crypt* and *cryptic,* and the combining form *crypt-, crypto-.*

The term *apocrypha* was used in reference to scriptural writings which were "hidden" from the general public. Some books were considered so important and precious that only an esoteric circle of believers was allowed access to them. Other books were hidden not because they were too good but because they were not good enough, that is, their authenticity was in doubt or they were heretical. In the fourth century, St. Jerome, who produced the Vulgate version of the Bible, used the term *apocrypha* in a different sense to designate those books and parts of books that were contained in the Septuagint (Greek) Bible but were not part of the Hebrew Bible. These included the following books: 1 & 2 Esdras (2 Esdras was not included in the Septuagint, however), Tobit, Judith, Wisdom of Solomon, Ecclesiasticus, Baruch, 1 & 2 Maccabees, and certain additions to Esther and Daniel. Their designation as *apocrypha,* however, was rejected by the Church, which accepted them as Holy Scripture.

In 1520 the German Protestant theologian Karlstadt sided with St. Jerome in designating these books as *apocrypha.* In Martin Luther's 1534 German version of the Bible, these books were not included in the Old Testament but were collected in a supplement with the heading "Apocrypha; that is, books which, although not estimated equal to the Holy Scriptures, are yet useful and good to read." Sixteenth-century English translations of the Bible followed Luther's example in including a separate Apocrypha section, as did the King James Version in 1611. The Puritans, however, objected strongly to the inclusion of these writings at all. In the Catholic Bible these works have continued to be an integral part of the Old Testament, although the Council of Trent (1545–63) officially designated them as "deuterocanonical," that is, constituting a second canon of equal authority.

When the adjective *apocryphal* was first used in English, around 1590, it described a writing or story that was 'of doubtful authenticity, spurious, or false'. By 1615 it was being applied, often capitalized, to the scriptural writings called the Apocrypha.

[ML, fr. LL, neut. pl. of *apocryphus* secret, uncanonical (said of writings not to be read to the congregation), fr. LGk *apokryphos,* fr. Gk, hidden, fr. *apokryptein* to hide away, fr. *apo-* away from + *kryptein* to hide]

apothecary See BOUTIQUE.
[ME *apotecarie,* fr. ML *apothecarius,* fr. LL, shopkeeper, warehouseman, fr. L *apotheca* warehouse (fr. Gk *apothēkē,* fr. *apotithenai* to put away, fr. *apo-* + *tithenai* to put, place) + *-arius* -ary]

appease See PAY.
[ME *appesen, apesen,* fr. OF *apaisier,* fr. *a-* (fr. L *ad-* to, at) + *-paisier,* fr. *pais* peace, fr. L *pac-, pax* peace]

applaud See PLAUDIT.
[MF or L; MF *applaudir,* fr. L *applaudere,* fr. *ad-* + *plaudere* to beat, clap, applaud]

apricot The *apricot* is native to China. It was probably late in the first century B.C. that the tree was introduced to the Mediterranean region. Whatever the route by which the tree came to the West, it could hardly be more circuitous than that by which *apricot* came to be its English name. The early Greek and Latin names of the tree, *Armeniakon* and *Armeniaca,* reflect the belief that the apricot had come from Armenia. (Even today the tree's scientific name is *Prunus armeniaca.*) Later the apricot was called *praecoquum,* 'early ripening', in Latin because it ripens earlier than the similar peach. In the first century A.D. the Greek physician Dioscorides mentioned *praecocia* as the Latin name for what the Greeks called *Armeniaka,* 'apricots'. The Latin word was borrowed into Greek as *praikokion.* Arabic *birqūq,* or *barqūq,* probably comes from this Greek word.

To the Arabic word (with the article *al-*) Europe owes its names for the apricot. *Al-birqūq,* or *al-barqūq,* became Spanish *albaricoque,* Portuguese *albricoque,* and Catalan *albercoc* or *abercoc.* From the Catalan word came Italian *albiococca,* French *abricot,* and probably English *abrecock,* the early form of *apricot.* The *t* that ends the present English word comes from the influence of the French *abricot.* The replacement of *b* by *p* is probably the result of a popular (and false) etymology. This etymological explanation stems from a long medieval tradition of trying to find a hidden and usually etymological connection between the form of a word and its meaning, and it is found in a lexicon published in 1617 by John Minsheu, an English teacher of languages. According to Minsheu, the fruit was so named because it was *"in aprico coctus"* (ripened in a sunny place). See also PEACH.

[alter. (prob. influenced by L *apricum* sunny place and MF *abricot* apricot) of earlier *abrecock,* prob. fr. obs. Catal *abercoc,* fr. Ar *al-birqūq* the apricot, fr. *al-* the + *birqūq* apricot, prob. fr. Gk *praikokion,* fr. L *praecoquum,* lit., one that is early ripening, fr. neut. of *praecoquus, praecox* early ripening, fr. *prae-* earlier, before + *-coc-, -cox,* fr. *coquere* to cook, ripen]

April   See JANUARY.

[ME *April, Averil, Aperil,* fr. OF & L; OF *avrill,* fr. L *Aprilis,* prob. of Etruscan origin; akin to Etruscan *apru* April, perh. fr. Gk *Aphrō,* short for *Aphroditē* Greek goddess of love, perh. orig. a goddess of the underworld]

apron   In Middle French a diminutive form of *nape,* 'a cloth or tablecloth', was *naperon,* 'a small cloth or apron'. This word appears in English of the fourteenth century as *napron.* Unfortunately it is often difficult to tell in rapidly spoken English just where the boundary between words falls when *an* precedes a word beginning with a vowel. So within the space of a hundred years *a napron* came to be apprehended as *an apron,* thus accounting for the form of the word today. Nor is this the only word in which such a change took place. The Old English *nædre,* a serpent, is found in translations of the Gospels dating from the tenth century. The Middle English form *nadder* was susceptible to the same sort of confusion as *napron,* and in the fourteenth and fifteenth centuries *a nadder* began to appear as *an adder.* See also AUGER. For the opposite change, from *an* to *a n-,* see NICKNAME.

[ME, alter. (resulting from incorrect division of *a napron*) of *napron,* fr. MF *naperon,* dim. of *nape* cloth, tablecloth, modif. of L *mappa* napkin]

aquavit See WHISKEY.
[Sw, Dan & Norw *akvavit*, fr. ML *aqua vitae*]

aqua vitae See WHISKEY.
[ME *aqua vite*, fr. ML *aqua vitae*, lit., water of life; prob. fr. the use of brandy as a medicine]

argon See XENON.
[Gk, neut. of *argos* lazy, idle, fr. *a-* not + *ergon* work]

argosy During the later medieval and early modern periods, the port of Ragusa in Dalmatia (now Dubrovnik, Yugoslavia) was a rich and powerful city. Ideally situated on an important trade route between Constantinople and Venice, Ragusa developed a vast sea trade, sending its merchant ships out over much of the world, even as far as India and America. *Ragusea* was the Italian word for a Ragusan merchant vessel. In England, too, Ragusan ships were familiar, and English borrowed the word *ragusye* from Italian *ragusea*. In sixteenth-century England, *Ragusa* was often called *Arragosa* or *Aragouse* or the like. This common variation on the city's name accounts for the modern form of our word *argosy*. The resemblance between *Argo*, the ship of Greek myth in which Jason and his companions sailed in quest of the golden fleece, and *argosy* is purely coincidental. The word *argosy* is often used figuratively for anything richly laden like the old Ragusan ships, a 'storehouse'.

[alter. of earlier *ragusye*, fr. It *ragusea* Ragusan vessel, fr. *Ragusa*, port of Dalmatia (now Dubrovnik, Yugoslavia)]

arrive See RIVAL.
[ME *ariven*, fr. OF *ariver*, fr. (assumed) VL *arripare* to land, come to shore, fr. L *ad-* to, at + (assumed) VL *-ripare* (fr. L *ripa* bank, shore)]

assail See SOMERSAULT.
[ME *assailen*, fr. OF *assaillir*, fr. (assumed) VL *assalire*, alter. (influenced by *salire*) of L *assilire*, *adsilire* to leap upon, fr. *ad-* to, at + *salire* to leap]

assassin The Arabic word *ḥashīsh* was originally applied to a number of grasslike plants and in time came to refer specifically to hemp. A product of the hemp plant was used as an intoxicant, and thus from Arabic we get our word *hashish*. The process whereby a general plant word came to be applied to a specific drug is replicated in English, where marijuana came to be known as *weed* or *grass*.

In the twelfth century, Europe learned of a murderous Ismaili sect in Syria, a sect that was part of the Shiite branch of Islam. Whether this sect regularly abused hashish is not known for certain; the colorful tales that are told about its members being held in thrall by visions of Paradise conjured up in a drug-induced trance or psyching themselves up for berserk attacks by smoking it are probably untrue. But it is true that they were

known as 'hashish-takers' (Arabic *ḥashīshī* or *ḥashshāsh*) by their fellow
Syrians. From one of these words or from their plurals with the ending *-in,*
the Romance languages acquired their words for the sect: French *assassin,*
Spanish *asesino,* and so forth. In all of these languages, the resulting term
came to be applied to murderers irrespective of religious or Eastern connotations. English borrowed its word *assassin,* probably from Middle
French, in the fourteenth century, when it first appeared (in the singular)
in the form *hassassis,* and later settled into the spelling *assassin* which had
also finally prevailed in French.

[ML *assassinus* or MF *hassassis,* from Ar *ḥashīshī* or its pl. *ḥashīshīyīn*
or Ar *ḥashshāshīn,* pl. of *ḥashshāsh* hashish abuser, fr. *ḥashīsh* grass,
hemp, hashish]

assault See SOMERSAULT.
[ME *assaut,* fr. OF *asaut, assaut,* fr. (assumed) VL *assaltus,* fr. *assaltus,*
past part. of *assalire* to assail]

assay See NOVEL.
[ME, fr. ONF *assai,* alter. (influenced by *a* to, fr. L *ad*) of OF *essai,* fr.
LL *exagium* act of weighing, weight, balance, fr. L *ex- + -agium,* fr.
agere to do, drive; influenced by L *exigere* to weigh, test, drive out]

assimilation *Assimilation* is the process whereby a sound becomes
more similar to a neighboring sound, typically an adjacent one. Thus the
prefix *in-* 'not', as in *inapplicable,* becomes *im-* in *immovable* (which
shows complete assimilation of the *n* to the *m* of *movable*). In *improbable*
assimilation of the *n* to the *p* of *probable* is partial; both *m* and *p* are bilabial sounds, involving closure made with the lips, whereas *n* involves closure
made between the tongue and the ridge behind the teeth. We can illustrate the process with the word *assimilate* itself: it is derived from the
Latin *ad-* 'to, towards' plus *similis* 'similar', and the *d* has assimilated to
the following *s.* (For the connoisseur, even *similis* is the product of assimilation: the original historically predicted form for Latin would have been
*semilis.)

The opposite of assimilation is *dissimilation,* where the difficulty of ar-
ticulating identical sounds in close succession causes one of them to
change to something different. Dissimilation is more circumscribed in its
action. A typical case in English would involve one of a pair of *r*'s changing
to *l;* for an example see PILGRIM.

Another phonetic process conditioned by contiguity of sounds is *epenthesis.* This is the insertion of a sound into a word to break up an awkward
consonant cluster or to provide a transitional sound between contiguous
consonants. The former function is seen in the occasional two-syllable pronunciation of *film* as \'fil-əm\. A bilabial transition sound *b* has often in the
history of English words been inserted between a bilabial *m* and a following liquid (*l* or *r*): thus *tremble* shows an epenthetic *b,* as against the more
original state of affairs that we may still see in *tremulous. Assemble* like-

wise shows an epenthetic *b:* the word is actually a doublet of *assimilate.*
See also DOUBLETS.

assumed   Etymological comparisons seem sometimes far-fetched: the
ped- of *pedal* is declared to be akin to *foot,* though the forms show no
sound in common. A cynic once quipped that etymology was the science
in which the vowels count for nothing and the consonants for very little.
The skeptical will be reassured upon learning that the sound correspon-
dences that are allowed to count as etymologically valid are in principle
regular and not arbitrary. As regards the above example, for instance, a
Latin *p- regularly* corresponds to English *f-* when the words are related
by common Indo-European ancestry rather than borrowing: for instances
compare Latin *piscis* with its English synonym *fish* and Latin *porcus* 'pig'
with English *farrow* 'young pig'. But skeptics may again feel that etymologists are playing tennis with the net down when they encounter etymologies like the following for the verb *chase,* which we print here in the
somewhat abbreviated form in which it appears in Webster's Ninth New
Collegiate Dictionary:

[ME *chasen,* fr. MF *chasser,* fr. (assumed) VL *captiare*—more at CATCH]

This says *chase* comes from the Middle English verb (here cited in its infinitive form) *chasen,* which was borrowed from a Middle French verb whose
infinitive form was *chasser,* which derives from a Vulgar Latin infinitive
captiare which we find nowhere written down but which we "assume" to
have existed in spoken Latin.

The reader may by now be prepared to accept that a phonetic bridge
of well-understood historical sound changes could be built from *captiare*
to *chasser;* a consideration even of such English doublets as *canticle* (borrowed from Latin) and *chant* (borrowed from French) will give a glimmer-
ing of the regularities involved. But what use is the bridge if the yonder
shore, here *captiare,* is merely "assumed"?

A look at the related entry for *catch,* to which reference is made in the
etymology at *chase,* provides some reassurance:

[ME *cacchen,* fr. ONF *cachier* to hunt, fr. (assumed) VL *captiare,* alter.
of L *captare* to chase, fr. *captus,* pp. of *capere* to take—more at HEAVE]

(ONF means Old North French; in this dialect, Latin *ca-* remained *ca-*
rather than changing to *cha-* as it did in Old French.) The existence of *cap-*
tare is quite certain, and an alteration of this to *captiare* seems indeed less
violent than the further evolution of the latter to French *chasser.* But why
posit a *captiare* at all—why not simply derive *chasser* from *captare?*

The answer is that the same roster of attested regular historical sound
changes which cause us not to blink an eye when a Latin *p* corresponds
to English *f* or Latin *ca-* becomes French *cha-* forbids us to derive, directly
from *captare,* either French *chasser* (and its earliest Old French form *cha-*
cier) or the other Romance cognates such as Spanish *cazar* or Italian *cac-*
ciare. For *captare* actually did leave descendants in the Romance languages, of regularly predictable form; for example, Italian *cattare* 'to obtain' and Spanish *catar* 'to watch'. To explain the medial consonants in

cacciare and *cazar* and the rest, we need to assume that they were palatal-
ized by the influence of an immediately following palatal vowel, namely
\i\. And here, the assumed form *captiare* does the trick. Now, a change
from *captare* to *captiare* is not a regular sound change within Latin, but
it is the kind of morphological tinkering of which we possess numerous
other Latin examples. And our confidence in the existence, albeit not directly recorded, of *captiare* is strengthened by the recorded existence of
captiosus 'preoccupied with hunting', found in written Latin of the sixth
century A.D., and *captia* 'the hunt', attested in the twelfth.

A standard term for such "assumed" forms is *reconstructed*, since often
we in effect construct them out of comparisons with attested forms in the
daughter languages (such as the Romance languages, daughters of Latin,
or the Indo-European languages, daughters of the reconstructed language
Proto-Indo-European). Quite commonly an asterisk is placed beside such
reconstructed forms to alert the reader that they are not actually attested,
thus **captiare*.

aster   See DISASTER.
[NL, fr. L, aster, fr. Gk *aster-, astēr* star, aster]

astrology   See DISASTER.
[ME *astrologie* astronomy, applied astronomy, fr. MF, fr. L *astrologia* astronomy, fr. Gk, fr. *astrologos* astronomer, fr. *astr-* (fr. *astron* star) +
logos speech, discourse]

atheist   See AGNOSTIC.
[MF *athéiste*, fr. *athée* (fr. Gk *atheos* godless, not believing in the existence of gods, fr. *a-* not + *theos* god) + *-iste* -ist]

atlas   *Atlas* was one of the Titans or giants of Greek mythology, whose
rule of the world in an early age was overthrown by Zeus in a mighty battle. Atlas was believed to be responsible for holding up the sky, a task
which he tried unsuccessfully to have Hercules assume. Thus in the sixteenth century the name *Atlas* was used in English to mean someone who
bears a heavy burden. In his published collection of maps, the sixteenth-
century Flemish cartographer Gerhardus Mercator included on the title
page a picture of Atlas supporting the heavens, and he gave the book the
title *Atlas*. Other early collections of maps subsequently included a similar
picture of Atlas and such books came to be called *atlases*. The name of the
Titans has itself contributed to English the adjective *titanic*. For other articles on words derived from mythology and legend see VOLCANO.

[after *Atlas*, a Titan of Greek mythology often represented as bearing
the heavens on his shoulders, fr. L *Atlant-, Atlas*, fr. Gk]

[fr. NL *Atlas*, title of a cartographical work (published in 1595) by Gerhardus Mercator (Gerhard Kremer) †1594 Flemish geographer; prob. fr.
the fact that the title pages of cartographical works of this period often
had a representation of Atlas bearing the heavens]

atonement   The adverbial phrase *at one,* meaning 'in a state of concord, harmony, or peaceful agreement' has been in use since the beginning of the fourteenth century. The noun *onement* was coined in the same century to denote such a state. John Wycliffe used this noun in the 1382 edition of his Bible. It later became commonly used in the phrase *at onement,* as exemplified in the following excerpt from William Watreman's 1555 translation of Boemus's *Fardle of Facions* ('Bundle of Manners and Customs'): "The redempcion, reconciliacion, and at onement of mankinde with God the father." The phrase in time coalesced to *atonement,* first used by Sir Thomas More in his *History of King Richard III* in 1513. Shakespeare, following More's lead, used it in ca. 1592 in his *Richard III:* "Ay madam. He desires to make atonement/Between the Duke of Gloucester and your brothers,/And between them and my Lord Chamberlain."

In sixteenth century theological works, *atonement* began to be used for 'the reconciliation of God and man as effected by the saving and redeeming work of Jesus Christ'. Regarding this usage, the *Catholic Encyclopedia* (1967 edition) states that *atonement* "is the only word of Anglo-Saxon origin that signifies a theological doctrine." *Atonement* appears in William Tyndale's Bible of 1526 and in the King James Bible of 1611. The word is also used in these Bibles in the sense 'reparation for an offense or injury'. The following modern use of this word by C. Day-Lewis (*The Poetic Image,* 1947) reveals its etymology: "the Mariner cannot begin to atone for his crime against love until he feels love again—his *atonement* starts when he feels *at one* with the beautiful water-snakes."

The verb *atone* also derives from the phrase *at one* and was first used around the middle of the sixteenth century. Although this verb does not appear in the Bibles of this period, it was used by Shakespeare, Milton, and Dryden in the sense 'to bring from a state of enmity or opposition to a state of friendliness, toleration, or harmony'. This use has since become archaic. Beginning in the seventeenth century, *atone* was also used in the sense 'to make reparation to; propitiate', as used by John Dryden in his 1697 translation of the *Aeneid:* "with prayers and vows the dryads I atone." This sense is also now archaic. The verb's main use in contemporary English is with the preposition *for* in the sense 'to make reparation or supply satisfaction; expiate'.

[ME *atonen* (fr. *at on*) + *-ment*]

attic   The ancient Greek city-state of Athens included the whole of the *Attic* peninsula, the region called Attica. Typical of the Attic or Athenian style of architecture is the use of pilasters, rectangular columns projecting from, but attached to, the wall. These take the place of the freestanding and usually rounded pillars common in other architectural styles. Occasionally the large columns and entablature that form the facade of a building are surmounted by a similar but smaller decorative structure, whose columns are usually pilasters, rather than pillars. Because this small upper order is in the Attic style, the French named it *attique,* and the English borrowed the name, respelling it according to a common pattern. From its originally specialized sense, *attic* was extended to cover the top story, just under the roof, of any building. So a word that was once associated with an architectural style of elegance and grace has come to designate what is usually no more than a lowly storage area. This *attic* is often a metaphor, as in James Russell Lowell's "Fable for Critics": "Here a gentleman present, who had in his attic/ More pepper than brains, shrieked—The man's a fanatic."

[F *attique*, fr. *attique* Attic, of Attica, fr. L *Atticus*, fr. Gk *Attikos*, fr. *Attikē* (Attica), region of ancient Greece]

attorney   A person calling himself an attorney for another but not licensed to practice law might be thought of as guilty of violating the law. But while the predominant use of the word *attorney* today is that of an "attorney-at-law," meaning 'lawyer', this is not always the case, and this use was not the original use of the word.

Attorney comes, by way of Middle English *attourney*, from Middle French *atorné*, a past participle of *atorner*, meaning 'to direct, appoint'. This derives from Old French *a* 'to' and *torner* 'to turn (in the sense of 'to turn to')'. Thus, in its original use, an attorney was someone you turned to or someone you let handle your affairs for you. The earliest use in English is from the late thirteenth century, and it distinguishes the action of a person acting "in person" or "in his own person" from the work of someone acting for another "by attorney." This use was prominent during Shakespeare's time, and the Bard used it more than once in his plays. In *As You Like It*, (ca. 1599), for example, Shakespeare has Rosalind (disguised as a boy, Ganymede) pretending to be Rosalind, the object of Orlando's love, so that Orlando can practice his wooing:

Ros.   . . . Am I not your Rosalind?
Orl.   I take some joy to say you are, because I would be talking of her.
Ros.   Well, in her person, I say I will not have you.
Orl.   Then, in my own person, I die.
Ros.   No, faith, die by attorney . . . in all this time there was not any man died in his own person . . . in a love cause.

In *Richard III* (ca. 1592), Richard is talking with the mother of the woman he loves and requests that the mother be his advocate or champion with her daughter, that she "be the attorney of my love to her. Plead what I will be, not what I have been. . . ."

This older use has not completely died out; it occasionally appears in modern-day writing:

. . . has received more approving treatment from his biographers, who like other biographers often view themselves as attorneys for their subject —Richard N. Current, *N.Y. Times Book Rev.*, 22 Apr. 1973

But it is now most often encountered in the phrase "power of attorney."

As the body of special professional legal agents became recognized in English law, there developed, beginning in the fourteenth century, the specific use to mean 'attorney-at-law' (one licensed to practice law in the courts). In the U.S. the terms *attorney* and *lawyer* are used interchangeably in this sense. In England, it is more common to talk of *solicitor* (a lawyer who advises clients and represents them in lower courts) and *barrister* (a lawyer qualified to plead in the higher courts).

The word *solicitor* derives ultimately from Latin *sollicitus*, an adjective meaning 'anxious, troubled' (and the origin of our word *solicitous*). From *sollicitus,* Latin derived the verb *sollicitare* with two distinct meanings: 'to disturb, agitate' and 'to entreat'. These two notions made their way into the Middle French verb *soliciter* and thence into the Middle French noun *soliciteur,* meaning both 'a prompter or agent' (in the sense of 'one who instigates or stirs up') and 'an advocate'. From here it was taken into Middle English as *solicitour,* with two senses, the now obsolete 'one who urges, provokes, or instigates' and 'one who conducts, negotiates, or transacts matters on behalf of another'.

Barrister is a purely English formation. In the Middle Ages the legal system in England was still based largely on Roman law. It was Roman law that was taught in the universities. The fundamentals of the growing body of everyday English common law were learned by personal service as the clerk of a judge or other high official in the courts. There existed several "Inns of Chancery" teaching students the knowledge of how to formulate writs and other legal documents presented to the civil courts on behalf of clients. These Inns of Chancery taught the rudiments but not the theory and refinements of the law. As the legal system became more complex, there came a need for a more thorough, practical grounding in the law, and from this need arose the Inns of Court. These four London societies, begun in the thirteenth century, provided extensive practical training to resident students and became the only route to becoming a lawyer capable of pleading a case in the courts. The training at the Inns included not only lectures but practice in conducting cases in mock trials presided over by real judges and established lawyers. In the practice courtrooms, as in the real ones, the judges and presiding officers were separated from the rest of the hall by a railing or barrier known as the *bar*. As students gained experience and advanced standing in their class, they were "called within the bar" and allowed to help preside over the mock trials. These students became known as *barristers* (a word formed from *bar* and the suffix *-ster*). (Today the legal profession as a whole is known as "the bar.") In England today, the distinction still exists between solicitors, who handle most of the direct client advising, trial preparation, and representation of clients in lower courts, and barristers, who represent the solicitor's clients in higher courts.

[ME *attourney,* fr. MF *atorné,* past part. of *atorner* to direct, dispose, attorn, fr. OF, fr. *a* to (fr. L *ad*) + *torner* to turn]

auger   Though the tool is not actually used to form what many call their belly button, the etymologies of *auger* and *navel* might seem to imply such a possibility. The Old English *nafela*, 'navel', is closely related to Old English *nafu,* 'nave'. The *nave* is the central part of a wheel from which the spokes radiate and through which a hole is pierced for the axle. (This is not the same word as the *nave* of a church.) The *navel* is the mark or depression more or less in the hub or center of a person's abdomen. In Old English a compound was formed from *nafu* plus *gār*, 'spear' (which is also the source of the first element of *garfish*, the name of various fishes with elongate bodies and long, narrow jaws). Thus *nafogār* was the 'nave spear', the tool used to pierce the hole in the hub or nave of a wheel. In Middle English the form *navegar* came to be spelled *nauger*, and finally in the fifteenth century *a nauger* began to be divided as *an auger*, giving the modern name of a tool used for boring holes. See also APRON, NICKNAME.

[ME, alter. (resulting from incorrect division of *a nauger*) of *nauger, navegar*, fr. OE *nafogār* (akin to OHG *nabugēr*, OS *nabugēr*, ON *nafarr*), fr. *nafu* nave (of a wheel) + *gār* spear]

August   See JANUARY.
[ME, fr. OE, fr. L *Augustus*, after Augustus Caesar †A.D.14 1st Roman emperor]

aunt   See COUSIN.
[ME *aunte*, fr. OF *ante*, fr. L *amita* father's sister]

auspices   See OSTRICH.
[pl. of *auspice*, fr. L *auspicium*, fr. *auspic-*, *auspex* bird seer, augur, fr. *au-* (fr. *avis* bird) + *-spic-*, *-spex* (fr. *spicere, specere* to look)]

autumn   In 1596 Edmund Spenser's *Faerie Queen* saluted the seasons through personification, portraying each season as a muse all dressed up in appropriate attire. Spenser first described how "lusty Spring is all dight [dressed] in leaves of flowres/That freshly budded and new bloosmes did beare/In which a thousand birds had built their bowers," fitting imagery for a season long associated with the bursting forth of new life. He continues:

> Then came the jolly Sommer, being dight
> In a thin silken cassock coloured greene,
> That was unlyned all, to be more light. . . .
>
> Then came the Autumne, all in yellow clad,
> As though he joyed in his plentious store,
> Laden with fruits that made him laugh, full
>   glad
> That he had banisht hunger, which to-fore
> Had by the belly oft him pinched sore. . . .
>
> Lastly came Winter, cloathed all in frize,
> Chattering his teeth for cold that did him
>   chill,
> Whil'st on his hoary beard, his breath did
>   freese. . . .

We still regard the seasons in much the same way, associating spring with new life, summer with airiness, autumn with harvest, and winter with bitter cold.

Many languages get their names for the seasons from characteristics of each season that have become symbolic of that particular time of the year. Our use of the word *spring* to describe the first season of the year derives from the sense of the noun *spring* which means a rising or springing into existence. The usual German word for this season, *Lenz,* is akin to our word *Lent,* which denotes the days of penitance and fasting observed by certain religions at this time of year.

Our word *summer* is very similar to the German word for this season, *Sommer.* Both words are related to the Sanskrit term *samā,* which means, aptly enough, 'season' or 'year'. The words *summer* and *winter* are still used occasionally to mean 'year' in statements like "She is a girl of seventeen summers" and "It happened ten winters ago."

Spenser's autumn muse wore a wreath decorated "With eares of corne of every sort," and he held a sickle for reaping "ripened fruits the which the earth had yold [yielded]." It seems that we have always regarded autumn as the season of plenty, during which all that has grown under the guiding hand of nature during the warm spring and summer months is finally ripe and ready for eating.

The German word for this season is *Herbst,* which is related to the English word *harvest* by way of Old English *hærfest.* Autumn was once even called *harvest* in English, and we still use this term to denote the season in which agricultural products are gathered. Our word *autumn* comes from Latin *autumnus,* whereas its synonym *fall* is native. We do in fact call the autumn season *fall* because of our association of autumn with the falling of the leaves. As far back as 1545, the seasons of the year were described as "Spring tyme, Somer, faule of the leafe, and winter." By the early eighteenth century, the phrase 'fall of the leafe' was replaced by the simpler 'fall', and ever since, we have used this word as a more informal means of describing the season in which the leaves fall from the trees. By the end of the sixteenth century, this term had assumed its own place in the annals of poetic discourse. In 1599 Sir Walter Raleigh wrote in a poem titled "Reply to Marlowe": "A honey tongue, a heart of gall/Is fancies spring, but sorrows fall."

Winter was represented by Spenser as a frigid season in which a man's breath freezes and sticks to his beard. The word is Germanic, of uncertain ulterior etymology—possibly deriving from an Indo-European root meaning 'wet' or from one meaning 'white'. So strong is the association between winter and hibernation that the term has come to denote a period of inactivity or decay, as epitomized by Shakespeare's famous phrase "the Winter of our Discontent. . . ."

[ME *autumpne,* fr. L *autumnus*]

average   One of the changes that signaled the reemergence of Europe from the Dark Ages was the burgeoning anew of European (and chiefly Italian) trade with the Levant. This important facet of Western history finds a modest reflection in the early history of this word. *Average* came into English from Middle French *avarie*, a derivative (by way of Italian) of Arabic *'awārīyah*, 'damaged merchandise'. French *avarie* originally meant damage sustained by a ship or its cargo. It came, by transference, to mean the expense of such damage, and later included other maritime expenses—especially the charges levied by a port on incoming ships. When the English borrowed the French word, they altered it to conform to the appearance of such English words as *pilotage* and *towage*. English *average* was first used in the later French sense of 'port charges', but later also in the sense of 'damage expenses'. When a ship or its cargo was damaged at sea, the owners (or insurers) of both ship and cargo had to share the expense or average. An average-adjuster determined an equitable division of costs among the parties held accountable. In this way an average became any equal distribution or division, like the determination of an arithmetic mean. Soon the arithmetic mean itself was called an average. Now the word may be applied to any mean or middle value or level.

[modif. (influenced by E -*age*) of MF *avarie* damage to ship or cargo, port dues, fr. OIt *avaria* damage to ship or cargo, fr. Ar *'awārīyah* damaged merchandise, fr. *'awār* defect, damage, fr. *'ār* to harm]

aviary See OSTRICH.
[L *aviarium*, fr. *avis* bird + -*arium;* akin to Gk *aetos* eagle, Skt *vi* bird]

avoirdupois See OUNCE.
[alter. (influenced by F *du* of the) of earlier *averdepois, avoir de pois,* fr. ME *avoir de pois, aver de peis* goods sold by weight, fr. OF, lit., goods of weight, fr. *aver* property, goods + *de* of (fr. L *de* from) + *pois, peis* weight]

awkward See LEFT.
[ME *awkeward* in the wrong direction, upside down, fr. *awke* turned the wrong way, left-handed (fr. ON *öfugr* turned the wrong way) + -*ward*]

aye-aye See PIGEON.
[F, fr. Malagasy *aiay,* of imit. origin]

azimuth See LUTE, ZENITH.
[ME *azimut, azimuth,* fr. (assumed) ML, fr. Ar *as-sumūt* the azimuth, pl. of *as-samt* the way, direction]

Aztec See INDIAN.
[Sp *azteca,* fr. Nahuatl, pl. of *aztecatl,* fr. *Aztlan, Aztatlan,* their legendary place of origin, lit., near the cranes (fr. *azta* — pl. of *aztatl* crane — + *tlan* near) + -*tecatl* (suffix denoting origin)]

B

Babbitt Since the 1920s *Babbitt* and *Babbittry* have endured as words
that encapsulate all of the values, attitudes, and mores of the complacent
American middle class. Both derive from the name of George F. Babbitt,
the protagonist of *Babbitt*, a satirical novel published by Sinclair Lewis in
1922. George Babbitt epitomizes the unimaginative and self-important
businessmen found in the provincial cities and towns of Middle America.
A real estate agent by profession and a conformist by nature, Babbitt is a
compulsive booster and joiner in his native Zenith, "The Zip City." Despite his evident prosperity and status in the community, he remains
vaguely dissatisfied. Although he makes tentative attempts at rebellion
through brief encounters with artists, bohemians, and socialists and by
having an extramarital liaison, Babbitt finds his need for social acceptance
greater than his desire for escape.

The impact of Lewis's book was immediate and great. Lewis had identified an enduring American type and had painted an incisive portrait. Almost overnight the word *Babbitt* was being used allusively, and soon it
became a generic synonym for an American conformist philistine. By the
end of 1922 a reviewer for the *Detroit Saturday Night Monthly Review
of Books* was taking notice of the *Babbitt* boom, observing that the word
had become the preferred term for "mentally-standardized businessmen
who are as short on original ideas as they are long on pep of the frothy and
hip-hip-hooray variety."

From the beginning *Babbitt* had definitely pejorative connotations. A
1925 issue of *Bookman* advised: "Still there always is something interesting everywhere, even in a Middle West Main Street town, if you can escape the Babbitts and find it." And in that same year *Harper's* promised
its readers that the periodical would be ". . . edited—as always—not for
Babbitts or morons or faddists but for the cultured minority." The pejorative use of the word *Babbitt* is not entirely in keeping with the spirit of
the book. In his novel Lewis paints a somewhat sympathetic portrait of the
protagonist. George Babbitt attempts to transcend his stifling, orthodox
values but is thwarted by his dread of social ostracism. He does encourage
his son to rebel, however.

Babbitt and *Babbittry* were not the only words derived from Lewis's
novel. The impact of the book was such that it inspired a whole host of
short-lived derivative words. Things relating to the lifestyle led by real-life
Babbitts were dubbed *Babbittical*. If one had joined the *Babbittian* class,
one had *Babbittized* oneself. Female Babbitts were *Babbittesses* and their

offspring were *Babbittinas,* and the whole family lived in the *Babbitt warrens* of *Babbittville.*

[after George F. *Babbitt,* stereotype Am. businessman portrayed in the novel *Babbitt* (1922) by Sinclair Lewis †1951 Am. novelist]

bacchanalia   We are prone, in our parochialism, to imagine that everything in the modern world is grander or more extreme than anything the past can offer. We assume that the modern-day drunken feasts or orgies that we call *bacchanalia* reveal human behavior at its wildest. In truth, our contemporary bacchanalia, such as Mardi Gras parades and fraternity parties, may be pallid imitations of the originals.

Bacchanalia derives from *Bacchus,* the epithet of the Greek god Dionysus and the name by which the god was known to the Romans. Dionysus was the greatest deity of the Hellenistic (i.e., later Greek) world. Introduced into Greece by way of Thrace and Phrygia, Dionysus was the subject of a multitude of conflicting traditions, which may have originally been associated with several deities from various countries and times. Dionysus came to represent the productive, life-giving, and intoxicating power of nature. His liberating power was most naturally and fittingly symbolized by wine, which was called "the fruit of Dionysus." Above all, Dionysus became known as the god of wine and ecstasy, the god who bestowed joy and dispersed sorrow. Dionysus's followers were the Bacchants or Maenads, roving bands of women who had abandoned their families and taken to the hills. They were usually represented in works of art as dressed in animal skins, wearing crowns of ivy in their disheveled hair, and waving leaf-entwined staffs. The Bacchants danced in torchlit frenzy to the rhythm of the flute and kettledrum. In myths the Bacchants tore their living victims to pieces and then partook of them in ritual feasts.

Dionysus was also regarded as the god of tragedy and as the protector of theaters. The development of Greek drama, especially tragedy, has been traced to the dithyrambic choruses recited at Dionysian festivals, which were orgies in the original sense of the word: secret ceremonial rites held in honor of the god and featuring ecstatic singing and dancing. The orgies honoring Dionysus probably originated as fertility rites. Gradually the festivals took on many forms, ranging from drinking feasts to festal processions and dramatic performances.

When the orgies were introduced into Rome, they became known as *bacchanalia,* after Bacchus. In Rome the rites for Bacchus started out as secret gatherings for women only. Later, after men were admitted, they became the sort of gatherings suggested by the contemporary meaning of *orgy.* The Bacchanalia of ancient Rome became increasingly notorious for drunkenness, debauchery, and licentiousness of all kinds. Things progressed to the point where the Roman senate felt the need to issue a decree prohibiting Bacchanalia in 186 B.C.

For other articles on words derived from ancient mythology and legend see VOLCANO.

[L, fr. neut. pl. of *bacchanalis*]

back-formation See SHERRY.

bad About the origin of *bad* there is little to say. It appears in English only in the thirteenth century, naming no relations and bearing no pedigree. It gradually takes over from such previously favored synonyms as *ill* and *evil*, and continues uneventfully as the basic antonym of *good* in various senses, down to our own day. But in the Black English vernacular by the mid-twentieth century and possibly earlier, the word took an interesting hop, coming to be used to mean 'good'.

Put so baldly, the change seems hopelessly paradoxical, but if examined more closely, it makes a kind of sense and even has parallels. In its most characteristic use, as in *bad dude*, the word has a connotation of 'potent, powerful': "Bein' a macho, strong young brother, I joined. I'm bad. It was exciting" (black serviceman quoted in Wallace Terry's *Bloods,* 1984). The word is further distinguished from *bad* in its traditional use by having its own peculiar comparative and superlative *(badder/baddest)* and some unusual possibilities in its grammar: "The Baxters relied on him as their baddest dude," and "Tong thought he was bad bad, but the little dude [his opponent] was a boxer and jabbed and hooked him dizzy" (these examples are from *The Autobiography of Leroi Jones,* 1984). A similar doubleness of meaning is found in *skookum,* which English borrowed from Chinook Jargon: on the one hand it denotes an evil spirit; on the other it is used adjectively to mean 'powerful, first-rate'. Finally we may compare *wicked,* used (especially in teenage slang) to mean 'nifty', and *vicious,* used similarly for 'terrific'. *Terrific* itself comes close to illustrating the same process, since it originally meant 'terrifying'. Just how chancy such sense-development is may be seen from the fact that *terrible,* which initially also meant 'terrifying', is now virtually an antonym of *terrific.*

[ME *badde;* prob. akin to OE *bæddel* hermaphrodite, *bædan* to defile]

bailiff See JUDGE.
[ME *bailif, bailiff, bailie,* fr. OF *baillif, bailliu,* fr. *bail* jurisdiction]

baize See KHAKI.
[MF *baies,* pl. (taken as sing.) of *baie* baize, fr. fem. of *bai* bay-colored]

balaclava See BLOOMER.
[fr. *Balaclava* (now usu. *Balaklava*), village in the Crimea, U.S.S.R., where a battle of the Crimean War was fought on Oct. 25, 1854]

ball See BALLOT.
[ME *bal,* fr. ON *böllr;* akin to OE *bealluc* testis, OHG *balla* ball, OE *bula* bull]

balloon See BALLOT.
[It dial. *ballone* (It *pallone*), aug. of It dial. *balla,* of Gmc origin; akin to OHG *balla* ball]

ballot   Abraham Lincoln insisted that "among freemen there can be no successful appeal from the ballot to the bullet . . . they who take such appeal are sure to lose their case and pay the cost." Etymologically speaking, there is little to choose between *ballot* and *bullet;* each is a little ball. But, in spite of their striking similarity in sound and sense, the two words are unrelated. *Bullet* is ultimately a descendant (via French *boule*) of Latin *bulla,* 'bubble', and *ballot* of a Germanic word related to English *ball* and *balloon.* Small balls, variously marked or colored, have often been used in secret voting. In ancient Athens, jurors voted with one kind of ball for acquittal and with another for condemnation. Even today, some clubs accept or reject candidates for membership on the basis of a vote taken with white and black balls, hence our word *blackball.* Renaissance Venice, a republic from the eleventh century, used this same kind of secret vote. A Venetian, being Italian, called the ball he voted with a *ballotta,* or 'little ball'. The English borrowed this name to use for a ball, or any other object, used in casting a secret vote.

[It *ballotta,* fr. It dial., dim. of *balla* ball, of Gmc origin; akin to OHG *balla* ball]

bandanna   The people of India are known for their love of colorful and decorative fabrics for both formal and casual attire. Often they go to great lengths to create a particular pattern or design on a fine piece of fabric. Other times, they find a way to make optimal use of a plain, coarse material. One example of their ingenuity in the design of fabric is the garment we call the *bandanna.* The term *bandanna* actually comes from the Hindi word *bādhnū,* which describes a process of tie-dyeing, whereby pressure is applied to certain areas of the cloth during dyeing to prevent those areas from receiving dye. The result is a splotchy effect caused by patches of undyed fabric. Large handkerchiefs are often tie-dyed to give them a more vibrant decorative appearance. For this reason, we call them bandannas. The association of the large handkerchief that is often worn on the head or around the neck with Indian tie-dyeing has been all but lost, and we now refer to all such handkerchiefs, even plain ones, as bandannas.

Another popular article of attire that we get from the Indian people is the cummerbund. In India, domestic servants and low-level citizens wear this waistband. The word *cummerbund* actually comes from the Hindi term *kamarband,* which in turn derives from Persian *kamar,* 'waist'. In the western hemisphere, the cummerbund is often worn by men in place of a vest with tuxedoes and other formal wear. Recently, women too have discovered fashion uses for the cummerbund, which has been adapted to suit various styles.

One of the most decorative and versatile fabrics to come out of India is the printed calico known as *chintz.* The word *chintz* has an interesting history. It comes from the Hindi word *chīṭ* (which in turn derives from Sanskrit). The word became *chintz* through an error in interpretation. The anglicized form of Hindi *chīṭ* came out as *chint.* But in commercial use it was most often in the plural form *chints.* Travelers hearing the plural and mistaking it for a singular form began spelling the sound as *chints* and then *chintz.*

Unlike the cummerbund, chintz was associated with wealth and prestige in India as well as in the West. In the first of his "Moral Essays," the Epistle to Sir Richard Temple (1733), Alexander Pope recalls the concern of a dying actress for the clothes she is to be buried in:

"Odious! in woollen! 'twould a Saint provoke,"
(Were the last words that poor Narcissa spoke)
"No, let a charming Chintz and Brussels lace
"Wrap my cold limbs, and shade my lifeless face:
"One would not, sure, be frightful when one's dead. . . ."

Not all Indian fabric is fancy or decorative. One of the more utilitarian fabrics we get from India is the material known as *gunny.* The Indian people used what they called *gani* as a material to hold merchandise being traded. *Gani* came from a Sanskrit word meaning, aptly enough, 'sack'. The coarse sacking material made from jute, another Indian product, was used in trading. Eventually the word came to be used in compounds, like *gunny cloth, gunnysack,* and *gunny-bag.*

[Hindi *bādhnū,* a variegated-color dyeing process involving tying the cloth in knots, cloth so dyed, fr. *bādhnā* to tie, fr. Skt *badhnāti* he ties]

baptist See CATHOLIC.
[ME *baptiste,* fr. OF, fr. LL *baptista,* fr. Gk *baptistēs,* fr. *baptizein* to baptize, dip]

barbaric Philology laments that the ancient Greeks, for all their scientific curiosity and historiographic distinction, left virtually no record of the languages of other peoples with whom they came in contact, languages now mostly lost forever to investigation. A hint of their linguistic insularism can be seen in the Greek word for 'alien, stranger': *barbaros,* a word of onomatopoeic origin, mockingly imitating foreign speech as though it were a babbling or stutter. In the derived Greek word *barbarophōnos* 'speaking a foreign language', the reference is purely linguistic; but *barbaros* came increasingly to take on connotations of 'rude, uncivilized', especially after the wars with the Persians. It is this sense we have inherited in our borrowed word *barbaric.*

Barbaros is also lurking, much less visibly, in our word *rhubarb.* In Greek, rhubarb was known both as *rhēon* (the source of rhubarb's genus name, *Rheum,* in Latin guise) and as *rha.* From these, Medieval Latin formed *rha barbarum* and *rheubarbarum*—'foreign *Rheum',* so to speak. Passing through Middle French, the word entered our language as *rhubarb.*

[L *barbaricus* foreign, barbaric, fr. Gk *barbarikos,* fr. *barbaros* foreign + *-ikos* -ic]

barnacle In Latin documents of twelfth- and thirteenth-century England, we find reference to a bird called the *bernaca,* said to be a goose with the singular quality that it is born on wood or rocks, by the shore, from which it hangs by its beak until mature—we might almost say "ripe"—then drops into the water and swims contentedly about its business. The English form of this word, *bernek* or *bernak,* was later altered to *barnacle.* Even as late as the mid-seventeenth century, Isaac Walton in his *The Compleat Angler* continues the belief in this wondrous creature: "The Barnacles and young Goslings bred by the Sun's heat and the rotten planks of an old Ship, and hatched of trees." Today we call this bird the *barnacle goose.*

The bird nests in such far-northerly places as Greenland and Novaya Zemlya, so in medieval times its mating habits were not readily observable by the amateur zoologists of the British Isles, where the bird winters. As if to compensate for the sketchiness of this belief, which grew up in the absence of observational fact, a further detail of origin was proposed: the actual bud from which the bird developed was said to be a crustacean often found clinging to shoreside objects and sporting a feathery feeding appendage suggestive of a wing. It is this crustacean which we call a barnacle today. A happy corollary of this genetic theory was that since the bird was not truly a bird, it could be enjoyed at Friday's dining table, when flesh was avoided. For another bird associated with a legend see HALCYON.

[ME *barnakylle,* alter. of *bernekke, bernake,* perh. of Celt origin; akin to W *brenig* limpets, Corn *brennyk,* Bret *bernic* barnacle, MIr *bairnech* limpet; fr. a popular belief in the Middle Ages that the goose grew from the shellfish]

barrister   See ATTORNEY.

[¹*bar* + -*i*- + -*ster*]

basilica   From their noun *basileus,* meaning 'king', the Greeks derived the adjective *basilikos,* meaning 'royal', and then the noun *basilikē,* meaning 'hall of the king'. In ancient Athens there was a public building called "Basilikos stoa" or Royal portico, the shape of which we do not know. It may or may not have been the prototype of the later Roman basilicas. The first of these was erected by M. Portius Cato, the censor, in 184 B.C., and was called after his name Basilica Porcia. Cato had recently visited Athens, so the Greek structure may have been imitated. By the time of Augustus there were five basilicas in the vicinity of the forum. They were used for public assembly, for transacting business, and for judicial proceedings. They were also built in various other cities throughout the empire. The typical basilica was an oblong building with a broad nave flanked by colonnaded aisles or porticoes and ending in a semicircular apse.

When the first Christian churches were built, they were often patterned after the civil basilicas. In the fourth century, the emperor Constantine had several Christian basilicas erected in Rome, which had a new feature: a transept crossing the nave just before the apse. This cross-shaped design became standard for churches in western Europe throughout the Middle Ages. Since the sixteenth century, the term *basilica* has been bestowed by the pope as a canonical title on particular churches, allowing them special liturgical privileges.

The Greek noun *basileus* also gave rise to another English term. The diminutive form, *basiliskos* 'little king, kinglet', was used in Greek legend in reference to a fabulous reptile that could kill any living thing with a mere look or breath. The Roman scholar Pliny attributed its name to a crownlike spot the *basiliscus* was believed to have on its head. This Latin word became *basilisk* when it was borrowed into English at the beginning of the fourteenth century.

In the sixteenth century, *basilisk* was also applied to a large cannon capable of throwing a 200-pound shot. It was named after the fabulous beast, presumably for its great power to kill. Another transferred sense began to appear early in the nineteenth century when biologists first applied *basilisk* to small tropical American lizards that had a crownlike crest at the top of their head.

[L, fr. Gk *basilikē*, fr. fem. of *basilikos* royal, fr. *basileus* king + *-ikos* -ic]

basilisk See BASILICA.
[ME, fr. L *basiliscus*, fr. Gk *basiliskos*, lit., little king, dim. of *basileus* king]

bead In Middle English *bede*, from Old English *gebed*, originally meant 'a prayer'. The number and order of a series of prayers are often kept track of with the aid of what is today called a *rosary*, a string of variously sized small round balls. Because each of these balls stands for a particular prayer, the name *bede*, Modern English *bead*, was transferred to the balls themselves. Today *bead* is used to refer to any small piece of material pierced for threading on a string or wire. The sense is also extended to refer to any small, round object, such as a drop of sweat.

Rosary is from Medieval Latin *rosarium*, which in earlier Latin had meant literally 'a rose garden'. It was used metaphorically to refer to a series of prayers, thought of perhaps as a garden of prayers and perhaps influenced by the association in Christian symbolism of the rose with the Virgin Mary and the rose garden with paradise. As with *bead*, the sense of *rosary* was applied by extension to the string of beads as well as to the prayers themselves. These senses of *rosary* first appeared in English in the sixteenth century.

[ME *bede* prayer, prayer bead, fr. OE *bed, gebed* prayer; akin to OHG *beta* request, *gibet* prayer, Goth *bida* prayer, OE *biddan* to entreat]

bear Two terms often used for stock-market traders are *bull* and *bear*. A *bull* is someone who buys securities or commodities in the expectation of a price rise, or someone whose actions make such a price rise happen. A *bear* is the opposite—someone who sells securities or commodities in expectation of a price decline. By extension both terms are used as adjectives, so a *bull* market is rising in value, while a *bear* market is declining. Depictions of the two animals are used for everything from market-report illustrations to gift items of porcelain and bronze. Certainly a majestic bull and a powerful bear present striking images. But there are other animals just as striking. How did these two come to be associated with the stock market?

The bear came first. A proverb that has been in use at least since the seventeenth century points out that it is not wise "to sell the bear's skin before one has caught the bear." By the eighteenth century the term *bear-skin,* apparently from this proverb, was being used in the phrase "to sell the bear-skin" or "to buy the bear-skin." The *bear-skin* element was quickly shortened to *bear,* and *bear* was then applied to stock that was being sold by a speculator. The speculator would sell a borrowed stock with a delivery date specified in the future. This was done with the expectation that stock prices would go down so that the stock could be bought back at the lower price and the difference from the selling price kept as profit. The word *bear* was also applied to the speculator selling stock in this fashion, with *bear-skin jobber* a slightly earlier synonym.

In 1720 England was rocked by a scandal known as the South Sea Bubble. This was a protracted scheme involving the South Sea Company, founded in 1711 to trade with Spain's colonies in the New World. South Sea stock became highly desirable when the king became governor of the company, and soon stockholders were enjoying returns of up to 100 percent. In 1720 the South Sea Company assumed most of the British national debt and convinced its investors to give up state annuities for company stock, which was sold at a very high premium. Many of the speculators were selling stock they did not own, and when the stock price suddenly fell nearly 1000 points, the result was a debacle for the company and tragedy for many investors. Although some realized great profits, most were ruined. A House of Commons inquiry revealed that some national office-holders had been involved in bribery and speculation. At least one was imprisoned; many of the South Sea Company's directors had their property confiscated.

The term *bear,* meaning the person who sells stock in expectation of a price decline, as well as the stock so sold, had been in use prior to the breaking of the South Sea Bubble. However, since this type of selling was used by many people involved in the scandal, the South Sea affair brought *bear* into widespread use. At about the same time the other animal symbol made its appearance. The term *bull* originally meant a speculative purchase in the expectation that stock prices would rise. Its earliest use was in 1714, and the word *bull* seems to have been chosen as a fitting alter ego to *bear.* Thus Alexander Pope wrote in 1720: "Come fill the South Sea goblet full;/ The gods shall of our stock take care:/ Europa pleased accepts the bull,/ And Jove with joy puts off the bear." The animal imagery caught on and has stayed with us.

[prob. fr. *bear* as used in the proverb about *selling the bearskin before catching the bear*]

bedlam   In 1247 a priory was founded in London for the order of St. Mary of Bethlehem. By 1330 this priory had become the Hospital of St.

Mary of Bethlehem, intended to serve the poor or homeless who were afflicted with any ailment. By 1405 this hospital, now under royal control, was being used, at least partly, as an asylum for the insane, the first such institution in England.

In popular speech the name *Bethlehem* had become telescoped to *Bedlam,* and in 1528 William Tyndale used *Bedlam* in his *The Obedience of a Christian Man* in reference to this particular hospital. Also in the sixteenth century, an inmate of this asylum came to be called a bedlam.

As with most such asylums of the time, abuses were prevalent when proper outside inspection was not maintained. Indeed, Bedlam had become infamous for its brutality. In his diary for 1657, John Evelyn noted that in Bedlam he "saw several miserable creatures in chains." By the latter part of the seventeenth century, the word *bedlam* had begun to be used in a generic way for any lunatic asylum. At about the same time the term was first applied metaphorically to a scene of wild uproar or confusion, its common meaning today.

In the eighteenth century, it became the custom of the upper classes to visit Bedlam to observe the antics of the insane patients as a form of amusement. It has been estimated that about 100,000 persons visited the hospital for this purpose in the course of a year. William Hogarth, known for his satirical paintings of society in this era, depicted fashionable ladies visiting Bedlam as a showplace. However, after an investigation in 1857, the hospital came under regular government inspection and has since been known for its enlightened treatment of the mentally ill.

[fr. *Bedlam,* popular name for the Hospital of St. Mary of Bethlehem, London, England, an insane asylum, fr. ME *Bedlem, Bethlem,* alter. of *Bethlehem,* town of Palestine]

beguile   See AMUSE.
[ME *begilen,* fr. *be-* + *gilen* to guile, deceive]

behemoth   See HIPPOPOTAMUS.
[ME *bemoth, behemoth,* fr. L *behemoth,* fr. Heb *běhēmōth,* pl. (expressing magnitude) of *běhēmāh* beast]

belfry   In our day, *belfry* denotes a bell tower; form and meaning seem to be serenely wed. But the word does not derive from *bell;* its immediate source is French, which got it from Germanic; and tracing its history will confront us with a welter of evidence and conjecture.

A centerpiece of medieval warfare was the siege tower, a wooden structure which could be rolled up against the wall of a defending fortification. In Middle High German of the early twelfth century, the structure was known by a term variously spelled *perfrit, bervrit,* and *berfrid.* In Modern German this has become *Bergfried* and in this form is closer to what many authorities postulate for the origin of *berfrid:* from the Germanic roots which appear in Modern German as *berg-* 'protect' and *fried* 'peace'. (An alternate view sees *berg* 'mountain' as the first element.) If this derivation is correct, then the Middle High German term or one of its Germanic cognates is the probable origin of a Medieval Latin term attested from around the same time, spelled *berfredus* and *belfredus*, with numerous variants. The forms with *l* in the first syllable would have resulted from dissimilation, a process of sound change whereby one of two closely related or identical sounds (in this case *r*'s) becomes a different sound (in this case *l*). Dissimilation of successive *r*'s often happened in Medieval Latin.

But the Latin forms do not neatly postdate the German, and it is also possible that it was rather German that borrowed the word from Medieval Latin, later using folk etymology to parcel out the Latin syllables into familiar-looking German forms. If so, the question arises of where Medieval Latin got the word, since nothing in classical Latin corresponds to it (as indeed we would surmise, given the great variety of the Medieval Latin spellings). It has been suggested that *berfredus* could be an echo of the Greek *pyrgos phorētos*, 'movable tower', a war tower mounted on the backs of elephants.

Whatever the precedence between the German and Latin forms, it is comparatively certain that the term was borrowed by Old French, where we find *berfroi* in the sense of 'siege tower' showing up in the mid-twelfth century. And again there were variant forms with *l* instead of *r* in the first syllable. (Modern French finesses the whole question by reducing the word to *beffroi*.) By the early thirteenth century, *berfroi* was being used to denote not a siege engine but a tower containing an alarm bell; by the fifteenth century, *beffroy* had come to denote the bell itself as well.

From French, the forms passed into English, thus repaying the Germanic loan to another branch of the same language family. *Belfrey* is attested in a Latin sentence written in England in 1272, in reference to an ordinary tower rather than a siege tower. The writer thus lapses into English at this one word, although *berefredum* was indeed used in the Latin of thirteenth-century England, in both the senses 'bell tower' and 'movable siege tower'. *Berefrei* first appears in an English document of uncertain date, from either the thirteenth or fourteenth centuries, and there means 'siege tower'. Both *belfrey* (with variant spellings) and *berfrey* (with variant spellings) came to be used in both the 'siege tower' and 'bell tower' senses.

Belfrey eventually won out, as did the sense 'bell tower', the other spelling and meaning being forgotten. Presumably the resemblance to *bell* aided the process, though it cannot be the whole story, for as we have seen, the 'bell tower' sense developed independently in French, where the word for 'bell' is *cloche* (related to our word *clock*).

[ME *belfray* tower, bell tower, alter. (influenced by ME *belle* bell or ML *belfredus* tower) of *berefreid, berfrey,* fr. OF *berfroi,* fr. MHG *bervrit,* prob. fr. ML *berfredus, belfredus, balfredus,* perh. fr. an (assumed) L word derived fr. Gk *pyrgos phorētos* movable war tower]

berserk   The Old Norse *berserkr* is a compound of *ber-,* the root of *björn,* 'bear', plus *serkr,* 'shirt' (related to the English dialect word *sark*). Thus a Norse *berserkr* was a warrior who wore a bearskin shirt. In battle these warriors would work themselves into a frenzy and, according to popular belief, at such times they even became invulnerable to the effects of steel and fire. The word was borrowed into English in the early nineteenth century when literary interest in Scandinavian history and myth was high, and from the sense of a Scandinavian warrior frenzied in battle the word became a general term for someone whose actions are marked by reckless defiance. Later in the nineteenth century *berserk* also began to be used as an adjective. In the United States this adjective began to gain considerable currency in the late 1930s, and in the *Chicago Daily Tribune* on 20 November 1940 an article headlined "America Goes Berserk" refers to "the recent addition of the word 'berserk,' as a synonym for crackpot behaviour, to the slang of the young and untutored. . . . American stenographers . . . are telling one another not to be 'berserk.'" Since then *berserk* has become a perfectly acceptable word no longer in the realm of slang.

Amok is similar in meaning to *berserk* and it has a similar origin. Surprisingly, however, it came into English from the other side of the world and at an earlier date, that is, in the seventeenth century from the Malay *amok* meaning 'a furious attack or charge'. A Malay would sometimes work himself into a frenzy of revenge and wildly attack his enemies, or even people at random when he was out of control. In English *amok* may be used to describe any action carried out or occurring in a violently raging or undisciplined manner, and is most common in the phrase "run amok."

[ON *berserkr*, from *ber-* (stem of *björn* bear) + *serkr* shirt]

Bible See VOLUME.
[ME, Bible, book, fr. OF, Bible, fr. ML *biblia*, fr. Gk, pl. of *biblion* book, dim. of *biblos, byblos,* book, papyrus, fr. *Byblos* (now Jubayl), Phoenician city from which papyrus was exported]

bier See SARCOPHAGUS.
[ME *bere*, fr. OE *bær, bēr;* akin to OS & OHG *bāra* bier; derivative fr. the stem of OE *beran* to carry]

Big Apple See KNICKERBOCKER.

bikini In July 1946 atomic bomb tests were carried out on the atoll of *Bikini* in the Marshall Islands. In the summer of 1947 another bombshell hit the beaches of the French Riviera, the bikini. It is not known who gave this name to the skimpy two-piece bathing suit, nor why he did so. One suggestion is that the effect achieved by a scantily clad woman appearing in public may be compared to the effect of an A-bomb blast. Another possibility put forward is that the bikini leaves its wearer nearly bare, the way the bomb tests stripped Bikini. A third suggestion is that the shape of the atoll suggested a bikinied figure, but after examining newspaper maps of the time we have had to conclude that even the most perfervid imagination would have had trouble connecting geography and anatomy in this case. There is no solid evidence for any of these guesses, and the reasons for naming a two-piece bathing suit after an atomic test site in the northern Pacific remain obscure, at least for the time being.

In any case, the bikini fashion mushroomed, and the word was borrowed from French into a number of other languages. Then in 1964 fashion-conscious bathers appeared in a new style, the topless bikini. Because of the relationship between this one-piece innovation and the two-piece bikini, someone coined the term *monokini* from *mono-*, a Greek prefix meaning 'single', plus part of *bikini,* thus punning on the first two letters of *bikini* as if they represented the Latin prefix *bi-*, meaning 'two'.

[F, fr. *Bikini,* atoll of the Marshall islands in the northern Pacific, site of atomic bomb tests of 1946]

billingsgate   Sailors have long been renowned for their seamanlike command of the vulgar tongue. Mule skinners have been championed for their ready facility with profane and obscene speech. None, however, has ever enjoyed the notoriety of fishwives for fluent, enthusiastic, and abusive vulgarity. Besides making their occupational name synonymous with a vulgarly abusive woman, fishwives have made the name of one of their historic gathering grounds a permanent part of the language.

From the time of the Roman occupation of Britain there stood on the north bank of the River Thames (near the site of latter-day London Bridge) a watergate that served as one of the two gates in the river wall giving access to the settlement now called London. Billingsgate, as it became known, originally was outfitted with quays. Over the centuries Billingsgate became a marketplace for all types of goods, but it evolved into a marketplace primarily for grain. Finally, in 1699, a government statute decreed that Billingsgate was to be the site for a free and open market for fish.

While Billingsgate was indeed famous for its fish, it achieved an equal measure of fame for the coarse vituperation that resounded throughout the fish stalls. The fishmongers, especially the women, enjoyed a reputation for unrestrained invective that was wittily inventive, vulgarly explicit, and vigorously conveyed. In Holinshed's chronicle (1577) of King Leir, which was probably the source that Shakespeare used for his tragedy, a messenger's tongue is said to be "as bad a tongue, if it be set on, as any oyster-wife at Billingsgate hath." The fame of the fishwives continued to reverberate throughout English letters. In a 1711 issue of the *Spectator,* Joseph Addison referred to the "Debates which frequently arise among the Ladies of the British Fishery." William Thackeray in *Vanity Fair* wrote that "Mr. Osborne. . .cursed Billingsgate with an emphasis worthy of the place." But Billingsgate became more than just a familiar reference; the word *billingsgate* itself became a synonym for coarse, abusive language. In 1712 Addison remarked: "Our Satyr [satire] is nothing but ribaldry and Billingsgate." The word had become generic and lowercase by the time (1799) Thomas Jefferson wrote: "We disapprove the constant billingsgate poured on them officially."

Its lexical legacy is about all that is left of the once boisterous Billingsgate. Market activities were moved in 1982 to a large modernized warehouse in the Isle of Dogs, overlooking the West India Dock near the

Thames. One wonders if the language of the marketplace has become as sanitized as the facilities.

[fr. *Billingsgate,* old gate and fish market, London, England, noted for the abusive language used there]

bimbo   *Bimbo* became something of a vogue word in the 1980s. With public figures having their careers destroyed as a result of indiscreet romantic liaisons, the word received a lot of "press." The cover of one top-selling magazine featured a photograph of a young woman involved in one such liaison, with the quote "I am not a bimbo." There is no doubt that the word *bimbo* is disparaging regardless of the context in which it appears. Typically it is used now of women whose sexual practices are regarded as less than respectable. Rarely would a man with a reputation for lascivious behavior be called a bimbo, though English novelist P. G. Wodehouse departed from typical modern chauvinistic use of the word *bimbo* in his 1947 work *Full Moon,* mentioning "bimbos who went about the place making passes at innocent girls after discarding their wives."

Originally, *bimbo* was a term of disparagement that applied to members of both sexes. As early as 1919, the term was used to describe a fellow who was unimportant or undistinguished, as in this example from *American Magazine:* "Nothing but the most heroic measures will save the poor bimbo." *Bimbo* is still used this way. Jay Stuller in a 1980 magazine article describing the "Toughest Job in Sports" says: "Likewise, a catcher must spend time positioning fielders and telling a thickheaded pitcher that the bimbo at the plate hasn't hit a curve in three seasons."

The exact derivation of the term *bimbo* has never been established, but the word is believed to come from an Italian word for 'baby'. It seems to have acquired its current meaning in much the same way that the English word 'baby' developed its meaning of 'girlfriend' or 'woman' and later simply 'person'.

The use of the word to mean a sexually promiscuous woman or 'tramp' goes back to around 1929 but did not really catch on in popular usage until the advent of the 1930s detective novel, which helped perpetuate the stereotype of the beautiful but dumb blonde who is taken out for a night on the town in exchange for sexual favors. As usage has increased in the latter half of the twentieth century, the term has taken on a more general notion of a beautiful woman viewed solely as a sex object, as illustrated by Richard Atcheson writing in *Holiday* (1968): ". . .and while you eat you can watch the bimbos frolicking on the high board at the pool."

It is interesting that *bimbo* started out as a term that was used in referring to men, for *bimbo* even in its "just another pretty face and no brains" sense seems now to be coming full circle, at least in part of its use. Cathleen Schine, writing in *Vogue* (1985), describes an actress who is "beautiful, with her vampy, heavy-lidded eyes and slight one-sided smile. Confident and dignified, she can make the guys on the show look a little like giggling *bimbos.*"

[prob. fr. It *bimbo* baby]

bindle stiff See TRAMP.

[*bindle,* prob. alter. of *bundle*]

bird See LEPRECHAUN, PATTERN.

[ME *brid, bird* young bird, bird, fr. OE *brid* young bird]

biscuit In earlier ages the preservation of food presented a greater problem than it does today, especially on long journeys. One expedient was to preserve flat cakes of bread by baking them a second time in order to dry them out. In Middle French the result of this process was called *pain bescuit,* literally 'twice-cooked bread'. In the fourteenth century, the second element of this phrase was borrowed into English, and, the notion of cooking twice having been lost, *biscuit* came to be used to designate any of various hard or crisp, dry baked products. (This is the sense that now prevails in England, while Americans would say *cookie* or *cracker.*) Similarities in shape and size led to the use of *biscuit* as the name for a small quick bread made from dough that has been rolled out and cut, or dropped from a spoon.

Remarkably similar etymologically is *zwieback.* This was borrowed directly from German and literally means 'twice-baked'. Zwieback is made by baking a sweetened bread enriched with eggs and then toasting slices of it until they are dry and crisp.

[ME *bisquite, besquite,* fr. MF *bescuit,* fr. *(pain) bescuit* twice-cooked bread, fr. *pain* bread + *bescuit* twice-cooked, fr. *bes-* twice (fr. L *bis-*) + *cuit,* past part. of *cuire* to cook, fr. L *coquere*]

bishop A *bishop*'s crosier or pastoral staff takes the form of a shepherd's crook as a visible sign that a primary duty of a bishop is to watch over the members of the church as a shepherd watches over his flock. The etymological significance of the word *bishop* parallels this symbolic function of the crosier very closely, for the Old English *bisceop,* along with the cognate forms in other Germanic languages, is derived from the late Latin *episcopus* meaning *'bishop'* or 'overseer'. This word in turn is derived from the Greek *episkopos,* formed from *epi,* meaning 'on' or 'over', plus *skopos,* 'one who watches'. Thus *bishop* literally means 'one who watches over others'. (See the discussion of *episcopal* at CATHOLIC.)

Another English word with a hidden etymological relation to *bishop* is *horoscope.* The second element is from the same Greek root *skopos,* and the first element, *horo-,* comes from the Greek *hōra,* meaning 'period' or 'time of day'. A *horoscope* is a diagram showing the relative positions of the planets and the signs of the zodiac by means of which an astrologer purports to foretell the future. Similarly a *telescope,* from Greek *tēle-,* meaning 'far, far off or distant', plus *skopos,* enables someone to view distant objects.

[ME *bisshop,* fr. OE *bisceop, biscop;* akin to OS *biskop* bishop, OHG *biscof,* MD *bisskop;* all fr. a prehistoric WGmc word borrowed fr. (assumed) VL *biscopus, ebiscopus,* fr. LL *episcopus* bishop, overseer, fr. Gk *episkopos,* fr. *epi* on, over + *skopos* watcher; akin to Gk *skopein* to view, watch]

bizarre With its odd spelling and un-English stress, *bizarre* is one of those words which, like *teensy* or *catawampus,* assists its meaning by its form. The word's history is likewise a bit on the odd side.

Bizarre was borrowed from the French in the seventeenth century and retains its French-style stress on the last vowel to this day. It was once held (and is still sometimes repeated) that the French word derived, via Spanish, ultimately from the Basque word for 'beard'. Anything involving a leap from Basque (a language historically unrelated to all the others in Europe) to English, and from beards to the bizarre, has the makings of a good story, but this one is short on veracity. *Bizarre* is attested in French from the first half of the sixteenth century, in Spanish not until the latter half, so French cannot have borrowed the word from Spanish. The source is rather the Italian *bizzarro,* which appears (in Dante) in the early fourteenth century, originally in the sense 'irascible'. *Bizzarro* has rather an unusual look in the lexicon of Italian as well, but Basque cannot be blamed; rather it is derived from Italian *bizza* 'fit of anger'. *Bizzarro* passed into Spanish (as *bizarro*), where it evolved the meaning 'brave'. The Spanish meaning managed to get borrowed by the French for a time during the sixteenth century, but French soon dropped this meaning and English never adopted it; so today English, French, and Italian stand together in having their respective versions of the word mean only 'strange', while in Spanish the word remains rather bizarrely distinct with the meanings 'brave' and 'generous'. The Spanish word is thus what is often called a 'false cognate': that is, a genuine cognate from the etymological standpoint, but with a meaning other than what one would predict on the basis of its relatives in other languages.

[F, fr. It *bizzarro*]

blackball See BALLOT.
[¹*black* + *ball*]

Blackfoot See INDIAN.
[trans. of Blackfoot *Siksika*]

blackmail Life was unfair for seventeenth-century Scottish farmers. Not only did they have to struggle to cultivate their land and produce good crops, but they also had to contend with corrupt chiefs who forced them to pay for protection of their land. If a farmer didn't pay the protection fee, these same extortionists would destroy his crops. It is this corrupt practice, not the post office, that has given us our word *blackmail.*

The *mail* of *blackmail* comes from a Scottish word meaning 'rent'. The *black* in *blackmail* probably derives from an age-old association between the color black and evil or "dirty deeds." It could also have something to do with the fact that the tribute paid by the farmers was in the form of cattle rather than in silver coins, known as "white money."

By 1601 the term had spread to England, where blackmail likewise existed in the form of tax or tribute. Eventually, the term came to describe anything extorted, be it money or some other favor. Today the noun *blackmail* denotes not only the booty exacted by extortion but also the act of extorting. Around 1880 *blackmail* became a verb as well and quickly spawned the noun *blackmailer,* which describes one who extorts by intimidation or by the unscrupulous use of an official or social position or of political influence.

Nowadays blackmail can be very subtle. We even hear from time to time of blackmail that acts upon personal feelings and actions, as in the following bit of a magazine article: "That old moan: 'You'll be sorry when I've gone' is a very common one. It's an emotional blackmail to keep loved ones on their toes."

[¹*black* + *mail* (tribute)]

blame   The English words *blame* and *blaspheme* are both descended from a single source, but they have come into the language by such different routes that their forms and meanings are distinct. Both words come from Late Latin *blasphemare,* 'to blaspheme', but whereas Middle English *blasfemen* was borrowed more or less directly from the Latin form, *blame* has a more complicated history.

During the development of the Late Latin word into Vulgar Latin and thence into French, a number of sound changes affected its form. The Vulgar Latin form was *blastemare,* a corruption of Late Latin *blasphemare.* Further changes took place in French, one of which was the loss of *s* in certain positions, and this gave Old French *blamer,* from which is derived Middle English *blamen,* modern *blame.*

The Late Latin *blasphemare* was borrowed from Greek *blasphēmein,* 'to speak ill of, blaspheme', from *blasphēmos,* 'evil-speaking'. The first element in this word is of obscure origin; the second element is from *phēmē,* 'speech'. This last element is also found in *euphemism,* derived from the Greek *euphēmos,* 'auspicious, sounding good'. The first part of this word is the Greek prefix *eu-,* meaning 'good'. For examples of the function of euphemism in English see JEEPERS.

[ME *blamen,* fr. OF *blamer, blasmer,* fr. (assumed) VL *blastemare,* alter. of LL *blasphemare* to revile, blaspheme, fr. Gk *blasphēmein* to speak ill of, blaspheme, fr. *blasphēmos* evil-speaking, fr. *blas-* (perh. akin to Gk *meleos* futile, unhappy) + *-phēmos* (fr. *phēmē* speech, fr. *phanai* to say)]

blanket   See KHAKI.
[ME, fr. OF *blanqete,* fr. *blanc* white + *-et* (dim. suffix)]

blarney   *Blarney* is the name of a town, a stream, and especially a castle, built in 1446, in County Cork, Ireland. The focus of attention in the ivy-covered ruin is the towering battlemented and machicolated keep. Embedded in the southern wall of the keep is a block of limestone, known as the Blarney Stone, inscribed in Latin with the castle builder's name and the date of construction. Tradition has it that anyone who kisses the Blarney Stone will be blessed with the gift of flattery or cajolery. The stone is several feet below the level of a walkway, and a person wishing to kiss the Blarney Stone must extend himself or herself downward and backward toward an opposite wall, with an accomplice holding onto his or her legs. Iron rods have been added as handrails.

The tradition of making a pilgrimage to the castle to kiss the Blarney Stone is supposedly based on a particular event in the castle's long history. The story goes that in 1602 the lord of the castle contrived an endless series of plausible excuses and words of flattery to forestall a promised surrender of the castle to attacking English forces until help could arrive. The lack of historical evidence for the story has failed to stifle the traditional claim that anyone who kisses the stone will be blessed with a similar gift of blarney. However long-standing the tradition is, references to *blarney* in print do not begin to appear until the late eighteenth century. The Irish-born writer Oliver Goldsmith gives the name Lady Blarney to one of his characters in *The Vicar of Wakefield*. Lady Blarney is a woman of the town who uses smooth flattery to insinuate herself into the company of the vicar's innocent family. Since much flattery, sincere or insincere, is at heart so much nonsense, *blarney* naturally developed a second sense synonymous with that word. This sense is first attested in a letter of 1796 by Sir Walter Scott: "I hold it (so to speak) to be all Blarney."

[fr. *Blarney stone,* a stone in Blarney castle, near Cork, Ireland, reputed to bestow talent for eloquent cajolery upon those who kiss it]

blaspheme   See BLAME.
[ME *blasfemen,* fr. LL *blasphemare*]

blends   The term *blend* is used in Merriam-Webster etymologies in a comparatively narrow and precise sense: a blend is a word made by combining other words or parts of words in such a way that they overlap (as *motel* from *motor* plus *hotel*) or one is infixed into the other (as *chortle* from *snort* plus *chuckle*—the *-ort-* of the first being surrounded by the *ch-.* . .*-le* of the second). In more general usage, *blend* is used of words like *brunch,* from *breakfast* plus *lunch,* in which pieces of the words are joined but there is no actual overlap. The essential feature of a blend in either meaning is that there be no point at which you can break the word with everything to the left of the break being a morpheme (a separately meaningful, conventionally combinable element) and everything to the right being a morpheme, and with the meaning of the blend-word being a function of the meanings of these morphemes. Thus, *birdcage* and *psychohistory* are not blends but compounds. And *anecdotage* in the sense 'anecdotes collectively' is an ordinary derivative of *anecdote* by means of the suffix *-age,* often used to form collectives. But in the punning use in which *anecdotage* refers to the garrulous retailing of warmed-over chestnuts (as though by one in his *dotage*) it is a blend, since now the meaning is not predictable from *anecdote* + *-age,* and no single division will give you *an-*

ecdote to the left and *dotage* to the right; phonetically both words are present in full, but overlapping.

Blends in our sense are typically deliberate and indeed often skillful creations. When a blend catches on, like *smog* (from *smoke* plus *fog*), it may become a useful and unobtrusive part of the language, its etymology forgotten by most speakers.

For cases of unconscious blending see CONTAMINATION. For further examples of blends, in the context of nonsense-poem coinages, see JABBERWOCKY.

bless   The Old English noun *blōd* 'blood' is believed to be the source of our word *bless*. From *blōd* the verb *blētsian, blēdsian* was derived. In pre-Christian England this verb was used to mean 'to make sacred or holy with blood'. The practice was to spread the blood of a sacrificial animal on something in order to ward off evil influences.

With England's conversion to Christianity, the verb *blēdsian* was used to translate the Latin verb *benedicere* 'to consecrate or hallow by religious rite or word'; more specifically, it referred to making the sign of the cross on or over something. The Latin verb itself was a translation of the Greek verb *eulogein* 'to speak well of; praise, eulogize'. This Greek verb was in turn a rendering of the Hebrew verb *bārak* 'to bend the knee in worship'.

During the Middle English period the verb *blēdsian* became *blessen* and by the fourteenth century had acquired the sense 'to invoke divine care for'. Shakespeare later used it in this passage from *Cymbeline* (ca. 1610):

> If you will bless me, sir, and give me leave,
> I'll take the better care; but if you will not,
> The hazard therefore due fall on me by
> The hands of Romans!

The sense 'to praise or glorify', echoing that of the Greek verb *eulogein,* was also acquired during this period. This use of *bless* is common in the King James Version of the Bible (1611): "Bless the Lord, O my soul: and all that is within me, bless his holy name" (Psalms 103:1).

'To make happy, successful, or prosperous' is yet another sense acquired by *bless,* probably as a result of the influence of *bliss.* S. T. Coleridge illustrates this use in this line from his poem "To Two Sisters" (1807): "You bless my heart with many a cheerful ray." One is more likely to find this sense in such contexts as "We are blessed with good health" and "The region is blessed with good soil and abundant water."

By the nineteenth century there is evidence of an euphemistic or ironic use of *bless* to mean 'curse' or 'damn', as in "I'm blessed if I know what went wrong" or "He impatiently blessed every driver who slowed him down on the highway."

[ME *blessen,* fr. OE *bletsian, blētsian, blēdsian,* fr. *blōd* blood; fr. the use of blood in consecration or sacrifice]

blizzard   There is a tradition of sorts in Iowa that the word *blizzard* for a severe snowstorm with high winds originated there. Allen Walker Read went to Iowa in 1926 to look into the tradition, and his findings, published in 1928, show that there is considerable evidence in its favor. The earliest printed citation for the use that is so far known appeared in the Estherville, Iowa, *Northern Vindicator* on 23 April 1870. It was spelled *blizards,* and was cautiously enclosed in quotation marks. One week later, in the 30 April edition, it appeared again, with the now familiar double -*z* spelling, but still in quotation marks. In June of 1870 the local baseball team adopted the name *Blizzards*—it must have been a memorably hard winter.

The Estherville tradition had it that the word itself was introduced by a local character named "Lightnin' " Ellis, who seems to have been one of a fairly numerous crowd of winter-idled men who, having perhaps worn out their welcome at the general store and barbershop, hung around to talk and keep warm at the newspaper office. According to interviews with several Estherville old-timers who remembered him, Ellis had a habit of using droll terms, and they associated *blizzard* with him.

All that the "Lightnin' " Ellis story really proves is that the word *blizzard* had some currency in everyday talk in Estherville in 1870 and probably earlier. After its appearance in print, *blizzard* spread during the next three to six years to several other newspapers in Iowa and neighboring states, becoming a well-known word in the Middle West. By 1888, when a still famous March storm paralyzed the Eastern seaboard for days, took 400 lives, and destroyed much property, it would become a well-known word nationally.

The relatively rapid spread of an unusual word has naturally excited some speculation about its origin, and a number of explanations have been offered for it. Since many of these appeared long after *blizzard* became common, it is impossible to verify them. Some claim credit for one locality or another, giving the speculations an air of home-town rivalry. The Dictionary of Americanisms has citations dated 1859 and 1861 from a diary published in the *Kansas Historical Quarterly* in 1932. The diary was kept by an army captain at Fort Leavenworth, Kansas. It turns out, however, that the diarist revised or enlarged or rewrote the diary about 1905, when *blizzard* was a common word, and we do not know whether he unconsciously used it in his revision, or if he had used it in the original, which was unfortunately thrown away. No printed evidence, however, has yet been found that antedates the *Northern Vindicator.*

If the 'violent snowstorm' *blizzard* can be fairly confidently ascribed to northwestern Iowa in the 1860–1870, it is more of a problem to explain where the word itself came from. We know *blizzard* was used earlier in this country in other meanings. In the 1830s the word is recorded twice in the works of Davy Crockett. Crockett used it once meaning a blast from a gun and once, figuratively, for a blast of words. From a shotgun blast to a verbal blast to a wintry blast would seem to be a reasonable enough development, but we cannot demonstrate it. The earlier uses appear to have been short-lived or local; the gun blast sense overlaps the snowstorm sense in time, but is attested only from other parts of the country. We have evidence of a 1770 *blizz* 'a violent rainstorm', but we cannot connect it to *blizzard.* The surname *Blizzard* is also attested, but it has not been connected to the snowstorm except in a fanciful account concocted in the 1920s which ascribes the coinage of the word to a Mother Wells of Spencer, Iowa. Mother Wells is supposed to have read a story about a violent-tempered Mr. Blizzard in her Free Baptist paper and then to have remarked of a terrific snowstorm in 1866, "My, this is a regular old man Blizzard of a storm."

[origin unknown]

bloomer   The billowing fullness of *bloomers* might be suggestive of flowers in full bloom, but they actually derive their name from a small-town feminist who unwittingly sparked a fashion revolution. A resident of Seneca Falls, New York—the site of an historic women's rights convention in 1848—Amelia Jenks Bloomer (1818–1894) was a feminist long before the cause was popular or the term even invented. Originally a temperance activist as well as a newspaper writer and editor, Bloomer soon expanded the scope of her reformist interests to include a number of women's issues, including suffrage. She first became involved with the right of women to liberate themselves from traditional clothing when, in 1849, she defended in her temperance paper the wearing of pantalets by the actress Fanny Kemble. The controversy really erupted the following year when visiting feminists appeared on the streets of Seneca Falls wearing full Turkish pantaloons under a shortened skirt. Bloomer took to defending the liberated attire in print, even calling it "sanitary attire." She noted that the then-fashionable long hoopskirts were both cumbersome and unsanitary, picking up dirt—and worse—from the unpaved streets. Her articles attracted the attention of big newspapers in New York City and elsewhere, and soon a fad of national proportions developed. Bloomer found herself at the center of attention and controversy, with correspondents soliciting her for patterns and information about the new attire, which was soon christened the "Bloomer Costume." Amazed at the furor that had been generated, she nevertheless took up the gauntlet and publicly supported the new attire—by 1851 known as the *bloomer*—by wearing it exclusively for the next several years. The vogue for bloomers survived through the end of the nineteenth century, being supported in part by the garb's suitability for women's bicycling. With changes in fashion, *bloomer* gradually came to be applied to other women's garments with similar full or baggy pants and elastic cuffs, from bathing suits to gymnasium shorts. Eventually the term was used of women's underpants.

Other garments that commemorate the names of individuals include the cardigan, raglan, and blucher. *Cardigan* derives from the seventh earl of Cardigan, James Thomas Brudenell (1797–1868). Largely remembered now as the leader of the disastrous Charge of the Light Brigade, Cardigan was known in his time for his sartorial savvy. The garment that bears his name was originally a knitted woolen vest that warded off the chill of a Crimean winter. By remarkable coincidence, *raglan* honors the name of Cardigan's commanding officer at Balaclava, the first Baron Raglan, Fitzroy James Henry Somerset (1788–1855). During the Crimean War, Raglan wore a loose-fitting overcoat with sleeves that extended all the way to the neckline. Originally *raglan* referred to the overcoat; it now can also mean the style of sleeve. The Crimean War was an unusually fertile breeding ground for new fashions, which were a response to the cold weather encountered by the British troops. The village of *Balaclava* itself, the site of a battle on 25 October 1854, is the namesake of the knitted hoodlike cap for the head and neck.

Blucher honors another example of a commanding officer taking sartorial charge of his troops, albeit in a different conflict. Prussian field marshal Gebhard Leberecht von Blücher (1742–1819) promoted a new style of half boot for his troops during the Napoleonic wars. Bluchers have since evolved into today's oxford shoes.

[after Mrs. Amelia *Bloomer* †1894 Am. pioneer in social reform who advocated such clothing]

blucher   See BLOOMER.
[after G. L. von *Blücher* †1819 Prussian field marshal]

bluestocking   The term *bluestocking* is usually used to mean 'a woman having or pretending to have intellectual interests or literary tastes'. Yet, the original "bluestocking" was a man and one of unimpeachable intellectual credentials. The origin of *bluestocking* goes back to the mid-eighteenth century to a circle of English ladies who decided to replace their social evenings of cardplaying and idle chatter to which tradition confined them with more intellectual pursuits. Taking the literary salons of Paris as their model, they decided to hold in the evening literary discussions—"conversations" as they called them—at which illustrious men of letters would be the honored guests. Samuel Johnson, David Garrick, Horace Walpole, the Earl of Bath, and Lord Lyttleton were a few of the invited notables. On one occasion, the ladies invited English botanist and sometime poet Benjamin Stillingfleet. Stillingfleet at first felt obliged to decline the invitation, as he was the typical poor scholar who lacked fancy evening clothes, including the de rigueur black silk stockings worn to such high society events. As the diarist Fanny Burney later recounted, Stillingfleet was assured that his ordinary clothes, including his blue worsted stockings, would be quite acceptable. Thus attired, Stillingfleet became a popular fixture at the evening conversations and was dubbed "blue stockings." The members of the coterie came to be called the "Blue Stocking Society" somewhat derisively, for it was considered ungraceful for women to aspire to learning. Though it was intended as a put-down, the participants in the conversations adopted the name *Bluestocking,* or its French equivalent *Bas Bleu*. One of their circle, Hannah More, composed the poem "The Bas Bleu, or Conversation," and in his biography of Samuel Johnson, James Boswell writes about the "Blue-stocking Clubs" without apology. Despite all of this, *bluestocking* was often used as a term of disparagement. In his *Table Talk* (1822) the English critic William Hazlitt stated his point of view: "I have an utter aversion to *blue-stockings*. I do not care a fig for any woman that knows even what *an author* means."

The term did not die out, nor has it been limited to historical reference.

It has acquired a new sense of 'a female scholar' without a hint of derision, as in this 1980s use by Margo Jefferson:

> Several generations of women had acquired the education to be *bluestockings* but had lacked the gumption or the encouragement to become more than unhappy wives.

[after *Bluestocking* society, 18th century literary clubs, some of whose members wore informal attire often including blue worsted stockings]

blurb   The practice of covering a book's jacket with effusive copy is an old one, and it is ubiquitous enough to have once been the target of American humorist Gelett Burgess's wit. The time was 1907, and the place was an annual dinner of the American Booksellers' Association, at which Burgess was one of the honored guests. It was the custom at these dinners for the guest authors to present to the assembled company souvenir copies of their latest books. For this particular occasion Burgess prepared a mock-solemn commemorative jacket of his latest, placing on the front cover a doctored picture of a fetching female that he had lifted from a dental advertisement. He dubbed his creation Miss Belinda Blurb and appended a self-congratulatory text. Seven years later in his work *Burgess Unabridged*, Burgess himself defined the word that he had coined:

> *Blurb* 1. A flamboyant advertisement; an inspired testimonial. 2. Fulsome praise; a sound like a publisher. . . On the 'jacket' of the 'latest' fiction, we find the blurb; abounding in agile adjectives and adverbs, attesting that this book is the 'sensation of the year'.

The coinage of *blurb* filled a widely felt need, and the word quickly took off. The very sound of the word was suggestive of the "mush, gush and tosh" (in the words of one writer) that book publicists favor. From the beginning, Burgess himself and others applied *blurb* to all dust jacket copy. Before long, *blurb* was commonly applied to advertising copy appearing elsewhere and then to advertisements or publicity notices of any sort. Within the publishing business itself, however, the self-promotional copy, which is found on the dust jacket and usually written by the publisher's PR department or advertising firm, is called "front-flap copy." A typical example, perhaps overly familiar to bookstore browsers, might be: "At once the monumental saga of one American family over three generations and a panoramic history of the West they helped to tame!" On the other hand, within the trade, *blurb* tends to be restricted to a commendatory quote—usually anything but unsolicited—about a book by another author or celebrity. Groucho Marx is said to have created what may be the last word in blurbs. When asked to supply a quotable quote, he accommodated with the line: "I've been laughing ever since I picked up your book. Some day I'm going to read it."

Burgess is responsible for popularizing another humorous term in the language, *bromide* in the sense 'tiresome person'. Bromides (compounds of the element bromine) were introduced as sedatives in the nineteenth century. In 1906 Burgess published a book titled *Are You a Bromide?*, doubtless striking anxiety into the hearts of millions. The metaphorical extension is similar to the more recent use (from the 1960's) of *downer* 'barbiturate' in the sense 'depressing person or situation'.

[coined 1907 by Gelett Burgess †1951 Am. humorist & illustrator]

bobby   See DERBY.
[fr. *Bobby,* nickname fr. *Robert,* after Sir *Robert* Peel †1850 Eng. statesman who organized the London police force]

bobolink   See PIGEON.
[fr. earlier *Bob-o-Lincoln, boblincon,* of imit. origin]

bobwhite   See PIGEON.
[imit.]

bodega   See BOUTIQUE.
[Sp, fr. L *apotheca* storehouse]

bodice   Not infrequently a singular word like *pease* is taken, because of its final consonant sound, to be a plural and a new word (like *pea*), more obviously singular in form, is created. The opposite process—the creation of a new word from a plural form assumed to be singular—is less common but not unknown in English. The word *bodice* represents such a derivation. One sense of the word *body* is 'the part of a garment which covers the body or trunk'. In the seventeenth and eighteenth centuries, a woman's corset was often called a "pair of bodies." The plural *bodies* or *bodice* was eventually interpreted as a singular. *Bodice* is now most often used to refer to the upper part of a woman's dress excluding the sleeves.
    Another singular plural is *chintz.* The original name for the fabric was *chint,* borrowed from its Hindi name *chīt.* The plural of *chint* was frequently used in business; merchants discussed the sale of "muslins, silks, and chints." *Chint* was less often met with in noncommercial contexts than such words as *muslin* and *silk,* with the result that *chints,* the most familiar form of the word, was assumed to be the singular. A very slight alteration has given us the modern spelling *chintz.*
    For the formation of new singulars from words which merely seem plural see SHERRY.

[fr. earlier *bodies,* pl. of *body* (part of a garment)]

boeotian   See PHILISTINE.
[*Boeotia,* district in ancient Greece (fr. L, fr. Gk *Boiōtia*) + E -*an*]

Boer   See VILLAIN.
[D, lit., farmer]

bohemian   See GYPSY.
[*Bohemia,* formerly a kingdom, now a province of western Czechoslovakia, thought of as the home of the Gypsies (trans. of F *bohème*) + E -*an*]

bombast   The original meaning of *bombast* (now obsolete) is 'cotton or any soft fibrous material used as padding or stuffing'. It is derived, through Middle French *bombace*, from Medieval Latin *bombax*, which means 'cotton', in spite of the fact that the original Latin *bombyx* and its Greek source refer to silk. According to one source, the shift was occasioned by an error going back to the Roman scholar Pliny, who had reported that cotton was produced by an insect analogous to the silkworm. *Bombast* has been retained in modern English because it took on the figurative sense of 'a pretentious or inflated style of speech or writing'. Thus the basic sense of 'stuffing or padding' has survived, but now the stuffing consists of words rather than cotton.

Another word that has undergone a similar development is *fustian*. In its earliest sense *fustian* is 'a fabric made from cotton and linen', but like *bombast* it too is now used to mean 'pretentious speech or writing'. The word itself is from Medieval Latin *fustaneum*, whose origin is disputed. One account traces it to Latin *fustis* 'club, staff', as a translation of Greek *xylinon*, literally meaning 'wooden' (from *xylon*, 'wood, club') but applied to cotton. That such an origin is at least semantically possible is shown by another Medieval Latin term referring to cotton, *lana de ligno*, literally 'wool of wood'. Such a conception lies at the basis of the German word for cotton to this day, *Baumwolle*, literally 'tree-wool'. Another account derives *fustaneum* from the Cairo suburb Fostat (Arabic *fusṭāṭ*), where fustian is said to have been manufactured. Even on that route we wind up back at Latin, since *fusṭāṭ*, literally 'camp', comes (via Greek transmission) from Late Latin *fossatum* 'ditch, fosse'. See also DENIM.

[modif. of MF *bombace*, fr. ML *bombac-*, *bombax* cotton, alter. of L *bombyc-*, *bombyx* silkworm, silk, fr. Gk *bombyk-*, *bombyx* silkworm, silk garment, prob. of Per origin; akin to Per *pamba* cotton]

bonfire   When Samuel Johnson brought out his great Dictionary of the English Language in 1755, he defined *bonfire* as "a fire made for some publick cause of triumph or exaltation", and derived the word from French *bon* 'good' plus English *fire*. Occasionally a correspondent writes us at Merriam-Webster, championing this etymology as against the rather gloomy one we give in our dictionaries, that it is from Middle English *bonefyre*, literally 'a fire of bones'. In support of the jollier etymology are cited such foreign words for 'bonfire' as German *Freudefeuer*, literally 'joy fire', French *feu de joie*, Italian *fuoco d'allegrezza*, and so forth.

There are several reasons for preferring the "bone fire" etymology. Among them are these:

(1) The creation posited by Johnson's etymology would be somewhat unusual, a French/Anglo-Saxon hybrid: for *fire* is purely native.

(2) Knowing that the word goes back to the fifteenth century, we might expect it to have evolved to *boonfire*, since *boon* (as in *boon companion*) is the form that developed from the French *bon* when it was borrowed at this early date.

(3) The spelling in our earliest attestation (ca. 1475) is *banefire,* and *bane* is a spelling of *bone* which long continued common in Scotland.

Even more telling, however, is the fact that the earliest appearance is glossed, in Latin, as 'fire of bones'—*ignis ossium.* And a citation from the fifteenth century confirms that this is not just a learned folk-etymology: "One is clene bones and no woode, and that is called a bone fyre."

[ME *bonefyre,* fr. *bone, bon* bone + *fyre* fire]

bonus See SALARY.
[L, good]

boojum See JABBERWOCKY.
[perh. fr. *boojum,* an imaginary creature in *The Hunting of the Snark* by Lewis Carroll (Charles L. Dodgson) †1898 Eng. mathematician and writer]

book The Old English noun *bōc* denoted both 'a written document' and 'beech'. It has been suggested that the bark of the beech might have been used for writing runic characters on, this giving rise to the 'written document' sense. The 'written document' sense is actually attested earlier than the 'beech' sense, however, thus casting the relationship into some doubt; indeed, the 'book' sense is already attested for the cognate of *book* in the earliest stages of the Germanic sisters of Old English (Gothic, Old High German, and Old Norse), so this meaning is very old. But it is certainly true that objects are often named for the materials from which they are made. For example, we find Old English *æsc* 'spear' named from the ash-tree, and Old English *lind* 'shield', named from the linden or lime-tree. Further evidence for the concretely material origin of the 'book' sense is the fact that in Old English and its Germanic sisters, the word for 'book' was originally a plural, evidently in reference to the separate blocks that were bound together to make a book.

Bōc in the sense of 'beech' did not survive past the twelfth century; it was replaced by *bēce. Bōc* in the sense of 'written document' dates from the ninth century, and although it is now obsolete it gave rise to the sense 'a set of written sheets of skin or paper or tablets of wood or ivory'. From this evolved the senses 'a set of written, printed, or blank sheets bound together into a volume' and 'a long written or printed literary composition'. By 1200 *book* was being applied to a section of a longer work, such as a book of the Bible or a book of Virgil's *Aeneid.* Its use for 'a record of commercial transactions' dates from the end of the fifteenth century.

The writing material used by Egyptians, Greeks, and Romans was the pith of the papyrus reed, which was cut into thin strips, pressed together, and dried to form a smooth, thin writing surface. For such writing material the Greeks used either of two words: *papyros,* which the Romans took as *papyrus,* and *chartēs,* which became *charta* in Latin. The Latin noun *liber,* originally denoting the inner bark of a tree, also came to be used for 'a sheet of papyrus used for writing' and then acquired the additional senses of 'book, volume, long document' and 'a division of a long literary work'.

From the Latin *liber* English derived *library* and *librarian,* and from the Greek *chartēs* English derived, through Latin and French, the words *chart, charter,* and *card.* (See also CARTEL.) The Greek *papyros,* after passing through Latin, was taken into early French as *papier* in the thirteenth century and then borrowed into English in the fourteenth century. A poet of that time, possibly Chaucer, used it in the *Romaunt of the Rose,* which is translated from French: "Sek the book of Seynt Austyn,/ Be it in papir or perchemyn." By Chaucer's time paper was probably being made from rag pulp, and so the connection between *paper* and *papyrus* became solely etymological.

[ME, fr. OE *bōc*]

boondoggle   *Boondoggle* sounds like one of those colorful concoctions so popular in the nineteenth century—*hornswoggle, sockdolager, rumbustious, tetotaciously, exflunctified*—but it didn't come to widespread public attention until 1935. On 4 April of that year it popped up in a headline in the *New York Times* over a story reporting an investigation by the Aldermanic Committee to Investigate the Relief Administration in New York City. A witness, Robert Marshall, testified that he taught boon doggles (the *Times* spelled it as two words) to relief recipients. The word caught the aldermen's interest, and they asked him about it. Here is how the *Times* reported it:

> "I spend a good deal of time explaining it," the witness said somewhat sadly. "Boon doggles is simply a term applied back in the pioneer days to what we call gadgets today—to things men and boys do that are useful in their everyday operations or recreations or about their home.
> "They may be making belts in leather, or maybe belts by weaving ropes, or it might be belts by working with canvas, maybe a tent or a sleeping bag. In other words, it is a chamber of horrors where boys perform crafts that are not designed for finesse and fine work, but simply a utility purpose."
> "Who gave it that outlandish name?" asked Chairman Deutsch.
> "That is an old-time name," the witness replied. "They catch it out West," he added hopefully.
> "Named for Daniel Boone?" inquired Vice Chairman Joseph E. Kinsley.
> "No, it is not named for Daniel Boone. It is boon doggles. It is spelled differently."

The *Times* story was picked up in many other newspapers, and *boondoggle* and *boondoggling* were quickly adapted by opponents of the New Deal as terms for money-wasting, unproductive projects.

If witness Marshall was vague about the sort of handicrafts he was teaching, he was even vaguer about the origin of the word. Its sudden widespread appearance in the press excited much speculation about its origin. The earliest explanation to surface—within four days of the original story—credited *boondoggle* to Robert H. Link, a Rochester, N.Y., man involved in the Boy Scouts, variously described as an Eagle Scout and as a Scoutmaster. Other explanations were offered. One traced the word to an Ozark term for 'gadget' and added speculation about Daniel Boone's supposedly having made playthings for his dog. Another claimed it was a northern British term. A retired colonel offered the explanation that *boondoggle* was derived from the same Tagalog word that gave us English *boondocks*. Another derived it from the iron-smelting industry, claiming the word was used to designate unprofitable attempts to produce good iron from slag.

The only one of these explanations to bear scrutiny was the first. The story of Link's coining the word had been written up in *Scouting,* a Boy Scout publication, in March 1930, five years before the New York City *boondoggle* surfaced. The occasion was an earlier flurry of interest in the word in connection with the World Jamboree of Scouts in England in 1929. The word had been applied to the Boy Scout plaited lanyard—a standard item of scouting handicraft—either by Link or someone else, and one of the lanyards so designated had been presented to the Prince of Wales at the Jamboree. What had been a local Rochester, N.Y., scouting word was thus, through the Jamboree, more widely diffused through the scouting world. The author of the *Scouting* article quotes a few paragraphs from the English magazine *Punch* from the fall of 1929 discussing the word; the occasion of the *Punch* notice was the presentation at the Jamboree of a boondoggle to Lord Baden-Powell, founder of the Boy Scouts.

Professor Harold H. Bender of Princeton, the chief etymologist of Webster's New International Dictionary, Second Edition, carried on considerable correspondence with the Boy Scouts in trying to pin down the origin. Various Scout executives in Missouri, Arkansas, and Texas were asked about *boondoggle* as an Ozark term; none of them knew it except as the lanyard, although one did turn up an informant who thought *boondoggling* meant 'piddling around'. (The word does not appear in the Ozark word list of Vance Randolph's *Down in the Holler.*) While they failed to find an Ozark connection, they did incidentally confirm the term's familiarity in Scouting circles.

[coined 1925 by Robert H. Link †1957 Am. scoutmaster]

boor See VILLAIN.

[D *boer* peasant, farmer, short for MD *gheboer, ghebuur,* fr. *ghe-* co- + *-boer, buur* dweller; akin to OHG *gi-* co- and to OE *gebūr* dweller, farmer, OHG *gibūro* peasant, fellow countryman, OE & OHG *būan* to dwell]

boss *Boss,* used as a designation for the person who gives the orders, came into English from the Dutch *baas* 'master' probably around the middle of the seventeenth century. It came in by way of New Amsterdam, or New York, as it was renamed when English colonists took it over. The treaty of Breda in 1667 between England, the Dutch republic, France, and

Denmark left New York and New Jersey in English hands and left us a number of Americanisms of Dutch descent including *boss.*

Our earliest citations for the word, dated around 1649 and 1653, are both poor approximations of the Dutch spelling. No one has yet turned up any eighteenth-century evidence, but we find the modern spelling *boss* current in 1806 when Washington Irving used it. It seems to have enjoyed considerable popularity among the lower orders of society, "propagated by the proletarian self-assertion that preceded the opening of the first Century of the Common Man, with Jackson's election in 1828," as H. L. Mencken put it. An English traveler named Captain Hamilton reviled *boss* along with many other Americanisms in 1833, and James Fenimore Cooper viewed it with distaste in 1838. Part of the success of *boss* seems to have resulted from an American aversion to *master,* which was common in British use.

About the time Fenimore Cooper was criticizing the noun, *boss* came into attributive use. It was first used in such combinations as *boss shoemaker, boss carpenter,* and *boss fiddler,* where it indicated a person of high skill and proficiency at a trade or craft. From such use it was easy to extract the notion of excellence, and in the second half of the nineteenth century *boss* was used as an all-purpose adjective of high approval. Mark Twain used it in *Huckleberry Finn:*

> Good land, duke, lemme hug you! It's the most dazzling idea 'at ever a man struck. You have cert'nly got the most astonishin' head I ever see. Oh, this is the boss dodge, ther' ain't no mistake 'bout it. . . .

We do not know how popular this adjective use was, since it must have been mostly a spoken use. But it cropped up from time to time in print; there are examples in the Merriam-Webster files from the 1920s and 1940s. It had a considerable revival in the 1960s, turning up almost simultaneously in the lingo of surfers, rock musicians, and car-racing enthusiasts. The Dictionary of American Regional English finds the revived *boss* most frequent in the speech of black Americans. Our earliest evidence associating the adjectival *boss* with blacks dates from around 1880; it may be that it was kept alive and transmitted through the medium of black speech.

Boss became a verb in the 1850s, and the noun was applied to the political boss in the 1860s. Both of these uses are still current. The political use got a big boost from the notoriety of Boss Tweed of New York in the 1870s, and it was probably also helped by its frequent appearance in *Time* magazine in the years following World War II. It may have been *Time*'s use that led Harry Truman to remark, "When a leader is in the Democratic Party, he's a boss; when he's in the Republican Party, he's a leader."

[D *baas* master, fr. MD *baes;* akin to Fris *baes* master]

botulism   See BOWEL.

[ISV *botul-* (fr. L *botulus*) + *-ism;* orig. formed as G *botulismus*]

boulevard   *Boulevard* is a borrowing from French, where the word first appeared (spelled *bolevers,* then *bollewerc*) in the fourteenth century in regions abutting Dutch-speaking territories. French had derived it from the Middle Dutch word *bolwerc,* which in turn was borrowed without change from the Middle High German. The German word, made up of *bole,* 'plank', and *werc,* 'work', had the same meaning as, and is the ultimate source of, the English *bulwark,* which itself first appeared in the fifteenth century as *bulwerke.*

The French *boulevard* was originally used for 'rampart of a fortification', and like our word *bulwark* was used in both a literal and a figurative sense of 'defense'. As the city of Paris outgrew its original walls, the old ramparts became simple promenades but retained the old name of *boulevard.* By the eighteenth century the word had acquired the sense 'a broad street lined with trees', and it was this sense that was borrowed into English in the eighteenth century. It has since taken on, in English, the additional sense 'a grassed or landscaped strip in the center or between the curbings and sidewalks of a boulevard'.

[F, modif. of MD *bolwerc*]

bourbon See WHISKEY.
[fr. *Bourbon* County, Kentucky]

boutique *Boutique* has been used in French for a retail shop since the thirteenth century. It has been knocking on the doors of English since the late eighteenth century, being used in travel literature and other writing as a word for a small shop in various parts of the world. It made its most successful penetration of English in the 1950s, in the milieu of the fashion industry. The large couturiers of Paris began setting up small specialty shops selling accessories and other fashion items in the street levels of their large and sumptuous buildings. These small shops were termed *boutiques.* The idea and the practice spread rapidly to New York and London and thence to the rest of the English-speaking world. Boutiques sprouted everywhere—sometimes small shops, and sometimes separate departments in large stores. In American English the word has been further extended to a number of small specialized businesses: small advertising agencies, small investment services, and even small specialized wineries in California.

The mention of wine brings us to the related word *bodega,* which comes to English through Spanish. It's a Spanish word for 'warehouse' and is often applied to the warehouses where sherry is aged. It is also applied to the winery and to places where wine (and other suitable beverages) can be drunk. All of these Spanish applications have been, from time to time, used in English. In the American Spanish from Cuba and Puerto Rico, *bodega* also means 'grocery', and it is in this use that it has most recently and commonly appeared in American English, applied to small groceries in the Hispanic neighborhoods of American cities. Some of these sell wine and beer, too, and partake of the earlier use of the word.

Both *boutique* and *bodega* are derived from Greek *apothēkē* 'storehouse', and *bodega* came by way of Latin *apotheca,* also meaning 'storehouse'. The Latin *apotheca* had a derivative *apothecarius* 'shopkeeper', which eventually found its way into English as *apothecary*. *Apothecary* was applied to both the person—more often *druggist, pharmacist,* or *chemist* now—who kept the specialized shop and to the shop itself—now usually *drugstore* or *pharmacy* in American English. In the seventeenth century Samuel Pepys could note matter-of-factly that he went "into London to Mr. Laxton's, my Lord's apothecary," but few people nowadays use the word unself-consciously.

The tail end of Greek *apothēkē* found its way into the French *bibliothèque* 'library', and that tail end of *bibliothèque* went into the modern coinage *discothèque* used first in French and then in English (spelled *discotheque,* without the accent) for the nightclubs where recorded music is played for the patrons to dance. Today's young people have shortened the word to *disco,* which severs our etymological connection right here.

[F, prob. fr. OProv *botica,* fr. Gk *apothēkē* warehouse]

bowdlerize   Editors usually work behind the scenes and remain in obscurity while authors bask in fame. Few editors have ever achieved the public attention gained by Thomas Bowdler (1754–1825). Although Bowdler was trained to be a physician, debilitating injuries and illnesses kept him from enjoying his chosen profession. From the 1780s on, he engaged in mostly extramedical pursuits. Some of his activities led him to various parts of Europe, and when he entered his literary phase, he took to warning English travelers against the uncleanliness of watering places in France. Expanding the scope of his interest in purification, he next tackled works of literature. In 1818 he published an edition of Shakespeare which he titled *The Family Shakespeare.* Its title page promised that "those words and expressions are omitted which cannot with propriety be read aloud in a family." Appropriating to himself the discretion he thought Shakespeare lacked, Bowdler reiterated his position in the preface: "Many words and expressions occur which are of so indecent a nature as to render it highly desirable that they should be erased." No play of Shakespeare's escaped Bowdler's broad eraser. Although Bowdler's edition met with adverse critical reaction almost immediately, it pleased the nineteenth-century public: four reissues were printed before his death, and at least four more afterwards. Having cleaned up Shakespeare, Bowdler proceeded to purify Gibbon's *History of the Decline and Fall of the Roman Empire.* Again, his title page promised a text marked by "the careful omissions of all passages of an irreligious or immoral tendency." In a display of supreme hubris, Bowdler even asserted that Gibbon himself would have approved of his deletions and that his edition would henceforth be the definitive edition of that classic work. When Bowdler was not attacking the classics of literature, he was an active participant in the Proclamation Society, which went about enforcing royal proclamations against impiety and vice. Bowdler's purification crusade was carried on by his nephew. A decade after his death Bowdler's name had become synonymous with expurgated works, and by 1836 the verb *bowdlerize* had been used to describe the purging of literary works.

[Thomas *Bowdler* †1825 Eng. editor + E *-ize*]

bowel   The Latin noun *botulus* denoted 'a sausage', and the diminutive form *botellus* was used for 'a small sausage'. During the Medieval Latin period *botellus* came to be used for 'intestine', presumably because of the physical similarity between the two. It was in this 'intestine' sense that *botellus* was taken into twelfth-century French as *boel* or *boiel*. In the fourteenth century, English borrowed the French word as *bowel*.

The Latin word for sausage has another descendant in English as well. In the nineteenth century, a type of food poisoning associated with improperly preserved sausages was called *botulismus* (from the Latin *botulus*) by German physicians. This term was taken into English and later anglicized to *botulism*. The poisoning has since been found to be caused by other, especially canned, foods containing the bacterium *Clostridium botulinum*.

Either *intestinum* or *interaneum* could be used in Latin for 'intestine'. The noun *intestinum* was derived from the adjective *intestinus*, meaning 'internal'. English borrowed the adjective as *intestine* in the early part of the sixteenth century, and used it to mean 'of or relating to the internal affairs of a country or people'. It was used chiefly in such phrases as "intestine feuds," "intestine wars," and "intestine conflicts." Toward the end of the sixteenth century, English also borrowed the noun *intestine* with its Latin sense.

The Latin *interaneum* was derived from the adjective *interaneus*, meaning 'interior'. This noun was usually used in the plural form *interanea* 'intestines', and this was altered to *intralia* in Medieval Latin. French took this noun as *entrailles* in the twelfth century, which English borrowed as *entrails* early in the fourteenth century.

[ME, fr. OF *boel, boiel*, fr. ML *botellus*, fr. L, small sausage, dim. of L *botulus* sausage; perh. akin to OE *cwith* belly, womb, OHG *quiti* vulva, ON *kvithr* belly, womb, Goth *qithus* stomach, womb]

bower   See VILLAIN.
[ME *bour* bedroom, dwelling, fr. OE *būr;* akin to OE & OHG *būan* to prepare, live, dwell, *būr* pantry, Goth *bauan* to live, dwell, OE *bēon* to be]

bowler   See DERBY.
[after John *Bowler* fl1861 Eng. hatmaker]

boycott   See DERBY.
[after Charles C. *Boycott* †1897 Eng. land agent in County Mayo, Ireland, who was ostracized in 1880 for refusing to reduce rents]

brandy   Brandy is a liquor distilled from wine or from fermented fruit juice. Thus it is not too surprising to learn that an earlier English form is *brandywine.* However, the earliest forms found in English are *brandwine* and *brandewine,* both used in the early seventeenth century. This word is derived from the Dutch *brandewijn,* earlier *brantwijn.* The second element in this compound is Dutch for 'wine', and the first element, *brant,* similar to English *brand* and *burnt,* is indeed derived from the Dutch verb *bernen,* 'to burn'. Thus the name 'burnt wine' refers to wine that has been distilled over a fire. In English the process of shortening *brandwine* or *brandywine* to *brandy* was already underway by the middle of the seventeenth century. See also GIN, WHISKEY.

[short for *brandywine,* earlier *brandwine,* fr. D *brandewijn,* fr. MD *brantwijn,* fr. *brant* (past part. of *bernen* to burn, distill) + *wijn* wine; akin to OE *biernan* to burn and OE *wīn* wine]

breakfast See JEJUNE.
[ME *brekfast,* fr. *breken* to break + *fast*]

bridal The second-oldest sense of *ale* is "a festival or feast" at which, as you might guess, a prominent activity was the drinking of ale. There were many kinds of ales in this sense—leet-ales, clerk-ales, bed-ales, soul-ales, dirge-ales. The historian G. M. Trevelyan tells us that in the fifteenth century church ales were a common means of raising funds for the parish church. One William Harrison, a traveling parson, reported with some satisfaction near the end of the sixteenth century that there were fewer of these and that the "heathenish rioting at *bride-ales*" was considerably diminished.

The bride-ale, or wedding feast—it seems to have been somewhat rowdier than the average reception today—is the earliest ale mentioned in English. It is mentioned in the Anglo-Saxon Chronicle for the year 1075. There the term refers to the wedding of the Earl of Norfolk to the daughter of the Earl of Hereford and is memorialized in a couplet (modernized):

> There was that bride-ale
> The source of man's bale.

The balefulness was not inherent in the bride-ale itself, but at this particular merrymaking the two earls and some others plotted a rebellion against William the Conqueror, then away in France putting down some other rebellion. The outcome was not fortunate for the earls.

The word *bride-ale* still has some use in historical reference, but it is not an everyday word. By the fourteenth century such shortened forms as *bridale, bridall,* and *bridal* were in use; the last of these is the living word today. Around the fourteenth century, too, the application of the word broadened to include the whole proceedings of the wedding and not just the wedding feast. And by the seventeenth century *bridal* was in frequent use as a modifier of other words—*dinner, chamber, bed, cake, bowl*—associated with the event. Since the *-al* ending looked and sounded the same as the *-al* ending of such adjectives as *natal, fatal,* and *mortal, bridal* was eventually—certainly in the eighteenth century—perceived as an adjective. This is its common use today.

On the other side of the aisle is the *bridegroom*. Back when Earl Ralph of Norfolk was the bridegroom, the second part of the word was *-guma*, meaning 'man', which became *-gome* in Middle English. But by the sixteenth century the spelling of *-gome* had become *-grome* or *-groom*. The intrusive *r* came by way of the word *groom*, more familiar by then than the old *gome:* folk etymology at work. *Bridegroom* revolted Noah Webster. In his 1828 dictionary he entered it with the etymological spelling *bridegoom*, saying "This word, by a mispronouncing of the last syllable, has been corrupted into *bridegroom*, which signifies *a bride's hostler;* groom being a Persian word, signifying a man who has the care of horses. Such a gross corruption or blunder ought not to remain a reproach to philology." Reproach to philology or not, *bridegroom* continued in use—no one except Noah seems to have used *bridegoom*. In his second edition, Webster went to *bridegroom*, but retained his complaint in the etymology.

For other examples of folk etymology see FOLK ETYMOLOGY.

[ME *bridale*, fr. *bridale*, noun, fr. OE *brȳdealu*, fr. *brȳd* bride + *ealu* ale]

bridegroom   See BRIDAL.

[by folk etymology fr. ME *bridegome*, fr. OE *brȳdguma;* akin to OHG *brūtigomo* bridegroom, ON *brūthgumi;* all fr. a prehistoric NGmc-WGmc compound whose first constituent is the word represented by OE *brȳd* bride and whose second constituent is the word represented by OE *guma* man]

brig   The Old Italian verb *brigare* 'to fight' gave rise to an interesting spectrum of English words. The most straightforward development came from the derived noun *brigata* 'company, troop', which French borrowed as *brigade* in the fourteenth century and passed on to English in the seventeenth. A further derivative, *brigadier*, is likewise still a military term. But another Old Italian derivative, *brigante* 'irregular soldier', had a different fate. French borrowed the word as *brigand* in the fourteenth century in the original sense, but by the fifteenth century the meaning had shifted to that of 'highwayman, robber': disbanded and irregular soldiers have at numerous times in history worn out their welcome in the towns on which they preyed. English got *brigand* from French in the fourteenth century, and the word shows the same sequence of meanings in our language, the earlier sense of 'irregular soldier' being now obsolete. However, a derivative of *brigand*, French *brigandine* (borrowed by English in the fifteenth century), still means 'body armor' in both languages, thus retaining a memory of the original military sense.

Italian *brigante* gave rise to another derivative in that language, *brigantino*, applied to a small, fast ship such as would be good for skirmishing. This came into French as *brigantin*, which English borrowed as *brigantine* in the seventeenth century. In the eighteenth century this was shortened to *brig* and denoted ships of various sorts. It is considered likely that *brig* in the sense 'military place of detention' is derived from this, from the image of prison ships.

[short for *brigantine,* fr. MF *brigantin,* fr. OIt *brigantino,* fr. *brigante* brigand + *-ino* -ine]

brigade   See BRIG.
[F, fr. MF, fr. OIt *brigata,* fem. of *brigato,* past part. of *brigare* to fight]

brigadier   See BRIG.
[F, fr. *brigade* + *-ier*]

brigand   See BRIG.
[ME *brigaunt,* fr. MF *brigand,* fr. OIt *brigante,* fr. *brigare* to fight, fr. *briga* strife, of Celt origin; akin to OIr *brīg* strength, virtue, W *bri* fame, honor]

brigandine   See BRIG.
[ME *brigandyne, brigantyn,* fr. MF *brigandine,* fr. *brigand* + *-ine*]

brigantine   See BRIG.
[MF *brigantin,* fr. OIt *brigantino,* fr. *brigante* brigand + *-ino* -ine]

Brobdingnagian   See GARGANTUAN.
[*Brobdingnag,* imaginary country inhabited by giants in *Gulliver's Travels,* by Jonathan Swift †1745 Eng. satirist + E *-ian*]

bromide   See BLURB.
[ISV *brom-* + *-ide*]

brontosaurus   Down through the ages people have been finding strange assemblages of bones in the earth. A number of different theories about the source of these bones were advanced in earlier times. The Chinese asserted that these were dragon bones and ground them up to use as a pharmaceutical. A popular Western idea was that the bones were the remains of the giants mentioned several times in the Bible. By the eighteenth century scientists were beginning to realize that the bones were the fossilized remains of ancient creatures, animals now extinct. By the nineteenth century paleontologists were systematically uncovering skeletons of the largest of these animals. In 1841, Sir Richard Owen, a British anatomist and paleontologist, originated the word *Dinosauria* as a group term for the extinct creatures. His new term combined the Greek words *deinos* 'terrible' and *sauros* 'lizard' as an evocative description of what he thought of as a group of huge, terrifying animals. From his formal word for the group came the general term *dinosaur.*

By the 1870s the hunt for dinosaur skeletons was on in earnest. American colleges and museums vied with wealthy private citizens like Andrew Carnegie to finance digging expeditions to the American West. Two men emerged the clear winners of a drive to discover the most dinosaur skeletons in the shortest amount of time. The two were Othniel Charles Marsh and Edward Drinker Cope. Both were professors and paleontologists, both were associated with the U.S. Geological Survey, and each bitterly disliked and distrusted the other. Before this rival pair began their excavations, only nine dinosaur species had been discovered in North America. Between them they added 136 species to the list and were responsible for the splendid dinosaur-skeleton collections that can be seen today in Yale's Peabody Museum and in the American Museum of Natural History in New York.

But in at least one instance, the confused situation of feuding expeditions not sharing information in the proper scientific manner resulted in the same dinosaur species being given two different names. Working in Wyoming, Marsh was the first to find two skeletons (without skulls) of a huge *sauropod* (from Greek *sauros* 'lizard' and New Latin *-poda* 'part resembling a foot') new to science. He named the animal *Apatosaurus,* meaning 'deceptive lizard'. Later on, another sauropod skeleton was uncovered, this time by an expedition working under Cope's direction, and this supposedly new species was dubbed *Brontosaurus,* or 'thunder lizard', a reference to the animal's earth-shaking size (it could weigh 30 to 40 tons and reach a length of 75 feet). It was not until the dust had settled and museums began the tedious, time-consuming job of classifying all the material that Marsh and Cope had feverishly dug up that they discovered the duplication. *Apatosaurus* and *Brontosaurus* were one and the same. Scientific rules of taxonomy are both clear and strict: the first name given to a new species is the correct one. By the time the mistake was uncovered, however, *Brontosaurus* was firmly entrenched not just in scientific literature but in the public's imagination as well. Modern publications usually call the plant-eating sauropod *Apatosaurus* but add that it was formerly called *Brontosaurus.* Some references still use *Brontosaurus,* but point out that the correct term is really *Apatosaurus. Brontosaur,* a general word for this group of slow-moving sauropods, is still in widespread use.

Apatosaurus has had to endure a double whammy: until recently even our conception of its appearance was wrong. Remember that Marsh's original discovery of the animal he named *Apatosaurus* consisted of two skeletons without skulls. He searched rather far afield for skulls that would complete his find. As it turned out, he did find two skulls and shipped them back East as part of the *Apatosaurus* skeletons. But these were not *Apatosaurus* skulls. They belonged to another sauropod, a related animal but certainly not the same creature. Based upon these skulls, artists' renderings of brontosaur skulls showed a massive, pleasantly rounded muzzle. The error was discovered in 1979, when a genuine *Apatosaurus* skull was found. It was much longer and more slender than the old, misidentified skull, and recent drawings of *Apatosaurus* not only give the dinosaur its correct name but finally depict its relatively slender, elongated head correctly.

[NL *Brontosaurus* (former genus name), fr. *bront-* + *-saurus*]

Brother Jonathan   See UNCLE SAM.
[¹*brother* + *Jonathan* (the name); prob. fr. the frequent use of Old Testament names among the English colonists in America]

brougham   See PHAETON.
[after Henry Peter *Brougham*, Baron Brougham and Vaux †1868 Scot. jurist]

brouhaha   In a fifteenth- or early sixteenth-century French farce, a priest disguised as the devil cried out, "Brou brou brou ha ha, brou ha ha!" By the mid-sixteenth century, French *brouhaha* was used as a noun meaning 'hubbub, uproar'. Some etymologists believe that *brouhaha* must be onomatopoeic in origin, but there is another possible explanation. The word may have come from the Hebrew phrase *bārūkh habbā'*, 'blessed be he who enters', from Psalm 118. This phrase has a fairly prominent place in Jewish worship because Psalm 118 is the last of the Hallel psalms, used at the great festivals. The twenty-sixth verse—"Blessed be he who enters in the name of the Lord! We bless you from the house of the Lord"—is a priestly benediction. The fact that an Italian dialect word *baruccaba* comes from this same phrase and also means 'hubbub' makes the suggestion of a Hebrew origin for *brouhaha* seem less farfetched.
   Another Italian word, *badonai,* has the same meaning and a parallel etymology; it comes from Hebrew *be adhōnāy,* 'by God'. The early appearance in the pseudo-devil's speech suggests that *brouhaha* may have been an intentional slight to the Jews. Good Christians of that time were only too willing to believe that the Jews were a diabolic people. The devil might well be expected to use words often heard at synagogues. However, a more innocent origin is also possible. *Bārūkh habbā',* frequently and rapidly spoken and not understood by worshipers whose knowledge of Hebrew was severely limited, could have come to stand for rapid, confused, or meaningless speech.
   The English word *patter,* 'to speak rapidly or chatter gibberish', has a similar history. It comes from the opening words of the Lord's Prayer, the Latin *pater noster.*

[F, perh. modif. of Heb *bārūkh habbā'* blessed be he who enters; fr. the frequent use in the synagogue of a passage containing these words, Ps 118:26 (RSV)]

buccaneer   Daniel Defoe, in his satire *The True-Born Englishman,* described that mongrel's ancestry: "Norwegian Pirates, Buccaneering Danes . . . with Norman-French compound the Breed." In 1700, when Defoe was able to speak thus cavalierly of "Buccaneering Danes," the general sense 'pirate' of the word *buccaneer* was quite new in English. A little earlier *buccaneer* had been limited to a particular kind of pirate—a freebooter of the seventeenth-century Spanish main. These men had adopted the eating habits of the French hunters living at that time in the West Indies, who were called *buccaneers* because they used the native Indian method of preparing and preserving meat by smoking it on a *buccan,* 'a wooden grid'. This type of grid was used by many South American Indians, but it was from the Tupi of Brazil that the French borrowed the name for it, *boucan*, which they carried with them to the West Indies.

[F *boucanier* French woodsman of the 17th century in the West Indies, pirate, fr. *boucaner* to smoke (meat) on a buccan, fr. MF *boucan* buccan, of Tupian origin]

buckaroo   When a word is borrowed into English from another language, the pronunciation is often changed to some degree, especially if in the language of origin the word contains sounds not normally used by native English speakers. A word may also be more readily naturalized if its form may be related to a familiar English word through folk etymology. Both of these processes have combined to give us the word *buckaroo*, which comes from the Spanish *vaquero*, 'cowboy'.

In Spanish a *v* in initial position as in *vaquero* is not pronounced with the upper front teeth and the lower lip as is English *v;* rather it is pronounced with both lips, resulting in a sound which English speakers might interpret as a form of *b*. Comparison of the word with some sense of English *buck* then gives rise to the form *buckaroo*.

Vaquero, which has also been borrowed directly into English with no spelling change, ultimately comes from Latin *vacca*, 'cow'. Another English word from this same source is *vaccine*. The Latin form *vaccinus*, 'of or from cows', gave English the word *vaccine*, originally used as an adjective with the same meaning as the Latin, but referring especially to something derived from cows infected with cowpox. In the late eighteenth century the English physician Edward Jenner discovered that inoculation with a form of cowpox was an effective preventative of smallpox. In honor of Jenner's work, the French chemist Louis Pasteur, who had been experimenting with other varieties of inoculation for a number of diseases, used the word *vaccination* for preventive inoculation in general and *vaccine* for the substance inoculated into the patient.

Pasteur's name has itself been immortalized in the word *pasteurize*. His discovery of a method for checking excessive fermentation and reducing disease in such liquids as wine, beer, and milk by heating them not only revolutionized the French wine and beer industries, but has since saved the lives of thousands of milk drinkers as well.

For other folk etymologies see FOLK ETYMOLOGY.

[by folk etymology fr. Sp *vaquero*, fr. *vaca* cow, fr. L *vacca*]

buckle   The diminutive *buccula* of Latin *bucca*, 'cheek', was also the name for the cheek-piece of a helmet. Its Old French descendant *bocle* or *boucle* designated the boss of a shield, which rather resembles a small cheek in being slightly protuberant on the face of the shield. The use of the word was later extended to belt fasteners. In this sense, the word was borrowed into Middle English. The first known use of *buckle* in English was in the poem "Most i ryden" (ca. 1325). This buckle was quite a costly article: "Hire gurdel of bete gold is al . . . the bocle is al of whalles bon."

(Her girdle is all of beaten gold . . . the buckle is all of whale's bone.) Dan Michel's *Ayenbite of Inwyt* (1340) made early use of *buckle* as a metaphor: "Thet chastete ssel bi straytliche y-loked . . . be abstinence . . . thet is the bocle of the gerdle." (Chastity shall be straitly locked . . . by abstinence . . . that is the buckle of the girdle.)

[ME *bocle*, fr. MF *bocle, boucle* boss of a shield, buckle, fr. L *buccula* small cheek, dim. of *bucca* cheek]

buddy   Young children often have trouble pronouncing certain combinations of letters in a word, particularly when an *r* and another consonant appear together. Many times, the *r* sound is replaced with a *w* or left out altogether. Occasionally, a word that is uniformly mispronounced becomes an established part of the language. Our word *buddy* is believed to be one such word that originated from a common mispronunciation. Children often have trouble enunciating the *r* in *brother,* so that the word comes out sounding more like *budda* or *buddy.* This version of the word stuck and has been used as an expression of endearment since at least the mid-nineteenth century. Later on, the word *buddy* came to have the more general meaning of "friend, companion, intimate partner."

Although this theory continues to prevail, it is not unchallenged. Many believe that *buddy* is much older. British coalminers used the word, variously spelled *buddy, buddie,* or *butty,* to designate a fellow worker as early as the late eighteenth century. Even if the "brother" use came first, there is a good chance that *butty* influenced the development of the meaning 'friend'. In any case, the term has become extremely popular in the United States, where it is also used casually as a form of address to any boy or man whose name is not known, as for example, "Say buddy, can you tell me how to get to Main Street?"

[prob. baby talk alter. of *brother*]

budget   From a word in an ancient Gallic language, the Romans formed the Latin noun *bulga,* denoting 'a leather bag or knapsack'. This noun became *bouge* when it was taken into twelfth-century French. By the end of that century, the diminutive form *bougette* was being used for 'a small bag'. English borrowed this word as *bowgette* in the fifteenth century and by 1611 or so had settled on the spelling *budget.* It was used for 'a usually leather pouch or wallet' and 'a leather or skin bottle'. Today these senses are found only in dialectal usage.

Near the end of the sixteenth century we find the earliest evidence of the use of *budget* for 'the contents of a pouch or wallet; a package, bundle, or collection'. This sense is also dialectal except when it refers to written or printed matter, as in "a budget of letters." The related sense of 'supply or quantity', such as "a budget of energy," can still be found in contemporary English.

The financial sense of *budget* is first attested in 1733, when it was used for 'a statement of the financial position of a government for the ensuing year based on estimates of expenditures and revenues'. Such a budget was prepared by the Chancellor of the Exchequer for the approval of the

House of Commons. By the 1850s, *budget* began being used nongovern-
mentally and more generally for a financial account of a family or individual. From this developed the sense of 'the money available, required, or
assigned to a particular purpose'.

[ME *bowgette,* fr. MF *bougette,* dim. of *bouge* leather bag, fr. L *bulga,*
fr. Gaulish; akin to MIr *bolg* bag, OE *bælg* bag, skin]

bug   A Middle English *bugge* was either a scarecrow or a hobgoblin. "As
a bugge either a man of raggis in a place where gourdis wexen kepith no
thing, so ben her goddis of tree." (As a bugge or a man of rags in a place
where gourds grow guards nothing, so are their gods of wood.) This was
John Wycliffe's rendering (in 1382) of the sixty-ninth verse of the sixth
chapter of the (Apocryphal) Book of Baruch. When the Douay Version of
the Old Testament was published in 1609, the "bugge . . . in a place
where gourdis wexen" had become "a scarecrow in a garden of cucum-
bers." A *bug* was by then no longer a scarecrow. That it was still a hobgoblin, Hamlet's "hoo! such bugs and goblins in my life—" (ca. 1600) indicates.
But this sense died early in the eighteenth century.

In the seventeenth century, the word *bug* was used to refer to insects,
especially to the bedbug. In Philip Massinger and Thomas Dekker's tragedy *The Virgin Martir* (1622), Spungius and Hircius, servants of Dorothea
(the virgin martyr), are tempted by Harpax, an evil spirit in human guise,
to desert Dorothea and the Christian faith to which she has converted
them·

> *Harpax.* . . . now that you see
>   The bonfire of your lady's state burnt out,
>   You give it over, do you not?
> *Hircius.*   Let her be hang'd!
> *Spungius.*   And pox'd!
> *Harpax.*   Why, now you're mine;
>   Come, let my bosom touch you.
> *Spungius.*   We have bugs, Sir.

The threat of bedbugs, however, is nothing to Harpax, and Spungius and
Hircius are won over.

Even in the seventeenth century, a *bug* was not always a bedbug. Daniel
Rogers, in *Naaman the Syrian, his disease and cure* (1642), wrote of "Gods
rare workmanship in the Ant, the poorest bugge that creeps." But the specific use of *bug* to mean 'bedbug' led to the word's becoming a name for
any member of the bedbug's order, Hemiptera. Entomologists insist that
no insect outside of this order is a true bug, though popular usage persists
in applying the word even to such creatures as spiders. *Bug,* 'insect', has
been extended to give us the other modern *bugs:* disease-causing germs,
enthusiasts (like "camera *bugs*"), concealed listening devices, and the like.

[ME *bugge* scarecrow, hobgoblin; akin to G dial. *bögge* hobgoblin, Norw
dial. *bugge* important man]

bull   See BEAR.

[prob. fr. the aggressive nature of the bull]

bulldog   The low-slung *bulldog* has bowed front legs that are so far apart that the dog looks as if it were eternally braced for trouble. Indeed its whole body has a sturdy, rock-solid appearance that suggests it could withstand a high wind and not blow over.

There was a time when the bulldog needed all the sturdiness it could muster. It also needed plenty of courage, as well as something the breed is not characterized by today: ferocity. The bulldog gets its name not from the fact that it resembles a domestic bull but from its use in the cruel and savage sport of bullbaiting. The bulldog was developed in England centuries ago specifically to attack an angry bull for the amusement of spectators, who could wager on the outcome. The bull was chained by the neck or leg to a stake in an open arena, and often it was roused to fury by being whipped or by having pepper blown into its nose. Then bulldogs were loosed in the arena. The dogs had been specially trained to grab the bull's sensitive nose. The most successful ones could slip past the bull's horns, seize it by the nose, and hold on, no matter how the bull tried to shake them loose. There were no winners in bullbaiting, for the bulldogs were often horribly injured or killed, and few bulls succeeded in shaking off the determined dogs. If one did, the spectators simply released more dogs into the arena.

When bullbaiting was finally outlawed by an act of the British Parliament in 1835, the bulldog's admirers suffered mixed feelings. As an attack animal the dog had outlived its usefulness. The bulldog's bred-in savagery could not be tolerated in a family pet. Yet, admirers did not want to lose the many desirable qualities of this old breed, such as determination and extraordinary courage. So the dog was developed into the compact, muscular creature that it is today, with its former aggressiveness completely eradicated.

Its four-square, low-center-of-gravity build has not changed. Nor has its undershot jaw. These characteristics helped its ancestors stand their ground and bite tenaciously and powerfully. Its determination remains unaltered, too. In fact, the breed's name is a synonym for tenacity. See also PIT BULL.

[*bull* + *dog*]

bullet   See BALLOT.

[MF *boulette* small ball, small missile & *boulet* cannonball, missile, diminutives of *boule* ball]

bulwark   See BOULEVARD.

[ME *bulwerke,* fr. MD *bolwerc,* fr. MHG, fr. *bole* plank + *werc* work, fr. OHG]

bum   See TRAMP.

[prob. short for *bummer,* prob. modif. of G *bummler,* fr. *bummeln* to loaf, dangle]

bunk   The word *bunk* in the meaning 'nonsense' is a shortened form of *bunkum,* a variant of *buncombe,* which in turn is the name of a county in North Carolina. So how did the name of a county come to be synonymous with *nonsense?* It may be said to have come about by an act of Congress. Around 1820 a congressman by the name of Felix Walker, who represented the district in which Buncombe County, North Carolina, was located, had stubbornly persisted in delivering an exceptionally long and wearisome speech to the sixteenth Congress despite the objections of his impatient colleagues. He later explained that he had been determined "to make a speech for Buncombe." His speech, then, was intended primarily to curry favor with his electors; whether or not it was relevant to the matter at hand was no concern of his. *Buncombe,* as well as its variant *bunkum,* quickly caught on as a synonym for meaningless political claptrap.

From political nonsense to any kind of insincere talk or action was but a short semantic step for *buncombe.* In *Pudd'nhead Wilson,* published in 1894, Mark Twain writes: "He said that he believed that the reward offered for the lost knife was humbug and buncombe." The shortened form, *bunk,* appeared about the year 1900 and is today the most common form.

[short for *bunkum,* var. of *buncombe,* fr. *Buncombe* County, North Carolina; fr. a remark made by Felix Walker *fl*1820, U.S. representative from the Congressional district including this county, who explained a seemingly irrelevant speech in Congress by the statement that he was speaking to Buncombe]

bureau   A word which today can apply to something as large and abstract as a division of government had its origins in a humble scrap of cloth. *Bureau* goes back to Old French *burel,* denoting a coarse woolen cloth such as the baize used to cover a desk. In form, *burel* seems to be a diminutive of *bure,* which has the same sense and is still used in Modern French. The problem is that *burel* is attested in the twelfth century, *bure* not till the fifteenth. It is possible that there is simply an accidental gap in the recording of *bure* in print and *burel* does indeed derive from it; alternately, *burel* may have been formed as a diminutive already in Vulgar Latin, from the word that later gave *bure.*

By a process of evolution typical of French, *burel* gave rise to a newer form *bureau,* which from denoting a coarse cloth came to denote the desk such a cloth often covered, a kind of semantic transfer known as metonymy. English borrowed the word in this sense in the seventeenth century— but the metonymy did not stop there, either in French or in English. *Bureau* was further extended (first in French, later in English) to denote the private office in which the desk stood and later came to apply abstractly to an office-based administrative unit.

Broad though this semantic span may be, it is matched exactly by the trajectory of another diminutive piece of cloth of Gallic and Latin etymology. In Latin, *pannus* meant a piece of cloth; this word is the source of our word *pane*, which originally had the same sense. From *pannus* Old French derived a diminutive *panel*, meaning a piece of cloth or specifically a saddle cushion. (It may be seen from these examples that "diminutive" here refers more to the presence of the ending than to the meaning of the word itself. Suffixes which in Latin functioned as true diminutive endings often became, in their Romance descendants, simply a handy way of beefing up the word, since many of the sounds of the Latin originals were being dropped. Thus the unsuffixed French descendant of *pannus* is simply *pan*, pronounced \pän\, a consonant followed by a single nasalized vowel.) Once again, *panel* gave rise to modern French *panneau:* but this time English borrowed the word early enough (in the fourteenth century) that it entered the language as *panel*, in which form it remained, unaffected by the sound change that affected its ancestor on the continent.

Panel first meant 'saddle-cloth' in English. Metonymy then took the word off in different directions. In the simplest, which would find little lasting influence, *panel* was applied to the saddle itself. But the real fortune of the word was made when, following an extended sense already existing in the legal French that was used in medieval England, *panel* was applied to a slip of parchment, particularly to one on which the names of jurors were inscribed. From this use it was extended to designating the jury, a use more commonly found today in the verb *impanel* (a jury), and it finally came to be applied to other collections of people with a common purpose.

[F, office, desk, cloth covering for desks and tables, coarse woolen cloth, fr. OF *burel* coarse woolen cloth (whence MF *bure*), fr. (assumed) VL *bura*, alter. of LL *burra* shaggy cloth, prob. of non-IE origin; akin to the source of Gk *berberion* shabby garment]

burke   On 28 January 1829, a crowd of some 30,000 people gathered in Edinburgh for the public hanging of a serial murderer. As the execution was about to begin, members of the throng cried out, "Burke him! Burke him!" So began the use of *burke* as a common verb meaning to kill by suffocation or strangulation. It was a matter of true justice that William Burke should die this way.

Burke was an Irish-born ne'er-do-well, who had drifted from job to job until 1827, when he turned up at an Edinburgh lodging house run by William Hare, a one-time traveling huckster. One night a fellow lodger, an elderly pensioner, happened to die in the house. Burke and Hare quickly saw this as an opportunity for personal gain and sold the body to a local surgeon, Robert Knox, for the purpose of dissection. The easy windfall inspired the men to conceive a plan whereby they would not have to leave the business of selling corpses to chance. Through their lodging house passed many anonymous wayfarers whose disappearance would attract scant attention. Over the next several months Burke and Hare, ably assisted by their wives, lured a number of such nameless wanderers into their house. There they got their hapless victims drunk and then proceeded to smother them—or strangle them, in the case of the feistier victims. They always did the deed in such a way as to leave no marks of violence. The bodies were then sold to Dr. Knox's school of anatomy for prices ranging from 8 to 14 pounds, considerable sums for the time. They disposed of at least 15 people in this fashion. Finally, on 31 October 1828, they made the mistake of choosing as their victim a poor old woman who was local. Her disappearance aroused the suspicions of the neighbors and the police and led to the exposure of their criminal enterprise. Although Burke was hanged, Hare escaped prosecution by turning king's evidence. Knox also was never charged, since Burke's confession had exonerated him of all knowledge of how the corpses had come into their possession. In an ironical twist of fate, Burke's own body was later dissected at the Edinburgh University Medical School.

The original sense of *burke,* popular in the aftermath of the execution but now little used, soon gave rise to the extended sense "to suppress (an inquiry) quietly or indirectly"—that is, to smother or hush up something. The notion of suppression is implicit in the concurrent sense of *burke* meaning "to set aside (an issue) without consideration or decision." Besides their lexical contribution, Burke and Hare were responsible for a liberalizing of the dissection laws so that anatomists could legally obtain corpses more easily. They are also said to have inspired another Edinburgh native, Robert Louis Stevenson, to write *The Body Snatchers.*

[after William *Burke* †1829 Ir. criminal, executed for this crime]

burlesque   In 1956 a license commissioner, in a report quoted in the *New York Times,* asserted that *burlesque* was "synonymous with the strip tease and the dialogue of unvarnished salaciousness." To this, many a would-be patron of the establishment in question doubtless replied: "Well, I certainly hope so!"

English borrowed *burlesque* intact from the French, which in turn had derived the word from the Italian *burlesco. Burlesco* itself was a derivative of *burla,* which in Italian and in Spanish (its language of origin) meant 'joke'. When *burlesque* was introduced into English in the seventeenth century, it was originally used of literary parodies. Increasingly, *burlesque* became associated with dramatic parodies as that form of theatrical entertainment developed and prospered. As with all parodies, theatrical burlesques derived their humor from the extreme disparity between the subject presented and the treatment it was accorded. The truly serious was treated with extreme levity, and the innately frivolous was treated with mock seriousness.

In the nineteenth century theatrical burlesques gradually ceased to be parodies of specific works or authors or of dramatic conventions or genres (such as heroic tragedy). Eventually, they became extravagantly absurd retellings of old, familiar stories. When burlesques were first mounted in the U.S., they generally followed the English pattern. Burlesques of Italian operas and romantic melodramas were especially popular. Many of these opera burlesques were performed by minstrel troupes, whose type of program strongly influenced the direction in which the burlesque show evolved.

Burlesque underwent a significant change in character in the 1860s. In 1868 Englishwoman Lydia Thompson introduced her troupe of provocatively dressed chorus girls, the British Blondes, to American theatergoers. At about the same time other stage entertainments, which were primarily spectacles, violated long-established standards regarding dress. A female ballet company in New York instituted the practice of having the women appear in costumes that bared their legs—something quite shocking in its time. By the 1870s New York theaters were routinely presenting, under the rubric of "burlesque," shows that were less concerned with parodying other theatrical or musical productions than with displaying the female figure. Unifying dramatic frameworks were discarded, as the shows became series of loosely connected songs and dances.

As burlesque continued to evolve, it assumed the varity-show format of vaudeville. Burlesque differed from vaudeville, however, in that its appeal was exclusively to males. Its humor was coarse and earthy: the comic monologues of baggy-pants comedians relied on dirty jokes, and double entendres abounded in the raucous skits. Above all, burlesque presented a plenitude of feminine pulchritude. The sensation created in 1893 by the belly dancing of Little Egypt at the World's Columbian Exposition in Chicago propelled burlesque to new frontiers of nudity. The striptease act became the main attraction and the identifying feature of burlesque in the first half of the twentieth century. If burlesque could still be regarded as parodying anything, it was probably the prevailing attitude of society concerning sex. Ironically, the change in that attitude—the sexual revolution—that occurred in the second half of the twentieth century brought about the eventual demise of burlesque. In a world of sexually explicit plays, films, and advertisements, topless bars, and minimal swimsuits, burlesque was an entertainment that no longer met a need.

See also VAUDEVILLE.

[F, fr. It *burlesco,* fr. *burla* joke, fr. Sp, prob. modif. of LL *burra* trifle, bit of nonsense, perh. fr. *burra* shaggy cloth]

burnsides   See SIDEBURNS.
[after Ambrose E. *Burnside* †1881 Am. general, who wore them]

bus   The Latin stem *omni-* meaning 'all' is familiar to English speakers through such compound forms as *omnipresent* and *omnipotent,* and in the English-Latin hybrid *omnium-gatherum.* The dative plural of the Latin word for 'all' is *omnibus,* with an *-ibus* ending Americans will recognize from the motto *E Pluribus Unum* ('from many, one'). French began using *omnibus* in 1828 to designate a vehicle, initially horse-drawn and later motorized, which carried passengers around town. English borrowed the word the next year. The reason for the designation was that this was the first such conveyance legally open "to all" social classes (*omnibus*); previous prototypes had been forbidden to many of humble station.

Omnibus seems to have an air of learned levity in its very makeup, and this was taken further in the short form *bus* that began to appear in English a few years later. The ancestry of *bus* is unusual on several accounts—in coming from a late borrowing of unmodified classical Latin, the Latin word being moreover a quantifier rather than a noun or verb or descriptive adjective; in being borrowed in the dative case; and finally in undergoing fore-clipping to *bus* rather than back-clipping, as is more usual for English, e.g. *auto* from *automobile*. The waggish career of *omnibus* continued further when, in the late nineteenth century, it was applied metaphorically to a waiter's assistant, scurrying about the premises like a bus around town; this is the ultimate origin of our term *busboy*.

[short for *omnibus*]

busboy See BUS.

bust See PASSEL.
[alter. of *burst*]

bustard See OSTRICH.
[ME *bustarde*, modif. (perh. influenced by MF *oustarde* bustard, fr. L *avis tarda*) of MF *bistarde*, fr. OIt *bistarda*, fr. L *avis tarda*, lit., slow bird, fr. *avis* bird + *tarda*, fem. of *tardus* slow]

buxom In England in the fifteenth century a bride promised to be *buxom* to her husband until death. But she was not making a vow, as an unwary modern reader might suspect, to remain either pleasantly plump or well endowed. Derived from the root of the Old English verb *bugan*, meaning 'to bend' or 'to bow', *buxom* originally meant 'easily bowed or bent, yielding, tractable'. John Milton uses *buxom* in a physical sense in *Paradise Lost* (Book II, line 842), when Satan says to Eve, ". . . thou and Death/ Shall dwell at ease, and up and down unseen/ Wing silently the buxom air. . . ." However, *buxom* was also used from an early period in a moral sense and came to mean 'obedient'. "To be *buxom*," a phrase used in the morning service, was the equivalent of the well-known and much debated phrase "to honor and obey" in the modern English marriage vow.

From the general sense of 'pliant' another sense of *buxom* arose in the sixteenth century: 'full of gaiety, blithe, lively'. Thus in Shakespeare's *Henry V*, Pistol describes Bardolph as "a soldier firm and sound of heart, and of buxom valor." A related sense, arising in the same period, of 'vigorously or healthily plump, sturdily formed' was used chiefly of a woman and led finally to the more specific modern sense of 'full-bosomed'.

[ME *buxom, buhsum*, fr. (assumed) OE *būhsum*, fr. OE *būgan* to bend, bow + *-sum* -some]

C

cab In the 1800s there was an abundance of cabs, of the horsedrawn variety. Our word *cab* is short for *cabriolet*, a light two-wheeled one-horse carriage with a folding leather hood, without doors but with a tall partition, known as a dashboard, in front of the seat, to protect its two riders from dirt and mud thrown up by the horse's hooves. The cabriolet, quite popular in Italy and France, where it was a carriage for hire, was introduced into London in 1820. By 1827 the shortened name *cab* had become established. Most of the London cabs were for hire, although they could only carry one passenger; the two-person seat had to accommodate the driver as well as the passenger. An improved design added an open seat for the driver beside the protected passenger section, allowing two passengers to ride together in private.

In the 1830s, an architect named Joseph Hansom introduced a further refinement of the cab, placing the seat for the driver in front and enclosing the passenger compartment. Thus we have the first *hansom cab,* which soon was shortened to simply *hansom.* However, it was not Hansom's original design that we associate with the word *hansom* but a later refinement offered by David Chapman in 1836. Chapman modified the design to put the driver's seat high at the rear so the passengers had a clear view over the horse and the driver looked over the passenger compartment. The driver, who came to be called a *cabby,* received instructions from the passengers through a trapdoor in the cab roof. It is this version we know today as the hansom cab.

The hansom quickly replaced the older hackney coaches as the most popular carriage for hire. *Hackney,* a term for any vehicle for hire, traditionally referred to a four-wheeled covered coach with room for six passengers and pulled by two horses. The name *hackney* is thought to be derived from the town Hackney outside London (now a borough of metropolitan London). The first use of the word was for a horse used for pleasure riding rather than one used as a draft animal or as a war charger. This use dates from the fourteenth century, and from almost the same time we have evidence of the use of *hackney* to refer to a horse let out for hire. From this use it was a natural extension to use of the word for a horsedrawn carriage kept for hire (a *hackney carriage* or *hackney coach* or simply *hackney*). The hackneys were first established as vehicles for hire in London in the early 1600s, and despite the restrictions on their number, the numbers grew until they were considered a nuisance. In 1635, John Taylor, known as the "Water Poet," wrote in his "The Olde Old Very Olde

Man" of how the coaches "have increased . . . to the undoing of the Watermen, by the multitudes of Hackney or hired Coaches: but they never swarmed so thick to pester the streets as they doe now. . . ." And diarist Samuel Pepys, writing in his journal in 1660, says: "Notwithstanding this was the first day of the King's proclamation against hackney coaches coming into the streets to be hired, yet I got one to carry me home."

From this early use of *hackney* to mean a horse or carriage for hire developed the more general sense, now obsolete, of one who does menial or servile work for hire, and then the verb use, 'to make trite, vulgar, or commonplace' by indiscriminate everyday use, and its derived adjective *hackneyed*. Through the process of shortening, *hackney* became *hack* in its original sense of a horse for hire, then for the hired cab, and ultimately as a derogatory word for 'one who forfeits individual freedom of action or initiative or professional integrity in exchange for wages or other assumed reward'.

Getting back to cabs, we find that near the end of the nineteenth century, just as motor cars were starting to take hold of the public's fancy, a mechanical device for recording distance traveled was a popular adjunct to the cabs used in the major cities of Europe. This device, used to calculate the fare due the driver, was known in German as a *taxameter* (derived from the Medieval Latin *tax* 'tax, charge' and the Greek-derived suffix *-meter* 'a measuring device'). The French called it a *taximetre* (which gave us our English spelling *taximeter*). These taximeters were tried in a few of the hansom cabs in London, but the device does not seem to have been widely used until the horseless carriage began to replace the hansom in the twentieth century. These motor cars for hire naturally took the name of their predecessor, *cab,* and with the addition of the taximeter became *taximeter cabs* and eventually *taxicabs*. Through a process of clipping, this has been further shortened to *taxi*. (This use of *taxi* later was taken over into the compound *taxi dancer,* 'a girl employed by a dance hall, café, or cabaret to dance with patrons who pay a certain amount for each dance or period of time'.) See also CLIPPING, PHAETON.

[short for *cabriolet*]

cabriolet   See CAB.
   [F, dim. of *cabriole, capriole* leap, caper; fr. its skipping lightness]

cad   See CADDIE.
   [short for *caddie*]

caddie   Gascon officers serving at the French court in the fifteenth century were called, in the Gascon dialect, *capdets*. The word *capdet* meant 'chief' or 'captain' and was derived from Latin *caput,* 'head'. But because most of these *capdets* were younger sons of noble Gascon families, the French *capdet* (later *cadet*) came to mean 'younger son'. It was common in all of France, and not just in Gascony, for the younger sons of the nobility to enter the army. So French *cadet,* established as meaning 'younger son', acquired a new sense, 'young gentleman in training for military service'. In the seventeenth century, English borrowed the French word in both senses.

In Scotland, in the eighteenth and nineteenth centuries, a *cawdy* or *caddie* (from *cadet*) was a person who made his living waiting about for odd jobs. The first of these *caddies* formed an organized corps in Edinburgh, and it may be that the quasi-military structure suggested the name. It is because golf is, in origin, a Scottish game that we have golf *caddies*. In England, *cad*, a shortening of Scottish *caddie*, 'odd-jobs man', was used by nineteenth-century students at schools or universities to refer contemptuously to local townsmen. Arthur Hugh Clough's *Dipsychus* gives some indication of the typical university scholar's attitude: "If I should chance to run over a cad, I can pay for the damage if ever so bad." The modern sense of *cad* comes from an Oxford University extension of the term to include any whose manners were considered ungentlemanly.

[F *cadet*]

cadence See CHANCE.
[ME, fr. OIt *cadenza*, fr. *cadere* to fall (fr. L) + *-enza* -ence]

cadenza See CHANCE.
[It]

cadet See CADDIE.
[F, fr. F dial. (Gascon) *capdet* chief, captain, fr. LL *capitellum* small head, dim. of L *capit-*, *caput* head]

cadmium See AMMONIA.
[NL, fr. L *cadmia* calamine (fr. Gk *kadmeia*, fr. fem. of *Kadmeios* Cadmean) + NL *-ium;* fr. the occurrence of its ores together with calamine]

calaboose See CLINK.
[modif. of Sp *calabozo* dungeon]

calcium See SCRUPLE.
[NL, fr. L *calc-*, *calx* lime + NL *-ium*]

calculus See SCRUPLE.
[L, pebble, stone in the bladder or kidneys, stone used in calculating, act of calculating, dim. of *calc-*, *calx* stone used in gaming, limestone, lime]

calliope To many listeners, the hyperactive set of steam whistles known as a *calliope* is more an instrument of torture than of music. To those who like their music melodic and not merely loud, the discovery that the instrument is named after a goddess whose name literally means 'beautiful-voiced' may constitute a case of adding insult to auditory injury. The calliope was named after *Calliope*, the foremost of the Muses—those nine sister goddesses who were seen in Greek mythology as presiding over poetry and song and the arts and sciences. Calliope was the muse of epic poetry and eloquence. Her Greek name, *Kalliopē*, derived from *kallos* ('beauty') and *ops* ('voice'). She was represented in art as holding an epic poem in one hand and a trumpet in the other and as wearing a laurel crown. Among the offspring variously attributed to her were Linus, a musician and the reputed inventor of melody and rhythm, and Orpheus. Orpheus played the lyre and sang so beautifully that all of nature joined him in dance. And he so moved Hades with his playing that he was allowed to return from the land of the dead with his beloved Eurydice. Like the other Muses, Calliope was a supposed source of poetic inspiration. Perhaps with this in mind, the steam-whistle organ invented around 1850 by A. S. Denny was named in honor of the goddess. Patented in 1855, the calliope once enjoyed great popularity in attracting patrons to river showboats, circuses, and carnivals, where its sound could be heard for miles around.

Although they are seldom invoked these days, the names of other Muses continue to enjoy an active lexical life. What better way to speak of the business of waltzing, fox-trotting, or even break dancing than to call it the *terpsichorean* art and thereby honor the goddess Terpsichore. Terpsichore, whose name derived from *terpsis* ('enjoyment') plus *choros* ('dance'), was the Muse of the choral dance and the dramatic chorus that evolved from it. Later, lyric poetry became her special province. In art she was usually represented as a graceful figure clad in flowing draperies and bearing a lyre.

Cliometrics, the application of statistics, principles of economics, and other quantitative methods to the study of history, perpetuates the name of the Muse of history. Clio, whose Greek name *Kleiō* means 'the proclaimer', was often represented in art as sitting with an open roll of papyrus or an opened chest of books. It may seem curious that this goddess of inspiration should lend her name to a discipline that is consciously committed to rigorously objective quantitative analysis. Stranger, still, is the fact that this muse of history has lent her name to the *Clio* awards, given every year for excellence in advertising.

For other articles on words derived from ancient mythology and legend see VOLCANO.

[fr. *Calliope*, chief of the Muses, fr. L, fr. Gk *Kalliopē*]

calque A *calque* is a creation using native elements to imitate a foreign pattern of meaning. The calque may be syntactic, as when *it goes without saying* was created in imitation of the French idiom *ça va sans dire;* purely semantic, as when English *foot,* long in the language as a body-part term, was extended to mean foot in the metrical sense, in imitation of Latin *pes,* which had both meanings; or lexical-compositional, as when *superman* was coined after German *übermensch* (literally 'over-man'). An alternate term for a calque is *loan translation,* a term which has the engaging feature of being itself a loan translation, namely, of German *Lehnübersetzung.*

In our etymologies, calques are indicated by "trans.," for "translation":

bread and circuses . . . [trans. of L *panis et circenses*]

Occasionally only part of a foreign formation is translated. Thus *liver-*

wurst is from German *leberwurst,* literally 'liver sausage', with only the first half of the compound being anglicized.

The word *calque* itself has an interesting etymology. It is from French *calque* meaning 'a copy or tracing of a design'. The French word goes back ultimately to Latin *calcare* 'to trample, tread', tracing being seen metaphorically as treading along a line. With a different aspect of treading being emphasized, *calcare* also gave rise to the English verb *caulk.*

[F, lit., copy, fr. *calquer* to trace, fr. It *calcare* to trace, trample, fr. L, to trample]

camera   See COMRADE.
[LL, chamber, room]

canapé   A mosquito was called *kōnōps* in ancient Greek, and a couch hung with curtains for protection against mosquitoes was a *kōnōpion.* This word for a useful piece of furniture was borrowed by the Romans (*conopeum*) and eventually made its way from Medieval Latin (*canopeum*) into Middle English (*canope*) and French (*canapé*). The English and the French have always seen things somewhat differently, and while the English attached the name to the covering curtain, now spelled *canopy,* the French attached it to the couch that it covered. Later, a piece of bread or toast topped with some savory food was felt to resemble a couch or sofa, and the French *canapé* gained a new meaning. We have borrowed the appetizer and its name from the French.

[F, lit., sofa, fr. ML *canapeum, canopeum* mosquito net; fr. the conception that the bread is a seat for the delicacy]

canary   Juba II (ca. 50 B.C.–ca. A.D. 24), king of Numidia and Mauretania, wrote prolifically on many subjects. Most of his work is long lost, but his writings were still available to the elder Pliny (A.D. 23–79), who retold Juba's account of an expedition to a group of islands off the northwest coast of Africa. The most outstanding feature of these islands, according to Pliny, was the multitude of large dogs (Latin *canes*) that Juba's expeditionary force found there. The islands were named *Canariae insulae,* 'dog islands'. Although neither Juba nor Pliny was aware of it, the dogs that gave the islands their names were probably not indigenous but brought by earlier invaders from Africa. Native to the islands, however, were small greenish-brown birds. Some of these birds were brought to Europe in the sixteenth century and were called, in England, *canary birds.* The dogs were long forgotten and the islands little remembered, and soon the birds' name was shortened to *canary.* The yellow domestic canary is a descendant of the wild greenish birds of the dog islands.

[*Canary* Islands, *Canaries* group in the Atlantic ocean southwest of Spain, fr. Sp *Islas Canarias,* fr. LL *Canariae insulae,* lit., dog islands]

cancel   To *cancel* something is to annul or destroy it. The original implication of cancellation was less broad. A document could be crossed out or canceled and hence made void. The cross-hatchings which sometimes cover a canceled document resemble a lattice. This resemblance was reflected in the formation of the Latin verb *cancellare*, 'to cancel', from the plural noun *cancelli*, 'lattice'. *Cancelli* (the singular, *cancellus*, is rare) is a diminutive of *cancri*, a rare and early plural form whose singular we would reconstruct as *cancer*. This *cancer* is not related to its homonym *cancer*, 'crab, disease'. Rather it is the word for the type of latticed barrier used to restrain a prisoner and is probably an altered form of Latin *carcer*, 'prison', the word which has also given us *incarcerate*.

[ME *cancellen*, fr. MF *canceller*, fr. LL *cancellare*, fr. L, to make like a lattice, fr. *cancelli* lattice, dim. of *cancer* lattice, prob. alter. of *carcer* prison]

cancer   The Latin word *cancer*, whose literal meaning is 'crab', is also the name of a number of maladies, including malignant tumors. Greek *karkinos* has the same double meaning. According to the second-century Greek physician Galen, the word owes its extended sense to the vague resemblance of the swollen veins that surround a cancer to the legs of a crab sticking out from its shell. For similar comparisons see RANKLE.

Latin *cancer*, or its Old North French development *cancre*, is the source of our word *canker*. *Cancer* itself was reborrowed from Latin in the fourteenth century, but now as \\'kan-sər\\, since by this time the standard pronunciation of Latin had a "soft" *c* (\\s\\) before *e*, rather than the "hard" *c* (\\k\\) of classical Latin. In French, meanwhile, Latin *c* before *a* had developed into *ch* (\\sh\\), yielding French *chancre*, which English borrowed in the seventeenth century. We thus have three words, *cancer, canker,* and *chancre*, all going back to Latin *cancer*, and each showing the effects of different vicissitudes of phonetic history.

Cancer is also, and has been since Roman times, the name of a constellation. Modern astrologers, disliking the connotations of the word *cancer*, occasionally refer to people born under the zodiacal sign of the crab as moon children, because the moon is the ruler of that sign.

[ME, Cancer (sign of the zodiac), fr. L, crab, cancer; akin to Gk *karkinos* crab, cancer, Skt *karkata* crab]

candelabra   See CANDIDATE.
[L, pl. (taken as sing.) of *candelabrum*, fr. *candela* candle]

candid   See CANDIDATE.
[F & L; F *candide*, fr. L *candidus* white, bright, fr. *candēre* to shine, be white; akin to LGk *kandaros* ember, Skt *candra* shining, moon]

candidate   A person campaigning for public office in ancient Rome customarily wore a white toga that had been rubbed with white chalk to make it bright and spotless. This white toga was worn to symbolize that the person did not have any stain on his character or reputation and thus was worthy of the office.

The Latin adjective for 'dressed in a white toga' was *candidatus*. In time this word also came to be used as a noun to denote the person campaigning for an office. *Candidatus* was formed from the adjective *candidus* 'shining white', which was derived from the verb *candēre* 'to be bright or white; glisten'.

This verb *candēre* is also the ultimate source of a few other English words. The words *candid, candor, candle, candelabra, chandelier,* and *incandescent* can all be traced back to this Latin verb.

When *candidate* was first used in English early in the seventeenth century, it referred to a person running for a public office, just as in Latin, the allusion to white togas having been lost. Its use was soon generalized to include an aspirant to any status or position, such as "a candidate for the priesthood" or "a candidate for a degree." In the eighteenth century, *candidate* acquired the additional sense of 'one that is likely to gain a position or to come to a certain place, end, or fate', such as "a candidate for the penitentiary" or more recently "a candidate for a heart attack."

[L *candidatus,* fr. *candidatus* clothed in white, fr. *candidus* white + *-atus* -ate; fr. the white toga worn by candidates for office in ancient Rome]

candle   See CANDIDATE.
[ME *candel,* fr. OE, fr. L *candela,* fr. *candēre* to shine]

candor   See CANDIDATE.
[F & L; F *candeur,* fr. L *candor,* fr. *candēre* to shine, be white]

canker   See CANCER.
[ME *canker, cancre,* fr. ONF *cancre* & OE *cancer,* fr. L *cancer* crab, cancer]

cannibal   When Christopher Columbus sailed to the West Indies, he found people in Cuba and Haiti who called themselves *caniba* and *carib* respectively. These words are dialect variants of Cariban origin, basically meaning 'strong men' or 'brave men'. Upon hearing the word *caniba,* Columbus, thinking he was not far from China, believed "que Caniba no es otra cosa sino la gente del Gran Can"; that is, "that the Caniba are none other than the people of the Grand Khan." Because these natives were believed by the Spanish to be man-eaters, the word *cannibal* in European languages came to mean a human being who eats human flesh. The form *carib* is the root of *Caribbean* as well as the name of the Carib or Cariban peoples and their languages. The name of *Caliban* in Shakespeare's last play, *The Tempest,* is also apparently derived from a related Carib form, perhaps from *galibi* meaning 'Carib'.

[NL *canibalis* Carib, fr. Sp *caníbal, caríbal,* fr. 15th cent. Arawakan *caniba, carib* (forms recorded by Columbus in Cuba and Haiti respectively), of Cariban origin; akin to Carib *calina, calinago, galibi* Caribs, lit., strong men brave men]

canopy See CANAPE.

[ME *canope, canape,* fr. ML *canopeum, canapeum* mosquito net, fr. L *conopeum, conopium,* fr. Gk *kōnōpion,* fr. *kōnōps* mosquito, gnat]

canter When the Romans invaded Britannia in A.D. 43, one of the towns they established in the southeastern area was called Durovernum. In the fifth century, when the Saxons invaded this area, they renamed the town Cantwaraburh 'the town of the men of Kent'. Late in the sixth century, the fourth king of Kent, Aethelbert I, made this town his metropolis. In 597 Pope Gregory I sent St. Augustine, a Benedictine monk, to convert the Anglo-Saxons to Christianity. He established a monastery in Cantwaraburh and, after his consecration as archbishop, founded the cathedral which has remained the chief ecclesiastical administrative center of England. (In time the name came to be Canterbury.)

In 1170 Archbishop Thomas à Becket was murdered in this cathedral by four knights of King Henry II's court. He was canonized as St. Thomas of Canterbury in 1173, and a shrine was established to him in a chapel of the cathedral. In 1174 Henry II did penance by being flogged at this shrine for whatever responsibility he bore for Thomas's murder. A few days later, Henry was victorious over the Scots at Alnwick in northern England. His victory was popularly believed to have been a result of his penance. Consequently, the martyr's fame and popularity became widespread, and his shrine was thronged for centuries by pilgrims of all classes, some of whom are depicted in Chaucer's *Canterbury Tales* (ca. 1386–1400). Many of these pilgrims traveled to Canterbury on horseback, and the easy, moderate gait of their horses came to be called the "Canterbury gallop." In the seventeenth century this term became shortened to *canterbury,* and then in the eighteenth century, to *canter.*

[short for *canterbury* n. (canter); fr. the supposed gait of horses ridden by pilgrims to the shrine of Thomas à Becket in Canterbury]

canvas, canvass *Canvas* cloth is often made of hemp. *Cannabis,* the Latin ancestor of *canvas,* was the classical Latin word for *hemp* and is, in modern scientific Latin, the generic name for the hemp plant, or marijuana. It probably also has the same non-Indo-European ancestor as *hemp.* At one time it was a popular sport or, when carried to extremes, an effective punishment to toss a person in a canvas sheet. The Duke of Gloucester, in Shakespeare's *Henry VI, Part I,* threatens the Bishop of Winchester with similar treatment:

> Thou that contrivedst to murther our dead lord,
> Thou that giv'st whores indulgences to sin.
> I'll canvass thee in thy broad cardinal's hat
> If thou proceed in this thy insolence.

It is not difficult to see how extended senses like 'to beat or buffet', 'to attack', or 'to thrash out or discuss' developed from figurative use of the verb *canvass.* The evolution of the familiar sense 'to solicit support', which appeared early, is unfortunately not clear.

[ME *canevas,* fr. ONF, fr. (assumed) VL *cannabaceus* hempen, fr. L *cannabis* hemp, fr. Gk *kannabis*]

cap   See CHAPEL, ESCAPE.
[ME *cappe,* fr. OE *cæppe,* fr. LL *cappa* head covering, cloak, perh. irreg. fr. L *caput* head]

cape   See CHAPEL, ESCAPE.
[prob. fr. Sp *capa* cloak, fr. LL *cappa* head covering, cloak]

caper   See CAPRICE.
[prob. by shortening & alter. fr. *capriole*]

cappelletti   See VERMICELLI.
[It, pl. of *cappelletto,* dim. of *cappello* hat, fr. ML *cappellus, capellus* cap, dim. of LL *cappa* head covering, cloak, perh. irreg. fr. L *caput* head]

caprice   *Capriccio,* in Italian, was originally a 'shiver of fear'. If we can manage to picture a person, utterly horrified, with his hair standing on end, his head will look rather like a hedgehog covered with spines. The word *capriccio* is a fine reflection of this resemblance; it comes from *capo,* 'head', and *riccio,* 'hedgehog'. The meaning of *capriccio* changed from 'sudden shiver' to 'sudden whim'. This shift in meaning was encouraged by the superficial similarity of *capriccio* to *capra,* the Italian word for 'goat'.

To the goat's reputation for friskiness we owe our *capriole* and probably *caper,* as well as the English sense of *caprice,* which comes by way of French from the later Italian sense. "I am heere with thee, and thy Goats," says Touchstone in *As You Like It,* "as the most capricious Poet honest Ouid [Ovid] was among the Gothes." Shakespeare was able to make a double play on the word *goats,* using the formal similarity of *Gothes* and the supposed etymological connection of *capricious* with Latin *caper,* 'goat'.

[F, fr. It *capriccio* caprice, shiver, fr. *capo* head (fr. L *caput*) + *riccio* hedgehog, fr. L *ericius;* basic meaning: head with hair standing on end, hence, horror, shivering, then (after It *capra* goat), whim]

capriole   See CAPRICE.
[MF or OIt; MF *capriole,* fr. OIt *capriola,* fr. *capriolo* roebuck, fr. L *capreolus* roebuck, wild goat, fr. *capr-, caper* goat; akin to OE *hœfer* goat, ON *hafr,* Gk *kapros* wild boar]

captain   See CORPORAL.
[ME *capitane, captein,* fr. MF *capitaine, capitain,* fr. LL *capitanus* foremost, chief, fr. L *capit-, caput* head]

captivate See CATCH.

[LL *captivatus,* past part. of *captivare,* fr. L *captivus* captive]

captive See CATCH.

[ME, fr. L *captivus,* fr. *captivus,* adj., fr. *captus* (past part. of *capere* to take, seize) + *-ivus* -ive]

capture See CATCH.

[MF, fr. L *captura,* fr. *captus* (past part. of *capere* to take, seize) + *-ura* -ure]

carat The idea that bigger is better when it comes to precious stones is not new. That idea has been around since long before our modern precision measuring instruments for gemstones. Hundreds of years ago people needed some standard for comparison when weighing precious stones that vary from very large to very tiny. They found that the seed of the coral tree or carob tree, which grows in the Mediterranean region, weighs approximately the same as the smallest gemstone, and they designated this seed one unit for weighing precious stones. Since the seed was called a *carat,* the name was used also for the unit of weight. Any stone that approximated the weight of one seed was deemed to weigh one carat. *Carat* derives, via a French or Medieval Latin intermediary, from Arabic *qīrāṭ,* 'bean pod', which is itself derived from Greek. Early in the twentieth century, the weight of the carat was set at 200 milligrams, and to this day we consider it the standard unit for gemstones.

Connoisseurs of fine jewelry know their *carats* from their *karats,* but for many other people, the terms are easily confused. *Karat* is defined as 'a unit of fineness for gold equal to 1/24 part of pure gold in alloy'. In other words, a 14-karat gold ring consists of fourteen parts gold and ten parts of some other metal, like copper. Further confusing matters is the fact that the term *carat* is also used to denote the proportion of gold in an alloy. In fact, *carat* was used in this sense in English before it was used to denote the weight of gemstones. Richard Eden, writing in his travelogue *The Decades of the Newe Worlde or West India* in 1555 says "The golde is of .xii. caractes or better in fynesse."

Both *carat* and *karat* come from the same source, but *carat,* which goes back to at least the fifteenth century, is significantly older than *karat,* which dates from around 1555. Today we frequently encounter both words in advertisements for fine jewelry, where size and quality are emphasized, with *carat* usually designating the size of a stone and *karat* designating the proportion of gold in the alloy. Often *karat* is abbreviated *K,* as in "18K gold case," but *carat* is always written in full.

[fr. MF, fr. ML *caratus,* fr. Ar *qīrāṭ* bean or pea pod, weight of four grains, carat, fr. Gk *keration* carob bean, small weight, carat, lit., small horn, dim. of *kerat-, keras* horn]

card See BOOK.
[ME *carde*, modif. of MF *carte*, prob. fr. OIt *carta*, lit., leaf of paper, fr. L *charta* leaf of papyrus, fr. Gk *chartēs*]

cardigan See BLOOMER.
[after James Thomas Brudenell, 7th Earl of Cardigan †1868 Eng. soldier]

cardinal The Latin noun *cardo* (and its stem *cardin-*) was originally used for 'a pivot or axis on which something turns; a hinge'. In extended uses, *cardo* acquired the senses of 'either of the pivots or poles on which the universe was supposed to rotate about the earth', 'any of the four points of the horizon' (north, south, east, west), and 'any of the four turning points of the year', that is, the solstices and equinoxes. The derived adjective *cardinalis* was used to mean 'serving as a pivot or hinge'.

In Medieval Latin *cardinalis* took on the sense of 'chief, principal'. The Church used it in this sense as a title given to prominent priests *(presbyteri cardinales)* and deacons *(diaconi cardinales)* of important churches. The pope also conferred the title on seven bishops *(episcopi cardinales)* of dioceses near Rome, who served as counselors in synodal meetings. The cardinal bishops, priests, and deacons in time formed an association or *collegium* called the Sacred College of Cardinals and in 1179 were given the exclusive right to elect popes.

The adjective *cardinalis* was also used to describe the four principal virtues *(virtutes cardinales)* on which the rest of the moral virtues 'turn' or are hinged, those being temperance, prudence, justice, and fortitude. Their designation as 'cardinal' can be traced to St. Ambrose in the fourth century. At the end of the fourth century we find occurrences of the term *cardinales venti* 'cardinal winds', and in the sixth century, *cardinales numeri* 'cardinal numbers'.

From early in the twelfth century the word *cardinalis* was often used as a noun for 'a cardinal bishop, priest, or deacon'. When taken into French, *cardinalis* became *cardinal,* which was borrowed into English, appearing in this ecclesiastical sense in the *Old English Chronicle* for the year 1125. The earliest appearance of the adjective in English was around 1300, when it was used in the term *cardinal virtues.*

The ecclesiastical robes of a cardinal have traditionally been of the color scarlet. In fact, this color is often referred to as *cardinal red.* An American songbird of this color has, since about the middle of the eighteenth century, been called a *cardinal.*

A major function of the Sacred College of Cardinals is the election of a new pope. The word *pope* derives from the Late Latin *papa,* which is a form of the Greek word *pappas.* This Greek word originated as baby-talk for 'father'. From the beginning, the Church in the East used *pappas* as an affectionate title for all its priests. When the title spread to the West in the third century as the Latin *papa,* it was usually reserved for bishops. It was apparently in the fourth century that it began to become a distinctive title of the Roman Pontiff. And the term *pontiff* itself derives from the Latin *pontifex,* which literally means 'bridgemaker', being made up of *pons* 'bridge' and a form of *facere* 'to make'. In ancient Rome's pagan religion, a *pontifex* was a member of the chief council of priests. The term was also used in Latin for a Jewish high priest. At first used as a title for bishops in the Western Church, *pontifex* seems, since the twelfth century, to have been reserved for the pope, especially in the titles *Pontifex Maximus* and *Pontifex Summus*.

[ME, fr. OF, fr. LL *cardinalis*, fr. L, of a hinge, fr. *cardin-*, *cardo* hinge + *-alis* -al]

Caribbean   See CANNIBAL.

[NL *Caribaeus*, *Caribbaeus* (fr. *Caribes* Caribs, fr. Sp *caribe* Carib, fr. 15th cent. Arawakan *carib*—form recorded by Columbus in Haiti) + E *-an*]

carnival
Carnival, the season or festival of merrymaking before Lent, originated in Rome, probably as a compromise that the Christian Church made with the annual pagan feast of Saturnalia. In its early celebrations carnival began on 6 January, the feast of the Epiphany, and lasted through Shrove Tuesday. The days of feasting and revelry that characterized carnival were enthusiastically welcomed as an offset to the upcoming days of fasting and penance to be observed during Lent. Some of the Renaissance popes were great patrons and promoters of carnival festivities, but later popes restricted the merrymaking to the last few days preceding Ash Wednesday, the beginning of Lent. The carnival spread to other Italian cities, and then to France and Spain, Germany and Austria. In modern France the merrymaking is more or less limited to Shrove Tuesday, or *mardi gras* (literally 'fat Tuesday'), when masked revelers sing, frolic, and parade in the streets. French colonists introduced Mardi Gras into America, where its most famous celebration is in New Orleans. In America the term *carnival* also applies to a traveling amusement enterprise that includes rides, sideshows, and games of chance.

The word *carnival* first appeared in English about the middle of the sixteenth century and is taken from the Italian *carnevale*. A popular and obvious-looking etymology would derive this from the Latin words *carne* and *vale*, thus meaning 'Farewell, O flesh!' But other considerations suggest a somewhat less colorful derivation, from the Old Italian *carne*, meaning 'flesh', and *levare*, 'to take away', which in turn come from the Latin *caro*, 'flesh', and *levare*. The practice of abstaining from meat during Lent, then, is the ultimate inspiration for *carnival*, but bidding it farewell does not enter into the story.

[It *carnevale*, *carnovale*, alter. of OIt *carnelevare*, lit., removal of meat, fr. *carne* flesh (fr. L *carn-*, *caro*) + *levare* to raise, take away, fr. L]

carol
The *carol* we associate with Christmas, and we use the word for a variety of songs in different styles, including religious hymns and traditional English Christmas songs. About the only thing these songs have in

common stylistically is their reference to the Christmas season. But originally the word *carol* referred to a more strictly defined song form.

The carol is related both etymologically and musically to *carole*, the name for a social dance that was highly popular with the courtly societies of western Europe during the twelfth and thirteenth centuries. *Carole* was borrowed into English from Old French. The earliest known instances of the Old French word *carole* occurred as translations of the Latin *chorus*. The etymology most commonly accepted is the one tracing it to *choraula*, which meant 'choral song' in Late Latin and 'one who accompanies a chorus on a reed instrument' in earlier Latin. *Choraula* is ultimately derivable from the Greek words *choros* ('chorus') and *aulos* ('reed instrument').

The earliest carol (or *carole* as it was then spelled in English too) was a dance in which the dancers sang the music, and it was a fixture of both courtly and popular festivities during the Middle Ages. Sometimes the dancers formed a circle and held hands; other times they formed a chain-like procession. The music of these early carols consisted of songs that made marked use of the refrain. The songs were sometimes led by a soloist who would sing the verses, while the dancers would reply in unison with the refrain.

At about the same time that the dance carols were flourishing in medieval courts, a genre of popular religious song was entering its golden age in England. Apparently because these songs too had refrains as their characteristic feature, they came to be known as *carols*. Although *carol* was originally used of any song making use of the verse-refrain format, regardless of subject matter, it came to be identified with a song of popular origin having a religious theme and especially one relating to the Virgin Mary or Christmas. Marked by simple language, stock phrasing, and traditional imagery, the medieval carol could be in English or Latin or frequently a mixture of both. Above all, the carol had uniform stanzas that were separated by a refrain. Although *carol* is now used of any strophic Christmas song, the refrain continues to be a prominent feature.

[ME *carole*, fr. OF, modif. of LL *choraula* choral song, fr. L, one that accompanies a chorus on a reed instrument, alter. of *choraules*, fr. Gk *choraulēs*, fr. *choraulein* to accompany a chorus on a reed instrument, fr. *choros* chorus + *aulein* to play a reed instrument, fr. *aulos* reed instrument like an oboe]

cartel   *Cartel* is ultimately derived from the Greek word *chartēs* 'a leaf of papyrus' and is thus a relative of *card, chart,* and *charter.* In Latin, the Greek *chartēs* became *charta* and referred to either the 'leaf of papyrus' or to 'that which is written on papyrus (such as a letter or poem)'. Early Italian took the word as *carta* and used it to denote 'a leaf of paper, a card'. The diminutive form *cartello* served to denote 'a placard or poster' and then acquired the sense of 'a written challenge or letter of defiance'. In the sixteenth century the French borrowed *cartello* as *cartel* with the meaning 'a letter of defiance'. From French the English language acquired *cartel* in this sense.

During the seventeenth century the word *cartel* took on the sense of 'a written agreement between belligerent nations especially for the treatment and exchange of prisoners'. This usage is exemplified by Bishop Gilbert Burnet, in his *History of His Own Time,* written about 1715: "By a cartel that had been settled between the two armies, all prisoners were to be redeemed at a set price."

German had borrowed the French word *cartel* as *kartell,* which was used in the same senses as those in English. However, by 1879 the Germans had found a new use for this word to denote the economic coalition of private industries to regulate the quality and quantity of goods to be produced, the prices to be paid, the conditions of delivery to be required, and the markets to be supplied. These German cartels were motivated by their industry's increasing desire to dominate foreign markets in the decade preceding World War I. During the world wars the German governments favored cartels to facilitate the transition to a war economy.

English took up this German usage around 1900 but applied it mainly to international coalitions of private businesses or governments. American antitrust laws ban such cartels or trusts as being in restraint of trade, but they exist internationally, with perhaps the most familiar one being the Organization of Petroleum Exporting Countries (OPEC).

[MF, fr. OIt *cartello* letter of defiance, placard, fr. *carta* card, leaf of paper, fr. L *charta* leaf of papyrus, fr. Gk *chartēs*]

Cartesian   See MACADAM.

[NL *cartesianus,* fr. *Cartesius* (René Descartes) †1650 Fr. scientist and philosopher + *-anus* -an]

Cassandra   *Cassandra,* daughter of King Priam of Troy, was given the gift of prophecy by Apollo; but because she spurned his advances, he ordained that her prophecies should go unheeded. She predicted aright the misfortunes that would befall from the stolen Helen and from the Trojan horse, but was scoffed at by her countrymen, to their doom.

In this figure she has passed into world literature. Shakespeare has her say, in *Troilus and Cressida:*

> Cry, Troyans, cry! A Helen and a woe!
> Cry, cry! Troy burns, or else let Helen go.

But Troilus dismisses her "brainsick raptures."

Cassandra came thus to be used generically for a prophet of doom, and this is the sense one finds entered in dictionaries. But what is interesting is how far modern writers, increasingly removed from the classical tradition, have strayed in their extension of the term. Occasionally the term is used with no doomsaying connotations:

> This January, the Cassandras of the commodity markets are tipping sugar as a sound gamble . . . —*Nature,* 4 Jan. 1969

Though the original Cassandra was a tragic figure, imprisoned for a madwoman by her own father and later dead by violence, the generic Cassandra may be portrayed as smug and comfy:

> . . . the smirking Cassandra who presides over the film
> —Penelope Gilliatt, *New Yorker,* 17 July 1971

The practicality of Cassandra—who made, so to speak, specific policy recommendations—may be minimized:

> . . . he does not, like Cassandra, leave us with nothing but warnings of doom —John Fludas, *Saturday Rev.,* 30 Sept. 1978

Finally, the generic Cassandra may be given attributes the precise opposite of the original, which were that she was dead on the money but could not make others believe her. In a great many instances now we see Cassandras depicted as being wrong:

> I found that the cuisine Cassandras could hardly have been more wrong —Roy DeGroot, *Esquire,* December 1973

Apollo's curse continues unabated.

[after *Cassandra,* daughter of King Priam of Troy, renowned as a prophetess of evil, fr. L, fr. Gk *Kassandra*]

catastrophe   When a catastrophe, such as an earthquake, strikes, its victims must surely think that their whole world has been turned upside down. In calling their misfortune a *catastrophe,* the victims are describing their sense of inversion even more aptly than they may realize. *Catastrophe* comes to us from the ancient Greeks and literally means "overturning." Its original context was classical drama. The catastrophe was one of the four parts of the dramatic structure into which the Greeks divided their plays. The introduction of the dramatic conflict was called the *protasis,* its continuance the *epitasis,* its heightening the *catastasis,* and its final outcome the *catastrophe.* The final outcome of the dramatic action was seen as an "overturning" because it usually marked a complete reversal, or inversion, of the status that the protagonist enjoyed at the beginning of the drama. In modern drama this final unwinding of the plot is usually known as the *denouement.* The term *catastrophe* was not restricted to tragedy, however. The resolution in a comedy was also known as a catastrophe and typically took the form of a marriage. When the classical sense of *catastrophe* first appeared in English contexts in the sixteenth century, *catastrophe* was indeed applied to the denouements of comedies as well as tragedies. In Shakespeare's *King Lear* there is a reference to "the catastrophe of the old comedy." And in Thomas Burnet's *The Theory of the Earth* (1684) there is this line, startling to modern readers: "That happy catastrophe and last scene which is to crown the work." To a modern reader who instinctively associates catastrophe with misfortune and misery, "happy catastrophe" seems oxymoronic. Yet the classical sense of *catastrophe* is still current in literary criticism. Allen Tate in discussing the dramatic structures of Dostoevsky's novel *The Idiot* terms the novel's resolution its "catastrophe."

By the time Shakespeare had written *King Lear*, the meaning of *catastrophe* had extended its scope beyond dramatic contexts. It came to be used of any kind of final event in a series, although the term tended to be used more often of unhappy conclusions. By the seventeenth century, *catastrophe* had come to be used of any event, whether final or not, that resulted in a subversion of the natural order of things. In 1672 the poet Andrew Marvell wrote of "the late war, and its horrid catastrophe." A century later, the scope of *catastrophe* had broadened to encompass any great misfortune and especially one that was sudden, widespread, or fatal.

[Gk *katastrophē*, fr. *katastrephein* to overturn, fr. *kata-* cata- + *strephein* to turn]

catawampus   See CATERCORNER.
[prob. by folk etymology fr. *catercorner*]

catch   *Catch*, in the form *cacchen* (with numerous spellings), was borrowed into English from the Old North French *cachier* sometime around 1200. Its original meaning was 'to chase', as in hunting. Very early in its history *catch* became used in its basic modern sense, 'to capture or seize after pursuit'. This development of our modern word *catch* came about through an interesting intertwining of the words *catch, chase,* and *latch*.

The Old North French ancestor of *catch, cachier,* is assumed to have derived from a verb *captiare* in Vulgar Latin, which is also the presumed ancestor of Medieval French *chasser*. (Vulgar Latin is so scantily recorded that many words must be assumed from a comparison of classical Latin and the descendant Romance languages.) It is *chasser* from which Middle English took *chasen,* which became our modern *chase*. *Latch,* meaning 'grasp, seize', as in "to latch onto something," is strictly a native word, coming from Old English *læccan* by way of Middle English *lacchen*. The closeness of the forms *cacchen* and *lacchen* apparently led to their ultimately sharing the sense 'grasp'. At about the same time *chasen* came into use and soon took over from *catch* the use they both had shared.

Catch is very unusual in being a verb imported from French but having a strong past tense inflection *(caught),* which is usually a characteristic of words of Old English origin. The form *caught* did not come into English from French but was formed by analogy with the original strong past tense of *latch,* which used to be *laught*. When *latch* came into modern English it lost its strong inflection; *catch* inherited it. Yet *catch* also had a weak-inflection form, like most verbs borrowed from French, and came into Modern English with two competing forms, *catched* and *caught*.

The fickleness of literary use with respect to *catched* and *caught* is curious. The King James Bible used *caught*. Shakespeare used mostly *caught,* but *catched* once in a while; so did Spenser. Ben Jonson used both, but Marlowe in his plays and Sidney in his poems used only *caught*. Milton used both, but *caught* more often than *catched*. Bunyan used *catched*. Donne used both. *Catched* can be found in Steele and Isaac Watts. Defoe seems to have used both about equally; Pope used both forms. But Dryden and Swift used only *caught*. Samuel Johnson used *caught* in his poetry and *catched* in his conversation. But after the time of Boswell and Johnson it is hard to find literary *catched*. The poets at the turn of the nineteenth century—Wordsworth, Coleridge, Byron, Shelley, Keats—all used *caught*, as did the novelists Jane Austen and Charlotte and Emily Brontë. *Catched* has now receded into dialectal use only.

Through their assumed Vulgar Latin source, which ultimately goes back to classical Latin *capere*, both *catch* and *chase* are related to *capture* and *captive* and *captivate*. The Middle French source of *chase* was also the source of a dance step called *chassé,* which in turn was altered to our verb *sashay.*

[ME *cacchen* to chase, catch, fr. ONF *cachier* to hunt, fr. (assumed) VL *captiare,* alter. of L *captare* to chase, strive to seize, fr. *captus,* past part. of *capere* to take, seize]

catch–22   Everyone knows that *catch-22* comes from Joseph Heller's novel *Catch-22,* published in 1961. The classic description is contained in this passage:

> There was only one catch and that was Catch-22, which specified that a concern for one's own safety in the face of dangers that were real and immediate was the process of a rational mind. Orr was crazy and could be grounded. All he had to do was ask; and as soon as he did he would no longer be crazy and would have to fly more missions. Orr would be crazy to fly more missions and sane if he didn't, but if he was sane he had to fly them. If he flew them he was crazy and didn't have to; but if he didn't want to he was sane and had to. Yossarian was moved very deeply by the absolute simplicity of this clause of Catch-22 and let out a respectful whistle.

Here Heller has created a rule for a person in a problematic situation that denies the only solution for the situation. Heller's novel was very popular, and his illogical concept caught the public fancy. *Catch-22* became the term for any number of equally baffling problems:

> . . . she ran into the show-business catch-22—no work unless you have an agent, no agent unless you've worked —Mary Murphy, *New York,* 9 Aug. 1976

> As one writer explains, "When a programer goes looking for ideas, he says, 'Give me something I haven't seen before.' So you create a really original show, and then you hear, 'Well, I'd feel better if I could see its track record.' Track record! How can an idea have a track record if it's never been done before? The whole thing's Catch-22. . . ."
> —Laurie Werner, *Cosmopolitan,* December 1977

And people also used it, as Heller had, for the rule or principle behind the situation:

> . . . this Catch-22 principle of the tax code: namely, that any transac-

tion which has no substantive object other than to reduce one's taxes—does not qualify to reduce one's taxes —Andrew Tobias, *New York*, 8 Mar. 1976

Heller did not set up Catch-22 as a narrow or precise principle of unlogic. He used it elsewhere in his novel as a name for any senseless or unreasonable rule; this aspect of *Catch-22* also caught the public fancy:

Continuing the Catch-22 logic, he explained that the agents busted in with guns drawn "to reduce the potential for violence." —Michael Drosnin, *New Times*, 2 May 1975

But once this genie had escaped the bottle, there was no forcing it back into its original confines, and its meaning has developed in several different directions. For instance, people have used *Catch-22* for a measure or policy having as its result the opposite of what was intended:

But there may be a medical catch-22: some experts now believe the examination, known as mammography, may actually cause more cases of breast cancer than it helps to cure —*Newsweek*, 2 Aug. 1976

And it has been used much like *dilemma*, to describe a situation in which either of two possible behaviors results in the same undesired result:

"Catch-22" If I don't jog, it's bad. If I jog in polluted city air, it's bad —Jim Berry, *Berry's World* syndicated cartoon, 1978

Nowadays we know this situation from another name it has—the *no-win situation:*

At the end, the ingenious Mr. Jeffries juggles his plot so that the murderer is faced with a no-win situation, his own lethal Catch-22 —Newgate Callendar, *N.Y. Times Book Rev.*, 8 Jan. 1984

Last and farthest from original Heller is the use of *Catch-22* as simply an emphatic version of *catch:*

. . . the puritanical Catch-22 that runs through our society—pleasure, it warns, must be paid for —Janet Spencer King, *Cosmopolitan*, February 1978

There is no telling where *Catch-22* will go from here. Americans, of course, are not immune to the effects of inflation. Accordingly, a few of them have moved beyond *Catch-22* to *Catch-23*, as in this remark on one of Heller's later novels:

In the new "Something Happened," there seems to be a Catch-23: coping with existence itself —Roderick Nordell, *Christian Science Monitor*, 9 Oct. 1974.

[fr. *Catch-22*, the paradoxical rule found in the novel *Catch-22* (1961) by Joseph Heller *b*1923 Am. author, fr. ²*catch* + *22*]

catercorner The medieval French were fairly casual about spelling. They took *quattuor* 'four' from Latin and spelled it *quatre*, the way the modern French do, and *catre*. Middle English picked up *catre*, spelling it many ways, the commonest of which was *cater*. The word still meant 'four', but to the English it mostly meant the four in dice, and sometimes cards. (The numbers in dice were all taken from French.) Four was an important number in two or three winning combinations (four and six seems to have been especially favored). False dice were sometimes made with the sides bearing the four and three slightly elongated in order to make favored combinations turn up more often. Such a die was known as a *cater-trey*.

The placement of the four spots on a die also can suggest an X, and by the second half of the sixteenth century there was a verb *cater* 'to move or place diagonally'. This in time produced an adverbial *cater* which occurs in dozens of compounds, most of them dialectal, meaning 'diagonal' or 'diagonally'. The most common and standard of these in the United States are *catercorner* and *cater-cornered*. Some commonly used variants are *catacorner*, *catty-corner*, and *kitty-corner*. Of the more fanciful variations, *catawampus* seems to be the most widespread, being attested almost everywhere except the Northeast. This folk term has completed an evolution from 'diagonal' through 'askew' through 'out of kilter', and is now often used figuratively to mean 'discombobulated, out of joint'.

[fr. obs. *cater* four-spot (fr. ME, fr. MF *quatre* four, fr. L *quattuor*) + *corner*]

catholic   In Greek, the words *kata* 'concerning' and *holou*, a form of *holos* 'whole', were compounded to form *katholou* 'in general', which gave rise to *katholikos* 'universal'. This Greek adjective was usually translated as *universalis* in Latin, but early Christian writers began using *catholicus*, the Latin form of the Greek word, for 'universal'. For example, the epistles of James, Peter, Jude, and John that were addressed to the Church at large and not to particular local communities were called the "Catholic Epistles." Around the year 110, St. Ignatius, Bishop of Antioch, used the term *katholikē ekklesia* 'Catholic Church'. In 325 the Council of Nicaea included this term in its formulation of the Nicene Creed. In its struggle against various heresies, the Church emphasized its universality, and its epithet *Catholic* took on the connotation of 'one and true' or 'orthodox'. In fact, after the Great Schism of 1054, while the Western Church continued to use *Catholic* in its title, the Eastern Church took *Orthodox* as its epithet.

Most of the Protestant churches arising out of the sixteenth-century Reformation eschewed the term *Catholic* for obvious reasons. Martin Luther even replaced the word *Catholic* in the Apostles' Creed with *Christian*. The Anglican Church, however, saw itself as "the Catholic Church in England," and thus referred to the Latin Church as "Roman Catholic." By analogy, since about 1835, the Anglican Church has often been called "Anglo-Catholic."

After Henry VIII's separation of the English Church from Roman authority in 1534, generic uses of *catholic* in the original sense of 'universal' begin to appear. Charles Lamb typifies this use in his *Essays of Elia* (1833): "I bless my stars for a taste so catholic, so unexcluding. . . ."

The American branch of the Church of England was reorganized in 1789 as the Protestant Episcopal Church in the United States. The word *episcopal* derives from the Late Latin *episcopus* 'bishop', which originated with the Greek *episkopos* 'overseer'. (See the article at BISHOP.) The word was chosen because bishops administer the Church's dioceses.

The Presbyterian Church, on the other hand, has no bishops; it is governed by presbyters or elders. The word *presbyter* can be traced back through Late Latin to the Greek *presbyteros* 'elder'. (See the article at PRIEST.)

The name of the Methodist Church derives, not from its methodical form of government, but from the methodical habits of study and prayer practiced by a small group of Oxford students, including John and Charles Wesley, in 1729. The epithet *Methodist* was applied derisively to them by their fellow students. This group began the movement that later led to the establishment of the Methodist Church.

In the early 1600s, religious persecution forced English separatists to flee the country. Amsterdam was a haven for such exiles, some of whom became the Pilgrims who settled in New England. (See the article at PILGRIM.) One group, led by John Smyth, formed a Baptist church while in Amsterdam. The word *baptist* derives ultimately from the Greek verb *baptizein* 'to dip or immerse in water'. This denomination is so called because its members profess belief in baptism only by immersion and only of adults.

In organization the Baptists are not much different from the Congregationalists, whose name derives from their belief in the right and duty of each congregation to make its own decisions about its affairs, independent of any higher human authority. The word *congregation* derives from the Latin verb *congregare* 'to collect into a group', which is made up of *com-* 'together' and *gregare* 'to collect', a derivative of *grex* 'flock'.

In 1708 a group of dissatisfied Baptists in Germany established a sect called the German Baptist Brethren; however, the members were more commonly called Tunkers, Dunkers, or Dunkards. These terms derive from the German verb *tunken* 'to dip'. The members were so called because their baptism involved immersing the candidate three times in water. The *Dunkards* are conscientious objectors, as are the Quakers and Mennonites.

The *Quakers,* more formally known as the Society of Friends, originated in the mid-1600s under the leadership of George Fox. Fox and his followers were derisively termed "Quakers" by a certain Justice Bennet at Derby in 1650, apparently from the physical manifestations of religious emotion characteristic of many of the early Friends.

The *Mennonites* owe their name to Menno Simons, a former Roman Catholic priest who was their early organizer in the Netherlands and Germany around 1550. Some German Mennonites emigrated to Pennsylvania in 1683, where their language was called "Pennsylvania Dutch." This is actually a misnomer, deriving from the misinterpretation of the German word *Deutsch* 'German' for *Dutch*.

In 1690 a group of Mennonites in Switzerland broke away from the main body because of disagreements concerning church discipline. These dissidents were then called *Amish* after their leader Jacob Ammann. Some Amish began emigrating to North America in the 1720s, first settling in eastern Pennsylvania.

In contrast to all the aforementioned sects, the Adventists were originally established in America. In 1831 in Massachusetts, William Miller began preaching of the second coming of Christ (*advent*, from the Latin verb *advenire* 'to come to'). He even set 1843 as the year of the second coming. When this prophecy failed, his loyal followers decided simply to await the imminent second coming. In 1845 a group of Adventists in New Hampshire adopted the belief that the seventh day of the week should be observed as the Sabbath. They were called, as you might guess, the Seventh-Day Adventists.

The *Unitarians* have a doctrine setting them apart from the other sects: their belief in the oneness or unity of God, which denies the doctrine of the Trinity (three persons in one God) and thus the divinity of Christ. Their name ultimately derives from the Latin *unitus* 'united', the past participle of the verb *unire* 'to unite'.

Another sect indigenous to America is the Church of Jesus Christ of Latter-day Saints, better known as the *Mormon* Church. The Church was founded by Joseph Smith in 1830 in western New York. Central to its belief is the *Book of Mormon*, which Smith claimed was the divinely inspired work of the fourth-century prophet and historian, Mormon.

Many Protestant churches call themselves *evangelical*. This comes from the Late Latin adjective *evangelicus*, which was taken from the Greek *evangelikos*, both meaning 'of or relating to or in agreement with the good news or gospel'. The Greek elements are *eu-* 'good' and *angelos* 'messenger'. The churches are so called because they stress the authority of the Bible.

Some Protestant churches call themselves *Pentecostal;* they believe that Christians should seek a postconversion religious experience called the baptism with the Holy Spirit, corresponding to the descent of the Holy Spirit upon the Apostles as recorded in Acts 1:12–2:4. This descent occurred about fifty days after Easter, hence the term *Pentecost*, from the Greek *pentēkostē* 'fiftieth day'.

[MF & LL; MF *catholique*, fr. LL *catholicus*, fr. Gk *katholikos* universal, general, fr. *katholou* in general, fr. *kata* down, concerning + *holou*, gen. neut. of *holos* whole]

caulk   See CALQUE.
[ME *caulken, calken*, fr. ONF *canquer* to trample, fr. L *calcare*, fr. *calc-, calx* heel]

causeway   A *causeway* is a raised road across wet ground or water. An earlier term for this, still sometimes used, is *causey*, and *causeway* is in fact originally a compound of this word and *way,* appearing in such spellings as *cauciwey, cawcewey,* and *cawcy wey. Causey* comes from the Old North French *cauciée,* cognate with Modern French *chaussée* as in *rez-de-chaussée* 'ground floor'. The weight of opinion is that the French forms derived, by way of Medieval Latin *via calciata,* 'paved highway', from Latin *calx*—the question is, *which* "calx," for there are two unrelated words of this spelling in Latin. One means 'limestone' (see the discussion of *calculus* at the article SCRUPLE), and one means 'heel'. The latter hypothesis leans on a passage from a tenth-century document which describes the *via calciata* as being made of "stone fragments trodden underfoot"—tamped down with the heel, it might be. But it is also true that the Romans used lime-based mortar, especially in boggy ground, and this 'lime' origin is today deemed the more probable.

Roman road making also gave us our word *street,* which goes back ultimately to Latin *(via) strata,* literally a 'spread-out way', applied to a paved road.

[alter. of ME *cauciwey,* fr. *cauci, cause* causey + *wey* way]

causey See CAUSEWAY.
[ME *cauci, cause,* fr. ONF *caucie, cauciée,* fr. ML *(via) calciata,* fr. *calciata,* fem. of *calciatus* paved, prob. fr. L *calc-, calx* limestone, lime + *-atus* -ate]

Celsius See FAHRENHEIT.
[after Anders Celsius †1744 Swed. astronomer who invented the centigrade scale]

cesarean See KAISER.
[by shortening and alter. fr. earlier *caesarean section,* prob. trans. of ML *sectio caesaria;* fr. the belief that Julius Caesar was so brought into the world]

cesspool This simple-looking word turns out to be a veritable reservoir of etymological murk. The simplest conjectures as to its origin take the *pool* part as original and self-explanatory and attempt to derive the first element either from *recess* or Italian *cesso* 'privy' or dialect words like *suss* 'hogwash'. Our earliest spelling (dating from the seventeenth century) of a form definitely ancestral to *cesspool* is *cestpool,* which has suggested a connection rather with *cistern* (whose initial syllable was formerly sometimes spelled with an *e* instead of *i*); at that time *cestpool* referred to a reservoir beneath a drain, not specifically for the collection of sewage. But about a hundred years earlier we find a form *cesperalle* denoting a cesspool in its modern sewage-collecting sense, and this has suggested an entirely different derivation in which *pool* was not an original part of the word, but was formed later by folk etymology.

Cesperalle is a variant spelling of *suspiral,* which in the sixteenth century denoted a cesspool. It earlier denoted a pipe or a vent. This last sense leads us to the Middle French source *souspirail (soupirail* in Modern

French). *Souspirail* is derived from Latin *suspirare* (from *sub-* plus *spirare* 'to breathe'), meaning 'to breathe' or 'to sigh'. *Suspirare* is the source of our poetic word *suspire*, far removed from the humble *cesspool*.

[prob. by folk etymology fr. earlier *cesperalle*, alter. of *suspiral* vent, pipe leading to a conduit, cesspool, fr. ME, fr. MF *souspirail* air hole, ventilator, fr. *soupirer, souspirer* to sigh, breathe, fr. L *suspirare*]

chablis   See LIEBFRAUMILCH.
[F, fr. *Chablis*, France, where it is made]

chamber   See COMRADE.
[ME *chambre*, fr. OF, fr. LL *camera*, fr. L, arched roof, fr. Gk *kamara* vault; akin to L *camur* curved, Av *kamarā* girdle]

champagne   See LIEBFRAUMILCH.
[F, fr. *Champagne*, region (formerly province) of northeastern France where it was first produced, fr. LL *campania* level country]

chance   A classic picture of the nature of chance was given by Epicurus, the ancient Greek philosopher. He imagined atoms as falling vertically through space in a uniform motion but for occasional uncaused swerving. The image of falling remains entwined with that of chance through several etymological metaphors.

Latin *cadere* 'to fall' gave us expressions for chance by two routes. Prefixation with *ad-* (whose consonant assimilated to the following *c*) yielded *accidere* (where the root vowel *a* also changed to *i* as a result of the prefixation), meaning literally 'to fall' and figuratively 'to happen' via a metaphorical extension identical to what we see in English *befall* and *fall out*. The present participle of this verb (nominative case *accidens*, accusative case *accidentem*) is at the origin of our English word *accident*. From *cadere* itself, Vulgar Latin seems to have derived a noun *cadentia*, literally 'falling'. The Italian correspondent of this word is *cadenza*, which did not develop the sense 'chance' but, via a different metaphor of 'falling off' suggesting 'ending', denoted a musical conclusion. It was borrowed by English in this sense. French also borrowed the Italian word, modifying it to *cadence*, which English in turn also borrowed, now in the sense of 'rhythm' (in effect, a succession of metrical endings). But French did not only borrow from Italian; it also developed its own native form of *cadentia*, first appearing in Old French as *cheance*, meaning 'accident' or, from the image of falling dice, 'luck, chance'. English borrowed this word as *chance*.

[ME, fr. OF *cheance, chance*, fr. (assumed) VL *cadentia* fall, fr. L *cadent-, cadens*, pres. part. of *cadere* to fall; akin to Skt *śad* to fall and prob. to W *cesair* hailstones]

chancre   See CANCER.
[F, chancre, canker, cancer, fr. L *cancer*]

chandelier   See CANDIDATE.

[F, lit., candlestick, modif. of L *candelabrum*]

chapeau   See CHAPEL.

[MF, fr. OF *chapel* hat, fr. *capellus* head covering, fr. LL *cappa* head covering, cloak]

chapel   St. Martin of Tours (died 397), while a soldier in the Roman army, is said to have divided his military cloak (Late Latin *cappa*) in half, giving one part to a shivering beggar at the gate of Amiens and wrapping the other part around his own shoulders as a cape. The word *cappa* was used in Late Latin for 'cloak' and 'head covering' and probably derived from the Latin *caput* 'head'. In Medieval Latin the diminutive form, *cappella*, was used for 'cape'. St. Martin's cloak was, after his death, kept as a relic by Frankish kings. They took it along on their wars and sheltered it in a tent, which was for this reason also called a *cappella* (or *capella*). The custodian of the relic was called a *cappellanus* (or *capellanus*), and this title passed into French as *chapelain*, which later became *chaplain* in English. During peacetime, the kings kept the relic in an oratory in their palace. This room set aside for private worship came to be called a *cappella* as well. By the seventh century *cappella* was being applied to any oratory where Mass was celebrated. In the eleventh century, the word was taken into French as *chapele*, which was borrowed into English early in the thirteenth century.

In the fifteenth century, *chapel* took on in English the extended sense of 'a choir of singers belonging to a chapel', such as that of a king or prince. By the 1660s we begin to find evidence of its use for 'a chapel service' and 'attendance at a chapel service'. In her novel *Mansfield Park* (1814), Jane Austen employs this sense: ". . . and after chapel he still continued with them. . . ."

The Late Latin *cappa* is also the source of the English words *cap, cape, chaplet* 'a wreath for the head', and *chapeau*, the last two having been borrowed from French. See also ESCAPE.

[ME, fr. OF *chapele*, fr. ML *cappella* chapel, short cloak, dim. of LL *cappa* cloak; fr. the preservation of the cloak of St. Martin of Tours as a sacred relic in an oratory specially built for that purpose]

chaperon   See ESCAPE.

[F, lit., hood, fr. MF, fr. *chape* cape, fr. LL *cappa* head covering, cloak]

chaplain   See CHAPEL.

[ME *chapeleyn*, fr. OF *chapelain*, fr. ML *cappellanus* chaplain, secretary of a king or noble, custodian of sacred relics, fr. *cappella* chapel, short cloak]

chaplet See CHAPEL.
[ME *chapelet*, fr. MF, fr. OF, dim. of *chapel* garland, hat, fr. ML *cappellus* head covering, fr. LL *cappa* head covering, cloak]

character "Amongst the ancients, there was a custom to make the character of a horse in the forehead of a bondslave." This item of information from Edward Topsell's *The Historie of Foure-footed Beastes* (1607) illustrates the original sense of the word *character* as 'a distinctive mark or impression'. The word itself can be traced back through French and Latin to the Greek noun *charaktēr*, which in turn is derived from the Greek verb *charassein* meaning 'to sharpen, cut in furrows, or engrave'. The noun was borrowed into English in the fourteenth century with essentially the same meaning it had in Greek, Latin, and French. In the fifteenth century *character* took on the sense 'a graphic symbol', such as a letter of the alphabet. By the seventeenth century the term acquired the transferred and generalized sense 'an aggregate of distinctive qualities'. Sherwood Anderson gives an example of this use of *character* when, in his novel *Poor White* (1920), he writes, "In all the great Mississippi Valley each town came to have a character of its own."

A related sense, also originating in the seventeenth century, referred to 'the aggregate of mental and moral traits marking a person or group'. This sense led to the use of *character* in the eighteenth century to mean 'one's reputation', which is exemplified in the following remark by Thomas Jefferson in 1786: "These debts must be paid, or our character stained with infamy." Also developing in the eighteenth century was its use to denote a person who is regarded as exemplifying distinctive or notable traits. An outgrowth of this sense is the use of the word to refer to a person depicted in fiction or drama. Still another offshoot is the pejorative sense of 'an odd or eccentric person', as illustrated when Oliver Goldsmith, in his play *She Stoops to Conquer* (1773), writes: "A very impudent fellow this; but he's a character, and I'll humour him a little."

It is clear that *character* has proved a most useful word to users of English since its introduction into the language. Its original single sense has now been all but buried by this complex set of later semantic developments.

[alter. (influenced by L *character*) of earlier *caracter*, fr. ME, fr. MF *caractère*, fr. L *character* mark, sign, distinctive quality, fr. Gk *charaktēr*, fr. *charassein* to sharpen, cut into furrows, engrave]

charisma The Greek word *charisma*, meaning 'favor, gift,' occurs several times in Greek translations of the Bible, chiefly in the New Testament books Romans and I Corinthians. It carries both the general sense of 'grace', equivalent to the Greek noun *charis*, and the more specific sense of 'a spiritual gift or talent divinely granted to a person as a token of grace and favor and exemplified by the power of healing, the gift of tongues, or prophesying'. Seventeenth-century English borrowed this theological term as *charism*, but by 1875 the form *charisma* was also in use.

The first secular use of *charisma* seems to have been its use by the German sociologist Max Weber in his 1922 publication *Wirtschaft und Gesellschaft*. This particular work was not translated into English until 1947, but even before this, Weber's use of *charisma* was being discussed:

> Charisma is, then, a quality of things and persons by virtue of which they are specifically set apart from the ordinary, the everyday, the routine —Talcott Parsons, *The Structure of Social Action,* 1937

The term was later applied to German leaders:

> . . . the strange German conception of the leader's "charisma," a combination of manliness, recklessness, and intellectualism —Louis L. Snyder, *Annals of the American Academy of Political and Social Science,* July 1947

By the 1950s, *charisma* was being used by literary critics:

> . . . for Paul radiates what the sociologists, borrowing the name from theology, call *charisma,* the charm of power, the gift of leadership —Lionel Trilling, *The Liberal Imagination,* 1950

The word was current in some intellectual circles when John F. Kennedy was elected president in 1960. Its frequent application to Kennedy by journalists served to popularize the term in the mass media. Since that time we can also find examples of the quality of *charisma* being applied to a thing:

> You can't hold a good look down, not when it's got the real charisma that classic tennis clothes do —*Glamour,* February 1967

The trend has been to use *charisma* almost synonymously with *appeal* or *magnetism.* In addition to magnetic political leaders, celebrities of all kinds have been described as having *charisma,* including evangelists, movie stars, athletes, generals, and writers. Some usage commentators have decried this devaluation or trivialization of *charisma,* but such a broadening and weakening of meaning is often the price of popularization.

> [Gk *charisma* favor, gift, fr. *charizesthai* to favor, fr. *charis* grace; akin to Gk *chairein* to rejoice]

charivari   In the past a curious tradition of some localities dictated that the wedding night of a newly married couple be accompanied by more than the usual confusion. The couple was treated by a motley band of revelers to a cacophonous serenade, delivered in derision on a battery of pots, pans, homemade musical instruments, and other noisemakers. The mock serenade was usually performed outside the windows of the home of the couple, who are presumed to be in the process of consummating their marriage. This travesty of a serenade, called a *charivari* (or *shivaree*), is known to date back as far as the fourteenth century in France, the birthplace of the word itself. The charivari was considered especially appropriate for second marriages or for marriages deemed incongruous. In one of his works, Washington Irving cites an example of a marriage that typically occasioned a charivari: "It was nothing more or less than a charivari to celebrate the nuptials of an old man with a buxom damsel." The charivari was brought by French settlers to Canada and to Louisiana, whence the custom spread throughout rural America. The variant spelling *shivaree* closely approximates the pronunciation of the word by English-speaking country folk. As the custom spread, so did its application: any unpopular marriage—or simply a marriage between unpopular people—was judged sufficient excuse for a charivari.

Since the nineteenth century the meaning of *charivari* has broadened considerably. In addition to its original meaning, it is now used of any babel of discordant noises or a confused mixture of incongruous elements. It is interesting that the spelling *shivaree* has developed an independent extended sense, 'celebration', one that has less of a derogatory nature than the original.

English borrowed *charivari* from French; the ulterior history of the word is obscure. Two wildly different hypotheses are that it comes from Late Latin *caribaria* 'headache' or from Hebrew *chaverim* 'comrades'.

[F *charivari*, perh. fr. LL *caribaria* headache, fr. Gk *karēbaria*, fr. *karē*, *kara* head + *-baria* heaviness (fr. *barys* heavy)]

chart   See BOOK.
[MF *charte* map, charter, fr. L *charta* document, piece of papyrus]

charter   See BOOK.
[ME *chartre*, fr. OF, fr. L *chartula* little paper, dim. of *charta*]

chase   See CATCH.
[ME *chacen, chasen*, fr. MF *chasser*, fr. OF *chacier*, fr. (assumed) VL *captiare*, fr. L *captare* to seize, strive after]

chassé   See CATCH.
[F, fr. past part. of *chasser* to chase, fr. OF *chacier*]

chauvinism   In the early nineteenth century the name *Chauvin* was used in France to denote an overzealous patriot. Nicolas *Chauvin*, who had the misfortune to lend his name to this sort of person, was a French soldier ridiculed for his extreme patriotism and fervent devotion to Napoleon. In the last third of the nineteenth century the French *chauvinisme*, meaning 'excessive or blind patriotism', was borrowed into English. Over the years the sense of *chauvinism* has extended from a political or national zeal to include undue partiality or attachment to any group or place to which one belongs or has belonged. "Male *chauvinism*," a topic of some notoriety beginning in the late 1960s, is first attested in the Merriam-Webster files as early as March 1950.

Another term for extreme nationalism, especially when marked by a belligerent foreign policy, is *jingoism*. This term originated during the Russo-Turkish War of 1877–1878. As British intervention seemed increasingly possible, the popular sentiment of many in England was expressed in a song with the words

> We don't want to fight, yet by jingo if we do,
> We've got the ships, we've got the men,
> We've got the money too.

A person holding the attitude implied by this song is referred to as a *jingo*, and the attitude itself is called *jingoism*. *Jingo* in the phrase "by jingo" is probably a euphemism for *Jesus*.

[F *chauvinisme,* fr. *chauvin* warmonger (after Nicolas *Chauvin* *fl*1815 Fr. soldier of excessive patriotism and devotion to Napoleon) + *-isme* -ism]

chemosurgery See SURGERY.
[*chemo-* chemical (fr. NL, fr. LGk *chēmeia* alchemy) + *surgery*]

Cherokee See INDIAN.
[prob. fr. Creek *tciloki* people of a different speech]

cherry See SHERRY.
[ME *chery,* modif. of ONF *cherise* (taken as a plural), fr. LL *ceresia,* fr. L *cerasus* cherry tree, cherry, fr. Gk *kerasos* cherry tree]

Cheyenne See INDIAN.
[CanF, fr. Dakota *Shaiyena,* fr. *shaia* to speak strangely, unintelligibly, fr. *sha* red + *ya* to speak]

chianti See LIEBFRAUMILCH.
[It, fr. the *Chianti* mt. area, Italy, where it was first made]

chickadee See PIGEON.
[imit.]

chieftain See CORPORAL.
[ME *cheftaine, chieftaine,* fr. MF *chevetain,* alter. (influenced by MF *chev-,* fr. ML *capi-,* fr. L *caput* head) of OF *chastain,* fr. LL *capitaneus* commander, fr. *capitaneus,* adj., outstanding, fr. L *caput*]

chiffchaff See PIGEON.
[imit.]

chimera The *Chimera* (Greek *Chimaira*) was one of the most fearsome creatures in Greek mythology. A fire-breathing female monster, it resembled a lion in the forequarters, a goat in the midsection, and a dragon in the hindquarters. In addition, works of art often showed a goat's head rising from its back. (The original meaning of *chimaira* is simply '(young) she-goat'.) The Chimera devastated all in her path until the heroic Bellerophon, astride his winged horse Pegasus, attacked her from on high, destroying her with a barrage of arrows. The specific classical reference gave rise in English in the fourteenth century to the extended use of *chimera,* especially in art and architecture, to refer to a representation of any grotesque monster constructed from the parts of various animals. By the sixteenth century the chimera had become a symbol of incongruity and of unrestrained fancy, and it acquired its current meanings of (1) 'a bizarre phantasm of incongruously joined parts' or (2) 'an unreal or unrealizable creature of the imagination'.

Another incongruously composite character from Greek mythology was Hermaphroditus, who was the son of the god Hermes and the goddess Aphrodite. He originally was a very handsome, but normal, young man. His beauty attracted the passionate attentions of a water nymph. Her amorous advances were unrequited. He made the mistake, however, of bathing in her pool, whereupon she rapturously embraced him and pulled him down into the lower depths. She prayed to the gods that he and she might forever be joined. Her wish granted, their bodies became one: the being that emerged had the breasts and proportions of a woman and the genitals of a man. Hermaphroditus then prayed that all men who bathed in that spring thereafter would suffer the same fate. Since the fourteenth century *hermaphrodite* has been used generically in English to refer to any animal or plant having both male and female reproductive organs. Since the seventeenth century *hermaphrodite* has been used figuratively to refer to anything having two diverse or incongruous elements. In fact, a two-masted sailing brig in which one mast is square-rigged and the other mast is fore-and-aft rigged is called an hermaphrodite brig.

[L *chimaera,* fr. Gk *chimaira* chimera, she-goat; akin to ON *gymbr* yearling ewe, L *bimus* two years (winters) old, *hiems* winter]

chintz   See BANDANNA, BODICE.
[earlier *chints,* pl. (taken as sing.) of earlier *chint,* fr. Hindi *chīt*]

Chi-Rho   See XMAS.
[*chi* + *rho,* names of the first two letters of Gk *Christos* Christ]

chiropractic   See SURGERY.
[*chiro-* hand (fr. L *chir-, chiro-,* fr. Gk *cheir-, cheiro-,* fr. *cheir* hand) + Gk *praktikos* effective, practical]

chirurgeon   See SURGERY.
[alter. (influenced by L *chirurgia* surgery) of ME *cirurgian,* fr. OF *cirurgien,* fr. *cirurgie* surgery + *-ien* -ian]

choleric   See HUMOR.
[ME *colerik,* fr. MF *colerique,* fr. L *cholericus* bilious, fr. Gk *cholerikos,* fr. *cholera* bilious disease (fr. *cholē* bile) + *-ikos* -ic]

chortle   See JABBERWOCKY.
[blend of *chuckle* and *snort*]

chrismon   See XMAS.
[ML, fr. *chris-* (fr. L *Christus* Christ) + *-mon* (fr. LL *monogramma* monogram)]

Christogram   See XMAS.
[*Christo-* (fr. LGk, fr. Gk *Christos* Christ) + *-gram*, fr. L *-gramma*, fr. Gk, fr. *gramma* letter, piece of writing]

chuck-will's-widow   See PIGEON.
[imit.]

ciao   See SLAVE.
[It, fr. It dial., alter. of *schiavo* (I am your) slave, fr. ML *sclavus* slave]

cinchona   See MACADAM.
[NL, after Doña Francisca Henriquez de Ribera, countess of *Chinchón* †1641 vicereine of Peru, who was said to have introduced the bark to Europe]

circumscribe   See SCRIVENER.
[L *circumscribere*, fr. *circum-* (fr. *circum* round, around, fr. *circus* circle) + *scribere* to write, draw]

clew   See CLUE.

cliché   Most modern writers shun clichés. But the cliché in its original sense was the livelihood of the eighteenth-century printer. The noun *cliché* is a French word meaning 'stereotype', that is, a plate used for making type in printing. In time, both *cliché* and *stereotype* came to be associated with a uniform, invariable way of creating something, like printing.

By the late nineteenth century, the idea of prefabrication had become distasteful, particularly in the creative world where originality is so highly valued. Both *cliché* and *stereotype* thus began to be used disparagingly to describe creative works that appeared to be cut from a mold. Not only literature but also dramatic presentations and works of art are susceptible to being deemed clichés.

Whereas *cliché* usually denotes a trite expression or a hackneyed theme, the word *stereotype* conveys a lack of originality in opinion, attitude, or judgment that shows itself in subscribing to a popularly held and oversimplified mental image of something. Frequently, a stereotype is a collection of qualities or traits all members of a particular group are assumed to exhibit, as illustrated in this use by James A. Michener in *Report of the Country Chairman* (1961): "He was about as far from the stereotype of a Hollywood star as I could imagine."

[F, fr. past part. of *clicher* to stereotype, of imit. origin; fr. the noise of the die striking the metal]

climate   In ancient Greek geography the word *klima,* meaning 'slope, inclination', referred to the supposed sloping of the earth from the equator to the poles. The Greeks attributed the various weather conditions found in different parts of the world to the earth's sloping. They methodically divided the earth into parallel belts or zones, corresponding to our concept of latitudes, each zone being called a *klima.* This term was later borrowed as *clima* into Late Latin in this sense, and eventually was taken as *climat* into Middle French and then into Middle English of the fourteenth century. *Climate,* in seventeenth century English, had come to refer to the condition of a region in relation to prevailing atmospheric phenomena, such as temperature and humidity. One of the early examples of this sense appears in Shakespeare's *Henry V* (ca. 1598), when the Constable of France asks, in regard to the climate of England: "Is not their climate foggy, raw, and dull,/On whom, as in despite, the sun looks pale,/Killing their fruit with frowns?" By the 1870s *climate* began to be applied additionally to any kind of prevailing condition or mood that affects something, such as the political climate, the intellectual climate, the business climate, a climate of unrest, and a climate of fear.

[ME *climat,* fr. MF *climat,* fr. LL *climat-, clima,* fr. Gk *klimat-, klima* inclination, the supposed slope of the earth toward the pole, region, clime, fr. *klinein* to slope, incline]

clink   There are many popular terms for jail, some of which are more or less self-explanatory, such as *lockup* and *slammer* or *slam.* Others, however, which come from a great variety of sources, are not as etymologically translucent. The term *clink,* for instance, comes from the name of a prison in the borough of Southwark in London. A part of the Manor of Southwark once bore the name *Clink,* and a prison situated there as early as the sixteenth century, also called *Clink,* had a widespread reputation as a rather dismal place. *Calaboose* has been in use in English since the late eighteenth century. It is a slightly modified borrowing of the Spanish *calabozo,* meaning 'dungeon'. Also from Spanish is *hoosegow,* in use in the United States since the early twentieth century. While the Spanish *juzgado* means 'a panel of judges', 'a tribunal', or 'a courtroom', its English derivative, *hoosegow,* seems to have been used only to mean 'jail'. *Pokey* has been used as a word for jail since the late nineteenth century, but its origin is obscure. It has been suggested that it is an alteration of earlier *pogie* meaning 'workhouse', itself of unknown origin. Another possibility is that it is related to the adjective *pokey* or *poky* meaning 'small', 'cramped', or 'dull and shabby'.

[fr. *Clink,* a prison in Southwark, borough of London, England, prob. fr. *Clink,* a part of the Manor of Southwark]

cliometrics   See CALLIOPE.
[*Clio*, muse of history + *-metric* + ¹*-s*]

clipping   By *clipping* (or *truncation*) we understand primarily the process whereby an appreciable chunk of a word is omitted, leaving what is sometimes called a *stump word*. When it is the end of a word that is lopped off, the process is called *back-clipping:* thus *examination* is docked to give *exam*. Less common in English are *fore-clippings*, in which the beginning of a word is dropped: thus *phone* from *telephone*. Very occasionally we see a sort of fore-and-aft clipping, such as *flu* from *influenza*.

Clipping is an ongoing process in the history of English. Its products tend to have a probational status at first—witness Swift's famous denunciation of *mob* when that word was newly clipped from Latin *mobile vulgus* ('fickle populace')—but may in time be absorbed wholly into the language. We may distinguish several stages in the process.

(A) The most solid state of acceptance of a clipped form comes when many speakers no longer even know what the earlier and longer form of the word was. Thus *chap*, meaning 'fellow', no longer evokes its antecedant *chapman*, an old term for a merchant. (For a similar semantic development, compare the use of *customer*, with approximately the same sense, in "a tough customer".) A *hack*, meaning a cab, has for most speakers cut its historical ties with *hackney*, which originally designated a kind of horse. (See also CAB.) Similar remarks apply to *pants* (from *pantaloons*), *cinema* (from *cinematograph*), and many others. Status as a completely independent word is further enhanced when the phonetic substance of the word is altered above and beyond the curtailment itself: thus *perambulator* ('baby carriage') yielded *pram*, not *peram*, and *geneva* gave rise to *gin*.

(B) The status of a clipping is more provisional when speakers can in general tell you right off what word it was clipped from. *Exam, gym, lab, ad, deb*, and *mike* are all very familiar words and must be considered part of the standard language, but anyone who knows the words at all can probably tell you where they come from (*debutante* and *microphone* in the last named cases), and the very availability of a recognizable longer source word makes their shorter offspring seem somewhat more informal. Just how breezily curtailed a word feels varies in ways not altogether predictable: somehow *math* sounds more formal, less an in-group clipping, than *chem* for *chemistry* or *sosh* for *sociology*.

(C) Finally, there are clippings that are frankly slangy and not, or not yet, seriously applying for citizenship in the standard lexicon. Such are *vac* for 'vacation', *caf* for 'cafeteria', and a host of P. G. Wodehouse Woosterisms ("So there you have the posish" and "I uttered an exclamash").

Fore-clipping may be neatly contrasted with back-clipping using a single form, *van:* as a back-clipping, it is a synonym of *vanguard*, but in the vehicle sense it was fore-clipped from *caravan*. (See also BUS.) Most cases in which an English word has been curtailed at the front and become standard, with memory of its ancestry largely lost, involve a relatively undrastic kind of curtailing known as *aphesis* or *aphaeresis*, in which an unstressed initial segment is dropped. (For a discussion see APHAERESIS.) An example is *cute*, from *acute*. More substantial fore-clippings, with antecedents increasingly forgotten, are *cello,* from *violoncello,* and *wig,* from *periwig.* Fore-clipped items for which the longer source word is known, like *zine,* from *magazine,* and *lytes,* from *electrolytes,* to most speakers tend to sound slangier than their back-clipped counterparts, like *auto,* from *automobile,* and *char,* from *charwoman.* There are also fore-clipped analogues of the back-clipped forms mentioned in our 'C' category above of frankly humorous or nonce forms, for instance *za* for *pizza.*

cloud-cuckoo-land   See UTOPIA.
[trans. of Gk *nephelokokkygia*]

clown   See URBANE.
[perh. fr. MF *coulon* settler, fr. L *colonus* colonist, farmer]

clue   The first *clue* ever tracked was not a murder weapon but a simple ball of yarn. The detective was not a police officer but a Greek hero out to exterminate, rather than arrest, his quarry, which was not a human being but a monster.

At first, *clue* and *clew* were simply two spellings of the same word which originally meant 'ball', then later, especially 'a ball of yarn or thread'. Our modern sense of 'guide to the solution to a problem' comes from a legend. According to Greek mythology, King Minos of Crete avenged the murder of his son by the Athenians by periodically sacrificing seven maidens and seven youths to the Minotaur, a monster that was half man and half bull and that lived on human flesh. The hero Theseus, Duke of Athens, volunteered to deliver the next serving so that he could kill the Minotaur. Ariadne, Princess of Crete and half sister of the monster, fell in love with Theseus and gave him a clew of thread so that he might unwind it behind him as he searched the labyrinth where the monster lived and thus find his way out. Theseus did just that, but after killing the Minotaur he abandoned Ariadne on the voyage home, in a decidedly unheroic move.

In time, *clew,* and later *clue,* came to designate anything that helps to solve a problem, particularly a mystery. In America, we still call a ball of yarn a clew. The spelling *clue* evokes a different image, usually of detectives attempting to unravel a mystery.

[ME *clewe,* fr. OE *cliewen;* akin to OHG *kliuwa* ball, ON *klō* claw, Gk *ginglymos* hinge, Skt *glau* round lump]

cobalt   Behind the gleaming façade of rationality presented by the names of metals as they appear today in the periodic table of elements may lurk a background of folk belief.

As a domestic sprite in German mythology, the *Kobold* could appear in the guise of anything from a helpful brownie to a troublesome poltergeist. As a mountain-dwelling gnome in miners' lore, he was essentially malicious. The word was borrowed into English, in these uses, as *kobold.*

A variant of the German term was *Kobalt,* which came to be applied to cobalt-containing ores by German miners as early as the sixteenth century. It was a depreciatory term, since the ore was worthless to preseventeenthcentury technology. Further, the arsenic contaminants often found with this ore could cause ulceration of the feet and hands of miners. The specific idea behind the transfer of the name of an injurious gnome to an injurious ore was that the cobalt ore was held to be harmful to neighboring silver ores, or actually to have been left as a kind of changeling by the mountain gnome who stole the silver. The mining term was borrowed by English as *cobalt* in the seventeenth century.

Another name for the kobold in German dialect is *Nickel,* sometimes described as a 'goblin' or 'demon'. It is apparently a special use of the nickname *Nickel,* from *Nicolaus.* (It is similar to English use of *Old Nick* for 'Devil'.) Niccolite, a frequent accompaniment of cobalt ores, was known in German as *Kupfernickel,* 'copper-nickel'. Just as cobalt ore was initially a disappointment to those who were after silver, so the copper-colored niccolite was an unwelcome substitute for valuable copper. *Kupfernickel* may have been named as a sort of "fool's copper" from the notion of malicious substitution by a sprite. Our English word *nickel* for the metal derives from a shortening of this word.

Wolfram may be of similar origin. Originally a German word, it is still the usual German term for tungsten and was formerly often used in this sense in English, a usage surviving in the chemical symbol for tungsten, *W.* (*Tungsten* itself is a Swedish word, meaning etymologically 'heavy stone'.) Although modern metallurgy has devised important uses for the metal, in former centuries it appeared mainly as an annoying obstacle to the extraction of tin. *Wolfram* may have been named after the voracious wolf, probably because it was viewed as robbing some of the tin from the ore.

It will be noticed that all three of the terms above derive from German. Although English has derived far fewer terms from German than from, say, French, the area of geology and extractive mineralogy has been comparatively fruitful in German borrowings. Other examples are *bismuth, gneiss, graben, graywacke, hornblende, kainite, karst, kieselguhr, kieserite, kunzite, kyanite,* and *langbeinite.*

[G *kobalt,* alter. (influenced by NL *cobaltum,* modif. of G *kobold*) of G *kobold* cobalt, kobold, fr. MHG *kobolt* kobold, fr. *kobe* hut, cage + *-olt* (prob. akin to OHG *holdo* spirit, fr. *hold* gracious); fr. its appearance in silver ore where it was believed to have been placed by silver-stealing goblins; akin to OE *cofa* den and to OHG *hald* inclined]

cobra   When the Portuguese navigator Vasco da Gama landed his fleet at Calicut, India, in 1498, he established the Portuguese Empire of the East. During the following period of contact with India, the Portuguese became aware of, among other things, a venomous snake with the remarkable ability to expand the skin of its neck to form a hood. The Hindi word the Indians used for the snake was *nāg,* but the Portuguese decided to rename it in their own language *cobra de capello,* 'hooded snake'. *Cobra* comes from the Latin word *coluber,* 'snake', and *capello* is derived from the diminutive form of the Late Latin noun *cappa,* 'hood'. The Portuguese name was borrowed into English in the seventeenth century, its first attested use being in 1668 in the *Philosophical Transactions of the Royal Society.* By the nineteenth century its name in English had become shortened to *cobra.*

[Pg *cobra* (*de capello*), lit., hooded snake, fr. L *colubra,* fem. of *coluber* snake]

cock See PIGEON.
[ME *cok,* fr. OE *cocc;* prob. akin to obs. D *cocke* cock, ON *kokr;* all of imit. origin]

cockney Hungry Piers Plowman, hero of a long fourteenth-century poem of social criticism and religious allegory, complained of not having either the eggs or the bacon to make a collop—a collop at the time was an egg fried on top of a piece of bacon. The word he used for the eggs was *cokeneyes. Cokeneye* or *cokeney* or *cokenay* (and there were even more spellings) is a word of easy derivation: it comes from *coken,* the genitive of *cok* 'cock', and *ey* or *ay,* common Middle English variations on our modern *egg.*

Well, what is a cock's egg? The etymologists are not certain. There seems to have been a folk usage of the fourteenth century (and since) in several European countries that applied *cock's egg* to small or misshapen eggs. These irregulars, so to speak, must have been the cheapest of all eggs—no wonder Piers thought himself in a deplorable condition.

The other possibility for *cokenay, cokeney* is that it was a child's word for an egg. Now why Piers Plowman would have used a child's term no one tries to explain, but the idea of the child's term, which has parallels in French and German, leads nicely into the development of the second sense.

Almost as old as the literal 'egg' sense in *Piers Plowman* is another fourteenth-century meaning, 'a pampered child', first found in Chaucer's *Canterbury Tales.* The word was not strictly limited to children; it was also used of pampered pets and of grownups—usually men—who gave the impression that they had been brought up in a rather over-sheltered way. This meaning was spelled *cockney*—the now familiar form—by the sixteenth century.

Now all of us know about the attitude of sophisticated city-bred folk toward the bewildered and unsophisticated countryman in the city. The slighting epithets are numerous: *rube, hick, bumpkin, clodhopper, yokel,* and more. Out in the country, the roles are reversed: the country folk have the barnyard sophistication and the city folk are the ones bewildered or revolted by country ways. In the late sixteenth century one of the words country people used for green, squeamish city people was *cockney,* from the 'pampered child' sense.

Perhaps typical of the seventeenth-century country person's idea of the gullibility of the city slicker is this punning attempt to explain the origin of *cockney* retailed by the lexicographer John Minsheu around 1617. He tells of the innocent city boy carried into the country for the first time by his father. The first strange sound he heard was made by a horse, and he asked his father what it was the horse did. The father told him that "the horse doth neigh." A little farther on, a rooster cut loose and the son asked the father "doth the *cocke neigh* too?"

Of course in the sixteenth and seventeenth centuries and before, the chief city that the English country folk were aware of was London, and *cockney* was therefore especially associated with Londoners, presumably as the city people least likely to be wise in the ways of the country. It has been broadly and narrowly applied. It seems first to have meant one born within the sound of Bow Bells—the bells of the church of St. Mary-le-Bow—which roughly means the area of the original city of London. Broadly, it is any Londoner, and for a while in early nineteenth-century New York, it designated any Englishman. Nineteenth-century American use kept alive for a time the old senses of a mollycoddled or effeminate man and an overprecious or effeminate city-dweller. But for most of us now, *cockney* refers to the people of London's East End and their characteristic *h*-dropping speech.

[ME *cokenay, cokeney* misshapen egg, spoiled child, effeminate person, lit., cock's egg, fr. *coken* (gen. pl. of *cok* cock) + *ey, ay* egg, fr. OE *æg*]

coffer   See SARCOPHAGUS.

[ME *coffre*, fr. OF *cofre, coffre*, fr. L *cophinus* basket, fr. Gk *kophinos*]

coffin   See SARCOPHAGUS.

[ME, basket, receptacle, fr. MF *cofin*, fr. L *cophinus*]

cognate   In the most typical use of the term, words of different languages are said to be *cognate* if they descend from a common source: thus Spanish *madre* and French *mère*, both meaning 'mother', are both descended from Latin *mater*. At a more remote time, *mater* and English *mother* are cognates, since both are believed to derive from a word in a language ancestral to Latin and English, called proto-Indo-European, of which direct record is lost. More broadly, the English words *mother* and *maternal* may be said to be cognate in relation to proto-Indo-European, although the latter must reckon borrowing and derivation in its ancestry.

Cognate etymologically means 'born together'. It comes from Latin *cognatus,* from *co-* 'together' plus *gnatus,* the old form of the past participle of *nasci* 'to be born'. The later form is *natus* without a *g* and is related to our words *natal* and *nativity*. We may wonder where the unfamiliar-looking *g* came from. *Nasci* and its derivatives are actually derived from a widespread Indo-European root meaning 'engender', which appears in the form *gen-* in Latin *genus* 'type' and a host of others that have made their way into English in some form (such as *genital* and *generate*), and which appears without the vowel *e* in *gnatus*. In Latin the initial *g* ceased to be pronounced before the *n*, much as English *gnaw* came to be pronounced \'nȯ\ (whereas the *g* was sounded in Old English times). But when protected by a preceding vowel, as in *gignere* and *cognatus*, it remained.

[L *cognatus,* fr. *co-* + *gnatus, natus,* past part. of *nasci* to be born; akin to L *gignere* to beget]

cohort   The *cohort* was a Roman military unit; in its most precise sense the cohort made up one tenth of a Roman legion. *Cohort* came into English via French from the Latin *cohors,* which had this meaning, but which originally meant 'farmyard'. *Cohors* through its *-hors* element is related to English *horticulture* and back through the mists of time to the ultimate sources of English *garden* and *yard.* By a somewhat different route through French, *cohors* yielded English *court*—a development that makes more sense in relation to cognates like *yard* and *garden* (the underlying sense is 'enclosed place') than does the military unit. The extension of *cohors* 'farmyard' to the military unit is supposed to have come about in this way: the 'farmyard' sense was applied to sections of an army camp, and was then applied to the unit quartered in that section.

The cohort was one of the tactical units that produced the Roman Empire, and hence it became a necessary word in English for translating or for writing about Roman history. Once established in English, it began to develop subsidiary senses—as, indeed, it had in Latin. One of the earliest developments in English was extension to any body of troops—a sense that in Latin had actually preceded the 'tenth of a legion' sense. One of the better known examples of this sense is in Byron's lines:

> The Assyrian came down like the wolf on the fold,
> And his cohorts were gleaming in purple and gold . . .
> —"The Destruction of Sennacherib", 1815

The Assyrians existed a lot earlier than the Roman cohort, but Byron didn't care; *cohort* sounded right to him.

Cohort by the early eighteenth century had come to be applied to any group or band, especially of friends, supporters, or adherents. This sense too existed in Latin. This meaning in English was at first used in the singular, but in the twentieth century it became used in the plural as well:

> . . . as Carrie Nation and her cohorts swarmed forward and pounded the panels with fists and stones —Herbert Asbury, *Carrie Nation,* 1929

When this meaning of *cohort* is used in the plural, it is easy for the reader to interpret it as 'adherents' or 'supporters' or 'colleagues'. By the 1940s and 1950s such use had become established in American English:

> The old poet had left, accompanied by two of his cohorts —Mary McCarthy, *The Groves of Academe,* 1952

For another case of a collective sense coming to denote a single person see COMRADE.

[MF & L; MF *cohorte,* fr. L *cohort-, cohors* enclosure, cohort]

colonel   One of the spelling-versus-pronunciation oddities in English is that *colonel* is pronounced the same as *kernel.* A review of the history of *colonel* shows how this discrepancy between spelling and pronunciation came about. In many languages when a word contains two identical or similar sounds, one of these sounds will often change over a period of time. A familiar example of this kind of change (called *dissimilation*) is the common pronunciation of *February* without the first *r*. For a similar reason when the Italian word *colonello,* denoting the commander of a column of soldiers, was taken into French it became *coronnel.* In the sixteenth century the word was borrowed by the English from French in the form *coronel.* Soon afterward, in writing, the spelling *colonel* came to be used in order to reflect the Italian origin of the word. However, by that time the pronunciation with *r* was well established, and today we still say "kernel" while we write *colonel.* For other differences between spelling and pronunciation see DEBT, ISLAND.

[alter. (influenced by MF or OIt; MF *colonel,* fr. OIt *colonello*) of earlier *coronel,* fr. MF, modif. of OIt *colonello* column of soldiers, colonel, dim. of *colonna* column, fr. L *columna*]

colony See URBANE.
[ME *colonie,* fr. MF & L; MF *colonie,* fr. L *colonia,* fr. *colonus* colonist, farmer, inhabitant (fr. *colere* to cultivate, dwell) + *-ia* -y]

Columbine See ZANY.
[It *Colombina,* dim. of *colomba* dove, fr. L *columba*]

companion See FELLOW.
[ME *compainoun,* fr. OF *compagnon,* fr. LL *companion-, companio* (prob. trans. of a Gmc word akin to Goth *gahlaiba* companion, fellow soldier, OHG *galeipo* companion), fr. L *com-* with, together + *panis* bread, loaf, food]

complexion See HUMOR.
[ME *complexioun* temperament, humor, combination of the humors, bodily constitution, fr. MF *complexion,* fr. ML *complexion-, complexio,* fr. L, combination, connection, complication, fr. *complexus* (past part. of *complecti* to entwine around, embrace, fr. *com-* with, together + *plectere* to braid) + *-ion-, -io* -ion]

compotation See SYMPOSIUM.
[L *compotation-, compotatio* (trans. of Gk *symposion* drinking party), fr. *com-* + *potatio* potation, act of drinking]

compunction See REMORSE.
[ME *compunctioun,* fr. MF *componction,* fr. LL *compunction-, compunctio,* fr. L *compunctus* (past part. of *compungere* to prick hard, sting, fr. *com-* with, together + *pungere* to prick, sting), + *-ion-, -io* -ion]

comrade Latin *camera* (also spelled *camara,* from Greek *kamara*) denoted a vaulted ceiling. In later Latin the word developed the senses of 'vault' and 'room in a dwelling'. The word developed into Old French *chambre* in these latter senses (the *b* appearing by the same process that produced the *b* in French *nombre* and English *number,* from Latin *numerus*), and was borrowed into Middle English as *chambre,* which has come to be spelled *chamber* in modern English.

Camera was also borrowed directly into English in the eighteenth century, in various technical Latinate senses. But the real fortune of the word was made by the phrase *camera obscura,* literally 'dark chamber', first applied in eighteenth-century English to a box with a lens in an opening for forming optical images. As techniques improved, the instrument developed into the modern photographic apparatus and the name was shortened back to *camera.*

Latin *camera*—or more precisely the variant *camara*—also continued its life on Spanish soil, as *cámara* 'room', and in a derivative collective noun *camarada,* literally 'roomful'. By a curious semantic development, *camarada* came to denote a roomful of persons (i.e., roommates) and finally a single person seen as a companion or fellow. This word gave rise (via French transmission) to English *comrade.* (For another case of a collective sense coming to denote a single person see COHORT.) Thus the *com-* of *comrade* has etymologically nothing to do with the Latin prefix *com-* 'together', appropriate though that would be semantically. For a synonym in which we do see the prefix *com-* see the discussion of *companion* at FELLOW.

[MF *camarade* group of soldiers sleeping in one room, roommate, companion, fr. OSp *camarada,* fr. *cámara* room, fr. LL *camera, camara*]

concierge   See SLAVE.
[F, fr. OF *cumcerges,* fr. (assumed) VL *conservius,* fr. L *conservus* fellow slave, fr. *com-* + *servus* slave]

concupiscence   See COVET.
[ME, fr. MF, fr. LL *concupiscentia,* fr. L *concupiscent-, concupiscens* + *-ia* -y]

condominium   When we hear the word *condominium,* we usually envision a modern dwelling of distinction not much larger than an apartment and yet spacious enough to comfortably accommodate the young upwardly mobile urban professional who owns it. Most of today's condos do fit that bill. But luxury living in a residential community was far from the mind of Bishop Gilbert Burnet when he wrote around 1715 in his *History of His Own Time,* "The Duke of Holstein began to build some new forts . . . this, the Danes said, was contrary . . . to the condominium which that king and the duke have in that duchy." At that time the word carried a very different meaning.

The word *condominium* itself comes from Latin *com-,* meaning 'with, together', and *dominium,* meaning 'domain'. As early as 1705, the term was applied especially to joint sovereignty exercised by two or more nations. To this day the word is occasionally used this way, as in this passage from *India International* (1951): "In the present shape of things, Egypt still has a voice in the Government of the Sudan which is known as a 'condominium.'"

It was not until 1962 that we began using the word in its more familiar sense 'individual ownership of a unit (as an apartment) in a multiunit structure or a unit so owned'. Since then, condominiums have sprung up all over the U.S. and in other lands, and they have become something of a symbol of middle-class affluence. An article in a 1983 issue of *The Geographical Magazine* describes the modern phenomenon known as the condominium: "Condominiums are simply a block of flats or a development of linked town houses where the individual owns his or her own unit outright while having a share of the joint ownership and responsibilities of the common parts, be they structural frames of the building, the lifts, boilers, swimming pools and gardens."

In recent years people have been quick to give the name *condominium* to a variety of structures that are owned by the occupants, including office buildings, town houses, and apartments. The word has even spread to the world of animals. A tower structure for cats to climb and play on has been referred to as a "kitty condominium," and a 1978 issue of *Massachusetts Wildlife* takes the condo craze a step further, describing a woodchuck's burrow as "a fantastic condominium providing free shelter for the woodchuck itself as well as skunks, snakes, rabbits and box turtles."

[NL, fr. L *com-* + *dominium*]

congregate   See EGREGIOUS.
[ME *congregaten*, fr. L *congregatus*, past part. of *congregare*, fr. *com-* with, together + *gregare* to collect, fr. *greg-*, *grex* flock]

congregation   See CATHOLIC.
[ME *congregacioun*, fr. MF *congregation*, fr. L *congregation-*, *congregatio*, fr. *congregatus* + *-ion-*, *-io* -ion]

conjugal   See YOGA.
[MF or L; MF, fr. L *conjugalis*, fr. *conjug-*, *conjux* husband, wife, consort, fr. *conjungere* to join together, unite in marriage]

conquer   See QUESTION.
[ME *conqueren*, fr. OF *conquerre*, fr. (assumed) VL *conquaerere*, alter. (influenced by L *quaerere* to ask, search) of L *conquirere* to search for, bring together, fr. *com-* + *quirere* (fr. *quaerere*)]

conquest   See QUESTION.
[ME *conquest*, *conqueste*, fr. OF *conquest*, *conqueste*, fr. (assumed) VL *conquaesitus*, *conquaesita*, alter. of L *conquisitus* (masc.), *conquisita* (fem.), past part. of *conquirere* to search for, bring together]

conquistador   See QUESTION.
[Sp, fr. *conquistado* (past part. of *conquistar* to conquer, fr. *conquista*

conquest, fr. fem. of *conquisto,* past part. of *conquerir* to conquer, fr. L *conquirere* to search for, bring together) + *-or*]

consarn   See ORNERY.
[alter. of ¹*concern;* prob. euphemism for *confound*]

consecrate   See SACRED.
[ME *consecraten,* fr. L *consecratus,* past part. of *consecrare* to consecrate, fr. *com-* + *secrare* to consecrate, fr. *sacr-, sacer* sacred]

consider   See DISASTER.
[ME *consideren,* fr. MF *considerer,* fr. L *considerare,* lit., to observe the stars, fr. *com-* with + *-siderare* (fr. *sider-, sidus* star, constellation)]

constable   When the word *constable* first came into English from French in the Middle Ages, a *conestable* was the chief officer of a king's household. His office was one of great power: he was commander of the army, supreme judge, subordinate only to the king himself. In *Sawles Ward* (1240), *wit* (what we would now call *reason* or *judgment*) is described as God's *constable:* "Wit the husbonde godes cunestable cleopeth warschipe forth ant makith hire durewart." (Wit, the manager of the household, God's constable, calls worship [honor or repute] forth and makes her gatekeeper.) Latin *comes stabuli,* which is the ancestor of *constable,* means, literally, 'officer of the stable'. But the title was transferred from stable to court; the chief officer of Frankish kings became the *comes stabuli.* The title's increase in prestige was not as great as it may seem. All the king's horses were scarcely less valuable to the king (probably in many cases more valuable) than all his men, and their charge was not an unimportant duty.

Another high officer who had his relatively humble beginnings in the stable is the *marshal.* The *steward,* however, although his name is etymologically equivalent to *sty-ward,* was never a keeper of pigs. See also MARSHAL, STEWARD.

[ME *conestable,* fr. OF, fr. LL *comes stabuli* officer of the stable, chief equerry, marshal, fr. *comes* officer, count + *stabuli,* gen. of *stabulum* stable]

contamination   As a term of philology, *contamination* refers primarily to unconscious blends, either syntactic, as when the synonymous *cannot help* and *cannot but* cross paths and give rise to *cannot help but,* or lexical, as when *regardless* and *irrespective* yield *irregardless.* These particular examples are considered ill-favored mongrels by many; but the effects of contamination may be more subtle and buried in history.

Consider for instance our word *grief.* It derives from the Old French *grief,* which meant 'heavy, troubled' and the like. The expected etymon would be Latin *gravis* 'heavy', which was also adapted into French in the learned form *grave* and is the source of our word *grave.* But Old French *grief* and its cognates, Italian *greve,* Rumanian *greŭ,* Provençal *greu,* etc., presuppose a form *grevis,* not attested in Latin but assumed for Vulgar Latin to account for the modern words. Now as Latin evolved, there was no regular sound change of such an *a* to *e,* so whence did we get *grevis?* The widely accepted postulate is that this form is due to the influence not of a synonym but of the antonym of *gravis,* namely *levis* 'light'.

An example closer to home is provided by *halyard,* a kind of hoisting tackle. The earlier form of this word was *halier;* and there is no general rule in the development of English that would have added a *d* at the end of such a form. The likely explanation is that *halier* was altered by contamination from *yard* (in the nautical sense, as in *yardarm*).

When contamination causes a word to be refashioned in such a way that the influencing word not merely colors the influenced, the way *levis* lends a vowel to *grevis,* but is actually present as a segment, like *yard* in *halyard* (at least in the spelling) or like *rail* in *taffrail* '(rail around) the upper part of the stern of a ship' (from Dutch *tafereel,* a cognate of *table*), the process shades over into what is known as FOLK ETYMOLOGY (which see).

convolute See VOLUME.
[L *convolutus,* past part. of *convolvere* to enfold, enwrap, fr. *com-* with, together + *volvere* to roll]

cool The adjective *cool* was first used for 'moderately cold' during the Old English period, when it was spelled *cōl.* In the fourteenth century we find Chaucer applying it to human attributes to mean 'not heated by passion, calm, dispassionate'.

In Shakespeare's time this sense was extended further to 'lacking ardor, enthusiasm, or hearty feelings; lukewarm'. This sense is evident in the following twentieth-century example from *Collier's Year Book* 1949: "Leaders . . . have been cool to the new government but have refrained from direct opposition."

In the 1720s *cool* was first applied to a large sum of money, as in "he won a cool hundred dollars." Here *cool* carries the intensive sense of 'whole, full'. Perhaps it derives from the fact that it was calmly or dispassionately counted.

By about 1825 we find *cool* extended a bit further to describe one that is 'marked by deliberate unabashed effrontery, presumption, or lack of due deference, respect, or discretion'. An example can be found in Willa Cather's *Death Comes for the Archbishop* (1927): "He took a cool pleasure in stripping the Indians of their horses or silver or bullets. . . ."

In the 1940s *cool* took on a new meaning in the world of jazz. 'Relaxed, restrained, and understated' describes the cool jazz that developed during this period in contrast to the swing and Dixieland styles. Within this world *cool* was then applied to anything that met with approval. It took the place of 'good, great, excellent'—the best was the coolest. This usage became widespread throughout the hip world and was even more loosely applied to anything acceptable, fashionable, or copacetic.

In his *Understanding Media* (1964), Canadian educator Marshall McLuhan redefined *cool* to fit his interpretation of the communications media. In dictionary style, his meaning may be stated as 'employing understatement and a minimum of detail to convey information and usually requiring the listener, viewer, or reader to complete the message'. Accordingly, he classifies radio and movies as hot media, and TV, the telephone, and speech as cool media.

Finally, in the 1980s, the original metaphor behind the hip use of *cool* was revived (*cool* itself having become hopelessly uncool) in the new slang expression *chill out,* meaning 'relax'.

[ME *cole,* fr. OE *col;* akin to OHG *knoli* cool, OE *calan* to get cold, *cald, ceald* cold]

cop   Several colorful stories circulate concerning the origin of *cop.* One is that *cop* was shortened from *copper,* a name given because the first London police (or members of some other early police force) wore large copper buttons on their uniforms. Another version has these officers wearing star-shaped copper shields. Details of such word origins vary freely, as the stories are their own justification and people who repeat them seldom see a need to offer supporting evidence. An entirely different approach to explaining *cop* is through the first letters of a phrase such as 'constable on patrol' or 'constabulary of police' or (least likely of all) 'chief of police'. This story has it that, in signing reports, policemen (presumably the same ones who wore the copper buttons or shields) abbreviated the official phrase beside the name, writing something like "John Smith, C.O.P." (See also AC-RONYMIC ETYMOLOGIES.)

The truth is simpler, if less entertaining. Around the year 1700 English gained a slang verb *cop,* meaning 'to get ahold of, catch, capture' and perhaps borrowed from Dutch. This word is somewhat unusual in having remained slang to this day, unlike most slang words which either die out or become more respectable over time. By 1844 *cop* is recorded in print as being used to refer to what police do to criminals, though it is probably somewhat older in speech. In very short order the *-er* agent suffix was added, and a policeman became a *copper,* one who cops or catches or arrests criminals. This usage first appeared in print in 1846. The connection with the metal copper must have been made almost at once in the popular mind, for a British newspaper reported in 1864 that "as they pass a policeman they will . . . exhibit a copper coin, which is equivalent to calling the officer copper." The noun *cop* shortened from *copper* appeared in print in 1859.

[short for ⁵*copper*]

coquette   "Little cock" is a singularly inappropriate name for a flirtatious female. But, etymologically speaking, a *coquette* is just that. The domestic cock is noted for his arrogant (or *cocky*) strut and for his promiscuity. A Frenchman who displayed similar amorousness and swagger earned the nickname of *coquet,* a diminutive of *coq,* 'rooster'. *Coquette* is simply the feminine form of *coquet.* Although both the masculine *coquet* and the feminine *coquette* have been borrowed by English, *coquette* is by far the more common. So much is *coquetry* considered a feminine trait, in fact, that men have been labeled "male *coquettes.*" The eighteenth-century English novelist Eliza Parsons felt strongly that "there is nothing more deserving reprehension . . . than a male coquette."

[F, fem. of *coquet*, dim. of *coq* cock, fr. OF *coc*, fr. LL *coccus*, of imit. origin like OE *cocc* cock]

corporal There are three *corporals* in present-day English; the first two we know are related, and the third may be, but the case is a bit iffy. The first noun *corporal* 'linen cloth on which the eucharistic elements are placed' was taken into Middle English from Medieval Latin *corporale*, which came from Latin, where it was the neuter form of the adjective *corporalis*, derived in turn from *corpus* 'body'. The religious corporal got its name from the doctrine that the consecrated bread is or represents the body of Christ.

The adjective *corporal* came by the same route from the same roots, Latin *corporalis* and *corpus*. *Corporal* has had two chief meanings in English: its present sense 'relating to the body' and a perhaps slightly earlier sense 'relating to the physical or material world'. This latter use has been taken over by the somewhat more recent adjective *corporeal*, itself derived from *corpus* via a different adjective, *corporeus*.

The third, military, *corporal* has a more checkered history. It was taken into English from Middle French *corporal*. In Middle French it was a variant form of *caporal*, which was derived from Italian *caporale*, in turn derived from *capo* 'head, chief', from Latin *caput* 'head'. The difficulty here is the *-or-* in the Middle French. Where did it come from? There are two schools of thought. One ascribes it to the influence of the words derived from Latin *corpus*. The other points to an early fifteenth-century Venetian *corporalis*—actually a Latin-like transcription form existing in the Venetian dialect of Italian. Middle French *corporal* could then have been derived from the Venetian form, which would ultimately go back to Latin *corpus*. The variants in *cap-* are then explained as due to the influence of the words derived from Latin *caput*. It is virtually impossible to know which of these theories is correct.

Certainly one of the influences toward the *cap-* spelling would be the forebears of English *captain*. *Captain* first appears in Middle English as *capitane*, borrowed from Middle French *capitain* or *capitaine* (it retains the *e* in Modern French). It was taken into French directly from Latin *capitaneus* 'chief' (both noun and adjective), which comes from *caput* 'head'.

The Middle French borrowing from Latin was a conscious and learned one. *Capitain, capitaine* apparently replaced earlier words of the same meaning, among them *chevetain, chevetaigne*, which had been derived by the less consciously scholarly French from the Late Latin *capitaneus*. Middle French *chevetain* became *chieftaine* in Middle English, and *chieftain* in Modern English. Our *captain* and our *chieftain* are therefore doublets.

[ME *corporale*, fr. MF *corporal*, fr. ML *corporale*, fr. L, neut. of *corporalis* of the body; fr. the doctrine that the bread of the Eucharist becomes or represents the body of Christ]

[ME *corporel, corporal,* fr. MF, fr. L *corporalis,* fr. *corpor-, corpus* body + *-alis* -al]

[MF, lowest noncommissioned officer, alter. (prob. influenced by *corps* body) of *caporal,* fr. It *caporale,* fr. *capo* head, chief (after such pairs as It *tempo* time: *temporale* temporal), fr. L *caput* head]

coupé *or* **coupe**   See PHAETON.
[F *coupé,* prob. fr. *carrosse coupé,* lit., cut-off coach, fr. *carrosse* coach + *coupé,* past part. of *couper* to cut, cut off]

court   See COHORT.
[ME, fr. OF, fr. L *cohort-, cohors* enclosure, court, thing enclosed, crowd, fr. *co-* + *-hort-, -hors* (akin to L *hortus* garden)]

cousin   Words of close kinship like *mother, father, sister, brother, daughter,* and *son* are among the oldest and most basic of the English vocabulary, tracing their ancestry back through the Germanic proto-language all the way to proto-Indo-European. But our terms for the next degree of kinship are mostly borrowed from French in historical times and were originally Latin, where they had a much narrower meaning.

The Latin *consobrinus* meant literally 'child of one's mother's sister'. It was formed by combination of *com-* 'with, together' and *sobrinus* 'cousin on the mother's side', a derivative of *soror* 'sister'. Its specific literal meaning notwithstanding, *consobrinus* was used by the Romans chiefly in the general sense 'the child of an uncle or aunt; a first cousin'. *Consobrinus* became *cousin* in Old French, from which it was borrowed into English in the thirteenth century. Its meaning has shown some variation through the years. It was once commonly used, for example, in the general sense 'a kinsman or kinswoman' when referring to a niece or nephew, as in Shakespeare's *Much Ado About Nothing:* "How now, brother! Where is my cousin your son?" But its principal sense has remained 'the child of an uncle or aunt'. It has also been used since the seventeenth century to denote a relative descended from a common ancestor but along a different line. Thus, the children of first cousins are second cousins to each other; the children of second cousins are third cousins, and so on. The child of one's first cousin is known as a first cousin once removed.

The Latin source of *uncle* also carries maternal overtones. It is *avunculus,* which in form is a diminutive of *avus* 'grandfather, ancestor' but was used primarily to mean 'mother's brother'. By the time it entered English through French as *uncle* in the thirteenth century, it had acquired the more general sense 'the brother of one's father or mother', and it was also used to mean simply 'an aunt's husband'.

For *aunt,* a similar story: it comes to us via French from Latin *amita,* which meant 'father's sister'. And similarly for *niece* and *nephew,* which descend, again via French, from Latin *neptis* and *nepos* respectively (though these originally meant 'granddaughter' and 'grandson'). Even the *grand-* of *grandfather,* etc., is a French-transmitted Latin borrowing.

[ME *cosin,* fr. OF *cosin, cousin,* fr. L *consobrinus* child of a mother's sister, cousin, fr. *com-* + *sobrinus* cousin on the mother's side, fr. *soror* sister]

covet   From its verb *cupere* 'to desire' Latin derived three nouns which have passed with minimal modification into English. *Cupiditas* meant 'yearning' and 'greed, avarice'; English borrowed this as *cupidity* in the same senses, though only the latter is now used. Latin *cupido* was a near synonym, but its fortunes diverged when it came to stand for the personification of specifically carnal desire, the counterpart of Greek *eros:* this is the source of our familiar (and rather domesticated) *Cupid.* A strengthened form of *cupere, concupiscere* 'to desire ardently', yielded a noun *concupiscentia* in the Late Latin of the Christian church and came specially to denote sexual desire, a meaning reflected in the English version *concupiscence.* In thus narrowing from the meaning 'desire in general' to 'sexual desire', *cupido* and *concupiscentia* parallel the development in our purely native word *lust:* in Old English it could refer to a wide range of desires. (To this day its German cognate *Lust* refers quite generally to pleasure.)

Cupiditas entered English by another and more devious route, disguised as a French verb. French is quite good at disguising Latin, owing to the extensive sound changes that Latin underwent on French soil: the Old French verb for 'desire avidly' was *coveiter* (later refashioned to *convoiter,* after the familiar but here unetymological prefix *con-*). This is the source of our word *covet.*

[ME *coveiten,* fr. OF *coveitier,* fr. (assumed) VL *cupidietare,* fr. (assumed) VL *cupidietat-, cupidietas,* alter. of L *cupiditat-, cupiditas,* fr. *cupidus* desirous (fr. *cupere* to desire) + *-itat-, -itas* -ity; perh. akin to MHG ver*wepfen* to become moldy, Icel *hvap* dropsical flesh, Goth af*hwapjan* to choke, extinguish, L *vapor* steam, vapor, Gk *kapnos* smoke, Skt *kupyati* he swells with rage, is angry; basic meaning: smoking, boiling]

coward   The tail is a very timid member. A frightened animal may draw its tail between its hind legs, or it may simply turn its tail and run. In such an animal as the hare (an early coward was *Coart,* the hare in the Old French version of the medieval beast-epic *Reynard the Fox*), the white flash of the fleeing tail is especially remarkable. But even a tailless animal like man can turn tail and flee when afraid. And it is in the tail of an army, unless that army is in retreat, that you can expect to find the *cowards.* Whether it is the idea of an animal's tail or an army's that is responsible, it is certain that the Old French *cuart* or *coart,* from which we get our *coward,* is a derivative of *coe* or *coue,* 'tail'.

[ME *coward, cuard,* fr. OF *coart, cuart,* adj. & n., fr. *coe, coue* tail (fr. L *cauda*) + *-art* -ard; prob. fr. the idea of a coward retreating to the tail end of an army, or fr. the idea of a frightened animal with its tail between its legs]

cowslip   Perhaps because the wild and dainty *cowslip* was to be found scattered throughout the pasturelands of England, the Anglo-Saxons took their name for this bright yellow flower from something else also found in pastures. The circular pattern formed by the low-lying leaves of the *cowslip* may also have suggested the name, for literally *cowslip* means 'cow dung', from Old English *cū*, 'cow', plus *slyppe* or *slypa*, 'pulp, paste'. In the United States the word *cowslip* has also been applied to other flowers, most notably the marsh marigold.

A hybrid of the British cowslip and the primrose is the *oxlip*. The etymological makeup of *oxlip* is similar to that of *cowslip*, with *ox* substituted for *cow*, perhaps because the oxlip is larger than the cowslip. The modern spelling somewhat disguises the second element from Old English *slyppe* or *slypa;* the sound of the *s* has been assimilated to the *s* sound of the *x*. The known history of the word *oxlip* provides a good example of the way words may survive for many years without appearing in print, being passed on orally from one generation to the next, perhaps only in a particular region or in some one or two dialects. In some medical recipes written down around the year 1000 this word appears in Old English as *oxanslyppe*, from *oxan*, the genitive singular of *oxa*, 'ox', plus *slyppe*. No subsequent use of the word is known for a period of about five hundred and fifty years, but then in William Turner's *A New Herball* (1568) we find, "Coweslippe is named in . . . Latin herba paralysis, and there are two kinds of them, . . . the one is called in the West contre of some a Cowislip, and the other an Oxislip, and they are both called in Cambridgeshyre Pagles." After this time *oxlip* begins to appear in print with some regularity, occurring twice, for instance, in the works of Shakespeare. Clearly *oxlip* remained in the vocabulary of at least some Englishmen during these five centuries even though no written occurrences are known throughout the period when Old English changed to Middle English and then to early Modern English. See also DAISY, HYACINTH.

[ME *cowslyppe*, fr. OE *cūslyppe*, lit., cow dung, fr. *cū* cow + *slyppe*, *slypa* pulp, paste]

creance   See FALCON.

[ME *creaunce* trust, confidence, leash for a hawk, fr. MF *creance*, fr. (assumed) VL *credentia* trust, belief (whence ML *credentia* promise, security given, credit, belief)]

credence   See FALCON.

[ME, fr. MF or ML; MF *credence* trust, confidence, fr. ML *credentia* promise, security given, credit, belief, fr. (assumed) VL *credentia* trust, belief, fr. L *credent-*, *credens* (pres. part. of *credere* to trust, believe) + *-ia -y*]

credenza   See FALCON.

[It, lit., belief, confidence, fr. ML *credentia* security given, belief; fr. the practice of placing a lord's food and drink on a sideboard or buffet to be tasted by a servant before being put on the lord's table in order to make sure that it contained no poison]

Creek See INDIAN.

[prob. so called fr. the numerous streams in the territory of the Creek Confederacy]

cretin The Alps, like other mountainous regions, cannot provide their inhabitants with an iodine-rich diet. An iodine deficiency in the mother may result in the birth of mentally and physically retarded children, dwarfish idiots when fully grown. Such dwarfs were once common in certain Alpine valleys of French Switzerland. They were called, in the local dialect, *cretins*. The word was used in kindness. A *cretin* was, originally, simply a 'Christian'. The term came to be used, as well, to differentiate human beings from other animals, since the possession of a Christian soul was considered to be what gave man dominion over the rest of creation. The specific use of *cretin* for these unfortunate idiots emphasized their humanity.

In the eighteenth century the dialect word was borrowed into standard French without this connotation, the etymological connection with standard French *chrétien* 'Christian' being no longer apparent. From French the word passed into English.

[F *crétin*, fr. F dial. *cretin* Christian, human being, kind of deformed idiot found in the Alps, fr. L *christianus* Christian; fr. the desire to indicate that such idiots were after all human]

cricket See PIGEON.

[ME *criket*, fr. MF *criquet*, of imit. origin]

crocodile *Crocodile* was taken into English in the fourteenth century from the Old French word *cocodrille*, which is derived from the Latin word *crocodilus*, a borrowing from the Greek word *krokodilos*, which originally denoted any of various lizards, and then came to be applied to the crocodiles of Egypt. According to the Greek historian Herodotus, who lived in the fifth century B.C., the word in its original form meant 'pebble-worm' etymologically, the lizards evidently being named for their habit of basking on pebbles on the river banks.

The expression *crocodile tears* for insincere or feigned sorrow derives from the mistaken notion that the crocodile sheds tears while devouring its prey. One medieval version of this story has it that the beast weeps over the head after having eaten the body not from repentance but from frustrated gluttony: the head is too bony to be a good morsel. Shakespeare makes reference to *crocodile tears* when he has Othello comment on his wife's weeping: "If that the earth could teem with woman's tears,/ Each drop she falls would prove a crocodile."

[alter. (influenced by L *crocodilus*) of ME *cocodrille*, fr. OF, fr. ML *cocodrillus*, alter. of L *crocodilus*, *corcodillus*, fr. Gk *krokodeilos*, *krokodilos*, alter. of (assumed) *krokodrilos*, fr. *krokē* pebble + *drilos* worm]

crocodile tears   See CROCODILE.
[so called fr. the ancient belief that crocodiles shed tears over their victims and make moaning sounds to attract prey]

crosier   See PASTOR.
[ME *croser*, fr. MF *crossier* staff bearer, fr. *crosse* pastoral staff (fr. OF *croce*, of Gmc origin; akin to OHG *krucka* crutch) + *-ier* -er]

cross   See CRUSADE.
[ME *cros, crosse*, fr. OE *cros*, fr. ON or OIr; ON *kross*, fr. (assumed) OIr *cross* (whence MIr *cross*), fr. L *crux*]

crucial   See CRUSADE.
[F, fr. L *cruc-, crux* cross + F *-ial*]

crucifix   See CRUSADE.
[ME, fr. ML & LL; ML *crucifixus* representation of Christ on the cross, fr. LL, the crucified Christ, fr. *crucifixus,* past part. of *crucifigere* to crucify, fr. L *cruci-, crux* cross + *figere* to fasten]

crucifixion   See CRUSADE.
[LL *crucifixion-, crucifixio*, fr. *crucifixus* + *-ion-, -io* -ion]

cruciform   See CRUSADE.
[L *cruci-, crux* cross + E *-form*]

crucify   See CRUSADE.
[ME *crucifien*, fr. OF *crucifier*, fr. LL *crucifigere*]

cruise   See CRUSADE.
[D *kruisen* to make a cross, move crosswise, cruise, fr. MD *crucen*, fr. *crūce* cross, fr. L *cruc-, crux*]

crusade   During the eleventh century, the enthusiasm of Western Christians for the pilgrimage to the Holy Land increased. The Holy Sepulcher was considered the most venerable of relics, and pilgrims of every class were ready to brave any peril in order to visit it. In 1077, however, Jerusalem was taken by the Seljuk Turks, and by 1092 not one of the great metropolitan sees of Asia remained in the possession of Christians. As a result, in 1095 Pope Urban II convoked a council at Clermont-Ferrand, in south central France. The pope addressed the assembled Christians and exhorted them to go forth and rescue the Holy Sepulcher from the infidels. The crowds responded with cries of "God wills it!" and eagerly received the red cross of cloth, which they wore on their breast to identify them as soldiers in this Christian army. The first crusade was launched.

The red cross badge was to give rise to the name *crusade* for this enterprise. The Latin noun *crux* 'cross, gibbet' was taken into Old French as *crois* and into Spanish as *cruz*. In the twelfth century, French formed the verb *croiser* 'to take the cross as a crusader'. From the feminine past participle of this verb, *croisée*, the French formed the noun *croisade* 'crusade'. Meanwhile, the Spanish formed the nouns *cruzada* 'crusade' and *cruzado* 'crusader'. Both the French and Spanish forms were borrowed into English, with *croisade* predominating into the eighteenth century. During that century, the blend *crusade*, with Spanish stem and French ending, began to appear, and was given as an alternate in Samuel Johnson's Dictionary (1755), along with the more common *croisade* and *crusado*. By the time of Noah Webster's Dictionary (1828), *crusade* had become the most common form, while *croisade* was included as an alternate form.

By the 1780s an extended sense became evident when *crusade* was used for 'any remedial activity pursued with zeal and enthusiasm'. Thomas Jefferson was one of the first to use it so, when, in 1786, he wrote "Preach, my dear Sir, a crusade against ignorance."

The original sense of *crux* in classical Latin was an instrument of torture, whether gibbet, cross, or stake. By extension it meant 'torture, trouble, misery'. With this in mind, English borrowed *crux* in the sense of 'a puzzling or difficult problem'. From this sense developed its use for 'an essential point requiring resolution', as in "the crux of a problem," and the sense of 'a main or central feature', as in "the crux of an argument."

The Latin *crux* is also the core of the English words *crucial, crucifix, crucifixion, cruciform, crucify,* and *excruciating.* The English *cross* derives from *crux* through either Old Irish or Old Norse. The English *cruise* also derives from *crux,* which became *crucen* 'to make a cross' in Middle Dutch and *kruisen* 'to sail crossing to and fro' in Modern Dutch before being borrowed into English in the seventeenth century.

[blend of earlier *croisade* + *crusado; croisade* fr. MF, modif. (influenced by OProv *crozada*) of OF *croisée*, fr. fem. of past part. of *croiser* to take up the cross, fr. *crois* cross; *crusado* modif. of Sp *cruzada* (after Prov *crozada*), fr. fem. of past part. of *cruzar* to take up the cross, fr. *cruz* cross; OF *crois* and Sp *cruz* fr. L *cruc-, crux*]

crux See CRUSADE.
[L, cross, torture]

cryosurgery See SURGERY.
[*cryo-* cold, freezing (fr. G *kryo-,* fr. Gk, fr. *kryos* icy cold) + *surgery*]

crypt See APOCRYPHA.
[L *crypta* vault, cavern, fr. Gk *kryptā,* fr. fem. of *kryptos* hidden, fr. *kryptein* to hide; akin to ON *hreysar* heap of stones, OIr *crāu* stable, hut, Lith *krauti* to pile up]

crypt- *or* **crypto-** See APOCRYPHA.
[NL, fr. Gk *kryptos*]

cryptic See APOCRYPHA.
[LL *crypticus,* fr. Gk *kryptikos,* fr. *kryptos* hidden + *-ikos* -ic, -ical]

cuckoo See PIGEON.
[ME *cuccu, cuckow,* of imit. origin like MLG *kukuk,* MD *coecoec,* OF *cucu,* L *cuculus,* Gk *kokkyx,* Skt *kokila*]

cudbear See MACADAM.
[irreg. (pron. spelling) after Dr. *Cuthbert* Gordon, 18th cent. Scot. chemist]

cummerbund See BANDANNA.
[Hindi *kamarband,* fr. Per, fr. *kamar* waist, loins + *band* band, bandage; akin to Av *bandō* band, fetter, Skt *bandha* binding]

Cupid See COVET, EROTIC.
[after *Cupid,* Roman god of love, fr. ME *Cupide,* fr. L *Cupido*]

cupidity See COVET.
[ME *cupidite,* fr. MF *cupidité,* fr. L *cupiditat-, cupiditas,* fr. *cupidus* desirous + *-itat-, -itas* -ity]

curfew See FOCUS.
[ME *corfeu, curfew,* fr. MF *cuevrefeu, covrefeu,* signal given in the evening to put out or bank the fire in the hearth, curfew, fr. *covrir* to cover + *feu* fire, fr. L *focus* fireplace, hearth]

cuss See PASSEL.
[alter. of ¹*curse*]

cynic In Aldous Huxley's short story "The Gioconda Smile," a young woman asserts: " 'Oh, you're cynical.' Mr. Hutton always had a desire to say 'Bow-wow-wow' when that last word was spoken. It irritated him more than any other word in the language." Mr. Hutton's apparently irrational impulse has a firm basis in etymology. English *cynic* is derived from the Greek word for 'dog', *kyōn.*
The philosopher Antisthenes, an Athenian contemporary with Plato, taught that virtue is the only good and that self-control and independence are the essence of virtue. Antisthenes and his followers were ostentatiously ascetic, contemptuous of wealth and pleasure. An adherent of this school of philosophy was called *kynikos,* which means, literally, 'doglike'. It is likely that one reason for this choice of appellation was that Antisthenes taught in a gymnasium outside Athens which was called *Kynosarges.* There is no doubt, however, that the literal meaning of *kynikos* was uppermost in the minds of most Greeks who so referred to the *cynic* philosophers. Indeed, *kyōn* became a popular nickname for 'cynic'.
Cynic has been used in English since the sixteenth century as a word for a philosopher of this school. We often find, especially in early remarks on cynics, a strange inclination to connect these philosophers with tubs. James Howell's *Instructions for Forreine Travell* (1642) refers to "the Cynique shut up alwaye in a Tub." John Brown, in his *Essays on the Characteristics of the Earl of Shaftesbury* (1751), speaks of "all the old philoso-

phers, from the elegant Plato walking on his rich carpets, to the unbred cynic snarling in his tub." The reference is to the most famous of the cynic philosophers of Athens, Diogenes, who carried his ascetic principles to extremes. According to tradition, Diogenes refused to live in a house, but slept in a large tub belonging to the temple of the goddess Cybele.

The word *cynic* had not been long in English before it was applied to any faultfinding critic, especially to one who doubts the sincerity of all human motives except self-interest.

[MF or L; MF *cynique,* fr L *cynicus,* fr. Gk *kynikos,* lit., doglike (prob. influenced in meaning by *Kynosarges,* a gymnasium where Antisthenes taught), fr. *kyn-, kyōn* dog + *-ikos* -ic]

czar   *Czar,* or *tsar,* is our English word for a pre-Soviet Russian emperor. *Tsar* is a straightforward borrowing from the Russian, but the form of *czar* is strange. It looks rather like a Polish word, and in fact there is a Polish *czar,* but it is pronounced like English *char* and means 'charm' or 'spell'. The Polish equivalent of Russian *tsar* is spelled *car*—Polish *c* is pronounced *ts.* We owe our peculiar spelling of *czar* to an Austrian diplomatist, Siegmund, Freiherr (Baron) von Herberstein (1486–1566). He was ambassador to the Russian court during the reigns of the German kaisers Maximilian I and Charles V. In 1549 he published *Rerum moscovitarum commentarii* (Commentaries on Muscovite Matters), one of the first Western books concerning things Russian and for many years the major source of information about Russia in Western Europe. Herberstein wrote in Latin, but his spelling of Russian *tsar* was influenced by his native German. The *c* in Herberstein's *czar* may have come from Polish, but his *z* was surely added as a pronunciation indicator—*z* in German, like *c* in Polish, is pronounced *ts.* The English word *czar* first appeared in a 1555 translation of Herberstein's work. See also KAISER.

[NL, fr. Russ *tsar',* fr. ORuss *tsĭarĭ, tsĕsarĭ* emperor, fr. Goth *kaisar,* fr. Gk or L; Gk, fr. L *Caesar*]

D

Dada *Dada,* a movement in art and literature which celebrated the irrational, was born in 1916 in tranquil, neutral Switzerland while the rest of Europe was engulfed in World War I. There in Zurich a group of aesthetes gathered at the Café Voltaire. This mixed bag of poets, painters, and war protesters included Marcel Duchamp, Jean Arp, Marcel Janco, Hugo Ball, Richard Hülsenbeck, and Tristan Tzara. They decided to respond to the madness around them by creating an art movement based on nihilism and irrationality, one that would repudiate traditional artistic values and conventions and would shock and outrage bourgeois sensibilities. Tristan Tzara, a Romanian-born poet and the group's leader, would later publish a series of seven manifestos ("I am neither for nor against, and I do not explain, for I hate sense") and the first poems and essays in the anarchically scrambled language that the movement espoused. One of his first acts, however, was to found, with Jean Arp and Richard Hülsenbeck, a review titled *Être sur son dada,* which is French for "On one's hobbyhorse." Like *hobbyhorse* in English, *dada* in French has the figurative sense of 'an idée fixe or obsession'. And like the English expression "riding one's hobbyhorse," *être sur son dada* is a well-established French phrase that means continually dwelling on or reverting to one's pet idea or favorite topic. It was probably the use of this figurative sense of *dada* in the title of the group's iconoclastic little review, first published in 1916, that was responsible for popularizing *Dada* as the name for this whole revolutionary movement in art and literature.

Years later, when recounting the birth of Dada, founding members of the movement gave varying embellished explanations for the actual source of the name. The basic story went that one day at the Café Voltaire the artists were groping for a name for their nascent movement when they decided to determine it in the most arbitrary way possible. They flipped open a Larousse dictionary and chose the word a cavalierly wielded paper knife pointed to. In another version of the story, the paper knife was merely used to flip open the book, and the page was then scanned for the most suitable word. In yet another version, a dictionary was thumbed through until the group found the word that best epitomized the spirit of the movement. Reportedly, they were delighted when they hit upon *dada,* a child's word for a plaything and a childish word that was suggestive of the way they wanted to thumb their collective noses at the adult world around them. Some of the supposed recollections of the participants regarding the moment of discovery are incredibly precise. Dadaist Jean Arp later claimed that Tristan Tzara pronounced *dada* for the first time at 6:00 p.m., 8 February 1916, at the Terrace Café. Arp proclaimed that *dada* perfectly suited a movement whose object was "to spit in the eye of the world."

[F, fr. (baby talk) *dada* hobbyhorse, hobby (arbitrarily chosen symbol of the movement), redupl. of *da, dia* giddap]

dairy See LADY.

[ME *dayerie, deyerie,* fr. *deye* female servant, dairymaid (fr. OE *dǣge* kneader of bread) + *-erie* -ery; akin to ON *deigja* dairymaid; derivative fr. the root of OE *dāg* dough]

dais See DOUBLETS.

[ME *deis, dees,* fr. OF *deis,* fr. L *discus* quoit, dish]

daisy The *daisy* doesn't just bud, blossom, and die like most other flowers. Rather, it performs a daily routine, much as people do, of "sleeping" at night by closing and "waking" in the morning by opening up again. Because of this unusual trait and because of the whorled appearance of the flower, the daisy was given the Old English name *dægesēage,* meaning literally 'day's eye'. The distinctive ray-like appearance of the daisy as it opens and closes with the sun reminds one of an eye that opens in the morning and closes at night. So it is that poet John Leyden paid tribute to the human quality of this simple flower in his 1803 poem "Scenes of Infancy": "When evening brings the merry folding hours, And sun-eyed daisies close their winking flowers."

The *dandelion* is another flower named for a resemblance to an anatomical feature. The name comes from Middle French *dent de lion,* which means literally 'lion's tooth'. The flower was given this name because of its jagged-toothed leaves. With its striking head, which is round and yellow and balances on a hollow stalk, the wildflower might look to some like a proud golden-maned lion stretching in the sun. See also COWSLIP, HYACINTH.

[ME *daisie, dayeseye,* fr. OE *dægesēge, dægesēage,* fr. *dæg* day + *ēage* eye]

Dakota See INDIAN.

[Dakota (Santee dial.) *Dakota,* lit., allies]

dame See DUNGEON.

[ME, fr. OF, fr. L *domina* mistress, lady, fem. of *dominus* master, lord; akin to L *domus* house]

damson See PEACH.

[ME *damascene, damesene, damson,* fr. L *(prunum) Damascenum,* lit., plum of Damascus, fr. neut. of *Damascenus* of Damascus, fr. *Damascus* Damascus, Syria]

dandelion   See DAISY.
[fr. earlier *dent de lion,* fr. MF, lit., lion's tooth; trans. of ML *dens leonis;* fr. its sharply indented leaves]

danger   See DUNGEON.
[ME *daunger* power, jurisdiction, liability, reluctance, fr. OF *dangier* power, jurisdiction, alter. (influenced by OF *dam* damage, fr. L *damnum*) of *dongier,* fr. (assumed) VL *domniarium, dominiarium* authority, fr. L *dominium* ownership (fr. *dominus* master) + *-arium* -ary]

darn   See JEEPERS.
[euphemism for *damn*]

darnation   See JEEPERS.
[euphemism for *damnation*]

date   The English word *date* in its temporal sense, in spite of semantic and phonetic similarity, has nothing to do etymologically with *day* but is descended from Latin *dare,* 'to give'. In ancient Rome, the date of a letter was written in this manner: "Dabam Romae Kal. Aprilis." (I gave [this letter] at Rome April 1—the kalends of April.) A later formula used *data Romae,* 'given at Rome', instead of *dabam Romae,* 'I gave at Rome'. *Data,* past participle of *dare,* 'to give', had the feminine case ending because it was understood to refer to the unexpressed feminine noun *epistula,* 'letter'. By the sixth century, *data* itself had become a noun, used for the formula indicating the date on a letter. In French, its descendant *date* was used not only for the formula on a letter, but also for the time that such a formula indicated or indeed for any given point in time. The Middle English borrowing from French also had these senses. It was not until the late nineteenth century that *date* began to be used for an appointment or engagement at a specified time. The further sense 'a person of the opposite sex with whom one has a date or appointment' is a twentieth-century extension.

The *date* that is the fruit of the date palm is unrelated to the temporal date. This *date* is descended from Greek *daktylos.* The primary meaning of *daktylos* is 'finger', but the word was also used to denote the fruit. The reason for this extension of meaning is debated. Some suggest that the pinnately divided leaves of the date palm look rather like fingers and that this fact gave the fruit its name. This account would be more convincing if the tree, rather than its fruit, had been named *daktylos.* It is more likely that the clustered dates themselves were felt to resemble fingers. It has also been suggested that Greek *daktylos,* 'date', is not the same word as *daktylos,* 'finger', but rather a folk-etymological alteration of some Semitic word. Such words for the date palm as Arabic *daqal* and Aramaic *diqlā* are quoted in support of this theory.

[ME, fr. MF, fr. LL *data,* fr. *data* (as in *data Romae* given at Rome), fem.

of L *datus,* past part. of *dare* to give; akin to Gk *didonai* to give, Skt *dadāti* he gives]

[ME, fr. OF, modif. of OIt *dattero* or OProv *datil,* fr. L *dactylus,* fr. Gk *daktylos,* lit., finger]

deacon See VICAR.

[ME *dekne, dekene,* fr. OE *diacon, dēacon,* fr. LL *diaconus,* fr. Gk *diakonos, diēkonos,* lit., servant, fr. *dia-, diē-* (alter. of *dia-*) + *-konos* (akin to Gk en*konein* to be active in service); akin to L *conari* to attempt]

dean See VICAR.

[ME *deen,* fr. MF *deien,* fr. LL *decanus,* lit., chief of ten, fr. L *decem* ten + *-anus* -an]

debt In a society having a high rate of literacy and such a dependence upon the printed word as is usual in our present state of civilization and technological competence, it is often difficult to realize that the principal domain of language is still largely the spoken word. Convincing evidence of this fact, however, may be found in the tenacity of many spoken items that rarely get into print or are stigmatized in the schools, such as *ain't* or a host of irrepressible scatological terms. Additional evidence may be seen in the failure of what we might call scholastic or academic spelling influences to affect the pronunciation of a number of words. For example, the word *debt* is derived through Middle English *dette* from Old French *dette* or *dete.* The letter *b* was added to the spelling in both French and English in the late Middle Ages by scholars who wished to reflect the ultimate origin of the word in Latin *debitum,* although no *b* was ever pronounced in either French or English. While Modern French spelling reform has eliminated the *b* in this position, the English form has become petrified, leaving schoolchildren with another silent letter that must be memorized. The artificial alteration of spelling under the influence of other forms can also be seen in *doubt, plumb, plumber, subtle, indict, receipt, island, isle,* and *aisle.* A glance at the etymology of the last of these will clearly show the extent to which such influence may reach. See also ISLAND, KILN.

[ME *debte,* alter. (influenced in spelling by MF *debte,* fr. OF, alter. — influenced in spelling by L *debitum* — of *dette, dete*) of *dette,* fr. OF *dette, dete,* fr. (assumed) VL *debita,* fr. L, pl. of *debitum* debt, fr. neut. of *debitus,* past part. of *debēre* to owe, fr. *de* from + *habēre* to have]

December See JANUARY.

[ME *decembre,* fr. OF, fr. L *december* (tenth month), fr. *decem* ten]

decimate Any Roman soldiers who pondered mutiny had good reason to think twice. A technique used by the Roman army to keep mutinous units in line was to select one-tenth of the men by lot and execute them, thereby encouraging the remaining nine-tenths to follow orders. The Latin verb for this presumably effective form of punishment was *deci-*

mare, literally 'to take a tenth of', which was derived from *decimus,* 'tenth', from *decem,* 'ten'.

The old Roman practice has not continued into modern times, of course, but its memorable ferocity has given us the verb *decimate,* which has been used in English since 1600. *Decimate* was originally used in historical reference to the Roman disciplinary procedure, but it soon came to be used more broadly in what is now its usual sense, 'to destroy a large part of', as in "the bombing decimated the city" or "the plague decimated the population." This new sense was first attested in 1667. Although it carries no suggestion of 'one tenth', it does retain clearly the overtones of extreme violence or terror associated with the original sense.

The Latin *decimare* was also used in the less ferocious sense 'to tax to the amount of one tenth', and *decimate* has sometimes had this sense in English, as when the poet John Dryden described someone as "poor as a decimated Cavalier." But the usual word describing a one-tenth tax in English is *tithe,* which functions as both a noun and a verb and which is derived from the Old English *teogotha,* a form of *tenth. Tithe* has had a strong religious connection throughout most of its history. Early use was in reference to the ten-percent tax paid (in money or in produce) by the ancient Hebrews in accordance with Mosaic law. A similar tax, also called a *tithe,* was required in support of parish churches in Britain until the middle of the nineteenth century. In current usage, *tithe* is perhaps most familiar in reference to voluntary contributions equal to one-tenth of one's income made in support of a church.

The meaning of the verb *tithe* has overlapped that of *decimate* more than once; it has had some use in describing the practice of putting to death every tenth man. And, more interestingly, *tithe* has also been used in a few instances in the opposite sense, in which every tenth man was spared. *Tithe* is also similar to *decimate* in having acquired an extended sense in which the etymological connection with 'one tenth' is lost; it is sometimes used to mean simply 'a small part'.

[L *decimatus,* past part. of *decimare,* fr. *decimus* tenth, fr. *decem* ten]

deer   The semantic development of words is often from the general to the specific. For instance, *deer* is used in Modern English to denote species, belonging to the family *Cervidae,* such as black-tailed and white-tailed deer, reindeer, caribou, elk, and moose. The Old English *dēor,* however, could refer to any beast or wild animal, or to wild animals in general, as in the Old English translation of Genesis: "God geweorhte thære eorthan deor æfter hira hiwum," where the King James Version reads, "God made the beast of the earth after his kind" (1:25). This sense of *deer* accounts for the reference in Shakespeare's *King Lear* to "rats and mice and such small deer." In time *deer* was restricted to denote the animal that was the primary object of the hunt in England, and from that usage the term has spread to other members of the same family. Old High German *tior,* like Old English *dēor,* means 'wild animal', as do the related terms in other early Germanic languages such as Old Norse *dȳr* and Gothic *dius*. The Old Norse word also was used especially for the animals we call deer today.

The evidence of cognate forms in more distantly related Indo-European languages gives us some indication of the very early semantic development of these words. For example, Lithuanian *dvėsti*, 'to breathe, expire', suggests that the Indo-European root from which *deer* is derived meant 'breathe', with the sense 'animal' deriving from the fact that animals are distinguished from the rest of nature by having breath. (For a similar sense development see ANIMAL.)

The young of the deer owes its name to a similar narrowing of meaning. *Fawn* derives (via Middle French *faon*) ultimately from Latin *fetus*, which referred to the young of any beast and occasionally to human babies.

[ME, deer, animal, fr. OE *dēor* beast; akin to OHG *tior* wild animal, ON *dȳr*, Goth *dius* wild animal, Lith *dvėsti* to breathe, expire, Skt *dhvaṁsati* he falls to dust, perishes]

defendant   See JUDGE.
[ME *defendaunt*, fr. MF *defendant*, pres. part. of *defendre*, fr. OF, fr. L *defendere*, fr. *de-* + *-fendere* to strike]

defenestration   See WINDOW.
[*de-* from + L *fenestra* window + E *-tion*]

Delaware   See INDIAN.
[fr. the *Delaware* river, after Thomas West, Lord *Delaware* (Baron *De La Warr*) †1618 colonial administrator in America]

delicatessen   Near the end of the nineteenth century the word *delicatessen* began to appear in English. Its earliest sense is 'delicacies' or 'ready-to-eat food products'. In this sense *delicatessen* is a plural noun, reflecting its origin in German *delikatessen*, the plural of *delikatesse*. The German is a borrowing from French *délicatesse*, meaning 'delicacy'. In English a second sense of *delicatessen* developed when it was understood as a singular noun used to designate a store where delicacies are sold. Just as German borrowed the French *délicatesse*, so did English long before *delicatessen* made its appearance. *Delicatesse*, meaning 'delicacy' or 'tact', was borrowed from French into English as early as 1698. It was used in 1704 by Jonathan Swift in *A Tale of a Tub* in which he mentions deducing faculties of mind from verbal behavior such as "agreeable conversation; . . . repartee; . . . humor; . . . [and] very good raillery: all which required abundance of *finesse* and *delicatesse* to manage with advantage. . . ."

Because of the widespread popular belief to the contrary, it seems worthwhile to point out directly that *delicatessen* has no etymological connection with the German verb *essen*, 'to eat'.

[G *delikatessen* (formerly spelled *delicatessen*), pl. of *delikatesse* delicacy, fr. F *délicatesse*, fr. MF *delicatesse*, prob. fr. OIt *delicatezza*, fr. *deli-*

cato delicate, dainty, tasty (fr. L *delicatus* pleasing to the senses, voluptuous) + *-ezza* -ess]

delirium See LEARN.
[L, fr. *delirare* to be crazy, fr. *de-* from + *lira* furrow, track]

Delphic The writers of daily horoscopes who supply their readers with such helpful advice as "Seek counsel but make your own decisions" or such prophetic announcements as "New lines of communications open" are following an ancient oracular tradition. Their deliberately vague pronouncements might be characterized, with historical justification, as *Delphic,* another word that is part of our cultural legacy from classical Greece. The word perpetuates the name of the ancient Greek town of Delphoi (better known now in its Latin form *Delphi*). Delphi was situated on the southern slopes of Mount Parnassus in central Greece and was the site of classical Greece's most important temple. The temple was believed to occupy the center of the world. Originally an oracle of the goddess Gaea, Delphi by the seventh and sixth centuries B.C. had acquired fame throughout the Greek world as the foremost oracle of Apollo. The oracular medium or priestess, known as a Pythia, was a mature matron who lived apart from her husband and dressed in the clothes of a maiden. Following an elaborate ritual, the Pythia and the visiting suppliant would first bathe in a spring, and then the priestess alone would drink from a sacred spring before entering the temple. There, seated on a sacred tripod positioned over a fissure in the rocks (from which vapors emanated), she would chew the leaves of a laurel, the tree sacred to Apollo. While in her divine ecstasy she would utter incoherent responses to the questions that the suppliant had previously posed. Her utterances were interpreted by attending priests, who then proceeded to recast the messages into verses that were often highly ambiguous or obscure. In religious matters the Delphic oracle was deemed the supreme authority in Greece and was regularly consulted concerning propitiation of the gods and the averting of evil. The oracle was consulted on public matters as well as private, and the Pythia was frequently called upon to forecast the outcomes of proposed wars and political actions. Forecasts of the future were so obscure or equivocal as to allow for just about any interpretation. The Delphic oracle became proverbial for the nature of its forecasts even in its own time. The fact that even today the word *Delphic* remains a synonym for *ambiguous* and *obscure* testifies to its enduring fame.

[fr. L *Delphicus,* fr. Gk *Delphikos,* fr. *Delphoi* town in ancient Greece + *-ikos* -ic]

delude See AMUSE.
[ME *deluden,* fr. L *deludere,* fr. *de-* + *ludere* to play]

demonstrate See MONSTER.
[L *demonstratus,* past part. of *demonstrare,* fr. *de-* + *monstrare* to show]

denim   The name of many a fabric is derived from the name of the place in which the fabric originated or in which it was manufactured. It is rather unusual, however, that two different names derived from the names of cities in different countries should be applied to the same material. *Denim* comes from the French *de Nîmes*, meaning 'of Nîmes', originally used in the phrase *serge de Nîmes*, which appeared in English in the seventeenth century as *serge denim*. *Serge*, from the Latin adjective *sericus*, 'of silk', is a durable twilled fabric, and Nîmes is a city of southern France where textiles are still an important industry. Today *denim* is not only a term for a type of cloth; in the plural it is used for overalls or trousers made of denim.

Another common name for these same garments is *jeans*, used in the plural like *denims*. In the singular *jean* is also a term for a durable twilled cotton and is short for the phrase *jean fustian*, which first appears in texts from the sixteenth century. *Fustian*, from Medieval Latin *fustaneum*, is a cotton or cotton and linen fabric, and *jean* is the modern spelling of Middle English *Jene* or *Gene*, from *Genes*, the Middle French name of the Italian city Genoa, where it was made and shipped abroad.

[F *(serge) de Nîmes* serge of Nîmes, France]

derby   The original *derby* is an annual horse race run at Epsom Downs, England. Epsom Downs, however, is nowhere near the town or county of *Derby* in north central England; it is a racetrack in Surrey, southwest of London. The *derby* got its name not from its location but from the title of its founder, Edward Stanley, the twelfth Earl of *Derby*, who established the race in 1780. *Derby* then became the term for a number of prominent horse races, usually restricted to three-year-olds, and today it has come to mean any race or contest open to all comers or to a specified category of contestants.

In the United States in the 1880s the name *derby* was also applied to a stiff felt hat with a dome-shaped crown and a narrow brim. Apparently, this type of hat was first made in the 1860s by a London hatter named *Bowler;* thus, it is called a *bowler hat* in England and in the United States either *derby* or simply *bowler.*

Another earl who lent his title to the general English vocabulary was John Montagu, the fourth Earl of *Sandwich*, who died in 1792. According to an account published in his lifetime, the earl was an inveterate gambler and would spend up to twenty-four hours at a stretch at the tables. Rather than interrupt his play for meals, he would have slices of cold beef between pieces of toast, and the *sandwich* was born.

Charles Anderson Worsley, the second Earl of *Yarborough*, who died in 1897, was also an avid card player. It was said that he bet a thousand to one against the dealing of a whist or bridge hand containing no card higher than a nine, and since then such a hand has been called a *Yarborough*. Actually, the earl was not risking much as long as he did not make this wager too often, for the odds against dealing a *Yarborough* are about 1,828 to 1.

The names of several Englishmen who were not peers have also passed into the lexicon. Sir *Robert Peel* organized the London police force in 1832, and from his nickname any London policeman came to be called a

bobby. In Ireland, whose constabulary Sir Robert also had a hand in organizing, a policeman was for a time called a *peeler*. Charles G. *Boycott* was
a nineteenth-century English land agent in County Mayo, Ireland, and
when he refused to lower the rents for his tenants, they in turn declined
to pay him any rent at all. Any similar refusal to have dealings with a person or organization is now called a *boycott*. See also GROG.

[fr. the *Derby*, famous horse race run at Epsom Downs, England; after
Edward Stanley †1834, 12th earl of *Derby*, who founded it in 1780]

derrick   The Tyburn, a short subterranean river in west London, gave
its name to the place of executions located until 1793 at the intersection
of Edgeware Road and Oxford Street, where Marble Arch now stands. In
the reign of Queen Elizabeth I there was an executioner named *Derick*
who achieved some notoriety because of his position. Among those he beheaded was the second Earl of Essex, Robert Devereux, the onetime favorite of the queen. According to a street ballad which was hawked about at
the time, it appears that the earl had previously saved the life of this same
Derick.
    While members of the nobility were accorded the courtesy of behead-
ing, it was the lot of condemned commoners generally to be hanged. Consequently the populace named the Tyburn gallows after the hangman
Derick. This usage spread, and throughout the seventeenth century *derrick* was a term for both a hangman and a gallows. These senses eventually
became obsolete, but in the next century *derrick* began to be used for a
gallowslike hoisting apparatus employing a tackle rigged at the end of a
beam. Subsequently, *derrick* has become a term for a framework or tower
over a deep drill (as for an oil well), used for supporting boring tackle or
for hoisting and lowering. See also GUILLOTINE.

[after *Derick fl ab*1600 hangman at Tyburn, London, England]

describe   See SCRIVENER.
    [L *describere*, fr. *de-* + *scribere* to write]

desecrate   See SACRED.
    [*de-* + *-secrate* as in *consecrate*, v.)]

desire   See DISASTER.
    [ME *desiren*, fr. OF *desirer*, fr. L *desiderare* to long for, miss, desire, fr.
    de- from, away + *-siderare* (fr. *sider-*, *sidus* star, constellation)]

desk   See DOUBLETS.
    [ME *deske*, fr. ML *desca*, modif. of It *desco* board, table, fr. L *discus* dish,
    disk, quoit]

deus ex machina   In Hollywood Westerns it is the U.S. Cavalry arriving
at breakneck speed just in the nick of time. In sentimental melodrama, it
is a disease, which once was usually consumption and now is cancer more
often than not. In stories from any of several genres it is a sudden change

of heart straight out of nowhere. In every case "it" is a *deus ex machina*—
the person, thing, or event that conveniently and usually very improbably
resolves a seemingly irresolvable dramatic situation. The origin of the
term, which comes from Latin and literally means 'a god from a machine',
can be traced back to Greek drama of the fourth century B.C. Even during
the nascency of the drama, playwrights were wrestling with the problem
of how to resolve the essential conflict that they had elaborately created
in their dramas. Euripides and Sophocles were two of the Greek playwrights who resorted to divine intervention to bring about the resolutions
of their dramas.

Sophocles used divine intervention in *Philoctetes*, a tragedy in which
the title character is a young Greek warrior who possesses a bow of divine
origin. The bow is the key to the success of the Greek cause in the Trojan
War. Odysseus and an accomplice are repeatedly thwarted in their attempts to engage the reluctant warrior in the siege at Troy. The stalemate
is resolved by the appearance in a vision of the god-man Heracles, who
simply commands Philoctetes to go to Troy. Since special effects were
then at an understandably primitive stage, the sudden appearance of a
god in the sky was effected by means of a cranelike machine (in Greek,
mēchanē).

The resolving of a tangled plot by the timely intervention of a god hoisted on a crane became a standard convention in the Greek and Roman theater. The extended application of the term for this stage effect to any
providential savior or improbable event also became established during
classical times. It was in this extended sense that *deux ex machina* first appeared in English contexts in the seventeenth century, and it remains a
favorite device of storytellers.

[NL, a god from a machine, trans. of Gk *theos ek mēchanēs*]

devil   In the Hebrew Old Testament, the word *śaṭān* (literally 'adversary') usually refers to a human adversary. But in some of the later books
(especially the Book of Job) where the *devil* plays a large part, *śaṭān* is the
devil himself, the major adversary of the Lord. In the Septuagint, the
Greek translation of the Old Testament, this superhuman adversary is usually called *diabolos* or 'slanderer' (from the Greek verb *diaballein*, 'to slander', which means literally 'to throw across'). But in the Greek New
Testament, the Hebrew word, which is *Satanas* or *Satan* in its Greek form,
is used as if it were the devil's proper name. The older Latin translation
of the Bible retains Greek *diabolos* as *diabolus*, but St. Jerome's version,
the Vulgate, calls the devil *Satan*. Both words were borrowed into Old English, and we now call our greatest adversary both *Satan* and the *Devil*.

The devil appears in a great many proverbs. We are often told that two
of these, "the devil to pay" and "between the devil and the deep (blue)
sea," do not refer to Satan at all but rather to a perfectly innocent nautical
devil. This *devil* is a seam in a ship's hull, on or below the waterline. "The
devil to pay" is supposed to be a short form of "the devil to pay and no
pitch hot." This interpretation depends on a homonym of the verb *pay*
which means 'to apply pitch'. Unfortunately for the nautical explanation,

both proverbs are attested much earlier than is the requisite sense of *devil*. We first find "the devil to pay" in a poem written about 1500: "Better wer be at tome for ay, than her to serue, the devil to pay." (*At tome* is apparently a scribal error for *at home*. The couplet becomes, in Modern English: "It would be better to stay at home forever than to serve here to please— or pay—the devil.") We have no evidence for the longer "the devil to pay and no pitch hot" until 1828. "Between the devil and the deep sea" goes back at least to 1637. Robert Monro, in *His Expedition with the Worthy Scots Regiment Called Mac-Keyes Regiment,* wrote: "I, with my partie, did lie on our poste, as betwixt the devill and the deep sea." The *devil* in a ship's hull, on the other hand, is first reported in William Henry Smyth's *Sailor's Word-Book: An Alphabetical Digest of Nautical Terms,* compiled about 1865. It is true that nautical terms are likely to enjoy a long oral use without being written down. But three and a half, or even two, centuries seems rather too long to be an acceptable assumption for the nautical explanation. It is more likely that this proverbial *devil* is the Devil himself. See also LUCIFER, PAY.

[ME *devel,* fr. OE *dēofol,* fr. LL *diabolus,* fr. Gk *diabolos,* lit., slanderer, fr. *diaballein* to throw across, discredit, slander, fr. *dia* through, across + *ballein* to throw]

devolve   See VOLUME.
[ME *devolven* to roll down, fr. L *devolvere,* fr. *de* down, away + *volvere* to roll]

dexterous *or* **dextrous**   See RIGHT.

[L *dexter* skillful, relating to or situated on the right + E *-ous*]

dextrose   See RIGHT.
[ISV *dextr-* (fr. L *dextr-, dexter* on the right) + *-ose,* fr. F, fr. glu*cose*]

diamond   The Greek and Latin for the hardest imaginable substance, whether applied to a legendary stone or an actual substance like diamond or steel, was *adamas,* from which is derived Old French *adamant.* This was borrowed into English in the fourteenth century with much the same range of meanings as its classical etymon. From the figurative use of this noun in English comes the adjective *adamant,* meaning 'unyielding', 'unshakable', or 'immovable'.

The hardest known substance occurring in nature is diamond, and thus when diamonds became known to the Western world sometime around the beginning of the Christian era the Latin *adamas* was applied to them as well as other very hard substances. In this way *adamant* also became a word for diamond in Old French and Middle English. In Late Latin, however, the form *diamas* began to be used to distinguish diamonds from other substances included previously in the term *adamas.* This distinction proved useful, and so in English we have the two terms *adamant,* used of an unbreakable or extremely hard substance, and *diamond,* used of the precious stone.

[ME *diamaunt, diamaunde,* fr. MF *diamant, diamande,* fr. LL *diamant-, diamas,* alter. of (assumed) VL *adimant-, adimas* hardest iron or steel, diamond, alter. of L *adamant-, adamas,* fr. Gk]

die See SKIRT.

[ME *dien, deyen,* fr. or akin to ON *deyja* to die; akin to OS *dōian* to die, OHG *touwen* to die, Goth *diwans* mortal, OIr *duine* human being, Arm *di* corpse]

diet The Diet of Worms, at which Martin Luther was condemned as a heretic, is surely one of history's least appetizingly named events. But Luther was not compelled to eat a plateful of squirming invertebrates. Worms is a city in Germany, and the *diet* in question is not nourishment but rather a formal assembly. The two words *diet* are unrelated.

The nourishing *diet* first appeared in English in the thirteenth century. Its original meaning was the same that it has in Modern English, 'habitually taken food and drink'. But *diet* was used in another sense too in the Middle and early Modern English periods, to mean 'way of living'. In the *Tale of Beryn* (ca. 1400) we find these words of comfort: "Ech day our diete shall be mery & solase & this shall be for-get [forgotten]." This is, in fact, the original meaning of *diet*'s Greek ancestor *diaita,* which is derived from the verb *diaitan,* which means 'to lead one's life' or 'to govern'. In the Greek, *diaita* had already come to be used more specifically for a way of living prescribed by a physician, a diet or other regimen. This was also the meaning of the Latin word *diaeta,* borrowed from the Greek.

The other *diet* is a derivative of the Latin word *dies,* 'day'. Medieval Latin *dieta* was used not only for a day's journey, a day's work, or a day's wage, but also for a particular day set for a meeting or assembly, and then later for the assembly itself. In particular, a formal assembly of the councillors of the Holy Roman Empire was called a *dieta.* It was at one of these assemblies, held at Worms in April of 1521, that Luther was condemned for heresy.

[ME *diete,* fr. OF, fr. L *diaeta* prescribed dietary regimen, fr. Gk *diaita,* lit., manner of living, fr. *diaitan* to arbitrate, govern, lead one's life, fr. *dia-* through + *-aitan* (akin to Gk *aisa* destiny, share)]

[ME *dyet,* fr. ML *dieta,* fr. L *dies* day]

dine See JEJUNE.

[ME *dinen,* fr. OF *disner, diner* to dine, breakfast, fr. (assumed) VL *disjejunare* to break one's fast, fr. L *dis-* + LL *jejunare* to fast, fr. L *jejunus* fasting, hungry]

dink See YUPPIE.

[*d*ouble *i*ncome, *n*o *k*ids]

dinosaur   See BRONTOSAURUS.
[NL *Dinosauria*, fr. *din-* (fr. Gk *dein-*, *deino-*, fr. *deinos* terrible) +
-sauria (fr. *saurus* lizard — fr. Gk *saura, sauros* lizard — + *-ia*)]

dire   See FURY.
[L *dirus;* akin to Gk *dedienai* to fear, *deos* fear, *deinos* terrible, Av
dvaēthā threat, Skt *dveṣṭi* he hates]

dirge   The meaning of English *dirge* is not directly related to the meaning of the Latin form from which it is derived. *Dirge* and its earlier form
dirige, meaning 'a song or hymn of lamentation', come from the first word
of a Latin antiphon used in the Office of the Dead: "Dirige, Domine deus
meus, in conspectu tuo viam meam." (Direct, O Lord my God, my way in
thy sight.) This adaptation from the Vulgate Bible of a portion of Psalm 5
opens the first nocturn of the service, and the first word of the Latin antiphon became the English generic term for a funeral hymn and subsequently for any slow, solemn, and mournful piece of music. (For other
words derived from the use of a foreign word rather than from its meaning
see PIANO, SHIBBOLETH.)
  The Latin *dirige* used in the Office of the Dead is a form of the verb
dirigere, 'to direct, make straight', and there are several words in English
that are derived in both form and meaning from this verb. For instance,
combination with the English suffix *-ible* gives the adjective *dirigible,*
meaning 'steerable'. A *dirigible* balloon, therefore, is a balloon that can be
steered or directed. From this application of the adjective, *dirigible* has
come to be used as a noun denoting the airship itself.
  Less obviously derived from *dirigere* is our common verb *dress.* The
considerable difference in the forms of these two words is due to the fact
that *dress* comes indirectly from the Latin via Middle French *dresser*
which can be traced through a series of sound changes to a Vulgar Latin
verb derived from the Latin *directus,* the past participle of *dirigere. Dress*
was first used in Middle English in the sense 'to make or set straight', which
is familiar to us today especially from the related sense 'to arrange troops
or equipment in a straight line and at proper intervals'. The implications
of arranging something in proper order or fashion led to such senses as 'to
put clothes on' and 'to kill and prepare an animal for market'.

[ME *dirige, derge,* fr. L *dirige* (sing. pres. imper. act. of *dirigere* to direct,
make straight), the first word of an antiphon adapted from Ps 5:9 (Vulgate) that opens the first nocturn in the Office of the Dead]

dirigible   See DIRGE.
[L *dirigere* to direct, make straight + E *-ible*]

disaster   "We make guilty of our disasters the sun, the moon, and the
stars; as if we were villains on necessity; fools by heavenly compulsion;
knaves, thieves, and treachers by spherical predominance; drunkards,
liars, and adulterers by an enforc'd obedience of planetary influences.
. . . ." When Shakespeare's Edmund in *King Lear* (ca. 1605) railed against

astrology rather than against the stars, the word *disaster* was quite new. It entered English from Middle French or Old Italian only in the late sixteenth century. But Shakespeare was fond of it and used it aptly. The word owes its very existence to astrology. Old Italian *astro* is 'star'; a *disastro* was due to the negative aspects of stellar influence.

The influence of the stars on our language did not stop with producing the large group of words—*stellar, astrology, aster, disaster, desire, consider,* and many others—related to *star*. We also owe the unrelated *influenza* to former astrological convictions. Italian *influenza* has the same meaning as its English cognate *influence*. But in the fifteenth century, sudden epidemics whose earthly causes were not apparent were blamed on the *influenza* of the stars. The report of a Roman epidemic which spread through much of Europe in 1743 brought the word to England.

[MF & OIt; MF *desastre*, fr. OIt *disastro*, fr. *dis-* dis- (fr. L) + *astro* star, fr. L *astrum*, fr. Gk *astron;* akin to OE *steorra* star, OHG *sterro, sterno,* L *stella*]

disco   See BOUTIQUE.
[short for *discotheque*]

discotheque   See BOUTIQUE.
[F *discothèque* collection of phonograph records, discotheque, fr. *disque* disk (fr. L *discus*) + *-o-* + *-thèque* (as in *bibliothèque* library, fr. L *bibliotheca*)]

discus   See DOUBLETS.
[L]

dish   See DOUBLETS.
[ME, fr. OE *disc* plate; akin to OS *disk* table, OHG *tisc* dish, table; all fr. a prehistoric WGmc word borrowed fr. L *discus* dish, disk, quoit, fr. Gk *diskos*, fr. *dikein* to throw]

disinformation   In a political cartoon published in the 1980s, a befuddled-looking man reads a sign that contains the words "U.S. Office of Disinformation" with an arrow pointing left. It is obvious to the reader that the man will certainly be lost if he follows the arrow; the reader can see what the man cannot, that the U.S. Office of Disinformation is really just around the corner to the right.

The man in the cartoon will not be severely affected by this encounter with disinformation. He may wander around until he stumbles upon the office he is seeking. In real life, of course, disinformation has much more severe repercussions, and it can be every bit as debilitating to public opinion as its cousin, propaganda.

Like propaganda, disinformation is associated with the covert system of public-opinion manipulation through the dispensing of selective information long believed to be practiced by the Soviet Union and its sophisticated intelligence network, known to us as the KGB. So strong is this association that the term *disinformation* is thought to be a literal translation of Russian *dezinformatsiya,* which means 'misinformation'. *Dezinformatsiya* is purported to have been the name of a department of the KGB formed in 1955, which oversaw the dispensing of propaganda to international media and government organizations.

The reported use by the Soviets of disinformation for purposes of international domination is worthy of our juiciest spy novels. According to one-time CIA director William Colby, the Soviet disinformation bureau would plant a fictitious story in a leftist publication. The story would circulate to a Communist journal, and eventually be printed by the Soviet news agency, which would subsequently attribute the information to undisclosed sources. In this way, a lie would circulate around the world in the guise of an officially documented news item.

Whether or not our word *disinformation* does indeed come from Russian *dezinformatsiya* is a matter open to speculation. As early as 1939, years before the *Dezinformatsiya* agency is reported to have been formed, the word *disinformation* appeared in a description of German intelligence activities prior to World War II: "The mood of national suspicion prevalent during the last decade in contemporary Europe is well-illustrated by Gen. Krivitsky's account of the German 'Disinformation Service', engaged in manufacturing fake military plans for the express purpose of having them stolen by foreign governments." The English word *disinformation* may even have developed independently of Russian *dezinformatsiya* out of our own mounting concern with the spread of propaganda and practices of misinformation that perhaps began in the years just before World War II. In that case, *disinformation* may have originated as a noun form of the verb *disinform,* which in turn is derived from the combination of *dis-* and *inform,* just as *misinform* is derived from the prefix *mis-* and the verb *inform.*

In this age of increased hostility between political factions at home and abroad, *disinformation* is becoming an increasingly popular word. No longer do we perceive the Soviets as having a monopoly on this form of deception. Increasingly, the word is being used in reference to alleged covert practices of U.S. government officials. Tad Szulc, writing in *The Washingtonian* magazine (March 1974) tells of a CIA agent in Thailand faking a letter from a guerrilla leader to the Bangkok government: "This is a classic example of the 'disinformation' technique, intended to embarrass the guerrilla leader . . . and thus weaken the subversive movement."

Regardless of which side of the Iron Curtain the term hailed from, disinformation is a powerful manipulative tool in the constant battle for world domination.

[prob. trans. of Russ *dezinformatsiya* misinformation]

disk   See DOUBLETS.
[L *discus* dish, disk, quoit]

dismal   Medieval calendars designated two days in every month *dies mali,* 'evil days', which were considered inauspicious. These days were also known as "Egyptian days," probably because their nature was supposed to have been discovered by ancient Egyptian astronomers. Some medieval writers, however, interpreted the name "Egyptian" as referring to the ten Biblical plagues which the Lord visited upon Egypt when Pharaoh refused to allow Moses to lead Israel out of the country. According to the thirteenth-century English encyclopedist Bartholomaeus Anglicus (as translated from his Latin by John of Trevisa, about 1398): "Dies egipciacus is that day in the whiche God sente som wreche in to Egipt, and for the dayes Egipciaci beth foure and twenty, hit suyth that god sente mo wrechis vppon the Egipcians than ten." (Dies egipciacus is the day on which God sent a plague into Egypt, and because there are twenty-four Egyptian days, it follows that God sent more than ten plagues upon the Egyptians.) Chaucer, too, believed that the unlucky days commemorated the Biblical plagues: "I trowe hyt was in the dismal,/ That was the ten woundes of Egipt." (I believe it was in the period of unlucky days, that was the ten plagues of Egypt.) Chaucer apparently interpreted *dismal* as being Middle French *dis mal*, 'ten evils'. But *dismal* comes from the Latin *dies mali*.

By the fifteenth century *dismal* was often being used attributively. A "dismal day" was one of the twenty-four that belonged to the *dismal*. It was not long before the word was reinterpreted as an adjective, meaning at first 'unlucky' but eventually 'gloomy' or 'miserable'.

[ME, fr. *dismal*, n., set of 24 days (two in each month) identified as unlucky in medieval calendars, fr. AF, fr. ML *dies mali*, lit., evil days, fr. L *dies* (pl. of *dies* day) + *mali* (pl. of *malus* evil, bad)]

dissimilation   See ASSIMILATION.
[¹*dis-* + *-similation* (as in *assimilation*)]

distaff   In a 1961 book on the joys of barbecuing, the authors put forth a statement regarding outdoor cooking and the proper role of women:

It is our belief that the cook should be male. Cooking over charcoal is a man's job and should have no interference from the distaff side of the family. If the man of the house prefers to have his wife do the cooking, just skip the whole idea of doing it outdoors.

The passage is full of sexual stereotyping, from the notion that outdoor cooking is macho to the suggestion that a woman's place is in the kitchen. And in referring to women as "the distaff side of the family," the cookbook authors carried the stereotyping even further.

A distaff was originally a short staff that held a bundle of fibers, flax or wool perhaps, that were drawn and twisted into yarn or thread either by hand or with the aid of a spinning wheel. The job of spinning customarily fell to the women, and since it was such a basic daily task, the distaff naturally came to be the symbol for woman's work. This symbolic use of the word *distaff* dates back to the time of Chaucer and is found a number of times in the works of Shakespeare. Eventually *distaff* came to be used figuratively for everything relating to the womanly domain and for womankind collectively. The women of a family became known as the *distaff* or the *distaff side*. The distaff became so closely identified with women that the day following the 12 days of Christmas was formerly known as *Distaff's Day* or *St. Distaff's Day*. On this day women were expected to quit their holiday baking and entertaining and get back to their spinning and other routine chores.

The task of spinning was formerly of such importance that it gave rise to another word now associated with women exclusively. The word *spinster* dates from the fourteenth century and originally meant a person who spins, especially as a regular occupation. Naturally, the word was usually applied to women. By the seventeenth century *spinster* had also become the established legal term for an unmarried woman. Not until the eighteenth century did *spinster* acquire its current sense: 'a woman who remains unmarried beyond the usual age for marrying'.

It is interesting that while the distaff has a long history as the female symbol, there has been no comparable tradition for a male symbol. The only male counterpart for *distaff side* is the rather obscure term *sword side*. *Sword side*, referring to the father's side of a family, is a literal translation of an older Germanic compound, but it did not exist in English before the nineteenth century.

[ME *distaf*, fr. OE *distæf*, fr. *dis-* bunch of flax (akin to MLG *dise* bunch of flax on a distaff) + *stæf* staff]

ditali *or* **ditalini**   See VERMICELLI.

[*ditali* fr. It, pl. of *ditale*, lit., thimble, fingerstall; *ditalini* fr. It, pl. of *ditalino*, dim. of *ditale*]

divert   See AMUSE.

[ME *diverten*, fr. MF & L; MF *divertir*, fr. L *divertere* (also *divortere*) to turn aside, go different ways, differ, fr. *di-* (fr. *dis-* away, apart) + *vertere* to turn]

djinn   See GENIUS.

[Ar *jinnīy* demon, spirit]

dog days   To the ancient Egyptians, the heliacal rising of the brightest star in the heavens signaled the annual inundation of the Nile, which renewed the fertility of the land. They called the star *Sothis* and worshiped it as a goddess. They also based their calendar on its rising, which marked the beginning of their new year. In later times, the Greeks called the same star *Seirios* (in English we use the Latin form *Sirius*), which means 'scorching' or 'burning', because its appearance was associated with the dry, hot days of summer. When the Greeks applied their mythology to the heavens, Sirius was conceived of as the hound of the hunter Orion, and thus was called *kyōn*, their word for 'dog'.

The Romans, as they did so often, adopted the Greek notion. They called Sirius *canicula*, the Latin for 'small dog', and the constellation to which it belonged was named *Canis Major*, the 'Greater Dog'. The dry, hot days of summer that were associated with the rising of *canicula* were called *dies caniculares*, which by the process of loan translation has survived in the Modern English expression "dog days."

[trans. of LL *dies caniculares*, trans. of Gk *hēmerai kynades;* fr. their being reckoned in ancient times from the heliacal rising of the Dog Star (Sirius)]

dollar   In the mountains of northwestern Bohemia, just a few kilometers south of the East German-Czechoslovakian border, is the small town of Jáchymov. In the early sixteenth century, when the town was known by its German name, Sankt Joachimsthal, a silver mine was opened nearby and coins were minted to which the name *joachimstaler* was applied. In German this was shortened to *taler.* Shortly afterward the Dutch or Low German form *daler* was borrowed into English to refer to the *taler* and other coins (such as the Spanish *peso*) that were patterned after it. In his autobiography Thomas Jefferson tells us that he "proposed . . . to adopt the Dollar as our Unit of account and payment." In doing so Jefferson was simply recognizing that the Spanish *dollar* was already an important medium of exchange here because of trade with the West Indies. Accordingly, we find the following resolution of the Continental Congress adopted on 6 July 1785, "Resolved that the money unit of the United States of America be one dollar."

[alter. of earlier *daler,* fr. D or LG, fr. G *taler,* short for *joachimstaler,* fr. Sankt *Joachimsthal* (Jáchymov), town in northwestern Bohemia, Czechoslovakia, where the first talers were made]

domain   See DUNGEON.
[ME *demaine, domaine,* fr. L *dominium,* fr. *dominus* master, owner]

dominate   See DUNGEON.
[L *dominatus,* past part. of *dominari* to rule, govern, fr. *dominus* lord, master]

domino   If you were invited to an eighteenth-century masked ball in England you would have gone dressed up as some sort of character, say, a shepherd, or you would have gone simply incognito, probably wearing a loose cloaklike garment with a mask. The name for this get-up was *domino,* a word borrowed from French where it had been used in the same meaning since the 1660s. The French *domino* 'ball costume' was developed by extension from an earlier *domino* which was the name of a hood worn by priests. The priestly hood sense is attested in French from early in the fifteenth century and is presumed to be derived from Latin *dominus* 'lord, master', but the exact means of transmission is uncertain; the general supposition is that it comes from the dative form *domino* as used in such standard religious phrases as *benedicamus Domino* 'let us praise the Lord'.

One of the purposes of the masked ball was to ease social discourse by disguising to some extent the external marks of class and the inhibitions they impose. Lady Mary Wortley Montagu in a letter written in March 1744 tells how several of her friends "almost by force" took her from Avignon, France, where she was then living, to Nîmes to attend some great social function. When she arrived she was visited by two socially prominent Huguenots and asked to intervene with the Duke of Richelieu in behalf of some other Huguenots who had just been imprisoned—the strictures of Louis XIV on the worship of the Huguenots still being in force then. Her letter goes on: "They moved my compassion so much I resolved to use my endeavours to serve them, though I had little hope of succeeding. I would not therefore dress myself for the supper, but went in a domino to the ball, a mask giving opportunity of talking in a freer manner than I could have done without it." As it turned out, Lady Mary was successful in her endeavors.

The domino was worn by men as well as women. The costume sense of *domino* was sometimes also applied to the person wearing the costume. It is used nowadays to refer to certain color patterns in dogs, such as Afghan hounds.

The *domino* of the game dominoes seems to be an independent borrowing, again from French. The French had begun using *domino* in this meaning in the later part of the eighteenth century. The game first turned up about that time in both France and Italy. It is believed that French prisoners of war brought the game to England. At any rate the word *domino* first appeared in English about thirty years after it had in French. The origin of the French word is again somewhat mysterious. There was a theory, now abandoned, that *domino* came directly from Latin *dominus* 'master' and was used in reference to the winner of the game. French etymologists appear to be fonder of the theory that the name came from a likening of the pieces—often ebony backs with ivory faces in the beginning—to priests wearing domino hoods.

One thing that a bored child with a set of dominoes learns early is that rows of them stood on end can be toppled in sequence by tipping over the first piece. It doesn't take long for the child to realize that with a proper set-up dominoes will fall in curves and circles too. This fortuitous characteristic of a set of dominoes has intrigued many people, including college students who set up elaborate arrays of thousands of dominoes to topple as a sort of exhibition, and mathematicians, who have calculated that a chain of dominoes will fall at a fixed speed after the first four or five fall no matter how hard or gently the first domino is pushed.

The chain-reaction characteristic of dominoes was carried into the realm of political science in the 1950s, when it was used metaphorically to illustrate the theory that one southeast Asian country's turning communist would inevitably cause its neighbor to become communist, and so forth. This metaphor soon became formalized as the *domino theory* and its results were known as the *domino effect*. Before many years had passed, the domino theory and domino effect were transferred from southeast Asia to other areas of interest—today, often that of international finance. And *domino theory* and *domino effect* have redounded on *domino: domino* is no longer just the flat rectangular game piece but now often refers to a single unit in a chain subject to the domino effect. Thus we find references to falling dominoes, teetering dominoes, shaky dominoes, even big ones:

> . . . so long as the few big dominoes that could suffer immoderate losses (eg, Texas banks and Mexico) are moderately propped up —*The Economist,* 29 June 1985

For other words derived from Latin *dominus* see DUNGEON.

[F, prob. fr. *domino* (in the prayer formula *benedicamus Domino* let us bless the Lord), dat. of *dominus* lord, master]

don See DUNGEON.
[Sp, fr. L *dominus* master, lord]

donjon See DUNGEON.
[ME *donjon, dongeoun*]

donnybrook The word *donnybrook* has been applied to just about every kind of tumultuous struggle, from baseball games to political contests. For political contests in which the politicians are Irish, the label might be especially apt. Donnybrook, now a part of Dublin, was once a suburb about a mile and a half from the city's center. In 1204 King John granted to the citizens of Dublin a charter to hold at Donnybrook an annual trading fair as a way of raising funds for the building and upkeep of the city's walls. For the next 651 years it was held in August on a flat green beside the River Dodder. In addition to horse trading, the fair featured the selling of trinkets and food. Entertainment took the form of dancing to pipes and fiddles and dramatic performances by strolling bands of players.

Donnybrook Fair became legendary for the vast quantities of liquor consumed. The fair also became locally infamous for the number of hasty marriages performed the week after the fair. But perhaps its best-known claim to fame was the frequent eruption of brawling. The fighting, which often involved the wielding of shillelaghs, was said by witnesses to be all in good fun. One nineteenth-century German visitor observed that for all the tumult, the general scene was one of genuine merriment and glee. Eventually Donnybrook Fair's reputation was its undoing. From the 1790s there were campaigns against the drunken brawl that the fair had become. The fair met its demise in 1855. By that time, however, the name *Donnybrook* had acquired the generic sense that would accord it an enduring place in the language.

[fr. *Donnybrook Fair,* an annual event known for its brawls held in Donnybrook, suburb of Dublin, Ireland]

doublets *Doublets* are words in a given language that go back to the same etymological source but look different because they arrived at their present state by different routes. Thus English *two* and Latin *duo* 'two' both go back to a root with this meaning in the ancestral Indo-European language—that is, the English and the Latin words are COGNATE (which see). When English borrowed *duo* (in the musical sense) from Italian, where it is the immediate offspring of Latin, *duo* became a doublet of *two*.

A curious case is that of *fresh*. The Germanic language ancestral to both English and German had a root meaning 'fresh', represented in Modern German by *frisch*. The Old English version of this root was *fersc*, which meant 'unsalted'. Middle English had both the expected *fersh* and a new form *fresh*. The spelling with -*re*-, which eventually won out, was probably influenced by Old French *freis* 'fresh' (the Modern French forms are *frais* in the masculine and *fraîche* in the feminine). Old French had borrowed this word from the Germanic. Italian, meanwhile, had made an analogous Germanic borrowing, appearing in Italian as *fresco*, applied in particular to fresh plaster, and English later repaid the compliment by borrowing *fresco* (in a specialized sense having to do with painting) from Italian. *Fresh* and *fresco* are therefore doublets.

Despite the etymological implication of 'two' in *doublets*, the term is also applied to sets of more than two cognates. Latin *discus* meant 'platter' or 'quoit' and was borrowed unchanged by English in the mid-seventeenth century in a sports sense similar to the Latin. *Discus* was re-borrowed a few years later as *disk*, now shorn of the Latin grammatical termination -*us*, for astronomical applications, referring to the round shape of the sun and moon. But *discus* had already been borrowed, more than a millennium earlier, appearing in Old English as *disc* 'platter' and evolving by regular sound change into *dish*. Latin itself, meanwhile, had not stood still, and the classical *discus* had spun off a Medieval Latin *desca* 'table', which English borrowed and which is the source of modern *desk*. *Discus* also underwent comparatively radical sound change as the Latin spoken in France evolved into French; the Old French version of *discus* is now reflected in English *dais* 'raised platform'. (For a similar case of multiple reflexes of a single Latin word see GENTILE.)

In most cases of English doublets, at least one of the forms is of foreign origin. But occasionally subtle effects will generate doublets entirely from within English. Thus Old English had a word meaning 'shade' whose nominative form was *sceadu* and whose oblique case form was *sceaduwe*. The former evolved into *shade*, the latter into *shadow*. *Shade* and *shadow* are thus inflectional doublets.

For English dialect doublets see ORNERY, PASSEL, RILE, SASS.

doubt   See DEBT.

[ME *douten* to fear, doubt, fr. OF *douter*, fr. L *dubitare* to doubt]

downer   See BLURB.

draconian   *Draconian* is still regularly used to refer to any law, measure, or rule of authority that is notably harsh or cruel. The word derives from the name of Draco, an Athenian lawgiver of the seventh century B.C., whose purpose was to reform the criminal justice system. Before Draco there was little justice in the system; punishment was largely carried out in the name of mere personal revenge. About 621 B.C. Draco issued the first comprehensive written code of laws. The purpose was to mandate particular penalties for any of an array of crimes. The harshness of the penalties became legendary. But what Draco lacked in compassion he made up for in consistency: almost all criminal offenses, both trivial and serious, called for the death penalty. According to a fourth-century B.C. orator, Demades, the Draconian laws were written in blood. He and later authors, including Aristotle, may have exaggerated the severity of Draco's code, but in 594 B.C. the Athenian statesman Solon repealed almost all of it. Solon retained Draco's laws concerning homicide, however, which placed the responsibility for justice with the state and not with the victim's family. It is appropriate that the latter lawgiver's name is preserved in English as *solon,* a synonym for a wise and skillful lawgiver. On the other hand, the proverbial severity of Draco's code has resulted in *draconian* being applied to various things, not just laws, that are extremely harsh or rigorous. According to one classical tradition, Draco died by being smothered in a shower of hats and cloaks, in what was ostensibly an expression of adulation on the part of the public. But you have to wonder.

[L *Dracon-, Draco* fl621 B.C. Athenian lawgiver (fr. Gk *Drakōn*) + E *-ian*]

drat See JEEPERS.
[prob. euphemistic alter. of *God rot*]

dream Not until the thirteenth century did *dream,* in the Middle English forms *drem* and *dreem,* appear in the sense of 'series of thoughts, images, or emotions occurring during sleep'; however, the word itself is considerably older. In Old English *dream* means 'joy', 'noise', or 'music'. Yet the shift in sense between Old and Middle English was not simply the result of an adaptation and specialization of the earlier senses. Rather it would appear that after many Scandinavian conflicts, conquests, and settlements in Britain the Old Norse *draumr,* meaning a dream during sleep, influenced the meaning of the similar and probably related English word. By the end of the fourteenth century the earlier meanings had been entirely replaced, and the modern extended senses of *dream* as 'an ideal' or 'something desirable' have since developed from the sense of a *dream* during sleep. See also NIGHTMARE.

[ME *dreem,* fr. OE *drēam* noise, joy, music, prob. influenced in meaning by ON *draumr* dream; prob. akin to OHG *troum* dream, ON *draumr,* Gk *thrylos* noise, din, Latvian *duñduris* gadfly, wasp]

dress See DIRGE.
[ME *dressen,* fr. MF *dresser,* fr. OF *drecier,* fr. (assumed) VL *directiare,* fr. L *directus* direct, past part. of *dirigere* to direct, fr. *di-* (fr. *dis-* apart) + *-rigere* (fr. *regere* to rule)]

dunce It seems strange that this word, which suggests dullness of wit and ignorance to us now, should have been derived from the name of one of the most brilliant thinkers of the later Middle Ages. The explanation is to be found in a profound shift of attitude toward the intricacies of scholasticism and especially toward the thought of John Duns Scotus, one of the luminaries of scholasticism. The *Duns* of his name was from the market town in Scotland where he was born in the mid-thirteenth century. So ingenious were the theological and metaphysical speculations of this thinker that informal contemporary usage conferred on him the title of *Doctor Subtilis* (the Subtle Doctor), just as it conferred *Doctor Angelicus* (the Angelic Doctor) on Thomas Aquinas. The influence of Duns Scotus continued well beyond his lifetime; indeed, his followers—*Scotists,* or *dunsmen,* as they were sometimes called—were a powerful conservative element in the English universities during the sixteenth century. They tended to resist both the new learning of humanism and the complaints of the reformers, with the result that *dunsman* and the shorter form *duns* (later respelled as we have it today) became terms of opprobrium and scorn meaning first 'sophist' or 'pedant' and gradually taking on the modern sense of *dunce.*

[alter. of earlier *duns,* after John *Duns* Scotus †*ab*1308 Scot. scholastic theologian, whose once widely accepted writings were strongly ridiculed in the 16th cent.]

dundrearies   See SIDEBURNS.
[after Lord *Dundreary,* character in the play *Our American Cousin* (1858), by Tom Taylor †1880 Eng. dramatist, as portrayed by Edward A. Sothern †1881 Eng. actor]

dungeon   *Dungeon,* in use in English since the fourteenth century, originally referred to the keep of a castle, which was its most securely located and protected part. During its early history this word had about a dozen different spellings, but nowadays, in the sense of a castle's keep, the usual spelling is *donjon.* The donjon was the stronghold to which the garrison and residents of the castle retreated if the outer walls had been scaled or breached in a siege. It was, then, the last line of defense.

The subterranean room of a donjon was also called a *dungeon,* which is the usual spelling for this sense. This dark, damp room was used as a cell for the confinement of prisoners.

Both *donjon* and *dungeon* come from the Middle French word *donjon.* The origin of the French word has been the subject of some dispute, but most likely it derives from an unrecorded but assumed ancestor, the Medieval Latin word *dominio,* in turn a derivative of the Latin *dominus,* meaning 'lord, master'.

Such superficially unrelated words as *dame, domain, dominate, don,* and *danger* can also be traced back to their ultimate origin in the Latin word *dominus. Dame,* meaning 'a woman of rank, station, or authority', came into English from Old French in the thirteenth century. *Domain* derives from the Middle French *demaine, domaine* to mean 'legal possession of land as one's own'. This sense, first attested in the fifteenth century, has since become obsolete. The sense 'landed property which one has in his own right' dates from the seventeenth century. *Dominate* is taken from the Latin *dominatus,* the past participle of the verb *dominari,* 'to rule, govern', and was first used in English in the seventeenth century. *Don*, meaning 'lord, sir', was borrowed into English from Spanish in the sixteenth century. *Danger* first appeared in Middle English as *daunger*, meaning 'power, jurisdiction', having been derived from the Old French *dangier* of the same meaning. The latter word came from the assumed Vulgar Latin word *domniarium*, which in turn was derived from the Latin *dominium*, meaning 'ownership'. The original sense of *danger*, viz., 'power, jurisdiction', is now archaic, having been replaced by the sense 'peril, risk' in the fifteenth century. It is not difficult to see how this sense development came about: one who stands within the *danger* (in the original sense) of an erratic man of power may well be in jeopardy and so in *danger* (in the derived sense).

For another word derived from Latin *dominus* see DOMINO.

[ME *donjon, dongeoun, dungeon,* fr. MF *donjon,* fr. (assumed) ML *dominion-, dominio,* fr. L *dominus* lord, master + *-ion-, -io* -ion]

Dunkard   See CATHOLIC.
[alter. of *Dunker,* fr. PaG, fr. *dunke* to dip + *-er*]

E

easel   An easel is a frame for supporting something, such as an artist's painting or a blackboard, at a particular angle. The word was borrowed into English in the seventeenth century from the Dutch *ezel,* which was used to designate the same piece of equipment. This sense of *ezel* was a metaphorical extension of the literal meaning 'ass, donkey,' probably from the fact that, like a beast of burden, an *easel* is used to hold things. If this metaphor seems at all odd, we need only to recall that since at least the eighteenth century English has used *horse* in a very similar way in the compound *sawhorse,* a framework used to support wood for cutting.

[D *ezel,* lit., ass, donkey, fr. MD *esel;* akin to OE *esol* ass, OS & OHG *esil,* Goth *asilus;* all fr. a prehistoric Gmc word borrowed with modification fr. L *asinus* ass]

eau-de-vie   See WHISKEY.

[F, lit., water of life, trans. of ML *aqua vitae*]

eavesdrop   The verb *eavesdrop* first appeared in the seventeenth century and is probably a back-formation by subtraction of its agent ending from the noun *eavesdropper,* which in turn is derived from the Middle English noun *evesdrop,* now spelled *eavesdrop.* Dating from the ninth century, *eavesdrop* and its variant *eavesdrip* referred to the water that falls in drops from the eaves of a house. Later the term was also applied to the ground on which water falls from the eaves. In English law the term came to denote a special permit that was formerly required before one could build so that water from one's eaves could fall directly on the land of another.

The original meaning of eavesdropper, as it was used in the fifteenth century, was one who stood within the eavesdrop of a house to overhear what is going on inside, as is evident in the following passage from *Termes de la Ley,* first compiled by John Rastell in 1527: "Evesdroppers are such as stand under walls or windows by night or day to hear news, and to carry them to others, to make strife and debate amongst their neighbours: those are evil members in the commonwealth, and therefore . . . are to be punished." From such beginnings sprang the word which has come to be applied to the sophisticated electronic eavesdropping carried on by governmental agencies today.

[prob. back-formation fr. *eavesdropper*, fr. ME *evesdropper*, fr. *evesdrop*, n. + *-er*]

echelon The Old French word *eschele* or *eschiele* was used for 'ladder', since it was the offspring of the Late Latin word *scala* of the same meaning. Beginning in the thirteenth century, *eschelon* (modern French *échelon*), a diminutive form of *eschele,* was used in French to mean 'a rung of a ladder.' Various figurative senses gradually developed from this, including the sense of *échelon* that was borrowed into English in the eighteenth century, namely, 'an arrangement of a body of troops with its units somewhat to the left or right of the one in the rear like a series of steps'. The term later came to be used for such arrangements of aircraft and ships as well as of troops. Subdivisions of a military organization were also termed *echelons.* Eventually the extended and transferred senses 'one of the levels or grades in a hierarchical organization' and 'the group of individuals occupying such a level' came into use. In fact, *echelon* has been applied to just about any structure or formation that resembles a series of steps.

The Late Latin word *scala,* which was itself derived from the Latin *scalae,* meaning 'stairs, ladder', is also the source of the English noun *scale* in the sense of 'a graduated or ordered series of marks, degrees, stages, or classes'.

[F *échelon,* lit., rung of a ladder, fr. OF *eschelon,* fr. *eschele, eschiele* ladder, fr. LL *scala* ladder, staircase, fr. L *scalae* (pl.) stairs, rungs of a ladder, ladder]

Edgar See OSCAR.
[after *Edgar* Allan Poe †1849 Am. poet and story writer known as the father of the detective story]

eerie See WEIRD.
[ME (northern dial.) *eri,* fr. OE *earg* cowardly, lazy, slow, wretched]

egregious The adjective *egregious* is derived from the Latin *egregius,* meaning 'distinguished,' 'eminent', a word whose most prominent elements are *e,* 'out of', and *grex,* 'herd, flock'. Thus an *egregious* person or thing has some quality that sets him or it apart from others. Originally this was a remarkably good quality that placed him eminently above others. In sixteenth-century English, however, an antithetical sense came into use when *egregious* was applied to one that was conspicuously or outrageously bad, as when in Shakespeare's *Cymbeline* Posthumus Leonatus refers to himself as "most credulous fool, egregious murtherer, thief. . . ."This shift to a pejorative sense may have resulted from the ironic use of the original sense, but in any case the pejorative meaning is the one which persists in common use today, as in such examples as "egregious blunders," "egregious brutality," and "egregious fools."

Gregarious is etymologically related to *egregious.* It derives from the Latin *gregarius,* 'of or relating to a herd or flock', which in turn comes from *grex. Gregarious* has been part of the English vocabulary since the seventeenth century with the meaning 'inclined to associate with others of one's kind'. First used of animals, by the eighteenth century *gregarious* had come to be applied to persons, and by the nineteenth century to plants.

Grex has been a very productive source of English words. Other words derived from it are *aggregate, congregate,* and *segregate.* The adjective *aggregate* is from the Latin *ad-,* meaning 'to' or 'toward', and *grex,* and means 'formed by the collection of units or particles into a body, mass, or amount'. The verb *congregate* comes from *com-,* meaning 'with' or 'together', and *grex,* and means 'to collect together into a group, crowd, or assembly'. *Segregate* derives from *se,* 'without', and *grex,* and means 'to separate or set apart from others'.

[L *egregius,* fr. *e* out of (fr. *ex*) + *greg-, grex* flock, herd]

elder   See ADOLESCENT.

[ME, fr. OE *yldra, ieldra, eldra,* compar. of *ald, eald* old]

éminence grise   From time immemorial there has been the power on the throne and the power behind the throne. One of history's most famous instances of unofficial power exercised without public acknowledgment was the case of Père Joseph. He is the one who was first described as an *éminence grise,* the term for a person who wields the real though not the official power. Born in 1577 and originally named François du Tremblay, Père Joseph joined the Capuchins in 1599. In 1612 Père Joseph met the politically ambitious Cardinal Richelieu, the chief minister of Louis XIII of France. Richelieu appointed Père Joseph his personal secretary, although the friar's power far exceeded what the position might suggest. The friar also served as the cardinal's confessor, general confidant, and secret agent. As the two became a power at court to be reckoned with and feared, their rivals called them by distinctive epithets behind their backs. For his resplendent cardinal's robes of scarlet, Richelieu became known as L'Éminence Rouge 'the red eminence'. The contrasting gray habit of the Capuchins earned Père Joseph the epithet L'Éminence Grise 'the gray eminence'.

Part of the mission of the Capuchin order was the conversion of heretics. With apostolic zeal, Père Joseph was determined to rid France of all heresy and then to have France lead a great crusade against infidels abroad. His grand scheme included a Counter-Reformation in Europe and an assault by a united Christendom against the Turks. As fate would have it, Père Joseph's determination to return European Protestants to Roman Catholicism coincided with Cardinal Richelieu's grand design to bring all of Europe under the domination of France. The two agreed that their plans required the destruction of the Hapsburg Austrian empire, and so they embarked upon a course that led to France's participation in the Thirty Years' War. Although he usually remained in the background, Père Joseph acquired at court powers akin to those of a foreign minister. It is still a matter of debate which of the two clerics was the dominant power and whether Père Joseph's immense power stemmed as much from his own personality as from his relationship with Richelieu.

Père Joseph's soubriquet was often cited by later historians. However, the historical reference did not pass into generic use, at least not in English contexts, until long after his era. There appears to be no documented use of *éminence grise* before the 1920s. Since that time, there has been sustained use of the generic sense. World wars and the Machiavellian machinations of international politics have fueled a continuing need for the word. *Gray eminence*, the English equivalent of *éminence grise*, was used in 1941 by Aldous Huxley as the title of his study of Père Joseph. Huxley's own prestige probably helped to establish the English equivalent as well as popularize the French original.

Although *éminence grise* and *gray eminence* were relatively late in establishing themselves in English, the story behind them appears to have now been forgotten. In the second half of the twentieth century a new meaning has been developing, influenced by erroneous assumptions regarding the origins of these terms.

One of the éminences grises of the French literary world was elected today to the French Academy —*N. Y. Times*, 15 Jan. 1971

. . . became the *éminence grise* of French filmmakers six years ago when he proved that talkiness was next to godliness —Paul Gardner, *New York*, 8 Nov. 1976

And editors have been working overtime on albums, portfolios, *memento mori* appreciations, and the annual reruns of the medium's [photography's] gray eminences —Margaret R. Weiss, *Saturday Rev.*, 26 Nov. 1977

In these examples the term obviously has the meaning of "an eminent senior member of a group" and thus is synonymous with *elder statesman, grand old man*, and *doyen*. Doubtless the writers have mistakenly assumed that *éminence grise* derived from the notion that eminent senior figures are typically gray-haired. Doubtless, too, the sinister Capuchin friar would have appreciated the irony that his derisive epithet had assumed a meaning so approving.

[F, lit., gray eminence, nickname of Père Joseph (François Le Clerc du Tremblay) †1638 French monk and diplomat who was confidant of Cardinal Richelieu †1642 Fr. statesman and cardinal who was styled *Éminence Rouge* red eminence; fr. the colors of their respective habits]

Emmy See OSCAR.
[fr. alter. of *Immy*, nickname for *image orthicon* (a camera tube used in television)]

enormous See NORMAL.
[L *enormis* (fr. *e* out of, out + *norma* rule) + E *-ous*]

enthuse   See SHERRY.
[back-formation fr. *enthusiasm*]

enthusiasm   "The sense of this word among the Greeks affords the noblest definition of it; enthusiasm signifies God in us" (Anna Louise de Staël, 1810). Madame de Staël was indeed familiar with the Greek roots of this word. The adjective *entheos, enthous* (formed from *theos* 'god'), was used to mean 'inspired or possessed by a god'. This adjective gave rise to the verb *enthousiazein* 'to be inspired by a god', from which the noun *enthousiasmos* 'inspiration or possession by a god' was derived.

When the Greek noun was borrowed into seventeenth-century English, its Greek sense was retained; however, by the nineteenth century this original sense had become archaic. It was replaced by the secularized sense 'impassioned emotion' and was often used for the intense emotion kindled by poetry. The word then became associated with religious zealots and took on the sense of 'excessive or extravagant display of religious emotions; fanaticism'. The philosopher and poet Henry More comments on this in his *Explanation of the Grand Mystery of Godliness* (1660): "If ever Christianity be exterminated, it will be by Enthusiasm."

By the eighteenth century, *enthusiasm*, especially in nonreligious contexts, acquired the sense 'ardent zeal for a cause or subject', its most common meaning today. In the twentieth century we also find occurrences of its use to mean 'something that inspires or is pursued with ardent zeal', as in "his current enthusiasm is racquetball."

[Gk *enthousiasmos*, fr. *enthousiazein* to be inspired, fr. *entheos, enthous* inspired, fr. *en-* ²en- + *-theos, -thous* (fr. *theos* god)]

entrails   See BOWEL.
[ME *entraille*, fr. MF, fr. ML *intralia*, alter. of L *interanea*, pl. of *interaneum* intestine, fr. neut. of *interaneus* interior, fr. L *inter* between + *-aneus* (as in *extraneus* external)]

entrée   Most of us would not regard the main course of a meal as the 'entrance' or beginning of anything, the exception, of course, being those children of all ages who tolerate the main course merely as a prelude to dessert. *Entrée*, which signifies the main course in the U.S., is in fact the French word for 'entry'. *Entrée* originated in Old French and first served as the source for the Middle English *entre*, which in the thirteenth century came into Modern English as *entry*. In the eighteenth century *entrée* was once again borrowed, this time in unaltered form, from the French. In this incarnation *entrée* originally had the sense, still current, of 'the act or manner of entering'. To this meaning was added the sense of 'permission or right to enter'. Today the latter sense is the more common: "Efforts to collect unpaid debts provided entrée for imperialistic actions by Britain and most of the countries of the European continent" (Joseph Kraft, *New Yorker*, 15 Oct. 1984).

In eighteenth-century Britain *entrée* also developed a distinct culinary sense. In those days the dining experience could be a test of one's stamina.

A typical formal dinner might have merely as its principal courses soup, fish, meat, and dessert. In addition, there were various side dishes, plus the salad and cheese courses. After the fish course and as a warm-up to the meat course—a roast, typically—came a small dish that was fancily concocted of several ingredients and often garnished and sauced. In the words of one old-fashioned culinary manual, it was supposed to be "easy to eat and pleasing to the appetite but not satisfying." Because it was served immediately preceding the centerpiece of the whole meal—the roast—it was called the *entrée*, being, in effect, the "entrance" to the really important part of the meal. As fashions and Anglo-American dining habits changed, meals gradually diminished in their elaborateness, and fewer and simpler courses were served. In the U.S. the course following the appetizer course continued to be known as the *entrée*, even if it did turn out to be a roast. The practice of referring to the main course as the *entrée* was apparently led by hotels and restaurants. Perhaps the preference for *entrée* lay in the fact that it was obviously French, and anything French was considered to have prestige.

[F *entrée*, fr. OF *entree*]

entry See ENTRÉE.

[ME *entre*, fr. OF *entree*, fr. fem. of *entré*, past part. of *entrer* to enter]

epenthesis See ASSIMILATION.

[LL, fr. Gk, fr. *epentithenai* to insert a letter, fr. *epi-* + *entithenai* to put in, fr. *en-* ²en- + *tithenai* to put, place]

epicure Today *epicure* refers to someone who takes keen and discriminating pleasure in eating and drinking. Synonymous with *gourmet, gastronome* or *bon vivant, epicure* suggests self-indulgent, voluptuous hedonism. Nothing could be more remote from the lifestyle and teachings of the man from whose name *epicure* derives.

The Greek philosopher Epicurus (341–270 B.C.) articulated an ethical philosophy of simple pleasure, friendship, and retirement. In 306 B.C. he established in the garden of his house at Athens a school of philosophy that came to be known as Ho Kepos ("The Garden"). Life at the school was serenely simple. Although his disciples were allowed to drink a half-pint of wine a day, the usual drink was water, and commonly the food consisted of barley bread. During a time of famine Epicurus and his disciples survived on a daily ration of a few beans. In contrast to the schools of Plato and Aristotle, Epicurus's Garden admitted women, thereby fostering later suspicions of sexual impropriety. At the heart of Epicurus's ethical philosophy was the pursuit of pleasure, but pleasure equated with tranquility of mind and freedom from pain rather than indulgence of the senses. Defining pleasure in those terms, he wrote that "we declare pleasure to be the beginning and end of the blessed life." Succeeding generations of his disciples debased his philosophy, however, reducing his lofty notion of pleasure

and happiness to material and sensual gratification and debasing his reputation in the popular mind.

When *epicure* entered the English language, probably in the sixteenth
century, its original sense (now obsolete) referred to a follower of Epicurus
or his philosophy. At about the same time the specific sense of "one devoted to sensual pleasure" developed and that gave rise to the closely related
sense of 'one with sensitive and discriminating tastes especially in food or
wine'.

[after *Epicurus* (fr. L, fr. Gk *Epikourus*) †270 B.C. Greek philosopher]

episcopal   See CATHOLIC.
　　[ME, fr. LL *episcopalis,* fr. *episcopus* bishop + L *-alis* -al]

erotic   Eros was the Greek god of sexual love. According to one tradition
in Greek mythology, Eros was the son of Aphrodite, the goddess of love,
and Ares, the god of war. In early classical art and literature Eros was depicted as a handsome young man of athletic build. He could tame wild
beasts, break the thunderbolts of Zeus, and battle the monsters of the sea.
The love that he symbolized was frankly sexual, thus the meaning of the
derived adjective *erotic.* In early classical times Eros was often seen as
something like a patron saint of homosexual love between men and
youths. Statues of Eros were commonly found in gymnasiums, academies
for athletics where men and boys exercised naked. At some shrines, however, he was worshipped as a god of fertility. Later, in Hellenistic times,
the concept of love became increasingly romanticized and the image of
Eros became accordingly sentimentalized. Eros gradually evolved into the
figure of a wanton infant or child sporting wings and equipped with a bow
and a quiver full of arrows. The Romans later called him Amor ('love') or
Cupido ('desire'). In Roman art and literature the cherubic avatar of the
god became the dominant version, and gave rise to the chubby cherub of
a *cupid* that now adorns our St. Valentine's Day cards. For other articles
on words derived from ancient mythology and legend see VOLCANO.

　　[F & Gk; F *érotique,* fr. Gk *erōtikos,* fr. *erōt-, erōs* sexual love + *-ikos* -ic,
　　-ical]

err   See EXTRAVAGANT.
　　[ME *erren,* fr. OF *errer,* fr. L *errare;* akin to OE *ierre, yrre* wandering,
　　angry, *iersian* to be angry, OHG *irri* gone astray, angry, *irrōn* to go
　　astray, OS *irri* angry, Goth *airzeis* led astray, deceived]

erratic   See EXTRAVAGANT.
　　[ME *erratik,* fr. MF or L; MF *erratique,* fr. L *erraticus,* fr. *erratus* (past
　　part. of *errare* to wander, err) + *-icus* -ic]

escape   English *escape* and its French equivalent *échapper* are tantaliz-
ingly close in form and meaning, but the phonetic difference is such as to
rule out direct borrowing. The actual historical link is provided by the Old
North French form of the language. Normally in the course of the devel-

opment of French, the *ca* part of Latin words became changed to *cha*. But in Old North French, a northern dialect form, the Latin *c* remained *c* before *a*. Thus the Old North French equivalent was *escaper* 'to escape', and this is the immediate source of our word. Similar forms in other Romance languages, such as Italian *scappare* and Spanish and Portuguese *escapar*, show that the word probably goes back to something in the Latin vocabulary from which the Romance languages evolved their words. But there is nothing in classical Latin that corresponds. Some form must have been coined in the later, spoken form of Latin, called Vulgar Latin, which subsequently showed up in the local phonetic costume of France and Italy and so forth. But what?

One early attempt at explanation noticed Italian *scampare* 'to rescue' and suggested that *scappare* 'to escape' may have come from that. (For a comparable semantic development, there is French *sauver* 'to rescue' and *se sauver* 'to escape', literally 'to save oneself'.) *Scampare* evidently derived from a Vulgar Latin **excampare*, meaning quite literally 'to decamp', as this is derived from Latin *ex-* 'out of' and *campus* 'camp, battlefield'. But this explanation, while semantically plausible, has two problems: the phonetic development posited is unusual; and other Romance languages with an equivalent of *scappare* lack an equivalent of *scampare* in the appropriate meaning. As consolation, we may note that *scampare* nevertheless did find its way into English, by an indirect route, winding up as our word *scamper*.

A second explanation, now generally accepted, assumes a Vulgar Latin **excappare*, from *ex-* plus *cappa* 'cloak', which is the ultimate source of both *cape* and *cap* in English. Here there are no phonetic problems, but the semantic development is somewhat surprising. The idea seems to have been that of casting off one's heavy cloak the better to flee. Or the image could even have been as in the scene from melodrama, in which a pursuer lays hand on the cloak of the fugitive, who then literally gives him the slip, leaving him holding an empty garment.

Whatever the true explanation, it is certain that Late Latin *cappa* (possibly derived from Latin *caput* 'head', and if so, then literally 'head-covering') has had a healthy number of offspring in English. Besides the ones already mentioned, we have *chaperon* from French—again showing the characteristic shift of *ca-* to *cha-*. In French, *chaperon* originally meant 'hood', but was applied metaphorically to someone who protectively accompanies a young lady. The metaphor is a familiar one: *protect* itself goes back to Latin *tegere* 'to cover'. (See also CHAPEL.)

[ME *escapen, ascapen*, fr. ONF *escaper, ascaper*, fr. (assumed) VL *excappare*, fr. L *ex-* + LL *cappa* head covering, cloak]

Eskimo   See INDIAN.
[Dan *Eskimo* & F *Esquimau*, fr. the name applied by the Algonquians to the tribes north of them; akin to Abnaki *esquimantsic* eaters of raw flesh, Cree *askimowew* he eats it raw]

esquire   In the chivalrous days of old, becoming a knight was no simple matter of matriculating at the nearest knight school. A boy being groomed for knighthood would begin his training as a page in the household of a nobleman. When he reached his teens, he would be elevated to the position of a knight's personal attendant, whose duties included carrying the knight's shield. The name given to such an attendant in English was *esquire* or, more often, *squire*, from the Old French *esquier*, 'shield bearer', a derivative of the Late Latin *scutarius*, which in turn was derived from the Latin *scutum*, 'shield'.

Knights began to go out of style in about the fourteenth century, when the introduction of gunpowder to European warfare made their methods obsolete. The title *knight* has since then been bestowed by English sovereigns on individuals to honor some meritorious achievement or service to the crown. *Esquire* has also continued in use as a title, denoting since the fifteenth century a member of the English gentry ranking below a knight. More familiar is its function as a title of respect following a man's name, used especially in addressing correspondence. *Esquire* has been used in this way since the sixteenth century. Originally it was used only for a man who had the rank of esquire, but courtesy eventually extended its use to any man who could otherwise be addressed as "Mr."—which now means just about any man at all, and it is still so used in British English. In American English, however, *esquire* has been largely appropriated by lawyers, who since the nineteenth century have used it when referring to or addressing each other in writing. It has recently begun to be used by some attorneys following the names of women as well as men.

The related *squire* has had a similar but more far-ranging career. It shares with *esquire* the sense relating to the English gentry, and it also has had some use in American legal circles. Probably its best-known senses, however, are 'the owner of a country estate', which dates from the seventeenth century, and 'a devoted attendant upon a lady; a gallant', which goes back to the sixteenth. *Squire* also retains some suggestion of its original 'attendant' sense in its use as a verb, meaning 'to attend (someone) as a squire; to escort'. This verb is actually quite old, dating back to the time of Chaucer.

[ME *esquire, esquier, squier*, fr. MF *escuier, esquier* shield bearer, squire, fr. LL *scutarius*, fr. L *scutum* shield + -*arius* -ary; akin to OHG *sceida* sheath]

essay   See NOVEL.

[MF *essai, assai*, fr. OF, fr. LL *exagium* act of weighing, weight, balance, fr. L *ex-* + -*agium*, fr. *agere* to do, drive; influenced by L *exigere* to weigh, test, drive out]

essence   See QUINTESSENCE.

[ME *essencia, essence*, fr. MF & L; MF *essence*, fr. L *essentia*, fr. *esse* to be + -*ent-*, -*ens* -ent + -*ia* -y]

essential   See QUINTESSENCE.
[ME *essencial,* fr. LL *essentialis,* fr. L *essentia* essence + *-alis* -al]

ether *or* **aether**   See QUINTESSENCE.
[ME *ether,* fr. L *aether,* fr. Gk *aithēr,* fr. *aithein* to blaze, kindle]

ethereal   See QUINTESSENCE.
[L *aetherius, aethereus* (fr. Gk *aitherios,* fr. *aithēr* ether) + E *-al*]

etiquette   When *estiquette* first appeared in fourteenth-century French, it was a post used as a target in certain games, or a mark, stuck on a post. It took its name from *estiquer,* 'to stick or attach', a verb the French borrowed from Middle Dutch *steken* (related to Modern English *stick*). *Étiquette* soon had several meanings in French: it was a document bearing military orders or a soldier's billeting orders; it was a label attached to something for description or identification (this, the source of English *ticket,* is still the primary meaning of *étiquette* in Modern French). Later, in royal palaces, there were notices that set down the proper forms to be observed at court. The *étiquette* of the court eventually became the court ceremonial itself as well as the document that described it. It was this sense that English borrowed. *Etiquette* is no longer confined to the high circles it began in but now includes the proper forms to be observed in any social situation.

[F *étiquette*]

Eucharist   See MASS.
[ME *eukarist,* fr. MF *eucariste,* fr. LL *eucharistia,* fr. Gk, Eucharist, giving of thanks, gratitude, fr. *eucharistos* grateful (fr. *eu-* + — assumed — *charistos,* verbal of Gk *charizesthai* to show favor, fr. *charis* favor, grace) + *-ia* -y]

euphemism   See BLAME.
[Gk *euphēmismos,* fr. *euphēmos* auspicious, sounding good (fr. *eu-* good + *-phēmos,* fr. *phēmē* speech, fr. *phanai* to say) + *-ismos* -ism]

eureka   Some of us perhaps wonder why we often exclaim "Eureka!" at the moment of a sudden discovery, whether it be the finding of a long-lost item or the determination of the solution to a problem. Some may even wonder if they are calling out the name of a city in California or a college in Illinois. Actually, the elated discoverer is reenacting an event, or least the legend of an event, that is supposed to have happened in the third century B.C. in the Greek city-state of Syracuse in Sicily. The famous Greek mathematician and mechanical inventor Archimedes (ca. 287–212 B.C.) was asked by Hiero II, the tyrant of Syracuse, to test the purity of the gold in a crown that he had commissioned. Hiero suspected that the crown had been adulterated with some other metal, such as silver. For a time the problem frustrated Archimedes. The solution arrived the day Archimedes patronized a public bath. Upon stepping into his bath, which was nearly full, he observed that some of the water ran over. The thought immediately struck the mathematician that a body must remove its own bulk of water when it is immersed; if silver is less dense than gold, then a given weight of silver would have more bulk than an equal weight of gold and consequently would remove more water. As the idea flashed through Archimedes' mind, he leaped out of his bath, exclaiming, "Heurēka! Heurēka! ('I have found')." Without thinking to dress himself, the euphoric mathematician raced home, eager to put his sudden discovery to the test. While the notion of an absentminded mathematician running naked through the streets has charmed many, that part of the story is in all likelihood pure fabrication. The anecdote of Archimedes' adventure in the baths is traceable to the Roman architect and engineer Vitruvius, who lived two centuries after Archimedes. (There is no contemporary source for the anecdote.) While Archimedes probably did determine the proportion of gold and silver in a crown for Hiero by weighing it in water, later writers have not been able to resist embellishing the tale.

Eureka or, as it may more accurately be transliterated from the Greek, *heurēka* derives from the same Greek root word as *heuristic*. *Heurēka* ('I have found') is the first person singular perfect indicative of the Greek verb *heuriskein* 'to discover, find'. From this verb the Germans derived, by way of New Latin, their word *heuristisch*. Adopted into English in the nineteenth century as *heuristic*, the word was originally used in logic to refer to assumptions or lines of reasoning that could not be justified but were useful as trial-and-error means of arriving at a truth. *Heuristic* is now used of any of a number of things, such as computer programs, that are involved in experimental problem solving.

[Gk *heurēka* I have found, 1st pers. sing. perf. indic. act. of *heuriskein* to find; fr. the exclamation attributed to Archimedes †212 B.C., Greek mathematician and inventor, on discovering a method for determining the purity of gold]

evangelical   See CATHOLIC.

[LL *evangelicus* (fr. Gk *euangelikos,* fr. *euangelion* + *-ikos* -ic) + E *-al*]

evolve   See VOLUME.

[L *evolvere* to unroll, unfold, fr. *e-* out (fr. *ex-*) + *volvere* to roll]

excruciating   See CRUSADE.

[fr. pres. part. of *excruciate,* fr. L *excruciatus,* past part. of *excruciare,* fr. *ex-* ¹ex- + *cruciare* to torment, crucify, fr. *cruc-, crux* cross]

execrate   See SACRED.

[L *execratus, exsecratus,* past part. of *execrari, exsecrari,* fr. *ex-* ¹ex- + *-secrari* (fr. *sacr-, sacer* sacred)]

exonerate See JUDGE.

[ME *exoneraten,* fr. L *exoneratus,* past part. of *exonerare* to relieve, free, unload, fr. *ex-* ¹ex- + *onerare* to load, fr. *oner-, onus* load]

explode See PLAUDIT.

[L *explodere, explaudere,* fr. *ex-* ¹ex- + *plodere, plaudere* to clap, applaud]

exquisite See QUESTION.

[ME *exquisit,* fr. L *exquisitus,* fr. past part. of *exquirere* to search out, seek, fr. *ex-* ¹ex- + *-quirere* (fr. *quaerere* to seek, gain, obtain, ask)]

extravagant The ghost of Hamlet's father disappears abruptly when a cock crows, and Hamlet then recalls that at the cock's warning of approaching dawn "Th' extravagant and erring spirit hies/ To his confine." Here Shakespeare is using both *extravagant* and *erring* in their literal senses. *Extravagant* is derived from Medieval Latin *extravagans,* formed from the prefix *extra-,* meaning 'outside' or 'beyond', plus the verb *vagari,* 'to wander about'. Thus an *extravagant* spirit is one that travels beyond the borders of his usual abode. Developing from its literal sense, *extravagant* came to mean 'exceeding the limits of reason or necessity' and 'lacking in moderation, balance, and restraint'. From these are derived the related prodigal senses of *extravagant,* that is, 'spending much more than necessary'.

Err is similar in that it is derived from Latin *errare,* 'to wander'. The earliest English sense of *err* is exemplified clearly in the general confession used in the Episcopalian service of Morning Prayer, which begins, "Almighty and most merciful Father; we have erred, and strayed from thy ways like lost sheep." The sense of *err* meaning 'to do wrong' derives fairly straightforwardly from this metaphor of wandering off the right path. Similarly the earliest sense of *erratic,* also from Latin *errare,* is 'having no fixed course, wandering'.

[ME *extravagaunt,* fr. MF *extravagant,* fr. ML *extravagant-, extravagans,* fr. L *extra-* outside, beyond + *vagant-, vagans,* pres. part. of *vagari* to wander about]

eyas See FALCON.

[ME, alter. (resulting fr. incorrect division of *a neias*) of *neias, nyesse,* fr. MF *niais* fresh from the nest, fr. (assumed) VL *nidax* nestling, fr. L *nidus* nest]

F

Fahrenheit   Gabriel Daniel Fahrenheit was born in 1686 in Gdansk, Poland, of German parents. In 1701 his parents died suddenly, and he was sent to Amsterdam to learn business. The business of making scientific instruments especially interested him. He learned about thermometers from the Danish astronomer Olaus Roemer, who probably designed them for meteorological purposes. Fahrenheit himself invented the alcohol thermometer in 1709 and the mercury thermometer in 1714. He also discovered that water can remain liquid below its freezing point and that the boiling point of liquids varies with atmospheric pressure. Fahrenheit originally took as the zero of his scale the temperature of an equal ice-salt mixture and selected the value 96° for normal body temperature. The final scale required an adjustment of this to 98.6°. Later, he based his scale on 32° for the freezing point of water and 212° for the boiling point of water. This scale was in general common use in English-speaking countries until the 1970s, since which time many countries have officially adopted the Celsius scale.

Anders Celsius was born in 1701 in Uppsala, Sweden, where his father was professor of astronomy at the university. He himself later became a professor of mathematics and then was appointed professor of astronomy at the same university. In 1736 he took part in the expedition which verified Newton's theory that the earth is somewhat flattened at the poles. Celsius is best known, however, for his thermometric scale, first described in 1742, for which he chose 100 as the freezing point of water and zero as the boiling point. In 1747, three years after his death, Celsius's scale was reversed. It is sometimes called the centigrade scale because of the 100 degrees between the defined points. The *Celsius* scale is in general use wherever the metric system is used and especially in scientific work.

   [after Gabriel D. *Fahrenheit* †1736 Ger. physicist]

falcon   Falconry is the sport of hunting with a trained bird of prey, usually a hawk or falcon. One of the world's most ancient sports, falconry or hawking was being practiced in Asia almost three thousand years ago. From Asia falconry spread across Europe and into England, picking up impetus from European contact with Asia Minor during the Crusades. Trained birds were being flown by the Saxons in Britain well before the Norman Conquest of 1066, but the invading Normans soon restricted the ownership of the most desirable falcons and hawks to the ruling class (to themselves, in other words). The Normans changed falconry in another decisive way: they imposed their native French on a conquered England, and the specialized language of falconry therefore shows a strong French influence.

The term *falcon* came into English by way of Old French. The source of the French word was the Late Latin word *falco,* for which the inflectional stem is *falcon-*. Originally only female birds were called falcons; the males were (and to this day, technically still are) known as *tiercels.* This term came into English from Middle French and traces back to Latin *tertius* 'third'. The term is appropriate, for male falcons are usually one-third smaller than females.

Falcons, hawks, eagles, and even owls have at one time or another been used in the sport of falconry. These birds are collectively referred to as *birds of prey* or *raptors.* The word *raptor* comes from the Latin verb *rapere* 'to seize'. That is precisely how raptors hunt—they seize their prey with immensely strong feet armed with dagger-sharp talons (the curved beak is used to pull off bite-sized pieces of meat once their quarry has been caught and killed). (See also RAPT.)

The birds used in falconry were not bred in captivity until very recently, so traditionally falconers have trained wild birds. These were either taken from the nest when quite young or trapped as adults. The term for a nestling bird is *eyas,* and a trained bird that was taken from the nest at this age is always referred to as an eyas bird. The word came into English as the result of an error. The Middle French word was *niais* 'fresh from the nest'. This in turn was derived from some Vulgar Latin derivative of Latin *nidus* 'nest' (*nest* is related to the same Latin source word). The *n* dropped away because early writers incorrectly divided *a neias* as *an eias,* perhaps influenced by such Middle English words as *ey* 'egg' and *eyry* 'aerie'. (For examples of a similar change see APRON, AUGER; for the opposite change see NICKNAME.) A bird trapped as an adult, on the other hand, is termed a *haggard,* from the Middle French *hagard.* A haggard bird is notoriously wild and difficult to train, and it wasn't long before this falconry sense was being applied in an extended way to a "wild" and intractable person. The next step was to use the word to express the way the human face looks when a person is exhausted, anxious, or terrified. The result is that the most common modern meaning of *haggard* is 'gaunt' or 'worn'.

Like other sports, falconry requires specialized equipment, but falconry is unique in centering around an animal and not a person. For this reason most hawking equipment is used on the bird, not on the falconer—with one major exception. Because birds of prey have sharp talons or claws, a falconer must wear a heavy leather glove to protect his hand and forearm when he picks the bird up. This glove is called a *gauntlet,* which came from Middle French *gantelet.* This word was a diminutive form of *gant* 'glove', unusual for French in being a word of Scandinavian origin. A gauntlet was originally a metal-reinforced leather glove used during the Middle Ages to protect the hand in combat. A falconer's glove serves the same purpose, to protect, so the word *gauntlet* was applied to the leather hawking equipment.

Hunting birds are controlled by means of supple leather straps attached to each leg by a wide leather cuff. Each cuff and its trailing strap is termed a *jess,* another word that entered English by way of French. The Middle French form was *gies,* from the plural of *jet* 'throw', from the verb *jeter* 'to throw'. The French verb in its turn comes ultimately from the Latin verb *jacere* 'to throw'.

When a bird is being trained, a long, light line is attached at one end to the jesses and held by the falconer at the other. This arrangement allows the bird some freedom of movement but still gives the falconer control over it so it cannot fly away. This line is called a *creance,* a name given it by some long-ago falconer with a wry sense of humor and a working knowledge of bird-of-prey psychology. Middle French *creance* traces back to Latin *credentia,* meaning 'trust' or 'belief'. A falconer, therefore, can trust his bird to come back to him after a flight—as long, of course, as it is tethered, and as long as he holds the other end of that tether. English *credence* 'belief' is based upon the same Latin source word, as is *credenza,* a type of sideboard or bookcase that originally was where a lord's food and drink were tested by a servant for poison. The latter comes to us by way of Italian.

Next to the gauntlet, a falconer's most essential piece of field equipment is the lure. This is a padded weight made of leather, and often of feathers as well, designed to look like a pigeon, a favorite prey of falcons. The lure can be swung on a cord by the falconer, and it is used to call in a bird. Early in training the bird is conditioned to associate the lure with food by being allowed to eat pieces of meat that have been tied to it. The word *lure* comes from Middle French *loire,* a word of Germanic origin. Its original meaning was the piece of falconry equipment, but in time the word began to take on extended senses.

When it is not being flown, a bird used for falconry is housed in a building or flight cage called a *mews.* The term comes from Middle French *mue,* from *muer* 'to molt'. The French word comes from Latin *mutare* 'to change', which also gives us *mutate.* It gives us *molt* as well, and this explains how the *mews* got its name. Raptors molt during the summer, shedding old feathers that have been broken in the course of the past season's hunting and growing new ones. During the molt the birds, whose bodies are undergoing significant changes, are moody and unpredictable. The new, growing feathers are also vulnerable to damage, so the birds are not flown during the summer months but instead are put up in the mews, the building or cage where they undergo the molt. Another, newer sense of *mews* is a stable often with living quarters built around a court. The word later came to refer to living quarters adapted from such stables. King Henry VIII of England was responsible for at least beginning the change from housing hunting birds to housing horses. During Henry's reign, the royal mews were converted to stables on his orders. Soon members of the nobility were following their sovereign's lead and converting cages to stables, thus bringing about a decline in the sport of falconry.

[ME *faucoun, falcon,* fr. OF *faucon, falcon,* fr. LL *falcon-, falco*]

fall   See AUTUMN.

[ME, fr. OE *feall;* akin to OFris, OS & OHG *fal* fall, ON *fall,* deverbatives fr. the root of E ¹*fall*]

fan   See FANATIC.

[prob. short for *fanatic*]

fanatic   In Latin the adjective *fanaticus* was originally used to mean 'of or relating to a temple', having been derived from the noun *fanum,* 'temple'. It was later used in reference to those pious individuals who were thought to have been inspired by a deity. In time the sense 'frantic, frenzied, mad' arose because it was thought that persons behaving in such a manner were possessed by a deity. This last sense was the first meaning of the word *fanatic* as it was used in English in the sixteenth century. This sense, which is now obsolete, led to the development in the seventeenth century of the sense 'excessively enthusiastic, especially about religious matters'. Jonathan Swift in his satire against corruption in religion, *A Tale of a Tub* (1704), illustrates this usage in the following comment: "The Two Principal Qualifications of a Phanatick Preacher are, his Inward Light, and his Head full of Maggots and the Two different Fates of his Writings are, to be burnt or Worm eaten." The adjective then became less specific in its application and came to mean simply 'excessively enthusiastic or unreasonable', which is the sense illustrated by Anson Mount in an article in *Playboy* (September 1968) in which he describes a football coach as having "a curious combination of paternal warmth and flinty hardness that elicits almost fanatic devotion from his players." The noun *fan,* meaning 'enthusiast', is probably a shortening of the noun *fanatic.*

The word *profane,* which comes from the Latin adjective *profanus,* is ultimately derived from the same source as *fanatic,* having as its elements *pro-* and *fanum,* which literally translates as 'before the temple', i.e., outside it. The Romans used *profanus* to mean 'unholy, not sacred' and later applied it in a more pejorative way to persons who were wicked or impious. It was borrowed into English as *profane* in the fifteenth century to mean 'secular, worldly' as opposed to 'religious, spiritual'. This usage is illustrated in the following comment by George Santayana: "The profane poet is by instinct a naturalist. He loves landscape, he loves love, he loves the humor and pathos of earthly existence. But the religious prophet loves none of these things." Beginning in the sixteenth century *profane* was also used to mean 'irreverent, blasphemous', in a development which rather parallels the sense development of *profanus* in Latin.

[L *fanaticus* frantic, inspired by a deity, fr. *fanum* sanctuary, temple]

farce   When the word *farce* was first used in English, it had to do with cookery, not comedy. In the fourteenth century the French word *farce* was borrowed into English as *farse* with its meaning, 'forcemeat, stuffing', unchanged. The French had derived the noun from the assumed Vulgar Latin word *farsa,* which had been formed from the past participle of the classical Latin verb *facire*, meaning 'to stuff'. This use of *farce* (so spelled in English since the eighteenth century) is still evident in cookbooks today.

The comedic use of *farce*, however, derives from another sense of the word in early French. From the thirteenth to the fifteenth centuries, especially in France and Spain, Latin liturgical texts (such as the chanted parts of the Mass) were frequently interpolated with explanatory or hortatory phrases, often in the vernacular language. Seeing a similarity between the culinary stuffing and the interlarding of liturgical texts, the French also called such an interpolation a *farce* (in this sense the word is usually spelled *farse* in English). Such farsing became abusive, however, and was officially abolished in 1570 when Pope Pius V issued his Roman Missal to supplant the multiplicity of missals then in use.

In fifteenth-century France this sense of *farce* was further extended to 'impromptu buffoonery interpolated by actors into the texts of religious plays'. Such farces included elements of clowning, acrobatics, reversal of social roles, and indecency. The farce developed into a dramatic genre and spread quickly, in time developing into the commedia dell'arte in Italy.

In England the farce became popular in the sixteenth century as a short dramatic work whose sole purpose was to provoke laughter. It continued to flourish as a broadly satirical comedy with absurdly laughable plots. Though it was successful in nineteenth-century music halls and vaudeville theaters, the farce attracted even larger audiences when it became a favorite motion-picture genre with slapstick routines, mad chases, and pie-throwing scenes.

For a similar culinary metaphor applied to a literary genre see SATIRE.

[ME *farse*, fr. MF *farce*, fr. (assumed) VL *farsa*, fr. L, fem. of *farsus*, past part. of *facire* to stuff]

farrow   See PORK.

[ME *farwen*, fr. (assumed) OE *feargian*, fr. OE *fearh* young pig; akin to OHG *farah* young pig, L *porcus* domestic pig, Lith *paršas* barrow]

fascinate   When we describe a person as bewitching, the historical connection to the darker arts of witchcraft is still discernible; the sense of *bewitch* was originally injurious. In *charm* as well (a descendant of Latin *carmen* 'song, incantation') there remain both a magical and a more light-hearted sense. But with *fascinate* in our day the connection is no longer obvious. To get at its necromantic background we must dig at the etymological roots.

Fascinate comes from Latin *fascinare*, 'to bewitch', a derivative of *fascinum*, which meant both 'evil spell' and 'penis'. The link between this rather startling pair of senses is that images of the latter were widely used as protection against the former. The notions were united in the figure of Fascinus, an early Latin godling worshipped as the author of sorcery, whose symbol was the phallus. Phallic amulets were in fact the favorite counter-charm among the Romans, worn about the neck to avert the evil eye.

A relation to Latin *fascis* 'bundle' (the root of Latin and English *fasces*) has also occasionally been posited, since the notions of hexing and binding are often connected, as in our word *captivate.* See also FASCISM.

[L *fascinatus,* past part. of *fascinare,* prob. modif. (influenced by L *fari* to speak) of Gk *baskainein* to bewitch, speak evil of, fr. *baskanos,* sorcerer, slanderer, prob. fr. a Thracian or Illyrian word akin to Gk *phaskein* to say, *phanai* to say]

fascism   For many, a fascist government has come to represent the authoritarian regime in its most repressive manifestation. Perhaps few are aware that the name *fascism* derives from an insignia of authority in ancient Rome. The fasces (a Latin plural meaning 'bundles') was a cylindrical bundle of elm or birch rods, held in place by red-colored bands and mounted on a pole. Projecting above the cylinder of rods was the blade of an ax. The fasces was borne on the shoulders of lictors, officers of the Roman courts who accompanied the magistrates in their public appearances. The rods and ax blade symbolized the authority to punish or execute criminals. A lowering of the fasces constituted a salute to a higher official. The removal of the ax blade from the fasces whenever it was borne within the city of Rome was a recognition of the sovereignty of its citizens. As a symbol of authority the fasces has endured up to modern times. The fasces has adorned government buildings, been used as a classical motif on furniture, and has appeared on U.S. military insignia and coins, including the dime.

The fasces also became a symbol of solidarity. Consequently, the Italian word *fascio,* which derived from the Latin singular *fascis,* came to mean 'a politically united group' as well as 'a bundle'. As an example, organizations of workers and peasants that functioned as agrarian trade unions in Sicily during the 1890s were known as *fasci siciliani.* The term *fasci* was also applied to the organizations of military veterans, who were often from the officer ranks, that formed in Italy following World War I. Originally intended to be watchdogs for the best interests of the combat veterans, the groups evolved into patriotic and nationalistic organizations that were violently opposed to Bolshevism and socialism.

In 1919 Benito Mussolini, a veteran and a former socialist, united in Milan a bunch of disgruntled socialists, anarchists, restless revolutionaries, and unemployed veterans into a force known as the *Fasci di Combattimento.* At the time of its founding the group adopted the ancient Roman fasces as its emblem, thereby signifying their solidarity and a belief in rigid allegiance to a central authority. At the same time they established an important symbolic link with the imperial grandeur of ancient Rome. As the Partito Nazionale Fascista, Mussolini and his followers culminated their grasp for power by forcing the Italian government to hand control over to them in October of 1922.

Fascismo, as Mussolini's movement was by then known, had established the main tenets of its political philosophy: the exaltation of the nation, the devaluation of the individual, the centralization of an autocratic government headed by a charismatic dictator, severe economic and social regimentation, and the ruthless suppression of opposition. Even before they had achieved total control of Italy, the rise of the Fascisti had been sufficiently chronicled to allow English-language publications to feel justified in anglicizing *Fascismo* by 1921. In June of that year the *Literary Digest* published an essay that today is as remarkable for its assessment of fascism as it is for its early use of the word itself:

> Not all the doings of the Fascisti can be commended, nor is Fascism free from disquieting symptoms; but without its daring energy Italy would probably have felt the grip of Asiatic Jacobinism and have gone through a period of terrible dissolution.

Fascisti was anglicized in the English-language press with equal readiness. The *Manchester Guardian Weekly* in its issue of 29 July 1921, referred to Mussolini as "the Fascist leader" and in its 12 August issue of that same year reported the signing of a "peace treaty between Fascists and Socialists."

What is perhaps even more surprising is the swiftness with which the meaning of *Fascism* became generalized. The Fascist regime in Italy was soon perceived as the prototype of a number of emerging right-wing authoritarian regimes. As early as November of 1923 the *Contemporary Review* discussed "Fascism in Germany." During the 1920s *fascism* was also applied to emerging right-wing movements in Hungary, Turkey, and elsewhere. In its issue of 8 October 1924, the American magazine *Nation* used the word to describe a strain of brutal authoritarianism in American society:

> Thousands of patriots were already parading in the nobler white robes, enforcing discipline by night, terrorizing communities, smashing the laws in the name of "The Law." No other performance could possibly compete with this in existence; no other fascism could win the limelight.

The meaning of *fascism* has steadily expanded since the 1920s. The term has come to be used without regard to actual political persuasions and sometimes even in contradiction to traditional political labels. In some circles on the left the practice of calling anyone on the right a "fascist" was established long ago. On the other side of the political spectrum, during the 1950s *Time* magazine and the FBI director J. Edgar Hoover in his book *Masters of Deceit* (1958) took to referring to Soviet Communists—leftists by traditional standards—as "the Red fascists." Deploring the use of *fascism* and *fascist* as generalized terms of opprobrium, E. B. White in an editorial in the *New Yorker* (published in 1946 as part of a collection titled *The Wild Flag*) noted that the meaning of *fascist* had degenerated to the point where "a Fascist is a man who votes the other way." Since the defeat of the Axis powers in World War II, *fascism* and *fascist* have fallen into such ill repute that even those whose political philosophy is in full accord with Mussolini's disavow the label of "fascist."

In its latest semantic development *fascism* has expanded even beyond politics. *Fascism* is now used of any kind of oppressive dictatorial control of another's personal affairs. Those who are intolerant in matters of religion and seek to impose their views on others are decried as "religious fascists" by their opponents. Rules and regulations regarding occupational safety that are deemed excessive by some are characterized as "health and safety fascism." Computer programs that limit the user's options are resentfully characterized as "software fascism." And, in an area of particular concern to some, health and fitness advocates who would deny the dietetically indifferent their enjoyment of junk food are castigated as "food fascists."

[It *fascismo,* fr. *fascio* bundle, political group + *-ismo* -ism]

faucet Unlikely as it may seem at first glance, our *faucet* is descended from Latin *falsus,* 'false'. In Late Latin a verb was formed from this adjective, *falsare,* 'to falsify', which became in course of time French *fausser.* In medieval French, *fausser* developed new meanings. As well as 'to falsify', *fausser* could be used to mean 'to be false to' or even 'to damage or break'. It is to this last sense that we owe our *faucet.* A cask which is made to contain liquids usually has a hole through which it may be emptied. Although this bunghole is present by intention, the stopper that plugs it may be looked upon a bit fancifully as piercing or breaking into the cask. For this reason such a stopper was called, in medieval France, a *fausset.* The word was borrowed into Middle English, and it was put to good use in a later version (ca. 1430) of a Wycliffe translation of the Book of Job. There Elihu expresses in forceful simile his compulsion to speak to Job: "Lo! my wombe is as must with out faucet ether a ventyng that brekith newe vessels" (Job 32:19). (The King James Version is probably clearer to modern ears: "Behold, my belly is as wine which hath no vent; it is ready to burst like new bottles.")

In Middle English *faucet* was used not only for the stopper in a cask but also for a fixture used to draw liquid from a cask or other vessel. This is the modern application of the word, though modern faucets, unlike medieval ones, most often draw water from pipes rather than wine from casks.

[ME, fr. MF *fausset,* fr. *fausser* to damage, be false to, fr. LL *falsare* to falsify, fr. L *falsus* false]

fawn See DEER.
[ME *foun,* fr. MF *faon, feon* young of an animal, fr. OF, fr. (assumed) VL *feton-, feto,* fr. L *fetus* offspring]

February See JANUARY.
[ME *februarie,* fr. L *februarius,* fr. *februa,* pl., feast of purification held on the 15th of February + *-arius* -ary; perh. akin to L *fumus* smoke, vapor]

fedora The world of literature has given the language some words that have far outlasted the literary works they came from. For instance, *fedora,* the name for the common soft felt hat with a creased crown, actually comes from *Fédora,* a tragedy by the nineteenth-century French playwright Victorien Sardou. First produced in 1882, *Fédora* was a triumphant comeback for Sarah Bernhardt in the title role of Fédora Romanoff, a Russian princess. The soft felt hat that she wore inspired a fashion trend that was adapted for use by both men and women. How quickly the fashion became established is evidenced by the fact that such mainstays of American culture as the Montgomery Ward and Sears & Roebuck catalogues were selling fedoras (under that name) by the 1890s.

Enormously popular in their time, Sardou's melodramas are rarely performed nowadays. George Bernard Shaw's dismissive appraisal of "Sardoodledom" sounded the death knell for that kind of theater. But those were halcyon days for haberdashery inspired by the stage. George Du Maurier published in 1894 a novel called *Trilby*, a story of Trilby O'Ferrall, who was an artist's model living in the Latin Quarter of Paris. In one of the book's illustrations her fiancé, Little Billee, is shown wearing a narrow-brimmed soft felt hat. The runaway success of the novel helped to create a vogue for the hat style known as the *trilby*. The vogue was fueled the following year by a popular stage version of the novel in which the hat was conspicuously sported.

The *Trilby* story made another lasting contribution to the language. Trilby O'Ferrall becomes mesmerized by a maleficent musical genius named Svengali. Svengali eventually persuades her to break her engagement, give up the life of an artist's model, and become his companion. Under his hypnotic power she develops a beautiful voice and becomes a celebrated prima donna. Upon his sudden death, she loses her voice and dies soon afterwards. In the years following the success of the novel and play, *Svengali* developed the generic sense of one who exercises a powerful or hypnotic influence over a youthful protégé, often for some sinister purpose.

Not every by-product of the *Trilby* fad lasted, however. For a few decades *trilby* was a semi-jocular synonym for "foot," and there was even something known as the *Trilby Shoe*. (Again, Montgomery Ward and Sears had them in their catalogues.) You see, the free-spirited Trilby O'Ferrall was admired for her feet, reputedly the most beautiful in all of Paris.

[*Fédora* (1882), drama by V. Sardou †1908 Fr. playwright]

fee   In earlier ages one of the primary evidences of a person's wealth was the amount of cattle—i.e., livestock in general—he owned. Thus, in a number of Indo-European languages words meaning 'cattle' developed the sense of 'personal property'. Old English *feoh*, literally meaning 'cattle', was one of these; and in our earliest written records it is used in the sense of 'wealth' or 'property', appearing in *Beowulf* and in King Alfred's translation of Boethius's *Consolation of Philosophy*. Though the term is now obsolete, it survived into the early modern English period. It occurs, for instance, in the description of a tree bearing golden apples in Edmund Spenser's *Faerie Queen*:

> The warlike Elfe much wondred at this tree,
> So fayre and great, that shadowed all the ground,
> And his broad braunches, laden with rich fee,

Did stretch themselves without the utmost bound
Of this great gardin. . . .

Though it is related, Old English *feoh* is not the source of the word *fee* used in current English. Middle English took the form *fee* from Old French *fé*, which had the variants *fié* and *fief*. (This last variant is the source of our word *fief*.) Originally, this word *fee* did not mean a sum of money. Like its Old French source, it denoted an estate granted to someone by a feudal lord. Later *fee* developed the sense of 'a perquisite or reward', and this led to the sense common today, 'a payment given for professional services'. Though French is a Romance language descended from Latin, it seems to have borrowed some form of *fé, fié, fief* from a Germanic source, and it is in such a root that the distant connection exists between the two English words both spelled *fee*. See also SALARY; and for another word showing the semantic development from 'cattle' to 'property' see PECULIAR.

[ME, fr. OE *feoh* cattle, property, money; akin to OHG *fihu* cattle, ON *fē* cattle, sheep, money, Goth *faihu* money, wealth, L *pecus* cattle, *pecunia* money, *pectere* to comb, Gk *pekein* to comb, *pokos* fleece, Skt *paśu* cattle; basic meaning: to fleece, pluck (wool)]

[ME, fr. OF *fé, fié, fief*, prob. of Gmc origin; akin to OHG *fihu* cattle]

feisty The word *fist* (pronounced \'fīst\) appeared as both noun 'a breaking of wind, a foul smell' and verb 'to break wind' around 1440. Because *fisting* is attested as early as the year 1000, there probably was a verb *fistan* 'to break wind' in Old English. By the sixteenth century the participle *fisting* had become common in contemptuous expressions for a small dog, such as "fisting cur," "fisting hound," and "fisting dog." Although *fist* and *fisting* have since become obsolete, a variant form of the noun, *feist*, continues in use chiefly in the Southern and Midland dialect areas of the U.S. in reference to a small mongrel dog. Since such dogs tend to be nervous and temperamental, *feist* gave rise to the adjective *feisty*, which was applied to lively, fidgety, or quarrelsome people. Such usage dates from about 1895. In general American usage, *feisty* is applied chiefly to someone who shows a lively aggressiveness, such as in this sentence by Sally Quinn in *We're Going to Make You a Star* (1975): "She's a feisty, gutsy, bright, funny dame who doesn't mince words." Another curious word developing from the discharge of gas is discussed at PETARD.

'A foul smell' is also the original meaning of the noun *funk*, which dates from the seventeenth century. This noun and the verb *funk*, 'to subject to offensive smell or smoke', probably derive from *funkier*, a French dialect verb meaning 'to give off smoke'. By the end of the nineteenth century the adjective *funky* had been formed from the noun to describe something or someone having an offensive odor, such as "a funky bar," or "a funky armpit." In the early 1950s this adjective was picked up by black jazz musicians who applied it to low-down, earthy, bluesy music. Further amelioration of *funky* occurred in the 1960s when it came to be used as a generalized term of approval for something unpretentiously or quaintly fashionable.

[*feist* (by shortening and alter. fr. obs. *fisting* \\'fīstiŋ\\, adj., breaking wind — in such expressions as *fisting dog, fisting hound* — fr. pres. part. of obs. *fist*\\'fīst\\, v., to break wind, fr. ME *fisten*, fr. *fist* flatus) + *-y*]

fellow   The Old Norse word for a partner, *fēlagi*, means literally 'fee-layer'. *Fēlagar* (the plural of *fēlagi*) were those who laid together their property (fee) for some common purpose. (See also FEE.) In medieval Iceland partnership was legally recognized and protected. In the eyes of the law, even marriage was a *fēlag* ('fee-laying' or 'partnership'). The proper formula to be used in pleading before a divorce court was, "Ek vil skilja vith fēlaga minn." (I want to separate from my fellow.) Old English borrowed *fēlagi* from Old Norse and called a partner (but not a marriage partner) a *feolaga*. This word has come down to us, through several centuries and the development of a number of senses, as Modern English *fellow*. A *fellow* may be a companion, one of a pair, the holder of a fellowship, a boyfriend, or, in its most general and probably most common sense, any man.

Companion is a partial synonym of *fellow*. Just as fellows, etymologically speaking, are those who share or lay together their property, companions are sharers of bread. The Late Latin *companio* is a compound formed of *com-*, 'together, with', and *panis*, 'bread, food'. A similar compound occurs in several old Germanic languages: Gothic *gahlaiba* (from *ga-*, 'together, with', and *hlaifs*, 'loaf, bread'), Old High German *galeipo* (*ga-*, 'together, with', and *hleib* or *leib*, 'loaf, bread'). The Latin *companio* is probably a loan translation from some such Germanic word, converting the individual constituents of the Germanic compound into their Latin equivalents. See also COMRADE.

[ME *felawe*, fr. OE *feolaga*, fr. ON *fēlagi*, fr. *fē* cattle, sheep, money + *-lagi* (akin to ON *leggja* to lay)]

female   In the fourteenth century *female* appears in English with spellings such as *femel, femelle,* and *female* and is used both as a noun and as an adjective. It is derived, through Middle French, from the Latin *femella*, 'young woman, girl', which is a diminutive of *femina*, 'woman'. In English, however, the similarity in form and pronunciation between the words *female* and *male* led to the retention of the spelling *female* and also to the popular belief that it is derived from, or somehow related to, *male*. Apart from the influence on the spelling there is no etymological connection between them. For other examples of this process of transforming a word to show an assumed relation to better understood words see FOLK ETYMOLOGY.

[ME, alter. (influenced by *male*) of *femel, femelle*, fr. MF & ML; MF *femelle*, fr. ML *femella*, fr. L, young woman, girl, dim. of *femina* woman]

ferret   The *ferret* is a semidomesticated breed of the European polecat. For centuries the ferret has been used in Europe in hunting rats and sometimes rabbits. Even the ancient Romans were fond of the sport of rabbit-hunting with ferrets. But both the wild polecat and his domestic relative have rather bad reputations, especially as poultry thieves. The *polecat*'s name (Middle English *polcat*) is of uncertain origin, but one suggestion is that it may be a compound of Middle French *pol* (or *poul*), 'cock', and Middle English *cat*. And the ferret is a 'little thief': Middle English *ferret* (or *furet*) comes from Middle French *furet*, earlier *fuiret*, an alteration of *fuiron*, which ultimately goes back to Latin *fur*, 'thief'. The sport of ferreting out rodents and rabbits gives us the common modern sense of the verb *ferret*, 'to find by persistent searching'.

[ME *feret, ferret, furet,* fr. MF *furet, fuiret,* alter. of *fuiron,* deriv. of L *fur* thief]

fester   See RANKLE.

[ME *festren,* fr. *festre, fester,* n., abscess, fr. MF *festre,* fr. L *fistula* pipe, tube, a kind of ulcer]

fetish   In fifteenth-century Portugal the term *feitiço* was applied to such religious objects as saints' relics and rosaries. Portuguese explorers of West Africa extended the term to functionally similar indigenous charms and idols. *Feitiço* comes from Latin *facticius* 'artificial, manufactured', a derivative of *facere* 'to do' and the source of the English word *factitious*. The sense in Portuguese, however, was not so much 'artificial' as 'artful' or (another derivative of *facere*) 'effective'. The African items, in particular, were not necessarily manufactured, but might be stones and the like.

In the early seventeenth century the word entered English from Portuguese, in such spellings as *fatisso* and *feitisso;* at the same time the Portuguese word for "fetisher" or medicine man was taken over as *fetissero*. In the meantime French had borrowed the Portuguese term, at first in the form *fetisso,* but it was soon gallicized to *fétiche.* It is this French form that gave rise to the current English spellings, *fetish* and (less commonly) *fetich.* (French was also the intermediary for a near-synonym, *gris-gris,* applied to specifically African talismans and amulets.)

In the nineteenth and twentieth centuries two interesting new currents of thought accorded a prominent place to the notion of *fetish* in extended senses. The first, deriving from Marxist theory, speaks of "commodity fetishization," thus actually harking back to the etymological root at *facticius.* An example in this vein is a reference to "more fetichism of our luxury goods and gadgets" (*Saturday Review of Literature,* 1949). The second derives from psychoanalytic theory and refers either to manufactured items like articles of clothing or to body parts, when they are the object of obsessive displaced sexual interest. Outside these special areas the term is also used in an attenuated sense to denote any sort of hobbyhorse, nostrum, or other preoccupation. It is in this latter sense that the word is used in a 1926 issue of the *Archives of Therapeutics:* ". . . those old fetiches of the medical profession, 'woolen underwear.' . . ."

See also FASCINATE.

[F & Pg; F *fétiche*, fr. Pg *feitiço*, fr. *feitiço*, adj., artificial, false, fr. L *facticius* factitious]

fettucini   See VERMICELLI.
[It *fettuccine*, pl. of *fettuccina*, dim. of *fettuccia* small slice, ribbon, dim. of *fetta* slice]

fiasco   The Italian *fiasco* means 'a glass bottle' and is related to the English *flask*. In English *fiasco* was first borrowed from Italian in this literal sense, referring especially to a long-necked, straw-covered bottle for wine. There is, however, a less literal sense that is harder to account for. Apparently the French adopted the Italian *fiasco* into the phrase *faire fiasco*, meaning 'to fail' (literally 'to make a bottle'). A similar phrase is found in Italian, *fare fiasco*, also signifying a failure; it is possible that the Italians borrowed back their own *fiasco* in its new sense from the French. Whatever is the case in these two languages, *fiasco* was borrowed into English in the late nineteenth century in its newly acquired sense of an utter and often ridiculous failure. Just what prompted the development of the sense 'failure' from 'bottle' has remained obscure. One guess that has been put forward a number of times to fill this gap is that when a Venetian glassblower discovered a flaw developing in a beautiful piece he was working on, he would turn it into an ordinary bottle to avoid having to destroy the object. The bottle would naturally represent a failure of his art to the glassblower. This theory (only one of several) remains without evidence to support it.

[It, of Gmc origin; akin to OHG *flaska* bottle, E *flask*]

fiddle   See VIOLIN.
[ME *fithele*, *fidel*, fr. OE *fithele*, prob. fr. ML *vitula*, perh. fr. L *vitulari* to celebrate, be joyful]

fief   See FEE.
[F, fr. OF *fief*, *fié*]

fifth column   From the early days of World War II through the height of the Red scare in the United States during the 1950s, the inevitable term for a group of domestic subversives or for the secret supporters and sympathizers of one's enemy was *fifth column*. Surprisingly, this word originated not in a world conflict or even in an English context. *Fifth column* is a translation of the Spanish *quinta columna* and was born of the Spanish Civil War in 1936. As reported in the *New York Times* for 16 October 1936, Emilio Mola, a general in the rebel forces of Francisco Franco, had predicted in a radio broadcast that Madrid would fall as the result of the four columns of troops approaching the city as well as through the efforts of another column of supporters who were hiding within the city and poised to join the invaders. In a report published on 17 October, the *Times* correspondent William P. Carney specifically alluded to these secret supporters as the "fifth column," thereby using *fifth column* in an English context for the first time. A dispatch from Valencia three days later related that *fifth column* had already become a catchword there. Soon *fifth column* became a battle cry of the Spanish Loyalists.

The transition of *fifth column* from historical reference to generic noun was undoubtedly influenced by several factors. Ernest Hemingway chose *The Fifth Column* as the title of a play about the Spanish Civil War that he wrote in Madrid in 1937 and saw produced the following year. His stature as a writer helped to give the term broad exposure. At the same time political journals such as the *New Republic* and *Nation* increasingly started to use *fifth column* as a generic term for a conspiracy of subversives or traitors. These journals contained references to "Hitler's Fifth Column in America," to "Labor's Fifth column," and to the " 'Fifth Column' in the Treasury." The term was widely applied as well to the Norwegian collaborators who assisted the Nazi invasion of Norway in 1940. Fifth columns were found in Holland, Belgium, France, and all the other countries that fell to Hitler's armies. *Fifth column* became synonymous with *Trojan horse* and largely superseded the latter during the war years. The word was then applied retroactively to historical events that predated the Spanish Civil War.

Apparently, there were no bounds to the applicability of *fifth column*. A 1941 yearbook on public health stated that "Venereal disease is a potent fifth column in national defense." Viewing the common cold in terms of total warfare, a 1953 syndicated newspaper article explained that "the cold virus acts as a 'fifth column' of advance enemy agents, 'softening up' your body for invasion by the germs that cause sinus trouble, pneumonia, bronchitis and ear infections." And a 1942 agricultural bulletin referred, apparently in all seriousness, to the plant sneezeweed as the "fifth columnist" in sheep production. Later, the mindset of the McCarthy era encouraged some to see the presence of fifth columns in every sector of American life. With somewhat decreasing frequency *fifth column* continued to do service during the Vietnam War. In the 1980s, an official of the U.S. State Department accused the Iranian government of treating its religious minorities as a "fifth column" requiring suppression. Ironically, the father of the word *fifth column*, General Mola, died in June 1937, never having joined up with the Fifth Column forces about which he had boasted.

[trans. of Sp *quinta columna;* fr. the fact that during the Spanish Civil War rebel sympathizers in Madrid were so called when in 1936 four rebel columns advanced against this city]

filbert See MACADAM.
[ME *filberd, filbert,* fr. AF *philber,* after St. *Philibert* †684 Frankish abbot whose feast day (Aug. 20) falls in the nutting season]

filibuster In the middle of the nineteenth century bands of adventurers organized in the United States were in Central America and the West Indies, stirring up revolutions. Such an adventurer came to be known in English as a *filibuster,* from the Spanish *filibustero.* The word had originated in Dutch, as *vrijbuiter.* Its travels on the way from Dutch to Spanish are not well documented, but it is likely that the Spanish borrowed the word from the French (*flibustier, fribustier*), who had it from the English (*flee-booter, freebooter*). Now the word was back in English again with a new form and meaning.

Early in the nineteenth century, John Randolph, a senator from Virginia, got into the habit of making long and irrelevant speeches on the floor of the Senate. Vice President John C. Calhoun refused to rule Randolph out of order, so the Senate soon voted to give the presiding officer explicit power to deal with such problems. In 1872, however, Vice President Schuyler Colfax struck a blow against the expeditious handling of Senate business with his ruling that "under the practice of the Senate the presiding officer could not restrain a Senator in remarks which the Senator considers pertinent to the pending issue." Within a few years the use of delaying tactics in the Senate was rife. Senators practicing such tactics were compared with military adventurers, *filibusters*, who wreaked havoc in other countries, and were said to be *filibustering*.

[Sp *filibustero* freebooter, prob. fr. F *filibustier, fribustier*, fr. E *flee-booter, freebooter*]

flamenco   The Spanish homonyms *Flamenco*, 'Fleming', and *flamenco*, 'flamingo' have both yielded English words. From the first of these we get our English word *flamenco*, 'a vigorous dance style of Gypsy origin'. What connection there may be between Flemings and Gypsy dance has been much disputed, but the most likely explanation is this. In the early sixteenth century the Holy Roman Emperor Charles V, who was also King Charles I of Spain, had several Flemish ministers who were not popular with the king's Spanish subjects. It was probably because these particular Flemings were so odious that *Flamenco*, the Spanish word for Fleming, became a disparaging term for any foreigner. Andalusians used the term derisively for the Gypsies who came into southern Spain in the sixteenth century. This particular application of the term may have been ironical in intent, for the short, swarthy Gypsy was almost the antithesis in appearance of the typical Fleming. Whatever the reason, the Gypsy's new name stuck, and *flamenco* was also applied to the dance style typical of these Andalusian Gypsies.

English *flamingo* is a derivative, by way of Portuguese, of the second Spanish *flamenco*, which may or may not involve a comparison with ruddy-faced Flemings. An alternate suggestion is that *flamenco* comes from the Old Provençal name for the bird, *flamenc,* said to be a derivative of Latin *flamma*, 'flame'. Most flamingos are pale pink or rosy white. When standing at rest or wading about in search of food, they do not seem to justify their vivid name. But when a *flamingo* takes flight, the sudden flash of his scarlet wing coverts against the coal black of his quill feathers is like a burst of flame.

[Sp, Fleming, Flemish, buxom and ruddy, resembling a Gypsy, being in Gypsy style, fr. MD *Vlaminc* Fleming]

flamingo See FLAMENCO.

[Pg, fr. Sp *flamenco*, prob. fr. OProv *flamenc*, perh. fr. *flama* flame (fr. L *flamma*) + *-enc* one of a (specified) kind, of Gmc origin; akin to E *-ing* one of a (specified) kind]

focus The Latin noun *focus* originally denoted 'a hearth or fireplace'. Mathematicians of the seventeenth century borrowed this noun and gave it a new life, defined in the Oxford English Dictionary as 'one of the points from which the distances to any point of a given curve are connected by a linear relation'. Scientists studying optics at this time also put the word to use for 'a point at which rays of light converge or from which they diverge or appear to diverge'. Both the mathematical and optical senses of the Latin word were used by the German astronomer Johannes Kepler in his book *Astronomiae Pars Optica* (The Optical Part of Astronomy) in 1604. Since the optical sense refers to the "burning point" of a lens or mirror, which is closer to the original 'fireplace' sense of the Latin *focus*, this particular sense of the word may have preceded its mathematical sense.

The medical profession also found a place in its vocabulary for this word to designate 'a localized area of disease or the chief site of a generalized disease or infection'. Early in the eighteenth century we find *focus* also used for 'the position in which an object must be situated in relation to a lens for clearness of image'. By the late eighteenth century the word had become part of the general vocabulary, denoting 'a center of energy, activity, attraction, or interest', such as the focus of a storm, volcanic eruption, or earthquake, as well as the focus of attention, research, conflict, effort, power, etc.

The Latin noun *focus* gave rise to the Medieval Latin *focarius*, meaning 'relating to a fireplace'. The latter was assimilated into French as *foyer*, meaning 'fireplace'. In time it took on extended senses for 'a family's home' and then 'a gathering place'. In particular, it was applied to a large room in a theater where performers could gather, in other words, a greenroom. Later it was used for a larger room where theatergoers or concertgoers could gather during intermissions, in other words, a lobby. It was in this sense that English borrowed *foyer* around the middle of the nineteenth century.

The Latin *focus* is also the source of the French word *feu* 'fire'. In Middle French the verb *covrir* 'to cover' was combined with *feu* to form the noun *covrefeu*, *cuevrefeu*, which denoted 'a signal given in the evening to put out or bank the fire in the hearth'. Such a signal (usually the ringing of a bell) was given because a hearth fire left unattended overnight might spread and destroy the house or even the town. Even when hearth fires were no longer regulated, many towns had other rules that called for the ringing of an evening bell, and this signal was still called *covrefeu*. A common regulation required that certain people be off the streets by a given time. In this sense English borrowed the word in the fourteenth century as *curfew*.

In the thirteenth century, French also compounded *feu* 'fire' with the collective noun suffix *-aille* to form *fuaille*, *fouaille*, which denoted 'material used to feed a fire'. In the fourteenth century, English borrowed this French noun as *fuel*.

[NL, fr. L, fireplace, hearth]

folk etymology *Folk etymology,* also known as *popular etymology,* is the process whereby a word is altered so as to resemble at least partially a more familiar word or words. Thus the Spanish word *cucaracha* entered English as *cockroach,* by influence of the already familiar native words *cock* and *roach.* Sometimes the process seems intended to "make sense of" a borrowed foreign word using native resources: a *gillyflower* is in fact a flowering plant, and thus seems more transparent than its Middle English ancestor *girofle,* a borrowing from Middle French; and the Late Latin *febrifugia* (a plant with medicinal properties, etymologically 'fever expeller') is nicely Englished as *feverfew.* But in most cases the product of folk etymology is objectively not much help towards understanding what the word means and may be downright misleading. A cockroach resembles neither a cock nor a roach (the latter being a kind of fish; *roach* in the sense 'cockroach' is a later shortening of *cockroach*).

The term *folk etymology* can give a somewhat misleading impression, particularly when it is illustrated with hoary examples like the dialectal *sparrow-grass* for *asparagus,* suggesting that folk etymology is typically the work of yokels. This is by no means necessarily the case. *Sovereign* (*soverein* in Middle English) goes back to a popular Latin form we reconstruct as **superanus* (a derivative of *super-* 'over'); it got its modern *g* by association with the etymologically unrelated *reign,* a distinctly literate influence.

For other instances of folk etymology and related processes see BELFRY, BUCKAROO, FEMALE, FRONTISPIECE, GRIDIRON, HANGNAIL, HELPMATE, HUMBLE PIE, JERUSALEM ARTICHOKE, PENTHOUSE, SHAMEFACED, TINKER, and WISEACRE.

forebear   See ANCESTOR.
[ME (Sc dial.) *forebear,* fr. *fore-* + *-bear* one that is (fr. *been* to be + *-ar, -er* -er)]

fornicate   See FORNICATION.
[LL *fornicatus,* past part. of *fornicare, fornicari,* fr. L *fornic-, fornix* arch, vault, arched basement (inhabited by people of the lower classes), brothel, prob. fr. *fornus, furnus* oven]

fornication   The Latin verb *fornicare,* which is the source of English *fornicate* and *fornication,* is derived from the noun *fornix,* 'arch, vault, arched basement'. Because brothels were sometimes established in the Roman vaults, *fornix* itself took on the sense 'brothel' and the derived verb *fornicare* was used with much the same meaning as modern English *fornicate.* The noun *fornication* appears in English at the beginning of the fourteenth century, some two hundred and fifty years before the verb *fornicate.* In 1303 Robert Mannyng of Brunne in his penitential manual

Handlyng Synne did his best to define the noun with the utmost discretion, and though his fastidiousness resulted in some vagueness it is dispelled in part by the context: " 'Fornycacyoun' [ys], whan two vnweddyde haue mysdoun." ("Fornication" is when two unmarried people have done wrong.)

[ME *fornicacioun,* fr. MF & LL; MF *fornication,* fr. LL *fornication-, fornicatio,* fr. *fornicatus* (past part.) + L *-ion-, -io* -ion]

found See ABUNDANCE.
[ME *founden* to mix, fr. MF *fondre* to mix, pour, melt, fr. L *fundere* to found, pour; akin to OE *gēotan* to pour, OHG *giozzan* to pour, ON *gjōta* to bring forth (young), Goth *giutan* to pour, Gk *chein* to pour, Skt *juhoti* he pours into the fire, sacrifices]

foyer See FOCUS.
[F, lit., fireplace, fr. ML *focarius* fireplace, fr. L *focus* fireplace, hearth + *-arius* -ary]

frank See VANDAL.
[ME, fr. OF *franc,* fr. ML *francus,* fr. LL *Francus,* n., Frank]

frankfurter See HAMBURGER.
[G *Frankfurter* of Frankfurt, fr. *Frankfurt* am Main, Germany]

freebooter See FILIBUSTER.
[part trans. of D *vrijbuiter,* fr. *vrijbuit* plunder (fr. *vrij* free — akin to OHG *frī* free, OE *frēo* — + *buit* booty, fr. *buiten* to exchange, plunder, fr. MD *būten,* fr. MLG) + *-er* -er; akin to MLG *būte* exchange, distribution]

fresco See DOUBLETS.
[It, fresh plaster on which one may paint, coolness, fr. *fresco,* adj., cool, fresh, of Gmc origin; akin to OHG *frisc* fresh]

fresh See DOUBLETS.
[ME *fresh, fersh,* fr. OE & OF; OE *fersc* fresh, not salt, unsalted; akin to OFris *fersk* fresh, MD *versch,* OHG *frisc* fresh, and perh. to Russ *presnyl* fresh, sweet, unleavened; OF *freis* fresh (fem. *fresche*), of Gmc origin; akin to OHG *frisc* fresh]

Friday See SUNDAY.
[ME, fr. OE *frīgedæg;* akin to OFris *frīadei, frigendei* Friday, OHG *frīatag;* all fr. a prehistoric WGmc compound formed from components represented by OHG *Frīa,* the Germanic goddess of love, and *tag* day; trans. of L *Veneris dies,* lit., day of Venus (the Roman goddess of love and the planet Venus)]

frontispiece The process of folk etymology very early obscured the true etymology of *frontispiece* in English, which has nothing to do with the word *piece* at all. The earliest known form of the word in English (1597 or 1598) is *frontispice,* though as early as 1601 *frontispiece* had appeared as well. *Frontispice* is derived, through the same form in Middle French, from the Late Latin *frons, frontis,* which originally meant 'forehead' or 'brow' and then came to mean 'front' in general, plus *-spicium,* from the verb *specere,* 'to look at'. The earliest sense of *frontispice* was architectural: 'the part of a building that is most easily seen, front'. By 1607 the English *frontispice* was also used to refer to the title page of a book, probably because of the practice of decorating title pages with columns, pediments, and other architectural details. From this sense developed the most current sense of 'an illustration preceding the title page of a book'. Even in its earliest known use in this sense (1682) the word appears as *frontispiece.* For other folk etymologies see FOLK ETYMOLOGY.

[alter. (influenced by *piece*) of earlier *frontispice,* fr. MF, fr. LL *frontispicium* front of a building, lit., view of the front, fr. L *front-, frons* forehead, brow, front + *-i-* + *-spicium* (fr. *specere* to look at)]

fuel See FOCUS.
[ME *fewel,* fr. OF *fouaille, fuaille,* fr. *feu* fire, fr. LL *focus,* fr. L, hearth]

funky See FEISTY.
[¹*funk* (offensive smell) + *-y*]

fur Animals can now, with any luck, walk around in their own *fur.* But there was a time when fur was not fur until it had been removed from its original inhabitant and used to adorn a human being. The well-to-do of the late Middle Ages wore robes *furred* (lined and trimmed) with the pelts of animals. These trimmings and linings were called *furs.* The word was soon used for the soft hair of animals, even of living animals which might be expected to yield such decorative furs. But when robes were first furred, it was the act of lining rather than the material used that the verb *fur* suggested. The Middle English *furren* was borrowed from Middle French *fourrer,* 'to line a garment'. The Middle French meaning had developed from an earlier meaning, 'encase'; *fuerre,* a Germanic loanword in Old French, meant 'a sheath'. The sheath which encases a knife or sword is a far cry from the fur in which an animal is encased, but the development of *fur* has occurred through a series of easily comprehensible steps.

[ME *furren,* fr. MF *fourrer* to line a garment, fr. OF *forrer,* fr. *fuerre* sheath, of Gmc origin; akin to OE *fōdder* case, sheath, Goth *fodr* sheath; akin to Gk *pōma* cover, lid, Skt *pāti* he watches over, protects]

fury No more fearsome figures darkened the nightscape of Greek mythology than those of the Erinyes. Born of the blood-drops from the emasculation of Uranus, with snakes coiled in their hair, they roamed the land avenging perjury and murder and carrying out the curses of parent against son. Neither prayer nor tears could sway them, nor sacrifice stave off their wrath. Often they were referred to by a euphemism meant to deprecate a visit from them, as the Eumenides, 'the well-disposed'.

The Romans eschewed the euphemism and called these vengeful goddesses the *Dirae*, from *dirus*, source of and synonymous with our word *dire*, or *Furiae*, from *furere* 'to rage'. The singular form *furia* gave rise to our word *fury*, via the intermediate stage of French *furie.* Rage reached us by the same route, though here French sound-changes have made the connection to the Latin etymon unrecognizable: French *rage* goes back to Latin *rabies* 'frenzy, ferocity', also the immediate source of our modern medical term.

[ME *furie*, fr. MF & L; MF, fr. L *furia*, fr. *furere* to be mad, rage + *-ia* -y]

fustian   See BOMBAST, DENIM.
[ME *fustane, fustian*, fr. OF *fustane, fustaine*, fr. ML *fustaneum*, prob. fr. ML *fustis* tree trunk, fr. L, club, staff; trans. of Gk *xylinon* cotton, fr. neut. of *xylinos* wooden, fr. *xylon* wood, club]

G

galaxy   The earliest known use in English of the words *galaxy* and *Milky Way* is in the following lines from a poem by Geoffrey Chaucer called *The House of Fame*, written sometime before 1385: "Se yonder, loo, the Galaxie,/ Which men clepeth the Milky Wey,/ For hit is whit." (See yonder, lo, the galaxy, which they call the Milky Way, because it is white.) These lines make it clear that *Milky Way*, at least, was a term in popular use in England before that time, though how early it may have been used is impossible to say. The idea of the whiteness of the *Milky Way* being similar to that of milk is considerably older than the English language, however, for *galaxy* derives through Latin from Greek *galaxias*, which is based upon the Greek *gala*, meaning 'milk'. Not until the nineteenth century was *galaxy* used as a generic term for other star systems as well as the one in which we live, and to distinguish our *galaxy* from others the name of *Milky Way* has proved useful in English. See also LETTUCE.

[ME *galaxie, galaxias*, fr. ML & L; ML *galaxia*, fr. LL *galaxias*, fr. Gk, fr. *galakt-, gala* milk; akin to L *lac* milk]

gallimaufry   See POTPOURRI.

[MF *galimafree, calimafree* ragout, hash]

galumph   See JABBERWOCKY.

[prob. alter. of *gallop*]

gamut   In the eleventh century, Guido d'Arezzo, a musician and former Benedictine monk, devised a system of musical notation that was subsequently adopted throughout Europe. Guido's system consisted of hexachords, and he named the six notes *ut, re, mi, fa, sol,* and *la*, all of which he derived from the initial syllables of six lines of a hymn to St. John the Baptist written about the year 770. The lines are as follows:

> *Ut* queant laxis
> *re*sonare fibris
> *Mi*ra gestorum
> *fa*muli tuorum
> *Sol*ve polluti
> *la*bii reatum
>   Sancte Iohannes.

(That with full voices your servants may be able to sing the wonders of your deeds, purge the sin from their unclean lips, O holy John.)

Guido called the first line of the bass staff Γ (gamma), and we can assume that *gamma ut* was the term his followers used for the note falling on this line, i.e., the first note of the lowest hexachord. This later was contracted to *gamut* and was used to denote the whole scale as well as the lowest note. The term was generalized further to mean the whole range of a voice or instrument. By the seventeenth century *gamut* had been generalized as fully as possible and was now applied to an entire range of any sort. This use is exemplified by T. S. Eliot when, in his essay "A Dialogue on Dramatic Poetry," he states: "Only prose can give the full gamut of modern feeling, can correspond to actuality."

About the middle of the seventeenth century, the Guidonian hexachords were replaced with octaves, and the syllable *si*, probably formed from the last words (*Sancte Iohannes*) of the aforementioned hymn, was added. Ultimately, the *ut* was replaced with the more singable *do*, and *si* was generally replaced by *ti*.

[prob. modif. of (assumed) ML *gamma ut*, fr. ML *gamma* lowest note of the Guidonian scale (fr. LL, third letter of the Greek alphabet) + *ut* lowest note of each hexachord in the Guidonian scale]

garden   See COHORT.
[ME *gardin*, fr. ONF, fr. *gart* garden, of Gmc origin; akin to OHG *gart* enclosure]

garfish   See AUGER.
[ME *garfysshe*, prob. fr. ME (northern) *gar, gare* spear (fr. OE *gār*) + ME *fysshe, fish* fish]

gargantuan   Gargantua was originally a benevolent giant of medieval French folklore. Above all he was famous for his enormous appetite, his name deriving from Spanish *garganta*, 'gullet'. Shakespeare includes a reference to Gargantua's proverbial voraciousness in his comedy *As You Like It*:

You must borrow me Gargantua's mouth first before I can utter so long a word; 'tis a word too great for any mouth of this age's size.

In 1532 the French satirist François Rabelais used a popular chapbook that was a compilation of tales about Gargantua to serve as a basis for his satiric epic *Gargantua* (1535). In Rabelais's work Gargantua is an athletic, good-natured, peace-loving prince. He is the son of Grandgousier and Gargamelle and the father of Pantagruel. Consistent with tradition, Gargantua is presented as an eater and drinker of prodigious proportions. The voraciousness of his appetite may be explainable in part by the fact that his mother, Gargamelle, endured an eleven-month pregnancy that was terminated only when an overindulgence in tripe induced her delivery of

Gargantua through her left ear. His first words upon entering the world were "Drink, drink, drink!" In one of his more memorable incidents, Gargantua inadvertently swallows five pilgrims, staves and all, while eating a salad.

All of the details of Gargantua's life befit a giant. He rides a colossal mare whose tail switches so violently that it fells the entire forest of Orléans. Around the mare's neck hang the bells of Notre Dame Cathedral that Gargantua has stolen. The scale of everything connected with Gargantua gave rise to the adjective *gargantuan,* which since Shakespeare's time has been used of anything of tremendous size or volume. Rabelais used the travels and adventures of Gargantua and his ribald companions as a vehicle to hold up to devastating ridicule the follies of the religious, educational, legal, and political institutions of his day. His name has become identified with gross and robust humor.

The human penchant for hyperbole is doubtless responsible for the plethora of words available for describing things of enormous size. Like *gargantuan, Brobdingnagian* comes from a satiric work. In *Gulliver's Travels,* the celebrated work by Jonathan Swift, Gulliver is at one point abandoned in the land of Brobdingnag. There the inhabitants are 12 times the size of normal people, and all other objects in the kingdom are proportionately large. Compared with the natives, Gulliver is but a pygmy. He is treated like a pet by the members of the court and is subjected to a number of embarrassing indignities. The great difference in size between Gulliver and the giants forces him to notice the grossness and physical imperfections of his hosts. The grossness of the Brobdingnagians is in sharp contrast to the overriding characteristic of another race encountered by Gulliver in his adventures. Before experiencing Brobdingnag, Gulliver had been shipwrecked on the coast of Lilliput. Here, he is the one who is gigantic, for the average Lilliputian is a mere six inches in height. Again, everything else in the kingdom is sized accordingly. The diminutive size of the Lilliputians mirrors their moral character. They are a petty, self-important, arrogant, warring race of twerps—not unlike human beings, in Swift's view. Soon after the publication of *Gulliver's Travels* in 1726, writers began to refer to things of great size as *Brobdingnagian* and to things unusually small as *lilliputian.* In addition, the marked small-mindedness of Swift's diminutive creatures is responsible for a second sense of *lilliputian* that is equivalent to 'petty'.

For other words denoting large size see HIPPOPOTAMUS, MONSTER.

[*Gargantua,* gigantic king who is the hero of the novel *Gargantua* (1535) by François Rabelais †1553 Fr. humorist and satirist + E -*an*]

garnet Names of gemstones can be misleading. The stone commonly known as *garnet* gets its name from Old French by way of Middle English *grenat;* ultimately it comes from an adjective meaning 'red like a pomegranate'. Red garnets do indeed resemble the pulp of the pomegranate in color. But many garnets are not red at all. Garnets actually come in a variety of colors from red to green, although we most often associate the color red with the stone. While garnets are valuable in their own right, they are not quite as popular as other gems, like the ruby. In fact, some red garnets from the Western U.S. are often given trade names like American or Arizona ruby, which confuse the issue even further.

Unlike the garnet, the *ruby* is a gem that is always true to its name. The word *ruby* comes from Middle French *rubi*, which in turn derives from Latin *rubeus*, meaning 'reddish'. Although they may vary in shade from pink to deeper red, all rubies have a reddish hue and a translucent quality that makes them extremely attractive for jewelry.

Long ago, writers used the term *ruby* for almost any red gem, and eventually *ruby* became synonymous with the color red. Over time, the red of the ruby has come to be associated with passion as well as health and has captured the imaginations of love poets on numerous occasions. As early as 1380, perhaps, Chaucer in "To Rosamounde" compares the lady's beauty to that of the ruby:

> Madame, ye ben of al beaute shryne
> As fer as cercled is the mapamounde [map of the world],
> For as the cristal glorious ye shyne,
> And lyke ruby ben your chekes rounde.

Among literature's favorite rubies are the human lips. In 1610, Shakespeare's *Cymbeline* contained these lines:

> Cytherea,
> How bravely thou becom'st thy bed! fresh lily,
> And whiter than the sheets! That I might touch!
> But kiss; one kiss! Rubies unparagon'd,
> How dearly they do't!

[ME *gernet, grenat,* fr. MF *grenat,* fr. OF, fr. *grenat,* adj., red like a pomegranate, fr. *grenate* (in *pome grenate* pomegranate)]

gauche   See LEFT.
[F, lit., left, on the left, fr. MF, fr. *gauchir* to turn aside, swerve, alter. of *guenchir,* of Gmc origin; akin to OHG *wankōn* to stagger, sway]

gauntlet   See FALCON.
[ME *gauntlette,* fr. MF *gantelet,* dim. of *gant* glove, of Scand. origin; akin to MLG & MD *want, wante* mitten, ON *vöttr* gloves and perh. to ON *vöndr* wand]

gay   More than four decades ago movie star Gene Autry, the Singing Cowboy, could ride across the silver screen in a Western titled *The Gay Cowboy,* and no one at the time was likely to think that the title character was anything more than merry and lively. For better or worse, since those more innocent times *gay* has acquired as one of its dominant senses the meaning 'homosexual'. Although the meanings of 'merry' and 'high-spirited' have certainly not vanished, the reality of the lexical marketplace is that the sexual sense of *gay* has made many writers cautious about using the earlier senses.

Gay was borrowed from the Middle French *gai* in the fourteenth century. The meaning 'happily excited, merry' was its original sense and the one in which Chaucer used *gay* in "The Miller's Tale" (ca. 1392). In a significant development in the seventeenth century, *gay* acquired the related but more sinister sense of 'given to unrestrained self-indulgence and the pursuit of pleasure'. It became synonymous with *devil-may-care, rakehell,* or *rakish.* This sense of *gay* gave birth to *gay blade* and *gay dog,* two bywords for the worldly-wise playboy in search of licentious pleasures. In fact, Lothario, a character in the eighteenth-century play *The Fair Penitent* and one whose name has become generic for a seducer, is called "Gay Lothario" by his creator, Nicholas Rowe. This sense of *gay* has almost always been applied to men and to men exhibiting definite and often vigorous heterosexuality.

In all probability, though, it was this 'devil-may-care' sense of *gay* that gave rise to *gaycat,* a term originating in hobo slang and meaning 'a young and inexperienced tramp'. Recorded as part of hobo cant as early as 1897, *gaycat* originally referred to a tenderfoot hobo who in a pinch was willing to break the code of conduct and to accept work. By the 1920s *gaycat* was recorded as having wide distribution throughout the hobo community. A fact of the hobo lifestyle was that the greenhorn hobo often needed to attach himself to a veteran of the road in order to survive. It was generally taken for granted that the relationship between the youth and the older man eventually turned into a sexual liaison. If such relationships were commonplace in the hobo community, it comes as no surprise to find in a 1935 handbook of underworld and prison slang the following entry: "*Geycat* . . . a homosexual boy." *Gay,* in its 'homosexual' sense, is not known to have surfaced as an independent adjective until the 1950s. Its earliest known occurrences are in hard-boiled fiction and in works specifically dealing with homosexuality, as Donald Webster Corey's *The Homosexual in America* (1951). *Gay* appears to have been confined to the homosexual subculture and those intimately acquainted with it throughout the 1950s and the early 1960s. From that time onward, the term made its frequent appearance in glossaries of slang and in works intended to acquaint heterosexuals with homosexual life. In such contexts *gay* was usually put in quotation marks and given a gloss, the implication being that it was an in-group usage that most people would not know. The ascendancy of *gay* matched the increasing visibility of the homosexual community and the rise of the homosexual theme in the arts. Furthermore, general awareness of the 'homosexual' sense of *gay* was undoubtedly advanced when organizations for homosexual rights chose such names as the Gay Liberation Front and the Gay Activist Alliance.

The use of *gay* in the names of homosexual rights organizations was also evidence of another semantic development: the use of *gay* not only to mean 'exhibiting homosexuality' but also to encompass 'relating to or used by homosexuals.' Thus, there were growing references to "gay bars," "gay newspapers," "gay hotels," and even "gay Christmas cards."

Coincident with the semantic expansion of *gay* was its functional shift from adjective to noun. As with the adjective, the noun *gay* made its first known appearance in the 1950s and in a piece of writing from the hard-boiled school of journalism. The May 1953 issue of *True Crime* related that "the city decided to crack down on the 'gays' and . . . padlocked a number of known homosexual hangouts."

The introduction of the word *gay* into the heterosexual community provoked a range of responses that tended to correspond to individuals' feelings about homosexuality itself. *Gay* was regarded by some as the disreputable slang of a despised subculture. Ignorant of the word's history, many commentators regarded it as a euphemism, with lingering connotations of merriness and high spirits, that was being foisted upon the heterosexual majority. Homosexuals themselves seemed to regard it as a positive designation, as evidenced by the militant slogan "Gay is good and I am proud." *Gay* was seen as a desirable alternative to the clinical-sounding *homosexual* and far preferable to a host of blatantly offensive words. Others saw *homosexual* as a valid complement to *heterosexual,* but they contended that *gay* was the proper counter term for the equally informal *straight.*

With the widespread adoption (if not always the willing acceptance) of *gay,* have come efforts to assign *gay* a variety of specific meanings. Some have attempted to discriminate between *gay* and *homosexual,* designating as *gay* persons having erotic or affectional preferences for members of their own sex and restricting *homosexual* to those who actually engage in sexual activity with members of their own sex. More widely observed is the distinction between *gay* and *lesbian.* The women's liberation movement has been concurrent with the homosexual liberation movement. As a consequence, homosexual females have often sought to assert their independence from males of either sexual preference. One of the ways in which they have done so is to insist that *gay* refer to males only and that *lesbian* be used for homosexual females. Indeed the distinction is adhered to by many, as evidenced by such institutions and organizations as Lesbian and Gay People in Medicine, the Institute for the Protection of Lesbian and Gay Youth, and the Lesbian/Gay Health Conference. Even when *gay* appears alone, there is usually the strong assumption that the reference is to males. By itself *gay* is rarely used to refer to females.

Perhaps the most intriguing development in the history of *gay* is one that suggests that its meaning may be moving beyond sexual orientation. In discussing the lifestyle of present-day Yuppie couples, *Time* magazine noted in 1984 that they typically have two incomes and no kids, are part of the gentrification movement, and display an avid interest in health, fitness, and food. In the words of *Time,* "Yuppies are in a sense heterosexual gays."

See also LESBIAN.

[ME, fr. MF *gai,* perh. fr. OProv, of Gmc origin; akin to OHG *gāhi* rapid, hurried, impetuous]

gecko See PIGEON.
[Malay *ge'kok,* of imit. origin]

geez See JEEPERS.
[alter. of *jeez*]

Gemini See JEEPERS.
[ME, fr. L, twins, pl. of *geminus;* prob. euphemism for LL *Jesu domine* Jesus lord!]

generate See COGNATE.
[L *generatus,* past part. of *generare* to beget, create, fr. *gener-, genus* birth, race, class, kind]

genie See GENIUS.
[F *génie,* modif. (influenced by *génie,* genius, fr. L *genius*) of Ar *jinnīy* demon, spirit]

genital See COGNATE.
[ME, fr. L *genitalis,* fr. *genitus* (past part. of *gignere* to beget) + *-alis* -al]

genius According to ancient Greek mythology a *daimōn* is a supernatural being whose nature is intermediate between that of a god and that of a man. It was believed that at birth each person is assigned one of these spirits to act as a guardian throughout his life. The standard Latin translation of *daimōn* was *genius,* from *gignere,* 'to beget'. Latin also borrowed the Greek word in the form *daemon,* 'spirit', which in Late Latin was often restricted to mean an evil spirit. *Genius* in the sense of 'attendant spirit' was borrowed from Latin into Middle English in the early fifteenth century.

Part of the role of the tutelary *genius* was to guard, if not actually determine, a person's character; thus, in the sixteenth century *genius* came to be used in direct reference to a person's inclination or bent of mind, as in Sir Philip Sidney's *Defence of Poetry* (1595): "A Poet, no industrie can make, if his owne Genius bee not carried vnto it." In the next century this led to the sense of 'a strongly marked aptitude'. This sense of *genius* was often used of poets and artists, and in England in the eighteenth century the Romantics began to use *genius* to mean 'an extraordinary native intellectual power', especially as manifested in an unusual capacity for creative activity of any kind.

The first translation of the *Arabian Nights* from Arabic into French rendered the Arabic *jinnīy,* meaning 'spirit' or 'demon', as French *génie,* meaning the same as English *genius.* The translators were no doubt influenced by the similarities between the Arabic and French words in both pronunciation and meaning. Thus it is from French that English gets the form *genie* for a spirit such as appeared to Aladdin when he rubbed his magic lamp.

A variant form, *jinni,* was borrowed directly from the Arabic. In that language the plural of *jinnīy* is *jinn,* and this has yielded (in differing styles of transliteration from the Arabic alphabet) the English variants *jinn* and *djinn.*

[L, fr. *gignere* to beget]

genteel   See GENTILE.

[MF *gentil*]

gentile   In the earliest Roman times, the *gens* (plural *gentes*) was a clan; the word is from the Indo-European root *gen-* 'beget' and is cognate with our word *kin.* The plural *gentes* was also used to designate the peoples of the world, particularly the non-Romans. The people that could be designated by *gens* thus ran a curious range, from those closest to home to those decidedly foreign.

The derived adjective *gentilis* was used with both these implications. In the later Latin of the Christian church, *gentilis* and *gentes* were used respectively to translate Greek *ethnikos* and *ta ethnē,* which meant 'pagan(s)'—*ta ethnē* was in turn a rendering of Hebrew *goyim* 'non-Jews'. It was by this route that English borrowed its word *gentile.*

But the borrowing of this word did not stop there. *Gentilis* became *gentil* in Old French, meaning originally 'high-born' (in modern French the word simply means 'nice'). The Old French word was borrowed into English and resulted in our word *gentle,* originally in the same meaning (as it still is in the phrase "of gentle birth"). Over the centuries *gentle* evolved its current principal sense of 'mild'. (Lest anything seem inevitable about the association of aristocratic birth and mild manners, you should know that a contrasting evolution is preserved in *surly,* from Middle English *sirly,* a derivative of *sir.*)

Nor did this exhaust the English appetite for the progeny of *gentilis.* From Middle French we borrowed *gentil* again, and it remains in our language as *genteel.* At first the word referred straightforwardly to gentle birth, with the particular implication of 'stylish'. But a complex play of snobbery and affectation has conspired over time to emphasize the ironical in its use, so that its chief uses today involve the false pretense of superior social standing or a prissy sort of delicacy.

There is a fourth scion of *gentilis* hiding in our lexicon, this one in better orthographic disguise. The latest of the borrowings of *gentil,* dating from the seventeenth century, it appears in our dictionaries now as *jaunty.* Like *genteel* with its last-syllable stress, *jaunty* attempts to render the sound of the French etymon, this time concentrating on the vowel quality of the first syllable. *Jaunty,* too, first meant 'genteel, stylish' but has evolved the sense of 'sprightly', nearly opposite the current implications of *genteel.*

[ME *gentil, gentile,* fr. LL *gentilis* foreigner, heathen, fr. L, member of the same family or gens, fellow countryman, fr. *gentilis,* adj.]

gentle   See GENTILE.
[ME *gentil,* fr. OF, fr. L *gentilis* of the same clan or family or race, fr. *gent-, gens* clan, family, race (fr. the stem of *gignere* to beget) + *-ilis* -ile]

geranium   Many of the plants in the geranium family have long, thin, tapering fruits that resemble birds' beaks. The Greeks, impressed by this resemblance, named the wild geranium *geranion,* 'little crane', diminutive of *geranos,* 'crane'. *Geranium* is now the scientific name of the genus that includes the wild geranium, whose common English name is *cranesbill.* Other members of the family have been given scientific names modeled on this one. *Erodium* was named for the long-billed heron (Greek *erodios*), but it is commonly called *storksbill* in English. The common or garden geranium is really a member of a related genus, *Pelargonium,* named for the stork (Greek *pelargos*).

[NL, fr. L *geranion, geranium,* any of several plants of the geranium family, fr. Gk *geranion,* dim. of *geranos* crane; akin to OE *cran* crane, OHG *krano,* Arm *krunk,* L *grus* crane, Skt *jarate* he cries, it sounds; basic meaning: croaking]

german   See GERMANE.
[MF *germain* brother, cousin, fr. *germain,* adj., having the same parents]

German   See GERMANE.
[ML *Germanus,* fr. L, any member of the Germanic peoples that inhabited western Europe in Roman times]

germane   The English homonyms *german,* 'having the same parents or the same maternal or paternal grandparents', and *German,* 'of Germany', can be traced to a pair of unrelated Latin homonyms: *germanus,* 'having the same mother and father', and *Germanus,* 'German'. The history of the second of these is obscure. It is apparently not Latin or even Germanic, but may have originated with the ancient Celtic people of Gaul, near neighbors of the *Germani.* The first *germanus* is a derivative of the word *germen,* 'bud, sprout, germ', children of the same parents being likened to buds of the same tree. It was in French that *germanus,* in the form *germain,* was extended from full siblings to full cousins. This *german* was borrowed into English in the fourteenth century and was for a while a free form not limited to occurrence in compounds. The *Ordynarye of Crysten Men* (1502) described the degrees of kinship: "Broder and syster make the fyrst, the chyldren the which ben germayne make the seconde." Later in English the range of meaning of *german* was still further extended to include all near relatives: "Wert thou a Leopard, thou wert Germane to the Lion" (Shakespeare, *Timon of Athens,* ca. 1607).

The form *german* survives today only in the frozen compounds *brother-german, sister-german,* and *cousin-german.* But the variant *germane* has a life of its own. In *Hamlet,* Shakespeare used *germane* figuratively—"The phrase would bee more Germaine to the matter: If we could carry Cannon by our sides"—and gave it what is now the standard meaning of *germane,* 'relevant and appropriate'. The spelling of these forms, which (as the quotations above show) was once unstable, has been solidified by convention only since the late nineteenth century.

[ME *germain, germane,* lit., having the same parents, fr. MF *germain,* fr. L *germanus,* irreg. fr. *germin-, germen* bud, sprout, germ + *-anus* -an]

gerrymander It is perhaps ironic that a man who signed the Declaration of Independence and attained the vice presidency of the United States should be chiefly remembered for a notorious bit of political flimflam. *Gerrymandering,* the now universal term for drawing the boundaries of electoral districts in such a way as to give one party an unfair advantage over its rivals, "honors" the name of Elbridge Gerry (1744–1814). A native of Marblehead, Massachusetts, Gerry was born into a family of maritime traders. While still a young man he became an avid supporter of the colonists' cause against the British and a protégé of firebrand Samuel Adams. An original member of his local Committee of Correspondence, Gerry went on to become a delegate to the second Continental Congress and one of the signers of the Declaration of Independence. As a Democratic-Republican he was elected to the governorship of Massachusetts in 1810 and reelected in 1811.

His second administration achieved lasting notoriety because of a measure of 11 February 1812 that has since become known as the "Gerrymander Bill." The purpose of the bill was to redistrict the state in such a way as to give the Democratic-Republicans a majority in the state senate. This was not the first time that redistricting had been exploited to give one side a political advantage, but never before had the manipulation been so blatant. Gerry's home territory of Essex County, in the northeast corner of Massachusetts, was subdivided into bizarrely shaped senatorial districts. During the campaign a map of Essex County was displayed at a meeting of the Federalist Party, the opposition. Onto an outline of the grotesquely configured district, one of the Federalists—perhaps the noted painter Gilbert Stuart himself—sketched an animal's head, wings, and claws. Upon completing his handiwork, the artist proclaimed, "That will do for a salamander!" Another party member quickly rejoined, "Gerrymander!" The caricature of the district as a winged monster—with Gerry's profile superimposed upon its back—was widely reproduced, and the coinage *gerrymander* immediately caught on, at first applied to the caricature itself and then to the actual act of redistricting. With equal alacrity *gerrymander* was turned into a verb. In its 28 December 1812 issue, the *New York Post* reported an attempt "to Gerrymander the State [of New Hampshire] for the choice of Representatives to Congress."

As far as the Democratic-Republicans of Massachusetts were concerned, the act of 1812 worked exactly as intended. In the election of April 1812, the Federalist candidates for the state senate received 51,766 votes to 50,164 for the Democratic-Republicans, but the Federalists won only 11 seats and the Republicans won 29. Their victory was neither complete nor enduring, however. Gerry himself was defeated in his reelection bid. and the Gerrymander Bill of 1812 was repealed on 16 June 1813.

Gerry, whose career had more than its share of ups and downs, experienced yet another reversal of fortune. A few weeks after his defeat for reelection, he was nominated by the Republicans for the U.S. vice presidency on a ticket headed by James Madison. The Madison-Gerry ticket won the general election of November 1812, although it failed to carry Massachusetts by a wide margin. Gerry died in office after having languished in the political graveyard of the vice presidency for a year and a half.

[Elbridge *Gerry* †1814 Amer. statesman + sala*mander;* fr. the fancied resemblance to a salamander (made famous by caricature) of the irregularly shaped outline of an election district in northeastern Mass. that had been formed for partisan purposes in 1812 during Gerry's governorship]

ghost   The word *ghost,* spelled *gost* or *gast* in Middle English, derives from the Old English noun *gāst.* Its original meaning was 'the soul regarded as the seat of life; the principle of life'. The chief surviving use of this sense is in the expression "give up the ghost" in reference to the act of dying. Chaucer, in recounting the tragic story of Pyramus and Thisbe in *The Legend of Good Women* (ca. 1385), gives us a good example of this sense:

> This woful man, that was nat fully ded,
> Whan that he herde the name of Tisbe cryen,
> On hire he caste his hevy, dedly yen [eyes],
> And doun agayn, and yeldeth up the gost.

Beginning in the eleventh century, we find examples of *ghost* being used for 'the spirit of man as distinguished from the body'. An example of this use can be seen in this couplet from one of Jonathan Swift's riddles published in 1729:

> "All Shapes and Features I can boast,
> No Flesh, no Bones, no Blood—no Ghost."

This sense has now become archaic.

By Chaucer's time the use of *ghost* for 'the soul of a deceased person that manifests itself to the living' had also become established. This sense is evident in Shakespeare's *Hamlet:* "There needs no ghost, my lord, come from the grave/To tell us this." This is now the most common sense of the word.

The third person of the Trinity has been called the *Holy Ghost* since the eleventh century. The roots of this name lie in the Old Testament. The Hebrew *ruah ha-qodesh* 'Holy Spirit' was the name given by the Jews to certain phases of the action of God upon nature and man. The word *ruah* originally meant 'breath' or 'wind'. Breathing was thought of as the vital force that animated and inspired human beings. The Holy Spirit (breath) of God was the source of the superhuman strength of Israel's heroes and the inspiration of its leaders, judges, and prophets.

When the Old Testament was translated into Greek (the Septuagint), the Hebrew name was rendered as *pneuma hagion*, the word *pneuma* meaning 'breath, wind'. In the New Testament, which was written in Greek, the Holy Spirit was conceived of as the source of graces and gifts, descending upon Jesus at his baptism and upon the Apostles at Pentecost. When the Bible was translated into Latin (the Vulgate) in the fourth century, the Greek *pneuma hagion* became *spiritus sanctus, spiritus* also meaning 'breath, wind'. In Old English this became *hālig gāst*, and in Middle English *holi gost*. The -*h*- in *ghost* first began to appear in the latter part of the sixteenth century. It was probably influenced by the Flemish spelling *gheest*.

Holy Ghost is the name used in the 1549 Book of Common Prayer and in the King James Bible (1611). The Catholic English version of the New Testament (Rheims, 1582) also uses Holy Ghost. However, twentieth-century English editions of the Bible prefer the designation Holy Spirit because *spirit* expresses the idea more clearly than *ghost*, which is now used chiefly of the soul of a deceased person. The word *spirit*, as we have seen, derives from the Latin *spiritus* and denotes 'breath, wind', as does the Greek *pneuma* and the Hebrew *ruah*.

[ME *gost, gast*, fr. OE *gāst;* akin to OS *gēst* spirit, OHG *geist* spirit, ON *geiska*fullr full of terror, Goth us*gaisjan* to frighten, Skt *heḍa* anger]

giddy   Before the nature of mental illness began to be understood, the cause of insanity was long thought to be possession by spirits or demons. The Old English *gidig*, meaning 'insane', was akin to Old English *god*, 'god', and had the underlying sense 'possessed by a god'. The Middle English derivative *gidy* retained overtones of madness, but its meaning tended more toward 'foolish, stupid'. Only a small semantic sidestep was then required to produce the sense 'dizzy', which was first recorded at the end of the fourteenth century. (*Dizzy* itself had made much the same step shortly before, from its earliest sense, 'foolish, silly', to its now usual sense, first attested in about 1340.) By the seventeenth century, the new meaning of *giddy*, as it had come to be spelled, had produced several extended senses, including 'causing dizziness' and 'rapidly whirling'. These senses are still in use, as is the sense 'lightheartedly or exuberantly silly', which first occurred in the middle of the sixteenth century and which may be said to combine elements of both the 'foolish' sense and the 'dizzy' sense, with perhaps even the suggestion of a little harmless craziness.

For a strikingly different semantic development taking off from the idea of being possessed by a god see ENTHUSIASM.

[ME *gidy, gedy* mad, foolish, dizzy, fr. OE *gydig, gidig* possessed, mad, fr. the stem of *god* + -*ig* -y]

gin   *Genever* (now spelled with an initial *j*), from Latin *juniperus* by way of Old French, was the Dutch word for a drink made of distilled spirits and flavored with juniper berries when this was still a fairly new concoction. British soldiers returning from wars in the Lowlands brought home the word along with the beverage. In its new land, however, the word was influenced by the similar-sounding name of a city in Switzerland, and thus the earliest English name for the drink is *Geneva*, which appeared in print in 1706.

In eighteenth-century England the popular creation of new slang or cant words by clipping longer words was just as common as it is today (as witness Jonathan Swift's disapproval of *mob, rep,* and *phiz*), and so there soon arose a shortened form, *gin,* to mean not only the Dutch drink but also a similar liquor made in Britain, not necessarily flavored with juniper but remarkably popular. So popular did it become, in fact, that gin drinking among the lower classes soon was a major social problem. In 1738 Alexander Pope included this note on *gin* in his *Satires and Epistles of Horace Imitated:* "A spiritous liquor, the exorbitant use of which had almost destroyed the lowest rank of the People till it was restrained by an act of Parliament in 1736." The problem was not then at an end, for Hogarth published his famous engraving *Gin Lane,* showing the horrific effects of gin on the lives of the urban poor, more than a decade later. The epidemic proportions of this menace are long past, but the drink which caused it is still very much with us and so is its abbreviated name. See also BRANDY, WHISKEY.

[by shortening and alter. fr. *geneva,* modif. (influenced by *Geneva,* city in Switzerland) of obs. D *genever* (now *jenever*), lit., juniper, fr. MD *geniver, genēver,* fr. OF *geneivre, genevre,* fr. (assumed) VL *jeniperus,* fr. L *juniperus*]

girasole   See JERUSALEM ARTICHOKE.
[It *girasole* sunflower, fr. *girare* to turn (fr. LL *gyrare,* fr. L *gyrus* gyre) + *sole* sun, fr. L *sol*]

girl   See MAN.
[ME *girle, gerle, gurle* young person of either sex]

glamour   In classical antiquity the Greek and Latin ancestors of the English word *grammar* were used in reference not only to the study of language but also to the study of literature in its broad sense. In the medieval period, moreover, the meaning of Latin *grammatica* and its derivatives in other languages was extended to include learning in general. Since almost all learning was couched in a language not spoken or understood by the unschooled populace, it was commonly believed that such subjects as magic and astrology were included in this broad sense of *grammatica.* Scholars tended to be viewed with awe and more than a little suspicion by ordinary men, a state of affairs which no doubt made it easier for many Elizabethan playgoers to accept the reality of Christopher Marlowe's Dr. Faustus and Robert Greene's Roger Bacon in their dealings with the devil and their mastery of the black arts.

This connection between *grammar* and magic was evident in a number of languages, and in Scotland by the eighteenth century a form of *grammar,* altered to *glamer* or *glamour,* meant 'a magic spell or enchantment'. As *glamour* passed into more extended English usage, it came to mean 'an elusive, mysteriously exciting, and often illusory attractiveness that stirs one's imagination and appeals to one's taste for the unconventional, the unexpected, the colorful, or the exotic'. Now the word has been further generalized to mean simply 'an alluring or fascinating personal attractiveness'.

[Sc *glamour, glamer,* alter. of E *grammar;* fr. the popular association of erudition with occult practices]

gnomon See NORMAL.
[L, fr. Gk *gnōmōn* interpreter, discerner, pointer on a sundial, carpenter's square, fr. *gignōskein* to know]

goatee See SIDEBURNS.
[*goat* + *-ee;* fr. the resemblance to the beard of a he-goat]

goatsucker See PIGEON.
[so called fr. the belief that it sucks the milk from goats]

golly See JEEPERS.
[euphemism for *God*]

good-bye In the Spanish *adios* and French *adieu* 'farewell, good-bye', we see an explicit wish that the person addressed should be in the care of God *(dios, dieu).* The same sentiment lies at the origin of *good-bye,* which comes from the phrase *God be with you.* The phrase gradually eroded over time, appearing in such versions as *God be wy you* (in the sixteenth century), *God b'y you* (in the seventeenth), and numerous other versions before settling on *good-bye* in the nineteenth century, the final form buttressed by the example of *good night* and *good day.* Such a process of gradual phonetic attrition has occasionally occurred elsewhere in English, producing, for instance, *hussy* from Middle English *houswif* 'housewife'. When this process occurs, the semantic connection with the source phrase is generally lost, and now *hussy* and *housewife, good-bye* and *God be with you,* exist side by side in the language with differing employments.

In time *good-bye* was further shortened simply to *bye,* at which point reduction could scarcely proceed further. To some speakers, indeed, this meager monosyllable seemed in need of fattening, so they produced the reduplication *bye-bye.* But *bye-bye* is again thick enough to shed a little poundage; accordingly you will sometimes hear this uttered as a breezy "b'bye."

[contr. of *God be with you*]

googol Mathematicians have long found it convenient to use scientific notation for large numbers in order to make their calculations less cumbersome. In the 1930s Professor Edward Kasner, an American mathematician, found himself working with numbers as large as 1 followed by a hundred zeros. While it is possible to write this number, using scientific notation, simply as 10^{100}, Dr. Kasner felt that it would be good to have a name for it, thus making it as easy to discuss as to write. According to his own account Dr. Kasner one day asked his nine-year-old nephew Milton Sirotta to give him a name for a number as large as 10^{100} guaranteeing that he would use the word in the future. Milton made up the word *googol,* and since Dr. Kasner kept his promise and used the word it has spread and been widely adopted by mathematicians. Dr. Kasner relates that his nephew went even further and provided him with a name for an unimaginably larger number, 1 followed by a googol of zeros or $10^{10^{100}}$. This number Milton called a *googolplex,* adding to his first creation the ending *-plex* as it is used in words like *duplex.* For another fanciful scientific name see QUARK.

[coined by Milton Sirotta *b ab*1929 nephew of Edward Kasner †1955 Am. mathematician]

goon   In the late twenties a journalist named Elzie C. Segar began drawing a comic strip called *Thimble Theater,* known to many of us today as *Popeye.* In this strip Segar created a character with a hulking body, enormous hands, a bald head but hairy shins and forearms, and a nose much like that of the Second World War's omnipresent Kilroy. He called his character Alice the *Goon,* and despite her subhuman appearance she was essentially goodhearted. As a word, *goon* gained wide currency and took on a darker color of meaning during the labor troubles of the late thirties when thugs hired to terrorize workers were called *goons.*

However, it would appear that Segar did not create the word *goon* itself. In December 1921, before Alice had ever appeared in *Thimble Theater,* Frederick Lewis Allen published an article in *Harper's* magazine titled "The Goon and His Style." In this article Allen writes, "A goon is a person with a heavy touch as distinguished from a jigger, who has a light touch. While jiggers look on life with a genial eye, goons take a more stolid and literal view. It is reported that George Washington was a goon, whereas Lincoln was a jigger." Thus an earlier source than Alice must be found for *goon,* and the likeliest possibility is that it is a shortened form of the dialect word *gooney,* 'a simpleton', a word of which one variant spelling (*gony*) is recorded in English as far back as the sixteenth century. Long ago sailors applied this word as an epithet to the albatross, and the name has stuck. See also JEEP.

[prob. short for E dial. *gooney* simpleton, var. of *gony, gawney*]

gorge   See GORGEOUS.
[ME, fr. MF, fr. LL *gurga,* alter. of *gurges,* fr. L, whirlpool; akin to OHG *querka* throat, ON *kverk* throat, Skt *gargara* whirlpool, L *vorare* to devour]

gorgeous   It is not hard to see why *gurges,* the Latin word for 'whirlpool', should have come in Late Latin (about the third century A.D.) to mean 'throat' as well. Similarity of form, function, or operation often leads the speakers of a language to transfer in informal situations the name of an object to a part of the body, as when we say "down the hatch!" or go on a diet to take off a "pot" or tell someone to shut his "trap." To speakers of Late Latin the notions of downward passage and voraciousness must have suggested the aptness of the transfer. *Gurges,* altered to *gurga,* eventually became Middle French *gorge,* which in turn came into English in the late fourteenth century, later developing such familiar meanings as 'a ravine with steep, rocky walls', by metaphorical extension from the original 'throat'. In Middle French, meanwhile, a new word, *gorgias,* had been derived from *gorge* as the name for an article of clothing. In the late Middle Ages, a standard article of feminine dress was the wimple, a cloth headdress that surrounded the neck and head, leaving only the face uncovered. The *gorgias* was, strictly speaking, the part of this garment that covered throat and shoulders (hence its derivation from *gorge*), but the word was also applied to the whole headdress. An elegant and elaborate *gorgias* was apparently so much the mark of a well-to-do and fashionable lady that *gorgias* became an adjective meaning 'elegant' or 'fond of dress'. The adjective passed into Middle English in the form *gorgayse,* which was reinterpreted after it had become thoroughly anglicized and was altered to fit the pattern of English adjectives in *-ous.*

[alter. (influenced by *-ous*) of ME *gorgayse,* fr. MF *gorgias* elegant, fond of dress, prob. fr. *gorgias* wimple, fr. *gorge* throat]

gorilla   In the days before modern technology had contracted our world into a "global village," men depended upon the reports of travelers for news of strange and wonderful things to be encountered in distant lands. Desdemona hung on Othello's words as he told her of "the Cannibals that each other eat,/ The Anthropophagi, and men whose heads/ Do grow beneath their shoulders." The Carthaginian navigator Hanno was such a man as Othello. He made a voyage along the west coast of Africa in the fifth or sixth century B.C., and an account of his journey was inscribed in Punic on stone tablets which have since disappeared. However, a Greek translation of this account has survived, and in it we find mention of an island on which the explorer saw what he described as a tribe of hairy women. According to the Greek translators, Hanno's interpreters on the expedition called these creatures *Gorillai.* Whether the travelers actually saw a species of anthropoid ape or something else we will never know, but when the *gorilla* of western equatorial Africa was discovered in 1847, Dr. T. S. Savage, an American missionary, suggested the scientific name *Troglodytes gorilla* for this new animal. Dr. Savage's name has been superseded by the binomial designation *Gorilla gorilla,* and the popular name has become simply *gorilla.* (See also ORANGUTAN.)

Though often pronounced like *gorilla,* the word *guerrilla* is not otherwise related; in Spanish *guerrilla* is a diminutive of *guerra,* 'war', and so means 'a small war' or 'a band of men who fight in such a war'. Since it entered English during the time of the Napoleonic wars in Spain, however, it has most often been applied to an individual engaging in irregular warfare rather than a band of men or the war itself, or used attributively in expressions like "guerrilla warfare."

[NL (specific epithet of *Troglodytes gorilla,* former binomial designation for the gorilla), fr. Gk *Gorillai,* believed to be the name of an alleged African tribe of hairy women]

gosh   See JEEPERS.
[euphemism for *God*]

gossamer   In late autumn when the year is moving along in an orderly manner toward winter, the weather often turns quite suddenly, but temporarily, around. In America a warm spell late in the year is usually called *Indian summer.* The American term is now common in England, but older names like *Saint Martin's summer* (Saint Martin's Day is November 11) and *Saint Luke's summer* (Saint Luke's Day is October 8) are still current there. It is likely that England once had still another word for this season: *gossomer* (Middle English *gos,* 'goose', and *somer,* 'summer').

Much writing of the Middle English period has not survived the passage of the centuries, and it happens that in what we do have the word *gossomer* is not attested in that sense. But we have a clue from German, where we find similar words. The German *Gänsemonat,* 'goose-month', was November, when the geese were at their best for eating. Two other German words for Indian summer, *Altweibsommer,* 'Old Wives' summer' (*Old Wives' summer* is also occasionally used for Indian summer in English), and *Mädchensommer,* 'Maidens' summer', are also names used, as Middle English *gossomer* was, for the cobweb film that floats in the warm autumn air. This cobweb film is also known by the dialectal term *summer-goose* in northern England. This is apparently an inversion based on the likeness (admittedly slight) of a downy cobweb to a goose's down.

[ME *gossomer* (prob. also 'Indian summer', the period when geese were eaten extensively), prob. fr. *gos, goos* goose + *somer* summer; fr. its prevalence at this season of the year]

gossip   In Old English *sibb* occurs as a noun meaning 'kinship' and as an adjective meaning 'related by blood or kinship'. A modern descendant of *sibb* is *sibling,* 'one of two or more persons who have the same parents'. By the eleventh century a compound had been formed from the noun *sibb* prefixed by *god,* the ancestor of Modern English *god.* A *godsibb,* therefore, was a person spiritually related to another, specifically by being a sponsor at baptism. Today we would call such a person a *godmother* or *godfather,* using *god* in the same way.

By the fourteenth century the *d* had begun to disappear in both pronunciation and spelling, and *godsibb* developed into *gossib* and then *gossip,* the form which is used today. The meaning, too, had begun to change, and the sense of *gossip* as a close friend or comrade developed alongside the sense of a godparent. Chaucer's Wife of Bath tells her fellow-pilgrims on the road to Canterbury of having once gone walking with a lover and "my gossib dame Alys." From there it was only a short step to the *gossip* of today, a person no longer necessarily friend, relative, or sponsor, but someone filled with irresistible tidbits of rumor.

[ME *godsib, gossib,* fr. OE *godsibb,* fr. *god* + *sibb* kinsman, fr. *sibb,* adj., related]

Gotham   See KNICKERBOCKER.
[fr. *Gotham,* a proverbial town in England noted for the folly of its inhabitants, fr. ME]

grammar   See GLAMOUR.
[ME *gramere, gramer, grammer,* fr. MF *gramaire,* modif. of L *grammatica,* fr. Gk *grammatikē,* fr. fem. of *grammatikos* skilled in grammar, fr. *grammat-, gramma* letter, piece of writing + *-ikos* -ic]

Grammy   See OSCAR.

Grand Guignol   Horror shows featuring sadistic murders may be thought of by some as a film style unique to the 1980s, but the genre is much older. For more than 60 years, dating from the turn of the century, the Theatre du Grand Guignol in Paris presented a series of one-act plays dealing largely with murder, mayhem, and molestation to twentieth-century audiences. It has been reported that there was a fair amount of swooning in the audience with more men than women fainting at the sight of the killings staged in gruesome detail. The theater was a major attraction in Paris and came to be considered one of Paris's main features. An article in *Time* magazine in 1950 talks of a famous painter in Paris being "as much an institution as the Eiffel Tower or the Grand Guignol."

In French, *guignol* refers to a puppet, named after a well-known character of the same name. Differing accounts have been given of where the puppet Guignol character got his name: he may have been named after an eccentric town character of Lyons, France, or, more likely, the verb *guigner,* meaning 'to give a sidelong glance'. In any event, in 1795 Lyons saw the establishment of the Guignol puppet theater. Short-nosed and round-eyed, the puppet Guignol wore the traditional garb of the French peasant—and an expression of perpetual surprise. A character of mercurial temperament, Guignol was quick to anger but equally quick to forgive his wife, Madelan, and to help his drinking companion, Gnafron. Guignol was endowed with the regional dialect and mannerisms of Lyons, but he proved to have an appeal for people all over France. Eventually he became France's most prominent puppet character. Part of his appeal undoubtedly stemmed from the stylized violence of the performances that bore some resemblance to the Punch and Judy shows of England. The association of Guignol with violence led at the turn of the century to the naming of a small theater on the Rue Chaptal in Montmartre, Paris, Le Grand Guignol. Just as the Guignol puppet theater presented shows incorporating violence for children, Le Grand Guignol presented similar shows for adults, featuring flesh-and-blood "puppets." Scaring people turned out to be quite profitable, and in a few years the theater had a regular clientele, including at one time members of several European royal families. Within a decade or so of the theater's founding, the term *Grand Guignol* had appeared in English and become synonymous with sensationally horrific entertainment and gratuitous violence:

> The play lacks a moral center, and since the dramatist penetrates but shallowly into the guiding motives of the actors, the effect seldom rises above poetic Grand-Guignol —*Times Literary Supp.*, 24 Aug. 1951

[fr. *Le Grand Guignol,* a small theater in Montmartre, Paris, specializing in short plays full of sensationalism and horror]

gray eminence   See ÉMINENCE GRISE.
[trans. of F *éminence grise*]

gregarious   See EGREGIOUS.
[L *gregarius* of or relating to a herd or flock, fr. *greg-, grex* herd, flock + *-arius* -ary; akin to OIr *graig* herd of horses, Gk *ageirein* to collect, *agora* assembly, Lith *gurgulỹs* thickening]

grid   See GRIDIRON.
[back-formation fr. *gridiron*]

griddle   See GRIDIRON.
[ME *gredil, gridel,* fr. ONF *gredil,* fr. LL *craticulum* fine wickerwork]

gridiron   In 1882 Walter Camp, often considered to be the father of modern American football, introduced into the game a rule requiring a gain of five yards in three downs or the surrender of the ball to the opponents. To facilitate enforcement of this rule the field was marked with horizontal white lines at five-yard intervals, and soon thereafter the descriptive term *gridiron* was widely used for a football field. *Gridiron* spread rapidly, even to Great Britain, where in December 1896 the *Daily News* observed, "The ground here is marked out by white lines . . . thus giving it the appearance of a gigantic gridiron—which, indeed, is the technical name applied to an American football field." Whether or not we would consider *gridiron* a "technical name," we can easily see why the term caught on, for the visual effect is very similar to that of a grate or griddle used for broiling food.

Yet the story is not complete, for *gridiron* is not a compound of *grid* plus *iron*. The Middle English forms *gredire* and *gridirne* developed from Middle English *gredil, gridel* (modern *griddle*), though it is not clear whether this replacement of an *l* by an *r* sound was a normal phonetic development or purely the result of folk etymology. It is probable in any case that the similarity of the ending of the Middle English form to Middle English *ire, iren,* 'iron', greatly encouraged the process of folk etymology. The word *griddle* is ultimately derived from the Late Latin *craticulum,* meaning 'fine wickerwork'. That the folk etymology of *gridiron* was widely accepted is evidenced by the fact that in the early nineteenth century the *-iron* was dropped to form the word *grid*. For other folk etymologies see FOLK ETYMOLOGY.

[ME *gredire,* prob. by folk etymology (influence of *ire, iren* iron) fr. *gredil, gridel*]

gringo The Medieval Latin proverb, "Graecum est; non potest legi" (It is Greek; it cannot be read), is the ancestor of the popular "It's Greek to me." In Spanish, *hablar en griego* (literally 'to talk in Greek') is to speak unintelligibly. *Griego,* slightly altered, became *gringo.* According to the *Diccionario Castellano* of P. Esteban de Terreros y Pando, published in 1787, *"Gringos,* llaman en Malaga a los estranjeros, que tienen cierta especie de acento, que los priva de una locucion facil y natural Castellana; y en Madrid dan el mismo, y por la misma causa con particularidad a los Irlandeses." (In Malaga, they call *Gringos* those foreigners who have a certain type of accent which keeps them from speaking Spanish easily and naturally; and in Madrid they give the same name, and for the same reason, particularly to the Irish.)

Gringo made its way into English because Mexicans sixty years later used it freely to refer to Anglo-Americans. The first English record of *gringo* is an entry in the diary of artist John James Audubon's son. J. W. Audubon's *Western Journal* for 1849 complains: "We were hooted and shouted at as we passed through, and called *'Gringoes'."*

A very popular explanation of the origin of *gringo* claims that during the Mexican War (1846–1848) Robert Burns's "Green Grow the Rashes, O!" was a favorite song of the American soldiers and that "Greengrow" became the Mexicans' *gringo.* The much earlier use of *gringo* in Spain disproves this theory.

[Sp, alter. of *griego* Greek, unknown language, stranger, fr. L *Graecus* Greek, fr. Gk *Graikos*]

gris-gris See FETISH.

[F *gris-gris,* of African origin; akin to Balante *grigri* charm, amulet]

grog The eighteenth-century English admiral Edward Vernon is reputed to have been in the habit of wearing a grogram cloak and to have won, for this peculiarity, the nickname "Old Grog" among the sailors under his command. The Royal Navy in the West Indies had been given by custom a daily ration of rum, but in 1740 Vernon, alarmed at damage to the physical and moral health of his men, ordered that the rum should be diluted with water. This mixture, not immediately approved, was christened *grog,* after its godfather. *Grog* eventually gained in popularity, however, and its name came sometimes to be used as a general term for any liquor, even undiluted. A drunkard could be called *groggy,* and now anyone, however sober, who acts drunk or shaky on his feet is *groggy.* See also DERBY

[fr. *Old Grog,* nickname of Edward Vernon †1757 Eng. admiral who ordered the sailors' rum to be diluted; *Grog* short for *grogram;* fr. his habit of wearing a grogram cloak in bad weather]

grotesque During the Italian Renaissance, Romans of culture took a great interest in their country's past. The remaining buildings of the ancient city of Rome were heavily excavated, exposing chambers that became known, familiarly, as *grotte*, 'caves'. The walls of many a *grotta* were covered with exotic paintings, *pitture grottesche*, and *grottesca* became the name for a later but similar type of painting representing fantastic combinations of human and animal forms interwoven with strange fruits and flowers. The Italian word soon worked its way into French and English. An inventory made in 1561 of the Scottish royal wardrobes and jewel houses included "Item, twa paintit broddis [boards] the ane of the muses and the uther of crotesque or conceptis." (The form with initial *c* is from the French.) The adjective *grotesque*, first applied only to decorative art of this kind, is now used to describe anything fanciful or bizarre. *The Gentleman's Magazine* in 1747 assured its readers that "a woman with her head peeping out of a sack, could hardly . . . make a more Grotesque figure." See also ANTIC.

[MF & OIt; MF *grotesque, crotesque*, fr. OIt *grottesca*, fr. (*pittura*) *grottesca*, lit., cave painting, ancient painting found in the ruins of Rome; *grottesca*, fem. of *grottesco*, adj., fr. *grotta* cave, fr L *crypta* vault, cavern]

grunt See PIGEON.
[so called fr. the noise it makes when taken from the water]

guerrilla See GORILLA.
[Sp, lit., small war, dim. of *guerra* war, fr OHG *werra* discord, strife, quarrel]

guillotine While to modern minds the guillotine appears to be a particularly gruesome machine of death, it was hardly thought so by its early proponents. In fact, the guillotine was the product of humanitarian and egalitarian intentions. The invention of the guillotine was necessitated by the French Revolution, during which period the frequency and number of executions called for new technology. Up to that time there were two methods of capital punishment. For the common criminal of the riffraff variety, there was hanging. For errant nobility, there was the privilege of decapitation, usually by a broadax. In actual practice, however, decapitation often proved to be a messy affair; nervous hands and sloppy technique often required more than one blow, thereby protracting the procedure and the agony of the victim. It was thus proposed that decapitation could most efficiently and humanely be performed by a machine. The proposer was Joseph Ignace Guillotin (1738–1814), a French physician and deputy to the Constituent Assembly in 1789.

Contrary to legend, the machine was not invented by Guillotin himself but by a German mechanic named Tobias Schmidt under the direction of French surgeon Dr. Antoine Louis. After several satisfactory experiments with corpses at a hospital, the new technology premiered—with admirable success—on 25 April 1792 for the expeditious dispatch of a notorious highwayman named Pelletier. The egalitarian spirit brought on by the French Revolution demanded an end to the old two-tier system of execution, and so the guillotine became a right to be enjoyed by all. The machine was initially identified with Dr. Louis and was called a Louison or Louisette, but quickly it became associated with its republican advocate, Guillotin. *Guillotine,* probably from "la guillotine" or "Madame Guillotine," had made its way into English by 1793, which was, coincidentally, the year in which Louis XVI and Marie Antoinette lost their heads. Also contrary to legend, Dr. Guillotin never fell victim to the guillotine but died a natural death—his head still attached. See also DERRICK.

[F, after Joseph Ignace *Guillotin* †1814 Fr. physician who in 1789 proposed its use]

guinea fowl See TURKEY.
[*guinea,* fr. *Guinea,* region in West Africa]

gun Early Scandinavian mythology celebrated the warlike virtues. Women as well as men of Norse legend were often brilliant warriors. Likewise many proper names of Old Norse women were borrowed from the battlefield. One of these, *Gunnhildr,* is a compound of *gunnr* and *hildr,* both words meaning 'battle'. The Scandinavian element had been increasingly prominent in the language and life of England since the raids and the settlement began in the ninth century. One reflection of this importance is that the English of the Middle Ages sometimes gave their daughters these old Scandinavian names. At the same time men of that era often named their weapons and other inanimate objects which were considered as belonging exclusively to men's domain with feminine names, just as modern men often name their cars or boats.

One ballista (a large missile-thrower rather like a crossbow) which defended Windsor Castle early in the fourteenth century was named in Latin *Domina Gunilda,* 'Lady Gunilda'. The same name may have been given to engines of war by the early Norsemen who knew its etymological significance. Or its use by the English may simply have been a fortunate coincidence. At any rate, the use of this particular name for the Windsor ballista was not an isolated instance. *Gonnylde* was the name of a cannon in an early fourteenth-century song. The word *gun,* which we also trace back to the fourteenth century, is probably a shortening of *Gunnilda.*

Gun as a slang term for a thief may come from Yiddish *ganef,* altered by folk etymology under the influence of the more familiar *gun.* A *gun moll* is usually a gangster's girl friend, but the original *gun molls* were female thieves, who owed their name to the Yiddish-descended *gun.* For other examples of folk etymology see FOLK ETYMOLOGY.

[ME *gonne, gunne,* prob. irreg. fr. *Gonnilda, Gunnilda, Gunilda,* fem. proper name (sometimes applied to an engine of war), fr. ON *Gunnhildr,* fem. proper name]

[prob. by folk etymology fr. *ganef* thief, rascal, fr. Yiddish *ganef, gannef,* fr. Heb *gannābh* thief]

gung ho The Chinese Industrial Cooperatives Society, whose Chinese name was *chung¹-kuo² kung¹-yeh⁴ ho²-tso⁴ she⁴,* was founded in 1938. Its long name was very soon abbreviated to *kung¹-ho²*. In 1942 Lt. Col. Evans Fordyce Carlson of the United States Marine Corps was in China organizing the Second Raider Battalion. Carlson, a fervent admirer of the ardent spirit of the Chinese Communists, used their example in trying to instill a sense of unity and purpose in his men. He explained to them that *Gung ho* was the motto of the Chinese cooperatives and that it meant 'work together'. In fact, although *kung¹* may be translated 'work' and *ho²* 'together', the two do not combine in Chinese to form a phrase 'work together', but are only the shortened form of an unwieldy name. But the misinterpreted motto caught on with the Second Raider Battalion. Soon they were proudly calling themselves and their spirit *gung ho*. Other marines began using *gung ho* to describe the raiders of this battalion, not as unified and hardworking, but as obnoxious; for many marines *gung ho* became a general disparaging adjective. The positive and negative seem to have reached a compromise as the word came into general, nonmilitary use. A person who is *gung ho* now is 'extremely or overly enthusiastic'.

[*Gung ho!*, motto (interpreted as meaning "work together") of certain U.S. marine raiders in World War II, fr. Chin (Pek) *kung¹-ho²*, short for *chung¹-kuo² kung¹-yeh⁴ ho²-tso⁴ she⁴* Chinese Industrial Cooperatives Society]

gunny See BANDANNA.
[Hindi *ganī, goṇī,* fr. Skt *goṇī* sack]

guy On 4 November 1605 in London, Guy Fawkes was arrested and later executed for having planted some twenty barrels of gunpowder in the cellars of the Houses of Parliament as his part in a conspiracy to blow up the Parliament buildings on the following day. The failure of this conspiracy, now known as the Gunpowder Plot, is still celebrated in England on 5 November, Guy Fawkes Day. On this day bonfires are lit and fireworks displayed, and on the bonfires are burned effigies of Guy Fawkes made from old tattered clothes stuffed with straw or rags. As early as 1806 these effigies had come to be called *guys*. On the days before 5 November children in England can still be seen in the streets with their *guys* asking passersby to give "a penny for the guy" in order to buy fireworks. The use of this word was extended to other similar effigies and then to a person of grotesque appearance or dress. In the United States by the middle of the nineteenth century *guy* had been generalized to mean simply 'man' or 'fellow' and its pejorative connotations were lost.

[after *Guy* Fawkes †1606 Eng. conspirator]

gymnasium The ancient Greeks placed a high value on both physical and mental fitness. Each important city in Greece had a public area set aside in which young men would gather to exercise, compete in sports, and receive training in philosophy, music, and literature. Living in a warm climate and not wanting to be encumbered in their activities by unnecessary clothing, the Greeks would typically do their exercising in the nude. The name given to the exercise area was therefore *gymnasion*, literally 'school for naked exercise', from the verb *gymnazein*, 'to exercise naked', a derivative of the adjective *gymnos*, 'naked'. The Greek *gymnasion* became the Latin *gymnasium*, which was used in two distinct senses to mean both 'an exercise ground' and 'a public school'. *Gymnasium* was first used in English at the end of the sixteenth century. As an English word, now often shortened to *gym*, it has entirely lost its original connotations of nakedness. Its principal use is to denote a large room with special equipment for various athletic activities (such as *gymnastics*, from the Greek *gymnastes*, 'trainer in a gymnasium') or for playing indoor sports (such as basketball or volleyball).

The English *gymnasium* has also lost the scholarly connotations of its Greek and Latin sources; very little training in philosophy, music, and literature is likely to occur in the typical American gym. In German-speaking countries, however, the 'school' sense of the Latin word has been kept alive through the use of *gymnasium* to mean 'a secondary school preparing students for the university'.

[L, gymnastic school, school, fr. Gk *gymnasion*, fr. *gymnazein* to train naked, exercise, fr. *gymnos* naked]

gymnastics See GYMNASIUM.
[pl. of *gymnastic* physical exercise, fr. MF *gymnastique*, fr. Gk *gymnastikē*, fr. fem. of *gymnastikos*, adj., fr. (assumed) *gymnastos* (verbal of *gymnazein* to train naked) + *-ikos* -ic]

Gypsy *or* **Gipsy** In the early years of the sixteenth century there began to appear in Britain some members of a wandering race of people who were ultimately of Hindu origin and who called themselves and their language *Romany*. In Britain, however, it was popularly believed that they came from Egypt, and thus they were called *Egipcyans*. This soon became shortened to *Gipcyan*, and by the year 1600 the further altered form *Gipsy, Gypsey* began to appear in print. The earliest known example is in Shakespeare's *As You Like It*, where two pages undertake to sing a ditty "both in a tune, like two gipsies on a horse."

In France it was thought that these same people came from *Bohemia* and thus they were called *Bohèmes*. This was translated into English as *Bohemian* and was originally used synonymously with *Gypsy*. In Sir Walter Scott's novel *Quentin Durward* (1823) one of the Gypsy characters says, "I am a Zingaro, a Bohemian, an Egyptian, or whatever the Europeans . . . may choose to call me; but I have no country." The extended sense of *bohemian*, 'a person living an unconventional life', was first introduced into literature in William Thackeray's *Vanity Fair* (1848): "She was of a wild, roving nature, inherited from father and mother, who were both Bohemians, by taste and circumstance."

[by shortening and alter. fr. *Egyptian*, earlier *Egipcien, Egipcian*, fr. MF *egipcien*]

H

hackney See CAB.

[ME *hakeney, hakenai,* prob. fr. *Hakeneye* Hackney, formerly a town, now a metropolitan borough of London, England]

haggard See FALCON.

[MF *hagard*]

halcyon According to Greek mythology, Alkyone, the daughter of Aeolus, god of the winds, was so distraught on learning that her husband had been killed in a shipwreck that she threw herself into the sea and was changed into a kingfisher. So this bird was called *alkyōn* or *halkyōn* by the Greeks. Legend had it that the bird built a floating nest on the sea about the time of the winter solstice in December. It charmed the wind and the waves so that for about a two-week period, while its eggs were incubating, the sea remained calm; hence the expression *halcyon days (alkyonides hēmerai),* used to describe a period of peace or prosperity. The Romans borrowed the Greek word as *halcyon* or *alcyon,* and eventually the word found its way into fourteenth-century English as a name for a species of kingfisher. By the sixteenth century, *halcyon* began to be used as an adjective for 'calm, peaceful, tranquil'. For another bird associated with a legend see BARNACLE.

[ME *alceon, alicion,* fr. L *halcyon, alcyon,* fr. Gk *halkyōn, alkyōn*]

halibut A Middle English term for a flatfish was *butte,* which still survives in the form *butt,* designating any of a number of flatfish including flounder and *halibut.* Because fish was frequently eaten on holy days and days of abstinence, *butte* was compounded with *haly,* a form of *holy,* thus giving Middle English *halybutte,* which became our modern *halibut.* Other languages have formed similar compounds: modern Dutch has *heilbot* and Low German *heilbutt* and *heilige butt,* all analogous to *halibut.* Norse has *heilag-fiski,* 'holy fish', while Swedish *helgeflundra* and Danish *helleflynder* both literally mean 'holy flounder'.

[ME *halybutte,* fr. *haly, holy* holy + *butte* flatfish, fr. its being eaten on holy days]

hamburger Why isn't there any ham in a *hamburger?* The source of the word provides the answer. The word itself has nothing to do with a type of meat. It comes from the name of the German city Hamburg, where what was originally called "Hamburg steak" originated. It was actually ground beef. In the 1850s, German immigrants brought the product and the term to the United States, where in a matter of a few decades Hamburg steak came to be considered an archetypal American food. By 1889, *Hamburg steak* was being replaced by *hamburger steak*, which by 1908 was being shortened to *hamburger*. In the 1930s, the term *hamburger* was beginning to be used for the sandwich as well as for the meat. Since the early 1950s, the shortened spelling *hamburg*, for both senses of *hamburger*, has been found in the Northeast, especially in New England. (Such clipping is also evident when *frankfurt*, and also *frank*, is used for *frankfurter*.)

While the hamburger has achieved a significant place in the American diet, the word itself has achieved prominence in the American vocabulary. It has given the language a new combining form, *-burger*, which has resulted in such compounds as *cheeseburger, porkburger, baconburger, nutburger*, and *mooseburger*, among many others. By about 1945, *burger* itself was being used as a familiar shortening of *hamburger*.

Another German import, *frankfurter*, ought to be mentioned here because, like *hamburger*, it derives from the name of its city of origin, Frankfurt am Main, where it was often served at beer gardens. The same linguistic process resulted in the English word *wiener*, which is a shortening of *wienerwurst*. The first element is derived from *Wien*, the German name for the city of Vienna, where the sausage originated.

[G *Hamburger* of Hamburg, fr. *Hamburg*, Germany]

handicap   "Here some of us fell to handicap, a sport that I never knew before, which was very good," Samuel Pepys reported to his diary on 18 September 1660. *Handicap*, from *hand in cap*, was an old form of barter. Two men who wished to make an exchange asked a third to act as umpire. All three put forfeit money in a hat or cap, into which each of the two barterers inserted a hand. The umpire described the goods to be traded and set the additional amount the owner of the inferior article should pay the other in order that the exchange might be equitable. The barterers withdrew their hands from the hat empty to signify refusal of the umpire's decision, or full to indicate acceptance. If both hands were full, the exchange was made and the umpire pocketed the forfeit money; if both were empty, the umpire took the forfeit but there was no exchange. Otherwise, each barterer kept his own property, and the one who had accepted the umpire's decision took the forfeit money as well.

A similar exchange was described by William Langland in *Piers Plowman* late in the fourteenth century. Hikke the hostler traded his hood for the cloak of Clement the cobbler. Robyn the ropemaker, as umpire, declared Hikke's additional obligation to Clement to be a cup of ale. Had either refused, he would have forfeited a gallon of ale.

As early as the late seventeenth century, there was in England a kind of horse race arranged in accordance with the rules of handicap. For this *handicap match* or *handicap race* (the name is not recorded before the mid-eighteenth century) the umpire determined the additional weight that the better horse should carry. Handicap horse races are still run today in this same manner. In time the term was extended to other contests, and *handicap* came to signify the advantage or disadvantage imposed.

[fr. obs. E, a game of forfeits and exchange in which the players held forfeit money in a cap, alter. of *hand in cap*]

handlebar mustache   See SIDEBURNS.

hangnail   *Hangnail* is derived by folk etymology from *agnail* or *angnail*, 'a sore or inflammation around a fingernail or toenail'. The earliest sense of *agnail* is not what we now call a hangnail; in the Old English form *angnægl* it was used as early as the tenth century to mean 'a corn on the foot'. The second element of the word, -*nail*, did not originally refer to the toenail or fingernail, but rather it meant an iron nail or something like it. Thus, in *agnail* a hard corn was likened to the head of a nail. The first element, *ag-* or *ang-*, is related to Old English *ange*, meaning 'painful'.

In the sixteenth century *agnail* began to be used as a term for a variety of ailments of the fingers or toes, and this usage led to the belief that the -*nail* of *agnail* meant 'toenail' or 'fingernail'. By then, however, the adjective *ange* was obsolete, and the first element of *agnail* was not readily interpretable. So the compound was re-formed to make sense to ordinary speakers of the language. By the last quarter of the seventeenth century the form *hangnail* had arisen and meant specifically 'a bit of skin hanging loose at the back or side of a fingernail'. For other folk etymologies see FOLK ETYMOLOGY.

[by folk etymology fr. *agnail, angnail*, fr. OE *angnægl* corn, fr. *ang-* (akin to *ange, enge* narrow, painful) + *nægl* nail (of iron)]

hansom   See CAB.
[after Joseph Aloysius *Hansom* †1882 Eng. architect who designed such a vehicle]

harass   We have all felt *harassed* at some time or other, and at such times it may seem that we are being hounded unmercifully by those who oppose us. In a strictly etymological sense this may be true. The French *harasser*, from which *harass* is derived and which has the same range of meanings as its English counterpart, is derived from the Middle French *harer*, meaning 'to set a dog on'. This verb is derived from Old French *hare*, a cry used to encourage hunting dogs during the chase. Though *hare* is of Germanic origin, akin to Old High German *hara, hera*, 'hither', and *hiar*, 'here', its specific source is not known.

[F *harasser*, fr. MF, fr. *harer* to set a dog on, fr. OF *hare*, interj. used to incite dogs, of Gmc origin; akin to OHG *hara, hera* hither, *hiar* here]

harbinger   The modern *harbinger* is simply a forerunner, like the inaus-

picious amphibian of Washington Irving's *Sketch Book:* "The boding cry
of the tree-toad; that harbinger of storm." The duties of an earlier harbinger were more clearly defined. In late medieval and early modern times
he was the person sent before an army, a royal progress, or the like, whose
job was to find lodgings for the whole company. Earlier the spelling was
herbergere, and the first English *herbergeres,* as early as the twelfth century, were the hosts themselves, the actual providers of lodgings. The Old
French word from which the English was borrowed was itself derived
from an early Germanic loanword. Old French *herberge* took from its Germanic ancestor both the literal meaning, 'army encampment', and the figurative extension, 'hostelry'. Modern English *harbor* is another
descendant of the same word, having the meaning of 'a place of comfort
or refuge' before developing the sense of 'a sheltered place providing an-
chorage for ships'.

The intrusive *n* which made *herbengar* of *herbergere* entered a number
of English words in late Middle English, especially before *-ger.* This accounts for such modern pairs as *messenger-message, passenger-passage,
scavenger-scavage,* and *porringer-porridge.* The same *n* appears in *popinjay.* See also POPINJAY, SCAVENGER.

[ME *herbergere, herbergeour, herbengar,* fr. OF *herbergere, herbergeor*
one that makes camp, one that provides lodgings, host, fr. *herberge* army
encampment, hostelry, of Gmc origin; akin to OHG *heriberga* army encampment, hostelry]

harbor   See HARBINGER.
[ME *herberge, herberwe, herber, harborowe;* akin to OHG & OS *heriberga* army encampment, hostelry, MLG *herberge* hostelry, ON *herbergi;*
all fr. a prehistoric WGmc-NGmc compound whose components are
akin respectively to OHG *heri* army and to OHG *bergan* to shelter,
hide]

harlequin   See ZANY.
[alter. (influenced by obs. F *harlequin,* fr. MF, fr. OIt *arlecchino*) of earlier *harlicken,* modif. of OIt *arlecchino;* fr. MF *Helquin, Hannequin, Hen-
nequin,* leader of a troop of malevolent spirits popularly believed to fly
through the air at night, fr. OF *Hellequin, Hielekin, Hierlekin,* prob. fr.
(assumed) *Herle king* (whence ML *Herla rex*) King Herle, mythical figure who may orig. have been identical with Woden, chief god of the
Germanic peoples]

harvest   See AUTUMN.
[ME *hervest* autumn, fr. OE *hærfest;* akin to OHG *herbist* autumn, ON
haust autumn, L *carpere* to gather, pluck, Gk *karpos* fruit, Skt *kṛpāṇa*
sword, Gk *keirein* to cut]

hashish   See ASSASSIN.
[Ar *ḥashīsh* dry herbage, hashish]

hazard   *Hazard* was once only a game played with dice. The French archbishop William of Tyre, writing his Latin history of the Crusades late in the twelfth century, explained the origin of this *hazard* and its name (*hasard* in Middle French). The game was invented, he said, to pass the time during the siege of a castle in Palestine called *Hazard* or *Azart.* Unfortunately for the credibility of this theory, the name of the castle seems really to have been *'Ain Zarba,* and the name of the game was certainly never that. The French word did originate in the time of the Crusades, however, and most likely comes from the post-classical Arabic *az-zahr,* 'the die' ('one of the dice'). *Hazard* was borrowed by the medieval English, and within a few centuries what had been a venture on the outcome of a throw of the dice could be any venture or any risk. Now 'chance' or 'venture' and 'risk' or 'peril' are the primary meanings of *hazard.* The game of *hazard* is played infrequently now, and the modern player probably assumes that the game is so called because of the chances taken in play.

[ME *hasard, hazard,* fr. MF *hasard,* fr. Ar *az-zahr* the die]

hearse   In Middle French the word *herce,* meaning 'harrow', was applied to a triangular frame that was used for holding a number of candles and was similar to the ancient form of a harrow. Both the literal and extended senses were used in Middle English when the word was borrowed. It was a widespread practice to erect an elaborate temporary or permanent framework over the coffin or tomb of a distinguished person. Such frameworks were often decorated with lighted candles, and thus the term *herse* (or *hearse* in modern orthography) was applied to them. A series of extensions subsequently led to the application of *hearse* to a bier and then to a vehicle for conveying the dead to the grave, this last the most familiar sense of *hearse* today.

An etymologically related word, *rehearse,* comes from the Middle French *rehercier,* meaning 'to repeat'. The likely original meaning of the French verb is 'to harrow again'. Thus when we *rehearse* something we cover the same ground we went over before, and, as in harrowing a field, we continue to do so until all the lumps and clods have been smoothed out.

[ME *herse,* fr. MF *herce* harrow, frame for holding candles, fr. L *hirpic-, hirpex* harrow, prob. of Oscan origin; prob. akin to Oscan *hirpus* wolf, L *hircus* he-goat]

heaume   See TARGET.
  [MF, fr. OF *helme*]

hector   In Homer's account of the Trojan War, Hector stands as the bravest Trojan of them all. He is the son of the Trojan king Priam, the husband of Andromache, and the brother of Paris, whose abduction of the Grecian queen Helen started the ten-year conflict. The foremost fighter among the Trojans, he is presented in Homer's *Iliad* as the ideal warrior: fearless combatant, loving son and husband, steadfast friend. His many exploits during the Trojan War include his combat with Ajax, his storming of the Greek ramparts, and his slaying of Patroclus, the friend of Achilles.

In revenge for the death of Patroclus, Hector is slain by Achilles, the greatest of the Greek warriors, and his body is dragged around the wall of Troy. After the Trojans ransom Hector's body, they find that it has been divinely preserved from corruption and mutilation, and they bury it with the highest honors.

It is not entirely certain how Hector declined from being the symbol of honor and bravery to being a synonym for a braggart and a bully. At least since the fourteenth century the name *Hector* has been used allusively in English for a valiant warrior. The word apparently acquired its pejorative sense in the latter half of the seventeenth century. At that time there appeared on the streets of London rowdy toughs who were known as Hectors. While they may have perceived themselves as gallant young blades, to the general populace they were blustering, swaggering bullies who brandished their swords, intimidated passers-by, and engaged in vandalism. *Hector* quickly acquired the generic sense of any bully or braggart. At the same time *hector* began being used as a verb, acquiring the senses of "to play the bully" and "to intimidate or harass by bluster or personal pressure."

The evolution of *hector* into a synonym for a blustering bully may have been influenced by the tradition of the boastful soldier in comedies since Roman times. Known as the *miles gloriosus,* he is a stock character in Roman comedies. One such example is Thraso in the comedy *Eunuchus* ("The Eunuch") by the Roman playwright Terence. Thraso is a vain, blustering captain whose attempts to gain the sexual favors of a courtesan meet with comedic results. From his name comes the adjective *thrasonical,* which means "boastful."

[after *Hector,* a Trojan warrior in Homer's *Iliad,* fr. L, fr. Gk *Hektōr*]

hedgehog See SWINE.
[ME *hegge hogge,* fr. *hegge* hedge + *hogge* hog]

heliotrope See JERUSALEM ARTICHOKE.
[L *heliotropium,* fr. Gk *hēliotropion,* fr. *hēlio-, hēlios* sun + *tropos* turn; fr. its flowers' turning toward the sun]

helium See XENON.
[NL, fr. Gk *hēlios* sun + NL *-ium,* suffix used to form names of chemical elements]

helm See TARGET.
[ME, fr. OE]

helmet See TARGET.
[MF *helmet, heaumet,* dim. of *helme, heaume* helmet, of Gmc origin; akin to OE & OHG *helm* helmet, ON *hjalmr,* Goth *hilms;* akin to OE *helan* to hide, conceal]

helpmate   Verse 18 of chapter 2 of Genesis in the King James Version of the Bible runs like this:

And the Lord God said, It is not good that the man should be alone; I will make him an help meet for him.

In the passage *meet* is an adjective that means 'suitable', and the help that the Lord God thought meet for Adam turned out to be Eve.

Now it is well known that when something is read aloud, the spaces are not pronounced. So "an help meet for him," as it turned out to be Eve every time it was read, could be interpreted so that *help meet* was one word, with a meaning that described Eve's relationship to Adam—that of wife or companion.

The King James Bible was published in 1611. The transformation from noun followed by adjective to compound noun took more than sixty years to become firmly enough established in the popular mind to be used in print. Its first printed appearance is in John Dryden's comedy *Marriage à la Mode,* published in 1673:

She's sick as aptly for my purpose as if she had contrived it so. Well, if ever woman was a help-meet for man, my spouse is so. . . .

You notice that Dryden's use echoes the Bible. It is generalized in such a way as to suggest that "Woman is a help(-)meet for Man" might well have been the subject of sermons over the years, perhaps not infrequently. Such a possibility is also suggested by the frequent appearance, italicized, of the Biblical phrase and variations on it in John Milton's religious prose works. He also echoes the phrase by turning it around and putting the adjective first: *a meet help.* None of Milton's uses suggests that he thought of *help meet* or *meet help* as a compound noun, however. The transfer to noun status had to occur in the head of the listener, not the preacher.

We can reasonably assume that Dryden's use represents socially acceptable speech. The speaker of the lines, Rhodophil, is half of the male love interest in the play; he is a captain of guards, a courtier, and not some ill-educated country bumpkin. And we can safely assume that the author was familiar with the cultivated speech of his day; he was Poet Laureate at the time he wrote the play.

Helpmate does not appear for almost half a century after Dryden's *help-meet.* We cannot be absolutely sure how it was formed. It may have been an independent formation from *help* and *mate*—some etymologists think so, and for what the fact may be worth, the earliest example of *helpmate* does not echo the Biblical original of *helpmeet.* But the next example does, and this suggests that *helpmate* may have been formed from *helpmeet* by folk etymology—and some etymologists (including ours) believe such is the case. In folk etymology something that is familiar and makes sense—here, *mate*—is substituted for something unfamiliar—and *meet,* once its adjectival use is forgotten, is unfamiliar.

Curiously, neither *helpmeet* nor *helpmate* received recognition as words until almost the middle of the nineteenth century, more than a century and a half after Dryden's original *help-meet* appeared in print. Samuel Johnson did not enter it in his dictionary of 1755. But Johnson based his dictionary on established and elevated literature. Dryden's nondramatic poems, his heroic tragedies, even his prose criticism would have been used by Johnson, but not his stage comedies. Johnson would have thought Restoration comedies too immoral to use.

Neither word was recognized by Henry Todd, who revised and expanded Johnson's dictionary at the end of the eighteenth century, nor were they recognized by Noah Webster in his 1828 unabridged. We do not know why Todd missed them, but we are fairly sure about Noah: he depended heavily on Johnson's second folio of 1755 except for American words.

Both *helpmate* and *helpmeet* are in current use, with *helpmate* the more common word. It is common enough to have led at least one modern editor of Dryden's play to insert it anachronistically. In the seventeenth century *meet-help* and *meet-helper* had some little use in the same sense. Neither survives today.

For other folk etymologies see FOLK ETYMOLOGY.

[by folk etymology (influenced by *mate*) fr. *helpmeet*, fr. *help*, n. + *meet*, adj. (fitting) in *I will make an help meet for him* (Gen 2:18 AV)]

hemp   See CANVAS, CANVASS.

[ME *hemp, hempe*, fr. OE *hænep, henep;* akin to MD *hennep* hemp, OHG *hanaf, hanif*, ON *hampr;* prob. all of non-IE origin; akin to the source of Gk *kannabis* hemp & Arm *kanap*]

heresy   In ancient Greek, the verb *hairein*, meaning 'to take', gave rise to the adjective *hairetos* 'able to choose' and the noun *hairesis* 'the act of choosing'. In time the noun developed the extended senses of 'a choice', 'a course of action', 'a school of thought', and 'a philosophical or religious sect'. Stoicism, for example, was a *hairesis*.

Within Judaism, a *heresy* (our Modern English equivalent and derivative of *hairesis*) was a religious faction, party, or sect, such as the Pharisees or Sadducees. Applied to such groups, *hairesis* was used in a neutral, nonpejorative manner. In fact, when this Greek noun is used in the New Testament, it is usually translated as *sect*. When the prosecutor Tertullus charged St. Paul with being the ringleader of "the sect of the Nazarenes," implying that Christianity was simply another party within Judaism, Paul responded: "But this I confess to thee, that according to the way, which they call a heresy, so do I serve the Father and my God . . ." (Acts 24:14, Douay).

When St. Paul used the term *hairesis* in a Christian context, its meaning was pejorative, designating a splinter group within the Christian community that threatened the unity of the Church. By the end of the second century, *haeresis* (the Latin equivalent) was being applied to an organized body holding a false or sacrilegious doctrine. From this use it took on the sense of 'a body of doctrine substantially differing in some aspect from the doctrine taught by the Church'. In the early centuries of the Church such heresies included Arianism, Donatism, Nestorianism, Manichaeism, Monophysitism, and Pelagianism, among others. Their adherents were often punished by excommunication.

In the twelfth and thirteenth centuries, the Church was vigorously engaged in supressing heresies. This led, in 1231, to Pope Gregory IX's establishing of the Inquisition, an ecclesiastical tribunal for combating heresy. Heretics who refused to recant after being tried by the pope's inquisitor were handed over to civil authorities for punishment.

The Church used the Latin *haeresis* (from the Greek *hairesis*) for 'heresy' and *haereticus* (from the Late Greek *hairetikos*, a derivative of *hairetos* 'able to choose') for 'heretic'. These two words were taken into early French as *heresie/eresie* and *heritique/eritique* and then into English in the thirteenth and fourteenth centuries, respectively, as *heresy* and *heretic*. Their religious senses passed into English as well.

In Chaucer's time the noun began to take on nonecclesiastical use, being applied to any dissenting opinion, belief, or doctrine in any field. In his *The Legend of Good Women* (ca. 1385), Chaucer writes: "That is an heresye ageyns my lawe." At about the same time we also find this noun being used for 'a school of thought, a sect', echoing the ancient Greek use of *hairesis*.

[ME *eresie, heresie,* fr. OF, fr. LL *haeresis,* fr. LGk *hairesis,* fr. Gk, action of taking, choice, sect, fr. *hairein* to take + *-sis;* perh. akin to Gk *hormē* assault, attack]

heretic   See HERESY.
[ME *eretik, heretik,* fr. MF *eretique, heretique,* adj. & n., fr. LL *haereticus,* fr. LGk *hairetikos,* fr. Gk, able to choose, fr. *hairetos* (verbal of *hairein* to take, *haireisthai* to choose) + *-ikos* -ic]

hermaphrodite   See CHIMERA.
[ME *hermafrodite,* fr. L *hermaphroditus,* fr. Gk *hermaphroditos,* fr. *Hermaphroditos,* mythological son of Hermes and Aphrodite who became joined in body with the nymph Salmacis]

hermetic   See QUICKSILVER.
[NL *hermeticus,* fr. *Hermet-, Hermes Trismegistus* Thoth, the Egyptian god of wisdom, fabled author of a number of mystical, philosophical, and alchemistic writings, fr. Gk *Hermēt-, Hermes trismegistos,* lit., thrice-great Hermes (with whom the Greeks identified Thoth) + L *-icus* -ic, -ical]

heuristic   See EUREKA.
[G *heuristisch,* fr. NL *heuristicus,* fr. Gk *heuriskein* to discover; akin to OIr *fūar* I have found]

hierarchy   The earliest examples of the use of *hierarchy* in Middle English are found in works of the late fourteenth century and refer to the ranks or orders of angels. The first element of the word is from Greek *hieros,* meaning 'supernatural', 'powerful', 'holy', or 'sacred'. The second element comes from *archos,* 'ruler' or 'leader'. A second sense of our word *hierarchy,* appearing only slightly later than the first, is 'a form of government administered by an authoritarian group, especially a priesthood'. Just as the sense devolved from angels to the priesthood, so too it was extended from the secular government to the classification of a group of people with regard to ability or economic or social standing, and finally to the arrangement of objects, elements, or values in a graduated series.

A number of other terms for various forms of government are also based on Greek *-archēs* plus *-ia:* for example, *monarchy,* 'undivided rule by a single person', from Greek *monos,* 'alone, single'; *oligarchy,* 'government by the few', from Greek *oligos,* 'few'; and even *anarchy,* 'the absence of government altogether', from Greek *an-, a-,* meaning 'without'.

[ME *ierarchie,* fr. MF *ierarchie, hierarchie,* fr. ML *hierarchia,* fr. LGk, fr. Gk *hierarchēs* (fr. *hier-, hieros* powerful, holy, sacred + *-archēs, archos* ruler, leader) + *-ia* -y]

hippopotamus   *Hippopotamos* was the name invented by the Greeks to describe the bulky, barrel-shaped animal that spends most of the day bathing in the rivers of Africa. The two elements of the word are *hippos,* 'horse', and *potamos,* 'river'. In fact, however, the hippopotamus is more closely related to the hog than to the horse. It may grow to a length of fourteen feet, to a height of five feet, and may weigh up to five tons. Biblical scholars equate the "behemoth" mentioned in Job 40:15–24 (Revised Standard Version) with the hippopotamus:

> Behold, Behemoth,
>   which I made as I made you;
> he eats grass like an ox.

*   *   *

> Under the lotus plants he lies,
>   in the covert of the reeds and in the marsh.
> For his shade the lotus trees cover him;
>   the willows of the brook surround him.
> Behold, if the river is turbulent he is not frightened;
>   he is confident though Jordan rushes against
>   his mouth.

Because of the portentous tone of this passage and its rather indefinite description, *behemoth* has come in English to mean 'something of oppressive or monstrous size'. See also GARGANTUAN, MONSTER.

[L, fr. Gk *hippopotamos,* fr. *hippos* horse + *potamos* river, fr. *petesthai* to fly, dart, rush]

history   See NOVEL.
[L *historia,* fr. Gk *historia* inquiry, information, narrative, history, fr. *historein* to inquire into, examine, relate (fr. *histor-, histōr* judge) + *-ia* -y; akin to Gk *idein* to see]

hobby   Back in the fourteenth and fifteenth centuries a *hobby*—or *hoby* or *hobyn*—was a small to medium-sized horse, apparently originally a pony-like horse of an Irish breed. The words *hobby, hoby,* and *hobyn* originated as some of the many nicknames for *Robert* (there were also *Rob, Robin, Robby, Bob, Bobby, Dobbin, Dobby*). For some reason two of these nicknames, *dobbin* and *hobby,* became permanently attached to kinds of horses. The word *hobby* is still occasionally associated with small Irish horses.

Hobby was used either with or without the associated word *horse.* In the sixteenth century the compound *hobby-horse* was applied to a horse costume used by morris dancers and to the dancer wearing it. Also in the sixteenth century it was used of the child's toy consisting of a stick with a horse's head.

By the end of the seventeenth century *hobby-horse* had been extended to any favorite topic, pursuit, or pastime of an adult—the adult's toy horse to play with, so to speak. This sense was given a great boost in popularity by the appearance in 1760 of the first two volumes of Laurence Sterne's *The Life and Opinions of Tristram Shandy, Gent.* Toward the end of the first volume, Sterne ventures upon a description of Uncle Toby:

> To avoid all and every one of these errors, in giving you my uncle *Toby's* character, I am determined to draw it by no mechanical help whatever; . . .—but, in a word, I will draw my uncle Toby's character from his HOBBY-HORSE.

We learn more about Uncle Toby and his hobby-horse in the second volume:

> He was one morning lying upon his back in his bed, the anguish and nature of the wound upon his groin suffering him to lye in no other position, when a thought came into his head, that if he could purchase such a thing, and have it pasted down upon a board, as a large map of the fortifications of the town and citadel of *Namur,* with its environs, it might be a means of giving him ease.—I take notice of his desire to have the environs along with the town and citadel, for this reason,—because my uncle *Toby's* wound was got in one of the traverses, about thirty toises from the returning angle of the trench, opposite to the salient angle of the demi-bastion of *St. Roch;*—so that he was pretty confident he could stick a pin upon the identical spot of ground where he was standing when the stone struck him.
>
> All this succeeded to his wishes, and not only freed him from a world of sad explanations, but, in the end, it prov'd the happy means, as you will read, of procuring my uncle *Toby* his HOBBY-HORSE.

As well as being very popular in England, *Tristram Shandy* enjoyed a considerable vogue on the continent, and was translated into German and French. As a result of these translations the German word *Steckenpferd,* which had designated the child's horse-toy, acquired the new meaning of 'favorite pastime' or 'pet idea', the Shandean sense. The same thing happened in French: *dada,* a child's word for a horse, acquired the new 'hobby-horse' sense too. (For further development of this word see DADA.)

In the nineteenth century the *hobby-horse* popularized by *Tristram*

Shandy was shortened to *hobby*, getting back to where it began. It is still *hobby* today.

[ME *hoby, hobyn*, perh. fr. *Hobbin*, nickname of Robert or Robin]

hobnob The earliest occurrence of the form *hobnob* is in Shakespeare's *Twelfth Night*. Sir Toby Belch is arranging a duel between Sir Andrew Aguecheek and a young gentleman who is really Viola disguised as a man. Sir Toby says to Viola that Sir Andrew's "incensement at this moment is so implacable, that satisfaction can be none, but by pangs of death and sepulcher: Hob, nob, is his word: giv't or take't." In this context *hobnob* means something like 'however it may turn out' or 'hit or miss'. *Hobnob* is an alteration of *habnab*, still used in some British dialects to mean 'in one way or another'. Although we have no written evidence for *habnab* or the phrase *hab or nab* earlier than the sixteenth century, the term must have survived in spoken form from the Middle English period. *Habnab* is fairly clearly derived from the Middle English dialect form *habbe*, a subjunctive form of *habben*, 'to have', plus the negative *nabbe* from *nabben*, 'not to have', which was formed in Old English as *nabban* from a contraction of the negative particle *ne* and *habban*, 'to have'. Modern English has lost this particle, but of course we still contract common negative verb phrases to produce forms like *isn't* and *won't*.

The modern sense of *hobnob* began to develop in the eighteenth century when it was used by persons drinking one another's health. *To drink hobnob* meant 'to drink alternately to one another', and *hobnob* soon came to mean 'to drink sociably'. Today *hobnob* is used even more generally and simply means 'to associate familiarly'.

Another word constructed on the same pattern as *hobnob* is *willy-nilly*, 'without choice'. Depending upon the contexts in which it was used in early examples, *willy-nilly* may have been an alteration of any one of three possible phrases, *will I nill I, will he nill he*, or *will ye nill ye*, or even all three. Similar to *nab, nill* was formed in Old English by blending the negative particle *ne* and the verb *wyllan*, 'to wish', thus producing *nyllan*, 'not to wish'.

[alter. of *habnab*, fr. (assumed) ME dial. *habbe nabbe, habbe or nabbe* whether he (she, I) has (have) or does (do) not have, fr. ME dial. *habbe*, 1st & 3d pers. sing. pres. subj. of *habben* to have (fr. OE *habban*) + ME *or* + ME dial. *nabbe*, 1st & 3d pers. sing. pres. subj. of *nabben* not to have, fr. OE *nabban*, fr. *ne* not + *habban* to have]

hobo See TRAMP.
[perh. alter. of *ho, boy*, a call used in the northwestern U.S. in the 1880s by railway mail handlers when delivering mail]

Hobson's choice In the late sixteenth and early seventeenth centuries in Cambridge, England, Thomas (or Tobias) Hobson plied his trade as the licensed carrier of passengers, letters, and parcels between Cambridge and London. He kept a stable of about forty horses for this purpose and rented them to the university students when he was not using them. Of course, the students wanted their favorite mounts each time, with the result that a few of Hobson's horses were overworked. To correct this situation, he began a strict rotation system for letting out his horses so that all of them would see equal service. When a customer came for a horse, Hobson gave him the choice of taking the one that stood nearest the stable door or none at all. In this way, every customer and every horse was treated alike. This rule of his became well known and was referred to as *Hobson's choice*. Soon, people began using this term to mean 'no choice at all', in all kinds of situations having nothing to do with horses. As the term spread from city to city, Hobson's name became fixed in the language.

Hobson's career as a carrier, however, came to an end in 1630 when, due to another outbreak of the plague in London, his journeys were suspended by the authorities. He died the following year. John Milton, who had known Hobson personally and had done business with him, wrote two poems in his memory. In one of these, "On the University Carrier," he suggests that if Hobson had been allowed to continue his journeys, death might have missed him.

In this century, *Hobson's choice* has been used in the additional sense of 'a dilemma', that is, a choice between equally undesirable alternatives. Purists argue that this is a misuse, for in a dilemma one has a real, albeit unpleasant, choice; Hobson offered none. The sense nonetheless persists.

[after Thomas Hobson †1631 Eng. liveryman; fr. his practice of requiring every customer to take the horse which stood nearest the door]

hock   See LIEBFRAUMILCH.
[short for *hockamore*, modif. of G *Hochheimer* of Hochheim, fr. *Hochheim*, Germany, its locality]

hodgepodge   An earlier form of *hodgepodge*, and still a form used commonly in Britain, is *hotchpotch*. This in turn is a rhyming alteration of *hotchpot*, which first appeared in Middle English as *hochepot*. The Old French *hochepot*, from which the English is derived, is formed from *hocher*, 'to shake', and *pot*, which has the same meaning as English *pot*. *Hochepot*, then, was a stew with many different ingredients all shaken (and presumably cooked) together in the same pot. An early English cookbook, dated around 1440, contains a recipe for "Goos in Hochepot," and various dishes are called *hotchpotch* even today. This mixture of many ingredients in one pot prompted the extension of the meaning to imply any heterogeneous mixture, and today *hodgepodge* and *hotchpotch* are generally used to mean 'a jumble of incongruous and ill-suited elements'. For a similar culinary metaphor see POTPOURRI.

[alter. of *hotchpotch*, alter. of *hotchpot*, fr. ME *hochepot*, fr. MF, fr. OF, fr. *hocher* to shake + *pot* pot]

hog   See SWINE.
[ME *hogge*, fr. OE *hogg*, perh. of Celt origin and akin to W *hwch* hog, Corn *hoch*]

Holy Ghost, Holy Spirit   See GHOST.
[*Holy Ghost,* fr. ME *holi gost,* fr. OE *hālig gāst,* trans. of LL *spiritus sanctus,* trans. of Gk *pneuma hagion,* trans. of Heb *ruaḥ ha-godesh* holy spirit; *Holy Spirit,* fr. ME *hooli spirit,* trans. of LL *spiritus sanctus*]

Homeric   See STENTORIAN.
[L *Homericus,* fr. Gk *Homērikos,* fr. *Homēros* Homer, traditional Greek epic poet who prob. lived *ab* the 8th cent. B.C. + Gk *-ikos* -ic]

honey   See MEAD.
[ME *hony,* fr. OE *hunig;* akin to OHG *honag* honey, ON *hunang,* L *canicae* bran, Gk *knēkos* tawny, and perh. to Skt *kāñcana* gold]

hooch   The Hoochinoo Indians of Alaska are a small Tlingit tribe. Their name, *Hutsnuwu* in their own language, means literally 'grizzly bear fort'. In the late nineteenth century, the Hoochinoo had a reputation for drunkenness. Sheldon Jackson, in *Alaska, and Missions on the North Pacific Coast* (1880), described a short visit: "Tuesday we reached Angoon, the chief town of the Hootznahoos . . . but we did not remain long, as the whole town was drunk." The Hoochinoo distilled their own alcoholic liquor from molasses. The art of making this liquor was not a native one; it must have been Americans of European descent who introduced the distillation process, which requires the use of metal coils. In the course of time, however, the drink became inextricably associated with the Indians who made it, and it took their name. This liquor was blamed, in the "Report on the Population of Alaska" published with the 1890 United States Census, for "nearly all the trouble in this country." We find in the same report the casual remark: "The cause of the disturbance was, as usual, hoochinoo."

By the end of the nineteenth century, a shortened form, *hooch,* was being used for the Hoochinoo liquor. During Prohibition in the 1920s, *hooch* became very popular as a name for any illegal alcohol. *Hooch* has remained in common, though seldom in formal, use as a word for alcoholic liquor, especially the illicit variety.

Another *hooch,* meaning 'hut', has entered the language through armed forces slang. This word, which first appeared as *hoochie,* may derive from the Japanese *uchi,* 'house'. The term became especially popular with servicemen in the Far East during the time of the American involvement in Viet Nam.

[short for *hoochinoo,* fr. the *Hoochinoo* Indians, a Tlingit people of Alaska that made such liquor, fr. Tlingit *Hutsnuwu,* lit., grizzly bear fort]

[prob. modif. of Jp *uchi* house]

hoopoe   See PIGEON.
[prob. imit. alter. of *hoop* (hoopoe), fr. MF *huppe,* fr. L *upupa,* of imit. origin like Gk *epop-, epops* hoopoe, G dial. *huppupp*]

hoosegow   See CLINK.
   [Sp *juzgado* panel of judges, tribunal, courtroom, fr. past part. of *juzgar* to judge, fr. L *judicare*]

Hoosier   The use of *Hoosier* to designate an Indianan is attested in print as early as 1826. *Hoosier* is the earliest spelling and the one used today, but *Hoosher* and *Hooshier* also had some use in the first half of the nineteenth century.

   Hoosier has no obvious affinity with any other word, and consequently many explanations of its origin have been offered. Some of these are interestingly far-fetched. Some would-be etymologist derived it from the "old Saxon" *hoo* meaning 'hill dweller, rustic'. The best description of old Saxon *hoo* in this connection is the more recent Anglo-Saxon *hooey:* the word in question was seldom spelled *hoo,* meant 'hill' rather than 'hill dweller', and never crossed the Atlantic. Even in Britain it survives chiefly in place names. Another theory connected it with *whoosher,* which someone found in a 1659 dictionary with the meaning 'a rocker, a stiller, a luller, a dandler of children asleep' (quoted in H. L. Mencken, *The American Language, Supplement II,* 1948); this possibility seems remote, to put the kindest possible construction on it.

   Other elderly recollectors derived it from *husher,* given two different meanings in two different recollections; one husher was a sort of vigilante while the other was a boastful and rambunctious river boatman. Neither sense of *husher* is otherwise attested. Another theory attributes the word to the inquisitiveness of early Hoosiers, who could not forbear calling out to each house they passed "Who's here?" or "Who's yere?" Another version of this cry is said to have been offered by James Whitcomb Riley. Fights among the early settlers were held to be so vicious that noses and ears were bitten off. Thus someone strolling into a tavern and finding an ear on the floor would nonchalantly kick it aside, asking "Whose ear?"

   And there are more. Another theory derives it from a mispronunciation of *hussar.* Or it is supposed to come from a French *houssière* 'holly plantation' or a dialectal *hoose* 'roundworm' or a supposed Indian word *hoosa* or *hooza* 'maize'; or from *huzza.*

   Or would you prefer a proper-name source? There is a story that a contractor named Hoosier—Samuel Hoosier in one version—working on a canal in Louisville, Kentucky—either the Louisville & Portland Canal or the Ohio Falls Canal in different versions—recruited his laborers from the Indiana side of the river. These laborers became known as *Hoosier's men* and then simply *Hoosiers.*

   The Indiana historian Jacob Piatt Dunn dismissed most of these explanations as hogwash as far back as 1907. His theory was that *Hoosier* was of English dialectal origin. Not that dialect had been overlooked: there was the earlier mentioned *hoose* (not recorded in the *English Dialect Dictionary*), and a magazine writer in 1945 asserted that *hoosier* came without change straight from Lancashire (it is not in the *English Dialect Dictionary* either). Dunn's most plausible source was a Cumberland dialect word *hoozer* which was applied to anything large of its kind. In support of this theory Dunn produced 1832 and 1834 citations using *hoosier* of a huge sturgeon and of giant pumpkins.

Dunn's *hoozer* theory at least has some vestige of plausibility. It is likely that a Cumberland dialect word could have been brought over from settlers from that region of England; there are certainly enough Cumberlands in the Southeast (and some in the Northeast, too) to suggest that immigrants came from there. And we know that most of the early immigrants to Indiana came from the South, and that in the early nineteenth century many came to Indiana from the Piedmont region of North Carolina, where *hoosier* in a different sense is still used.

The Indiana frontiersman was presumably no larger than the frontiersman of any other state at the time; the designation could have arisen in the sort of local tall-talk that spawned the image of the *ten-gallon hat* in the West. But what is larger than usual can also be considered ungainly, and many students and authorities—from as far back as 1835—believe that *hoosier* had a pejorative meaning when it was first hung on Indianans. Certainly many state nicknames began as terms of disparagement, as *Puke* (Missourian), *Crawthumper* (Marylander), *Sucker* (Illinoisan), *Yahoo* (Arkansan), *Leatherhead* (Pennsylvanian), *Mudhead* (Tennesseean), *Tar Heel* (North Carolinian), *Cracker* (Georgian), *Clam-catcher* (New Jerseyan), and so forth, would suggest. At least some of these names were defiantly adopted by the people so disparaged, and *Hoosier* may be such an adoption.

As plausible as such a development of senses would seem, it is only conjecture, for we have no written evidence to support it. We know that *Hoosier* was adopted by Indianans themselves in the 1830s, but there are no written examples of a generally pejorative *hoosier* until we find the expression "a Hoosier Texan" in 1846.

The disparaging use of *hoosier*—almost always lowercased while the Indiana *Hoosier* is almost always capitalized—seems to have three parts. The first of these is a general term of disrespect for an untutored and not too swift country person or farmer. It is pretty well attested in the nineteenth century and in the first part of the twentieth. At this period, when a much larger proportion of the population lived on farms than at present, there were numerous disparaging terms for farmers used by the presumably more sophisticated city slickers: Harold B. Allen's dialect survey of the upper Midwest turned up eighty-six such terms still surviving in the 1950s. *Hoosier* was one of these, but it seems not to have been much used by then. The same use is well attested in the specialized jargon of such groups as lumbermen, sailors, vagabonds, and members of the I.W.W. These uses undoubtedly derived from the earlier general pejorative use, although one theorist claims the lumbering use to derive directly from the Indiana *Hoosier*—West Coast lumbering operators were supposed to have recruited green farm boys from Indiana. The story smacks of after-the-fact invention.

The second disparaging *hoosier* use is found chiefly in the Appalachians, where it denotes the mountaineer or backwoodsman farthest removed from the gentling hand of civilization. This use would be the one that in theory would have been the forerunner of the Indiana *Hoosier*. It seems to be attested as early as 1857, when it was coupled with the pejorative *cracker. Cracker* and *hoosier* are, in the twentieth century, in what linguists call complementary distribution; *cracker* is the disparaging word of choice in Southern lowlands and *hoosier* in the more mountainous regions. This *hoosier* is frequently found in combinations like *mountain hoosier*. It is generally pronounced as if spelled *hoojer*, and we have examples, from people unfamiliar with the conventional spelling, spelled *hoojer*, *hoojee*, and *hooger*. If this indeed is the forebear of the Indiana *Hoosier*, the pronunciation has changed from the early nineteenth century to the present.

The third disparaging *hoosier* seems to have migrated from the Appalachians to St. Louis, Missouri, but it did not retain its Appalachian pronunciation. This local use is regularly associated with the uncultured and uneducated country person, and St. Louisans seem to associate such folk with the Ozarks of southern Missouri. It is also commonly used as a generalized term of abuse for any person of either sex and any color who irritates the speaker in some way.

The generally disparaging *hoosier* seems to have dwindled along with the farm population. The later two are rather restricted geographically, and even they may be receding in use as they appear to be most commonly used by older speakers (younger ones tend to prefer the all-too-common vulgar epithets that everyone knows). The Indiana *Hoosier* continues to flourish, as it has all along, and has no pejorative connotations in that use today.

[perh. alter. of E dial. *hoozer* anything large of its kind]

Hopi   See INDIAN.
[Hopi *Hópi*, lit., good, peaceful]

horoscope   See BISHOP.
[MF, fr. L *horoscopus*, fr. Gk *hōroskopos*, fr. *hōro-* (fr. *hōra* period of time, time of day) + *skopos* watcher, observer; akin to Gk *skopein* to view, watch]

horticulture   See COHORT.
[L *hortus* garden + E *-i-* + *culture*]

hospice   See HOST.
[F, fr. L *hospitium* hospitality, lodging, inn, fr. *hospit-*, *hospes* host, stranger, guest]

hospitable   See HOST.
[NL *hospitabilis*, fr. L *hospitare* to be a guest, lodge + *-abilis* -able]

hospital   See HOST.
[ME, fr. OF, fr. LL *hospitale*, fr. L, bedroom, fr. neut. of *hospitalis* of a guest, hospitable, fr. *hospit-*, *hospes* host, stranger, guest + *-alis* -al]

hospitality See HOST.

[ME *hospitalite*, fr. MF *hospitalité*, fr. L *hospitalitat-*, *hospitalitas*, fr. *hospitalis* of a guest, hospitable + *-itat-*, *-itas* -ity]

host The words *host* (meaning 'innkeeper' or 'one who entertains guests'), *hospice*, *hospital*, *hospitality*, *hospitable*, *hostel*, *hotel*, and *hostage* all share a common origin—the Latin noun *hospes*, meaning both 'a guest or visitor' and 'one who provides lodging or entertainment for a guest or visitor'. All of these English words passed through and were altered by French before entering our language, with the exception of *hospitable*, which was taken directly from the New Latin *hospitabilis*, a derivative of *hospes*. *Host, hostel, hotel* (which was *hostel* in Old French), and *hostage* lost the *-p-* in passing from Latin to French. The *-t-* in these words owes its presence to the declensional stem *hospit-* of *hospes*. The French took *hospice* from the Latin *hospitium* 'hospitality, lodging' (another derivative of *hospes*), the Latin *-tium* being represented by *-ce* in French (in the same manner Latin *servitium* became French *service*). All of these etymologically related words have retained their common semantic core: they all relate to guests or visitors of one kind or other.

The noun *host* meaning 'an army' or 'angels' or 'a multitude' can be traced back to the Old French *ost, host* 'army', which was taken from the Medieval Latin *hostis* 'army', an extended sense of the Latin *hostis*, originally used for 'stranger, foreigner' and then for 'enemy'. It has been suggested that this *hostis* derives from *hospes*, since they both can refer to 'a stranger', but there is no evidence of this derivation. Our word *hostile*, borrowed from the French in the sixteenth century, developed from the Latin adjective *hostilis* 'relating to or characteristic of an enemy', a derivative of *hostis*.

A third *host*, used for 'the eucharistic bread', was borrowed from the Middle French *oiste, hoiste* (modern French *hostie*) of the same meaning. The source of the French word and usage is the Late Latin *hostia*, which extended the 'sacrificial victim' sense of the Latin *hostia* to 'the consecrated eucharistic bread', from the doctrine that it is or represents the body of Christ, the sacrificial victim of the Mass.

[ME *oste, hoste* host, guest, fr. OF, fr. L *hospit-, hospes* host, stranger, guest]

[ME *ost, oost, host, hoost*, fr. OF *ost, host*, fr. LL *hostis*, fr. L, stranger, enemy]

[ME *oste, hoste*, fr. MF *oiste, hoiste*, fr. LL & L; LL *hostia* Eucharist, fr. L, sacrifice]

hostage See HOST.

[ME *ostage, hostage*, fr. OF, fr. *oste, hoste* host, guest + *-age*]

hostel See HOST.

[ME *ostel, hostel*, fr. OF, fr. LL *hospitale* hospice]

hostile   See HOST.

[MF or L; MF, fr. L *hostilis*, fr. *hostis* stranger, enemy + *-ilis* -ile]

hotchpotch   See HODGEPODGE.

[alter. of *hotchpot*]

hotel   See HOST.

[F *hôtel*, fr. OF *ostel, hostel*]

Hugo   See OSCAR.

[after *Hugo* Gernsback †1967 Am. (Luxembourg-born) author, inventor, and publisher]

Huguenot   The German word *Eidgenoss(e)* 'confederate' was applied on Swiss soil to the Genevan citizens who, in the sixteenth century, resisted the annexationist designs of the duke of Savoy, preferring to join forces with the already confederated Swiss cantons. The Genevan French form of the German word was *eidgnot* or *eydgenot* or *eygenot*. And while the German word went on to become in our own time a synonym of 'Swiss', the French form underwent a very different evolution.

From the standpoint of Catholic France, what was most notable about Geneva was its preeminence as a center of the Protestant Reformation, particularly under the leadership of the Frenchman Jean Calvin, who arrived in Geneva as a refugee in 1536. By 1552, the French form was used in France to mean 'Calvinist'. During the second half of the sixteenth century, a modified form *huguenot* arose, probably in the region of Touraine in northwest central France, and soon achieved a premier position among a welter of local variants. It is not certain whether the Tourangeaux had altered the word in reminiscence of Besançon Hugues, a Swiss Protestant leader who died in 1532, or after some more local celebrity. In any case, *huguenot* came to be applied pejoratively to all French Protestants in an attempt to tar them with the foreign brush. English took up the term in the sixteenth century, in the sense 'French Protestant'. When, in 1685, the French king Louis XIV revoked the Edict of Nantes, which had provided some measure of protection to the Huguenots, a massive Protestant emigration began, and England and America began to receive Huguenots as well as the word.

[MF, fr. (Geneva dial.) *huguenot* Genevan partisan of an alliance with Fribourg and Bern as a means of preventing annexation by Savoy, alter. (prob. after Besancon *Hugues* †1532 leader of the movement in Geneva to prevent annexation by Savoy) of *eidgnot*, fr. G (Swiss dial.) *eidgnoss* confederate, fr. MHG *eitgenōz*, fr. *eit* oath (fr. OHG *eid*) + *genōz* comrade, fr. OHG *ginōz;* akin to OHG *noizzan* to use, enjoy]

humble   See HUMBLE PIE.

[ME *umble, humble,* fr. OF, fr. L *humilis* low, slight, humble, fr. *humus* earth, ground + -*ilis* -ile; akin to Gk *chthōn* earth, *chamai* on the ground, Skt *ksam* earth, ground]

humble pie   Let us suppose that you are a great Anglo-Norman baron of, say, the thirteenth century. You go out to hunt deer on your estate taking with you a considerable party of friends, guests, and retainers. After you have shot a few deer, you return, and the retainers butcher the animals for use. The better cuts belong to you, the lord of the manor; the rest—head, skin, shoulders, chine, and what the dictionaries delicately call edible viscera—are left for the gamekeeper, the huntsmen, and the other servants.

Those edible viscera—liver, heart, kidneys, and so forth—were known in Norman French as *nombles*, a word the French in their mysterious way had derived from Latin *lumbulus*, denoting a cut of meat, from *lumbus* 'loin'. By the fourteenth century, *nombles* had passed into English as *numbles*, by the fifteenth it was *umbles*, and by the sixteenth *humbles*. The usual way to prepare the umbles or humbles was to make them into a meat pie—really a thick rich stew with a crust. So while the lord and the rest of the gentry were feasting on a splendid haunch of venison, the gamekeeper and other servants were dining on shoulder and umble pie.

Actually the earliest spelling we find for the pie itself is *humble pie*, attested from before 1642, but little used subsequently, although it has been revived in the twentieth century. *Umble pie* has been recorded since 1663 and has been the more common spelling ever since. *Numble-pie* seems to have been attested only once:

> Robin helped him largely to numble-pie and cygnet and pheasant, and the other dainties of his table; and the friar pledged him in ale and wine, and exhorted him to make good cheer —Thomas Love Peacock, *Maid Marion,* 1822

Peacock undoubtedly used the *numble* spelling as most appropriate to the time of Robin Hood.

If on the great estates only the servants ate the umble pie, in the city it was a different matter. Samuel Pepys, a thrifty middle-class London dweller—the sociologists today would call him upwardly mobile—made this note in his diary for 5 July 1662: "I having had some venison given me a day or two ago, and so I had a shoulder roasted, another baked, and the umbles baked in a pie, and all very well done." Pepys seems not have found the gift of some of the gamekeeper's parts of the deer the least bit demeaning, and he served them for dinner to Sir William Penn, the admiral, and Sir William's son, William, whom we remember as the founder of Pennsylvania. Pepys again mentions umble pie with considerable approbation the following year:

> . . . and Mrs. Turner came in, and did bring us an umble pie hot out of her oven, extraordinary good, and afterwards some spirits of her making, in which she has great judgment, very good, and so home, merry with this night's refreshment —diary, 8 July 1663

We do not find the figurative *humble pie* until about 1830, when it turns up in a book on the vocabulary of East Anglia. It is used in the phrase "make one eat humble pie," which is defined there as "To make him lower his tone, and be submissive." The learned compiler of this book suspected that the phrase derived from the pie made of deer umbles, and in that case, he thought, it should be written "*umble-pie, the food of inferiors.*"

Quite a few learned and casual commentators since 1830 have concurred, at least in part, with the 1830 opinion that stuff fit only to be served to servants was the probable origin of the figurative *humble pie.* Some will allow the influence of the adjective *humble* too. But the evidence of Pepys and Peacock suggests that umble pie was not inferior stuff. Peacock calls it a dainty, and Pepys obviously relished his. Nothing suggests that they considered it socially stigmatized either.

Now let's consider the adjective *humble,* originally (in the thirteenth century) *umble.* It too is a borrowing from French, where it was used in Old French both with and without the *h.* It had earlier been borrowed as *humele* from the Latin *humilis,* derived in turn from *humus* 'earth'. The French added the *b* gratuitously, as they were wont to do in certain phonetic environments (they gave us another in *number*). In English *humble* was often pronounced without the *h* even when it was spelled with it. So we have *humble, umble, umbles, humbles, umble pie, humble pie,* and a situation ripe for punning.

While we cannot be sure of East Anglian attitudes in the 1820s and 1830s, the figurative *humble pie* looks to us like a simple pun in which the adjective, commonly pronounced without the *h* (Dickens spelled it without the *h* to show Uriah Heep's pronunciation in *David Copperfield*), has been substituted for the *umble* of the same sound. *Humble pie* appears to be the contribution of some unknown East Anglian wit.

[*humbles,* by folk etymology fr. *umbles,* fr. ME, alter. (prob. influenced by *umble* humble) of *noumbles, nombles* numbles, fr. MF *nombles,* pl. of *nomble* muscle from the thigh of a deer, fillet of beef, pork loin, modif. of L *lumbulus* small loin, fr. *lumbus* loin + *-ulus* -ule]

humor   Throughout the Middle Ages it was believed that everything on Earth was made of different combinations of four elements: earth, air, fire, and water. These elements in turn were thought to be composed of combinations of what were known as the Four Contraries: hot, cold, moist, and dry. Fire derived from the combination of hot and dry; air from hot and moist. Earth was believed to be composed of cold and dry, and water of cold and moist. In men these same four contraries were thought to combine into the four *humors,* and the balance or imbalance of these humors in a particular person determined his temperament.

The four humors were derived as follows: choler from hot and dry, blood from hot and moist, melancholy from dry and cold, and phlegm from cold and moist. Because of the similarities in their composition, the humors were related metaphorically to the four elements; thus a *choleric* person is fiery, hot-tempered, irascible, and vindictive. A *sanguine* person, in whom blood predominates, is generally cheerful, confident, and optimistic, while a *phlegmatic* person is stolid, sluggish, and inclined to be rather dull. *Melancholy,* in the Middle Ages, meant more than simply 'thought-ful' or 'sad'. A melancholy man was apt to be extremely dejected and prone to protracted anger, as well as being liable to nightmares. The ar-chetypal melancholy character is Hamlet, who complains of his bad dreams and who even diagnoses his own melancholy. In this sense also must we understand the archangel Michael's warning to Adam, in Milton's *Paradise Lost,* that lacking temperance,

> . . . in thy blood will reign
> A melancholy damp of cold and dry,
> To weigh thy spirits down, and last
>   consume
> The balm of life.

Coming from a Latin word meaning 'moisture' or 'fluid', *humor* originally reflected the appropriate combinations of heat and moisture that account-ed for a person's disposition, as we have seen. After becoming a general term for 'disposition' or 'temperament', *humor* came to mean 'a mood or temporary state of mind'. From this developed the sense of 'caprice, whim, or fancy', from which are derived the senses of *humor* relating to persons or things which are comic or amusing.

The words *temper* and *temperament* also referred originally to the com-bination and balance within the body of the four humors, for they derive from the Latin *temperare,* 'to mix, blend, or regulate'. *Complexion,* from the Latin *complexio,* 'combination', was originally synonymous with *tem-per* and *temperament.* Because a person's temper or temperament was often thought to be revealed in his coloring, *complexion* came to mean simply 'the hue or appearance of the skin' and this meaning has persisted into our own day.

See also STOMACH.

[ME *humour,* fr. MF *humeur,* fr. ML & L; ML *humor* humor of the body, fr. L *humor, umor* moisture, fluid; prob. akin to L *ūvēre* to be moist, MD *wac* damp, wet, ON *vökr* damp, Gk *hygros* wet, Skt *uksati* he sprinkles, he moistens]

Huron   See INDIAN.
[F, lit., boor, fr. MF, fr. *hure* disheveled head of hair, head of a wild ani-mal]

hussy   See GOOD-BYE.
[alter. of *housewife,* fr. ME *houswif,* fr. *hous* house + *wif* woman, wife]

hustings   For most people, the hustings—whatever they may be—are where babies are kissed, the flesh is pressed, and media events are staged. What are these hustings that U.S. presidential candidates must be on for two or more years in order to claim residency at 1600 Pennsylvania Ave-nue? Originally hustings were assemblies. In fact, our modern word *hust-ing* derives from the Old English *hūsting,* which in turn comes from the Old Norse *hūsthing,* a compound literally meaning "house assembly." A husting was a council held by a leader, such as a king or earl, and attended by his immediate followers. The practice of a husting acting as a judicial body dates back to Anglo-Saxon times in England. It may well have originated as a means of settling disputes between Danish and English merchants. By Norman times *hustings* referred to a court that assembled regularly for the settling of various kinds of civil suits. The court of hustings also served as a court of record. With greatly reduced powers, the court of hustings still exists in the City of London, where it is irregularly convened and presided over by the lord mayor and the aldermen. In London the court was traditionally convened in the Guildhall. In time the platform upon which the lord mayor and the aldermen were seated also came to be known as the *hustings*. By the eighteenth century the court also had come to serve as a site for the nomination of members of Parliament, the nomination taking the form of a speech delivered from another platform specially constructed for the occasion. By custom the new nominees addressed their electors from this same platform. (The whole arrangement was done away with by the Ballot Act of 1872.) In due course the platform came to be used for all manner of political speechifying, and *hustings* likewise came to mean any platform from which a political speech was delivered. In a natural semantic development, *hustings* came to refer on both sides of the Atlantic to the campaign process itself. In the U.S. especially, *hustings* has come to be used of the places, elevated or otherwise, along the campaign trail at which candidates make their pitch for public office.

Coincidentally, the political folklore of the U.S. has provided politicians with an alternative to going out "on the hustings." Politicians from rural areas, or merely those with pretensions to log-cabin origins, can go "on the stump," recalling those mythic days when politicians from the backwoods used tree stumps as speaker's platforms. And *stump* in this context has developed the verb use, 'to go about making political speeches or supporting a cause'.

[ME, fr. OE *hūsting,* fr. ON *hūsthing,* fr. *hūs* house + *thing* assembly]

hyacinth   The gods of ancient Greek mythology had some of the same foibles we think of as human failings. Both Apollo and Zephyros, the gentle West Wind, adored the handsome young man Hyakinthos. The youth led a charmed life safe from all earthly danger. But when Zephyros found his love was not returned and Hyakinthos was devoting too much attention to Apollo, he felt neglected and ultimately flew into a jealous rage, allowing a discus thrown by Apollo during a friendly game to hit and kill the young Hyakinthos. Apollo was devastated by the death of his friend. To commemorate the loss, he caused a deep red flower to spring up at the place where the slain youth's blood mixed with the earth. The flower (so the legend ran) was called a *hyacinth,* after Hyakinthos.

From this mourning for the youth emerged the Lakonian festival, the Hyakinthia, the first days of which are spent grieving and the last day, celebrating. The day of mourning marks the dying of Hyakinthos and the celebration commemorates the regrowth of vegetation, as symbolized by the hyacinth.

The name of another well-known flower has its origin in mourning. The 'passion' in *passionflower* is a reference to the Passion of Christ. Portions of the flower resemble the cross upon which Christ was crucified, and so we call it a passionflower. Many wrongly assume that the flower is an aphrodisiac, thus misinterpreting the meaning of *passion* within the name. See also COWSLIP, DAISY.

[L *hyacinthus*, a precious stone, a flowering plant, fr. Gk *hyakinthos*]

hydrargyrum   See QUICKSILVER.
[NL, alter. of L *hydrargyrus*, fr. Gk *hydrargyros*, fr. *hydr-* (fr. *hydōr* water) + *argyros* silver]

hydromel   See MEAD.
[alter. (influenced by LL *hydromel*) of ME *ydromel*, fr. MF & LL; MF *ydromel*, fr. LL *hydromel*, fr. L *hydromeli*, fr. Gk, fr. *hydr-* water + *meli* honey]

hyena   See SWINE.
[L *hyaena*, fr. Gk *hyaina*, fr. *hys* hog]

hypnosis   While *hypnosis* and *morphine* might seem quite unrelated, in fact both words have their roots in the same classical myth. In Greek mythology Hypnos (in Latin, Somnus) was the god of sleep. The brother of Thanatos (Death) and the son of Nyx (Night), Hypnos lived, according to one tradition, in a land of perpetual darkness and mist. The god's home was a cavern, through which the waters of Lethe, the river of forgetfulness, flowed. Surrounding Hypnos, who reclined on a couch, were numerous sons—the Dreams. Prominent among the sons was Morpheus. Hypnos and Morpheus were occasionally called upon to exercise their powers when the chief gods wished to intervene in mortal affairs. Hypnos could induce a state of sleep, and Morpheus had the power to make human forms appear to dreamers.

In 1843 Scottish surgeon James Braid (1795–1860) used the name of the Greek god of sleep to create the term *hypnotism,* which he introduced in his treatise *Neurypnology, or the rationale of nervous sleep. Hypnotism* (also known in the nineteenth century as *Braidism*), the science or practice of artificially inducing a sleep-like trance, gave rise to the coinage of *hypnosis,* the term for the sleep-like trance itself. (See also MESMERIZE.)

Morphine was first isolated in 1806 by the German pharmacologist Friedrich Wilhelm Adam Sertürner (1783–1841). Sertürner named the derivative of opium *morphium,* after the god of dreams, for the deep sleep it induces in addition to relieving pain.

For other articles on words derived from ancient mythology and legend see VOLCANO.

[NL, fr. *hypn-* + *-osis*]

hypochondria Many ancient theories of pathogenesis, attractive though they are, have been discarded. That dire humor, black bile (or melancholy), was said to be a secretion of the spleen or kidneys and to produce a morbid state of bleak depression and with it an excessive concern with one's health. This "disease" was named for the region below the breastbone in which it had its origin, the *hypochondria.* This Late Latin word is a derivative of Greek *hypo,* under', and *chondros,* 'cartilage of the breastbone'.

Another disease, *hysteria,* more commonly observed in women than in men, was once supposed to be an exclusively feminine disorder and was blamed on a disturbance of the womb. This belief is reflected in the Greek *hysterikos,* meaning 'hysterical' or 'of the womb' (from *hystera,* 'womb'), and in an archaic sense of English *mother,* 'hysterical fit'. *Mother* was once a standard term for the womb, and *rising of the mother, fits of the mother,* and even simply *mother* were hysterical fits brought on by disturbance of the womb. Shakespeare's King Lear, distressed by his daughters' "unnatural" behavior, puts himself figuratively into a maternal position: "O, how this mother swells up toward my heart! Hysterica passio! Down, thou climbing sorrow!" See also HUMOR.

[NL, fr. LL, pl., abdomen, belly (formerly supposed to be the seat of hypochondria), fr. Gk, fr. *hypochondria,* neut. pl. of *hypochondrios* under the cartilage of the breastbone, fr. *hypo-* under + *-chondrios,* fr. *chondros* cartilage, cartilage of the breastbone, granule, grain]

hysteria   See HYPOCHONDRIA.
[NL, fr. E *hysteric* (fr. L *hystericus* of the womb, fr. Gk *hysterikos,* fr. *hystera* womb + *-ikos* -ic; fr. its being originally applied to women thought to be suffering from disturbances of the womb) + NL *-ia*]

I

icicle The Old English *gicel* is found as early as the beginning of the eighth century glossing (translating) the Latin *stiria*, 'icicle'. The Old English form became Middle English *ikyl* or *ikel* and later Modern English *ickle*, which still survives as a Yorkshire dialect word. In the late seventeenth century we find Charles Cotton writing in *The Joys of Marriage*, "Be she constant, be she fickle,/ Be she fire or be she ickle." The word for *ice* in Old English is *is*, and in a manuscript of about the year 1000 we find *stiria* glossed somewhat redundantly as *ises gicel*, that is, 'an ice icicle'. Some three hundred years later in Middle English this became the compound which we know today as *icicle*, which means precisely what it did a thousand years ago.

[ME *isikel*, fr. *is* ice + *ikel* icicle, fr. OE *gicel;* akin to OHG *ihilla* icicle, ON *jökull* icicle, glacier, *jaki* piece of ice, MIr *aig* ice, W *iâ*]

idiot To say a person is "his own man" is certainly not to insult him. To call him an *idiot* is quite another thing. The Greek adjective *idios* means 'one's own' or 'private'. The derivative noun *idiōtēs* means 'private person'. A Greek *idiōtēs*, however, was not "his own man" in the way we mean that phrase today. He was simply a person who was not in the public eye, who held no public office. From this sense came the sense 'common man', and later 'ignorant person'—a natural extension, for the common people of Greece were not, in general, particularly learned. The word was borrowed from Greek into Latin as *idiota*, whence French has *idiote*, which in turn became a loanword in English in the thirteenth century.

The milder meaning of *idiot*, 'ignorant person', is obsolete. But John Capgrave, in the middle of the fifteenth century, could speak of Christ's apostles as *idiots* and never fear the wrath of the church: "Ryght as be twelue ydiotes, sent Austin [Saint Augustine] seyth, hee meneth the apostellis, for thei not lerned were." By carrying ignorance to extremes, we arrive at the *idiot* who is mentally deficient. An English lawyer, Henry Swinburne, defined this *idiot*, in 1590: "An *Idiote*, or a naturall foole is he, who notwithstanding he bee of lawfull age, yet he is so witless, that hee can not number to twentie, nor can tell what age he is of, nor knoweth who is his father, or mother, nor is able to answer to any such easie question."

The word *private* itself, though in some uses it suggests the sign on the boss's office, has fallen to a low estate in the military sphere, where it denotes the lowest rank. *Private* comes from Latin *privatus*, which as a noun is a near synonym of the Greek *idiōtēs.* In formation the word is a past participle of *privare,* 'to deprive, relieve'. *Privatus,* used as an adjective, had already in Latin the more or less contrary connotations of our own *private.* It could refer to private property (cut off from the public) or to unofficial, merely individual, and thus often subordinate status (cut off from public office).

[ME, fr. MF *idiote,* fr. L *idiota,* fr. Gk *idiōtēs* person in a private station, person without professional knowledge, ignorant person, common man, fr. *idios* one's own, private, peculiar]

ignoramus   See LOTHARIO.
[after *Ignoramus,* an ignorant lawyer in *Ignoramus* (1615), play by George Ruggle †1622 Eng. playwright, fr. NL *ignoramus* endorsement on a bill of indictment, fr. L, we do not know, 1st pl. pres. indic. of *ignorare* to be ignorant of]

IHS   See XMAS.
[LL $\overline{\text{IHS}}$, $\overline{\text{IHC}}$, fr. Gk $\overline{\text{IHC}}$, $\overline{\text{IH}\Sigma}$ (the capitalized forms of the Greek letters iota, eta, and sigma), short for *Iēsous* Jesus]

Iliad   See STENTORIAN.
[fr. the *Iliad,* ancient Greek epic poem dealing with the siege of Troy and attributed to Homer, fr. L *Iliad-, Ilias,* fr. Gk *Iliad-, Ilias,* lit., of Troy, fr. *Ilion* Troy]

Illinois   See INDIAN.
[F, of Algonquian origin; akin to Miami *alänia* man, Shawnee *hilenawe*]

immaculate   See MAIL.
[ME *immaculat,* fr. L *immaculatus,* fr. *in-* ¹in- + *maculatus,* past part. of *maculare* to spot, stain]

immediate   See MEDIUM.
[LL *immediatus,* fr. L *in-* ¹in- + *mediatus* mediate]

imp   Today the word *imp* usually refers to either a small demon or a mischievous child. However, the origin of the word is, oddly enough, rooted in the field of horticulture. In Vulgar Latin the verb *putare* 'to trim, prune' was, we assume, compounded to form the unrecorded verb *imputare* 'to graft into or on'. This assumed verb was later taken into Old High German and became *impian* in Old English, *impen* in Middle English, and *imp* in Modern English, keeping its original Latin sense.

In the Old English period the noun *impa* was formed from the verb *impian* and was used for 'a young shoot of a plant, a seedling'. In Middle English this noun was usually spelled *impe* or *ympe.* In *The Romaunt of the Rose,* a fourteenth-century translator, perhaps Chaucer, gives us an example of this sense: "Nay, thou planten most elleswhere/Thyn ympes, if thou wolt fruyt have." (No, you must plant your imps elsewhere, if you want to have fruit.) This sense became obsolete in the eighteenth century. In the fourteenth century the noun was also put to metaphorical use to mean 'offspring, child'. Edmund Spenser illustrates this use in *The Faerie Queen* (1590), when he writes "Fayre ympe of Phoebus and his aged bryde." In Modern English this 'offspring' sense has become archaic. In the sixteenth century the noun acquired the pejorative sense 'a small demon or wicked spirit'. In his poem "A Long Story" (1753), Thomas Gray describes such an imp:

> . . .thereabouts there lurk'd
> A wicked Imp they call a Poet,
> Who prowl'd the country far and near,
> Bewitch'd the children of the peasants,
> Dried up the cows, and lam'd the deer,
> And suck'd the eggs, and kill'd the pheasants.

By the seventeenth century we have occurrences of the now most common sense, 'a mischievous child'. Jonathan Swift mentions one such child in *Gulliver's Travels* (1726): "I once caught a young male of three years old, . . . but the little imp fell a squalling, and scratching, and biting."

In the fifteenth century the verb took on a transferred sense in the sport of falconry. It was used to mean 'to graft or repair (a wing, tail, or feather) with a feather in order to improve a falcon's flying capacity'. This specialized usage is the only sense of the verb surviving in contemporary English. In the seventeenth century this falconry sense gave rise to the related but now archaic sense 'to fasten wings on or to a person'. This use is illustrated in George Herbert's poem "Easter Wings" (1633): "For if I imp my wing on thine, Affliction shall advance the flight in me." By the end of the sixteenth century, we have evidence of the verb's use to mean 'to add on a piece to, eke out, extend'. George Chapman provides a good example of this in his play *Monsieur d'Olive* (1606): "All my care is for Followers to Imp out my Traine." This sense has also become archaic.

[ME *impe,* fr. OE *impa,* fr. *impian;* akin to OHG *impfōn* to graft; both fr. a prehistoric OHG-OE word derived fr. (assumed) VL *imputare* (whence OF *enter* to graft), fr. L *in-* ²in- + *putare* to cut, prune]

impecunious See PECULIAR.

[*in-* not + obs. E *pecunious* rich, fr. ME *pecunyous,* fr. L *pecuniosus,* fr. *pecunia* money + *-osus* -ose]

implode See PLAUDIT.

[²*in-* + *-plode* (as in *explode*)]

incandescent See CANDIDATE.

[prob. fr. F, fr. L *incandescent-, incandescens,* pres. part. of *incandescere* to become white, to become hot, fr. *in-* ²in- + *candescere* to become white, to become hot, incho. of *candēre* to shine, be white]

incarcerate See CANCEL.
[L *incarceratus,* past part. of *incarcerare,* fr. *in-* in, within + *carcer* prison]

inch See OUNCE.
[ME *inch, inche,* fr. OE *ince, ynce,* fr. L *uncia* twelfth part, ounce, inch]

Indian In Europe in the Middle Ages, the name *India* was not only applied to the land we now call *India* but was also often extended to the whole of the distant East, India and beyond. Trade with the Far East was lucrative, but the overland journey was long and difficult. Christopher Columbus, in the late fifteenth century, believed that he could find an easier way of getting at the wealth of the Orient. According to his calculations the westward distance by sea was less than one-third of the eastward distance. When he was finally able to test his theory, Columbus was delighted to find land just about where he had said it would be. Reaching the Bahamas in 1492, he believed that he had arrived at the outer islands of "India." He was confirmed in his belief when he came to the large island of "Japan" (he had, in fact, discovered Cuba). Because of Columbus's mistake, the newly discovered lands were called *India* or the *Indies,* even after the realization that they were geographically distinct from the *India* or *Indies* of Asia. The two were later distinguished as East Indies and West Indies. But *Indian,* the inaccurate name given to the inhabitants of the new "India," remained.

Just as the general name we use for the American aborigines is European, so are a number of our names for particular Indian peoples European in origin. The *Delaware* nation of eastern North America is named for the Delaware River, whose valley they inhabited. The river itself was named for an Englishman, Thomas West, Lord Delaware, who was colonial governor of Virginia in the early seventeenth century. Southeastern North America, the home of the *Creek* peoples, is rich in streams and rivers. It was probably for this reason that they were given their English name.

The name *Huron* reflects the low opinion of Indians that was common among the French who explored the St. Lawrence valley. French *huron* means 'boor' and is derived from *hure,* 'disheveled head of hair'. The Nez Percés of the Pacific Northwest also have a French name. Why these people should have been given a name whose literal meaning is 'pierced nose' we do not know. Some Indian tribes do practice nose piercing for the insertion of ornamental shells, but there is no evidence that this custom existed among the Nez Percés. Perhaps the name was extended to them from another tribe; perhaps a few Nez Percés did wear nose shells. Another European name for an Indian tribe is that of the *Blackfoot.* The English name, in this case, is simply a translation of *Siksika,* the Blackfoot's own name. It was probably because they wore black moccasins that the Blackfoot gave themselves this name.

Many of our standard English names for Indian tribes are not European but Indian in origin. Often English has borrowed a tribe's own name without translating it as we did *Siksika.* Some Indians simply called themselves "men." *Illinois* comes from a word meaning 'man, person'. *Leni-Lenape,* the Delaware's name for themselves, which is sometimes used in English, means 'real person'. The *Dakota,* a large group of allied tribes of the northern Mississippi valley, named themselves 'allies'. The *Hopi* of northern Arizona spoke of themselves as 'the good' or 'the peaceful'. Perhaps it was because of their peace-loving character that some of their neighbors doubted that they could survive. One author in an 1877 *Bulletin* of the Buffalo (New York) Society of Natural Sciences reported that "the title of *'Moquis'* has been applied to this confederacy by its enemies, and signifies the dying race. I understand that they usually speak of themselves as *'Hopees.'* "

Some Indian peoples named themselves for the places where they lived, and these names have often been adopted in English. Both the *Massachuset* and the *Narraganset* were so named. The literal meaning of the place name *Massa-adchu-es-et* is 'about the big hill'. The related *Narraganset* once inhabited most of what is now Rhode Island, but their name probably reflects an original association with a small point of land extending into the ocean—*naiagans* means 'small point of land'. The name of the *Aztecs,* too, comes from a locality. According to Aztec legend, the original home of this people was a place called *Aztlan,* 'place of the cranes'.

The names people give themselves are generally flattering or, at worst, neutral. But they cannot always expect their neighbors to be so kind. For the *Apache* and *Sioux* we use names chosen by their enemies. *Apache* probably comes from Zuñi *apache,* 'enemy'. The Zuñi called the Navajo, who were their particular enemies, *Apachu.* The Spanish, from whom we borrowed the word *Apache,* sometimes used the term for the Navajo as well as for their relatives, the *Apache. Sioux,* another name for the Dakota, comes from an Ojibwa word for 'enemy', *nadoweisiw,* whose literal meaning is 'little snake'.

It is only human nature to ridicule the foreign speech and other peculiar characteristics of other people. *Cheyenne* and *Cherokee* reflect this fact. The Dakota considered their own speech "white"; unintelligible speech was "red." Their name for the Cheyenne, *Shaiyena,* comes from *shaia,* 'to speak red, or unintelligibly'. The Creek word *tciloki,* 'people of a different speech', is probably the source of English *Cherokee.* The Dakota gave the *Iowa* their mocking name, which means 'the sleepy ones'.

Some names reflect eating habits or supposed eating habits. The *Mohawk* of New York were suspected by their Algonquian neighbors of cannibalism; their name means literally 'they eat animate things'. The *Eskimo* are not usually classified as an Indian people, but their name has an Indian origin. The Algonquian peoples often lumped together all the tribes north of them as 'eaters of raw flesh'. A word related to Cree *askimowew,* 'he eats it raw', became our *Eskimo.*

[*Indian* inhabitant of India or of the East Indies, prob. fr. (assumed) ML *Indianus,* fr. ML *indianus,* adj., fr. L *India* subcontinent in Southern Asia + *-anus* -an; fr. the belief on the part of Columbus that the lands discovered by him in 1492 and later were part of Asia]

indict   See DEBT.

[alter. (influenced by ML *indictare* to indict, fr. AF *enditer*) of earlier *in-dite, endite,* fr. ME *inditen, enditen,* fr. AF *enditer,* fr. OF, to write down, compose, make known, fr. (assumed) VL *indictare* to make known, proclaim, fr. L *indictus,* past part. of *indicere* to proclaim, fr. *in-* in + *dicere* to say]

infant   Latin *infans* means literally 'not speaking, incapable of speech'. In classical Latin the noun *infans* designated a very young child who had not yet learned to talk. But later *infans* became the most common word for any child, however talkative. In the Romance languages, too, the descendants of Latin *infans* are words that mean 'child'. In English the word *infant,* which was borrowed from the French, was originally used as the French used *enfant,* for any child. *The Boke of Curtasye* (ca. 1450) gave advice to the young: "Yf that thou be a yong enfaunt, And thenke tho scoles for to haunt. . . ." (If you are a young child and plan to go to school. . . .) But the word is seldom used now except in the earlier Latin sense 'a very young child, a baby'. It is obviously this *infant* that Tennyson uses in *In Memoriam* (1850):

> . . . but what am I?
> An infant crying in the night,
> An infant crying for the light,
> And with no language but a cry.

In the Middle Ages in France, a young soldier of good family who had not yet been made a knight was called *enfant.* Similarly, in Italy one of the soldiers who followed a mounted knight on foot was an *infante.* Soon foot soldiers collectively became *infanteria,* which was borrowed into French as *infanterie* and into English as *infantry.*

[ME *enfaunt, infaunt,* fr. MF *enfant,* fr. L *infant-, infans,* fr. *infant-, infans,* adj., incapable of speech, young, fr. *in-* not + *fant-, fans,* pres. part. of *fari* to speak]

infantry   See INFANT.

[MF & OIt; MF *infanterie,* fr. OIt *infanteria,* fr. *infante* infant, boy, footman, foot soldier (fr. L *infant-, infans* infant) + *-eria* -ry]

influence   See DISASTER.

[ME, fr. MF, fr. ML *influentia,* fr. L *influent-, influens,* pres. part. of *influere* to flow in (fr. *in-* in + *fluere* to flow) + *-ia* -y]

influenza   See DISASTER.

[It, influence, epidemic, influenza, fr. ML *influentia* influence; fr. the fact that epidemics were formerly attributed to the influence of the stars]

influx See ABUNDANCE.

[LL *influxus,* fr. L *influxus,* past part. of *influere* to flow in, fr. *in-* ²in-
+ *fluere* to flow]

innuendo "Verbum sapienti sat," the Latins had it: a word to the wise
suffices. Sometimes less than a word: a nod.

Latin *nuere* meant 'to nod', and a couple of its compounds have been
preserved for the English-speaking world. *Adnuere* and its assimilated
variant *annuere* meant literally 'to nod to', thus by extension 'to nod assent, to grant favor, to give the nod to'. The phrase *annuit coeptis,* 'He
(God) has smiled on our undertakings', stares out at us from the back of
every dollar bill. *Innuere* was 'to nod meaningfully, to intimate or signify'.
The ablative case of this verb's gerund was *innuendo,* literally 'by nodding
(or hinting)', used in Medieval Latin documents to introduce parenthetical
remarks. This use was borrowed into English prose, particularly legal
prose, as in the following sixteenth-century example cited in the Oxford
English Dictionary: "What-soeuer thinge it is, that knave your sonne—
innuendo this deponentes sonne—made it & brought it to the Church."
In this particular example *innuendo* is equivalent to another adverbial
Latin borrowing, *scilicet* 'namely'; but unlike *scilicet, innuendo* found use
also as a noun, referring to an interpolation in a text, and more broadly to
any indirect suggestion or veiled allusion. The notion of the invidious possibilities of this kind of remark came to predominate so that today an *innuendo* typically refers to an insinuation that is at best catty, at worst
defamatory.

[L, by hinting, abl. of *innuendum,* gerund of *innuere* to hint, intimate,
fr. *in-* ²in- + *nuere* to nod]

inoculate In both Latin and English, the word for 'eye' (*oculus* in Latin)
has been used metaphorically to denote something that looks like or is suggestive of a person's organ of sight. The circular markings on a peacock's
tail and the underdeveloped buds on a potato are common examples of
this use of *eye.* In horticulture, as the Roman poet Virgil explains in his
Georgics (36–29 B.C.), an *oculus* from one plant can be grafted onto another plant for propagation. The Latin verb *inoculare* and the noun *inocula-
tio* were derived from *oculus* to refer to this procedure. The verb was
borrowed into English in the fifteenth century as *inoculaten* with the same
meaning.

In the eighteenth century, medical researchers discovered that introducing a small amount of an infective agent into a person made that person immune to a normal attack of the disease. By analogy with the
implanting of a bud, the inserting of an infective agent into the body was
also referred to by the words *inoculate* and *inoculation.* This medical use
of these words is by far the most common use today.

By the nineteenth century, writers were making figurative use of these
words in reference to introducing something into the mind. In 1824, for
example, Washington Irving, in *Tales of a Traveller,* confesses, "My parents had tried in vain to inoculate me with wisdom." And a century later,

H. L. Mencken, in *Prejudices* (1923), observes, "The theory . . . is that a taste for music is an elevating passion, and that if the great masses of the plain people could be inoculated with it they would cease to herd into the moving-picture theaters."

[ME *inoculaten,* fr. L *inoculare,* fr. *in-* ²in- + *oculus* eye, bud]

inquest   See QUESTION.
[ME *enquest, inquest,* fr. OF *enqueste,* fr. fem. of (assumed) *enquest,* fr. (assumed) VL *inquaestus,* past part. of *inquaerere* to inquire]

inquire   See QUESTION.
[ME *enquiren, inqueren, inquiren,* alter. (influenced by L *inquirere* to inquire) of *enqueren,* fr. OF *enquerre,* fr. (assumed) VL *inquaerere,* alter. (influenced by L *quaerere* to seek, ask) of L *inquirere,* fr. *in-* ²in- + *-quirere* (fr. *quaerere*)]

inscribe   See SCRIVENER.
[L *inscribere,* fr. *in-* ²in- + *scribere* to write]

intermediary   See MEDIUM.
[prob. fr. F *intermédiaire,* fr. L *intermedius* + F *-aire* -ary]

intermediate   See MEDIUM.
[ML *intermediatus,* fr. L *intermedius* intermediate (fr. *inter-* + *medius* mid, middle) + *-atus* -ate]

internecine   The Latin noun *nex* 'violent death' gave rise to the verb *necare* 'to kill' and *internecare* 'to kill without exception, massacre'; on the latter the adjective *internecinus* 'fought to the death, devastating' was formed. In Latin the prefix *inter-* did not always carry the meaning 'between' (as in *interponere* 'to place between, insert') or 'mutual', but was used in some words to denote the completion of an action, which in the case of *internecinus* means 'to the death'. Other examples of this use of *inter-* include *interbibere* 'to drink dry, drain' and *intermori* 'to die off or down completely'.

When Samuel Johnson was preparing his Dictionary (1755), however, he was either unaware of the completive meaning of *inter-* or (more likely) misconstrued its meaning in the available examples of *internecine,* since he defined it as 'endeavouring mutual destruction'. On the other hand, when Noah Webster came to define *internecine* for his Dictionary (1828), he gave only the original sense of 'deadly, destructive'. It was not until the 1864 revision of Webster's Dictionary that the Johnsonian sense 'mutually destructive' was added. This latter sense gained acceptance among the literati of the nineteenth century, superseding the word's original meaning. In the twentieth century still another sense evolved and not without controversy. Writers began using *internecine* to mean 'of, relating to, or involving conflict within a group'. "Internecine warfare" no longer refers to bloody massacres but to the internal bickering that goes on within a political party, a trade union, a government, an alliance, a profession, an ethnic group, a nation, a business, a movement, or a family. This sense has become predominant despite the repeated protests of some linguistic purists.

[L *internecinus*, fr. *internecare* to destroy, kill (fr. *inter-* + *necare* to kill, fr. *nec-*, *nex* violent death) + *-inus* -ine]

intestine See BOWEL.
[MF *intestin*, fr. L *intestinum*, fr. neut. of *intestinus*, fr. *intus* within]

inveigle To *inveigle* is not to blind, yet when we permit ourselves to be inveigled we are, in a sense, blinded by our seducer's wiles. The ancestor of our word *inveigle* is probably a Medieval Latin phrase meaning 'blind'. Literally, *ab oculis* is 'lacking (or away from) eyes'—the Latin preposition *ab* expressed separation. From *ab oculis* are derived the French adjective *aveugle*, 'blind', and the verb *aveugler*, 'to blind'. French *aveugler*, like its English equivalent, *blind*, is often used figuratively. When English borrowed the French verb in the late Middle Ages, only the figurative use was taken. English *inveigle* originally meant 'to blind or delude in judgment'. This sense is now obsolete, but the present meaning, 'to win over by wiles', is not very far removed.

The form of the English word is apparently due to an English misapprehension of the construction of French *aveugler*. Treating *aveugler* as if it were a compound of a prefix *a-* and a root *veugler*, English modified the word to fit a familiar pattern of its own. The supposed prefix *a-* was replaced by a common English prefix *in-*.

[modif. (influenced by E ²*in-*) of MF *aveugler* to blind, hoodwink, fr. OF *avogler*, fr. *avogle*, *avugle* blind, prob. fr. ML *ab oculis*, fr. L *ab* from + *oculis*, abl. pl. of *oculus* eye]

involve See VOLUME.
[ME *involven*, fr. L *involvere* to wrap, envelop, fr. *in-* ²*in* + *volvere* to roll]

iota See JOT.
[L *iota*, *jota*, fr. Gk *iōta*]

Iowa See INDIAN.
[Dakota *Ayuhwa*, lit., sleepy ones]

irregular derivation The user of our dictionaries will sometimes come across an etymology like the following:

> **urinalysis** *also* **uranalysis** [*urinalysis* fr. NL, irreg. fr. *urin-* + *analysis*; *uranalysis* fr. NL, fr. ¹*ur-* + *analysis*]

Given that, by the mysteries of sound change, such disparate forms as *come* and *venue*, or *pedal* and *foot*, are considered to be etymological kin, the reader may wonder why we jib at such a transparent-looking connection as that between *urinalysis* on the one hand and *urine* and *analysis* on the other and call the derivation "irregular."

The answer is that sound change, however dramatic its effects may appear after the course of centuries, tends on the whole to be regular, as do the patterns of word-formation in a given language. If an Indo-European **p* appears in a Latin word beginning with *p*, we expect that any natively developed English cognate will begin with *f* (Latin *pes*—English *foot*, for instance). And we expect that compounding in Old English can have certain effects on the quality of vowels, so that we are not surprised at the short vowel sound in the first syllable of *husband* as against the diphthong in the cognate *house*. But there is no general model which requires the lopping of the *an-* in *analysis* when the word is combined with something else. Rather there is a tendency, acting sporadically in various languages, to avoid repeated sounds in certain configurations: thus Old English *Englaland* 'land of the Angles' was reduced to *England*. A more regular formation *urinanalysis* would, in the usual casual articulation, have come out \ˌyuṙ-ən-ən-ˈal-ə-səs\. The coiner kindly spared us such a potential tongue twister by offering \ˌyuṙ-ə-ˈnal-ə-səs\. In a similar fashion, we say *mineralogy* rather than the more "logical" *mineralology* (the science or "ology" of minerals).

A subtle aspect of the matter is this: the variant *uranalysis* does not rate as irregular, since we have a prefix *ur-* or *uro-* (from Greek *our-, ouro-*) 'urine', appearing regularly in such words as *uremia* and *urogenital*.

"Irregular from" can also apply to formations within a foreign language. At *clandestine* we have, in our Webster's Ninth New Collegiate Dictionary, an etymology that includes the following:

[. . . fr. L *clandestinus,* irreg. fr. *clam* secretly . . .]

There is no suffix **-destinus* in Latin to explain this formation. *Clandestinus* was probably modeled on *intestinus* 'internal, personal', a word of related meaning.

There are as many types of irregular formation as there are ways of not following a rule. Some of the ways are themselves recurrent and have earned special names: see BLENDS, CLIPPING.

Islam   See SALAAM.

[Ar *islām* submission (to the will of God), fr. *aslama* to surrender]

island   Oddly enough the words *island* and *isle* are etymologically distinct. *Island* can be traced back to the Old English *īgland*, composed of the two elements *īg* and *land*. *Land,* as we might expect, means 'land', but it is surprising to note that *īg* is found in Old English as a distinct word meaning 'island'. In a sense, then, we can interpret *īgland* as 'island-land'. Remains of *īg* can be found today in a number of British place names. For instance, it is represented by the last syllable of Chertsey, Lindsey, and Mersea, and by the *y* in Runnymede, the meadow where King John reluctantly granted the Magna Charta to his barons in 1215.

However, we have not yet accounted for the *s* in the modern spelling of *island*. To do so we must first look at *isle*. In early Old French the form was *isle*, but when the *s* was no longer pronounced it was eventually deleted from the spelling. At this stage it was borrowed into Middle English as *ile*. In the fifteenth century the French again restored an *s* to the orthography (though not to their pronunciation) in order to represent the Latin *insula*, from which it springs. In the fifteenth century the *s* was also included occasionally in English for the same reason, and from the time of Edmund Spenser (1552–1599) *isle* began to appear with increasing regularity, completely displacing *ile* around 1700.

Also in the fifteenth century we find the first instances of *ile-land*, showing that the first element of the word was even then thought to be a derivation of Old French *ile*. From there it was only a short step to the addition of *s* under the influence of *ile, isle,* and in the sixteenth century we find the first appearance of such forms as *isle-land, ysle-land,* and *island.* For other similar alterations in spelling see COLONEL, DEBT.

[alter. (influenced by E *isle*) of earlier *iland,* fr. ME, fr. OE *īgland;* akin to OFris *eiland* island, ON *eyland;* all fr. a prehistoric NGmc-WGmc compound whose first constituent is represented by OE *īg, īeg* island and whose second constituent is represented by OE *land;* OE *īg, īeg* island akin to OE *ēa* river, OHG *ouwa* land by water, meadow, *aha* river, ON *ey* island, *ā* river, Goth *ahwa* river, L *aqua* water]

isle See ISLAND.
[ME *isle, ile,* fr. OF, fr. L *insula,* perh. fr. *in* + *-sula* (akin to L *salum* sea, *sal* salt)]

J

jabberwocky   A number of words originally coined or used as nonsense words have taken on specific meanings in subsequent use. Renowned among such words is *jabberwocky*, used by Lewis Carroll in *Through the Looking Glass* as the title of a nonsense poem about a fantastic monster called a *jabberwock*. A meaningless nonsense word itself, *jabberwocky* appropriately enough became a generic term for meaningless speech or writing.

In *The Hunting of the Snark*, Carroll warns against the *boojum*, a variety of another imaginary creature, the snark. When British ecologist Godfrey Sykes was traveling in the Lower California peninsula in 1922, he spied from a distance a strange-looking, spiny tree; and as the story goes he remarked, "Ho ho, a boojum, definitely a boojum!" The name stuck and this tree, known to scientists as *Idria columnaris,* is more popularly called a *boojum* or *boogum.*

Carroll was very fond of coining blends or, to use his term, *"portmanteau"* words, so called because blending words is like packing them into the same traveling bag. Thus Carroll not only added to the English language a number of blend words, he also gave us a new sense for *portmanteau,* and we can now use it as an adjective to mean 'combining more than one use or quality'. Among the portmanteau words coined by Carroll which have become useful members of the language are *chortle* and *galumph. Chortle,* a blend of *chuckle* and *snort,* means 'to sing, chant, laugh, or chuckle exultantly'. *Galumph,* probably an alteration of *gallop,* may also be influenced by some such word as *triumphant.* Today it is used with the sense 'to move with a clumsy heavy tread'.

Runcible was coined by another noted writer of nonsense verse, Edward Lear. He used *runcible* with obscure meaning in various contexts, perhaps the most famous of which is from "The Owl and the Pussycat": "They dined on mince and slices of quince,/ Which they ate with a runcible spoon." Subsequently the term *runcible spoon* was applied to a fork with three broad, curved prongs and a sharpened edge used with pickles or hors d'oeuvres, thus assuring *runcible* some life, admittedly limited, outside the poetry of Lear.

[*Jabberwocky,* nonsense poem in *Through the Looking Glass* by Lewis Carroll (Charles L. Dodgson) †1898 Eng. author and mathematician]

Jacobean   See MACADAM.
   [NL *jacobaeus* Jacobean (fr. *Jacobus* — James I — †1625 king of England)
   + E -*an*]

jade   Gemstones were once believed to have magical and medicinal
properties. *Jade* was supposed to be especially effective in combating kidney disorders, and the stone owes its name to this belief. The sixteenth-
century Spanish, who brought jade home with them from their possessions
in the New World, named the powerful green stone *piedra de la ijada,*
'loin stone'. Not only in Spain but throughout western Europe jade became popular both as an ornament and as a cure or preventive of internal
problems. Sir Walter Raleigh mentions jade and its use in his *Discoverie
of the Large and Bewtiful Empyre of Guiana* (1596): "A kinde of greene
stones which the Spaniards call *Piedras Hijadas,* and we vse for spleene
stones." The term *spleen stone* did not survive in English; our modern
word *jade* was borrowed from the French, who had so transformed Spanish *ijada.*
   Two kinds of stone are called *jade.* The rarer and more valuable *jadeite*
takes its name from *jade,* but the more common *nephrite* was named, like
jade itself, for its supposed curative powers. *Nephros* is the Greek for 'kidney'.
   An earlier English homonym of *jade* is used for either a horse or a
woman. The origin of this word is uncertain. It was first used in Middle English to mean 'a broken-down horse'. In Chaucer's *Canterbury Tales* the
host encourages the nun's priest:

> Be blithe, though thou ryde upon a jade.
> Wht thogh thyn hors be bothe foul and lene?
> If he wol serve thee, rekke [care] not a bene [bean].
> Look that thyn herte be murie [merry] evermo."

In the early Modern English period the word for a worthless horse was
often applied derogatorily to a woman (or, very rarely, to a man) considered worthless. Now a jade is more often a disreputable woman than a broken-down horse.
   Jaded, meaning 'worn out' or 'dulled by excess', is also derived from the
equine *jade.* Originally, to jade a horse was to make a *jade* of it, to wear
it out or break it down by overwork or abuse. It was not long before people
were jaded as well.
   See also AMETHYST.

   [F, fr. obs. Sp (*piedra de la*) *ijada,* lit., loin stone; Sp *ijada* loin, fr. L *ilia*
   pl. of *ilium, ileum* groin, viscera; fr. the belief that jade cures renal colic]

   [ME, a broken-down horse, of unknown origin]

Jahveh   See JEEPERS.
   [NL, fr. Heb *Yhwh*]

January   The earliest Roman calendar supposedly was introduced about
738 B.C. by Romulus, the legendary founder of Rome. The year consisted

of 304 days divided into ten months, each month being the period between one full moon and the next. These Romans seemed to have ignored or at least left uncounted about two months during the winter. The year began with the vernal equinox, which signaled the beginning of the growing season.

The first month was named *Martius* after Mars, originally a god of agriculture before becoming the god of war. *Martius* was taken into Old French as *march*, which Middle English borrowed as *March* at the beginning of the thirteenth century.

The second month was named *Aprilis*, a word of unknown origin but with a folk etymology that goes back to the Roman scholar Varro (116–27 B.C.), who said it was likely formed from the verb *aperire* 'to open', since this is the period when the buds of leaves and flowers begin to open. *Aprilis* became *avrill* in Old French, which was borrowed into Middle English as *Averil, Aperil,* and finally *April.*

The third month, *Maius,* was probably named for the goddess Maia, the mother of Mercury by Jupiter. In Old French this name became *mai,* which was taken into Middle English as *May.*

Junius, the fourth month, was probably named in honor of the goddess Juno. Old English used the Latin form *Junius* for this month, which became *June* in the fourteenth century.

Quintilis, the name of the fifth month, was formed from the adjective *quintus,* meaning 'fifth'. In 44 B.C. the Roman senate renamed this month *Julius* in honor of Gaius Julius Caesar, the general and statesman who was born in this month. Old English kept the Latin form *Julius,* which eventually became *July* in late Middle English.

Sextilis, the name of the sixth month, was appropriately formed from the adjective *sextus,* meaning 'sixth'. In 8 B.C. the senate renamed this month *Augustus* in honor of Augustus Caesar, the first emperor of Rome. In Old English the Latin form was anglicized to *August.*

September, being the seventh month, was formed from *septem,* meaning 'seven'. This name became *septembre* in Old French and then *Septembre* in Middle English. Eventually the influence of Latin fixed the spelling as *September.* In like manner, *October* was formed from *octo,* meaning 'eight', *November* from *novem* 'nine', and *December* from *decem* 'ten'.

The second king of Rome, Numa Pompilius (715?–673? B.C.) decided to fill in the two-month winter gap with *Januarius,* which was derived from *Janus,* the god of gates and later of beginnings, and *Februarius,* so named because the *Februa,* the feast of spiritual cleansing and expiation, took place during this period.

This calendar was basically a lunar reckoning and had become increasingly out of phase with the seasons. To correct this, Julius Caesar, in 46 B.C., employed the astronomer Sosigenes to review the calendar and suggest ways of improving it. His suggestions included using the sun instead of the moon as the basis for reckoning, allowing for a leap year, and moving the beginning of the year from March 1 to January 1. These suggestions were adopted to devise the Julian calendar, which began on 1 January 45 B.C. Since January was now the first month, September, October, November, and December were no longer the seventh, eighth, ninth, and tenth months. However etymologically inappropriate these names had become, they were retained.

For other articles on words derived from ancient mythology and legend see VOLCANO.

[ME *Januarie,* fr. L *Januarius,* first month of the ancient Roman year, fr. *Janus,* two-faced god or numen of gates and doors and therefore of beginnings (fr. *janus* arch, gate) + *-arius* -ary]

jaunty See GENTILE.
[alter. of earlier *jentee,* fr. F *gentil*]

jean See DENIM.
[short for *jean fustian,* fr. ME *Jene, Gene* Genoa, Italy (fr. MF *Genes*) + *fustian*]

jeep In March 1936 in newspapers across the country, Popeye's girl-friend, Olive Oyl, was delivered a box labeled "Eugene the Jeep" and containing a small animal. Eugene turned out to be a friendly little creature which made the sound "jeep." He was able to foretell the future, and when asked a question he always gave a truthful answer, indicated by wiggling his tail. Elzie C. Segar, creator of the comic strip *Thimble Theater* into which Popeye was introduced in 1929, continued the story of the Jeep throughout much of the year 1936. In 1937 work was begun by several manufacturers to develop an all-purpose vehicle for military use. When the vehicle was ready, it was apparently designated *g.p.* for *general purpose.* Probably under the influence of the famous Eugene the Jeep the pronunciation of the letters *g.p.* became shortened to one syllable and the spelling *jeep* was adopted. For a similar alteration compare the spelling and pronunciation of *veep,* from *v.p.,* an abbreviation of *vice president.* See also GOON.

[prob. alter. (influenced by Eugene the *Jeep,* a fanciful animal in the comic strip *Thimble Theater* by Elzie C. Segar †1938 Am. cartoonist) of *g.p.* (abbr. of *general purpose*)]

jeepers, jeepers creepers All languages and cultures seem to have words or practices that are taboo and hence are not mentioned in polite society. Perhaps because of the shock produced when such words are used, many of them have come to function as interjections, the meaning of which is subordinated to their emotional impact. Another result of the social restrictions against using taboo words is the creation of euphemisms that can be used more freely, though naturally much of the intended force may be lost by this substitution.

Many religions prohibit the utterance of the true names of their particular deities. For instance, out of reverence or for fear of desecration, the Jews about 300 B.C. ceased to pronounce the divine proper name. Because their language was written without any indication of the vowels, the original pronunciation of this name was forgotten in time, though the consonants continued to be used in written texts. These four consonants, which in English we transliterate as YHWH, came to be known as the *tetragrammaton*, from the Greek meaning 'having four letters'. When vowels began to be transcribed in Hebrew several reconstructions of this word were suggested and various possible pronunciations of the tetragrammaton have given us such words as *Jehovah, Yahweh, Jahveh,* and other similar spellings for the name of God.

There are similar prohibitions against the irreverent use of the name of God or Jesus Christ in Christian cultures. Thus, to satisfy what seems to be a need for invective, a number of euphemisms are substituted for those in English. Today *golly* and *gosh* are considered harmless euphemisms for 'God'; and *jeepers* and *jeepers creepers* are used instead of 'Jesus' and 'Jesus Christ'. Slightly more complicated are the terms *jiminy, jiminy crickets,* and *jiminy Christmas. Jiminy* is an alteration of *Gemini,* the name of the third sign of the zodiac, literally meaning 'twins', which was itself apparently used as a euphemism for the Late Latin phrase *Jesu domine,* 'Jesus lord'. *Jiminy crickets* and *jiminy Christmas* then conflate this with the initial sounds of 'Jesus Christ'. Another euphemism for 'Jesus' is *jeez,* sometimes with the spelling altered even further to *geez.*

A number of phrases once used as oaths were also telescoped into a single interjection by leaving out 'God' as in *zounds* from *God's wounds,* or *struth,* sometimes spelled *strewth,* from the phrase *God's truth.* The rather mild imprecation *drat* is probably a euphemistic alteration of *God rot.*

As can be seen from many of the examples above, the initial sounds of the taboo words are often retained, and the euphemism is created by changing other parts of the word or by using other words that are not taboo and which begin with the same sounds. Thus we have *darn* and *darnation* as euphemisms for *damn* and *damnation. Shoot* used as an interjection is a euphemism for *shit,* as are *shucks* and *sugar.*

See also BLAME.

[*jeepers* euphemism for *Jesus; jeepers creepers* euphemism for *Jesus Christ*]

jeez, geez   See JEEPERS.
[euphemism for *Jesus*]

Jehovah   See JEEPERS.
[NL, intended as a transliteration of Heb *Yahweh,* the vowel points of Heb *'ădhōnāy* my lord being substituted for those of *Yahweh;* fr. the fact that in some Heb manuscripts the vowel points of *'ădhōnāy* (used as a euphemism for *Yahweh*) were written under the consonants *yhwh* of *Yahweh* to indicate that *'ădhōnāy* was to be substituted in oral reading for *Yahweh*]

jejune   For a word whose core meaning in Modern English is 'insipid', *jejune* has led a remarkably robust and varied semantic life.

The trail begins with Latin *jejunus*—rather abruptly, as the Latin word is of uncertain parentage. Its primary and original meaning was 'on an empty stomach, fasting'. Applied to the neuter word *intestinum* 'intestines', it took the form *jejunum*, and in this form was borrowed into English, to denote a section of the small intestine. The section was so named because it was said to be found always empty at death.

Already in Latin, various metaphorical extensions of *jejunus* were in use, much as in English we may describe either a child or a style as "undernourished." Applied to land or prose, it meant 'barren'. In English, *jejune* is first attested in the 'fasting' sense in the early seventeenth century, but in time the connotations radiating out from the further sense of 'undernourished', such as 'flat, vapid', came to predominate. In our own century especially, *jejune* seems often to be used with the specific implication of 'sophomoric' or 'callow', so that Webster's Third New International Dictionary added a further subsense, 'immature, juvenile, puerile', not recorded in earlier editions. Such uses have led some observers to speculate that the users may be confusing *jejune* with the unrelated French word *jeune* 'young', from Latin *juvenis* (the French descendant of *jejunus* is the similar-looking *jeun* 'on an empty stomach'). Since 'puerile' is not an implausible semantic development from the sense 'insipid', we cannot be certain that such contamination has played a role; but suspicion is strengthened when one reads (in the *N.Y. Times Book Rev.* for 12 Aug. 1984): "There is so little other decent fiction around to tickle a jejune man's fantasies."

In Vulgar Latin, *jejunus* gave rise to a compound verb reconstructed as *disjejunare*, literally 'to break one's fast'. The first meal of the day is named for this notion: English *breakfast*, where the spelling but not the pronunciation makes the etymology clear, and the French descendant of the Vulgar Latin verb, (*petit*) *déjeuner*. Under different accentual conditions, *disjejunare* yielded French *dîner*, the source of our verb *dine*.

[L *jejunus*]

jeopardy In French *jeu parti* means literally 'divided game'. In Old French, the major criterion for a *jeu parti* was the involvement of alternative possibilities or opposed viewpoints. A *jeu parti* could be a poem in dialogue form representing the discussion or argument of problems, especially amorous problems. Or it could be a situation in a game like chess in which the relative worth of alternative plays is uncertain. It was in this sense that the word was borrowed into Middle English. In any undertaking, a position that provides equal chances of success and of failure can be described in terms of a similar position in chess and called a *jeopardy*. But the word was very early used in its present sense: *jeopardy* is 'risk or danger, with a greater probability of losing than of winning'. Chaucer knew both *jeopardies*. He wrote of "Ieupardyes . . . at ches" and of the hopeless peril of besieged Troy: "For Troy is brought in swich a Iupartye/ That it to save is now no remedye."

Another descendant of Old French *jeu* is *jewel*. *Jewel* comes from the diminutive *juel* and so is, etymologically, a 'little game' or 'little plaything'.

[ME *jupartie, jeopartie, jeopardie*, fr. AF *juparti, jeu parti*, fr. OF, alternative, poem treating amorous problems in dialogue form, fr. *ju, jeu* game, play (fr. L *jocus* joke, jest, game) + *parti,* past part. of *partir* to divide]

jeremiad   Jeremiah, known in Hebrew as Yirmeyahu and in Late Latin as Jeremias, was a Biblical prophet, a reformer, and the author of the Old Testament book that bears his name. Living from about 650 B.C. to about 570 B.C., he was intimately involved in the political and religious events of his time. He witnessed the capture of Jerusalem by the Babylonians in 586 B.C. and the exile of many Judaeans to Babylonia. From the beginning of his prophetic career, Jeremiah's messages were condemnations of his people for their false worship and social injustice. He continually called upon his people to quit their wicked ways, to give up their idols and false gods, and to honor their covenant with Yahweh. During the reign of Jehoiakim, Jeremiah denounced the ruler for his selfishness, materialism, and inequities. The prophet also persistently rebuked his ruler and fellow countrymen for not readily submitting to the yoke of the Babylonians. (He claimed that God willed it.) Even when he and other Jews were exiled in Egypt, he continued to rebuke his fellow exiles. (According to tradition, his exasperated companions stoned him to death in Egypt.) When Jeremiah was not inflicting his lamentations on his country and people, he was inflicting them upon himself. A portion of the Book of Jeremiah is devoted to the "confessions" of Jeremiah, a series of individual laments reflecting on the hardships endured by a prophet with an unpopular message.

Jeremiah made his way into the English language by way of French. From the Late Latin *Jeremias* the French derived *Jérémie* and used the personal name as the root for *jérémiade,* which means the same as the English *jeremiad:* a prolonged lamentation or complaint.

[F *jérémiade,* fr. *Jérémie* Jeremiah †*ab* 585 B.C. Heb. prophet known for his pessimism (fr. LL *Jeremias, Hieremias,* fr. Gk *Hieremias,* fr. Heb *Yirmĕyāh*) + *-ade* -ad]

Jerusalem artichoke   The *Jerusalem artichoke,* also called *girasole,* does not come from Jerusalem or anywhere else in the Middle East, nor is it an *artichoke;* it is a widely cultivated perennial American sunflower. The tubers are edible and are used as a vegetable and as a livestock feed. The fact that the flavor of these tubers is reminiscent of the flavor of the *artichoke* accounts for this element of the name. *Jerusalem* is here the result of folk etymology from Italian *girasole,* 'sunflower', so that a familiar comprehensible word has been substituted for what was probably taken to be foreign gibberish. A sunflower is called *girasole* in Italian because many sunflowers turn to face the sun as it crosses the sky. *Girasole* is formed from Italian *girare,* 'to turn', plus *sole,* 'sun'.

Heliotrope, a member of the forget-me-not family, also turns toward the sun, and although it is biologically unrelated to the *girasole* it has a similar etymology. Latin *heliotropium* is from Greek *hēliotropion. Hēlios* is the Greek for 'sun' and *tropos* means 'turn'.

For other folk etymologies see FOLK ETYMOLOGY.

[*Jerusalem* by folk etymology fr. It *girasole* sunflower, fr. *girare* to turn + *sole* sun, fr. L *sol*]

jess See FALCON.
[ME *ges, gesse,* fr. MF *gies, giez,* fr. pl. of *giet, get, jet* throw, fr. *jeter* to throw, fr. L *jactare,* fr. *jactus,* past part. of *jacere* to throw]

jewel See JEOPARDY.
[ME *juel, jowel, jewel,* fr. OF *juel, joel, joiel,* dim. of *ju, jo, jeu* game, play]

jiminy See JEEPERS.
[alter. of *Gemini*]

jingo See CHAUVINISM.
[fr. *Jingo* supporter of the British belligerent attitude toward Russia in 1878, fr. *jingo* (a mild oath), prob. euphemism for *Jesus;* fr. the fact that the phrase *by jingo* appeared in the refrain of a chauvinistic song sung by the Jingoes]

jingoism See CHAUVINISM.
[*jingo* + *-ism*]

jinn, jinni See GENIUS.
[Ar *jinnīy* demon, spirit]

join See YOGA.
[ME *joinen,* fr. OF *join-, joign-,* stem of *joindre,* fr. L *jungere*]

jonquil See JUNKET.
[NL & F; NL *junquilia,* fr. F or Sp; F *jonquille,* fr. Sp *junquillo,* dim. of *junco* rush, reed (fr. the appearance of the leaves), fr. L *juncus*]

jot "Till heaven and earth pass, one jot or one tittle shall in no wise pass from the law, till all be fulfilled." This is the King James Version of Christ's assurance (Matthew 5:18) that He was not "come to destroy the law or the prophets." Not the smallest letter, not a single stroke of a letter, we are told, will be lost. The word *jot* first appeared in English in William Tyndale's translation of Matthew's Gospel, in 1526: "One iott or one tytle of the law shall not scape." Tyndale simply put into an anglicized shape the Latin word *jota* (or *iota*), itself simply a transliteration of the Greek name of the ninth letter in the Greek alphabet.

The original Aramaic version must have referred to *yōdh,* the smallest letter in the Hebrew alphabet. The transfer across language boundaries was easily made because the Greek equivalent, *iōta,* was also the smallest letter in its alphabet. John Wycliffe, when he translated St. Matthew in 1382, did not try to anglicize the word *iota* but used instead the English letter *i:* "Till heuen and erthe passe, oon i, or titel, shal nat passe fro the lawe." He glossed *i:* "That is leste [least] lettre."

By the seventeenth century *iota* itself came to be used in English in the sense 'jot, whit', as in this passage by Daniel Featley in *Clavis Mystica,* a treatise on the scriptures (1636): "Shall we lose, or sleightly pass by, any *iota* or tittle of the Booke of God?"

The English word *tittle (titel)* was first used in this translation of Wycliffe's. *Titel,* which he used in this passage to translate the Latin Bible's *apex,* 'point' (the Greek New Testament has *keraia,* 'point', 'hook', literally 'horn'), comes from Middle Latin *titulus,* a 'title' or 'diacritical mark'. A *jot* or a *tittle* is now simply 'a very small part'.

[L *jota* iota, jot, fr. Gk *iōta,* of Sem origin; akin to Heb *yōdh* yodh]

joust   See YOGA.
[ME, fr. OF *joste, juste, jouste,* fr. *joster, juster, jouster* to gather, unite, joust, fr. (assumed) VL *juxtare,* fr. L *juxta* near, nearby; akin to L *jungere* to join]

jovial   In the astrology of ancient Rome it was believed that life on earth was subject to the influence of the planets. Thus, a person born during the ascendancy of a particular planet was subject to that planet's influence on his life, character, and fortune. Five planets (besides Earth) were known at that time, and they were named after major Roman deities: Jupiter, Saturn, Mars, Venus, and Mercury. Each deity possessed particular attributes of character, which also characterized those persons born under the planet bearing that deity's name.

The largest planet was named after the chief god, Jupiter (also called Jove). He was characterized as majestic and authoritative and was considered the source of joy and happiness. The Latin adjective *jovialis* was used to mean 'of or relating to Jupiter'. In Middle French this had become *jovial,* which was borrowed into English in the seventeenth century in the sense of 'majestic'. Michael Drayton, in his poem "The Owle" (1604), exemplifies this use in referring to the eagle: "When this princely jovial fowl they saw." Today, *jovial* is more often used for 'good-natured, jolly', reflecting another of Jupiter's attributes. Astrologers consider being born under the planet Jupiter a most auspicious sign.

Saturn, the god of agriculture and father of Jupiter, was conceived of as a bent old man having a stern, sluggish, and sullen nature. A person born under the planet Saturn was supposed to have such a disposition. The Latin *Saturnius* 'Saturn' yielded the assumed adjective *saturninus* 'of Saturn' in Medieval Latin, which was borrowed into English as *saturnine* in the fifteenth century. Robert Browning made use of this adjective in *The Ring and the Book* (1868): "Mimic the tetchy humour, furtive glance,/And brow where half was furious, half fatigued,/O' the same son got to be of middle age,/Sour, saturnine,—your humble servant here."

Mars, the god of war, was originally conceived of as a god of agriculture. Later he was associated with the Greek god of war, Ares, taking on his warlike character. Mars thus became a god of death and devastation. The color red (for blood) was associated with him, which is probably the reason that the reddish planet was named after him. The Latin adjective *Martialis* 'of or relating to Mars' was taken into English in the fourteenth century as *martial* and was used to mean 'of, relating to, or suited for war'. In reference to a person it meant 'given to fighting, warlike'. In astrology, *Martial* describes the evil or pernicious influence of the planet Mars on all those born under it.

The Romans honored Venus, goddess of love and beauty, by naming the brightest planet after her. Latin poets used her name as a synonym for 'sexual love, venery'. The adjective *venereus,* derived from her name, meant 'relating to sexual pleasure' and 'lascivious, wanton'. This adjective was borrowed into Middle English as *venereal* and used in the sense 'relating to sexual desire or intercourse'. In astrology, one born under the planet Venus was supposedly inclined to be lascivious or lustful. While the astrological sense has become obsolete, *venereal* is still used, mainly in reference to sexually transmitted diseases.

Mercury (Latin *Mercurius*), messenger and herald of the Olympian gods and himself the god of merchants and thieves, was noted for his eloquence, swiftness, and cunning. In honor of this fleet-footed messenger, the Romans named the fastest moving planet Mercury. The derivative adjective *mercurialis* 'of or relating to Mercury' was taken into English in the fourteenth century as *mercurial* with its original Latin meaning. In astrology, one born under the planet Mercury was expected to be eloquent, ready-witted, sharp-dealing, sprightly, or thievish. A modern example of this use appeared in the journal *English* (October 1921): "He is mercurial, sprightly in mind as in body, because the jester of the gods presided over his birth."

For other articles on words derived from ancient mythology and legend see VOLCANO.

[MF & LL; MF, fr. LL *jovialis* of the god Jupiter, fr. *Jov-, Juppiter* Jupiter, ancient Roman god of the sky + L *-alis* -al]

jubilee "And ye shall hallow the fiftieth year, and proclaim liberty throughout all the land unto all the inhabitants thereof: it shall be a jubilee unto you" (Leviticus 25:10, AV). Ancient Hebrew law established every fiftieth year as a year of emancipation and restoration. All Hebrew slaves were freed; lands were restored to their former owners; fields were left uncultivated. This year took its name, *yōbhēl,* from the ram's horn trumpets used to proclaim its advent. When the Old Testament was translated into Greek and later into Latin, the translators borrowed the Hebrew name, since neither Greeks nor Romans had any comparable semicentennial celebration to lend its name to the *yōbhēl.* The Greeks simply put the Hebrew word into Greek form, *iōbēlaios.* But the borrowing of the Greek word into Latin was less straightforward. It could not be denied that a *iōbēlaios* was a joyful time, and Latin had already a remarkably similar word, *jubilare,* 'to raise a joyful shout'. The influence of *jubilare* gave the Greek word its Latin form, *jubilaeus.*

Since *jubilee* came into English with John Wycliffe's translation of the

Bible, it has acquired several new meanings. Any fiftieth anniversary, or even another special anniversary, may be called a *jubilee*. A *golden jubilee* is a fiftieth anniversary, *silver jubilee* is a twenty-fifth, and *diamond jubilee* a sixtieth or seventy-fifth. The pope declares a *jubilee* year for Roman Catholics every twenty-five years. *Jubilation* and *jubilant*, English descendants of Latin *jubilare*, have also influenced the extended meanings of *jubilee*, and *jubilee* may be used as a simple synonym of *jubilation*.

[ME, fr. MF & LL; MF *jubilé*, fr. LL *jubilaeus*, modif. (influenced by L *jubilare* to jubilate) of LGk *iōbēlaios*, fr. Heb *yōbhēl* ram's horn, trumpet, jubilee]

judge   A study of English legal terms reveals the great influence of the French language in this area. For more than a century after the Norman Conquest in 1066, England's legal language was French; thus, most of the technical terms of the law, especially of the private law, are of French (and ultimately Latin) origin.

In Roman law the Latin noun *judex* denoted 'an individual appointed to hear and determine a case; a judge'. This noun was formed from *jus* 'law, right' and *-dic-*, *-dex*, from the verb *dicere* 'to say'. From *judex* (declensional stem *judic-*) the verb *judicare* 'to judge, decide' was formed, which is the source of our verb *adjudicate* 'to pass judgment on; settle judicially'. *Judex* passed into French as *juge*, which was than taken into English around 1300, becoming the noun *judge* in modern English. The Latin verb *judicare* became *jugier* in early French and was borrowed into English also around 1300 as *juggen*, later becoming the verb *judge*.

From *judex* was also derived the Latin noun *judicium*, used for 'legal proceedings, a trial; a panel of judges; a judgment, verdict; a considered opinion'. *Judicium*, in turn, became the source of the Latin adjectives *judicialis* 'judicial' and *judiciarius* 'judiciary'. In French *justicium* was used to form the adjective *judicieux*, which English borrowed in the late sixteenth century as *judicious* 'having or exercising sound judgment'.

In Saxon England guilt or innocence was often determined by a trial by ordeal in which the suspected person was subjected to a physical test. This might involve taking up in the hand a piece of red-hot iron, walking barefoot over red-hot plowshares, plunging a bare arm into boiling water, or being cast into water. If the person passed the test unhurt, he was adjudged innocent; if otherwise, he was condemned as guilty. Trial by jury can also be traced back to the Saxons. An accused person might be *vindicated* (from Latin *vindicare* 'to set free') or *exonerated* (from Latin *exonerare* 'to free from a burden') if a number of persons (*juratores* 'sworn witnesses') came forward and swore to a *veredictum* 'an answer or decision given to a court', that they believed him innocent. *Veredictum* was formed in Medieval Latin from *vere* 'truly' and *dictum* 'said', a form of the past participle of *dicere* 'to say'. This noun was taken into Anglo-French and thence into Middle English as *verdit*. The Latin word later influenced the English to alter the spelling to *verdict*, which then became the Modern French form as well.

Though trial by jury existed among the Anglo-Saxons, the word *jury* itself is not of Old English origin. Early French took the Latin verb *jurare* 'to take an oath, swear' as *jurer*. From this verb, Anglo-French formed the noun *juree,* which was used for 'a body of persons sworn to give a verdict on some matter submitted to them'. *Juree* became *jure, jurie* in Middle English and *jury* in Modern English.

In addition to judge and jury, several other persons figure prominently in our courts of law. The term *plaintiff* goes back to the Latin verb *plangere* 'to beat, beat one's breast, lament'. The past participle, *planctus,* used as a noun for 'a beating of the breast, lamentation', was taken into Middle French as *plaint* and used for 'an audible expression of woe, lamentation'. From this noun, French formed the adjective *plaintif* 'lamenting, complaining'. French law then used *plaintif* as a noun for 'the initiator of a lawsuit', which English borrowed as *plaintiff* about 1400.

Opposed to the plaintiff is the *defendant,* the party being sued or charged. This term derives from the substantive use of the present participle, *defendant,* of the early French verb *defendre,* a gallicization of the Latin *defendere* 'to ward off, refute, make a defense in a legal action'.

In criminal cases, the *prosecutor* 'pursues' the defendant for redress or punishment for a crime. His title ultimately derives from the verb *prosequi* 'to follow, pursue', whose past participle is *prosecutus.*

In U.S. courts, a *bailiff* announces the entrance of the judge usually with the cry *oyez.* This word *oyez* is the imperative form of the Anglo-French verb *oir* 'to hear'. The French derived it from the Latin *audire* 'to hear'. *Bailiff* can also be traced back through French to a Latin origin. The Latin noun *bajulus,* meaning 'one who bears burdens for pay; porter', gave rise to the verb *bajulare* 'to carry a burden, keep in custody'. From this verb the French formed *baillier,* meaning 'to bear, manage, take charge of' and 'to hand over, deliver'. In early French, the noun *bail* 'custody, jurisdiction' was derived from *baillier,* and it led to the noun *baillif* 'a king's officer having jurisdiction in a certain district'. This term was borrowed into English toward the end of the thirteenth century.

[ME *juge,* fr. MF, fr. L *judic-, judex* judex, judge, fr. *ju-* (fr. *jus* right, law) + *-dic-, -dex* (fr. *dicere* to determine, say)]

judicious   See JUDGE.
[MF *judicieux,* fr. L *judicium* judgment + MF *-eux* -ous]

juggernaut   In the early fourteenth century Friar Odoric, a Franciscan missionary, published a journal of his travels to the Far East. In this account he brought to Europe from India for the first time the story of the enormous carriage or car on which devotees of *Jagannāth,* an avatar of the god Vishnu, draw his image in procession from the temple at Puri. Some of the worshipers of *Jagannāth,* whose name means 'Lord of the World', would allow themselves to be crushed beneath the wheels of the car in sacrifice to their god. However, reports of the frequency of this practice have often been exaggerated, and many of the deaths probably were a result of accidents which inevitably occur in the press of celebration. In any event, Friar Odoric's story spread throughout Europe, and as a result the

English form *juggernaut* began to be used in the nineteenth century in the sense of a massive inexorable force or object that crushes everything in its path.

Not surprisingly, *juggernaut* was also used to refer to such massive vehicles as the steam locomotives of the nineteenth century and the armored tanks developed during the First World War, and now can stand for any vehicle which threatens to run down anything in its way. Even in the early years of the automobile this new machine was viewed with alarm and foreboding by many, and we find in the Merriam-Webster files a citation taken from the *Automobile Review* of 15 April 1903 referring to the rapid spread of these horseless carriages: "It increases the number of fast travelers on the road, and gives the weight of numbers to the whole automobile movement, and removes from the sport the absurd criticism of 'rich men's juggernauts.' "

[Hindi *Jagannāth* lord of the world (i.e., Vishnu, one of the principal Hindu gods), fr. Skt *Jagannātha*, fr. *jagat* world (fr. *jagat*, adj., moving, living) + *nātha* lord; fr. a belief that some devotees of Vishnu allowed themselves to be crushed beneath the wheels of the car on which his image was being drawn in procession; akin to Skt *jigāti* he goes]

jugular See YOGA.
[LL *jugularis*, fr. L *jugulum* collarbone, neck, throat; akin to L *jungere* to join]

July See JANUARY.
[ME *julie*, fr. OE *julius*, fr. L, after Gaius *Julius* Caesar ₁44 B.C. Roman general and statesman who was born in this month]

junction See YOGA.
[L *junction-*, *junctio*, fr. *junctus* (part part. of *jungere* to join) + *-ion-*, *-io* -ion]

June See JANUARY.
[ME *Junius, Juyn, June;* ME *Junius,* fr. OE & L; OE, fr. L, prob. fr. *Junius,* name of a Roman gens; ME *Juyn, June,* fr. MF & L; MF *juin,* fr. OF, fr. L *Junius;* prob. akin to L *Juno,* ancient Italian goddess]

junket *Juncus* is the Latin word for a rush, a marsh plant whose stems and leaves are useful for making mats and baskets. Long ago a type of cream cheese was prepared in baskets made of rushes or reeds, and the cheese took its name from its container. In Italy in the Middle Ages this cream cheese was called *giuncata,* a derivative of Latin *juncus.* It was probably from this Italian source that Middle English borrowed *ioncate.* English *ioncate,* later *junket,* was first used for cream cheese but later became the name of a dessert made of sweetened curdled milk. In the early modern period, indeed, *junket* became a popular term for any sweet dish. William Adlington's sixteenth-century translation of *The Golden Ass of Apuleius* (1566) lists a few: "Bread pasties, tartes, custardes and other delicate ionckettes dipped in honie." From this sense of *junket* developed the extended sense 'a feast or banquet'. Perhaps two centuries ago, *junket* began to be used for a large picnic or outing at which eating and drinking are a major part of the entertainment and later for any pleasure outing or trip. The most common contemporary *junket* is a trip made by a public official at public expense.

Another descendant of Latin *juncus* is our *jonquil*. This flower was named for the resemblance of its long, narrow leaves to those of rushes.

[ME *ioncate,* prob. fr. OIt *giuncata* cream cheese, fr. (assumed) VL *juncata,* fr. L *juncus* rush]

junta See YOGA.
[Sp, fr. fem. of *junto* together, joined, fr. L *junctus,* past part. of *jungere* to join]

jury See JUDGE.
[ME *jure, jurie,* fr. AF *juree,* fr. OF *jurer* to swear, fr. L *jurare, jurari,* fr. *jur-, jus* law, right]

juxtaposition See YOGA.
[L *juxta* near + E *position*]

K

kaiser The name of Gaius Julius Caesar, the famous Roman general and statesman, became synonymous with the office of emperor of the Roman Empire, and later emperors adopted his name to indicate their right to the imperial title. Subsequently other European languages borrowed this name from Latin as a word for emperor, and forms appropriate to each language developed. Middle English *keiser* appears in this sense in the twelfth and thirteenth centuries, and even earlier its Old English cognate *cāsere* is used with the same meaning. The word was also used in Gothic in the form *kaisar* from which derives the Russian form *tsar'*. This is the source of *czar* and *tsar* in English.

Caesar's name is also perpetuated in the English term *cesarean,* 'the surgical incision of the walls of the abdomen and uterus for the delivery of offspring'. The name was given to this operation because of the belief that, like Macduff in Shakespeare's *Macbeth,* Julius Caesar was "from his mother's womb/ Untimely ripp'd." For another word derived from Julius Caesar's name see *July* at JANUARY.

[ME *keiser,* fr. ON *keisari;* akin to OE *cāsere* emperor, OHG *keisur,* Goth *kaisar;* all fr. a prehistoric Gmc word borrowed fr. L *Caesar,* cognomen of Gaius Julius *Caesar* †44 B.C. Roman general and statesman]

kamikaze In about 1274 Kublai Khan made the mistake of sending a fleet against Japan. The Japanese took warning and began to prepare their defenses, and the attack was unsuccessful. The great Khan then sent envoys, inviting the Japanese ruler to pay him homage, but the Japanese beheaded these envoys and continued to build up their defenses. Finally, in 1281, Kublai Khan sent an immense fleet. Although Japan was prepared and her defenders were determined, the Mongol horde was not easy to resist. But after some weeks of inconclusive fighting, a great and sudden storm arose and destroyed the Mongol fleet. To the Japanese this salvation was *kamikaze,* 'divine wind'.

In the Second World War Japan sent out pilots willing to give up their lives to help save their country by destroying American ships. These were the members of a special corps named *kamikaze* after the storm that had saved Japan some seven centuries earlier. The kamikaze's drastic methods made a greater impression on Americans than did his patriotic goal. *Kami-*

kaze, originally borrowed into English as a name for the suicidal pilot, is now an adjective meaning 'suicidal'.

[Jp, lit., divine wind, fr. *kami* god + *kaze* wind]

kaput   To win all of the tricks in the card game piquet is *faire capot*, 'to make capot', in French, while *être capot*, 'to be capot', is to have lost all of the tricks in a game. *Capot* was borrowed into English directly from French as early as the seventeenth century as a noun signifying the winning of all the tricks in piquet and other games. In German this same *capot* was transliterated as *kaput*, and from the sense of having lost a game German *kaput* developed the senses of 'finished' and 'broken'. *Kaput* began to appear in English writing in the late nineteenth century, generally in contexts where a German word would be appropriate or else printed in italics or glossed to show that it was not yet a fully anglicized word. However, during and after the Second World War *kaput* gained greater currency in English and is now widely used to mean 'utterly finished', 'useless', or 'hopelessly outmoded'.

[G, fr. F *capot* not having made a trick at piquet]

karat   See CARAT.
[prob. fr. MF *carat*, fr. ML *caratus* unit of weight for precious stones]

katydid   See PIGEON.
[imit.]

keloid   See RANKLE.
[F *kiloïd, chéloïd*, fr. Gk *chēlē* claw + F *-oïde* -oid]

khaki   *Khaki* is ultimately derived from the Persian word for 'dust'. It originally meant 'dust-colored' but was soon applied to a fabric of this color, used for uniforms. The military connotation is at the forefront of the way the word is usually used today, but the 'dust' connection remains in that a uniform of another color would not be described as khaki. In a couple of other cases, however, the color name that lies at the origin of a fabric word has been quite forgotten. A *blanket* may today be of any color, though the word comes ultimately from French *blanc* 'white'. *Baize* is now typically green, but derives from Middle French *bai* 'bay-colored'—bay being reddish brown. (The *z* in *baize*, incidentally, is an oddity: it actually represents the plural ending of the immediate French source word *baies*. For other instances of a plural noun reinterpreted as a singular see BODICE.)

[Hindi *khākī* dusty, dust-colored, fr. *khāk* dust, fr. Per]

kibitz   Pewits, or lapwings, gather in flocks in fields and pastures, crying "pewit," or "kiebitz," or the like. (The variation is not in the birds' call, of course, but in human interpretations of it.) These creatures seem to show a general curiosity about the world, although they are really merely inquiring into the edibility of some part of it. The pewit's German name, *kiebitz*, came to be applied to human busybodies as well as the inquisitive birds. This sense of the noun gave rise to a new verb by functional shift: an offensively nosy onlooker at cards could be said to *kiebitzen*, 'to kibitz'. The word passed from German into Yiddish as *kibitsen*, and thence to English as *kibitz*.

[Yiddish *kibitsen*, fr. G *kiebitzen*, fr. *kiebitz* pewit, busybody, fr. MHG *gībitz* pewit, of imit. origin]

kiln   Most of us who have nothing professionally to do with kilns pronounce the word \'kiln\, sounding the *n*. The *n* is indeed fully etymological, as *kiln* derives from Latin *culina* 'kitchen, cookstove', which also lies at the root of our word *culinary*. But those who work with kilns traditionally pronounce it \'kil\, rhyming with *pill*. The dropping of final *n* after *l* is in fact a very old change in English, dating back to the fourteenth century. Our modern word *mill* was frequently spelled *milne* in the Middle Ages, reflecting its origins in Latin *molina*. (*Miln* still exists as a dialect variant of *mill*.) And *ell*, an old measure derived from the length of the arm, was *eln* in Middle English, and is related to Latin *ulna* 'arm, forearm' (itself borrowed into English as the name for one of the forearm's bones).

Another loss of a stop consonant after a nasal in the course of the development of English was the loss of final *b* after *m*. In this case the process has been carried through across the board as regards pronunciation, but the spelling recalls the old state of affairs: *climb, comb, dumb, lamb, womb*. See also DEBT.

[ME *kilne*, fr. OE *cyln, cylen*, fr. L *culina* kitchen, fr. *coquere* to cook]

kitty-corner   See CATERCORNER.
[by folk etymology fr. *catercorner*]

kiwi   See PIGEON.
[Maori, of imit. origin]

kiwifruit   The plum-sized, brown-skinned, hairy *kiwifruit* takes its name from the nickname for New Zealanders, who in turn derive their name from the kiwi, a flightless bird native to New Zealand. The kiwifruit actually grows on a shrub called a *Chinese gooseberry*. It is called this despite being grown commercially, for the most part, in New Zealand and California and despite being unrelated to the true gooseberry.

Although the kiwifruit is relatively new to the United States, it has been eaten in China for hundreds of years. The Chinese call it, and the plant that produces it, *yang tao*. When the plant was introduced into New Zealand in 1906, it was renamed *Chinese gooseberry* by New Zealand horticulturists, partly for its country of origin and partly for its superficial resemblance to the gooseberry. The New Zealanders changed more than just the plant's name, however. After extensive testing and development, particularly by a nurseryman named Hayward Wright, a hybrid form that bore large, luscious fruit was produced. In 1953 New Zealand began exporting the improved fruit, still called the Hayward variety in honor of its developer. At that point the fruit was being sold as the *Chinese gooseberry,* but without much appeal for shoppers and without any association with New Zealand. With a change of name came a change in fortunes for the growers and shippers, and the new fruit quickly became popular. No one is sure who first came up with the name *kiwifruit*—New Zealand growers or American merchants and consumers. What is known is that the name caught on, just as the fruit that tasted of strawberry, lime, and a dash of banana caught on.

The new name was a good choice for another reason besides that of associating it with New Zealand, where it was first developed as a commercial crop. The long-billed kiwi bird appears to have no wings and is covered with long, grayish-brown plumage that looks more like hair than feathers. The brown fuzz on the outside of a *kiwifruit* looks something like the hair-like feathers of the flightless kiwi bird.

[*kiwi,* nickname for New Zealanders; fr. the fact that it was first established as a commercial crop in New Zealand]

knee See YOGA.
[ME *kne, knee,* fr. OE *cnēow, cnēo;* akin to OHG *kneo* knee, ON *knē,* Goth *kniu,* L *genu,* Gk *gony,* Skt *jānu*]

knickerbocker In 1809 Washington Irving published *A History of New York from the Beginning of the World to the End of the Dutch Dynasty.* Presented as the work of a fictional historian Diedrich Knickerbocker, *History of New York* is at once a parody of the pretentious guide books of the times and a genial satire of the early Dutch settlers of the New Netherlands. As promised in the title, the book begins with the Creation, leaps ahead to the Dutch exploration of America, and settles into a portrait of Dutch New York. There are humorously affectionate descriptions of Dutchmen dressed in baggy breeches, wide-brimmed hats, and oversized boots and puffing at long-stemmed clay pipes. Along with seriocomic recountings of early Dutch legends and traditions, there are racy passages detailing the moral peccadilloes of the staid settlers. Irving probably chose *Knickerbocker* as the name for his fictional alter ego because it was a Dutch name with a long and proud history, the Knickerbocker family having been established in the Hudson River valley since the seventeenth century.

Knickerbocker's History of New York (as the work came to be known) was an instant success. Its enduring popularity resulted in many printings and several revisions. In the preface to the 1848 edition, Irving noted that New Yorkers of Dutch descent had taken to calling themselves "genuine Knickerbockers." Irving's good-natured burlesque of early New York apparently struck a responsive chord in many nineteenth century New Yorkers, whether of Dutch descent or not. *Knickerbocker* soon became a byname for any native or resident of New York—city or state. Attributive use of *Knickerbocker* also became popular. By 1856 the Yankee poet Longfellow was privately complaining of "the dreadful Knickerbocker custom of calling on everybody." The popular practice of attaching *Knickerbocker* to anything related to New York survives today perhaps most conspicuously in the name of New York City's professional basketball team, commonly known by the shortened form of the name, Knicks.

Knickerbocker also survives in an entirely different sense. In the 1850s the English caricaturist George Cruikshank illustrated an edition of the work with a depiction of the eponymous Knickerbocker and his fellow Dutch burghers as wearing loose-fitting breeches gathered just below the knee. The renewed interest in sports and outdoor activities, such as bicycling and golfing, in the mid-nineteenth century sparked a revival of the fashion for knee breeches. The resemblance between the latest interpretation and the style worn by the Dutch colonists in Cruikshank's illustrations was enough to inspire the adoption of *knickerbockers* for knee breeches. Before very long *knickerbockers* was shortened to *knickers,* the name by which they are best known today.

Knickerbocker is not the whole of Washington Irving's legacy to the people of his beloved New York. They also owe to him one of New York City's most frequently applied nicknames, *Gotham.* During 1807 and 1808 Irving, his brother William, and James Kirk Paulding published a humor periodical known as *Salmagundi; or, The Whim-Whams and Opinions of Launcelot Langstaff, Esq. and Others.* The title, taken from the name of a salad plate variously concocted from an assortment of ingredients, was intended to suggest the miscellaneous nature of the collection. Under the cover of imaginative pseudonyms, the writers unleashed their wit on contemporary politics, theater, fashion, and manners in order to "instruct the young, reform the old, correct the town, and castigate the age." It was in an issue of *Salmagundi* that Irving gave the name *Gotham* to New York City. *Gotham* had long been proverbial for a place where fools resided. The story behind this goes all the way back to the Middle Ages. According to legend, when King John threatened to visit the town of Gotham, in Nottinghamshire, the villagers attempted to discourage such a visit by acting like fools and madmen before the king's heralds. The ploy worked, and Gotham was spared the visit—but supposedly acquired a reputation for foolishness. During the reign of Henry VIII a collection of popular tales of stupidity—perhaps the medieval equivalent of ethnic jokes—was published as *Merry Tales of the Mad Men of Gotham.* The collection inspired many other stories of stupidity to be associated with the inhabitants of Gotham. Irving dubbed his own hometown *Gotham* in the belief that it, too, was populated by fools.

Since a metropolis like New York is continually reinventing itself, it is perhaps not surprising that the popularity of the nickname *Gotham* has been eclipsed in recent years by another, the *Big Apple.* Since the 1970s it has become almost the de rigueur nickname for New York. While *Gotham* can be traced with certainty to Washington Irving, the history of *Big Apple* is much less certain. The ascendant popularity of *Big Apple* in the 1970s can be traced to Charles Gillett. In 1970, as head of the New York Convention and Visitors Bureau, he started a promotional campaign to have New York known as "the Big Apple." While he did not coin the term, and was not even the first to apply it exclusively to New York, he is now generally credited with popularizing it.

So when and how did New York acquire the nickname of the *Big Apple?* In the 1 October 1967 issue of the *New York Times,* John S. Wilson made the following observation:

> Even though New York has been the Big Apple for several decades—the goal of hopeful jazz musicians not only in this country but around the world—it does not have the kind of positive identity with jazz that a number of other cities have.

It is worth noting that while Wilson states that New York has been thought of "for several decades" by jazz musicians as the *Big Apple,* that is, "the big time," there is no indication that musicians, or jazz musicians in particular, actually called New York the *Big Apple.* Rather, a close reading indicates that jazz musicians used *Big Apple* as a synonym for *big time* (an old vaudeville term) and that New York was naturally considered in the top rank.

We find that the word *apple* was common in the jazz world as far back as the 1930s. Robert S. Gold, in *Jazz Talk,* quotes Cab Calloway in *Hi Di Ho* (1938) as stating that *apple* means "the big town, the main stem, Harlem" as the place musicians strive for. In 1937 a new jazz dance, reported to have begun in South Carolina, became a craze in New York. It was known as the Big Apple even before it made its appearance "up north." And in a 19 December 1938 issue of *Time* magazine, a sports item mentions that big-time racetracks and especially New York tracks were known by horsemen and jockeys as the Big Apple. By whatever route it made its way to the Convention and Visitors Bureau, the nickname *Big Apple* appears to have been embraced by New Yorkers and has become known around the world.

[after Diedrich *Knickerbocker,* pretended author of *History of New York* (1809), by Washington Irving †1859 Am. author]

knickers   See KNICKERBOCKER.
[short for *knickerbockers*]

kobold   See COBALT.
[G]

krypton   See XENON.
[Gk, neut. of *kryptos* hidden]

kudo   See KUDOS.
[back-formation fr. *kudos* (taken as pl.), fr. Gk *kydos*]

kudos   The Greek noun *kydos* was borrowed into English as *kudos* around 1830 and was used in the sense of 'the praise or prestige one gains by having accomplished something noteworthy'. The Oxford English Dictionary notes that its earliest use was in British university slang and labels it a colloquialism. In print, it was usually italicized to indicate its nonstandard status. For university slang, it eventually became more widely popular than one might have expected.

In construction, *kudos* is originally a mass noun and, like *glory, acclaim, renown,* or *prestige,* it takes a singular verb:

> . . . they had acquired much kudos among the pilgrims —John Buchan, *The Last Secrets,* 1924

> . . . the kudos of our first glassmakers is not to be ascribed to their acceptance of ancient influences —R. W. Smith, *The New-England Galaxy,* Winter 1965

Like *renown* or *praise, kudos* was often used without a verb that would signal its singular status.

> . . . the Office of War Information has come in for kudos on the work it has done —*Newsweek,* 17 Aug. 1942

> . . . spend their time in competition for kudos and influence —Elizabeth Janeway, *N.Y. Times Book Rev.,* 19 Mar. 1967

Since the *-s* ending is like the regular plural ending of count nouns, those not familiar with Greek endings could easily misconstrue this as a plural form. In 1925 we found our first example of the unambiguously plural use of the noun in print:

> Colonial mechanics have very few kudos thrown in their path —letter to editor, *Rand Daily Mail* (Johannesburg), 23 Dec. 1925.

Once *kudos* was perceived as a plural, it was inevitable that someone would prune the *-s* to create the singular *kudo,* taken to mean 'award, compliment, accolade'. This was done in the 1940s. Here is a more recent example:

> I would rather get qualified approval from this gentle man . . . than any kudo from any other person in this field —J. P. Driscoll, *Trans-Action,* October 1971

Although some usage commentators inveigh against the form *kudo,* which is probably why it is not usually found in scholarly writing, this back-formation is certainly not without precedent: *cherry* was formed from the Old North French noun *cherise,* which was misconstrued as a plural; and *pea* was formed from the Middle English *pease,* also misconstrued as a plural noun.

The original sense of *kudos* is synonymous with *prestige,* which itself has had a fascinating history. The Latin verb *praestringere,* meaning 'to bind fast' and later 'to blind', gave rise to the noun *praestigiae,* meaning 'illusions, juggler's tricks, feats of legerdemain', from the notion that these blind the eyes to reality. In Late Latin this noun became *praestigium,* which was taken into sixteenth-century French as *prestige.* Its first appearance in English was in a 1656 glossary of "hard words" compiled by Thomas Blount, who defined *prestiges* as 'deceits, impostures, delusions, cousening [cozening] tricks'. While this 'deceit' sense has become archaic in Modern English, an extended sense of 'influence, esteem, or honor' arose in the early nineteenth century to become the predominant use of *prestige* today. The link between the senses may lie in the presumed power of prestige to blind people to the real merits and demerits of those who possess it.

[Gk *kydos;* akin to OSlav *čudo* wonder, Gk *akouein* to hear]

L

lackadaisical *Lackadaisical,* commonly used today in the sense of 'languid, lacking in life, spirit, or zest', might once have been rendered more literally as 'characteristic of one who often says, "Lackaday!" ' *Lackaday* is an interjection now archaic or rarely used, a headless form of *alackaday* or *alack the day,* formerly used to express sorrow or deprecation. *Alack,* itself an interjection used similarly, is probably a compound of the Middle English interjection *a,* 'ah', plus *lack,* 'fault, loss'. In addition to the now infrequent *alack,* Middle English had a similar interjection, *alas,* which is still used to express unhappiness, pity, sorrow, or concern. Though borrowed from Old French, the structure of *alas* is similar to that of the native *alack* since it was formed as a compound of Old French *a,* 'ah', plus *las,* 'weary, wretched'. The source of Old French *las* is Latin *lassus,* 'weary', which is also the root of English *lassitude.*

[irreg. fr. *lackaday* + *-ical*]

lackaday See LACKADAISICAL.
[short for *alackaday*]

lady Over the centuries the meaning of *lady* has become more and more generalized, and it is now widely used as a courteous term for a woman. As is evidenced by its continuing use as the title of various women of the upper classes in Great Britain, *lady* was formerly used to refer primarily to women of superior social standing, hence the connotations of courtesy that the word retains. Instances of the Old English form *hlǣfdige* from around the year 1000 show that the word was then used where today we would say *queen.* The earliest known sense to appear in Old English, however, attested as early as 825, is 'female head of a household' or 'a mistress of servants'. This sense reflects something of the ultimate etymology, for *hlǣfdige* is composed of Old English *hlāf,* 'loaf', plus *-dige,* which is akin to Old English *dǣge,* 'a kneader of bread' or 'a maid'. This same *dǣge* is the etymon of modern English *dairy* from the Middle English form *deye,* meaning 'maid' or 'dairymaid', plus *-ery.* Thus a dairy is the place where the (dairy)maid works.

  Lord is etymologically similar to *lady.* The Old English *hlāford* or *hlāfweard* is formed from *hlāf* plus *weard,* meaning 'keeper' or 'guard', the Old English form of modern *ward.* The earliest known instances of *hlāford* show the sense of 'head of a household'. It would appear that in

Old English the *hlāf-* element in *hlǣfdige* and *hlāford* was to be taken no more literally than is the first element of the modern term *breadwinner*.

Both *lord* and *lady* show the effects of that process of sound change called *syncope* or *syncopation* by linguists. Both words have lost the internal sound represented by *f* in the Old English forms. The Middle English spellings given in the etymology of *lady* below show the loss taking place. The ancestor of *lord* eventually lost a whole syllable in this way.

[ME *lady, lavedi, lafdi,* fr. OE *hlǣfdige,* fr. *hlāf* bread, loaf + *-dige* (fr. root of a prehistoric verb meaning to knead); akin to OE *dǣge* maid, kneader of bread]

lammergeier See OSPREY.
[G *lämmergeier,* fr. *lämmer* (pl. of *lamm* lamb, fr. OHG *lamb*) + *geier* vulture, fr. OHG *gīr*]

landau See PHAETON.
[fr. *Landau,* Bavaria, Germany, where it was first manufactured]

landaulet See PHAETON.
[fr. *landau* + *-let*]

lasagna See VERMICELLI.
[It, fr. (assumed) VL *lasania,* fr. L *lasanum* cooking pot, fr. Gk *lasana* (pl.) trivet, *lasanon* (sing.) chamber pot]

lassitude See LACKADAISICAL.
[MF, fr. L *lassitudo,* fr. *lassus* weary]

last English *last* has several homonyms. The verb *last* means 'to continue' or 'to endure'. In Old English, *lǣstan* was used like its modern descendant to mean 'to continue', but it also had the senses 'to follow' and 'to perform'. An Anglo-Saxon could last a leader or last a command or promise. It is the original Old English meaning 'to follow' which best reflects the source of the verb. The Germanic ancestor of Old English *lǣstan,* as well as its cognates Old High German *leisten,* 'to perform', and Gothic *laistjan,* 'to follow', probably meant 'to follow a track' and was derived from a noun meaning 'footprint' or 'track'.

This same noun was the source of another of our Modern English homonyms. Old English *lāst* meant 'footprint'. This word did not survive the Old English period, but its derivative *lǣste,* which was used for the model of a foot on which shoemakers shape their wares, endures today as modern *last.* (For other relatives of the verb and noun *last* see LEARN.)

The very common adjective and adverb *last,* which mean 'after the others', are not related to the noun and verb. They are descended from Old English *latost,* superlative of *lǣt* 'late, slow', by processes of sound change in which several internal sounds were gradually lost.

[ME *lasten,* fr. OE *lǣstan* to last, follow, perform; akin to OHG *leisten* to perform, Goth *laistjan* to follow; denominative fr. the root of OE *lāst* footprint]

[ME *laste*, fr. OE *lǣste*, fr. *lāst* footprint; akin to OHG *leist* shoemaker's last, ON *leistr* sock, Goth *laists* footprint, L *lira* furrow, track]

[ME *last, latst*, fr. OE *latost;* akin to OHG *lezzisto* last, ON *latastr* slowest; superl. of the adjective represented by OE *læt* late, slow]

latch   See CATCH.

[ME *lachen, lacchen*, fr. OE *læccan;* akin to Gk *lambanein, lazesthai* to take, grasp]

learn
One of the many distinctions we are taught to make in school is that between *learn* and *teach*. Such a sentence as "A thousand more mischances than this one have learn'd me how to brook this patiently" would wound the tender sensibilities of the prescriptive grammarian. But Shakespeare did not hesitate to use it in *Two Gentlemen of Verona*. Old English *leornian*, the ancestor of *learn*, meant 'to learn' or 'to study', never 'to teach'. But during the Middle English period the word came to be used in the last sense as well. It was only with the prescriptivism of the eighteenth century that this use of the word came to be frowned on. Samuel Johnson, in his Dictionary of the English Language (1755), could not, with the example of such respectable authors as Spenser and Shakespeare before him, call this usage wrong; he said rather, "This sense is now obsolete." Since that time, however, grammarians have not hesitated to brand it "illiterate."

The meaning of Old English *leornian*, we have said, was 'to learn' or 'to study'. It is also possible to surmise, by examining cognates of this word in other Indo-European languages, the original meaning of its ultimate source. This meaning seems to have been 'furrow' or 'track'. Apparently the sense 'to learn' developed from the idea of following a track. If we cease to follow the track, not only do we stop learning, but we are also in danger of graver consequences. *Lira*, a Latin cognate of *learn*, retains the ancestral meaning 'furrow' or 'track'. The verb *delirare* means 'to deviate from a straight line' or, etymologically speaking, 'to go out of the furrow'. *Delirare* came eventually to refer to another kind of deviation as well—madness. The derivative noun *delirium*, 'madness', was borrowed into English in the late sixteenth century. See also LAST.

[ME *lernen*, fr. OE *leornian;* akin to OHG *lirnēn, lernēn* to learn; prob. akin to OHG *-leisa* track, L *lira* furrow, track, Russ *lekha* garden bed, furrow; basic meaning: furrow, track]

lectern   See LEGEND.

[ME *lectorne, lectrun*, alter. (influenced by ML *lectorinum, lectrinum* lectern) of *lettorne, letrune*, fr. MF *letrun, letrin*, fr. ML *lectorinum, lectrinum*, fr. LL *lector* + L *-inum* (neut. of *-inus* -ine)]

lector See LEGEND.

[LL, fr. L, one that reads, fr. *lectus* (past part. of *legere* to read) + *-or* -er]

lecture See LEGEND.

[ME, fr. MF, fr. L *lectura,* fr. *lectus* (past part. of *legere* to gather, select, read) + *-ura* -ure]

left People who are right-handed often find it difficult to do things with their left hand, which is liable to be the weaker. Apparently the basic meaning of *left* in Old English is 'weak', although the evidence is scanty. *Left* appears as a gloss, or translation, of the Latin *inanis,* 'empty or weak', and the same word is the first element of *lyftādl,* 'paralysis or palsy', which translates literally into Modern English as 'the weak disease'.

This basic 'weak' sense of *left* was applied to the weaker hand by the majority of people, who are right-handed, with the result that the senses of *left* relating to direction developed from the Middle English use of *left* to refer to the hand on the same side of the body as the heart. By the twelfth century Middle English had developed many of the senses of *left* familiar to us today. A relatively recent development derives from the customary practice in European legislative chambers for the more liberal members of a governing body to sit on the left side of the presiding officer, thus giving us the political implications of *left.*

The earliest occurrences of Latin *sinister* mean 'left' or 'on the left side', but probably because of the left-handed ineptness of most right-handers *sinister* too developed the meaning 'awkward'. From this it came to mean 'injurious', 'evil', or 'unlucky', and even today many widespread superstitions relate to the left or sinister side, such as throwing salt over the left shoulder. *Sinister* was borrowed into English in the fifteenth century, and though the earliest instances reflect the senses of 'evil and inauspicious', it was also used during the same century with the directional senses of *left.*

Awkward is another word with a primary sense of 'left' which has taken on other implications. Middle English *awke* means 'from the left' or 'backhanded'; *awkward* thus means in an *awke* direction. So a backhanded blow with a sword, not necessarily a clumsy or ineffective one by any means, was called an awkward stroke. Today *awkward* means 'lacking in skill or *dexterity* (literally, "right-handedness")'. An awkward person might also be described as *gauche,* which is borrowed directly from the French *gauche,* meaning 'left' or 'on the left', and which has taken on a similar range of meanings.

Southpaw, 'left-handed', began to appear in the late nineteenth century, usually in a baseball context. One theory is that it developed from the fact that baseball diamonds were oriented so that the batter would not face the afternoon sun; thus the pitcher faces west with south to his left. This may be a fanciful explanation, however, since *southpawed,* 'left-handed', has been recorded in northern England where baseball is rarely played.

See also RIGHT.

[ME *luft, lift, left,* fr. OE *left, lyft-* (as in *lyftādl* palsy) weak; akin to MD *lucht, luft, loft* left, MLG *lucht*]

legend   The Latin verb *legere* originally meant 'to gather, collect'. In the course of time this verb came to be used in a figurative sense, namely, 'to gather with the eye, see', which in turn led to the particularized sense 'to read'. In Medieval Latin the word *legenda,* the gerundive of *legere,* meaning literally 'a thing to be read', was used in specific reference to 'the story of the life of a saint'. One of the popular books of the later Middle Ages was the *Legenda Aurea* of Jacobus de Voragine, a collection of saints' lives that incorporated a generous measure of fanciful material along with solid fact. Vernacular translations into most of the languages of Europe appeared over the centuries, including one into English by William Caxton in 1483. In the twelfth century the French borrowed this word as *legende* with the same meaning, and in the fourteenth century the word became part of the English vocabulary as *legend.*

This sense is now uncommon in English except in historical studies, but a later sense originating in the seventeenth century survives as 'a story handed down from early times by tradition and popularly regarded as historical although not entirely verifiable'. The development of this later use was a natural consequence of the less than fully historical nature of many saints' legends. Subsequently, 'one who is the subject of a legend' became an accepted sense. Also in the seventeenth century, *legend* came to denote 'an inscription on an object (as a coin)', which in turn led to the later sense 'an explanatory list of symbols appearing on a map or chart'. The words *lecture, lector, lectern,* and *legible,* all relating to reading, are some of the other derivatives of the Latin verb *legere.*

[ME *legende,* fr. MF & ML; MF *legende,* fr. ML *legenda,* fr. *legendus,* gerundive of *legere* to gather, select, read; akin to Gk *legein* to collect, gather, choose, speak, *logos* word, reason, speech, account, Alb mb-*leth* I collect]

legible   See LEGEND.
[ME *legibille,* fr. LL *legibilis,* fr. L *legere* to read + *-ibilis* -able]

Leni-Lenape   See INDIAN.
[Delaware, lit., real person, fr. *leni, lenni* real + *lenape* person, Indian]

leprechaun   The little people of Irish folklore known as *leprechauns* have a name that is descriptive of their size. The English word is borrowed from the Irish Gaelic *leipreachān,* or *luprachān.* The origins of this word in Middle Irish have been obscured somewhat by metathesis, the process of sound-transposition which also created Modern English *bird* from Old English *brid.* The letters *p, r,* and *ch* have shifted their position from that in the Middle Irish *lūchorpān.* Once this etymological puzzle has been solved, the meaning of the word becomes clear, for *lūchorpān* is a compound of Middle Irish *lū* 'small' and *corpān,* a diminutive of *corp,* 'body', from Latin *corpus*. Thus *leprechauns* are literally 'little people'. For more on metathesis see PATTERN.

[IrGael *leipreachān*, fr. OIr *lūchorpān*, fr. *lū* small + *corpān*, dim. of *corp* body, fr. L *corpus*]

lesbian Nothing about the present-day inhabitants of the Greek island of Lésvos off the Turkish coast would cause one to associate the island with female homosexuality. But a centuries-old literary tradition, which may or may not be historically correct, has made a persistent link. The most celebrated figure ever to have lived on the island was Sappho, who flourished from about 610 to 580 B.C. The wife of a man of wealth, Sappho lived in Mytilene, the island's principal city. It was the fashion of the time for women from the upper classes on Lesbos (as the island was then known) to form informal societies and to spend their many leisure hours in artistic pursuits, especially in the composing and reciting of poetry. One of these literary coteries was presided over by Sappho. Since early classical times her lyric poetry has been praised for its power and beauty. Classical critics celebrated her unique ability to establish a rapport with the reader. Sappho's poetry was particularly concerned with personal relationships, especially the friendships and rivalries that were common within her social circle. One of the recurrent themes of her poetry was the love of one woman for another, love ranging from gentle affection to sexual passion. Because of the intimacy conveyed by her poetry, it has been traditionally assumed that Sappho was expressing personal feelings. Ancient critics, who knew her poetry from a large body of work that is now mostly lost, say that Sappho herself was homosexual. There is no evidence outside of the poetry itself, however, that indicates her sexual preference and no evidence that the women who formed those poetry societies were homosexually inclined. Nothing more is known about Sappho's personal life, and today her works survive mostly in fragments. The alleged sexual proclivities of Sappho and her companions fostered development in the nineteenth century of a homosexual sense for the English word *lesbian*, which is centuries older in its strict geographical application, and also to a new word *sapphism*, synonymous with *lesbianism*.

See also GAY.

[L *Lesbi*us of Lesbos (fr. Gk *Lesbios*, fr. *Lesbos*, island in the Aegean Sea) + E -*an;* so called fr. the reputed homosexual band associated with Sappho *fl ab*600 B.C. Greek lyric poet of Lesbos]

lettuce Surprisingly enough, there is an etymological connection between the words *lettuce* and *galaxy*. Many types of *lettuce* have a milky white juice, and it is this property that accounts for the word. The earliest known Middle English form, *letuse*, comes from Old French *laitues*, the plural of *laitue*. This Old French form derives in turn from Latin *lactuca*, which is still used as the scientific name for the genus of composite plants of which many possess succulent leaves used in salads. The root of *lactuca* is Latin *lac,* meaning 'milk'. This is akin to the Greek word for milk, *gala,* which is the root of *galaxy.* See also GALAXY.

[ME *letuse,* fr. OF *laitues,* pl. of *laitue,* fr. L *lactuca,* fr. *lact-, lac* milk; fr. its milky juice]

libel   The ancient Romans used the Latin noun *liber* to denote 'the inner bark of a tree'. Since the books of this period were written on the inner bark of the papyrus plant, the word *liber* came to be applied to a book as well. To refer to a little book, the diminutive suffix *-ellus* was appended to give *libellus.* When this word was taken into French, it was usually spelled *libelle,* which in fourteenth-century English was borrowed as *libel.* Both French and English originally used the word with its Latin sense, 'a little book'. John Wycliffe so used it in his 1382 translation of the Bible: "And the priest shall write in a libel these cursed things" (Numbers 5:23).

The word was also used to mean 'a written declaration or statement', but by the nineteenth century this sense had become obsolete. However, the legal profession made particular use of this sense in applying the word to 'the written statement made by the plaintiff of his cause of action and the relief he seeks'.

In the sixteenth century, handbills and leaflets, being likened to little books, were also called libels. They were a popular means of spreading gossip and defamatory statements about famous people. At that point the term *libel* started being applied to such a defamatory statement that was published without just cause and tended to expose another to public contempt, ridicule, or hatred. Writers and publishers were often sued for their libels, and the word *libel* took on the added sense of 'the act or crime of publishing a libel'.

See also SLANDER.

[ME, fr. MF, fr. L *libellus,* dim. of *liber* book]

liberal   The Latin adjective *liber* was used to describe a person who is 'free, unrestricted, or independent'. It contrasted with *servus,* which meant 'slavish, servile, subject'. The combination of *liber* and the suffix *-alis* produced *liberalis,* which was used in the senses 'of or relating to freemen' and 'worthy of a freeman, fine, noble'. It was also applied to someone who is 'free in giving, generous' and to something that is 'plentiful or abundant'.

The Greek system of education was also that of Rome. Subjects were classified as 'liberal arts' (*artes liberales* in Latin) and 'servile arts' (*artes serviles*). The 'liberal arts' were those befitting a freeman. They required the exercise of mental faculties rather than physical abilities. The 'servile arts' were those befitting the lower classes and involved manual labor. Traditionally, the liberal arts consisted of the *trivium,* Grammar, Logic, and Rhetoric, and the *quadrivium,* Arithmetic, Music, Geometry, and Astronomy. The servile arts, by contrast, were occupational or mechanical in nature.

Artes liberales passed into early French as *arts libéraux* and then in the fourteenth century into English as *liberal arts. Liberal* then began to be used in such phrases as "liberal education," "liberal profession," and "liberal pastime," where it took on the sense of 'befitting a person of superior social status'. The Latin sense of 'free in giving, generous' began appearing in English in the 1380s. In his English translation of Ranulph Higden's Latin history *Polychronicon* in 1387, John de Trevisa gives an example: "In fighting he was strong, in giving liberal." In the fifteenth century we find *liberal* used for 'bestowed in a generous and openhanded way', as in "a liberal offer" and "a liberal quantity."

In the latter part of the eighteenth century, we find *liberal* used for 'not strict or rigorous; not confined to the exact or literal'. Alexander Hamilton, in a 1792 letter, wrote of "a disposition on my part towards a liberal construction of the powers of the national government." This sense gave rise to use of *liberal* to mean 'free from convention, tradition, or dogma; broadminded, open-minded'. In his book *Education and the Good Life* (1926), philosopher Bertrand Russell illustrates this usage: "Some people who themselves hold liberal views are willing that their children shall first acquire conventional morals, and become emancipated only later, if at all."

Early in the nineteenth century, there was in England a movement for change in the direction of freedom and democracy. This eventually led to the Reform Act of 1832, after which the two traditional political parties (Whigs and Tories) regrouped to form the Liberal Party and the Conservative Party. The Spanish and French had already applied the adjective *liberal* to their own revolutionaries at that time, and opponents of the Whig reformers pejoratively applied this word to the reformers, suggesting a kinship with the French revolutionaries. Nonetheless, the Whigs unreluctantly adopted "Liberal Party" as their new name.

In the U.S. the word *liberal* has not been as politically prominent as in Europe, though a few local parties in the nineteenth century did call themselves "Liberal." In the twentieth century, *liberal* has been applied to progressive groups within both Republican and Democratic Parties. More recently, however, Republicans have been associated with conservatism, while the Democrats have been associated with liberalism. In the 1980s the word took on associations at odds with its etymology. Geoffrey Sampson, writing in the *Times Literary Supplement* of 19 November 1982 comments on this turn: "A few years ago the Professor of Jurisprudence at Oxford (an American) defined a liberal as someone who values equality over freedom when the two ideals conflict. 'Liberal' in the U.S., in fact, commonly functions as a euphemism for 'socialist', still an unmentionable word in much of American society." Indeed, some conservatives have humorously derided it as "that l-word," implying that even *liberal* is becoming "unmentionable."

[ME, fr. MF + L; MF, fr. L *liberalis* of or constituting liberal arts, of freedom, of a freeman, noble, generous, fr. *liber* free + *-alis* -al; prob. akin to OE *lēodan* to grow, *lēod* people, OHG *liotan* to grow, *liut* person, people, ON *lothiun* shaggy, Goth *lindan* to grow, Gk *eleutheros* free, Skt *rodhati, rohati* he climbs, grows; basic meaning: growing]

librarian   See BOOK.
[*library* + *-an*]

library   See BOOK.
[ME *librarie,* fr. ML *librarium* & *libraria,* fr. neut. & fem. respectively of L *librarius* of books, fr. *libr-, liber* book + *-arius* -ary]

liebfraumilch   *Liebfraumilch* has long been the archetypal German wine for most Americans and for neophyte wine drinkers in general. In the Rhineland city of Worms, site of the famous Concordat of Worms in 1122 and the equally famous Diet of Worms in 1521, stands the historic Gothic structure known as the Liebfrauenkirche ('Church of Our Lady'), which was consecrated in 1467. Hundreds of churches throughout Germany have the name *Liebfrauenkirche,* but the one in Worms has achieved distinction for the 26-acre vineyard, called the *Liebfrauenstift* ('Endowment of Our Lady'), that surrounds it. The wine produced by this church-owned vineyard has long been known as *Liebfraumilch* (literally, 'Milk of the Blessed Mother'). The curiously charming name must account for the wine's renown, for, connoisseurs have asserted, the wine itself is less than outstanding. Nevertheless, the name *Liebfraumilch* became so widely and popularly known that other German winegrowers and shippers began selling their wines as *Liebfraumilch,* regardless of whether the grapes were grown in the yard of a local Liebfrauenkirche. Often the cheapest and poorest wines of the Rheinhessen (a region south and west of the Rhine river stretching west and south of Mainz), these Liebfraumilchs usually carried—and still do—labels with lavish illustrations of Madonnas and Gothic churches. Over the years wine producers all along the Rhine followed suit, and *liebfraumilch* eventually became one of the most recognized of all wine names and vaguely synonymous with wine from the Rhine. The German wine laws of 1971 more or less legalized the existing state of affairs. The name *liebfraumilch* can be used of wine produced in any of several wine-growing divisions of the Rhine and made from any of several grapes. The regulations do prescribe that the wine be "of pleasant character." Ironically, the wines from the vineyards of the church in Worms are no longer sold under the name *liebfraumilch;* as a way of asserting their individuality and authenticity, the growers have labeled them *Liebfrauenstiftswein.*

The names of most European wines have traditionally derived from place names, not from the grapes that went into them. *Hock,* which is the generic name for Rhine wine, especially among the English, derives from Hochheim, a major wine-producing and -exporting town on the Main River in the Rheingau (a region north of the Rhine west of Wiesbaden). *Chablis,* one of the most famous of all wine names, derives from the town of the same name in the old French province of Burgundy. Chablis is actually made from the chardonnay grape. The wine is named for the town rather than the grape because the historic reputation of the town's winegrowers is considered a better guarantee of quality. *Chianti,* another one of the wine world's most widely recognized names, similarly derives from the name of a mountain range near Florence, in Tuscany, where the wine originally was—and still is—made. France, Italy, Germany, and a number of other European countries precisely define the geographical areas that are entitled to the placement of *Chablis, Chianti,* and other wine names on labels. However, the fact that wine boards have no jurisdiction outside of their own national boundaries has resulted in the giving of different meanings to established wine terms in other parts of the world. In the United States, for example, *chablis* has been used of any number of highly variable white wines. In France *Sauternes* is used precisely with reference to a French village in Bordeaux and the sweet white wine produced there, while in the U.S. the name *sauterne* is used for white wines of every conceivable type. And for most Americans, *champagne* is simply any sparkling white or pink wine, any strict association of the wine with the Champagne region of France being lost. It was the realization of the value of an established name that many years ago prompted vintners along the Rhine to label every anonymous bottle of wine *liebfraumilch.*

[G, alter. of *liebfrauenmilch,* fr. *Liebfrauenstift* (lit., foundation of the Virgin Mary), religious foundation in Worms, Germany, where the wine was first produced + *milch* milk]

lilliputian See GARGANTUAN.
[*Lilliput,* imaginary country in Swift's *Gulliver's Travels* (1726) inhabited by people six inches high + E *-ian*]

lily-livered White is a color associated with fear. A badly frightened person may turn pale—"white as a sheet." But the sudden fright that drains the blood from one's face is quite different from the habitual cowardice of one who is *lily-livered.* Although the liver does not turn pale with fear, it was once believed that a deficiency of choler or yellow bile—the humor that governed anger, spirit, and courage—would leave the liver colorless. A person deficient in choler, and so white-livered, would be spiritless and a coward. Shakespeare, in *Henry V,* described a cowardly braggart: ". . . hee is white-liuer'd, and red-faced: by the means whereof a' faces it out, but fights not." Though lacking courage, he was sanguine, his red face indicating ample blood. *Lily-livered* and *white-livered* have been used synonymously since the sixteenth century; but *lily-livered,* probably because of its alliteration, is now the more popular term. See also HUMOR.

[*lily* + *livered;* fr. the whiteness of the lily and fr. the former belief that the choleric temperament depends on the body's producing large quantities of yellow bile]

limousine See PHAETON.
[F, lit., cloak, fr. *Limousin,* region in west central France]

litter English *litter* is a word of divers meanings, but all are ultimately derived from that of Latin *lectus,* 'bed', the ancestor of the English word. From *lectus* comes the French *lit,* 'bed'. *Litiere,* an Old French derivative of *lit,* was used not only for a bed but also for the type of vehicle we call a *litter,* a curtained couch on which a passenger reclines in comfort while being carried about on the shoulders of his retainers. In the fourteenth century, the spellings *litere* and *liter* appeared in English. The Middle English word, like the French, originally meant 'bed' or 'litter (vehicle)'; but the first sense, 'bed', did not survive into Modern English. Before its obsolescence, however, this sense gave rise to other senses of *litter*. The straw, hay, or like material laid down or strewn about to serve as bedding was called *litter*. So were the offspring of an animal which were born, or "bedded," at one time. Once *litter* had been applied to straw laid down for bedding, it was not farfetched to use the word for any odds and ends of rubbish lying scattered about. This eighteenth-century development yielded what is probably the most common sense of *litter* today.

[ME *litere, liter* bed, litter, fr. OF *litiere,* fr. *lit* bed, fr. L *lectus;* akin to OE *licgan* to lie, OHG *ligen,* ON *liggja* to lie, Gk *lechos* bed, *lechesthai* to lie down, OIr *lige* bed, grave, OSlav *ležati* to lie]

livid   The history of *livid* might be well described as "mottled." The Latin adjective *lividus* means 'dull, greyish or leaden blue', like the color of a dark bruise. The derivative adjective in French is *livide,* which was borrowed into English in the seventeenth century as *livid.* Early use of *livid* was primarily in describing flesh discolored by or as if by a bruise; it functioned more or less as a synonym of *black-and-blue.* A slight extension of meaning had by the end of the eighteenth century given it the sense 'ashen or pallid', as in describing the appearance of a corpse. *Livid* came eventually to be used in this sense to characterize the complexion of a person pale with anger—"livid with rage." In the twentieth century, two further extensions of meaning have caused *livid* to both gain color and to lose it. In part, presumably, because of association with words like *lurid* and *vivid,* and in part because an angry person is at least as likely to be red-faced as pallid, *livid* has acquired the sense 'reddish'. Its frequent occurrence in phrases like "livid with fury" has also given rise to a sense entirely unrelated to color, with *livid* now commonly functioning simply as a synonym of *furious* or *enraged.*

[F *livide,* fr. L *lividus,* fr. *livēre* to be blue; akin to OIr *lī* color, W *lliw* color, OE *slāh* sloe, OHG *slēha* sloe, Russ *sliva* plum]

loafer   See TRAMP.
[perh. short for *landloafer,* modif. of G *landläufer* vagabond, tramp, fr. *land* + *läufer* runner, walker]

loan translation   See CALQUE.
[trans. of G *lehnübersetzung*]

lord   See LADY.
[ME *lord, loverd,* fr OE *hlāford,* fr. *hlāf* bread, loaf + *weard* keeper, guard]

lothario   *Lothario, ignoramus,* and *abigail* are three words that have been used generically for so long that their origins in dramatic literature have been almost completely obscured. They all derive from the names of characters in now-forgotten plays that held the boards in the seventeenth and eighteenth centuries.

Lothario comes from *The Fair Penitent* (1703), a tragedy by Nicholas Rowe (1674–1718). In the play Lothario is a notorious seducer who is described as "haughty, gallant, and gay." He seduces Calista, an unfaithful wife and later the fair penitent of the title. Since the eighteenth century *lothario* has been a synonym for a foppish, unscrupulous rake. The character of Lothario has become a stock figure in English literature. For his novel *Clarissa Harlowe* (1748), Samuel Richardson (1689–1761) specifically modeled the character of Lovelace on Lothario.

Ignoramus is the title of a Cambridge University farce by George Ruggle (1575–1622) that was first produced in 1615. The title character, whose name in Latin literally means 'we do not know', is a magistrate for the town of Cambridge who fancies himself to be quite shrewd but is actually foolish and ignorant. In the course of the play he is subjected to a series of humiliations. He is denied the woman he loves, saddled with a shrew, subjected to a sound drubbing, judged to be possessed by evil spirits, subjected to exorcism, and packed off to a monastery. Ruggle based the character of Ignoramus on an actual Cambridge magistrate who was embroiled in an ongoing feud between town and gown at Cambridge. Because of the play's instant success, almost immediately *ignoramus* was used allusively for any woefully ignorant person. Ruggle may have been inspired in his choice of name for his title character by a proceeding in the English judicial system. The term *ignoramus* was written on bills of indictment by grand juries in England when the evidence presented seemed to be insufficient to justify prosecution. In these cases *ignoramus* indicated "we take no notice of, we do not recognize this indictment." Such a reference would have been familiar to Ruggle's university audience and would have been most appropriate for his satire of the judiciary.

Abigail, as a name for a lady's personal maid, comes to us from *The Scornful Lady* by Francis Beaumont (ca. 1584–1616) and John Fletcher (1579–1625), two of the leading dramatists of the Jacobean stage. A comedy of domestic life, the play was first produced around 1613. The leading characters include Abigail, a spirited lady-in-waiting. Beaumont and Fletcher may have been inspired in the choice of their character's name by Abigail, the wife originally of Nabal and later of David in the Bible. The biblical Abigail humbly refers to herself as "thine handmaid" (I Samuel 25:24, AV). The popularity of the generic use of *abigail* may have been further enhanced by a later example from history. Abigail Hill, who became Lady Abigail Masham, superseded the Duchess of Marlborough as Queen Anne's personal favorite. She served as the queen's lady-in-waiting from 1704 to 1714. During her tenure she attained considerable notoriety for her imperious manner, her powerful influence over the queen, and her repeated abuses of power.

[after *Lothario*, seducer in the play *The Fair Penitent* (1703) by Nicholas Rowe †1718 Eng. dramatist]

Lucifer *Lucifer*, 'bearer of light', is a strange name for the Prince of Darkness. Yet *Lucifer* is one of the devil's aliases. Latin *Lucifer* (from *lux*, 'light', and *ferre*, 'to carry') was the name of the morning star (the planet Venus) that heralds, if it does not exactly carry in, the dawn. The Prophet Isaiah recounts the fall of Babylon. He compares the king of Babylon for his former glory and his present degradation to the morning star: "How art thou fallen from Heaven, O Lucifer, son of the morning!" (Isaiah 14:12, AV). Later, Christians compared this Old Testament passage with Christ's words: "I beheld Satan as lightning fall from heaven" (Luke 10:18, AV). They then interpreted Isaiah's description of the downfall of Babylon as an allegory for the fall from heaven of the rebel archangel Satan. *Lucifer*, they concluded, must have been the devil's original name in his former position of respectability.

The *lucifer* match, a friction match invented in the early eighteenth century, was not considered a device of the devil. It was named for its ability to bring light.

See also DEVIL.

[ME *lucifer* morning star & *Lucifer* fallen rebel archangel, devil, fr. OE, fr. L *lucifer* morning star, fr. *lucifer*, adj., light-bearing (prob. trans. of Gk *phōsphoros* light-bearing, morning star), fr. *luci-* (fr. *luc-*, *lux* light) + *-fer*, adj. comb. form, fr. *ferre* to bear, carry]

Lucullan Lucius Licinius Lucullus, born about the year 117 B.C., was a Roman general and consul who gained fame by defeating Mithridates VI Eupator, the king of Pontus (in Asia Minor), who had waged three wars against Rome. Lucullus had acquired immense wealth during his military and administrative career in Asia Minor, and his attainments were, in spite of his detractors, triumphally celebrated after his return to Rome. He then retired in splendid luxury, surrounded by poets, artists, and philosophers, whom he liberally patronized. Lucullus entertained on such a sumptuous scale that his name became the basis of an adjective to describe a banquet of extravagant luxury and elegance.

Cicero, Plutarch, and Pliny, among others, wrote of Lucullus, and Sulla entrusted him with the revision of his *Memoirs*. Plutarch, in his *Parallel Lives*, describes Lucullus's life-style as follows:

> Lucullus's daily entertainments were ostentatiously extravagant, not only with purple coverlets, and plate adorned with precious stones, and dancings, and interludes, but with the greatest diversity of dishes and the most elaborate cookery, for the vulgar to admire and envy.

From the Latin adjective *lucullanus* or *lucullianus*, English formed *Lucullian*, *Lucullean*, and *Lucullan*, the last now being the most common form. The 'lavish, luxurious' sense in English dates from the 1890s. A typical example of its modern use is the following quotation from an article by Caroline Bates in *Gourmet*, March 1980: ". . . little buckwheat pancakes surmounted by smooth and buttery slices of smoked salmon and avocado, sour cream, and spoonfuls of caviar, made a blissfully Lucullan dish that I wouldn't want to indulge in regularly—just every other day perhaps."

[L *lucullanus, lucullianus,* fr. Lucius Licinius *Lucullus,* 1st cent. B.C. Roman general, patron of learning, and epicure + L *-anus, -ianus* -an]

lunatic The ancient Romans believed that some people's minds and behavior were affected by the different phases of the moon and that they were at their worst during a full moon but normal during a new moon. The Latin adjective describing such a person was *lunaticus,* which was derived from the noun *luna* 'moon'. This adjective became *lunatique* in Old French and passed into thirteenth-century Middle English as *lunatik.* Since the eighteenth century it has been spelled *lunatic.* Until the middle of the nineteenth century, *lunatic* was used for people who were insane some of the time yet had periods of normal behavior.

In the medical and legal literature of the eighteenth century a distinction was often made between the lunatic and the insane. The insane person suffered from chronic dementia, while the lunatic had lucid intervals and his condition was exacerbated by phases of the moon. While it is no longer used in medical and legal contexts, in the general vocabulary *lunatic* remains as a common term for a crazy or wildly foolish person.

The word for 'lunatic' in several other languages has a similar etymology. The Italian *lunatico,* the Spanish *alunado,* and the German *mondsüchtig* all mean 'moonstruck'.

[ME *lunatik,* fr. OF or LL; OF *lunatique,* fr. LL *lunaticus,* fr. L *luna* moon]

lure See FALCON.
[ME, enticement, falconer's lure, fr. MF *loire, loirre* falconer's lure, fr. OF, of Gmc origin; akin to MLG *lōder* bait, MHG *luoder;* akin to OE *lathian* to invite, OHG *ladōn,* ON *latha,* Goth *lathon* to call, invite, and perh. to Gk *laimos* wanton, impudent, greedy]

lust See COVET.
[ME, fr. OE; akin to OHG *lust* pleasure, desire, ON *losti* sexual desire, Goth *lustus* desire, L *lascivus* wanton, playful, Gk *lilaiesthai* to yearn, Skt *laṣati* he yearns, *lasati* he plays]

lute The Arabic word *'ūd* has the basic meaning 'wood, stick' and also the extended use of referring to a stringed musical instrument similar to a mandolin, perhaps because of its wooden sounding board. (In the word *'ūd,* the rightward curving apostrophe transcribes a consonant more or less unique to Arabic, consisting of a voiced constriction of the pharynx, and the macron over the *u* means that the vowel is long, rhyming approximately with *food.*) This word was borrowed into English in the eighteenth century, in various transcriptions, settling finally into the not surprising spelling *oud,* which in English refers to this Middle Eastern instrument.

But *'ūd* already had come into English much earlier, via Romance-language transmission, this time in the late thirteenth century as our word *lute.* Just as the instrument evolved from the Middle Eastern one, so did the word. The prefixed *l* came from the Arabic definite article *al-*, which is normally attached to nouns, as in *al-'ūd* 'the oud'. Languages normally borrow a foreign noun without any accompanying article, but since the Arabic *al-* is so intimately wedded to its noun (you cannot, for example, interpose an adjective between *al-* and *'ūd* the way you might in English), it frequently comes along as part of the word. We see this particularly in the English words *alchemy, alcohol, alfalfa, algebra,* and *almanac,* all coming to us from Arabic with the *al-* intact.

Yet in a number of instances the *al-* has undergone assimilation in Arabic, with the *l* changing to match a following consonant. Thus we also have less obvious borrowings from Arabic, such as English *acerola,* the name of a shrub, from Arabic *az-za'rura* (where the *al-* became *az-* under the influence of the first consonant of *za'rūra*) and English *azimuth,* ultimately from Arabic *as-sumūt.*

[ME, fr. MF *lut, leut,* fr. OProv *laut,* fr. Ar *al-'ūd* the oud, fr. *al* the + *'ūd* oud]

lynch   There have been so many claimants for the source of the eponymous word *lynch* that one might almost think that it is a term of approbation and not a verb describing a nefarious practice. The first person on whose behalf claims have been made apparently was James Lynch Fitzstephen, the mayor of Galway, Ireland. According to tradition—if not historical fact—in 1493 he was forced to carry out the hanging execution of his own son, a convicted murderer, when no one else would. Adherents to the story have failed to explain why *Lynch* and not *Fitzstephen* survived as the eponym and why *lynch* did not enter the language until centuries later. Another unfounded claim has been made in behalf of a certain John Lynch, who followed Daniel Boone into Kentucky and engaged in horse thievery; unlike other claimants, this Lynch was the victim of a summary execution and not a perpetrator. Another story maintains that the source is Lynch's Creek in South Carolina, where in the eighteenth century a band of "Regulators" would meet to carry out their vigilante justice. More serious claims have been made in behalf of Charles Lynch (1736–1796), a Virginia planter, justice of the peace, and colonel in the militia. His fame rests on his presiding, with others, over an extralegal court to suppress Tory activity in Virginia during the Revolution. Although of questionable legality, this court was not identified with execution without due process of law or as a result of mob action.

The blame—or at least the weight of evidence—for *lynch* now seems to fall on Captain William Lynch (1742–1820). Captain Lynch served with the Virginia militia and presided over a self-created tribunal that was organized to rid Pittsylvania County of a band of troublesome ruffians that had eluded the proper civil authorities. On 22 September 1780, Lynch and others entered into a compact stating their goals, reasons, and methods. Captain Lynch and his vigilantes soon became known as "lynch-men," and by 1782 their judicial code had become known as *lynch's law* and subsequently *lynch law.* By 1836 *lynch law* had given rise to the verb *lynch* in its current meaning: 'to put to death (as by hanging) by mob action without legal sanction'. While William Lynch and his cohorts were not the first vigilantes to take the law into their own hands, they were perhaps the first to proclaim and justify their methods in a formal, written compact.

[fr. *lynch law;* fr. William *Lynch* †1820 Am. militiaman; fr. his leadership of a band of vigilantes]

lyric   The harp-like stringed instrument known as the lyre played a central role in the poetic arts for the ancient Greeks. The lyre was the traditional accompaniment for the singing of songs and the recitation of poetry. An attribute of Apollo, the god of poetry and music, the lyre came to symbolize these arts.

Lyric derives from *lyre,* and its original meaning is 'suitable for singing to the lyre or for being set to music and sung'. From the adjective *lyric* evolved the noun *lyric,* which became the term for any short composition in verse that was either intended to be sung or was suggestive of song, especially in its expression of intense personal emotion.

One Greek poet whose name is commemorated in a type of lyric poetry is Anacreon (ca. 582–ca. 485 B.C.). While he apparently wrote a number of different kinds of poetry (now mostly lost), Anacreon was remembered and quoted by later writers for his good-humored works celebrating love and wine. According to ancient critics well versed in the body of his works, his songs often made claims of having been composed in moments of drunken revelry. The Roman author Pliny relates that Anacreon died by choking on a grape seed. While the story is apocryphal, it has served to enhance Anacreon's reputation as a consummate voluptuary who was given to carefree carousing. His amatory poems generally expressed his feelings for the beautiful youths gathered at the court of his benefactor. From antiquity onward, Anacreon had many imitators, both stylistically and thematically. Since the seventeenth century, a poem or song, and especially one celebrating the pleasures of love and drinking, has been called an *anacreontic.* A convivial music society formed in London in the 1760s called itself the Anacreontic Society. For this group the English composer John Stafford Smith later wrote the drinking song "To Anacreon in Heaven." The melody of this drinking song, or anacreontic, was eventually borrowed to serve as the music for Francis Scott Key's lyric "The Star-Spangled Banner."

[MF or L; MF *lyrique,* fr. L *lyricus,* fr. Gk *lyrikos,* fr. *lyra* lyre + *-ikos* -ic]

M

macadam Many words have obvious eponymous origins. The origins of *Freudian* and *Jeffersonian* are transparent, and although one may not know the specifics behind *Alzheimer's disease* or *Murphy's Law,* one does not doubt that they derive from the surnames of people. A number of other eponymous words, however, have had their origins obscured, and in some cases the name of the eponym has been distorted considerably. Probably few are aware that the paving stone surface known as *macadam* derives from the name of a now obscure Scottish engineer, John L. McAdam (1756–1836). As his fame faded and as *macadam* evolved into a lowercase, generic noun, the eponymous origin of the word was forgotten and the spelling was altered to produce a more conventional-looking word. McAdam's name survives even more tenuously in *tarmac,* shortened from *tarmacadam,* which designates a road surfacing that incorporates a tar binder.

Another Scotsman named John Macadam (this one spelling his surname differently) has his name living on in the name of a prized tropical nut, the *macadamia* nut. Macadam (1827–1865) spent his entire career as a physician in Australia, after a brief time as a chemist and teacher in Scotland. It was in Australia that Macadam met the famous botanist Ferdinand von Mueller, who discovered the unique species of nut tree while on an expedition in the 1850s and named the new discovery after his physician friend. Legend has it that Macadam never tasted the nut that was to immortalize his name. He died aboard ship on a trip to New Zealand after contracting pleurisy.

Cinchona, the tree bark yielding quinine and other alkaloids, was named after the countess of *Chinchón,* the wife of an obscure viceroy of seventeenth-century Peru. When the tree and its bark were named in her honor by the Swedish botanist Linnaeus, he misspelled her name (in New Latin) as *Cinchona.* Linnaeus's error was perpetuated by others, the countess was forgotten, and *cinchona,* not *chinchona,* became the standard spelling.

In all likelihood people who enjoy filberts are similarly unaware that *filbert* honors a seventh-century Frankish abbot. St. Philibert was neither a known grower nor a connoisseur of hazelnuts. His connection with the nut is based on the fact that his feast day falls on 20 August, which happens to be the peak of the nutting season in France and England. The Anglo-French word *philber* was borrowed into Middle English as *filbert.*

Dunce is another word whose present form disguises its eponymous origin from John Duns Scotus. (See also DUNCE.) Just as the casual user of *dunce* is unaware that he is defaming a theologian's good name, a chemist is likely to be ignorant of the fact that *cudbear,* a red coloring matter from lichens, is named after the Scottish chemist Dr. Cuthbert Gordon. *Cudbear* is a respelling of the doctor's first name. A similar, much more famous example is *maudlin,* which derives from *Magdalene,* the appellation of the penitent sinner known as Mary in the New Testament. *Maudlin* more accurately suggests how *Magdalen* (as in Magdalen College) is actually pronounced in England. (See also MAUDLIN.)

Sometimes eponymous derivations are obscured in pedantic ways. Things relating to the reign of King James I of England are called not *Jamesean* but rather *Jacobean,* which derives from the New Latin *Jacobaeus.* Similarly, *Cartesian,* the word for things relating to the French philosopher René Descartes, derives from the Latin equivalent of the philosopher's surname. Curiously enough, George Bernard Shaw, who lived when Latin had long ceased to be an international language, witnessed the Latinization of his surname to Shavius, from which comes the eponymous adjective *Shavian.*

Top honors for the most ingeniously disguised eponym go to industrial engineer Frank Gilbreth. He coined *therblig,* the term for any of the elementary subdivisions of a cycle of motions in a time-motion study, by spelling his own name backwards.

[after John L. *McAdam* †1836 Brit. engineer]

macadamia See MACADAM.
[NL, fr. John *Macadam* †1865 Australian chemist born in Scotland + NL *-ia*]

machine Scraps of the history of ancient dialects lie frozen in the layers of English, like jumbled bone fragments in fossil strata. Let us do a little linguistic paleontology now.

Mechanic is a straightforward borrowing of Greek *mēchanikos* 'relating to a machine', via the Latin intermediary *mechanicus.* The Greek *mēchanikos* is derived from *mēchanē* 'machine'. English *machine* is a cognate of *mechanic,* but how do we account for the difference in form?

The immediate source of English *machine* \mə-'shēn\ is French *machine* \mä-'shēn\. This accounts for the \sh\ sound we give to *-ch-* in this word. Although French is a descendant of Latin, French *machine* is not a word that evolved gradually out of Latin the way our *mechanic* did. Rather it is a learned fourteenth-century borrowing of Latin *machina,* lightly Gallicized. (Had *machina* undergone the usual French sound changes over centuries of uninterrupted evolution from Latin to French, it would look quite different.) Latin *machina* is in turn borrowed from Greek—but why is there a difference in form from *mēchanē?* How did all the vowels get changed?

The answer lies in the fact that ancient Greek, like most languages, was divided into dialects. When we say "Greek" without qualification, we normally mean the Ionic dialect of Greek, which includes Attic, the language of Athens. This is the dialect whose literary fortunes assured it preeminence in history. But the Doric dialect also had a certain importance, being for instance the language used by the seventh-century B.C. poet Alcman. And in Doric the form used for 'machine' was *machana*. Latin borrowed this Doric form early in its history, at a time when Latin words were regularly stressed on the first syllable, yielding presumably \\'mä-kä-nä\\ in very early Latin. This stress permitted the variation between *me-* and *ma-* to exist between Greek and Latin as it had earlier between dialects of Greek. Another sound process in early Latin was the weakening of vowels in certain circumstances in syllables after the stressed syllable. This process yielded *machina* \\'mä-kē-nä\\, explaining the *-chi-* variation. When *machina* was borrowed into French, the middle syllable, originally the product of weakening, was thrown into prominence because of French stress patterns, and this explains the stressed \\ē\\ of *machine* in English.

[MF, fr. L *machina*, fr. Gk (Doric dial.) *machana* (Attic *mēchanē*), fr. (Doric dial.) *machos* means, expedient (Attic *mēchos*)]

machismo See MACHO.
[MexSp, fr. Sp *macho* male + *-ismo* -ism]

macho The Latin word *mas* 'male' found no posterity, either in the Romance daughter languages (apart from a possible dialect word for 'ram' in Picardy) or as a learned loan; perhaps it was too terse for its own good. But the derivatives *masculus* and *masculinus*, with essentially the same meaning as *mas* despite both having the formally diminutive suffix *-cul-*, had many descendants. From *masculinus*, by the learned route, English acquired *masculine*. In popular Latin speech *masculus* was early syncopated (by dropping an unstressed sound) to *masclus*—we know this happened because a sort of usage document from around the third century A.D., the *Appendix Probi*, admonishes us to abstain from this vulgarism. And on French soil *masclus* melted further to *masle* and finally *mâle*, which English borrowed as *male* in the fourteenth century. *Masculus* assumed an even more disguised form on the Iberian peninsula, where it became *macho* in Spanish and was primarily used with reference to animals. As reapplied to human males, particularly in Mexican Spanish, the word retains some of its zoological connotations and denotes a he-male. The derived Spanish abstract noun *machismo* denotes the associated cult of virility.

Macho entered English from (Mexican) Spanish in the 1920s, both as an adjective and as a noun denoting a macho man. *Machismo* is first attested in English a couple of decades later. For several decades *macho*, when used at all, was typically used in a Latin American context, and the Hispanic connection is occasionally recalled today in such uses as "rodeo is a muy macho sport" (*N.Y. Times*, 5 Dec. 1977) and "Spain, land of mucho macho matadors" (*Atlanta Journal*, 16 Sept. 1984). But in the 1970s and 1980s the popularity of *macho* mushroomed dramatically as part of the rethinking of sexual politics going on in the United States. The term was sometimes used favorably or at least tolerantly: "mature macho, taciturn, taut, amused, self-confident" (Stanley Kauffmann writing about the actor Charles Bronson in *Before My Eyes,* 1974); "the wholesome macho vices— smoking, drinking and swearing" (*People,* 7 Mar. 1983). More often there was an implication of disapproval or of needing to get beyond earlier stereotypical behavior: "the macho assertiveness and swagger that became Hemingway's personal legend" (Alfred Kazin, *N.Y. Times Book Rev.,* 26 Oct. 1980); " 'When I went to Buffalo in 1969,' says O. J. Simpson, 'I thought I had to show my macho, to go all out and play fierce.' " (quoted in *Sports Illustrated,* 23 Aug. 1982). The semantic evolution was precisely summed up by G. Gordon Liddy in a 1980 *Playboy* interview:

> *Macho* was originally a perfectly respectable Spanish term for a manly man, a designation I'd feel perfectly comfortable with, but in recent years it's been expropriated as a code word by the women's liberation movement and twisted into a pejorative Archie Bunkerish caricature of the loutish, leering male who believes that the only natural position for women in this world is horizontal.

In addition to the use of *macho* in the sense of *machismo,* i.e., 'macho quality', illustrated in the Simpson remark above, we also sometimes hear *machismo* being used as an adjective meaning 'macho':

> He was being machismo and verbally abusive —American soldier, quoted by Wallace Terry, *Bloods,* 1984

The use of *macho* has been extended in various ways, keeping a core sense of bravura assertiveness and drawing away from any specific sexual reference. For instance, doing the Sunday *New York Times* crossword puzzle in ink has been described as "intellectually macho." Most startling from an etymological standpoint is the use of *macho* and *machismo* in reference to women: "The women exude an exhilarated pride that some might call female machismo" (*Town & Country,* June 1980); "another career-minded Hollywood powerhouse who might well be described as the modern macho woman" (*Elle,* August 1986).

There was a stillborn attempt to introduce a term *facho* to mean 'female macho'. But again recalling the Spanish origins of the word, writers in the late 1970s who applied the concept to women began using a variant *macha* with the Spanish feminine *-a* ending: "This is a terrific *macha* book for women who want to get stronger, physically and psychologically" (Carol Troy, *N.Y. Times Book Rev.,* 7 May 1978); "the new, assertive, risk-taking macha woman" (*Publishers Weekly,* 17 Apr. 1981). And extending the grammatical analogy beyond the bounds of Spanish grammar, Grace Lichtenstein in 1981 published a book titled *Machisma.*

[Sp, male, fr. L *masculus,* adj. & n., dim. of *mas,* adj. & n., male]

madeleine See MAUDLIN.
[F, prob. after *Madeleine* Paulmier, 19th cent. Fr. pastry cook]

maelstrom See MEAL.
[obs. D (now *maalstroom*), fr. *malen* to grind, turn (fr. MD) + *strom*

stream, fr. MD *strōm;* akin to OHG *malan* to grind, and to OHG *stroum, strōm* stream]

magazine   In Arabic, *makhzan* and its variant *makhzin* denote a storehouse (here the *kh* represents a single sound, that of *ch* in Scottish *loch* or German *Bach*). From one of these, or more probably from the plural *makhāzin* (variant *makhāzīn*), Middle French derived *magasin* 'storehouse' in the fourteenth century. English borrowed the word from French in the sixteenth century, in the same sense. The term then underwent disparate specializations of meaning, depending on what was being stored. An early development was the designation of specifically military depots and ammunition dumps; a further extension applied *magazine* not to a building but to a chamber or clip to hold cartridges in a gun. *Magazine* was also used in the titles of books with the implication 'storehouse of knowledge'. This was a rather common sort of metaphor: the Latin *promptuarium,* 'storeroom', was used in the title of a number of English reference works, for instance (in a variant *promptorium*) the celebrated fifteenth-century English-to-Latin dictionary *Promptorium Parvulorum* (as it were, 'a storeroom for young minds'), and the use of Latin *thesaurus* 'storehouse, treasure-chamber' in such titles led to its eventual generic use in English for a kind of book. (See also TREASURE.)

But for *magazine* was reserved still another fortune. In 1731 there appeared *The Gentleman's Magazine: or, Monthly Intelligencer. Magazine* at this time carried no implication of 'periodical': the title was structurally similar to that of the *Promptorium Parvulorum,* and the editors used the word in its earliest sense when they announced their intention "to promote a Monthly Collection to treasure up, as in a Magazine, the most remarkable Pieces. . . ." But the burgeoning field of periodicals had more need of new terminology than the old one of books, and *magazine* came firmly to acquire the sense of a periodical publication. The new sense proved so useful that later in the eighteenth century, French, having lent us *magasin* in the first place, collected on the debt by borrowing *magazine* in its new English spelling and signification.

Despite their likely derivation from an Arabic plural, French *magasin* and English *magazine* have always been singular (the Arabic plural forms are not easily recognized as such). Similar examples of English singulars derived from Arabic plurals include *carrack* 'merchant ship', from Arabic *qarāqīr,* plural of *qurqūr; fluce* 'Persian coin', from *fulūs,* plural of *fals;* and *azimuth,* from *as-sumut,* plural of *as-samt* 'path, way'.

[MF, fr. OProv, fr. Ar *makhāzin,* pl. of *makhzan* storehouse, fr. *khazana* to store up]

magdalen   See MAUDLIN.
[after Mary *Magdalen* or *Magdalene,* woman whom Jesus healed of evil spirits (Lk 8:2), considered identical with a reformed prostitute (Lk 7:36 ff.)]

mail   Latin *macula* meant 'blemish, blotch' and was borrowed unaltered into English in related medical senses; more familiar is its negative deriva- tive *immaculate* 'having no spot'. The Latin word had an extended sense, 'mesh of a net', retained in the Old French descendant of *macula, maille*. English borrowed the word around 1300 with particular reference to the links in chain-work armor, and later applied the word to the armor itself. This sense survives in our expression "coat of mail."

Unrelated is the *mail* which the postman brings. This goes back to an old Germanic word meaning 'bag'—but by a roundabout route. As was so often the case with Latin-derived words, with this Germanic borrowing French was again the transmitter. In the eleventh century Old French borrowed the word from Frankish, an early Germanic language of what is now France, as *male* 'leather sack' (nowadays it is spelled *malle* and means 'box, trunk'). Middle English borrowed the word around 1200, spelling it first as *male* and eventually as *mail*. In the mid-seventeenth cen- tury the word came to be applied specifically to a bag of letters or mailbag and then to the letters themselves.

For a third unrelated *mail* see BLACKMAIL.

[ME *maile, maille,* fr. MF, fr. OF, fr. L *macula* spot, mesh of a net]

[ME *male,* fr. OF, of Gmc origin; akin to MD *māle* bag, traveling bag, OHG *malaha, malha* wallet, bag]

male   See MACHO.

[ME, fr. MF *male, masle,* adj. & n., fr. L *masculus,* adj. & n., dim. of *mas,* adj. & n., male]

mall   The word *mall* is a shortened form of *pall-mall*, the name of a game played in Italy and France from the sixteenth century and in En- gland in the seventeenth century. The game's Italian name was *palla- maglio,* which is made up of *palla* (a form related to Old High German *balla*) meaning 'ball' and *maglio* (derived from the Latin noun *malleus* 'hammer') meaning 'mallet'. The French took the name as *pallemaille,* which became *pall-mall* in seventeenth-century English.

The object of this game was to drive a wooden ball about four inches in diameter with a mallet (called a *mall*) through an iron ring suspended above the ground at the end of an alley. The player doing so with the fewest strokes won. In time, the alley on which the game was played was called a *mall,* and even after the game was no longer popular, the word *mall* continued to be used for such alleys, many of which became walks or streets. One of these walks, called "The Mall," was located in St. James's Park, London. It was landscaped with trees and flowers and became a fash- ionable place to walk. Other similar places came to be called *malls,* too.

In the mid-twentieth century, the word was put to new uses. The grassy strip of land separating the directional lanes of roadways is called a *mall.* In urban districts *mall* is applied to a shopping area featuring a variety of shops usually surrounding an open-air concourse reserved for pedestrian traffic. And in suburban districts the term is used for a large building or group of buildings that contain a variety of shops, businesses, and restaurants with associated passageways (often containing trees or plants and benches on which shoppers can relax) as well as parking facilities.

[fr. The *Mall,* fashionable promenade in St. James's Park, London, that was originally a pall-mall alley, by shortening & alter. (influenced in pronunciation by ¹*mall*) fr. *pall-mall,* a game played with a ball and mallet, fr. MF *pallemaille,* fr. It *pallamaglio,* fr. *palla* ball (of Gmc origin; akin to OHG *balla*) + *maglio* mallet, fr. L *malleus*]

man   As you might well suspect, *man* is one of the oldest words in our language, attested very early in Old English in a number of spellings including *man, mann, mon,* and *manna.* Unsurprisingly it goes deep into the roots of the Germanic languages and has cognates in every Germanic language you can think of. So deep are those roots that there are even cognates in Slavic languages, such as Russian *muzh* 'husband' and *muzhchina* 'man', and in other groups within the Indo-European family.

The prevailing meaning of *man* in Old English is 'human being', used both in a particular and a collective way, that is, meaning 'human being' and 'humanity'. In Old English the sex-marked words were *wer* 'male person' (related to Latin *vir*) and *wif* 'female person'. Sometime around 1000 *man* began being used in the sense 'male person' and after a couple of centuries its use drove poor old *wer* into permanent retirement. *Wer* survives today only in the ever popular compound *werewolf.*

In English *man* kept both its 'male person' and its 'human being, humanity' senses. The cognate Germanic languages in general developed derivatives like the German *mensch* and the Swedish *människa* for the 'human being' sense. English has a compound derivative for the abstract sense: *mankind* (Old English had a similar word *mancynn,* literally 'mankin'). But *mankind* has not replaced the parallel abstract sense of *man.*

It is a curious fact that many of the Romance, Germanic, and Slavic words meaning 'male person'—Spanish *hombre,* Italian *uomo,* French *homme,* German *mann,* Russian *muzhchina*—developed in a fashion similar to that of *man,* being first sex-neutral words (the Romance trio are all descended from Latin *homo,* which was also sex-neutral).

Another curiosity is *girl,* which developed similarly. In Middle English, *girle, gerle, gurle* around 1300 meant 'young person of either sex'; it did not develop its present 'female child' sense until around 1375. The sex-neutral sense of *girl* has long been obsolete, however.

For more on the derivatives of Latin *vir* see VIRTUE; for Old English *wif* see WOMAN.

[ME, fr. OE *man, mon;* akin to OS & OHG *man* human being, man, ON *mathr,* Goth *manna,* Skt *manu* human being, man, OSlav *mǫžĭ* man, and perh. to OE ge*mynd* mind]

maneuver   We owe both *manure* and *maneuver* to the same French source, although they entered our language at different times. The Old French verb *manovrer* came from Latin *manu operare,* 'to do work by hand'. The French word developed from this literal meaning the more specific sense 'to cultivate (land)'. In the late Middle Ages (the earliest evidence is from about 1400), the English borrowed the word *manouren*, 'to cultivate'. From this verb we get the noun *manure* for the dung used to fertilize the land. *Manovrer* continued to go its own way in French. The older sense 'to work by hand' gave way to a more general 'to work or operate'. By the middle of the eighteenth century, *manovrer* (now pretty well settled down in the spelling *manœuvrer*) had developed a new specific meaning, 'to perform military or naval movements', and English reborrowed the word.

[F *manœuvrer*, fr. OF *manovrer, manuvrer* to do work by hand, fr. L *manu operare*, fr. *manu* (abl. of *manus* hand) + *operare* to work]

mankind   See MAN.
[ME, fr. ¹*man* + *kind*]

manure   See MANEUVER.
[ME *manouren*, fr. MF *manouvrer*, lit., to do work by hand, fr. L *manu operare*]

marathon   Runners regard as sacred writ the story of the very first marathon. In 490 B.C. the Athenians had miraculously defeated a much stronger force of invading Persians on the plains of Marathon. The runner Pheidippides was selected to carry the good news back to Athens. The fleet runner ran the grueling 25 miles as fast as he could. Upon reaching the walls of the Acropolis, Pheidippides cried out, "Rejoice, we conquer!"—and promptly dropped dead. Ever since, many marathon finishers have felt like doing exactly the same thing.

Spoilsport historians tend to regard that story as apocryphal. They point out that the only contemporary account of events surrounding the battle of Marathon is found in Herodotus. According to that historian, upon the landing of the Persians at Marathon, the Athenians sent Pheidippides to Sparta to request their participation in the forthcoming battle. The round-trip distance between Athens and Sparta was 150 miles, and fleet-footed Pheidippides ran it in two days flat. The heroic effort was all for naught, for the Spartans gave the excuse that for religious reasons they could not set out before the next full moon. The story of the post-battle run to announce victory is based upon a later, dubious tradition. The notion that the runner was again Pheidippides was the conceit of the poet Robert Browning in his *Dramatic Idyls*. Having never run a marathon himself, Browning could assume that a runner who had made the round-trip between Athens and Sparta before the battle would be the likely person for the post-victory jog.

When the Olympic Games were revived at Athens in 1896, the marathon footrace was intended as a re-creation of the dramatic 25-mile dash from Marathon to Athens. Fittingly, the winner of the first modern marathon was a Greek, Spiros Louis. The founding of the annual Boston Marathon the following year greatly helped to establish the marathon as a major sporting event. The marathon's eccentric distance of 26 miles, 385 yards, standard since 1924, stems from a decision made during the 1908 Olympics held in London. In order for the race to finish at the royal box in the London stadium, an extra 385 yards was added to the 26-mile distance then in effect.

Before the concept of running as a mass-participation sport arose in the 1970s, a certain mystique had evolved around the marathon, and it had become proverbial as a feat requiring almost superhuman endurance. The word *marathon* thus came to be used of any inordinately long competition, contest, or other activity that severely tested the stamina of its participants. Inspired by the grueling footrace, people have staged so-called marathon dance contests, marathon fundraisers, marathon theatrical and musical performances, and even marathon group-encounter sessions.

[*Marathon,* ancient town in east central Greece where in 490 B.C. the Greeks won a victory over the Persians of which the news was carried to Athens by a long-distance runner]

March   See JANUARY.
[ME, fr. OE *march, marz,* fr. L *martius,* fr. *martius* of Mars, fr. *Mart-, Mars,* Roman god of war and agriculture]

Mardi Gras   See CARNIVAL.
[F, lit., fat Tuesday]

mare (horse)   See NIGHTMARE.
[ME *mare, mere,* fr. OE *mere;* akin to OHG *merha* mare, ON *merr* mare, OE *mearh* horse, OHG *marah,* ON *marr,* W *march*]

marionette   Puppet shows have been widespread in the world since ancient times, but the elaborately jointed and intricately wired figure known as the *marionette* was not perfected until the nineteenth century. At the time the word entered English from French in the seventeenth century, the puppet known as a marionette was comparatively crude, often being operated by a single rod to the head. Performances involving these figures were nonetheless quite popular in France in the sixteenth century when *marionette* is first attested in this sense in French. Puppet plays were performed in particular at the Feast of the Assumption of the Virgin Mary into heaven. This led to the puppets being called by a diminutive form of *Marie,* the French name of the Virgin Mary. Similar diminutives, such as *mariotte* and *mariole,* had been used to designate other objects associated with the Virgin, such as a fifteenth-century coin bearing her image.

Our word PUPPET (which see) is also of French origin.

[F *marionnette,* fr. MF *maryonete,* fr. *Marion* (dim. of the name *Marie* Mary) + MF *-ete* -ette; prob. fr. the conception that a puppet resembles an image of the Virgin Mary]

maroon   The verb *maroon,* which means 'to abandon on a desolate island or coast', and the name of the dark-red color *maroon* are unrelated, but both have their origins in the vegetable kingdom.

Latin *cyma,* 'young cabbage sprout', is the probable ancestor of the earlier verb *maroon*. Because the young sprout is at the top of the cabbage plant, the Spanish *cima*, a descendant of the Latin word, came to mean 'top' as well as 'sprout'. The *cima* may be the top of anything—a treetop or the summit of a mountain, for instance. Its American Spanish derivative *cimarrón* means 'wild' or 'savage', apparently because wildness was thought to be characteristic of dwellers on mountaintops.

In the seventeenth and eighteenth centuries, the word was borrowed into English and modified to *maroon*. Maroons were Negroes who had been brought to the West Indies and Guiana to serve as slaves but had fled to freedom in the mountains. John Davies, in his *History of the Caribby Isles* (1666), said of these people: "They will run away and get into the Mountains and Forests, where they live like so many Beasts; then they are call'd Marons, that is to say Savages." The verb *maroon* was derived from this noun. Men who were abandoned by buccaneers on desolate islands and coasts were left to live, as the *maroons* had lived, "like so many Beasts."

The color takes its name from *marron*, the French word for the Spanish chestnut, which is a dark and shiny reddish brown.

[modif. of AmerSp *cimarrón*, fr. *cimarrón*, adj., wild, savage, lit., living on mountaintops, prob. fr. Sp *cima* top, summit, sprout, fr. L *cyma* young sprout of cabbage, fr. Gk *kyma* wave, young sprout, fetus, anything swollen, fr. *kyein* to be pregnant; akin to *koilos* hollow]

[F *marron*, lit., Spanish chestnut]

marshal   The French language is a direct descendant of Latin, but it has included since its early days a number of Germanic words. The Franks, a Germanic people, occupied Gaul in the third century A.D. and left their name and some traces of their own Germanic tongue to France. Old French *mareschal* is one of these early Germanic words. A *mareschal* is etymologically 'a horse-servant'; the compound is related to Old English *mere* (Modern English *mare*) and *scealc*, 'servant'. In addition to its original sense of 'a groom or keeper of horses', Old French *mareschal* became the title of a high official in a royal court. In England the Anglo-Saxons used the word *hors-thegn* ('horse-thane', once again literally 'horse-servant') in the same two senses. The Old English word did not survive, and in the Middle English period, the English borrowed the Old French *mareschal*, 'high official'. The earlier sense, 'keeper of the horses', was borrowed a little later but is now obsolete.

Although *marshal* in a number of its modern uses has a military flavor, it is in no way related to its homophone *martial*, a derivative of Latin *Mars*, the name of the Roman god of war. See also CONSTABLE, STEWARD.

[ME *marshal, mareschal*, fr. OF *mareschal*, of Gmc origin; akin to OHG *marahscalc* keeper of the horses, marshal, fr. *marah* horse (akin to OE *mere* mare, OHG *merha* mare, ON *merr* mare, OE *mearh* horse, ON *marr*, W *march*) + *scalc* servant; akin to OE *scealc* servant, OS *skalk*, Goth *skalks*; perh. akin to MHG *schel* jumping, angry, OHG *scelo* stal-

lion, ON *skelkr* fear, Skt *śalabha* grasshopper, Lith *šuolỹs* gallop; basic
meaning: to jump]

martial See JOVIAL.
[ME, fr. L *Martialis* of the god Mars, fr. *Mart-*, *Mars*, Roman god of war
and agriculture + *-alis* -al]

martinet Although the fictional Captain Queeg and the fictionalized
Captain Bligh have become familiar types of the obsessive, cruel taskmas-
ter, neither one has attained the status of Colonel Jean Martinet, whose
name has become a generic byword for an autocratic disciplinarian. Between 1660 and 1670 King Louis XIV of France and his war minister, the
Marquis de Louvois, undertook the creation of Europe's first regular army.
The new army of regulars was designed to replace the old army, which had
long been a hodgepodge of free-lance soldiers of fortune and self-
contained units of mercenary forces. Basic to the reorganization was the
introduction of highly standardized methods of training and drill. Jean
Martinet was appointed inspector general of infantry and accorded the
rank of lieutenant colonel in the king's own foot regiment. As drillmaster
of the French troops, Martinet trained his troops to advance into battle in
linear formations and to fire in volleys only upon command. The system
of linear warfare devised by Louvois depended upon precision of movement, and Martinet's task was to train the troops to move forward in unison and at exactly 80 paces a minute. The rigid discipline imposed by the
autocratic drillmaster helped to make Europe's first regular army the best
on the continent. The colonel was also highly regarded as a military tacti-
cian and engineer. He developed battle formations and introduced the use
of the bayonet as a combat weapon. During a campaign of 1672 he devised
transportable copper pontoons to bridge the Rhine River. In that same
year he was fatally struck by French artillery fire while leading an infantry
assault at the siege of Duisburg in Germany.

Martinet's name first appeared in English four years after his death in
William Wycherley's play *The Plain Dealer* (1676). In the play *Martinet*
is used in a sense, now obsolete, referring to a particular military drill. The
sense of *martinet* that generically denotes a strict disciplinarian is not
known to have appeared in print until a century later. By that time the
word was being used in all sorts of contexts, not just military. Curiously,
no comparable sense of *martinet* developed in French. As for the other
countries of Europe, they paid the colonel their highest honor in adopting
his methods of training and his standards of discipline.

[after Jean *Martinet*, 17th cent. Fr. army officer who devised a new system of military drill]

mascot The Medieval Latin noun *masca*, meaning 'witch', was borrowed as *masco* into the Provençal language of southern France. *Mascoto*,
a diminutive form of this Provençal noun, was used to mean 'charm, sorcery'. In the latter half of the nineteenth century the word became part
of the French language as *mascotte*, and was popularized in the title of the

operetta *La Mascotte,* composed by Edmond Audran in 1880. In this operetta *"la mascotte"* is the beautiful maiden Bettina, whose beneficent influence brings victories to the army of the prince of Pisa. The appearance of *mascot* in English followed soon afterward, when it was used generically to mean 'a person or thing held to bring good luck'. Today many athletic teams have mascots such as a pretty girl or a small boy to bring good luck to the team or to lend color to the game. A college mascot may be the animal symbolic of the institution, such as the Army mule or the Yale bulldog.

For other words originally associated with charms and sorcery see FAS-CINATE, FETISH.

[F *mascotte,* fr. Prov *mascoto* charm, sorcery, fr. *masco* witch, fr. ML *masca, mascha* witch, specter]

masculine   See MACHO.
[ME *masculin,* fr. MF, fr. L *masculinus,* fr. *masculus,* adj. & n., male (dim. of *mas,* adj. & n., male) + *-inus* -ine]

masochism   *Masochism* and *sadism* are so clinical sounding that one would suspect that their eponyms were clinical psychologists rather than upper-class writers who novelized their sexual fantasies and histories. *Masochism* derives from the name of the Chevalier Leopold von Sacher-Masoch (1836–1895), an Austrian novelist whose preoccupation with the sexual pleasure of pain was mirrored by his characters. From his early childhood, Sacher-Masoch was weaned on tales of violence and cruelty told to him by his wet nurse and his father, a chief of police. The tales of cruel, dominating females inspired him to fantasize, and as he grew to maturity, he began to act out his fantasies. He entered into slave-master relationships with a number of women. Sacher-Masoch's most widely read novel, *Venus im Pelz* ("Venus in Furs"), typically reflects the author's obsessive interest in beatings, studded whips, and other instruments of sexual cruelty. Sacher-Masoch was a well-known literary figure of his day, his notoriety being such that even before his death in an asylum to which he had been committed by his second wife, medical dictionaries were entering *masochism* as the term for the psychosexual disorder in which a person derives pleasure through having his sexual partner inflict physical or emotional pain.

Sadism, the opposite of *masochism* and its almost inevitable companion, derives from the name of an author whose life parallels Sacher-Masoch's in several respects. The Marquis de Sade, the byname of the Count Donatien Alphonse François de Sade (1740–1814), had a brief military career before devoting his life to debauchery and perversion. Shortly after his marriage into a wealthy family, de Sade began a series of liaisons with prostitutes, luring them to one of his residences for sessions of sexual abuse. After each scandal became public, de Sade was confined for a time to one fortress or another. And with each release, the marquis resumed his pursuits. For his scandalous crimes de Sade was sentenced to death in absentia in the 1770s and narrowly escaped the guillotine during the Revolution. During his periods of imprisonment he wrote the novels and plays that center on the sexual compulsions that consumed his own life. De Sade's works had an underground reputation throughout the nineteenth century. Before the century was over, *sadism* had become the established term for the sexual perversion in which gratification is obtained through the infliction of pain on others.

[ISV *masoch-* (fr. Leopold von Sacher-*Masoch* †1895 Ger. novelist) + -*ism*]

mass   In early Christianity, when Greek was still the Christian language at Rome, the Greek word *eucharistia* 'the giving of thanks' was used both for the consecrated bread and wine and for the whole service commemorating the Last Supper. By the third century, Latin had become the language of the Roman Church, and *eucharistia* was simply borrowed into Late Latin for the name of the service. (It has come into Modern English as *Eucharist*, referring to the sacrament commemorating the Last Supper as part of the overall service.) However, other Latin terms were also used for the service, including *gratiarum actio* 'the act of giving thanks', *divina sacrificia* 'divine sacrifice', *Coena Domini* 'the Lord's Supper', and *Oblatio* 'Oblation'.

St. Ambrose (339–397), bishop of Milan, is the earliest writer known to have used the word *missa* for the eucharistic service. He used the word as one already in familiar and in common use. By the end of the sixth century, *missa* had become almost the exclusive word for the service. (An adjectival derivative of this word, meaning 'pertaining to the Mass', is the source of our word *missal.*)

The word *missa* comes from a form of the past participle of the verb *mittere* 'to send, dismiss'. The eucharistic service was divided into two parts; during the first part the catechumens (those receiving instruction in the faith) were allowed to be present, but during the second part only the faithful (those already baptized) were allowed. There were thus two dismissals during the service: one of the catechumens just before the Offertory, the other of the faithful at the end of the service, usually with the formula *Ite missa est* (freely, 'Go, [you are] dismissed'). The word *missa* came to refer to such a dismissal. In time the first part of the service came to be called the *missa catechumenorum* and the second part the *missa fidelium*. When the practice of dismissing the catechumens was discontinued, the single, connected service was simply called *missa.*

In Vulgar Latin *missa* took a form we reconstruct as *messa* (the source of French and German *messe* 'Mass') and was taken into Old English as *mæsse*, which in Middle English was spelled *messe* or *masse*. In *The Canterbury Tales* ("The Summoner's Tale," ca. 1395), Chaucer gives us an example in these words of a preaching friar: "I have to day been at youre chirche at messe,/And seyd a sermon after my symple wit."

Cognate with this word *mass* is the word *mess*, originally meaning 'a portion of food'. Both words ultimately derive from the Latin verb *mittere* 'to send'. In Late Latin *mittere* was used in a greatly extended sense to mean 'to put, place'. The past participle, *missus*, was used as a noun to denote 'a course at a meal'. Early French took *missus* as *mes* (modern French *mets*) in the twelfth century, and in the fourteenth century *mes* was borrowed into English with the same meaning. In the fifteenth century the word acquired the sense of 'a group of persons who regularly take their meal together', and later it came to refer to 'the place were such meals are regularly served to a group'. In his 1828 Dictionary, Noah Webster recorded the added sense 'a medley; a mixed mass'. From this use developed the sense of 'a disordered, untidy, or unpleasant state or condition'.

The noun *mass* meaning 'a quantity or aggregate of matter' is unrelated to the religious *mass* or to *mess*. In the fourteenth century, *masse* was borrowed into English from Middle French, which derived it from the Latin noun *massa* 'that which adheres together like dough, a lump'. In the sixteenth century, *mass* took on the sense of 'a large quantity, amount, or number'. Since about the 1830s, *masses* has been used to refer to 'the body of people as contrasted with the elite'. The British prime minister, William E. Gladstone, illustrated this usage in 1886, when he proclaimed "all the world over, I will back the masses against the classes."

[ME *masse* mass, feast day, fr. OE *mæsse*, modif. of (assumed) VL *messa*, mass, dismissal at the end of a religious service, fr. LL *missa*, fr. L, fem. of *missus*, past part. of *mittere* to send, dismiss]

[ME *masse*, fr. MF, fr. L *massa* lump, mass, fr. Gk *maza* lump, mass, barley cake; akin to Gk *massein, mattein* to knead]

Massachuset   See INDIAN.

[Massachuset *Massa-adchu-es-et*, a locality, lit., about the big hill, fr. *massa* big + *wadchu* hill + *-es*, dim. suffix + *-et*, locative suffix]

maudlin   *Maudlin* derives from an alteration of *Magdalene*, also spelled *Magdalen*, the appellation of Mary, the woman mentioned in the Gospel of Luke (8:2, AV): ". . . Mary, called Magdalene, out of whom went seven devils." In the Gospel of John (20:11–13) we find a well-known passage in which Mary Magdalene is portrayed as weeping: "But Mary stood without at the sepulchre weeping: and as she wept, she stooped down, and looked into the sepulchre, And seeth two angels in white sitting, the one at the head, and the other at the feet, where the body of Jesus had lain. And they say unto her, Woman, why weepest thou?" Medieval representations of Mary Magdalene customarily showed her weeping, and thus by the seventeenth century *maudlin* had come to mean 'tearful, weeping, lachrymose'. During that century *maudlin* began to be used more generally to mean 'tearfully or weakly emotional' and was used as especially apropos of anyone drunk enough to be emotionally silly, fuddled, or sentimental. The pronunciation represented by the spelling *maudlin* is used of both Magdalene College, Cambridge, and Magdalen College, Oxford, thus providing the present-day English speaker with a link between the name of Mary Magdalene and the adjective *maudlin*.

Mary's byname also survives in English in less disguised form as *magdalen*, denoting a refuge for reformed prostitutes, and in the proper name *Madeline* or *Madeleine*, found generically now as *madeleine*, a pastry.

[fr. *Maudlin* Mary Magdalene, fr. ME *Maudeleyn*, fr. OF *Madelaine*, fr. LL *Magdalene*, fr. Gk *Magdalēnē;* fr. the practice of representing Mary Magdalene as a weeping penitent sinner]

mausoleum   Mausolus (died 353/352 B.C.) was a satrap (governor) of the Persian empire who exercised virtually autonomous rule over Caria, a region in what is now southwestern Turkey. As a ruler he is remembered chiefly for his part in the revolt of the satraps of Anatolia against the Persian king Artaxerxes II and for backing the islands of Rhodes, Cos, and Chios in their war against Athens. Probably his most significant decision was moving his capital to Halicarnassus, for it was there that he conceived a project that would assure the immortality of his name. Mausolus began the planning of his own burial monument. At his death, his queen Artemisia completed the design of the monument and directed its construction. The edifice that she built in honor of her late husband towered about 135 feet. It had a rectangular base of white marble with a periphery of 411 feet. The upper level of the building was bounded by a colonnade of 36 columns, with colossal statues placed between the columns. The structure, which also housed colossal statues of Mausolus and Artemisia, was known in Greek as the *mausōleion* after the ruler entombed there. It was one of the Seven Wonders of the Ancient World. It is believed to have been destroyed by an earthquake at some time during the period known as the Middle Ages in the West, and its stones used in other buildings. From the time of its construction the fame of the tomb of Mausolus was such that it became a generic term for any large and imposing burial structure. Our English word *mausoleum*, in use since the fifteenth century, derives—by way of Latin—from the Greek *mausōleion.*

Perhaps the most celebrated and majestic mausoleum still standing is the Taj Mahal. Fittingly, the Taj Mahal, like the tomb at Halicarnassus, was built in loving memory of a spouse.

[L, fr. Gk *mausōleion*, fr. *Mausōlos* Mausolus †*ab*353 B.C. ruler of Caria commemorated by a magnificent tomb at Halicarnassus]

maverick   In south Texas in the middle of the nineteenth century lived a lawyer, Samuel A. Maverick, who was to have his name immortalized because of some cattle that happened to come into his possession. He was not a cattleman himself, but a client of his gave him four hundred head of cattle in lieu of cash to settle a $1,200 debt. Maverick had no use for the cattle, and so left them in the care of one of his men. The cattle were never branded and were allowed to room at will. Inclined to take advantage of this situation, neighboring cattlemen burned their own brands on the strays, which were then herded with their own. Although Maverick eventually sold his depleted herd, the term *maverick* to designate any unbranded cattle caught on and spread throughout the West.

By 1890 the term had acquired the transferred sense 'a rootless wanderer'. American travelers abroad carried this sense of *maverick* with them, and the British were quick to adopt the useful appellation. Rudyard Kipling became familiar with it and entitled one of his stories "A Mutiny of the Mavericks" (1890). He was referring to the members of the Irish regiment of Her Majesty's Royal Loyal Musketeers, whom he termed *mavericks* because they were, as he put it, "masterless and unbranded cattle— sons of small farmers in County Clare, shoeless vagabonds of Kerry, herders of Ballyvegan, much wanted 'moonlighters' [night raiders] . . . and the like."

About the same time, *maverick* was applied to a member of a group who refused to accept one or more of the policies espoused by that group. Political mavericks have bolted their parties, religious mavericks have been tried for heresy, and intellectual and artistic mavericks have set independent courses of pursuit, refusing to be "branded" with restrictive or conformist labels. Also about 1890 *maverick* began to be used as a verb with the sense 'to brand and take possession of (an animal) as a maverick', which in turn gave rise to the generalized sense 'to obtain by dishonest or questionable means'.

[after Samuel A. *Maverick* †1870 Am. pioneer in Texas who did not brand his calves]

May See JANUARY.

[ME, fr. OF & L; OF *mai*, fr. L *maius*, fr. *Maia*, Roman goddess associated with Vulcan]

mead Before sugar was discovered, honey was the principal substance used to satisfy our ancestors' sweet tooth. Three different Indo-European roots for this delicacy are represented in English. The first appears in *honey* itself and is the general term in the Germanic languages. Another appears in *mead*, a drink of fermented honey, the oldest alcoholic beverage among the peoples north of the regions where the grapevine flourishes. Readers of *Beowulf* will recall the scenes of thanes quaffing from mead-cups on the mead-bench, as their cries filled the mead-hall. The word is cognate with Greek *methy* 'wine'. (See also AMETHYST.)

In the ancient Greek and Roman worlds, the closest equivalent to mead was *hydromeli* (Englished as *hydromel*), a drink made from honey and water. And here we meet the third Indo-European root for 'honey', reflected in Latin *mel* 'honey'. The root shows up in English in *mellifluous*, borrowed from a Late Latin word that literally meant 'honey-flowing'. It also appears, disguised, in *molasses*, where the initial vowel has been altered from that in Late Latin *mellaceum* 'must, new wine'.

Honey in Rome was mixed not with water alone, but with wine, the resulting beverage being known as *mulsum*, a word related to *mel*. (From the Greek word for the equivalent drink we get a learned English word for it, *oenomel*.) A Late Latin feminine relative of this word, *mulsa*, was used for mead or hydromel. This word passed into Old French as *mousse* 'froth', and was eventually borrowed by English, where *mousse* denotes a pudding-like desert, thus shedding all alcoholic associations and returning to the etymologically earliest implication of sweetness.

[ME *mede*, fr. OE *medu;* akin to OHG *metu* mead, ON *mjöthr*, Gk *methy* wine, Skt *madhu* sweet, honey, mead]

meal It may be natural to suppose that the *meal* of "three meals a day" has some relation to the *meal* of "ground meal," since both words pertain to food, but in fact they are unrelated. The *meal* of "ground meal" is derived from the Old English *melu*, a term akin to the Old High German verb *malan*, 'to grind', and also to Latin *molere*, 'to grind'. *Molere* is related to Latin *molina*, the source of the English noun and verb *mill*. A relative of this "ground meal" *meal* is *maelstrom*, which originated in early Dutch, where it was formed from *malen*, 'to grind', and *strom*, 'stream' (the modern Dutch word is *maalstroom*). *Maelstrom* in its oldest use is the name of a strong and dangerous current flowing between two of the Lofoten islands off the northwest coast of Norway. The word became established in the general vocabulary of English in the sense 'a powerful whirlpool' in the nineteenth century, following its use by writers like Edgar Allan Poe in stories describing, with some exaggeration, the dangers of the Norwegian current.

The "three meals a day" *meal*, on the other hand, is from the Old English *mæl*, 'measure, appointed time, mealtime'. It is akin to the Old High German *mal*, 'time', and to the Latin verb *metiri*, 'to measure', which is the source of the English word *measure*. In Middle English, as *mæl* became *meel* the word became more closely associated with food than with time or measurement. The modern spelling and modern senses were established by the end of the seventeenth century. An interesting relative of this *meal* can be seen in *piecemeal*, in which -*meal* is a suffix having the sense 'by a (specified) portion or measure at a time'. This suffix is traceable to Old English *mælum*, the dative plural of *mæl*. *Mælum* was quite productive as a suffix in Old English, forming such adverbs as *dropmælum*, 'drop by drop', *fotmælum*, 'foot by foot', and *gearmælum*, 'year by year'. The derivative suffix -*meal* was widely used in Middle English as well, producing adverbs like *cupmeal*, *littlemeal*, *pennymeal*, and *poundmeal*, as well as *piecemeal*, the only one of these words to have survived in common use in Modern English. The suffix -*meal* had pretty much fallen into disuse by the eighteenth century, although it can still be rarely encountered in a few words other than *piecemeal*, including *inchmeal*, 'inch by inch', and the now dialectal *limbmeal*, 'limb from limb', an old example of which can be found in Shakespeare's *Cymbeline* (1610): "O that I had her here, to tear her limbmeal!"

[ME *mele*, fr. OE *melu;* akin to OHG *melo* meal, ON *mjöl* meal, OHG & Goth *malan* to grind, ON *mala*, L *molere* to grind, Gk *mylē* mill]

[ME *meel* mealtime, meal, fr. OE *mæl* appointed time, mealtime, meal; akin to OHG *māl* time, ON *māl* measure, mealtime, Goth *mel* time, L *metiri* to measure]

[ME -*mele*, fr. OE -*mælum*, fr. *mælum*, dat. pl. of *mæl* appointed time]

measure See MEAL.
[ME *mesure*, fr. OF, fr. L *mensura*, fr. *mensus* (past part. of *metiri* to measure) + *-ura* -ure; akin to OE *mǣth* measure, Gk *metron* meter, measure, Skt *māti* he measures]

mechanic See MACHINE.
[prob. fr. MF *mechanique, mecanique*, adj. & n., fr. L *mechanicus*, fr. Gk *mēchanikos*, fr. *mēchanē* machine + *-ikos* -ic]

media See MEDIUM.
[NL, fr. L, fem. of *medius* middle]

medial See MEDIUM.
[LL *medialis*, fr. L *medi-* + *-alis* -al]

median See MEDIUM.
[MF or L; MF, fr. L *medianus*, fr. *medius* middle + *-anus* -an]

mediate See MEDIUM.
[ME *mediat*, fr. LL *mediatus*, past part. of *mediare* to be in the middle, fr. L *medius* middle]

medium The Latin word *medium* is the neuter form of the adjective *medius*, meaning 'middle'. It is also a neuter noun meaning 'the middle'. When *medium* was first borrowed into English late in the sixteenth century, it was used for 'something lying in a middle or intermediate position'. It was quickly picked up by logicians for 'the middle term of a syllogism' and by mathematicians for 'a geometrical or arithmetical mean', but both these senses have since become archaic.

By 1595, however, we find *medium* used for 'a means of effecting or conveying something'. It was at first applied to the air, as the medium of sight and sound. By the nineteenth century the word was being broadly applied to 'a condition, atmosphere, or environment in which something may function or flourish'. A good example of this sense is given by the English historian George Grote in his 1865 publication *Plato and the Other Companions of Sokrates:* "You cannot thus abstract any man from the social medium by which he is surrounded."

Early in the seventeenth century another sense developed: 'an intermediate or direct instrumentality or means'. Francis Bacon provides an example in his 1605 book *Of the Advancement of Learning:* "But yet is not of necessity that cogitations be expressed by the medium of words." More recently, Havelock Ellis, in his *The Dance of Life* (1923), writes: ". . . he occupied himself much with painting, the common medium of self-expression in his day. . . ." By the mid-eighteenth century we find the first use of the phrase *medium of exchange* for 'something commonly accepted as the instrument of commercial transactions'. By 1919, A. J. Wolfe (*Theory and Practice of International Commerce*) was writing of the "media of communication such as telegraphs, cables, telephones, the post. . . ." The term *mass media* for 'the means of communication (as newspapers, radio, and films) designed to reach the mass of the people' dates from 1923, while *news media* is attested from about 1946.

The middle of the nineteenth century saw the rise of another extended sense in an entirely different field: 'an individual through whom other persons seek to communicate with the spirits of the dead'.

By 1885 *medium* was also being used in biology for the nutrient system used for artificially cultivating bacteria or cells. More specifically this is also referred to as a *culture medium*. The sense is, in origin, a special application of the 'fostering environment' sense of the late sixteenth century, mentioned earlier.

By about 1890 the 'means' sense was picked up in the world of art to denote the material means of artistic expression, such as the medium of oil, watercolor, or fresco. This sense came to be applied to literary and musical forms as well. Photographers also borrowed the term, using it for the varnish that is spread on a negative before retouching. And in the theater, *medium* is the common name for a color filter used in stage lighting.

Whether to pluralize *medium* as *media* or *mediums* has been unsettling to some writers. The Latin plural has been used for all senses except the spiritualist sense, where *mediums* is firmly entrenched. Although *media* is the only plural used in the biological sense, the plural *mediums* has had some use in the other senses.

Since the 1920s there has been a trend toward using *media* as a singular count noun, a usage which seems to have originated in advertising jargon. This usage has since extended to other fields, and we have found such phrases as "a suitable media," "one media," "a new recording media," and "an optical disc media" in recent publications.

There is also a trend toward using *media* as a collective noun, which can take either a singular or a plural verb. When *media* takes a singular verb, it almost always refers to the mass media: television, radio, the press. In addition, it has come to refer to the people representing these organizations. Jesse Jackson, for example, was quoted in *Esquire*, December 1979, as saying: "I understand the media . . . and it apparently understands me."

Perhaps adding to the confusion is the occurrence of another *media* in English. This *media* is used in phonology for 'a voiced stop' and in anatomy for 'the middle coat of the wall of a blood vessel'. Its plural is *mediae*, the Latin plural of the feminine form (*media*) of the adjective *medius*.

The Latin *medius* is also the source of the English words *medial* and *median*, both referring to 'being in the middle'. The verb *mediate*, 'to interpose between two parties in order to reconcile them', was formed from the Latin *mediatus*, the past participle of the verb *mediare*, a Late Latin derivative of *medius*. Our words *intermediate, intermediary,* and *immediate* can also be traced back to the Latin *medius*.

[L, fr. neut. of *medius* middle]

megrim See MIGRAINE.
[ME *migrene, migrein, migreime,* fr. MF *migraine*]

melancholy See HUMOR.
[ME *malencolie,* fr. MF *melancolie,* fr. LL *melancholia,* fr. Gk, fr. *melan-, melas* black + *cholē, cholos* bile, gall + *-ia* -y]

mellifluous See MEAD.
[LL *mellifluus,* fr. L *melli-* (fr. *mell-, mel* honey) + *-fluus* (fr. *fluere* to flow); akin to OE *milisc* sweet, mild, *mildēaw, meledēaw* honeydew, OS *milidou* mildew, OHG *milituo* mildew, Goth *milith* honey, Gk *melit-, meli,* OIr *mil,* Arm *meɫr,* Alb *mjal,* Hitt *milit*]

Mennonite See CATHOLIC.
[G *Mennonit,* fr. *Menno* Simons †1561 Frisian religious reformer + connective *-n-* + G *-it* -ite]

mentor See STENTORIAN.
[after *Mentor,* tutor of Telemachus in the Odyssey of Homer, fr. L, fr. Gk *Mentōr*]

menu A *menu* is a list of the foods available at a restaurant or served at a particular meal. In these senses *menu* was borrowed in the nineteenth century from French, where the noun was created from the adjective *menu,* 'small, slender, detailed'. Presumably the last sense is the one that gave first the French and then us the noun, since a menu is a detailed list. The French adjective is derived from the Latin adjective *minutus,* 'small', which is also the source of the English adjective *minute.*

Just as French pressed the adjective *menu* into service as a noun, so too Latin had earlier adapted from *minutus* the feminine form *minuta* as a noun. The sense of *minuta* was specialized to mean 'the sixtieth part of a degree' and was later used in Medieval Latin to mean 'the sixtieth part of an hour'. It is from the latter that the English noun *minute* is derived. The sense of the noun which we mean when we speak of "the *minutes* of the last meeting" developed directly from Latin *minuta,* possibly short for *minuta scriptura,* 'draft in small writing'. This designation presumably distinguished the draft from the full, round hand of the final copy of the document.

[F, fr. *menu,* adj., small, slender, detailed, fr. L *minutus* small]

mercurial See JOVIAL.
[L *mercurialis* of the god Mercury, of the planet Mercury, fr. *Mercurius* Mercury, ancient Roman god of commerce and messenger of the gods & *Mercurius* Mercury, the 1st planet from the sun (fr. *stella Mercurii,* lit., star of Mercury, after *Mercurius,* the god Mercury; trans. of Gk *astēr tou Hermou,* lit., star of Hermes, Greek messenger of the gods) + *-alis* -al]

mercury See QUICKSILVER.
[ME *mercurie,* fr. ML *mercurius,* fr. L *Mercurius* Mercury, ancient Roman god of commerce and messenger of the gods; prob. fr. the com-

parison of the mobility of the metal to the traditional fleet-footedness of the god]

mercy *Mercy* is not something that can be bought or sold; yet it does have a connection with the marketplace. It was borrowed into Middle English from Old French *mercit, merci,* which had the same range of senses as English *mercy.* It is ultimately derived from Latin *merces,* meaning 'the price paid for something', 'wages', 'reward', or 'recompense'. *Merces* is derived from Latin *merx,* 'ware' or 'merchandise'. The roots of what is now the primary sense of *mercy* are to be found in the Latin of Christian writers in the sixth century, who began to use *merces* for the spiritual reward that derives from kindness to those who do not necessarily have a direct claim to such mercy and from whom no recompense is to be expected. Thus, in a sense, the dispensation of mercy is a figurative form of trade, transacted in a less mundane currency than our daily negotiations. While English has retained most of the senses of Old French *merci,* by and large these senses have not survived in French itself, where today *merci* is used primarily to express thanks.

[ME *merci, mercy,* fr. OF *mercit, merci,* fr. ML *merced-, merces,* fr. L, price paid for something, wages, reward, recompense, fr. *merc-, merx* ware, merchandise]

mesmerize Denounced as a quack by some and hailed as the discoverer of a great medical breakthrough by others, Franz Anton Mesmer (1734–1815) was the sensation of late eighteenth-century Europe. A graduate of a traditional medical school in Vienna, Mesmer early on developed unorthodox medical beliefs. In his doctor's thesis he asserted that the planets have a direct influence upon all the tissues of the human body. He claimed the existence of a mysterious fluid that permeates all matter, both living and nonliving. Eventually calling this force "animal magnetism," he cited as precedent for his theories the belief of the ancient Greek physician Galen that the moon affected epilepsy and hysteria. Around 1775 there were others about central Europe effecting seemingly miraculous cures, either by using magnets or by exorcizing demons. Studying these various cases, Mesmer reached the conclusion that in every case it was his "animal magnetism" at work. Despite a few astounding cures, Mesmer was denounced by several prominent physicians for practicing "magic" and was forced to leave Vienna. After a false start or two, Mesmer made a name for himself in Paris, especially after attracting the attention and support of Queen Marie Antoinette. He became the rage of Paris, and to his treatment rooms flocked all levels of society. For their treatment, patients joined hands and sat in a circle around a large tub of dilute sulfuric acid from which iron bars protruded. These iron bars had been previously charged with animal magnetism by Mesmer's magic touch. As the patients touched the bars, a current of animal magnetism flowed through them. Mesmer then proceeded to personally touch each person with his wand, causing each to twitch and writhe, continuing until the whole circle became agitated. The necessary crises having thus been produced, Mesmer effected the individual cures by having the animal magnetism flow from his body to the patient's. In 1784 King Louis XVI appointed a joint committee from the Société de Medicine and the Académie des Sciences to investigate Mesmer's claims. The committee included Benjamin Franklin and Antoine Lavoisier. The special commission concluded that Mesmer "cures" were entirely due to the imagination, stating that "imagination without magnetism produces convulsions and that magnetism without imagination produces nothing." Yet, Mesmer's popularity increased.

But Mesmer fled Paris in the face of the French Revolution, settling in Meersburg, Austria, where he faded into obscurity. What Mesmer had discovered—or rediscovered—was the technique once called "artificial somnambulism" and now known as hypnotism. He had unwittingly contributed to the notion that the faith of the patient goes a long way toward effecting recovery. One of Mesmer's disciples, Puységur, in 1784 developed a technique for inducing hypnosis and was the first to apply his mentor's name to it. By 1802 *mesmerism* was an English word. From *mesmerism* evolved the verb *mesmerize*, which originally was applied to hypnotic induction and now has the broad sense of 'to bind or hold by or as if by a spell or charm, fascinate'. See also HYPNOSIS.

[*mesmer*ism (fr. F. A. *Mesmer* †1815 Austrian physician + E *-ism*) + *-ize*]

mess See MASS.
[ME *mes,* fr. OF, fr. LL *missus* course at a meal, fr. *missus,* past part. of *mittere* to put, place, fr. L, to send]

message See HARBINGER.
[ME, fr. OF, fr. ML *missaticum,* fr. L *missus* (past part. of *mittere* to send) + *-aticum* -age]

messenger See HARBINGER.
[ME *messager, messangere, messengere,* fr. OF *messagier,* fr. *message,* fr. ML *missaticum,* fr. L *missus,* past part. of *mittere* to send]

Methodist See CATHOLIC.
[*method* + *-ist*]

mews See FALCON.
[pl. of *mew* cage, fr. ME *muwe, mewe,* fr. MF *mue,* fr. *muer* to molt, change, fr. L *mutare* to change]

migraine Greek *kranion* 'skull, brainpan' gave rise straightforwardly, via Latin transmission, to English *cranium,* a learned loanword. The word also entered English in phonetic disguise by a more popular and roundabout route. Using the prefix *hēmi-* 'half' (familiar to us from such scholarly borrowings as *hemisphere*), Greek formed *hēmikrania* to denote a pain on one side of the head, and this entered Late Latin as *hemicrania.* Old French took up the word as *migraigne* and *migraine,* using it sometimes in the original physical sense and sometimes in an extended sense of 'spite' or 'foul mood'. English borrowed the word (in a variety of spellings) around 1400. It was still often used in its strictly etymological sense, as in this passage from a fifteenth-century document (recorded in the Oxford English Dictionary): "a fervent mygreyn was in the ryght syde of hurre hedde." And the modern form *migraine* is still used, mostly literally, for a severe, often unilateral headache. But extended senses also developed, favored first by the circumstance that the affiliation to *hemi-* and *cranium* was now opaque, and second by the fact that some of the variant spellings coalesced around a second standard variant, *megrim*, which stabilized in the language as a doublet of *migraine*. *Megrim* was often used in a physical sense:

> She sighs for ever on her pensive bed,
> Pain at her side, and Megrim at her head
> —Alexander Pope, "The Rape of the Lock," 1712

Yet, even this was subject to variation, and *megrim* has been attested in the sense 'earache' in modern Scots dialect. The word also took off in a figurative direction, meaning things like 'troubling or unbidden thought' and, when plural, 'low spirits', a development reminiscent of the state of affairs in Old French. Something of the flavor of the word may be gleaned from a poem by Lord Byron ("Hints from Horace," written in 1811), defending the freedom of drama from spoilsport critics:

> Yet Chesterfield . . . fought for freedom to our plays;
> Uncheck'd by megrims of patrician brains,
> And damning dulness of lord chamberlains.
> Repeal the act! again let Humour roam
> Wild o'er the stage—we've time for tears at home

And James Joyce in *Ulysses* (1922) uses this 'low spirits' sense: "It was an ancient and a sad matron of a sedate look and christian walking, in habit dun beseeming her megrims and wrinkled visage."

[F, fr. LL *hemicrania* pain in one side of the head, fr. Gk *hēmikrania*, fr. *hēmi-* hemi- + *kranion* skull]

Milky Way   See GALAXY.
[ME, trans. of L *via lactea*]

mill   See MEAL.
[ME *mille*, fr. OE *mylen;* akin to OHG *mulī, mulin* mill, ON *mylna;* all fr. a prehistoric NGmc-WGmc word borrowed fr. LL *molina, molinum* mill, fr. fem. and neut. of *molinus* of a mill, of a millstone, fr. L *mola* mill, millstone + *-inus* -ine; akin to L *molere* to grind]

milliner   Since the end of the second World War, the reputation of the city of Milan as a center for international fashion has risen steadily. In the opinion of many, Milan now rivals Paris as an arbiter of what is fashionable and what is not. The current preeminence of Milanese fashion has several historical precedents, one of which was the occasion for an enduring contribution to the English language. Sixteenth-century England witnessed one such vogue for finery from Milan. Milan bonnets, Milan gloves, Milan jewelry, Milan needles, Milan point lace, Milan ribbons—all represented the best in Renaissance finery. The purveyors of these luxury goods imported from Milan were called *milaners* or *millaners* or, in the variant that survives today, *milliners*. Originally, the word *millaner* or *milliner* meant a native or inhabitant of Milan. We find an excellent example of this in John Rastell's 1529 work *The Pastyme of People, the Cronycles of Dyvers Realmys* (quoted in the Oxford English Dictionary): "He was encountered by the Mylleners and the Venicyans." Only a few of these early purveyors were, in fact, from Milan. Eventually, *milliner* was extended to all merchants specializing in fancy accessories, regardless of the actual origin of the merchandise. For several centuies *milliner* could refer to a purveyor of luxury items of any kind. In *The Winter's Tale* (ca. 1610), for example, Shakespeare uses *milliner* to refer to a vendor of fine gloves: "He hath songs for man or woman, of all sizes. No milliner can so fit his customers with gloves." Apparently, not until the nineteenth century was *milliner* reserved exclusively for makers or retailers of women's hats.

[irreg. fr. *Milan,* city in northern Italy + E *-er;* fr. the importation of women's finery into England from Italy in the 16th century]

miniature Before the art of printing was introduced in Europe, books were written by hand; and often titles, headings, and initials were written in red to contrast with the black ink of the text. The red pigment often used for this purpose and for decorative embellishments and drawings was made from cinnabar or red lead. The Latin word for this red coloring is *minium,* which English borrowed in the same meaning. Related to this noun is the Latin verb *miniare,* meaning 'to color with cinnabar or red lead'. In early Italian *miniare* became generalized to mean 'to illuminate a manuscript', and the noun *miniatura* was formed from the verb to denote a manuscript illustration done not necessarily in red alone but in any variety of colors.

Because the illuminations in manuscript books are small by comparison with paintings done on canvas, board, or wall, the word *miniature,* borrowed into English from the Italian *miniatura,* came to mean not only a manuscript illumination but any small portrait or painting, and eventually the sense was extended to denote anything very small. This last sense is also the most common sense of both the noun and adjective forms today. See also RUBRIC.

[It *miniatura* picture on a small scale, art of manuscript illumination, fr. *miniato* (past part. of *miniare* to illuminate a manuscript) (fr. L *miniatus,* past part. of *miniare* to color with cinnabar or red lead) + *-ura* process, act]

mint See MONEY.

[ME *mynt,* fr. OE *mynet;* akin to OHG *munizza* coin; both fr. a prehistoric WGmc word borrowed fr. L *moneta* mint, coin, money, fr. *Moneta,* epithet of Juno, ancient Italian goddess, wife of Jupiter; fr. the fact that the Romans coined money in the temple of Juno Moneta]

minute   See MENU.
[ME, fr. MF, fr. ML *minuta* minute, 60th part of an hour, brief note, fr. LL, 60th part of a degree, fr. L, fem. of *minutus* small]

[L *minutus* small, minute, past part. of *minuere* to lessen]

missal   See MASS.
[ME *messel, missall,* fr. MF & ML; MF *messel,* fr. ML *missale,* fr. neut. of *missalis* of mass, fr. LL *missa* mass + L *-alis* -al]

mob   See CLIPPING.
[short for ³*mobile,* fr. L *mobile (vulgus)* changeable crowd, the movable common people, neut. of *mobilis,* adj.]

Mohawk   See INDIAN.
[of Algonquian origin; akin to Narraganset *Mohowaùuck* Mohawk, lit., they eat animate things]

molasses   See MEAD.
[Pg *melaço,* fr. LL *mellaceum* must, fr. neut. of (assumed) *mellaceus* resembling honey, fr. L *mell-, mel* honey & *-aceus* -aceous]

molt   See FALCON.
[alter. of ME *mouten,* fr. (assumed) OE *mūtian* to change (as in *bimūtian* to exchange), fr. L *mutare*]

monarchy   See HIERARCHY.
[ME *monarchie,* fr. MF, fr. LL *monarchia,* fr. Gk, fr. *monarchēs, monarchos* monarch (fr. *monos* alone, single + *archos* ruler) + *-ia* -y]

Monday   See SUNDAY.
[ME, fr. OE *mōnandæg, mōndæg;* akin to OFris *monendei* Monday, MD *maendach, manendach,* MLG *māndach, mānendach,* OHG *mānatag;* all fr. a prehistoric WGmc compound formed from components represented by OE *mōna* moon and *dæg* day; trans. of L *dies lunae,* trans. of Gk *hēmera Selēnēs*]

money   One of the epithets of the goddess Juno, the wife of Jupiter in Roman mythology, was *Moneta.* When the Romans established a mint at the temple of Juno Moneta, this epithet became a generic Latin term for a place where money is made. The English words *mint* and *money* are both derived from Latin *moneta.* The considerable difference between the two words may be accounted for by the widely different routes by which each came into English.

Mint, attested in Old English in the form *mynet,* has been in the language since it first developed and comes from a primitive Germanic borrowing from Latin *moneta* which is also the source of Old High German *munizza*, 'coin'. A few sound changes for the vowels over the course of time since the Old English period, and we have the modern form *mint*. In Middle French, however, Latin *moneta* became *moneie*, which was then borrowed into Middle English in the form *moneye*. For other words derived from the names of ancient gods and goddesses see VOLCANO.

[ME *moneye*, fr. MF *moneie*, fr. L *moneta* mint, coin, money]

monokini   See BIKINI.

[*mono-* (fr. Gk *monos* alone, single) + *-kini* (as in *bikini*)]

monster   Children sometimes awaken from nightmares, frightened of the *monsters* of their dreams. Parents usually are quick to reassure them that these monsters are not real. But there are many monsters that are very real. The earliest recorded sense of the word is 'an animal or plant departing greatly in form or structure from the usual type of its species'. This sense has been in use from about 1300, and we read in the tale of the voyages of Sir John Mandeville from around 1400 that "a monstre is a thing difformed agen Kynde [deformed against nature] both of Man or of Best." By the seventeenth century, *monster* had taken on the figurative sense of someone or something that is bizarre or unnatural. In 1604 Shakespeare had Othello complain of his friend Iago: "By heaven, he echoes me,/As if there were some monster in his thought/Too hideous to be shown." And in 1837 Ralph Waldo Emerson in an address to the Phi Beta Kappa society of Harvard (quoted in the Oxford English Dictionary) said: "The state of society is one in which the members have suffered amputation from the trunk, and strut about so many walking monsters."

Chaucer was among the first to use the term *monster* in its familiar sense of a mythical creature of nonhuman or not fully human form. In his *Legend of Good Women* (ca. 1385) he describes the Minotaur, a half man, half beast kept by Minos in the underworld:

> This Mynos hadde a monstre, a wiked best,
> That was so crewel that, withoute arest [delay],
> Whan that a man was brought in his presence,
> He wolde hym ete; ther helpeth no defence.

In the sixteenth century, the word acquired the less terrifying but nevertheless ominous meaning of 'a person of inhuman cruelty or wickedness'. And at about the same time an equally common extended sense developed, that of something 'unusually large for its kind' often with the added notion of 'unwieldy'. In 1759 Oliver Goldsmith in his *Inquiry into the Present State of Polite Learning in Europe* used the word in this sense: "From these inauspicious combinations proceed these monsters of learning, the Trevoux, Encyclopedies, and Bibliotheques of the age." And in a more recent example, Donal Henahan writing in the *New York Times* of 19 February 1974 talks about an overlong Brahms sonata as "a five-movement monster that few pianists program." It is this sense which has yielded a familiar adjective use, first encountered in the nineteenth century and epitomized by this more recent example: "Ten thousand copies is a monster best-seller for a book of poetry" (Ben Pesta, *Rolling Stone,* 17 February 1972).

Regardless of the form a monster takes, all monsters have one thing in common: they are all awe-inspiring, even frightening, by virtue of some aspect of their physicality or personality. In fact, the word *monster* comes from the Latin *monstrum,* meaning 'an evil omen', which in turn seems to be a derivative of the verb *monēre,* meaning 'to warn, remind'. This same Latin verb *monēre* has yielded other modern English words in which the notion of reminding or warning can be seen. One is *demonstrate,* from Latin *demonstratus,* a past participle of *demonstrare,* which comes from *de-* 'away' and *monstrare* 'to show, point out'. *Monstrare* itself comes ultimately from *monēre.* Another is *premonition,* a warning of something about to happen. It comes, through several intermediaries, from Latin *praemonēre* 'to warn in advance', from *prae-* 'before' and *monēre.*

For other words denoting large size see GARGANTUAN, HIPPOPOTAMUS.

[ME *monstre,* fr. MF, fr. L *monstrum* evil omen, monster, monstrosity, prob. fr. *monēre* to remind, warn]

Mormon   See CATHOLIC.
[after *The Book of Mormon* (first published 1830), sacred scriptures of the Latter-day Saints]

morphine   See HYPNOSIS.
[F *morphine,* fr. *Morpheus* god of dreams + F *-ine*]

Moslem   See SALAAM.
[Ar *muslim,* fr. *aslama* to surrender (to God)]

mosquito   See MUSKET.
[Sp, fr. *mosca* fly, fr. L *musca*]

mother   See HYPOCHONDRIA.
[ME *moder,* fr. OE *mōdor;* akin to OHG *muoter* mother, ON *mōthir,* L *mater,* Gk *mētēr,* Skt *mātṛ*]

mousse   See MEAD.
[F, lit., froth, fr. LL *mulsa* hydromel, fr. L, fem. of *mulsus* mixed with honey, sweet as honey]

muckraker   John Bunyan's religious allegory *Pilgrim's Progress* (1678) includes a character identified as "a man . . . with a Muckrake in his hand," who busies himself so much with raking the muck—that is, with attending to worldly things—that his gaze is always downward and he never sees a celestial crown held above him. The metaphor inspired some occasional uses of *muckrake* in the nineteenth century, most notably in American political circles where, according to Maximilian Schele de Vere's *Americanisms* (1872), *muckrakes* was "a slang term . . . for persons

who 'fish in troubled waters,' from the idea of their raking up the muck
to see what valuable waifs and strays they may find in it."

Muckrake received its greatest boost when it was used by President
Theodore Roosevelt in an April 1906 speech criticizing the excesses of
journalists who had achieved great popularity by exposing the corruption
of public figures and institutions. Said Roosevelt, "The men with the
muckrakes are often indispensable to the well-being of society; but only
if they know when to stop raking the muck."

The term *muckraker* became almost immediately established in popular
use as a name for reform writers like Lincoln Steffens, Ida M. Tarbell,
Edwin Markham, and Upton Sinclair. Although originally meant to be pejorative, the name was adopted by the writers themselves, and it acquired
connotations of courageous honesty and social conscience. The muckraking movement did not last beyond 1912 however. Yet *muckraking* itself
is alive and well; the term is frequently pejorative but often acquires admiring connotations in a "watchdog" context:

> . . . a muckraking newsletter . . . regularly exposes expense-account
> padding, mismanagement and political favoritism by HUD execu-
> tives —Burt Schorr, *Wall Street Jour.*, 16 June 1975

[fr. *muckrake*, v., (fr. obs. E *muckrake*, n., rake for gathering dung into
a heap, fr. ¹*muck* + *rake*) + -*er*]

mugwump When James G. Blaine received the Republican Party's
nomination for the presidency in 1884, many Republicans refused to have
anything to do with his candidacy, supporting instead the Democratic candidate, Grover Cleveland. Those Republicans who remained loyal to their
party accused the bolters of a lofty and supercilious attitude and nick-
named them *mugwumps*. The word had previously been used as a jesting,
slightly derogatory term for someone who considered himself a great man.
The name given to Republican dissidents in 1884 came later to be used
for anyone who could not make up his mind. This is the sense of *mugwump*
that is now most common.

Mugwump came originally from Natick, a dialect of the language of the
Massachuset Indians. Roger Williams, in 1643, translated *muckquomp* as
captain. John Eliot, the "Apostle of the Indians," rendered English *duke*
by *mugquomp* in his Indian version of the Bible (1653). But for years a popular, pseudo-etymological "definition" of *mugwump* has persisted, credited to Congressman Albert J. Engel, who in a speech made in 1936
explained a mugwump as "a bird who sits with its mug on one side of the
fence and its wump on the other." But the explanation is older and anonymous. Two years earlier the *Minneapolis Journal*, on 15 October 1934, reported discovery of this "definition" by the *Blue Earth* (Minnesota) *Post*.

[Natick *mugquomp*, *mugwomp* captain, prob. fr. *mogki* great + -*omp*
man]

muscle Diminutives like Latin *musculus*, 'little mouse' (diminutive of *mus*), are used not only to name small things but often to express such diverse feelings as endearment and ridicule or to project a humorous attitude as well. Some muscles, especially the major muscles of the arm and leg, look a little like stylized mice, their tendons playing the part of a mouse's tail. This fancied resemblance accounts for the Latin word *musculus*, the ultimate source of English *muscle*. The word came through French into English, losing along the way its original Latin connotations.

Latin *musculus* was also applied to a creature of the sea; this is the source of the English word *mussel*. It is not certain whether the basis of the comparison is directly to a muscle, since this mollusk looks like little more than a muscle in a shell, or again to a mouse, which a mussel resembles in general outline. The latter comparison may not seem especially striking to us today, but Greek *mys* shows a similar semantic development, meaning both 'mouse' and 'mussel'. And Latin was sufficiently fond of its *musculus* metaphors that it applied the word to a small boat, a cover used in siege warfare, and a couple of other sea creatures as well.

[MF, fr. L *musculus,* dim. of *mus* mouse]

music   After experiencing a particularly moving performance, a music lover might be tempted to ascribe the composer's achievement to divine inspiration. Etymologically speaking, the appreciative listener would not be off the mark. The ancient Greeks seem to have believed that achievement in the arts was divinely inspired. The source of the inspiration was the Muses, the goddesses of poetry and song. Originally there were three of them, but as the myth of the Muses developed, the number expanded to nine. According to the most common tradition, the Muses were the daughters of Zeus and Mnemosyne, a Titaness. As goddesses of song, the Muses were naturally associated with Apollo, the god of the lyre and a mentor of the bards. As the myth of the Muses evolved, they became divinities whose purview expanded from just song to a variety of poetic modes and arts and sciences. In the full development of the myth, these were the nine Muses: Calliope, the Muse of epic poetry; Clio, the Muse of heroic poetry or history; Euterpe, the Muse of music, especially when produced by wind instruments; Melpomene, the Muse of tragedy; Terpsichore, the Muse of choral song and dance; Erato, the Muse of erotic poetry; Polyhymnia, the Muse of sacred poetry and hymns; Urania, the Muse of astronomy; and Thalia, the Muse of comedy and of merry or idyllic poetry. The Muses were invoked by mortal poets for their power to revive the memory and to bestow gracefulness to the poet's words. While the early Greeks beseeched the Muses for inspiration in all seriousness, the invocation became for the later Greek and Roman poets a mere formality. From *Mousa*, the Greek original for one Muse, came the term *mousikē*, which literally meant 'the art of the Muse'. Applied in general to any of the arts presided over by the Muses, *mousikē* came to be used especially of the art of producing a pleasing arrangement of tones. It is in this specific sense that *mousikē* ultimately gave rise to our word *music*.

For words derived from the names of other Muses see CALLIOPE.

[ME *musik,* fr. OF *musique,* fr. L *musica,* fr. Gk *mousikē,* any art presided over by the Muses, esp. music, fr. fem. of *mousikos* of the Muses, musical, fr. *Mousa* Muse + *-ikos* -ic]

musket The musket was originally a Spanish weapon, first used by the Spanish army in the sixteenth century, for Spain had, at that time, Europe's finest military force. The musket was introduced to France through her conflict with Spain, fought in Italy. Although the French borrowed the new weapon from their enemy, they took the name *mousquette* (or *mousquet*) from the Italians. Italian *moschetto*, diminutive of *mosca*, 'fly', was the word for the arrow of a crossbow. When the new weapon appeared, the name of the old one was taken over for it. The Spanish word *moschete*—*mosquete* in Modern Spanish—has a parallel history. The weapon soon reached England from France. The earliest appearance in English of the word *musket* is Sir Richard Knyghtly's order about 1587 that "Muskettes . . . shall be provided for this company."
By one of those coincidences in which the history of English words abounds, at about the same time the diminutive of Spanish *mosca*, 'fly', was providing Englishmen with a new word in an entirely different realm of experience: *mosquito*.

[MF *mousquet, mousquette*, fr. OIt *moschetto, moschetta* arrow for a crossbow, musket, dim. of *mosca* fly, fr. L *musca*]

mussel See MUSCLE.
[ME *muscle*, fr. OE *muscelle, muscle, musle;* akin to OS & OHG *muscula* mussel, MD *mosschele;* all fr. a prehistoric WGmc word borrowed fr. (assumed) VL *muscula*, alter. of L *musculus* small mouse, muscle, mussel]

mustache See SIDEBURNS.
[MF *moustache*, fr. OIt *mustaccio, mostaccio, mostacchio*, fr. MGk *moustaki*, fr. Gk (Doric) *mystok-, mystax* upper lip, mustache; prob. akin to Gk (Attic) *mastax* mouth, jaws, OE *mūth* mouth, OHG *mund*, ON *munnr, muthr*, Goth *munths* mouth, L *mandere* to chew, Gk *masasthai* to chew]

mutate See FALCON.
[L *mutatus*, past part. of *mutare* to change]

muttonchops See SIDEBURNS.
[so called fr. the shape]

N

nadir See ZENITH.
[ME, fr. MF, fr. Ar *naẓīr* opposite (in the phrase *naẓīr as-samt* opposite the zenith)]

namby-pamby

> Timely blossom, infant fair,
> Fondling of a happy pair,
> Every morn and every night
> Their solicitous delight

The charm of these lines may be lost on the reader of today. In the early eighteenth century, however, the verses of Ambrose Philips (1674–1749) were more likely to be met with approval and admiration. Philips, now vaguely remembered and largely unread, was in his day a poet celebrated for his pastoral poems, his poems in praise of children, and his verse composed for public occasions. He was a poet who could pen such lines as "Dimpley damsel, sweetly smiling" and the following adulatory verse to Sir Robert Walpole:

> Votary to public zeal,
> Minister of England's weal
> Have you leisure for a song,
> Tripping lightly o'er the tongue,
> Soft and sweet in every measure,
> Tell me, Walpole, have you leisure?

Ambrose Philip's name might well be as dead as his poetry had he not managed to incur the enmity of fellow poet Alexander Pope, who was legendary for the venom in his quill. Pope had a natural antipathy for Philips's political affiliations as well as envy for his critical acclaim, so the publication by Philips of poems eulogizing the children of friends merely served as the occasion for a war of wits. Henry Carey, a close ally of Pope, decided to publish a parody of Philips's infantile poetry and to devise from his name the rhyming pet name *Namby Pamby*. Using this baby-talk nickname as the title of his 1726 poem, Carey wrote:

> Namby-Pamby's doubly mild
> Once a man and twice a child . . .
> Now he pumps his little wits
> All by little tiny bits.

Pope delighted in the aptness of the contemptuous pet name and adopted *Namby Pamby* for the 1733 edition of *The Dunciad,* his epic poem satirizing the popular authors of the day. The enduring success of *The Dunciad* did much to ensure that the name *Namby Pamby* would forever be associated with the weakly sentimental. Before a score of years had passed, compositions that were insipidly precious, simple, or sentimental were said to be written in the "Namby Pamby style." Soon afterwards *namby-pamby* was used to stigmatize anything or anyone pathetically weak or indecisive. Doubtless Carey and Pope little realized that in coining *Namby Pamby* they were serving to perpetuate, albeit mockingly, the name of an author whose poems are (in the words of one critic) "flies in the amber of English verse."

[fr. *Namby Pamby,* nickname given to Ambrose Philips †1749 Eng. poet by some satirists of his time to ridicule the style of his verse]

narcissism   Our Modern English word for the love of oneself or one's own body has its source in one of the most beguiling, if peculiar, episodes of Greek mythology. Narcissus was the supposed offspring of a river and a water nymph. While he was still an infant, his mother asked a seer if her son would live a long life. In the time-honored tradition of myths, the seer responded enigmatically: "He will, if he never knows himself." Understandably, no one was able to discern the meaning of that dark saying. Narcissus grew to be a youth so strikingly beautiful that he attracted many would-be lovers, both male and female. He spurned the attentions of them all. Finally, after other would-be lovers had come and gone, one rejected lover prayed to Nemesis, the goddess of retribution. The goddess contrived that Narcissus would indeed "know himself" and had him catch sight of his own reflection in a pool on Mount Helicon. Narcissus became entranced with his own beauty. The more he looked, the deeper he fell in love with what he saw. He could not bear to tear himself away. Held in the grip of passion for himself, he lay beside the pool day after day until he wasted away and finally expired. By an act of the gods his body was metamorphosed into the flower now known as the *narcissus.*

The myth of Narcissus served as a source of inspiration for modern psychologists as they began applying the new science to the study of individuals who are morbidly interested in themselves or sexually attracted to their own bodies. Psychologist Havelock Ellis cited the Roman poet Ovid's retelling of the myth in an 1898 issue of a professional journal. As with the story of Oedipus, modern science found a psychological truth in an ancient myth. A year later a German psychologist coined the term *Narzissismus* to describe this form of self-love. In 1905 Ellis in his *Studies in the Psychology of Sex* accepted the recent coinage and used *narcissism* as the English equivalent.

For other articles on words derived from ancient mythology and legend see VOLCANO.

[G *narzissismus,* fr. *Narziss* Narcissus (fr. L *Narcissus*) + *-ismus* -ism]

Narraganset   See INDIAN.
[prob. modif. of Narraganset *naiaganset*, lit., people of the small point, fr. *naiagans* small point of land (dim. of *naiag* point) + *-et* locative suffix]

natal   See COGNATE.
[ME, fr. L *natalis*, fr. *natus* (past part. of *nasci* to be born) + *-alis* -al]

nativity   See COGNATE.
[ME *nativite*, fr. MF *nativité*, fr. ML *nativitat-*, *nativitas* birth, birth of Christ, fr. LL, birth, fr. L *nativus* native + *-itat-*, *-itas* -ity]

naughty   In Old English, the adjective *nā*, *nō* 'no' was combined with the noun *wiht* 'creature, thing' (the source of our word *wight*) to produce the pronoun *nāwiht*, *nōwiht*, meaning 'nothing'. In Middle English this word became *naught*, *nought*, and by around 1400 the suffix *-y* 'character-ized by' was added to it to form the adjective *naughty*, which was used to describe a morally bad or wicked person. We find an example in Proverbs 6:12 (AV): "A naughty person, a wicked man, walketh with a froward mouth." Although this sense of *naughty* is seldom used anymore, the word is commonly applied in a much weakened sense to children who are disobedient or who misbehave.

In the 1530s *naughty* took on the sense 'of inferior quality'. Jeremiah 24:2 (AV) provides a good illustration of this use: ". . . the other basket had very naughty figs, which could not be eaten, they were so bad." Also at about this time we find occurrences of the sense 'violating the accepted standards of morality, good taste, or polite behavior'. Shakespeare, in his *Merchant of Venice* (ca. 1596), illustrates this use: "How far that little candle throws his beams!/ So shines a good deed in a naughty world."

While nowadays *naughty* is most often applied to children, a person who commits a slight offense against propriety may also be mildly or play-fully censured with this adjective. The slight offense itself may be called a *peccadillo*. English borrowed this noun from the Spanish *pecadillo* 'little sin' toward the end of the sixteenth century. This diminutive form of *peca-do* 'sin' derives from the Latin noun *peccatum* 'sin'. In his poem "Epilogue to the Pilgrim" (1700), John Dryden makes use of this noun: "I pass the peccadilloes of their time;/ Nothing but open lewdness was a crime."

[ME *naught*, *nought* nothing (fr. OE *nāwiht*, *nōwiht* — fr. *nā*, *nō* no + *wiht* creature, thing) + *-y*]

nausea   *Nausea*, one of the more unpleasant symptoms of seasickness, is generally used in English today to mean 'stomach distress that is accom-panied by an urge to vomit', but the connection between nausea and sea-sickness is more than just physical. Both Latin *nausea* and its Greek source *nausia* or *nautia* referred to a general stomach distress but also meant 'sea-sickness' in particular. The Greeks gave the name to this illness from the

root word *naus,* meaning 'ship', which is related to the English words
naval and *nautical.*

The commotion and complaints so often associated with sufferers of sea-
sickness provided us with *noise* as another derivative of *nausea.* The form
noise developed in Old French with the senses of 'noise, noisy strife, quarrel'. Today in English *noise* may refer to any sound in general, but typically
it denotes undesirable sound.

[L, lit., seasickness, nausea, fr. Gk *nausia, nautia,* fr. *nautēs* sailor, fr.
naus ship]

nautical   See NAUSEA.
[L *nauticus* (fr. Gk *nautikos,* fr. *nautēs* sailor — fr. *naus* ship — + -*ikos*
-ic) + E -*al*]

naval   See NAUSEA.
[L *navalis,* fr. *navis* ship + -*alis* -al]

nave (of a church)   See AUGER.
[ML *navis,* fr. L, ship; akin to OE *nōw*end skipper, sailor, OHG *nuosc*
trough, ON *nōr* ship, Gk *naus,* Skt *nau*]

nave (of a wheel)   See AUGER.
[ME, fr. OE *nafu;* akin to OHG *naba* nave, ON *nöf* nave, OE *nafela*
navel]

navel   See AUGER.
[ME *navel, navele,* fr. OE *nafela;* akin to OHG *nabalo* navel, ON *nafli,*
L *umbili*cus navel, *umbo* boss of a shield, Gk *omphalos* navel, Skt *nab-
hya* hub of a wheel, *nābhi* navel, hub of a wheel]

necrophilia   See AMBROSIA.
[NL, fr. *necr-* + -*philia*]

necrosis   See AMBROSIA.
[LL, fr. Gk *nekrōsis,* fr. *nekroun* to make dead, mortify, fr. *nekros* dead
body]

nectar   See AMBROSIA.
[L, fr. Gk *nek-* (perh. akin to L *nec-, nex* death) + -*tar* (perh. akin to Skt
tarati he crosses over, overcomes)]

neon   See XENON.
[Gk, neut. of *neos* new]

nephew   See COUSIN.
[ME *nevew* nephew, grandson, fr. OF *neveu,* fr. L *nepot-, nepos* grandson, nephew, descendant; akin to OE *nefa* grandson, nephew, OHG

nevo grandson, kinsman, ON *nefi* nephew, kinsman, Gk *nepodes* children, Skt *napāt* grandson, descendant]

nephrite See JADE.
[G *nephrit,* fr. *nephr-* (fr. Gk *nephros* kidney) + -*it* -ite]

newt See NICKNAME.
[ME *newte,* alter. (resulting from incorrect division of *an ewte*) of *ewte, evete,* fr. OE *efete*]

Nez Percé See INDIAN.
[F, lit., pierced nose]

nice This bland-looking, workaday word has undergone a remarkable semantic evolution over the course of its history. The word was borrowed from Old French, in which it was used for 'simpleminded, stupid'. (French had formed *nice* from the Latin adjective *nescius* 'ignorant, not knowing', which was derived from the verb *nescire* 'not to know'.) The poet John Gower in his *Confessio Amantis* (ca. 1390) gives an example of this 'foolish' sense (now obsolete) in speaking of drunkenness: "He can make of a wisman nyce,/ And of a fool, that him schal seme/ That he can al the lawe deme" (He can make a wise man seem foolish and a fool think that he is able to administer the law). In the fourteenth century there developed the now obsolete sense of 'wanton, lascivious'. Chaucer provides an illustration of this sense in *The House of Fame* (ca. 1380): "Al this seye I be Eneas/ And Dido, and hir nyce lest,/ That loved al to sone a gest" (All this I say about Aeneas and Dido, and her wanton desire, that loved all too soon a stranger).

In the fifteenth century, *nice* acquired the meaning 'coy, reserved, diffident'. Shakespeare provides an example of this use in *The Two Gentlemen of Verona* (ca. 1594): "There is a lady in Milano here/ Whom I affect; but she is nice and coy/ And naught esteems my aged eloquence." Such use has been obsolete since the eighteenth century.

In the sixteenth century another sense developed: 'showing fastidious, particular, or finical taste'. In Milton's *Paradise Lost* (1667) we find an example of such use: " '. . . and to taste/ Think not that I shall be nice.' So down they sat,/ And to their viands fell." This sense is still in use today. Also in the sixteenth century we find *nice* beginning to be used in the sense 'requiring or involving great precision and delicacy'. William Cowper, in his poem "Hope" (1782), illustrates this use: "By this, with nice precision of design,/ He draws upon life's map a zigzag line,/ That shows how far 'tis safe to follow sin,/ And where his danger and God's wrath begin."

Not until the eighteenth century did *nice* come to be employed in the variety of uses generally meaning 'pleasing', 'pleasurable', or 'agreeable'. This sense was not included in Noah Webster's Dictionary (1828). Even in the 1864 revision of his dictionary, which at least recognized this generalized sense, a somewhat nationalistic editorial note stigmatized it:

Of late, a new sense has been introduced, . . . namely, *pleasing; as,* a *nice* girl, a *nice* party, a *nice* excursion, etc. We even hear it for *beautiful;* as, a *nice* morning, a *nice* day, etc. This use of the word, though sanctioned by no lexicographer, is extremely common among the English; and if *Americans* overdo as to "fine," *they* overdo as to "nice," but with this difference, that we always give the former its true sense [see FINE], while they rob the latter of its appropriate and distinctive meaning.

In succeeding editions this usage was labeled *colloquial* until the 1934 publication of Webster's New International Dictionary, Second Edition. Since about the middle of the nineteenth century there has been an ironic use of this generalized sense to mean 'bad' or 'inappropriate' as in "you're a nice one to talk" and similar contexts.

[ME, foolish, wanton, fr. OF, simpleminded, stupid, fr. L *nescius* ignorant, not knowing, fr. *nescire* not to know]

nickel   See COBALT.
[prob. fr. Sw, short for *kopparnickel* niccolite, part trans. of G *kupfernickel*, prob. fr. *kupfer* copper (fr. OHG *kupfer*) + *nickel* goblin, demon, fr. *Nickel*, nickname for *Nikolaus* Nicholas]

nickname   The earliest sense of *nickname* is a descriptive name given to a person, or even a place, in addition to the proper name, while today it can also mean a shortened or familiar form of a proper name. In Middle English the word expressed the first of these senses very explicitly. The noun *eke*, meaning 'an addition or extension', was combined with *name*, and thus an *ekename* was an additional name. By the fifteenth century *an ekename* began to be written as *a nekename*, in modern spelling *a nickname*. The noun *eke* involved in the history of *nickname* is related both to the verb *eke*, as in "eke out a living," and to the once common but now archaic adverb *eke*, 'too, also'.

A similar "incorrect" division gave us the modern *newt*, a salamander. The Old English *efete*, a small lizard, became Middle English *evete* or *ewte*, and eventually *an ewt* became *a newt*. The older form is preserved in *red eft*, the name of a North American newt that is brick red in color. Similarly, when we speak of "a *nonce* word" the *n* which begins *nonce* originally belonged to the preceding word in Middle English expressions like *to then anes*, 'for the one purpose'. See also OMELET. For examples of a similar change but in the opposite direction see APRON, AUGER.

[ME *nekename*, an additional name, alter. (resulting from incorrect division of *an ekename*) of *ekename*, fr. *eke* (n.) + *name*]

niece   See COUSIN.
[ME *nece*, fr. AF *nece* niece & OF *niece* granddaughter, niece, fr. LL *neptia*, fr. L *neptis* granddaughter; akin to L *nepos* grandson, nephew]

nightmare   Because of the similarity in form between the second element of the compound *nightmare* and *mare*, meaning 'a female horse', many people have assumed a connection between the two. Actually the -*mare* of *nightmare* is a survival of another word *mare* found in Old English as early as the eighth century but obsolete by the eighteenth. Old English *mare* means 'an evil spirit or incubus thought to oppress people during sleep'. The compound *nightmare* first appears in Middle English in the thirteenth century, in a sense much the same as *mare* in Old English. Not until the sixteenth century was the meaning of *nightmare* extended to refer to a frightening or oppressive dream, probably from the belief or suggestion that such dreams were caused by evil spirits. See also DREAM.

[ME, fr. *night* + *mare* (spirit), fr. OE; akin to OHG & ON *mara* incubus, Croatian *mora*]

niobium   See AMMONIA.
[NL, fr. *Niobe*, daughter of Tantalus + NL -*ium;* fr. its occurrence in tantalite]

niton   See XENON.
[L *nitēre* to shine + ISV -*on* (suffix used to form names of inert gases), fr. Gk, neut. of -*os* (nom. sing. masc. ending of many adjectives); fr. its phosphorescent properties]

noise   See NAUSEA.
[ME, fr. OF, noise, noisy strife, quarrel, fr. L *nausea* seasickness, nausea]

nonce   See NICKNAME.
[ME *nones*, fr. *nanes*, alter. (resulting from incorrect division of *then anes* in such phrases as *to then anes* for the one purpose, fr. *to* + *then* — dat. sing. neut. of *the*, def. art. — + *anes* one purpose) of *anes* one purpose, alter. (prob. influenced by *anes* once) of *ane*, dat. sing. neut. of *an* one, fr. OE *ān*]

noon   *Noon* has not always indicated that time of day at which the sun is most nearly overhead. According to the Roman method of reckoning time, the hours of the day were counted from sunrise to sunset; the night was divided into four watches. English *noon* is derived from Latin *nona*, from the feminine form of *nonus*, which means ninth. *Noon*, therefore, was the ninth hour of the day, or about three P.M. In Mark's account of the crucifixion of Christ, the King James Version of the Bible, published in 1611, reads, "there was darkness over the whole land until the ninth hour" (15:33). However, the corresponding passage from Wycliffe's translation of the New Testament, written in 1382, is "Derknessis ben maad . . . til in to the nynthe our, that is, noon." A church service which was held daily at this time of the day is also called *none* or *nones,* and perhaps in anticipation of this service or possibly of a mealtime, the time denoted by *none* or *noon* shifted to the hour of midday. A similar shift also took place in Dutch *noen* and French *none.* Thus, during the fourteenth century Middle English *noon* became an increasingly regular term for the middle of the day.

Also during the fourteenth century the prepositional phrase *after noon* gave rise to the noun *afternoon*. Of course, the institution of daylight savings time, first suggested jokingly by Benjamin Franklin and made a reality in the twentieth century, means that once again *noon* is not invariably the time when the sun is at its highest point.

In the Roman scheme of telling time, *sexta* designated the sixth hour or midday. In Spanish the adjective *sexta* underwent sound change and became *siesta*, which developed the meaning 'midday heat' and then 'afternoon nap'. English borrowed the word in the latter sense.

[ME, ninth hour of the day counting from sunrise, noon, midday, fr. OE *nōn* ninth hour of the day counting from sunrise, fr. L *nona*, fr. fem. of *nonus* ninth; akin to Skt *navama* ninth, L *novem* nine]

norm   See NORMAL.
[L *norma* carpenter's square, pattern, rule]

normal   The basic sense of the noun *norm* is 'an authoritative standard or model'. This is derived from the Latin *norma* which means 'rule or pattern' as well as 'a carpenter's square', for a square provides a standard or rule which ensures that a carpenter can regularly reproduce corners and edges that are straight and that form right angles. The Latin adjective *normalis*, formed from *norma*, originally meant 'forming a right angle' or 'according to a square', and it is from this Latin sense that we get the earliest attested sense of *normal* in English, 'perpendicular'. Latin *normalis*, however, was also used in more extended senses, and by the Late Latin period its usual meaning was 'according to rule'. Most of the senses of our word *normal* are derived from this Late Latin usage.

The term *normal school*, a school for training teachers, is not directly related to the above senses; it is one step removed from Latin, coming to us through French. *Normal school* is a translation of *école normale*, and the term derives from the fact that the first school named *école normale* was intended to serve as a standard or model for other teaching schools.

In Latin, the *norm-* root appeared after the prefix *e-* (variant of *ex-*), meaning 'out of', to produce *enormis*, literally 'abnormal, irregular'. The adjective acquired the specific sense of departing from the norm by being much larger in size than usual (i.e., 'huge'). 'Huge', of course, is the most common sense of its English descendant *enormous*.

The Latin *norma*, 'carpenter's square', is probably derived from Greek *gnōmōn*, which also means 'carpenter's square'. Additional senses are 'the pointer on a sundial', 'interpreter', and 'discerner'. All of these senses reflect in varying degrees the origin of the word in the verb *gignōskein*, 'to know'. *Gnomon* was borrowed into English directly from Greek and is still used to mean 'the style of a sundial' as well as other senses derived from or related to this.

[LL *normalis* according to rule, fr. L, according to a square, forming a right angle, fr. *norma* carpenter's square, pattern, rule (prob. fr. Gk *gnōmona,* accus. of *gnōmōn* interpreter, discerner, pointer on a sundial, carpenter's square) + *-alis* -al]

normal school   See NORMAL.

[trans. of F *école normale;* fr. the fact that the first school so named was intended to serve as a model for other teaching schools]

nostril   See WINDOW.

[ME *nostrill, nosethirl,* fr. OE *nosterl, nosthyrl, nosthyrel,* fr. *nosu* nose + *thyrel* hole]

notion   The Latin noun *notio* (with a declensional stem *notion-*) was used to mean 'a becoming acquainted, an examination or investigation' and then 'an idea or concept'. It is a derivative of the word *notus* 'known', which is the past participle of the verb *noscere* 'to come to know, become acquainted with'.

When the noun was borrowed into English as *notion* in the sixteenth century, it was used for 'an individual's conception of something known, experienced, or imagined'. George Herbert in his poem "Colossians 3.3," published in 1633, gives an example of this sense: "My words and thoughts do both express this notion,/ That Life hath with the sun a double motion."

Early in the seventeenth century, we find the first examples of the sense 'an idea, theory, or belief held by a person or group'. In his book *Plutarch's Philosophie* (1603), Philemon Holland employs this sense: "See how these philosophers maintain ordinary custom, and teach according to common notions." Also during the seventeenth century, *notion* was used to refer to 'mind, intellect, imagination'. Although this sense has fallen into disuse, it may have given rise to the eighteenth-century sense of 'a product of invention', which is evident in this quotation from John Evelyn's *Diary* (ca. 1700): "Machines for flying in the air, and other wonderful notions." This sense has also become obsolete.

The eighteenth century also saw the emergence of the use of *notion* for 'a personal inclination, desire, or fancy'. When Jane Austen wrote "I have no notion of loving people by halves, it is not my nature. My attachments are always excessively strong" (*Northanger Abbey,* 1817), she was using this sense.

In the 1790s, a new use was developing in America. *Notions* was being applied to 'small articles of trade', such as buttons, pins, ribbons, combs, and other clothing and personal items. Such notions came to be sold in a separate department in large stores. The idea here may have been that such items could give one the fancy, or notion, to buy, or the sense may have developed out of the "product of invention" sense. By 1805 another American use was emerging, in which *notions* referred to 'an assortment of various wares making up a cargo'. In his adventure narrative *Two Years Before the Mast* (1840), Richard Henry Dana makes use of this sense: "A cargo of fresh provisions, mules, tin bake-pans and other notions."

[L *notion-*, *notio* idea, conception, act of coming to know, fr. *notus* (past part. of *noscere* to come to know) + *-ion-*, *-io* -ion]

nought See NAUGHTY.
[ME, fr. OE *nāwiht, nōwiht,* fr. *nāwiht, nōwiht,* pron., fr. *nā, nō* + *wiht* creature, thing]

novel 'New, young, fresh' were the senses originally conveyed by the adjective *novel* when it was borrowed from French in the fifteenth century. It derives from the Latin adjective *novellus,* a diminutive form of the word *novus* 'new, young', a cognate of English *new.* Soon thereafter *novel* was being used as a noun for 'something new' and 'news', a usage that is now obsolete.

The Latin *novellus* was taken into Italian as *novella* and from the thirteenth century had been used as a noun for 'tale, fable, narrative'. In the sixteenth century, English needed a literary term for a short narrative dealing with local events that were humorous, political, or amorous in nature. This need was met when the Italian *novella* was borrowed as *novel.*

The first novels were simple, realistic, satiric tales or short stories. In the seventeenth century, the novel grew into a longer story with a more complex plot involving realistic characters and actions. In eighteenth-century England, the novel became the most popular literary form. The term *novel* thus contrasted with *romance,* a term borrowed from the French *romans* in the fourteenth century. *Romance* originally referred to 'a medieval tale in verse based on legend, chivalric love and adventure, or the supernatural' and then later to 'a prose work of fiction whose characters were usually heroic, adventurous, or mysterious, and whose events were remote in time'.

Early in the nineteenth century, the long short story (or the short novel) became popular and was called by the diminutive term *novelette.* Novelettes tended to be light, romantic, and melodramatic in nature. Not much later, the Italian word *novella* was taken unchanged into English with its Italian reference to the tales of such writers as Boccaccio. By the end of the nineteenth century it was being applied to any story with a compact and pointed plot. During the twentieth century, it has come to be used more or less interchangeably with the word *novelette.*

The name of another literary genre, the *essay,* can also be traced back to a Latin source. The noun *exagium,* formed from the prefix *ex-* 'out' and the verb *agere* 'to do, act, drive', was used for 'an act of weighing' and 'weight, balance'. The meaning of *exagium* was probably influenced by the verb *exigere,* meaning 'to drive out, exact, weigh, measure'. French took the Latin *exagium* in the twelfth century as *essai, assai,* and used it to mean 'an effort to do or perform; an attempt or endeavor'. English borrowed the French word in the late sixteenth century with the same meaning. In 1580, however, the word was put to a new use in French: Michel Eyquem de Montaigne published his collection of short compositions, which he titled *Essais.* He considered his compositions as "attempts" toward expressing his personal thoughts and experiences. This genre greatly influenced both French and English literature. Francis Bacon published his *Essayes* in 1597, and many English and American writers have since followed with their own essays.

Another literary form is the narrative of events connected with a real or imaginary subject, which was the first sense of the word *history* as used in the late fourteenth century. The English word was taken from the Latin *historia*, which was, in turn, borrowed from the Greek *historia*, a derivative of the verb *historein* 'to inquire into, examine, relate'. By the end of the fifteenth century, the term took on the more formal sense of 'a chronological record of significant events often with an explanation of their causes'. In the sixteenth century it was also applied to 'a treatise presenting systematically related natural phenomena', which is the original sense of the term *natural history*. In Shakespeare's time, *history* was also used for a drama that was based on actual historical events. In the twentieth century we also find the term used for an account of a patient's medical background.

In the twelfth century, French borrowed the Latin *historia* as *estorie, estoire,* which was used for 'a record of the events in a person's life' and then for 'a record of the events relating to a people or to mankind in general'. In the thirteenth century, English took the French *estorie* as *story,* using it in much the same way as the early sense of *history.* Early in the sixteenth century, *story* came to be used for 'a usually fictitious narrative of events designed to be entertaining', that is, 'a tale'. However, it was not until the nineteenth century that the *short story* emerged as a distinct literary genre. Unlike the novel or romance, the short story accomplishes its purpose with a calculated economy of action, description, and character development.

[ME, fr. MF *novele,* fr. fem. of *novel* new, fr. L *novellus,* fr. *novus* new]

novelette   See NOVEL.
  [*novel* + *-ette*]

novella   See NOVEL.
  [It, fr. fem. of *novello* new, fr. L *novellus,* fr. *novus* new]

November   See JANUARY.
  [ME *novembre,* fr. OF, fr. L *november* (ninth month), fr. *novem* nine]

O

oaf The elves, like their relatives the fairies, had a fondness for human children and fell into the bad habit of stealing them from their homes. It was probably once thought a kindness to a human parent's vanity to consider a deformed or retarded child a changeling rather than call it "the image of his father." The changeling was an *oaf* (spelled variously in earlier times *oph, aufe,* or *aulfe*); his name is related to that of his true parents, the elves. The name in its strictest sense should be applied only to genuine changelings, but it was soon given to any misshapen or idiot child, even one of undoubtedly human parentage. From the sense 'idiot child' it was a short and easy step to the present, somewhat weakened meaning, 'simpleton, lout'.

[of Scand origin; akin to ON *alfr* elf; akin to OE *ælf* elf, MLG *alf* incubus, MHG *alp* incubus]

October See JANUARY.
[ME *octobre,* fr. OF, fr. L *october* (eighth month), fr. *octo* eight]

octothorp This recent word refers to the symbol #, especially as found on pushbutton phones. First appearing in the mid-1960s, the term seems to have sprung up among telephone engineers.

Any such strange-looking word as this one inevitably excites the ingenuity of amateur etymologists. The *octo-* part would normally mean 'eight', and the symbol has eight points on the periphery. So far so good. But the *-thorp* part is not a Greek or Latin ending, as you would expect given the prefix, nor does it make sense as an independent English word. There is a somewhat rare word *thorp,* meaning 'village', but that will not work here.

Enter the etymological irregulars. A tale you will sometimes hear concerns a man Thorpe who had eight children and. . . . The story's plausibility goes down from there. But it represents one of the commonest types of popular explanation, the eponymous etymology.

Two points militate against the theory of origin in this touching parental scene, apart from general plausibility. First, it has no connection with telephone engineering. Second, the earliest form of the word seems to have been *octotherp,* which may then have been modified by vague association with the aforementioned English word, through CONTAMINATION (which see). How *octotherp* was coined is still a mystery, though we are told by a correspondent from the engineering community that it was coined as a lark, *octo-* for 'eight' as previously mentioned, and *-therp* when somebody burped. Such a tall-sounding tale is not entirely out of the question, given the arbitrariness of some modern scientific coinages. *Gas, radar, mho, livetin, athodyd,* and *ellagic acid* were all coined using non-classical procedures such as acronymy and anagrams; and some recent coinages have a decidedly humorous side to them: *byte, googol, therblig* and *quark.*

Octothorp still has not taken the country by storm. Its extent of use was for many years restricted enough that it was not entered in the Addenda Section of Webster's Third New International Dictionary until 1986. The # sign is still known by a wide variety of other names. Among them are *number sign, pound sign, space mark, sharp, crosshatch, hashmark, hachure, tic-tac-toe slashes,* and from computer hackers' slang *crunch* and *splat* (the latter term sometimes also is used for 'asterisk').

[*octo-* + *thorp,* of unknown origin; fr. the eight points on its circumference]

odd   Old Norse had two words for a triangle. One of these, *thrī-hyrningr,* was analogous to our word. *Hyrningr* (related to modern English *horn*), the word for an angle, was a standard element used in the formation of the names of polygons such as *fer-hyrningr,* 'square', *ātt-hyrningr,* octagon'. Although a triangle is certainly a three-angled figure, it is possible, by concentrating attention on the apex, to look at it as a single point. An arrowhead, after all, is basically a triangle, and likewise a point of land reaching out into a body of water is roughly triangular in shape.

The Old Norse word *oddi* was used both for a point of land and for a triangle. And this word is the ancestor of English *odd* with all its variety of meanings. Even in Old Norse *oddi* developed the meaning 'odd (as opposed to even) number', since the apex of a triangle is the unpaired angle and an odd number is a sum of pairs and one unpaired unit. The *oddamathr,* 'odd man', was the third (or any unpaired) man, the one who could cast a deciding or tie-breaking vote. English never called a triangle *odd,* but it did borrow the *odd* number and the *odd* man. From these it was no great step to considering *odd* as referring to anything singular or different.

[ME *odde,* fr. ON *oddi* point of land, triangle, odd number (as in such compounds as *oddamathr* odd man, *oddatala* odd number); akin to OE *ord* point of a weapon, OHG *ort,* ON *oddr,* and prob. to Lith *usnis* thistle, hawthorn, Alb *usht* ear of grain]

odyssey   See STENTORIAN.
[fr. the *Odyssey,* long epic poem recounting the adventures of Odysseus on his way home from the siege of Troy and attributed to Homer, fr. L *Odyssea,* fr. Gk *Odysseia,* fr. *Odysseus,* its hero + Gk *-ia* *-y*]

oenomel   See MEAD.
[LL *oenomeli,* fr. Gk *oinomeli,* fr. *oino-* oen-, wine + *meli* honey]

ofay   There are many words whose origins we do not know. But human nature abhors a vacuum, and people will devise etymological stories to explain these words. Many such tales are extremely fanciful and improbable, but almost any good story can find an audience willing to believe. The origin of *ofay*, a term used by black Americans to denote a white person, has not been satisfactorily explained; but several explanations have been proposed. One theory has it that *ofay* comes from the phrase "ole fay" or "old fay." The *fay* in question is, like *ofay*, a black dialect word for a white person. Unfortunately, the proponents of this theory never offered an etymology for *fay* itself. At any rate, it is most likely that *fay* is simply a shortening of *ofay*. The earliest evidence for *fay* supports this conjecture. In the *American Mercury* for August 1927 we find: "I drew a deep breath and looked about, seeking familiar faces. 'What a lot of 'fays,' I thought, as I noticed the number of white guests." The apostrophe before *fay* indicates that the author of this passage, at least, believed *fay* to be a truncated form. Our earliest evidence for *ofay* also dates from 1927, and comes from the December issue of *American Mercury:* "Here is the real melting-pot, and a glorious sight it is to see. Ugly people there are, certainly, but the percentage of beautiful folk is unquestionably larger than among the ofay brethren. One has but to venture abroad in a crowd of whites and then go immediately to a fashionable Negro thoroughfare. . . ."

Another suggestion is that *ofay* comes from French *au fait*, 'to the point', 'in the know', 'in a powerful position'. According to this theory, blacks recognized whites as being in power or *au fait*. This suggestion has nothing to support it but the almost certainly accidental resemblance in sound of English *ofay* and French *au fait*. Proponents of the theory would like *ofay* to have originated in New Orleans, where French was at least commonly spoken, though not as a standard black tongue. But the little evidence we have points to a more probable origin in New York's Harlem.

By far the most popular etymological theory is that *ofay* is pig latin for *foe*. There are several reasons for rejecting this theory. For one thing, we have been unable to find evidence that white people as a group were referred to by Negroes as "foes" at any time before 1927, the earliest date that we have for the written use of *ofay*. Further, the word *foe* in Modern English is used chiefly in poetic or figurative contexts—in writing, that is—and its occurrence in speech is rare save in the alliterative military expression "friend or foe." The sound of *ofay* might easily suggest that the word is pig latin. H. L. Mencken, in *The American Language, Supplement I*, reported having heard this explanation as long ago as 1937. Its very picturesqueness is reason enough for many to consider as a fact what is really an unsubstantiated theory.

[origin unknown]

office   In ancient Rome, the noun *officium* at first denoted 'a helpful act or service, a kindness' and then acquired the senses 'duty, obligation' and 'a person's regular employment, job, position, or post'. Etymologically, the word is composed of the noun *opus* 'work, task' and the verb *facere* 'to do, make'.

In Medieval Latin *officium* took on additional meanings, such as 'an official', 'an area ruled by an official', 'a craft or craft guild', and 'an office or countinghouse'. In religious contexts it referred to 'an ecclesiastical charge', 'a divine service, especially the Mass', and 'liturgical prayers'.

In twelfth-century French the word became *office*, which was borrowed into English in the fourteenth century. Chaucer used *office* in his *Canterbury Tales* in various senses: 'role, function, duty, occupation, place of occupation or business, religious service'. In "The Friar's Tale" (ca. 1395), he uses the 'duty' sense when he has a minor devil disguised as a yeoman explain to his companion, a corrupt church official, "My lord is hard to me and daungerous [demanding],/ And myn office is ful laborous,/ And therefore by extorcions I lyve." Since the eighteenth century, *office* has also been applied to a branch or subdivision of a government's administration, such as the Patent Office or Great Britain's War Office.

In Latin, the adjective suffix *-osus* 'full of' was combined with *officium* to produce *officiosus*, which was used to mean 'eager to serve, help, or perform a duty'. When this adjective was taken into English in the sixteenth century as *officious*, it carried the same meaning. Early in the seventeenth century, however, *officious* began taking on a negative sense to describe a person 'volunteering his services where they are neither asked nor needed'; thus, it became a synonym of *meddlesome*. This pejorative sense has driven out the original 'eager to help' sense to become the predominant meaning of the word in Modern English.

Also arising in the early seventeenth century was the use of *officious* to mean 'relating to an office or business; official, formal'. Roger North, in his *Lives of the Norths* (1742–44) illustrates this use: "He put off officious talk of government or politicks with jests." This sense, however, could not compete with its rival *official* and lapsed into desuetude. Furthermore, especially in the language of diplomacy, *officious* came to be used in opposition to the word *official* to mean 'of an informal or unauthorized nature, unofficial'. This sense, while not especially common, seems to be the one intended by George N. Shuster, in an article appearing in the *New Republic* of 17 January 1955: "Nevertheless his commentary . . . is an antidote to the official and officious writing on the German and the European situation."

Official itself was formed in Latin by combining the suffix *-alis* 'relating to' with *officium* to produce *officialis*. This adjective was used to describe something 'relating to duty or obligation'. By functional shift it became a noun to denote 'a magistrate's assistant', that is, 'an official'.

In Medieval Latin the noun *officialis* found many uses, especially for 'a person holding an office or post'. Such an *officialis* could have been a royal official, a court dignitary, a bishop's official, a household servant, a bailiff, a magistrate, or an officiating priest. When it was borrowed into fourteenth-century English as *official*, it was used to denote 'the presiding officer of an ecclesiastical court'. By the sixteenth century it had taken on the secular sense 'one who holds a public or government office', which is still its main use. In our own century it has also been applied to 'one who administers the rules of a game or sport', such as an umpire or referee.

[ME, fr. OF, fr. L *officium* service, kindness, activity, duty, office, alter. of (assumed) *opifacium,* fr. *opus* work + *-i-* + *-facium* (fr. *facere* to do, make)]

official   See OFFICE.
[ME, fr. MF, fr. ML *officialis,* fr. LL *officialis,* adj., fr. L *officium* duty, office + *-alis* -al]

officious   See OFFICE.
[L *officiosus,* fr. *officium* service, kindness, duty, office + *-osus* -ous]

OK   *OK* is considered by many observers of the language to be the most successful of all Americanisms, used around the world. But in spite of its wide recognition, the origin of *OK* is shrouded in mystery. We know nothing at all of it before its appearance in the Boston *Morning Post* on 23 March 1839 in this context: ". . . he of the Journal, and his *train*-band, would have the 'contributions box,' et ceteras, *o.k.*—all correct—and cause the corks to fly. . . ." This is a facetious suggestion by a Boston editor that a Providence editor (the *Journal* mentioned was in Providence) sponsor a party. How *OK* came from *all correct* and how it spread from here requires setting forth some background.

First, there were the newspapers. Before the existence of wire services, an American newspaper got most of its out-of-town news from others with which it exchanged copies. Interesting items would simply be reprinted from other newspapers. And early nineteenth century newspapers were not like their utterly serious modern counterparts: there was plenty of room in them for humor, poetry, fiction, and jabs at other newspapers. The first *OK* example is part of a humorous reply to an item reprinted from the Providence newspaper.

Second, there was the abbreviation fad. Among the young and fashionable set in American cities in the late 1830s, the thing to do was to reduce phrases to initials. A New York newspaper in 1839 reported an au courant young lady as remarking to her escort, "O.K.K.B.W.P." The young man paused, then kissed her. The reporter interpreted the initialism as "One Kind Kiss Before We Part." What the fashionable set says and does often turns up in the newspaper, and the fad for initials did turn up in Boston newspapers in the summer of 1838, in New York in the summer of 1839, and in New Orleans in the fall of 1839. Probably the exchange of newspapers helped spread the fad.

Third, there was the tradition of deliberate misspelling in humorous writing. Many American humorists from the 1820s on adopted as public personas uneducated bumpkins who communicated their observations in dialect made more dense by pointless misspelling. It is this tradition that turns *no go* into *know go* and *no use* into *know yuse.*

At the height of the initials craze it became fashionable to alter some of the abbreviations on the basis of such misspelling. Thus *A.R.* for *all right* was transformed to *O.W.* on the basis of *oll wright* and *N.G.* for *no go* to *K.G.* These altered abbreviations were often glossed with the straight spelling of the full phrase: a fanciful *K.K.K.* would turn out to stand for *commit no nuisance.* The first *OK* is glossed *all correct;* it is in this context that the *OK* is assumed to be based on the deliberately misspelled *oll korrect.*

Even though *OK* became one of the more commonly used initialisms, it might well have passed into oblivion with the equally popular *OFM (our first men)* when the fad passed, had it not been for the presidential election of 1840. In that year the Tammany Democrats in New York created a Democratic O.K. Club. The *O.K.* in this name was derived from *Old Kinderhook,* after Kinderhook, New York, the birthplace of Martin Van Buren, the Democratic candidate. It is rather likely that Old Kinderhook was selected with an eye to the currently popular *OK,* much as the expressions that make up modern acronyms are chosen with an eye to making a catchy set of initials.

The O.K.'s seem to have been mostly a bunch of bullyboys and rowdies whose purpose was to harass or break up Whig meetings (both sides retained plenty of rowdies). The activities of the O.K.'s kept them in the newspapers, and both sides made use of the currency of *OK* by contriving expansions with which they could slur each other. The heat of the campaign carried *O.K.,* in one signification or another (often 'oll korrect'), across the country. When Van Buren lost the election, the Whigs flaunted *OK* for his departure: "Off to Kinderhook."

The campaign gave another boost to *OK.* A Whig journalist floated the story that *OK* was used by Andrew Jackson as standing for *Ole Korrek* (later *oll korrect*), which was supposed to be Jackson's spelling of *all correct.* This was a reference to the presidential campaign of 1828 in which Jackson's bad spelling was a campaign issue. (But *oll korrect* was not part of that campaign.) Quite a few newspapers reprinted this story in one form or another, and one enterprising journalist laid the story to Jack Downing, the popular creation of humorist Seba Smith. Through frequent reprinting of the tale, *OK* and *oll korrect* and Andrew Jackson became fixed in American folklore. Jackson was frequently named as the originator of the abbreviation in later nineteenth-century explanations.

The practice of concocting fanciful expansions of *OK* continued in the newspapers for some years after the 1840 campaign. One of the results of this journalistic playfulness was that the real origins—so far as we know them—were forgotten, except for the persistence of the Andrew Jackson tale. Consequently, interested writers of letters to the editor offered many explanations of the origin. Several origins were supposedly discovered in other languages: Latin, Greek, Scottish, French, Finnish, Anglo-Saxon via Swedish, Mandingo, and Wolof were offered. One of the most persistent of these was Choctaw *okeh.* This etymon was suggested in 1885, and Andrew Jackson was involved in the story again—this time not through bad spelling but through his borrowing from the Choctaw Indians. This origin was believed by Woodrow Wilson, who wrote *okeh* on papers he approved. He was asked why he did not use *O.K.* "Because it is wrong," he replied.

This is what we know of *OK* so far. It is largely based on the research of Allen Walker Read as set forth in much greater detail in several issues of *American Speech* in 1963 and 1964. Professor Read seems rather to expect earlier evidence to be unearthed—a small-town Illinois newspaper in 1840 claimed that the abbreviation craze originated in Chicago in 1835—but it has not been discovered yet. The earliest unequivocal *O.K.*'s are found in Elizabethan English—one in a work written by Gabriel Harvey in 1593 that calls "H.N. an O.K." and repeating of the same in a 1596 work by Thomas Nashe, replying to Harvey. No one has figured out what this *O.K.* stands for, but it is clearly a noun and not the American *OK.*

[abbr. of *oll korrect*, alter. of *all correct*]

old See ADOLESCENT.

[ME *ald, old,* fr. OE *eald, ald;* akin to OS *ald* old, OHG *alt* old, ON *aldr* age, *ala* to bring up, nourish, Goth *alds* period of time, age (of a person), *altheis* old, *alan* grown up, L *alere* to feed, nourish, *alescere* to grow, *altus* high, Gk *aldēskein* to grow, an*altos* insatiable, Skt an*ala* fire (lit., the insatiable one), *r̥dhnoti* he flourishes, succeeds; basic meaning: to grow, nourish]

oligarchy See HIERARCHY.

[Gk *oligarchia,* fr. *olig-* (fr. *oligos* few) + *-archia* -archy (fr. *-archēs, archos* ruler + *-ia* -y)]

olla podrida See POTPOURRI.

[Sp, lit., rotten pot, fr. *olla* pot (fr. L *aulla, aula, olla*) + *podrida* rotten, putrid, past part. of *podrir* to rot, fr. L *putrēre*]

ombudsman In 1979 the producer of "60 Minutes," the television magazine known for its tenacious investigations into wrongdoing and its championing of individuals' rights, posed to an interviewer the rhetorical question and answer: "You know what we are? We have become America's ombudsman!" In choosing *ombudsman* to describe the role of his program, the producer was using a word which most Americans had never heard of two decades earlier but which can be traced back to the days when Vikings reigned and spoke the language known as Old Norse. One of the Old Norse words they were using was *umbothsmathr.* Compounded from *umboth* ('commission') and *mathr* ('man'), *umbothsmathr* had the meaning of 'commissary' or 'manager'. The Old Norse *umbothsmathr* evolved into the Modern Swedish *ombudsman,* acquiring the generic sense of 'representative' or 'commissioner'.

In 1809 the Swedish government established the office of *justitieombudsmannen.* The *justitieombudsman,* or justice commissioner, was empowered to investigate and redress the complaints of private citizens regarding abuse and maladministration on the part of public officials and bureaucrats. This functionary established a reputation as the one person to whom the victim of bureaucratic abuse or neglect could resort when all other channels failed. The concept of an ombudsman spread to Finland in 1919, to Denmark in 1954, and to Norway in 1962. The word *ombudsman* got a foothold in the English language when, also in 1962, New Zealand decided to appoint a comparably empowered official and to confer upon him the title of "ombudsman." The establishment of the office of ombudsman in New Zealand occasioned in other English-speaking nations a flurry of interest in *ombudsman* and ombudsmen. The mid-1960s witnessed a spirited discussion on the need for creating in the U.S. government an office of ombudsman with national jurisdiction. The rise of the civil rights movement in the U.S. no doubt helped to spur interest in an official who was perceived above all as the guardian of the rights of the private citizen. Interest was further fueled in 1966 when Great Britain appointed its first ombudsman, although he was officially known as the Parliamentary Commissioner for Administration. Although the proposal for a national ombudsman was never adopted by the U.S., several individual states created their own ombudsmen, as did West Germany, Israel, and some provinces of Canada and states of Australia.

The proliferation of governmental ombudsmen seems to have caused the job title of a number of people to suddenly become "ombudsman." A person who might previously have been known as a complaint adjuster, an arbitrator, a liaison, a troubleshooter, or a watchdog inevitably became an ombudsman. A hospital ombudsman was one who investigated the complaints of patients and advised them of their rights. A university ombudsman served the faculty and student body in the same capacity. A newspaper ombudsman was an in-house watchdog who investigated and reported on charges of error or unfairness against the paper. A corporate ombudsman was likely to be an executive in charge of the complaint department. Eventually *ombudsman* came to be applied to activists of any stripe whose chief concern was the redressing of grievances.

The popularity of *ombudsman* inspired a plethora of derivatives. The practice or profession of being an ombudsman became *ombudsmanry,* and the office or function of such a person became *ombudsmanship.* Since women were also attaining such positions, there arose the need for *ombudswoman* (or *ombudslady* among the nonfeminists). That development in turn raised the question of a need for a gender-neutral term, and so *ombudsperson* was born. When several ombudspersons acted as a unit, they became, of course, an *ombudscommittee.*

[Sw, lit., representative, commissioner, fr. ON *umbothsmathr,* fr. *umboth* commission (fr. *um* around + *bjōtha* to command) + *mathr* man]

omelet   Although the word *omelet* bears little resemblance to the Latin word *lamina,* the shape of an omelet does resemble a thin plate, which is what *lamina,* the etymon of *omelet,* means. The orthographic dissimilarity between the two words is due to the various alterations that took place in both Latin and French.

The Romans used the noun *lamella,* the diminutive form of *lamina,* to mean 'a small metal plate'. This diminutive became, in Old French, *le-*

melle, meaning 'blade of a sword or knife'. By a process somewhat similar to that which produced our *apron* from an earlier *napron* and changed the form of other English words as well, *la lemelle,* 'the blade', was misinterpreted as *l'alemelle,* which accounts for the appearance of the initial vowel. In Middle French the word *alemelle* became *alumelle* and then was altered to *alumette,* having been influenced by the common suffix *-ette.* It also acquired the additional meaning 'eggs beaten and cooked without stiring until set', since such a dish resembled a thin plate or blade. In turn, *alumette* was altered to *amelette,* and finally altered again (probably influenced by *œuf* 'egg') to *omelette,* the form used in Modern French. The word, now usually written *omelet,* has been used in English since the seventeenth century, when an omelet was described as 'a pancake of egges'. See also APRON, AUGER, NICKNAME.

[F *omelette,* fr. MF, alter. of *amelette,* alter. of *alumette,* alter. (influenced by *-ette*) of *alumelle,* lit., blade (of a sword or knife), fr. OF *alemelle, alemele,* alter. of *lemelle, lemele,* fr. L *lamella* small metal plate, dim. of *lamina* thin plate]

omnibus   See BUS.
[F, fr. L, for all, dat. pl. of *omnis* all; perh. akin to L *ops* wealth]

opéra comique   See VAUDEVILLE.
[F]

opt   The region of Alsace–Lorraine in what is now northeastern France has changed hands many times down through the centuries. One such change occurred in 1871, when the Treaty of Frankfurt ending the Franco–Prussian War stipulated that Alsace–Lorraine be ceded by France to Germany. (The French got it back again after World War I, then lost and regained it one more time during World War II.) Because many of the inhabitants of Alsace–Lorraine remained loyal to France, they were given a choice: they could stay in Alsace–Lorraine as German citizens or they could emigrate to France. It was apparently this opportunity to choose that gave us the verb *opt,* derived from the French *opter,* 'to choose'. The earliest uses of *opt* in English had to do specifically with Alsace–Lorraine, for example, in George Sala's *Paris Herself Again* (1879): "He was supposed to be a native of Alsace–Lorraine, who had 'opted' to become a French subject." From such usage *opt* acquired the meaning 'to make a choice of citizenship', which remained its principal sense until the 1950s, when it came into more common use in the general sense 'to choose'. The surge in its popularity following World War II seems to have begun through widespread use of its original sense to describe the decisions about citizenship and forms of government being made by individuals and nations at that time.

[F *opter* to choose, desire, fr. L *optare*]

orangutan   The *orangutan,* native to Borneo and Sumatra, has been known in western Europe since the seventeenth century. The name of the animal has been borrowed into most European languages, in a form similar to English *orangutan,* more or less unchanged from Malay *orang hutan,* which is a descriptive term for this primate meaning 'man of the forest', from *orang,* 'man', plus *hutan,* 'forest'. There is a tendency to rhyme the second and last syllables of *orangutan* (as if \raŋ\ and \taŋ\) and in a number of European languages including English a *g* is sometimes added to the last syllable, both in pronunciation and spelling. See also GO-RILLA.

[Malay *orang hutan,* fr. *orang* man, person + *hutan* forest]

orient   The noun *orient* is derived from the Latin adjective *oriens,* derived from the present participle of the verb *oriri,* 'to rise or come forth'. Its earliest English sense is 'the place on the horizon where the sun rises when it is near one of the equinoxes', i.e., the east. Thus it has come to be used today, most often capitalized, to refer to the Asian countries to the east of Europe.

With the spread of Christianity into Europe it became customary to build churches with their longitudinal axes pointing eastward toward Jerusalem. This practice gave rise to the use of *orient* as a verb meaning 'to cause to face or point toward the east'. This sense then became generalized to yield the sense 'to set or arrange in any determinate position, especially in relation to the points of the compass'. Nowadays we say that maps are *oriented* toward north, but before the widespread use of the magnetic compass enabled people to determine readily the direction of north, many European maps had east at the top, since this direction could be established by watching the sun rise, or on cloudy days simply by noting the orientation of the nearest church.

[ME, fr. MF, fr. L *orient-, oriens,* fr. pres. part. of *oriri* to rise, come forth]

ornery   English has quite a few doublets—words having a single source in, say, Latin, and arriving in English by differing routes as different words. For instance, *discus* and *dish* and *disk* and *dais* all spring from Latin *discus.* (See the discussion at DOUBLETS.) The same phenomenon is observable within English itself through the operation of dialectal pronunciations. An ordinary word will have a peculiar way of being pronounced in a dialect, that pronunciation will be given a more or less descriptive spelling so it can be represented in print, and then the pronunciation spelling will become perceived as a separate word. *Ornery* is one of these.

Ornery began simply as a dialectal pronunciation of *ordinary.* It is attested in both British and American English during the nineteenth century. Its earliest use seems to have been as a substitute for *ordinary;* this sense is attested here and there for about a century:

> Poor shotes thet ye could n't persuade us to tech,
> Not in ornery times, though we're willin' to feed 'em
> With a nod now and then, when we happen to need 'em; . . .
> —James Russell Lowell, *The Biglow Papers,* 2d series, 1867

Early in its history *ornery* became tinged with "a spice of contempt,"

as one glossarist put it. This use, close to *common* or *mean* or *low* in meaning, is the one we hear from Huck Finn when he cannot figure out how
his going to heaven would improve it:

> . . . seeing I was so ignorant, and so low-down and ornery —Mark
> Twain, *Huckleberry Finn,* 1884

Mark Twain had used the same sense twenty years earlier in "Those Blast-
ed Children," a sketch in which he proposed a number of outrageous treatments for children's ailments. One of his more severe recommendations
was the cure of stuttering by removal of the child's lower jaw. To this draconian treatment he appended an effusive testimonial after the manner
of patent medicine publicity of that day. This reads in part:

> But in a blessed hour you appeared unto me like an angel from the
> skies; and without hope of reward, revealed your sovereign remedy—
> and that very day, I sawed off my Johnny's under-jaw. May Heaven
> bless you, noble Sir. It afforded instant relief; and my Johnny has
> never stammered since. I honestly believe he never will again. As to
> disfigurement, he does seem to look sorter ornery and hog-
> mouthed . . .

Ornery gradually came to connote bad temper, bad behavior, or general
cantankerousness:

> A parcel of ornery cusses in that luvly sity bustid inter the hawl durin
> the nite and aboosed my wax works —*Artemus Ward: His Book,* 1862

It is this sense that has survived in modern use:

> . . . outlived and outsmoked her two husbands. The first one was an
> ornery scalawag named Griffin, who, we were given to understand
> when we were young, had gone to Hell for his sins —James Thurber,
> *New Yorker,* 16 Feb. 1952

Another word that developed as a pronunciation spelling is *tarnal,*
which was a dialectal pronunciation of *eternal* with the initial *e* lopped off
and the sound of *ar* substituted for that of *er. Tarnal* is found in print as
early as 1775. Its principal use has been as an intensive:

> (Come, thet wun't do, you landcrab there, I tell
>   ye to le' go my toe!
> My gracious! it's a scorpion thet's took a
>   shine to play with 't,
> I dars n't skeer the tarnal thing fer fear he'd
>   run away with 't.)
> —James Russell Lowell, *The Biglow Papers,* 1st series, 1848

> The 'Squire's wife didn't jine in the festiverties. She said it was the
> tarnulest nonsense she ever seed —*Artemus Ward: His Book*

Tarnal simply took this intensive use over from *eternal:*

> I will be hang'd if some eternal villain. . .
> Have not devis'd this slander
> —Shakespeare, *Othello,* 1604

Tarnal sounds rather like a euphemism, and it was soon grafted onto *damnation* to produce the euphemistic *tarnation,* attested as early as 1784. *Tarnation* is primarily a mild expletive, and a noun used in such contexts as "where in tarnation" or "what in tarnation." It has also been used as an intensive just like *tarnal:*

> 'I'm in a tarnation hurry. . .' —Thomas Chandler Halliburton, *The Clockmaker,* 1837

Intensive use is attested as late as the 1930s, but we have no later evidence. *Tarnal* and *tarnation* have an old-fashioned sound to them, and are seldom seen except in historical novels and such.

Tarnal and *tarnation* may have played a part in the development of the euphemism *darn,* according to the linguist Louise Pound. The theory is that the initial *d* of *damn* became attached to *tarnation* to give *darnation* (first attested in 1798), which was then clipped to *darn.* However Noah Webster knew *darn* before 1789, so there may or may not be a causal relationship.

The same sound change that produced *tarnal* produced *varmint* from *vermin.* (Here we have, in addition, a sound tacked on at the end rather than lopped off at the beginning.) The earliest examples date back to the sixteenth century and show *varmint* used like *vermin* as a collective noun. In the nineteenth century *varmint* began being used as a count noun, applied both to persons and animals.

> . . . on t'other side lived Jake Simpson—a sneakin, cute varmint
> —John S. Robb, "The Standing Candidate," 1846

> The fence was alluz up good, the gate shut, and not the track of varmints could be seen nor smelt —Hardin E. Taliaferro, "Larkin Snow the Miller," 1859

Varmint has retained both these uses in current English, but it is most frequently used for small predatory or nuisance animals and birds, for the hunting of which special small-caliber rifles have been designed.

Varsity is produced by the same change in the first vowel of *versity,* a seventeenth-century shortening of *university.* In British English *varsity* can still be used for *university,* but in American English it is used in reference to college and school sports. The same sound change also produced the imprecations *consarn* and *consarned* from *concern.*

For more on dialectal variants that have become standard see PASSEL, RILE, SASS.

[alter. of *ordinary*]

Oscar   In the spring of 1929 the Academy of Motion Picture Arts and Sciences made its first presentation of annual awards for excellence in motion pictures, giving the awards that year for pictures released in the

1927–1928 seasons. Up to that time the award, a ten-inch gold-plated bronze statue of a man with his arms in front of him resting on the handle of a sword, was known only as "the statuette." On her first day of work as a librarian at the Academy in 1931, Margaret Herrick, on seeing one of the statues on the desk of an executive and being told that the statue was the Academy's "foremost member," remarked, "He reminds me of my Uncle Oscar," referring to Oscar Pierce, a Texas fruit and wheat grower (who in reality was her mother's first cousin). What happened next ranks with the best of Hollywood stories. A Hollywood columnist overheard Mrs. Herrick's remark, and the next day his column made the statement: "Employees have affectionately dubbed their famous statuette 'Oscar.' "

Mrs. Herrick, who later became executive director of the Academy, came to regret the remark that she made in a mad moment of whimsy. In a 1959 letter to a Merriam-Webster editor, Mrs. Herrick admitted:

> Unfortunately, I must confess to having named the Oscar in 1931 in a thoughtless quip about an uncle of my mother's whom I have never met. I have regretted it more times than I care to remember because the family seemed strangely devoid of humor in relation to the distant uncle, and I have always felt that the Academy loses something in dignity every time the statuette is referred to as Oscar.

The founding of the Motion Picture Academy and its attendant awards served as an obvious model for the fledgling television industry two decades later. Soon after the founding of the Academy of Television Arts and Sciences came the annual ritual of awarding statuettes for achievement in the television industry. Artist Louis McManus was commissioned to design a distinctive award. The Motion Picture Academy had established the tradition of bestowing a catchy moniker on the trophy, and so the television academy followed suit. The academy's third president, Harry R. Lubcke, was a television engineer by profession. He bestowed on television's highest honor the name *Emmy,* after *Immy,* the slang term among television engineers for the image orthicon camera tube. The Emmys were first awarded in 1949 and have been known by that name ever since.

Professional organizations in the other arts have also followed the lead of the Motion Picture Academy. In 1947 the American Theatre Wing instituted the annual Antoinette Perry Awards for outstanding achievement in the theater. The awards were named after the actress and theatrical director Antoinette Perry (1888–1946). The awards have always been popularly known as the *Tonys,* after the nickname of the actress-director.

The National Academy of Recording Arts and Sciences has been awarding its *Grammy* Awards for outstanding achievement in the recording industry since 1959. The name of the award derives from the fact that the trophy is a model of an old-fashioned grammophone.

In the field of popular literature, the Mystery Writers of America annually award the *Edgars* for excellence in mystery writing. The trophies are miniature busts of Edgar Allan Poe (1809–1849), who is regarded as the father of the detective story. Not to be outdone, the World Science Fiction Convention annually presents its *Hugos* for achievement in the field of science fiction. The trophies, which are silver-plated miniature rocket ships, honor the memory of Hugo Gernsback (1884–1967), who was an American editor, publisher, inventor, and founder of *Amazing Stories*, the first magazine devoted to science fiction.

osprey   The osprey is a large, fish-eating bird that is in a class by itself. Scientists classify it as a hawk, and it is sometimes referred to as the fish hawk. However, the osprey is quite different from other hawks because it has evolved many unique features to help it catch fish. For example, the undersides of the bird's feet are covered with hundreds of spiny bumps that effectively hold slippery, struggling prey.

Since the osprey is superbly adapted to hunt fish, one might logically assume that its name means "fish catcher," or something like it. However, *osprey* actually comes from the Latin word *ossifraga*, which translates into 'bone-breaker', from *ossi-* 'bone' and *frangere* 'to break'. This is puzzling, since the osprey eats its catch whole; it is not noted for bone-breaking behavior. As it turns out, the bird was saddled with an inappropriate name through a literary mix-up.

The word *ossifraga* was used by the Roman author Pliny in his work *Natural History*. Pliny (a scientifically-minded man who met his end in 79 A.D. while investigating the eruption of Mt. Vesuvius at too close a range) does not go into detail about the bird he calls the *ossifraga*, although he does call it "another kind of eagle," so clearly our mystery bird is a bird of prey, probably a large one. Exactly why early French and English writers identified the *ossifraga* with the osprey cannot be determined now. The fact is that they did. *Ossifraga* was taken into Middle French as *osfraie* and applied to the fish hawk. In Middle English this became *ospray*, and today the word *osprey* and the fish-catching bird are irrevocably linked together, even though etymologically the linkage is inaccurate.

If the osprey was not Pliny's *ossifraga*, what bird was? In all probability, the "bone-breaker" he had in mind was the lammergeier, a big, eagle-like vulture found in Europe and Asia. *Lammergeier* is German for 'lamb vulture'; at one time the bird was thought to carry off lambs. That belief has no basis in fact, because the lammergeier feeds on carrion. Something that *is* true, however, gives us a clue to *ossifraga's* identity. The lammergeier specializes in eating bones. This specialty can present the bird with a problem, for while it is impressively large, with a wingspan that approaches 10 feet, it has a slender, relatively weak bill. In order to break large bones into pieces it can consume, it has developed the habit of flying aloft with a potential meal and then dropping the too-large bone onto the rocks below. If the lammergeier is successful, the bone breaks and it can eat. If the bone fails to break on impact, the bird simply retrieves it and tries again elsewhere. Occasionally it may drop something other than a bone. The Greek dramatist Aeschylus was supposedly killed when a large bird flying overhead mistook his bald head for a rock and dropped a tortoise on it. If this story is true, the culprit was probably a lammergeier.

Another reason for identifying the lammergeier with Pliny's bird is the fact that an old name for it is *ossifrage*, taken directly from Latin. But in recent times the distinction between the lammergeier and the osprey has been maintained, although at least one recent writer has begun muddying the issue by calling the osprey an ossifrage.

[ME *ospray,* fr. (assumed) MF *osfraie,* fr. L *ossifraga* sea eagle, fr. fem. of *ossifragus* bone-breaking, fr. *ossi-* + *-fragus* (fr. *frangere* to break)]

ostracize The Greek word *ostrakon* and its relatives *ostreon,* 'oyster', and *osteon,* 'bone', name hard, brittle objects. The *ostrakon* was a shell or an earthen vessel or a broken fragment of such a vessel. Such potsherds served ancient Athens as ballots in a particular kind of popular vote. Once a year the citizens could gather in the agora or marketplace of Athens to decide who, if anyone, should be banished temporarily for the good of the city. Each voter wrote a name on his *ostrakon.* If at least six thousand votes were cast and if a majority of them named one man, then that man was banished or *ostracized.*

When the word *ostracism* first appeared in English in the sixteenth century, it was used only to refer to the old Athenian custom. The earliest known figurative use was John Donne's, in a verse letter written to the Countess of Bedford early in the seventeenth century: "I have been told, that vertue in Courtiers hearts/ Suffers an Ostracisme, and departs." Of course, figurative use of the word is now common; the ostracism most frequently practiced is social ostracism, exclusion from acceptance by a group.

[Gk *ostrakizein* to banish by voting with potsherds, fr. *ostrakon* earthen vessel, potsherd, shell + *-izein* -ize]

ostrich In the seventeenth century, Latin *avis* 'bird' was borrowed into English unchanged in the phrase *rara avis,* literally 'rare bird' but used in the same sense as in Latin, to mean 'a marvel'. *Avis* crops up again in the Latin derivative *aviarium,* the source of our word *aviary.* But *avis* was a phonetically rather undernourished word, as one sees in particular when one realizes that the *v* was pronounced like *w* in classical Latin times, and the *-s* was an ending that would be changed in different cases of the noun. As a result, the word hides, virtually unrecognizable, in a number of words that have come down to us from Latin forms that have *avis* as part of a fixed phrase or compound. *Ostrich* is one such. It was borrowed from Old French *ostrusce,* which comes from an unattested Vulgar Latin form we may reconstruct as something like *austruthio,* deriving from *avis* and the Late Latin *struthio,* the latter a loan from Greek. The *avis* is more cleverly hidden in *bustard,* which derives ultimately from Latin *avis tarda.* Within classical Latin itself, *avis* appears in a stump form in *auspex* 'one who divines omens from the behavior of birds'. (Here the second part of the compound is from a root meaning 'see', familiar to us from our words *spectacle* and *spectator.*) The auspex held an important position, and his title was extended to mean 'patron, supporter of an enterprise'. His activity was called the *auspicium,* in a generalized sense 'patronage or leadership', and this word is the source of our word *auspices.*

[ME *ostriche*, fr. OF *ostrusce*, fr. (assumed) VL *avis struthio*, fr. L *avis* bird + LL *struthio* ostrich]

oud See LUTE.
[Ar *'ūd*, lit., wood]

ounce The difficulty in determining and establishing any standardized system of weights and measures is evidenced by the great variety of systems used in both ancient and modern times. The Romans used a system based on units that were divided into twelve parts. Thus the Latin *uncia*, meaning 'a twelfth part', was used to designate the twelfth part of a *pes* or 'foot'. From this is derived Old English *ince* or *ynce* and Modern English *inch*. The Roman pound, called *libra* in Latin (hence the English abbreviation *lb.* for pound and the symbol £ for the pound as a unit of currency), was also divided into twelve parts similarly designated by the word *uncia*. In this sense *uncia* followed a different path. It first became Middle French *unce*, and that form was borrowed into Middle English as *unce* or *ounce*. How, then, does it happen that we have sixteen ounces in a pound? The *troy* system of weights, today used primarily in weighing gold and other precious metals, was developed in the medieval period, probably in the French city of Troyes. The troy system, like the system used by the Romans, has twelve ounces. However, another system, also developed in the Middle Ages, has a larger pound as its unit. This is the *avoirdupois* system, widely used today in the United States, which has sixteen ounces per pound. Originally the same ounce was used in both troy and avoirdupois, but subsequent modifications in both systems have resulted in a troy ounce of 480 grains and an avoirdupois ounce of 437.5 grains.

[ME *unce, ounce*, fr. MF *unce*, fr. L *uncia* twelfth part, ounce, inch, fr. *unus* one]

oxlip See COWSLIP.
[earlier *oxislip, oxelip, oxslip*, fr. OE *oxanslyppe*, fr. *oxan*, gen. of *oxa* ox + *slyppe, slypa* pulp, paste]

oyez See JUDGE.
[ME *oyez!*, fr. AF *oyez!* hear ye!, fr. OF *oiez, oyez*, imperative pl. of *oir* to hear]

P

pacify See PAY.
[ME *pacifien,* fr. L *pacificare,* fr. *pac-, pax* peace + *-ificare* -ify, fr. *-ficus* -fic, fr. *facere* to make, do]

palace The word *palace* conjures up images of kings and queens and princes and princesses living in huge homes of splendor and luxury, often situated on high ground far above the common people. Although this image comes from fairy tales, it is not far removed from the first "palaces" of history. Residences were being built on the Palatine Hill in Rome from around 330 B.C. This hill, called the *Palatium* in Latin, was associated with power and prestige and held the homes of several of Rome's most prominent rulers, including the emperors Augustus, Tiberius, and Nero. Consequently, the word *palatium* came to be associated with living amid the splendor of unlimited wealth and prestige—specifically, in a large luxurious home on a hill. *Palatium* eventually began to denote such a royal house itself and later named any house that was large, ornate, and costly. In ensuing years, the term *palatium* passed into Old French and eventually into Middle English as *palais.* Today, any large, extravagant dwelling place can be called a *palace,* and the word is often used as an adjective meaning 'showy and luxurious', in such expressions as "palace car" or "palace hotel."

[ME *palais, paleis,* fr. OF, fr. L *palatium,* fr. *Palatium* Palatine Hill in Rome on which the residences of the emperors were built]

palaver See PARLOR.
[Pg *palavra* word, speech, fr. LL *parabola* speech, parable]

palimony See ALIMONY.
[blend of *pal* and *alimony*]

palmer See PILGRIM.
[ME *palmere,* fr. MF *palmier, paumier,* fr. ML *palmarius,* fr. L *palmarius,* adj., of palms]

pamphlet *Pamphilus, seu De Amore* ("Pamphilus, or About Love"), written in the late twelfth century by an author now unknown, was a poem detailing a series of amusing amorous adventures. *Pamphilus* was very popular in its day and one mark of the regard in which it was held was the widespread belief that it came from the pen of the great Roman poet of love, Ovid. Students at the University of Paris had to be reprimanded for neglecting serious works to read this erotic comedy.

In the late Middle Ages, the names of short literary works were often given diminutive forms. *Esopet* was a familiar name of *Aesop's Fables*. *Pamphilus* became *Pamphilet* (at least in French—the name, although probably used, is not attested in English). And *pamflet* was soon the word for any written work too short to be called a book. As early as 1344, the English scholar Richard de Bury in his *Philobiblon,* a Latin treatise on the love of books, wrote of preferring books to pounds, codices to florins, and thin *panfletos* to fat palfreys. A bit later (about 1387) Thomas Usk expressed in English his hopes for his *Testament of Love:* "Christe . . . graunte of thy goodnes to euery maner reder, full vnderstanding in this leud [unlearned] pamflet to haue."

[ME *pamflet,* fr. *Pamphilus (seu De Amore*) Pamphilus or About Love, popular Latin amatory poem of the 12th century + -*et*]

panache   The flamboyance and heroic flourish of manner conjured up by the word *panache* is aptly exemplified in the character of the long-nosed hero of *Cyrano de Bergerac,* by the French playwright Edmond Rostand. In the final moment of the play, the dying Cyrano declares that he has one thing left without spot or wrinkle that he can call his own: *"Et c'est . . . mon panache."* (And that is . . . my panache.)

Panache originally meant 'a plume or tuft of feathers on a helmet or hat' and is derived from the Late Latin *pinnaculum,* meaning 'a small wing' or 'a gable'. The figurative sense of *panache* developed from the verve and swagger exhibited by those bold enough to wear such a distinctive mark both in battle and among the ranks of polite society. Modern English *pinnacle* is also derived from *pinnaculum,* which is a diminutive of Latin *pinna,* meaning 'feather', 'wing', or 'battlement'. Thus the final word of the dying Cyrano, with his remarkable profile turned heavenward, can be seen as a multifaceted pun which works equally well in French and English and which draws upon the whole history and etymology of *panache.*

[earlier *pennache,* fr. MF, fr. OIt *pennacchio,* fr. LL *pinnaculum* small wing]

pandemonium   In Book I of *Paradise Lost,* the fallen Satan has his heralds proclaim "A solemn Councel forthwith to be held/ At Pandaemonium, the high Capital/ Of Satan and his Peers." Milton coined this name for the capital of hell from the prefix *pan-,* meaning 'all', plus the Late Latin *daemonium,* 'evil spirit', thus aptly naming the place where he gathered together all the demons. Later writers borrowed this word and used it more generally as a name for hell. Hell has often been described as a place where noise and confusion abound, and beginning in the late eighteenth century *pandemonium* was used of any wicked, lawless, or riotous place. After the middle of the nineteenth century *pandemonium* began to appear as a term for the uproar itself and not simply for the place where such tumult occurs.

[NL, fr. *Pandaemonium,* capital of Hell in *Paradise Lost* (1667) epic poem by John Milton †1674 Eng. poet, fr. *pan-* all (fr. Gk, fr. *pan,* neut. of *pas* all, every) + LL *daemonium* evil spirit, fr. Gk *daimonion,* fr. *daimōn* spirit, deity]

pander

Pan. . . . If ever you prove false one to another, since I have taken such pain to bring you together, let all pitiful goers-between be call'd to the world's end after my name; Call them all Pandars. Let all constant men be Troiluses, all false women Cresids, and all brokers-between Pandars! —Shakespeare, *Troilus and Cressida,* ca. 1601

At least part of the prophecy of Shakespeare's Pandarus came true. Shakespeare's character, however, is very different from the Pandarus of the original myth. In Greek mythology, Pandarus was a Lycian archer who fought with the Trojans in the Trojan War. He is remembered as the one who broke the truce between the Greeks and the Trojans by shooting an arrow at Menelaus, the king from Sparta. Pandarus is depicted in Greek myth as an admirable figure who is honored as a hero-god among his people. In medieval retellings of the story of Troy he becomes a player in the ill-fated love affair between Troilus, a Trojan prince, and Cressida, the daughter of a Greek priest. Pandarus acts as a go-between for the two lovers. This characterization of Pandarus first appeared in Boccaccio's *Il Filostrato* (ca. 1338), which was based on a twelfth-century French work that introduced the story of Troilus and Cressida to medieval romance. In Boccaccio's version, Pandarus is Cressida's young cousin. Boccaccio's work served as the source for Chaucer's fourteenth-century poem *Troilus and Criseyde,* but in Chaucer Pandarus becomes Criseyde's uncle. He is portrayed as a worldly-wise but sympathetic character. Shakespeare based his drama on Chaucer's version, but makes Pandarus more of a procurer than a benevolent go-between and in so doing makes him a less honorable character.

Pander actually dates from the early sixteenth century, first in the meaning of one who acts as a go-between for lovers, a direct development from the proper name *Pandar (Pandare, Pandarus),* then in an extended sense of one who acts as a procurer or pimp. Even before writing *Troilus and Cressida,* Shakespeare alludes to this pejorative sense in an earlier play, *Henry V* (ca. 1598) when he has the Duke of Bourbon, seeking to rally the French for one last stand against Henry's invading English forces, say:

> Let's die in honour. Once more back again!
> And he that will not follow Bourbon now,
> Let him go hence, and . . .
> Like a base pander hold the chamber door
> Whilst by a slave . . .
> His fairest daughter is contaminated.

Another extended sense soon arose, one who assists another in evil designs or who exploits the weaknesses of others. Again Shakespeare provides us with a good example of this use, this time from *The Winter's Tale* (ca. 1610). Leontes, King of Sicily, believing he has uncovered a plot in which his trusted aide Camillo has helped a would-be enemy, says:

> Camillo was his help in this, his pander;
> There is a plot against my life, my crown;
> All's true that is mistrusted. That false villain
> Whom I employ'd was pre-employ'd by him.

Concurrent with the rise of the extended senses was the creation of the verb *pander*. The verb's intransitive sense, meaning 'to minister to the baser desires, appetites, or motives of others', is now perhaps how the word *pander* is most commonly used. We speak of politicians who pander to voters or of motion-picture and television shows that pander to popular tastes for violence. Curiously, the original spelling *pandar* evolved into *pander* for both the noun, through an association with the *-er* ending of agent nouns, and for the verb, paralleling a common spelling for verbs. Thus, even though *pander* was an agent noun to begin with, the functional shift from noun to verb allowed for the development of the somewhat redundant agent noun *panderer*.

[alter. (influenced by *-er*) of ME *Pandare,* character who procured for Troilus the love of Cressida in *Troilus and Cressida* (1374) poem by Geoffrey Chaucer †1400 Eng. poet]

panel   See BUREAU.
[ME, fr. MF, prob. fr. (assumed) VL *pannellus,* alter. (influenced by L *-ellus* -el) of L *pannulus* small piece of cloth, fr. *pannus* cloth, rag, ribbon + *-ulus* -ule]

panhandler   See TRAMP.
[prob. fr. ¹*panhandle* + *-er;* fr. the extended forearm]

panic   The ancient Greek god *Pan* is often represented playing the *panpipes,* so called because he was believed to be the inventor of this instrument. Pan was very lustful and fond of chasing the nymphs. A nymph named Syrinx was once being chased by him and, finding herself unable to escape across the River Ladon, asked the nymphs of the river for help. They changed her into a bed of reeds by the riverbank. When Pan saw these reeds, the story goes, he cut pieces of different lengths and made a panpipe, which is also called a *syrinx* even now. The name of this nymph also survives in English in the word *syringe.*

Pan did not spend quite all his time playing his pipes or chasing nymphs, however. For instance, it was believed that he gave a great shout which instilled fear into the giants during their battle against the gods, and in Athens Pan was worshipped because the citizens believed that it was he who caused the Persians to flee in fear from the battle of Marathon. Thus from this more awesome aspect of his nature comes the word *panic.* For other articles on words derived from ancient mythology and legend see VOLCANO.

[F *panique*, fr. Gk *panikos*, fr. *Pan*, ancient Greek god of woods and shepherds who was regarded as the cause of the panic among the Persians at Marathon and of any sudden and groundless fear + *-ikos* -ic]

panpipe See PANIC.
[*Pan*, the ancient Greek god of woods and shepherds who was regarded as its inventor + E *pipe*]

pantaloons See ZANY.
[MF *Pantalon*, stage character wearing pantaloons, fr. OIt *Pantalone*, *Pantaleone*, fr. San *Pantaleone* 4th cent. A.D. physician and patron saint of physicians formerly often identified with Venice and Venetians]

paper See BOOK.
[ME *papir*, fr. MF *papier*, fr. L *papyrus* paper, papyrus, fr. Gk *papyros* papyrus]

papyrus See BOOK.
[ME *papirus*, fr. ML, fr. L *papyrus*]

parable See PARLOR.
[ME, fr. MF *parable*, *parabole*, fr. LL *parabola*, fr. Gk *parabolē* juxtaposition, comparison, parable, superposition (in geometry), parabola, fr. *paraballein* to throw or set alongside, compare, superpose (in geometry), fr. *para-* beside + *ballein* to throw]

parabola See PARLOR.
[NL, fr. Gk *parabolē*]

parasite Modern commentators on etiquette would probably agree that it is poor form to refer to a dinner guest as a *parasite*. Still, the description would be etymologically apt in some cases. *Parasite* is derived ultimately from the Greek *parasitos*, from *para-* 'beside' and *sitos* 'food'. *Parasitos* means literally 'one who eats at the table of another'. By extension it gained the meaning 'one who gains the hospitality or patronage of another through flattery'. The derivative noun in Latin was *parasitus*, which became the English *parasite* in the sixteenth century. In English, *parasite* has continued to denote a person who lives off or gains favor with another through flattery and obsequiousness, and all of its use is derogatory. The word may now be better known in a scientific sense, dating from the eighteenth century, 'an organism living in or on another organism from which it benefits and to which it usually causes injury'.

[MF, fr. L *parasitus*, fr. Gk *parasitos*, fr. *para-* ¹para- + *sitos* grain, bread, food]

parchment See VOLUME.
[ME *perchement, parchement,* alter. (influenced by ML *pergamentum,* alter. of L *pergamena*) of *parchemin, perchemin,* fr. OF *parchemin,* alter. (influenced by *parche, parge,* a kind of leather, fr. L *Parthica pellis,* fr. *Parthica,* fem. of *Parthicus* Parthian + *pellis* leather) of *pargamin,* fr. ML *pergamina,* alter. of L *pergamena,* fr. Gk *pergamēnē,* fr. fem. of *Pergamēnos* of Pergamum, fr. *Pergamon* (Pergamum), ancient city in Asia Minor (now Bergama, western Turkey)]

parlance See PARLOR.
[MF, fr. OF, fr. *parler, parlier* to speak, talk + *-ance* -ance]

parley See PARLOR.
[MF *parler* to speak, talk, fr. ML *parabolare,* fr. LL *parabola* speech, parable]

parliament See PARLOR.
[ME *parliament, parlement,* fr. OF *parlement,* fr. *parler, parlier* to speak, talk + *-ment* -ment]

parlor In medieval monasteries where silence was the rule, a room was set aside where monastics could converse with one another or with visitors. This room was designated the *parlor.* By Chaucer's time in the fourteenth century, parlors had become rooms in private dwellings as well. They were often handsomely furnished and served as reception rooms for visitors and as ceremonial rooms for family gatherings on Sundays and at times of weddings, funerals, and other important occasions.

The word *parlor,* a part of English since the thirteenth century, is taken from the Old French *parleor, parlour,* which is derived from the verb *parler,* meaning 'to speak, talk'. This verb can be traced back to the Late Latin *parabola,* 'speech, parable', a borrowing from the Greek *parabolē,* meaning 'juxtaposition, comparison, parabola'. The two elements making up this Greek word are *para-,* 'beside, alongside of', and *ballein,* 'to throw'.

The Greek *parabolē* is also the ultimate source of *palaver, parable, parabola, parlance, parley, parliament,* and *parole. Palaver,* 'profuse, idle, or worthless talk', was borrowed from the Portuguese word *palavra* in the eighteenth century as a result of contact between Portuguese and English sailors in the African coastal trade. *Parable,* 'an allegorical story told in simple terms', is a fourteenth century borrowing from Middle French. *Parabola,* which designates a particular kind of geometric curve, came into English from the New Latin word *parabola* in the sixteenth century, while *parlance,* 'manner or mode of speech', was taken from Middle French in the fifteenth century. *Parley,* 'a conference', is a sixteenth-century derivative of the French *parler,* and *parliament,* 'a formal conference for the discussion of public affairs', came from the Old French word *parlement,* which in turn derives from *parler.* The French word *parole,* meaning 'word, formal promise', was often used in the phrase *parole d'honneur,* 'word of honor', and when *parole* was borrowed into English in the seventeenth century, it was used especially for 'the promise of a prisoner of war upon his faith and honor to fulfill stated conditions in consideration of special privileges'.

[ME *parlour*, fr. OF *parleor, parlour* parlor, reception room in a convent, fr. *parler* to speak, talk]

parole See PARLOR.
[F, word of honor, word, speech, fr. OF, fr. LL *parabola* speech, parable]

parson See PERSON.
[ME *persone*, fr. OF, fr. ML *persona*, lit., person, fr. L]

passage See HARBINGER.
[ME, fr. OF, fr. *passer* to pass (fr. — assumed — VL *passare*, fr. L *passus* step) + *-age* -age]

passel *Passel* comes from *parcel* chiefly through the loss of the *r*. Loss of the sound of *r* after a vowel and before another consonant in the middle of a word is common in many widely used varieties of spoken English, including standard British and the English of New England, New York City, and the southern U.S. Both *passel* and *passell* are attested from the second half of the fifteenth century, so the form is not recent. But the modern use of *passel* as a collective noun for an indefinite number is a nineteenth-century Americanism.

> . . . they shook hands with the duke and didn't say nothing, but just kept a-smiling and bobbing their heads like a passel of sapheads —Mark Twain, *Huckleberry Finn*, 1884

> . . . Rousseau, Hobbes, Marx and a passel of other post-16th century thinkers —Ezra Bowen, *Time*, 6 May 1985

Loss of *r* also produced *cuss* from *curse* and *bust* from *burst*. *Cuss* is first attested in 1775 from an American source. It is applied to a person, who is characterized as "a damn cuss." Nobody is quite sure how this meaning developed. Two or three theorists in the past suggested it might have been influenced by a shortening of *customer*, but the theory seems to have no modern takers. Early uses of this noun are markedly dialectal in flavor:

> I thought I seed that Jake, the sneakin cuss, were gettin a mite ahead of me —John S. Robb, "The Standing Candidate", 1846

Modern printed uses in this country are not dialectal, and *cuss* can even be found now and again in British prose:

> Mr. David Lange is an awkward *cuss*, to use a New Zealand expression —*The Economist*, 5 July 1986

Cuss 'curse', both as a noun and as a verb, is first attested in early nineteenth-century American English, but it seems to have existed nearly simultaneously in British English. W. M. Thackeray used it as a conscious Americanism in *Pendennis* (1849), but as early as 1841 both he and Charles Dickens had used *cuss* in purely English settings. There is no real difference between Thackeray's 1841 "cuss me, I like to see a rogue" *(The History of the Great Hoggarty Diamond)* and John S. Robb's 1846 "cuss me if I know whether that were the right answer or not" ("The Standing Candidate"). *Cuss* 'curse' is no longer dialectal; present-day printed evidence suggests that it is now a not-too-serious euphemism:

> On the farm and in the Army he learned to cuss—but Mama Truman didn't raise her boy to swear in the presence of ladies —Clifton Daniel, *N.Y. Times Mag.*, 3 June 1984

Bust from *burst* crops up in 1806—again, in an American source, the *Journals of Lewis and Clark.* But by 1839 it turns up in the novels of Charles Dickens, so it is fairly likely that it existed in British speech as well. *Bust* has had quite an active life of its own, independent of *burst.* It quite early began to differentiate itself by a preference for a regular past and past participle *busted*—invariable *bust* is not frequent—which contrasts with *burst's* preference for the uninflected *burst*—*bursted* is not frequent.

> Would go down like a busted balloon —James Russell Lowell, *The Biglow Papers,* 1st series, 1848

> It most busted them, but they made up the six thousand clean and clear —Mark Twain, *Huckleberry Finn,* 1884

Mark Twain's use shows that *bust,* like *passel* and *cuss,* developed senses not shared with its original. Such uses as *trust-busting, union-busting,* and *budget-busting* are not shared with *burst* nor is the sense of *bust* 'arrest, raid'. *Bust* is a vigorous offshoot.

For more on dialectal variants that have become standard see ORNERY, RILE, SASS.

[alter. of *parcel*]

passenger   See HARBINGER.
[ME *passyngere, passager,* fr. MF *passager,* fr. *passager, passagier,* adj., passing, fr. *passage* + *-ier* -ary]

passionflower   See HYACINTH.
[trans. of NL *flor passionis,* lit., flower of the Passion, fr. the fancied resemblance of parts of the flower to the instruments of Christ's crucifixion]

pasta   See VERMICELLI.
[It, fr. LL, dough, paste, perh. fr. Gk *pastē* barley sauce, fr. fem. of *pastos* sprinkled, salted, fr. *passein* to sprinkle]

pasteurize   See BUCKAROO.
[Louis *Pasteur* †1895 Fr. chemist and bacteriologist + E *-ize*]

pastor   In both the Old Testament ("The Lord is my shepherd; I shall not want" —Ps. 23:1, AV) and the New Testament ("I am the good shepherd. The good shepherd lays down his life for the sheep" —Jn. 10:11, AV) we find the word *shepherd* used metaphorically for the deity. The word for 'shepherd' in Latin is *pastor*, and in the Latin of the Vulgate, "I am the good shepherd" is rendered as "Ego sum pastor bonus." The Latin *pastor* is derived from *pastus*, the past participle of *pascere*, meaning 'to pasture, feed, graze'. The English word *pasture* is, thus, also derived from this verb.

In the early centuries of Christianity, the role of shepherd/pastor was assumed by the bishop, who took direct responsibility for the spiritual well-being of the faithful committed to his care. As his flock increased in numbers, however, the bishop had to share his responsibility with other members of the clergy. By the fourth century, local churches were being presided over by a priest who was designated as the pastor.

Old French took the Latin *pastor* as *pastur* or *pastor*, and in the four-teenth century English borrowed it as *pastour* from Anglo-French. Both the literal 'shepherd' sense and the figurative 'parish priest' sense were in use. Except in dialect use in the American Southwest, the literal sense has all but disappeared from modern English.

As the shepherd has his crook or staff for guiding his sheep, a bishop has his pastoral staff symbolizing his role as "shepherd of souls." In Medieval Latin his staff was called a *crossa* (with several variant spellings). Old French took this Latin word as *croce*, which became *crosse* in Middle French. The derivative *crossier* was then formed to denote 'a staff bearer'. This French noun was borrowed into English in the fourteenth century as *croser*, which later came to be spelled *croiser* and then *crosier* in the six-teenth century. It was originally used in the same sense 'a staff bearer', but by the beginning of the sixteenth century had also come to refer to the pastoral staff itself. The 'staff bearer' sense has since become obsolete.

[ME *pastour*, fr. AF, fr. OF *pastur, pastor*, fr. L *pastor*, fr. *pastus* (past part. of *pascere* to pasture, feed, graze) + *-or*]

pasture See PASTOR.
[ME, fr. MF, fr. LL *pastura*, fr. L *pastus* (past part. of *pascere* to pasture, feed, graze) + *-ura* -ure]

patron See PATTERN.
[ME *patroun, patron*, fr. MF *patrun, patron*, fr. ML & L; ML *patronus* patron of a benefice, patron saint, master, pattern, fr. L, defender, pro-tector, advocate, fr. *patr-, pater* father]

patter See BROUHAHA.
[ME *patren, patern*, fr. *pater*noster Lord's Prayer, fr. ML, fr. L *pater noster* our father, the first two words of the Lord's Prayer]

pattern Latin *patronus* is derived from *pater*, 'father', and the duties of a Roman so designated were comparable to those of a father. He was a pro-tector of his city or province; a defender in a court of law was his client's *patronus;* the man who freed his slave became that slave's *patronus* and retained some legal rights over his freedman or freedwoman, like those of a father over his child. The use of *patronus* in Medieval Latin shifted to suit the new requirements of the Christian era. Such a father figure as a patron saint or the patron of a benefice was called a *patronus*, as was anyone who served like a father as a model or pattern to be emulated. Middle English *patroun* or *patron* (borrowed from Middle French) had a range of meaning similar to that of its Medieval Latin ancestor. A patron, in spite of the word's etymology, was not necessarily a man. Chaucer wrote of a woman who was nature's "chefe patron [pattern] of beaute, And chefe ensample of al her werke."

During the sixteenth century, another pronunciation of *patron* appeared, represented by such spellings as *pattern, paterne,* and *patarne* (similarly, we sometimes hear *apron* pronounced as though spelled *apern* even today). This transposition of sounds is called *metathesis,* and the effects of its working can be seen in such common words as *bird* (from Old English *brid*) and *task* (ultimately from the Latin word that also gives us *tax*). By the beginning of the eighteenth century, *patron* was no longer used of a person or thing which served as a model; the two forms, *patron* and *pattern,* were identified with separate senses and became two distinct words. See also LEPRECHAUN.

[ME *patron,* fr. MF, fr. ML *patronus*]

pawn   See PIONEER.
[ME *pown, poune,* fr. MF *poon,* fr. ML *pedon-, pedo* foot soldier, fr. LL, one who has broad feet, fr. L *ped-, pes* foot]

pay   Just as parents, in hopes of having a quiet home, give their babies pacifiers, so employers *pay* their employees, in an effort to avoid the difficulties of a discontented work force. Etymologically as well, to pay is to pacify. The Latin verb *pacare,* 'to pacify', is derived from *pax,* 'peace'. In the Middle Ages, *pacare* was used specifically to mean 'to pacify a creditor by paying a debt' and eventually, more generally 'to pay'. The Romance derivatives of the Latin word, including Old French *paier,* had both the original sense 'to pacify, please, or appease'—*appease,* like *pay* and *pacify,* is a descendant of Latin *pax*—and the later sense 'to pay'. Middle English *payen,* borrowed from the French in the late twelfth or early thirteenth century, was similarly used in both senses. In the treatise *Dives and Pauper,* a dialogue between a rich man and a poor man written in the fifteenth century, we find the familiar complaint of the worthy and well-to-do against the greedy poor: "Poore folke be not payed with suffycyent lyuynge but couete more than theym nedeth." (Poor people are not satisfied—or appeased—with a sufficient living, but covet more than is needful for them.) But this sense of *pay* is now long obsolete.

A nautical homonym of *pay* means 'to smear with pitch'. This word, descended from Latin *pix,* 'pitch', rather than *pax,* was borrowed from the French (*peier*) in relatively modern times; it is first attested in English in the early seventeenth century. See also DEVIL.

[ME *payen* to pacify, appease, please, pay, fr. OF *paier,* fr. L *pacare* to pacify, fr. *pac-, pax* peace]

[obs. F *peier,* fr. OF, fr. L *picare,* fr. *pic-, pix* pitch]

pea See SHERRY.
[back-formation fr. *pease* (taken as plural), fr. ME *pese,* fr. OE *pise, peose,* fr. L *pisa,* pl. of *pisum,* fr. Gk *pisos, pison*]

peach Like the apricot, the *peach* is a native of China. In the first century when the fruit was new to the classical world, it was named in Greek *mēlon Persikon* and in Latin *malum Persicum.* Both names mean literally 'Persian apple'. The tree was known to have originated in the East, and *Persian* served as a convenient catchall term for anything from the distant Orient.

In time *persicum* came to be used elliptically for *malum Persicum.* The feminine form *persica* of the classical Latin neuter adjective *persicum* then replaced the neuter form as the name of the peach in later Latin. The gradual transformation of *persica* by many tongues over the years yielded the Old French *pesche* and Middle French *peche,* which was borrowed into Middle English and became our modern *peach.*

Another fruit whose name comes from its place of origin is the *damson* plum. *Damson* is the descendant of Latin *Damascenum.* The *prunum Damascenum* was literally the 'plum of Damascus'.

See also APRICOT.

[ME *peche,* fr. MF (the fruit), fr. LL *persica,* fr. L *persicum,* fr. neut. of *Persicus* Persian]

peccadillo See NAUGHTY.
[Sp *pecadillo,* dim. of *pecado* sin, fr. L *peccatum,* fr. neut. of *peccatus,* past part. of *peccare* to sin]

peculate See PECULIAR.
[L *peculatus,* past part. of *peculari* to embezzle, fr. *peculium* private property]

peculiar The most common meaning of *peculiar* today is 'strange' or 'unusual'. The statement in *Fardle of Facions* (1555), William Watreman's translation of a Latin travel book, that "it was a peculier maner of the Kynges of the Medes, to haue many wiues" would now be taken to mean that the royal custom was an odd one, but the meaning intended was 'a manner peculiar to (or characteristic of) the kings of the Medes'. The sense 'strange' developed naturally from the earlier sense 'exclusively one's own, distinctive'. The earliest evidence we have for the word *peculiar* clearly intended to mean 'unusual' comes from Topsell's *Serpents* (1608): "The tongue of a serpent is peculiar; for . . . it is also cloven at the tip."

Middle English *peculier* came from Latin *peculiaris,* 'privately owned' or 'special', a derivative of *peculium,* 'property', from *pecu,* 'cattle'. The early habit of considering property in terms of its value in cattle is responsible for a number of English words descended from words for cattle, like Latin *pecu* and its cognates in other Indo-European languages. Among

these are *peculiar, peculate, pecuniary, impecunious,* and *fee.* See also
FEE.

[ME *peculier,* fr. L *peculiaris* of private property, owned privately, special, extraordinary, fr. *peculium* private property (fr. *pecu* cattle) + *-aris*
-ar; akin to L *pecus* cattle, OHG *fihu,* OE *feoh* cattle, property, money]

pecuniary   See PECULIAR.
[L *pecuniarius,* fr. *pecunia* money + *-arius* -ary]

peeler   See DERBY.
[Sir Robert *Peel* †1850 Eng. statesman who instituted the Irish constabulary + E *-er*]

pen   That *pen* 'enclosure' and *pen* 'writing implement' are etymologically unrelated may not be surprising, since the meanings are so distinct. The
'enclosure' *pen* traces its ancestry obscurely back to Old English *penn* and
has no known relatives in other languages. Its homophone, by contrast,
goes back to Latin *penna* 'wing, feather', for the original reference was to
a quill pen.
   Pen and *pencil* look close in both form and meaning, but again the resemblance is accidental. When *pencil* entered English in the early fourteenth century (as *pinsel,* among other spellings), it denoted an artist's
paintbrush. This was the meaning of its ultimate source in Latin, *penicillus.* English later also borrowed this Latin word unchanged, referring to
a tuft-like structure; the root is more familiar in our word *penicillin,* produced by the *Penicillium* mold, which is named for its brush-like shape.
Latin *penicillus* has an anatomical etymology: it is a diminutive of Latin
penis, which meant both 'penis' and 'tail'.

[ME, fr. OE *penn*]

[ME *penne,* fr. MF, feather, wing, pen, fr. L *pinna,* alter. of *penna* feather, wing; akin to Gk *pteron* wing, feather]

pencil   See PEN.
[ME *pensel, pencel,* fr. MF *pincel,* fr. (assumed) VL *penicellus,* fr. L
penicillus brush, pencil, lit., little tail, dim. of *penis* tail, penis]

penicillin   See PEN.
[*penicill-* (fr. NL *Penicillium* — fr. L *penicillus* brush — + NL *-ium*) +
-in]

penicillus   See PEN.
[NL, fr. L, brush, pencil]

Pentecost   See CATHOLIC.
[ME *Pentecost,* fr. OE *Pentecosten,* fr. LL *Pentecoste,* fr. Gk *pentēkostē*

fiftieth day, Pentecost, fr. *pentēcostos* fiftieth, fr. *pentēkonta* fifty, fr. *penta-* + *-konta* (akin to L *-ginti* in *viginti* twenty)]

penthouse   In Middle English *pentis* meant primarily 'a shed or roof attached to and sloping from a wall or building'. Its earliest known appearance is in an anonymous metrical sermon of around 1325: "Thar was na herberie/ To Josep and his spouse Marie,/ Bot a pendize that was wawles,/ As oft in borwis tounes es." (There was no shelter for Joseph and his wife Mary, except a lean-to that was wall-less, as is frequent in borough towns.) *Pentis* is derived through Middle French and Medieval Latin from Latin *appendix*, meaning 'appendage' or 'supplement'. (A direct borrowing from Latin gives the English *appendix* in its various senses.) Thus a *pentis* was a smaller building or structure attached to a larger one.

It was widely though mistakenly believed that *pentis* was related to Middle French *pente*, 'slope', and this belief was very likely encouraged by the fact that many such structures did in reality have sloping roofs. The beginning of the word thus being supposedly accounted for, its second syllable was then altered by folk etymology to *-house*. A subsidiary structure on the roof of a building to cover a stairway, a water tank, or other equipment is still called a *penthouse*, as is a dwelling on the top of a building, a common sense of the word today. For other folk etymologies see FOLK ETY-MOLOGY.

[by folk etymology (influence of MF *pente* slope — fr. *pendant* — and E *house*) fr. ME *pentis*, fr. MF *appentis*, prob. fr. ML *appendicium* appendage, lean-to, fr. L *appendic-*, *appendix* appendage, supplement, fr. *appendere* to append]

peon   See PIONEER.
[Pg *peão* & F *pion*, fr. ML *pedon-*, *pedo* foot soldier]

peregrination   See PILGRIM.
[MF or L; MF, fr. L *peregrination-*, *peregrinatio*, fr. *peregrinatus* (past part. of *peregrinari*) + *-ion-*, *-io* -ion]

peregrine falcon   See PILGRIM, FALCON.
[ME *faucon peregrin*, trans. of ML *falco peregrinus*]

peripatetic   See STOIC.
[ME *perypatetik*, fr. L *peripateticus*, fr. *peripateticos*, adj., fr. Gk *peripatētikos*, irreg. fr. *peripatos* place for walking, covered walk in the Lyceum where Aristotle taught]

person   The Latin noun *persona* was originally used for 'an actor's mask'. It was probably derived from the Etruscan word for 'mask', *phersu.* In time its use extended to 'a character in a play, a dramatic role'. By Cicero's time it was also being used outside dramatic contexts to refer to one's actual character or role in life and then to one's individual personality or being. In his grammar, *De lingua Latina*, Roman scholar Varro (116–27 B.C.) used *persona* for the grammatical 'person' that identifies the subject as the speaker, the one addressed, or the one spoken about. By the second century, *persona* was being used in Christian contexts for 'one of the three modes of being in the Trinity'.

In Medieval Latin *persona* was used for 'a human being, a person'. Later it meant 'a person of importance' and then was applied to 'a parish priest', probably from his being the most important man in the parish. It then passed into Old French as *persone* with these meanings. When Middle English borrowed the word, its evolution took two different paths. As *person*, it was used, as in Latin and French, for 'a human being'. It also took on the Latin senses of 'a character assumed in a play or in actual life' and 'one of the beings in the Trinity'. In the fifteenth century, *person* came to be used in legal terminology for 'one (as a human being, a partnership, or a corporation) that is recognized by law as the subject of rights and duties'. By the sixteenth century, we find the first application of *person* in English grammar. On another path, the French *persone*, meaning 'a parish priest', developed into *parson* in English and was used for 'a rector of a parish'. In fact, Chaucer's *Canterbury Tales* concludes with "The Parson's Tale" (ca. 1400). In modern English, parson has come to be used as a synonym for *clergyman* or *minister,* especially in Protestant churches.

Early in the eighteenth century, the Latin plural *personae* came to be used in English for 'the characters of a fictional representation'. It is in this sense that it is commonly found in theater programs in the phrase "dramatis personae," which heads a list of characters in a drama.

In diplomatic language, *persona* can be found since the 1880s in the phrase *persona grata* 'an acceptable person', which is used to express approval of another country's representative, and in the correlative phrase *persona non grata.* The latter has also developed considerable use outside diplomacy to express disapproval of a person.

In 1909 a book of Ezra Pound's poems was published with the title *Personae.* It is from Pound's use, and criticism of Pound's work, that *persona* acquired its use as a term in literary criticism. We are told by Lee T. Lemon, in *A Glossary for the Study of English* (1971), that "a persona is a mask or an alter-ego of the author; the term is used most frequently in this sense in the discussion of literature written in the first person and of lyric poems when it is advisable to distinguish between the author of the piece and the narrator he has created."

By 1917 the works of the Swiss psychologist Carl Jung were being translated into English. *Persona* was a term Jung used to denote 'an individual's social facade that reflects the role in life the individual is playing'. In Jung's *Psychological Types* (translated by H. G. Baynes, 1924), we find his explanation: "I term the outer attitude, or outer character, the *persona;* the inner attitude I term the *anima,* or *soul.*"

After Jung's use, *persona* started on an independent life of its own as a term for a person's public personality. J. F. Bernard, writing in *New Yorker* (12 November 1973), uses the word in this sense:

. . . despite vast differences in background, [the two diplomats] have certain traits in common so far as personal and diplomatic style are concerned. Their public personae are similar.

[ME *persone, person, persoun,* fr. OF *persone, persoune,* fr. L *persona* mask (esp. one worn by an actor), actor, role, character, person, prob. fr. Etruscan *phersu* mask]

persona   See PERSON.
[L]

pest   A modern *pest* is likely to be no more than a nuisance. The original *pest* was far more serious. In the sixteenth century England borrowed the French word for the plague, *peste.* The word could be used for any epidemic disease associated with high mortality. But the *pest* was usually, specifically, the bubonic plague. Those who had contracted the plague were often segregated in a hospital that bore the blunt designation *pesthouse.* Thus Daniel Defoe in his *Journal of the Plague Year* (1722) speaks of "some people being removed to the pesthouse beyond Bunhill fields." Such people would likely be in the charge of a *pest-man* or *pest-master* and would be removed in a *pest-coach,* while the bodies of dead victims were carried off in a *pest-cart.* The French *peste* retains its old significance today, but English *pest* is not very often used in this sense anymore. Albert Camus's novel *La Peste* had to be translated as *The Plague* rather than *The Pest* to give English readers a proper notion of its contents.

   The word *pest* had not been long in English before anything destructive or troublesome could be called a *pest.* The person who merely makes a nuisance of himself is the most common *pest* of all. See also PESTER.

   [MF *peste* plague, fr. L *pestis*]

pester   Although a person who *pesters* is called a *pest,* the two words are etymologically unrelated. *Pest* is a derivative of Latin *pestis,* 'plague', and *pester* of Latin *pastor,* 'herdsman, shepherd'. The Middle French word *empestrer* meant 'to hobble (an animal)'. It is derived, via a hypothetical popular Medieval Latin verb *impastoriare,* from *pastoria,* a term found in the seventh- and eighth-century Latin of the Germanic laws, where it designated a tether for a grazing horse. *Pastoria* in turn comes from the Latin adjective *pastorius,* 'of a herdsman', which would take the form *pastoria* when modifying a feminine noun such as *chorda* 'cord' or *catena* 'chain'.

   The Middle French word *empestrer* developed, from the original meaning 'to hobble', the extended sense 'to impede'. This was the meaning of the sixteenth-century English borrowing *pester.* Under the influence of the remarkably but accidentally similar noun *pest, pester* acquired the further sense 'to annoy'. See also PEST.

[modif. of MF *empestrer* to hobble (an animal), impede, embarrass, fr. (assumed) ML *impastoriare* to hobble (an animal), fr. L *in-* in- + ML *pastoria,* n., hobble, fr. L, fem. of *pastorius* of or belonging to a herdsman, fr. L *pastor* herdsman, shepherd + *-ius* -ious]

petard Shakespeare's *Hamlet* (ca. 1600) contains, among other well-known lines, this: "For 'tis the sport to have the enginer/Hoist with his own petar." Three words of Shakespeare's are spelled a bit differently today. *Enginer* we now spell *engineer*. Shakespeare's *hoist* is the past participle of *hoise*, a verb whose ordinary uses have been transferred to modern *hoist* (whose past tense and past participle are *hoisted*); *hoise* lives on only as the past *hoist* in Shakespeare's phrase or echoes of it.

Petar seems to have been a variant spelling or to have represented the French pronunciation of the French source word *petard*. The petard was an explosive device used in siege warfare. It was shaped like a bucket or bell and crammed full of gunpowder. The open end was firmly fastened to a stout plate of iron-bound wood. The idea of the device was to have your engineers—*petardiers* was the more precise term—sneak the device up to the fortress being besieged, under cover of darkness one rather assumes, hang it on or lean it against the gate, light the fuse, and run. When the petard went off, the explosion would break through the door and the casing, in strict accordance with Newton's third law of motion, was shot in the direction of the retreating petardiers. You can see then that the petardier was likely to be blown up by his own petard if it went off prematurely or if he was not shrewd in plotting his direction of retreat. The petard seems to have scored its first success in 1580, when Henry of Navarre used it to open holes in the gates of Cahors, which he then captured.

Petard was borrowed into English from the French. The French word was derived from the verb *péter* meaning 'to break wind'. The related French noun *pet*, whose primary meaning you can readily divine, is reported in the French-English dictionary of Abel Boyer (1699) to have a secondary meaning 'the report of a firearm'. So the bomb was not the only fighting connection of these words. *Péter* is derived from Latin *pedere*, of the same signification, and *pedere* is cognate with terms in Greek and other ancient languages going back all the way to the original Indo-European. These cognates may look different, but they all designate the same act of dubious social desirability.

For another curious word developing from the discharge of gas see FEISTY.

[MF, fr. *peter* to break wind (fr. *pet* expulsion of intestinal gas, fr. L *peditum*, fr. neut. of *peditus*, past part. of *pedere* to break wind) + -*ard;* akin to Gk *bdein* to break wind silently, Russ *bzdet*]

petit See PETTICOAT.
[ME, fr. MF, fr. OF]

petit bourgeois See PETTICOAT.
[F, lit., small bourgeois, fr. *petit* + *bourgeois* (fr. MF, fr. OF *borjois*, fr. *borc* burgher, fr. L *burgus* fortified place, of Gmc origin)]

petit four See PETTICOAT.
[F, lit., small oven]

petit jury   See PETTICOAT.
   [ME, lit., small jury]

petticoat   Since a *petticoat*, as the term is used today for a woman's garment, is neither petty nor a coat, the canny word enthusiast, having
learned to beware the pitfalls of folk etymology, might imagine that the
term derives instead from some recondite Latin source and that the resemblance to the shorter English words is accidental. But in fact a petticoat was originally and literally a small coat or tunic, worn in the fifteenth
century beneath the doublet (a style of jacket). *Petty* originally meant
'small', the sense retained by its French source word *petit* to this day. The
reference of both *petty* and *petticoat* subsequently traveled downwards,
so to speak, until *petty* came to mean 'small' normally only in the sense
'of small importance' or 'small-minded' and *petticoat* to refer to a skirt usually worn as underclothing.
   The French loanword *petit* survives in English under that spelling,
alongside the more anglicized *petty*. Semantically, the twins have gone
their separate ways, with *petit* escaping general pejoration. The *petit jury*
is a cornerstone of the Anglo-American legal system, a *petit four* (literally
"little oven" in French) is a dainty treat, and the feminine form *petite* is
an appreciative term. Awkwardly straddling these divergent paths is *petit
bourgeois*. In its actual reference, the term designates precisely that class
which is neither invidiously wealthy nor dangerously poor: the hardworking, lower-middle layer. But the term was largely an academic one
until the communists gave it a vigorous vernacular use. In that milieu, the
term is invariably pronounced "*petty* bourgeois" and is used as a term of
abuse.
   As for the French form *petit* whose progeny we have been examining,
its own ancestry is somewhat cloudy and does not stretch back as far as
classical Latin. It seems to spring from one of a number of popular formations from the post-classical Latin period, such as *pittittus* and *pitinnus*
and *pitulus*, all meaning 'small'. These are evidently of expressive origin,
perhaps in reminiscence of the pitter-patter of tiny feet.

   [ME *petycote*, lit., small coat, fr. *pety* small + *cote* coat]

petty   See PETTICOAT.
   [ME *pety* small, minor, alter. of *petit*]

phaeton   In Greek mythology, Phaeton is the son of Helios (the god of
the sun) who persuades his father to let him drive the chariot of the sun
across the sky for a single day. Helios is bound by a promise to grant his
son's one wish and agrees, although not without grave concern. His concern proves well-founded, for Phaeton, no match for the mighty horses,
loses control and the fiery chariot wanders in its course and flies too near
the earth. It scorches the northern part of Africa, turning it to desert and
darkening the skin of the people there. Fearing that the entire earth will
be burned up, Zeus is forced to destroy Phaeton with a thunderbolt. The
name Phaeton lives on in literature. The Roman poet Ovid tells the story

in his *Metamorphoses,* and we find it also in English literature. Shakespeare alludes to the story in *The Two Gentlemen of Verona* (ca. 1594): "Why, Phaeton . . ./ Wilt thou aspire to guide the heavenly car/ And with thy daring folly burn the world?"

This association of Phaeton with the speeding chariot of the sun made *phaeton* a good choice by coach builders seeking a dynamic name for a light, fast horse-drawn carriage. (For articles on other words derived from ancient mythology and legend see VOLCANO.) The first phaetons were made in France in the early 1700s, and the name spread to England, with the carriages, by the year 1743 (the word *phaeton* was actually in earlier use in English in a sense of 'a rash or adventurous charioteer'). The original phaeton was a fast, sporting four-wheel open carriage with a seat for two people; later designs developed it into a vehicle for four passengers. With the coming of the "horseless carriage," *phaeton* eventually was taken over as the name of a large touring automobile. The classic motor phaeton was a large car with a body that extended only up as high as the four doors, a folding fabric top, and side curtains that could be hung to keep out the rain. This car had two permanent seats for four or five riders, and some versions even had a jump seat to accommodate two more. The phaeton was a popular body style up to the early 1930s, when it was replaced by the fully enclosed automobile with a permanent top and roll-up glass windows.

A number of other names for automobiles or automobile styles were first the names of carriages: *coupe, landau, brougham,* and *station wagon. Coupe* or *coupé* is the term for a small automobile with two doors and a single seat for two people. As the name for a carriage, it referred to what was thought of as a "cut-down" version (hence the name, from French *coupé,* the past participle of *couper* 'to cut', but probably more immediately from *carrosse coupé,* literally, 'cut-off coach'). The horse-drawn coupe or coupé was a small, enclosed carriage with four wheels, a door on either side, a single seat for two facing forward, and a driver's seat outside separated from the passenger section by a glassed partition.

The *landau* carriage takes its name from Landau, Bavaria (in what is now West Germany), where it was first made, probably as early as the seventeenth century (although the name appears in English only from the mid-1700s). The landau was a full-size carriage accommodating four or six passengers on two full-width seats, the rear one facing forward and the front one facing aft. All early carriages were essentially open models that gradually developed into enclosed models to protect the riders from rain and cold. The landau was distinctive in being an enclosed carriage with a top that could be folded down (in essence, the first "convertible"). The top was made in two sections so that one part folded forward and the other folded back. The landau soon spawned a cut-down version, known as the *landaulet.* This model was similar to the coupe, with a solid body and roof above and forward of the door, while over the seat was a fabric top that could be folded back. Both the names *landau* and *landaulet* were taken over in the twentieth century as names for automobile styles. The motor landaulet was essentially an enclosed sedan or coupe with a folding top at the extreme rear quarter, over the rear seat. The early landaulets had an external S-shaped hinge mechanism supporting the folding top, and this hinge mechanism was one of the distinctive features of the body style. The name *Landau* has been used on automobiles, even into the second half of the twentieth century, but since the 1920s mostly as an advertising device to indicate a fixed roof style without a rear quarter window and, most recently, often with a vinyl section over only the rear quarter of the roof or with nothing more than the stylized S-shaped "landau hinge" as a decorative device on the side of the roof.

Another carriage name that has become part of the automobile lexicon is *brougham*. The brougham originated in England in the late 1830s when Henry Peter Brougham, former lord chancellor of England and later Baron Brougham and Vaux, commissioned a London coach builder to build a special four-wheel coupe of his own design. The driver sat in a high position on an uncovered seat in front and was separated from the enclosed passenger section by a glassed partition. It was intended to be a luxurious gentleman's carriage, and ultimately it came to be used for public cabs, soon the most popular cab design in America. (See also CAB.) The automobile called a *brougham* was quite similar to the carriage in having an enclosed section for the passengers separated from the uncovered driver's or chauffeur's section in front. This automobile style was popular in the 1920s. The name, however, has been revived and in more modern use usually designates a luxurious version of a manufacturer's car line.

Another vehicle in our look at automobile names that have derived from horse-drawn vehicles is the *station wagon*. The original station wagons, earlier known as *depot wagons*, were boxy enclosed wagons for conveying passengers to and from the train depot or station. Like the modern motorvehicle station wagon, the earlier versions had collapsible rear seats and a tailgate or rear door that allowed for carrying a large load of luggage.

Finally, this history would not be complete without a look at one example that runs counter to the trend of naming cars after carriages, the *limousine*. The limousine, originating in France, was named from a French word meaning, literally, 'cloak', deriving ultimately from Limousin, a region in France. It was originally a motorcar with an enclosed passenger section for up to seven riders separated by a glassed partition from a covered driver's or chauffeur's section in front. The original limousine was similar to the brougham except in the limousine the driver's seat was covered by the roof, perhaps suggestive of the hood of the limousine cloak. Don Berkebile, in his *Carriage Terminology: An Historical Dictionary* (1978), tells the rest of the story:

> In 1902 the editors of the French trade journal, *Le Guide du Carrossier,* suggested that since automobile designers borrowed automobile ideas from the carriage trade, the idea should also be reversed, with the carriage builders borrowing automobile designs. Accordingly, a two-wheel, horse-drawn LIMOUSINE was designed, having a body just like the auto, but minus the hood, and having its door in the rear. No evidence has been found to indicate that the idea gained acceptance.

[L *Phaeton,* son of Helios who attempted to drive the chariot of the sun with the result of setting the earth on fire, fr. Gk *Phaetōn*]

philistine   In the twelfth century B.C., the *Philistines* settled on the southern coast of what we know as Palestine. These inhabitants of Philistia, who gave their name to Palestine (from the Greek version of the ancient Hebrew name for Philistia), eventually came into conflict with the neighboring Israelites. In the Bible the Philistines are portrayed as a crude and warlike race. On a good day the Hebrew hero Samson slew a thousand of them with the jawbone of an ass (Judges 15). At least since the seventeenth century, *Philistines* was a humorous reference in English for one's enemies, into whose hands one had fallen or was in imminent danger of doing so. Another, more current sense of *philistine* entered the English language as the result of a dispute between the town and the university in the German town of Jena in 1687. The confrontation had left several people dead and prompted a local clergyman to address the issue in a sermon. For his sermon to the townspeople on the value of education, he chose his text from Judges 16:9(AV): "The Philistines be upon these. . . ." *Philister,* the German word for *Philistine,* soon caught on with the students as a catchword for an ignorant townsman opposed to education. *Philister* became an established term in German university slang for an outsider, for one (especially a townsman) who was not a member of the university community and thus not one of the chosen people. Familiar with it from this context, as were other English writers, the poet and critic Matthew Arnold borrowed it for his book *Culture and Anarchy* (1869). Translating *Philister* to *Philistine,* Arnold wrote in the first chapter:

> The people who believe most that our greatness and welfare are proved by our being very rich, and who most give their lives and thoughts to becoming rich, are just the very people whom we call Philistines.

Since Arnold, *philistine* has become widely used of any person who is highly materialistic, indifferent or hostile to art and literature, and smugly acceptant of conventional values.

Just as the ancient Hebrews considered their neighbors the Philistines crass and barbaric, the ancient Athenians held some of their neighbors in similar regard. Boeotia was an agricultural district in central Greece. To outsiders it was known chiefly for the abundance of its cattle and the moist heaviness of its air. The Boeotians were said to have little appreciation for the arts and culture that the people of Athens prized so highly. To the Athenians the Boeotians were as dense as their air and as dull and stupid as their cattle. The proverbial character of the Boeotians followed the word into the English language, where the adjective *boeotian* means boorishly stupid and the noun *boeotian* is roughly synonymous with *philistine.*

[ME, fr. LL *Philistinus,* fr. Gk *Philistinos,* fr. Heb *Pĕlishtī*]

phlegmatic   See HUMOR.

[ME *flaumatike,* fr. MF *flaumatique,* fr. LL *phlegmaticus,* fr. Gk *phleg-*

matikos, fr. *phlegmat-, phlegma* flame, inflammation, phlegm + *-ikos* -ic]

piano A harpsichord is played by means of a mechanism that plucks the strings, and so it is not possible to achieve fine gradations of loudness, although a number of stops do allow the dynamics of the instrument to be controlled in steps. Feeling the need to overcome this drawback in the harpsichord, a Florentine by the name of Bartolommeo Cristofori around the year 1709 invented a mechanism or "action" by means of which the strings of the instrument are struck by felt-covered hammers. This device allows the player more control over the loudness of his playing. Cristofori called his new instrument a *gravicembalo col piano e forte,* that is, 'a harpsichord with soft and loud'; *piano* means 'soft' in Italian musical terminology and *forte,* 'loud'. Similarly, the earliest known pieces written expressly for the new instrument are sonatas that Lodovico Giustini published in 1732 for the *cembal di piano e forte detto volgarmente di martelletti,* 'the soft and loud harpsichord commonly called the one with little hammers'. The instrument came to be designated by this term *piano e forte* or by contraction *pianoforte,* which was subsequently shortened to the form *piano.* (For other words derived from the use of a foreign word rather than from its meaning see DIRGE, SHIBBOLETH.)

[It, short for *pianoforte,* fr. *piano e forte* soft and loud, fr. *piano* soft (fr. LL *planus* smooth, graceful, fr. L, even, level, flat) + *e* and (fr. L *et*) + *forte* loud, strong (fr. L *fortis* strong); fr. the fact that its tones can be varied in loudness]

picayune The remarkable eating habits of the woodpecker, who drills holes in trees in his search for insects, are responsible for the derivation from *picus,* his Latin name, of a verb meaning 'pierce' or 'prick'. The derivative Provençal verb *pica* had a wide range of senses including 'to jingle or chime' as well as 'to prick'. This 'jingle' sense may have been responsible for the Provençal term *picaio* 'money', reflecting a time when coins were a relatively more prominent part of money, although another explanation would derive *picaio* from Latin *pecunia* 'wealth, property'. A small copper coin came to be called *picaioun,* and this appeared in French as *picaillon.* In nineteenth-century Louisiana, the French name, respelled in English as *picayune,* was transferred to the Spanish half-real piece, which was then in common use in some states of the American South. The *picayune* went the way of other small sums of money, and the word came to be used adjectivally (like *two-bit* or *twopenny*) to mean 'paltry'.

[F *picaillon* old copper coin of Piedmont, halfpence, fr. Prov *picaioun,* fr. *picaio* money, prob. fr. *pica* to strike, prick, sound, jingle (fr. — assumed — VL *piccare* to prick, pierce, fr. — assumed — *piccus* woodpecker, fr. L *picus*) + *-aio* -al (fr. L *-alia*)]

piecemeal See MEAL.
[ME *pece-mele,* fr. *pece* piece + *-mele* -meal]

pig   See SWINE.
  [ME *pigge*]

pigeon   Some animal names, especially those of birds, have been created through onomatopoeia, or imitation of sound. Since birdsongs are convenient ways of distinguishing the various species, they are often the source of the birds' names. The Romans used the noun *pipio* for a young bird from the sound of its shrill piping cries. In Middle French this became *pijon*, which was borrowed into Middle English as *pigeon*. Although pigeons generally coo, their young squab can be heard piping, especially when hungry.

Other birds whose names derived from the imitation of their characteristic songs include the *bobolink*, whose bubbling musical call is known over much of North and South America; the *bobwhite*, a favorite game bird of eastern and central United States; the *chickadee*, whose "chicka-dee-dee-dee" song enlivens the forests of North America; the *chiff-chaff*, a monotonously singing European warbler; the *chuck-will's-widow*, denizen of southern United States and a relative of the whippoorwill; the *cock*, whose "cock-a-doodle-doo" often serves as an alarm clock; the European *cuckoo*, whose call is suited for a less alarming kind of clock; the *hoopoe*, whose "hoo-hoo-hoo" call and handsome crest are familiar in Europe, Africa, and Asia; the *kiwi*, whose thin, piping cry can be heard in the swampy forests of New Zealand; and the *whippoorwill*, a North American bird more often heard than seen from nightfall to sunup. The chuck-will's-widow and the whippoorwill belong to a family of birds whose members are called *goatsuckers*. *Goatsucker* originated from the ancient belief that these widemouthed birds sucked milk from goats; actually they live by hunting for insects.

In addition to these birds, a few other creatures have had their names derived from imitations of characteristic sounds made by them. Examples include the *aye-aye*, a rodentlike lemur which agilely frolics in the trees of Madagascar; the *cricket*, whose chirping calls are produced by rubbing certain parts of its forewings together; the *katydid*, a grasshopper whose song "katy-did, katy-didn't" is also produced by rubbing its forewings together; and the *gecko*, a tropical reptile noted for its ability to run up walls and across ceilings. The name *grunt* is applied to a variety of tropical fishes that produce grunting noises when taken from the water.

  [ME *pejon, pijon, pigeon,* fr. MF *pijon* young bird, pigeon, fr. LL *pipion-, pipio* young bird, fr. L *pipire* to chirp; akin to L *pipare* to peep, chirp, of imit. origin like Gk *pipos, pippos* young bird, Skt *pippakā* a kind of bird]

piker   Missourians of the early and middle nineteenth century must have been an unprepossessing lot, to judge from some of the unflattering nicknames they acquired. As early as 1835 Missourians were referred to as *Pukes* or *Pukers*, for reasons that we do not now know. The term *puke* is known in Irish English as a term for a puny or unhealthy looking person; perhaps someone of Irish extraction hung the name on them. H. L. Mencken in the second Supplement to *The American Language* (1948) notes that there was at one time an attempt to explain away *Puke* as a misspelling or misprint for *Pike*. No one believed the explanation, however.

The association of *Pike* and *Piker* with Missourians seems to date from about the time of the 1849 Gold Rush. A county or two to the north of St. Louis on the Mississippi is Pike County, Missouri, and directly across the river from it is Pike County, Illinois. Mencken says that both Pike counties had a reputation for singularly backward yokels in "the early days." Mark Twain makes special mention in his prefatory note to *Huckleberry Finn* of four or five varieties of Pike County dialect that he used in the book. Hannibal, where Mark Twain grew up, was just two counties north of Pike County.

You can probably assume that the economic conditions in a locality noted for its unprepossessing yokels were not especially attractive, and when the Gold Rush started, many Pike Countyans headed for California to seek a better life. This migration was memorialized in folk songs like "Sweet Betsey from Pike":

> Oh don't you remember sweet Betsey from Pike,
> Who crossed the big mountains with her lover Ike,
> With two yoke of cattle, a large yellow dog,
> A tall Shanghai rooster, and one spotted hog;
> > Saying goodbye, Pike County,
> > Farewell for a while;
> > We'll come back again
> > When we've panned out our pile.
> —Carl Sandburg, *The American Songbag* (1927)

We have no way of knowing whether the unflattering characterization of Pike Countyans as yokels was deserved or not, and we have no way of finding out what incidents caused them to be despised by Californians. But we do know that for whatever reason, Californians developed a marked antipathy for Missourians. More than a decade later Mark Twain attests to the friction (his own aversion to Californians at that time sharpened by a border dispute between California and the Nevada territory):

> How I *hate* everything that looks, or tastes, or smells like California!— and how I hate everybody that loves the cursed State! Californians hate Missourians,—consequently I take great pains to let the public know that "Mark Twain" hails from there. I never let an opportunity slip to blow my horn for Missouri—*you bet*—as these rotten, lop-eared, whopper-jawed, jack-legged California abscesses say—*blast* them! —Mark Twain, letter, 11 April 1863

Californians expressed part of their dislike for Missourians by using *Pike* and *Piker*—which might well have been understood as mere geographical nicknames—as pejorative terms: an 1857 publication explained *Pike* as "a household word" in San Francisco used to designate persons with "a happy compound of verdancy and ruffianism."

From being a term for a Missourian or other immigrant to California exhibiting undesirable social characteristics, *piker* was broadened in use as a general term of contempt for many immigrants to California and later was applied, still pejoratively, to various kinds of small-time gamblers. Today it is most likely to be used of a person of mean and petty habits or outlook and to persons noted for their unwillingness to spend money or pay their fair share. The connection with Pike County, Missouri, is all but forgotten except by etymologists.

> All you have to do . . . is to stand in the street with an open bag marked, "Drop packages of money here. No checks or loose bills taken." You have a cop handy to club pikers who try to chip in post office orders and Canadian money, and that's all there is to New York
> —O. Henry, "Innocents of Broadway" in *The Gentle Grafter,* 1920

[Pike county, Missouri (thought to be the original home of many shiftless farmers who migrated to California) + E *-er*]

pilgrim   In Latin, the words *per* 'through' and *ager* 'land, field' were combined to form the adjective *pereger,* which was used to describe a person who is traveling abroad. From this adjective, the adverb *peregre* 'abroad' was derived, which in turn gave rise to the noun *peregrinus* 'a foreigner'.

From early Christian times it was the custom to undertake journeys to places of religious significance, and especially to Palestine and Rome. Such a journey or pilgrimage was called *peregrinatio* in Latin. These pilgrimages were made to venerate places made holy by the life of Christ, by the saints, or by miracles or apparitions. Through such veneration the Christian sought to remove the taints and penalties of sin. A person making such a pilgrimage was known as a *peregrinus,* which in Late Latin was altered (by dissimilation of the first *r* to *l*) to *pelegrinus.* Old French took this noun as *peligrin* (modern French *pèlerin*), which was borrowed into English around 1200 as *pelegrim, pilegrim,* becoming *pilgrim* in modern English.

In fact, during the Middle Ages pilgrimages were imposed as canonical punishments for certain crimes. The hardships of the journey made the pilgrimage a real penance. Pilgrimages also served to further international communication and to build up towns and roads. From the idea of the pilgrimages arose the idea of the Crusades and the religious orders founded to care for the pilgrims.

Many pilgrims to the Holy Land were anxious to bring home proof of their pilgrimage. This usually consisted of an emblem of crossed palm leaves taken from trees around Jerusalem. A pilgrim displaying such an emblem was called a *palmer.* Palmers are mentioned in the works of Chaucer, Spenser, Shakespeare, and Scott, among others.

The Puritans who journeyed across the Atlantic in 1620 to establish their own religious colony in Plymouth, Massachusetts, did not call themselves Pilgrims at first. It was later that William Bradford, one of their number and governor of the colony, referred to them (in 1630) as "pilgrimes." Cotton Mather also used the term in his *Magnalia Christi Americana* (an ecclesiastical history of New England, 1702). At the 1820 bicentennial of

Plymouth, Daniel Webster spoke eloquently of "our homage to our Pilgrim Fathers," and this name has since become common usage.

The Latin *peregrinus* also gave rise to the verb *peregrinari* 'to travel abroad, wander about', which led to the noun *peregrinatio*, originally meaning 'a traveling abroad'. In the twelfth century, French took this noun as *pérégrination*. English either borrowed the French word as *peregrination* or took it directly from the Latin and used it for 'an act of traveling or traversing'.

The name *peregrine falcon* is an anglicization of the Medieval Latin *falco peregrinus*, first used by Albertus Magnus in 1225. This 'pilgrim falcon' was so called because its young were caught while on their passage or 'pilgrimage' to their breeding place, and not, like other birds of its kind, taken while still in their nests, which were usually inaccessibly located in crags.

[ME, fr. OF *peligrin*, fr. LL *pelegrinus*, alter. of L *peregrinus* foreigner, fr. *peregre* abroad, fr. *pereger* being abroad, fr. *per* through + *agr-, ager* land, field]

pinnacle   See PANACHE.
[ME *pinacle*, fr. MF, fr. LL *pinnaculum* gable, small wing, dim. of L *pinna* battlement, feather, wing, alter. of *penna* feather, wing]

pioneer   In the game of chess, the pawns are the least valuable and most numerous pieces. They are the foot soldiers of the king's army. Their name *pawn* is derived from a Medieval Latin word *pedo*, which means 'foot soldier'. *Pedo*, a derivative of Latin *pes*, 'foot', had occasionally been used as an epithet for a person with broad feet; but in the Middle Ages, as a word for a foot soldier, it became much more common. *Pedo* is also the ancestor of *peon* and *pioneer*. Its descendants, Portuguese *peão* and French *pion*, both mean 'footman' or 'servant' as well as 'foot soldier'. The English borrowing *peon* was first used in India in these same senses in the seventeenth century. Two centuries later Englishmen in Spanish America called the working classes *peons:* the Spanish *peon* has the same meanings as its Portuguese and French cognates.

The *pioneers* Americans are most familiar with are people like Daniel Boone who opened up the American West. But a *pioneer*, like a *pawn* and a *peon*, was originally a foot soldier. Old French *peonier* was used at first for any foot soldier, but by the Middle French period the word (now spelled *pionnier*) had come to designate a particular type of foot soldier, a member of a unit that marched ahead of the army preparing the way by excavation and construction—an early Corps of Engineers, in effect. Because of the *pionnier's* position in advance of the main body of the army, anyone who helps to develop something new, to prepare a way for others to follow, came to be called a *pionnier*. English borrowed the word from French both in its military meaning and in its more general sense.

[MF *pionier, pionnier*, fr. OF *peonier* foot soldier, fr. *peon, pion* foot soldier (fr. ML *pedon-, pedo*) + *-ier* -er]

piquant See PUNGENT.
   [MF, fr. pres. part. of *piquer* to prick, sting, nettle, pique]

pit bull   There were 29 fatalities from dog attacks in the U.S. between 1983 and 1987; 14 victims were children under the age of six. Those grim statistics were responsible for a considerable public outcry. An alarming fact that swiftly became the focus of attention was that one type of dog, the pit bull, was the cause of 21 of the 29 deaths. The resulting publicity was so intensely negative that a few cities considered banning pit bulls outright. Many places contemplated legislation that would force owners to keep the dogs under strict control. But the threatened ordinances soon bogged down in a welter of confusion because of the difficulty in defining precisely what a *pit bull* was.
   The term has been applied to three different dog breeds: the American Staffordshire terrier, the Staffordshire bull terrier, and the roman-nosed bull terrier. In addition, *pit bull* is used as a generic term for non-purebred dogs that conform to a general type. The four groups resemble one another in several ways. All are compact, muscular, medium-sized dogs with powerful jaws and a courageous, tenacious spirit. All were originally bred to fight—first bulls, then badgers, and finally each other. By the early 1800s the cruel sport of bull-baiting, which involved setting specially bred dogs on a tethered bull, was disappearing, and dog-fighting evolved to take its place. Instead of being unleashed on bulls, dogs were trained to attack each other in pits, constructed so that crowds could watch and wager on the outcome. Violent action combined with the lure of betting made dog-fighting a popular sport, first in England and then in the United States. The dogs used were bulldog-terrier crosses, and were originally called "bull-and-terrier," "half and half," "pit dog," and "pit bullterrier." Over time, since they were being bred for a specific purpose, the dogs began to conform to a general standard. As interest in dog-fighting waned, owners became interested in showing their dogs. In 1935, The Kennel Club of England gave these dogs a breed standard and the name of Staffordshire bull terrier.
   Meanwhile fighting dogs had also been bred in the United States. Here they were known by various names, among them "pit dog," "pit bull terrier," and "Yankee terrier." In 1935, the same year that the Staffordshire bull terrier was recognized as a breed in England, the American Kennel Club bestowed breed status on American dogs, calling them the Staffordshire terrier. The dogs were heavier than their British counterparts and are now considered to be a different breed. In 1972 the name was revised to American Staffordshire terrier. Another ruling body, the United Kennel Club, had recognized essentially the same breed as the American Staffordshire terrier several years earlier. The canine movie star "Pete," who sported a ring around one eye and appeared in the *Our Gang* comedy series, was registered as an American pit bull terrier. So, confusingly enough, what is called an American Staffordshire terrier by one ruling body is called an American pit bull terrier by another.
   Thus two slightly different breeds, both originally bred for fighting, developed on opposite sides of the Atlantic (and, as we have seen, developed

two different names in the United States). During the 1860s, the British dog, now referred to as the Staffordshire bull terrier, was crossed with a white terrier. The result was a stylish white fighting dog that came to be called the "bull terrier." The bull terrier is the third of the purebred trio that are sometimes called "pit bulls."

Owners of these three breeds strongly object to having their dogs referred to as "pit bulls." They are quick to point out that most of the dogs responsible for fatal attacks on people have not been representatives of their breeds, but dogs of mixed ancestry bred for fighting. Dog fighting is still considered a sport by some in the United States, although there are widespread legal sanctions against it. Pit bulls bred for this blood sport are strongly marked by gameness, and, some would say, viciousness. The pit bull has recently become a kind of status symbol in inner cities, where the dog is apparently both admired for its fearless attitude and utilized as a personal guard dog. It is these dogs, whether they are kept in the city or in rural areas, that are predominantly responsible for human fatalities caused by so-called "pit bulls." It is also these dogs that many places have sought to either ban or control. But because the term *pit bull* can be applied to three purebred breeds, as well as to dogs of mixed ancestry bred as fighting and guard dogs, that has proved very difficult.

Lately the term has begun to acquire an extended meaning. Since the dogs are noted for their fighting ability, *pit bull* is sometimes applied to people who seem to be spoiling for a fight. Thus one particularly contentious television interviewer has been described as the "pit bull of talk-show hosts."

See also BULLDOG.

plagiarism The Latin noun *plaga* denoted a hunting net or snare used for capturing game. The netting of such animals was termed *plagium*. By extension, this word was also used for the crime of kidnapping children or freemen and selling them as slaves, the kidnapper being called a *plagiarius*. We know that by the time of the poet Martial, who died about A.D. 103, *plagiarius* was also being used to refer to a literary thief or plagiarist.

The Latin *plagiarius* became *plagiary* in seventeenth-century English and was used for 'kidnapper' (a sense now obsolete), 'plagiarist' (now considered archaic), and 'plagiarism' (still occasionally found in modern English). The noun *plagiarism* itself was formed from *plagiary* and was used to denote 'the practice of stealing the ideas or words of others and passing them off as one's own'. The verb *plagiarize* was also formed from *plagiary*, being first used early in the eighteenth century.

[earlier *plagiary* (fr. L *plagiarius* kidnapper, plagiarist, fr. *plagium* netting of game — fr. *plaga* hunting net — + -*arius* -ary) + -*ism*]

plaintiff See JUDGE.

[ME *plaintif,* fr. MF, fr. *plaintif* lamenting, complaining, fr. *plaint* (fr. L *planctus,* fr. *planctus,* past part. of *plangere* to strike, beat, beat one's breast, lament) + -*if* -ive]

planet In studying the sky, ancient astronomers observed that while most of the stars maintain fixed relative positions there are a few heavenly bodies that quite obviously change their positions in relation to each other and to the greater number of fixed stars. The most notable of these, of course, are the sun and the moon; but five others were observed that seemed to revolve about the Earth at different rates. These five—Mercury, Venus, Mars, Jupiter, and Saturn—were called by the Greeks *asteres planētai*, 'wandering stars', or simply *planētai*, 'wanderers'. The corresponding Latin term was *stellae errantes*, which also means 'wandering stars'; but Late Latin borrowed the Greek term in the plural form *planetae*, the singular of which was *planeta*. Through Old French, Middle English borrowed this word in the fourteenth century to give us the modern *planet*. An occurrence of the word in an Old English treatise of the eleventh century shows clearly that at the time it was not considered an English word: "Tha steorran the man hæt planete on lyden." (Those stars that are called *planets* in Latin.) In more recent centuries not only has the word become completely anglicized but three more *planets* have been discovered, Uranus in the eighteenth century, Neptune in the nineteenth, and Pluto in the twentieth. See also EXTRAVAGANT.

[ME *planete*, fr. OF, fr. LL *planeta*, modif. (influenced by Gk *planētēs* wanderer) of Gk *planēt-*, *planēs*, lit., wanderer, fr. *planasthai* to wander; prob. akin to ON *flana* to rush around]

plaudit The Latin verb *plaudere*, of uncertain origin, meant 'to strike with a flat surface', or specifically 'to clap'. In its composed form *applaudere* (from the common prefix *ad-* plus *plaudere*), it is the straightforward ancestor of our verb *applaud*, via the usual expedient of dropping the infinitive ending.

Plaudere also entered our language in a much less usual guise, retaining an inflectional ending, in this case *-ite*, the inflection for plural imperative. The inspiration for this offbeat borrowing was the practice of Roman playwrights of exhorting the audience to applaud at the end of a play. "Spectatores, bene valete, plaudite atque exsurgite!" cries Plautus (as much as to say, "You've been a great audience—now get up on your feet and clap!"). The first known English reflex of this usage is in a 1567 translation by Thomas Drant of Horace's *Art of Poetry*, recorded in the Oxford English Dictionary:

"That when the Epilogue is done   we may with franke intent
  After the plaudite strike up   our plausible assent."

Notice that *plaudite* here has three syllables. But by 1624 it had been shortened to *plaudit*. Nowadays the word usually occurs in the plural and simply means 'commendation', the specific connection to the theater having receded into the background.

Latin verbs often had different stems in different tenses, rather like English *write, wrote, written,* and in the case of *plaudere* there was a form, *plodere*, in the infinitival/present-tense system. English, with its appetite for Latin borrowing, has preserved several of these variant stems, but their connection is no longer transparent to the average English speaker. In Latin, after the prefix *ex-*, *plodere* was more commonly used, yielding *explodere* 'to drive from the stage' (by clapping and whistling), and by extension 'to reject'. From this we borrowed our word *explode*, at first in the Latin senses and later in the modern sense of violently expansive detonation. (*Implode* was not directly derived from Latin, but formed in modern English as an analog of *explode*.) Again in Latin, the participial stem *plaus-* formed *plausibilis*, 'applause-worthy', which was borrowed into English in this sense in the sixteenth century. The resulting *plausible* suffered a decline in fortune as it came to be applied to arguments seemingly commendable or convincing—but only seemingly. (*Specious*, a Latin-derived word which we now use in exactly this sense, traversed a similar path, from 'pleasing to view' to 'superficially or deceptively beautiful' to 'having only the appearance of being right or proper'. Etymologically it means 'beautiful'.) *Plausible* has recovered somewhat, being applied to arguments that may well be correct insofar as the speaker knows, though they may not ultimately prove "applause-worthy."

[L *plaudite* applaud!, 2nd pers. pl. imper. of *plaudere* to applaud]

plausible   See PLAUDIT.

[L *plausibilis* deserving applause, pleasing, acceptable, fr. *plausus* (past part. of *plaudere* to applaud) + *-ibilis* -ible]

plumb   See PLUMBER.

[ME *plom, plum, plumbe,* fr. (assumed) OF *plomb* lead, plummet (whence MF *plomb*), fr. OF *plon* lead, fr. L *plumbum*, of non-IE origin; prob. akin to the source of Gk *molybdos* lead]

plumber   The symbol for the chemical element lead is Pb, abbreviated from Latin *plumbum*, meaning 'lead'. Through Old French *plon* the root of the Latin form was borrowed into Middle English as the name of a weight (originally lead) attached to a line and used to indicate a vertical direction, or a weight of lead or other material used for various other purposes, such as a mariner's sounding lead or a fishline sinker. From the use of *plumb* and *plumb line* to determine or indicate a vertical direction, *plumb* developed the adverbial senses of 'vertically', 'exactly', 'completely', and even 'immediately', as well as the related adjectival senses of 'downright' and 'complete'. From the use of *plumb* as a sounding lead is derived the verb *plumb*, meaning not only literally 'to measure the depth of something by sounding', but also more figuratively 'to ascertain the quality of something by examining it minutely and critically'. Because the pipes and fixtures that assist the distribution and use of water in a building were formerly often made of lead, this apparatus came to be called *plumbing*. A person who installs, repairs, or maintains such fittings, then, is naturally called a *plumber*, from Latin *plumbarius*, because originally plumbers were primarily workers in lead. In many places in Europe archaeologists have unearthed lead pipes surviving from Roman times which reveal that Roman plumbers had considerable skill at their trade and that many buildings even then were equipped with running water.

The verb *sound* as used above is not the word derived from Latin *sonare* meaning 'to make a noise or sound'. It is from Middle English *sounden*, from Middle French *sonder*. *Sonder* is of disputed origin. One theory posits an unattested Latin form *subundare*, from *sub-* 'under' plus *unda* 'wave', as the source. Another would derive it from Middle French *sonde* 'sounding line' and derive *sonde* from some Germanic source. It is usually not possible to specify exactly the form of an etymon in the dialects of Germanic that influenced French, but comparisons can be made to similar forms in related Germanic languages such as Old English, where we find *sundlīne* 'sounding line', and Old Norse *sund* 'swimming, strait, sound'. Thus the Germanic theory seems plausible.

[ME *plummer, plumber,* fr. MF *plommier, plombier,* fr. L *plumbarius,* fr. *plumbarius,* adj., of or relating to lead, fr. *plumbum* lead + *-arius* -ary]

poignant See PUNGENT.
[ME *pugnaunt, poinaunt,* fr. MF *poignant,* pres. part. of *poindre,* fr. L *pungere* to prick, pierce, sting]

point See PUNGENT.
[ME, partly fr. OF *point* prick, sting, small spot, dot, item, point in time or space, fr. L *punctum* small hole, spot, point in time or space, fr. neut. of *punctus,* past part. of *pungere* to prick, sting, pierce; partly fr. OF *pointe* sharp end, fr. (assumed) VL *puncta,* fr. L, fem. of *punctus,* past part.]

poison See VENOM.
[ME *poisoun, poison,* fr. OF *poison* drink, philter, poisonous drink, poison, fr. L *potion-, potio* drink, fr. *potus* (past part. of *potare* to drink) + *-ion-, -io* -ion]

pokey See CLINK.
[alter. of earlier *pogie* workhouse, of unknown origin]

polecat See FERRET.
[ME *polcat,* perh. fr. MF *poul, pol* cock + ME *cat;* prob. fr. its habit of feeding on poultry]

pontiff See CARDINAL.
[F *pontif,* fr. L *pontific-, pontifex,* lit., bridgemaker, fr. *pont-, pons* bridge + *-fic-, -fex* (fr. *facere* to make, do)]

pope See CARDINAL.
[ME, fr. OE *pāpa,* fr. LL *papa,* fr. Gk *pappas, papas* title of bishops, lit., papa]

popinjay   Arabic *babghā'*, with its variants *bab(b)aghā'*, is the apparent ancestor of many of Europe's names for the parrot: Germans call the bird *Papagei*, Italians *pappagallo*, Spaniards *papagayo*, Portuguese *papagaio*, Danes *papegøje*. *Popinjay*, borrowed in Middle English from Middle French *papegai*, is the distant descendant of *babghā'*. (French *papegai* is not obsolete like English *popinjay* in the sense of 'parrot', but it has been largely replaced in contemporary French by the more recent *perroquet*.)

To be compared with a parrot or popinjay in the Middle Ages, when the bird was a beautiful rarity, was a high compliment. John Lydgate in 1430 addressed the Blessed Virgin Mary in this way: "O popinjay, plumed with al clennesse." But when the bird became more common, his coat could be considered merely gaudy, his mimicry vulgar. The modern popinjay is a vulgarly ostentatious person. For other words that have the intrusive *n* see HARBINGER, SCAVENGER.

[ME *papejay, papengay*, fr. MF *papegai, papejai*, fr. Ar *babghā'*]

porcelain   See PORK.

[MF *porcelaine* cowrie shell, porcelain (fr. the resemblance of its finish to the surface of the shell), fr. It *porcellana*, fr. *porcello* little pig, vulva (fr. L *porcellus*, dim. of *porcus* pig, vulva) + *-ana* -an; fr. the resemblance of the shell to the female pudenda]

porcupine   See PORK.

[ME *porke despyne, porkepin*, fr. MF *porc espin*, fr. OIt *porcospino*, fr. L *porcus* pig + *spina* thorn, prickle]

pork   *Pork*, the English word for the meat of swine, is a French loanword (Middle English *pork*, from Old French *porc*, 'pig'), a descendant of Latin *porcus*, 'pig'. The native English cognate is *farrow*, 'litter of pigs', a noun created by functional shift from the verb *farrow*, but ultimately derived from the Old English noun *fearh*, 'young pig'. But *pork* has other modern English kin. The *porpoise* was called, in classical Latin, *porcus marinus*, 'pig of the sea'. In Medieval Latin he was sometimes referred to as *porcus piscis*, 'pig fish'. The Middle French form *porpeis* or *porpois* became Middle English *porpeys* or *porpoys*. The *porcupine* is etymologically, like the hedgehog, simply a prickly pig, his name a derivative of *porcus* and Latin *spina*, 'thorn'. The variant *porpentine* was popular in the sixteenth and seventeenth centuries. Shakespeare's Hamlet was told by his father's ghost: "I could a tale unfold whose lightest word/ Would . . . make . . . each particular hair to stand an end/ Like quills upon the fretful porpentine."

Porcelain too is a derivative of Latin *porcus*. In classical Latin the word *porcus* was occasionally used as an informal term for the vulva (Greek *choiros*, 'young pig', was employed similarly). This double meaning survived in Italian *porcello* (literally 'little pig'). The side of a cowrie shell that contains the opening looks somewhat like a vulva, so the shell was called *porcellana* in Italian. The ceramic ware called *porcelain* took its name from the cowrie shell, whose shiny surface it resembles.

For other words that owe their being to the lowly pig see SWINE.

[ME *pork, porke,* fr. OF *porc* pig, hog, fr. L *porcus*]

porpoise   See PORK.
[ME *porpeys, porpoys,* fr. MF *porpeis, porpois,* fr. ML *porcopiscis,* fr. L *porcus* pig + *piscis* fish]

porridge   See HARBINGER.
[alter. (prob. influenced by ME *porray,* a kind of pottage, fr. MF *poree,* fr. ML *porrata,* fr. L *porrum* leek + LL *-ata* -ada) of *pottage,* fr. ME *potage,* fr. OF, fr. *pot* pot (of Gmc origin; akin to MD *pot,* OE *pott*) + *-age* -age]

porringer   See HARBINGER.
[alter. of *pottinger,* fr. ME *potinger,* alter. of *poteger,* fr. AF *potageer,* fr. MF *potager,* adj., of or relating to pottage, fr. *potage* pottage]

portmanteau   See JABBERWOCKY.
[MF *portemanteau,* fr. *porter* to carry (fr. L *portare*) + *manteau* mantle, fr. L *mantellum*]

posh   We do not know the precise origin of the adjective *posh,* meaning 'elegant, fashionable', but nearly everyone else seems to. Every year we get dozens of letters informing us that *posh* comes from the first letters of the phrase "port out, starboard home," which designated the most desirable accommodations on a steamship voyage from England to India and back. The most elaborate version of the story associates the practice with the Peninsular and Oriental Steam Navigation Company, which from 1842 to 1970 was the major steamship carrier of passengers and mail between England and India. The P. & O. route went through the Suez Canal and the Red Sea. The cabins on the port side on the way to India got the morning sun and had the rest of the day to cool off, while starboard ones got the afternoon sun, and were still quite hot at bedtime. On the return trip, the opposite was true. The cooler cabins, therefore, were the more desirable and were reserved for the most important and richest travelers. Their tickets were stamped *P.O.S.H.* to indicate these accommodations— in large violet letters, according to one recollection. This account of the origin of *posh* was even used in advertising by the P. & O. in the 1960s.

But the story won't float. The first appearance of the acronymic origin in print that we know of was a letter to the editor of the London *Times Literary Supplement* of 17 October 1935. The writer, an Englishman, wanted to enlighten the editors of the Oxford English Dictionary Supplement, who had marked its origin obscure; he identified *port out, starboard home* as "an American shipping term describing the best cabins." Why this phrase described the best cabins he does not say. The earliest association of the acronym with the P. & O. seems to come from *A Hundred Year His-*

tory of the P. & O., by Boyd Cable, which was published in 1937. The author calls it a "tale." And as late as 1962 the librarian of the P. & O. was unable to find any evidence that *P.O.S.H.* was actually stamped on anything.

The most detailed and colorful account of the acronym in our files is a letter from a retired mariner who recalled in considerable detail (including the violet letters) how in 1913 he had seen such a P. & O. round-trip ticket in the possession of a man returning to Hong Kong. He had missed his P. & O. ship in Italy and was thus a passenger on the same ship (of a different steamship line) as the letter writer. This man, a European official employed by the Chinese government, had booked his trip in Hong Kong and was thus making the round-trip in a direction opposite to that of the English gentry on their way to the Raj. According to the theory, his ticket should have been stamped *S.O.P.H.* to assure him cool accommodations. But the writer recalls a violet *P.O.S.H.*

And come to think of it, why would the P. & O. clerks have to stamp anything on the tickets? Surely they must have known the location of every cabin by its number. We therefore conclude that if the practice of preferring cabins on the cooler side of the ship did exist—and it certainly seems reasonable—no acronymic *P.O.S.H.* (or its unmentioned opposite *S.O.P.H.*) was necessary on the tickets for such accommodations. And no evidence of its use has yet appeared. We further conclude, then, that the acronymic theory of the origin of the adjective *posh* is simply a modern invention.

There are other theories to account for *posh*, one of which has been accepted by a few dictionaries. This explanation connects *posh* with English university slang from around the turn of the century. The earliest example of *posh* in print comes from a cartoon in *Punch*, 25 September 1918. It shows an RAF officer talking to his mother and has this bit of dialogue: "Oh, yes, Mater, we had a posh time of it down there."—"Whatever do you mean by 'posh', Gerald?"—"Don't you know? It's slang for 'swish'!" This exchange is not incompatible with an origin in university slang, but earlier evidence is lacking.

The most tantalizing earlier connection is in a 1903 story by P. G. Wodehouse in his *Tales of St Austin's*. In the story a character remarks of a bright yellow waistcoat that it is "quite the most push thing of the sort at Cambridge." Unfortunately for *posh*, Wodehouse spelled it *push*. In the much later Penguin paperback edition of the stories, the editor, Richard Usborne, changed *push* to *posh*. When queried, he replied that he suspected the original *push* to have been a misprint. If it was not a misprint, he thought it might have been a mistake by Wodehouse, who had never attended a university and who had made a number of small factual errors about Oxford and Cambridge in other stories. If Usborne's surmise is correct, *posh* would have been university slang. But it is only a surmise, and we are left with the intractable *push* originally printed.

Another possible source is a turn-of-the-century noun *posh* meaning 'a dandy'. This meaning is listed in two slang dictionaries of the period but without corroborative evidence. The Oxford English Dictionary Supplement could find nothing better for the sense than the nickname of a fisherman friend of Edward FitzGerald and a character Murray Posh, described as "a swell," in an 1892 novel. We don't know if this *posh* was ever used in print as a generic word.

[origin unknown]

Potemkin village   In 1980, at the time of the Olympic Games in Moscow, some of the Western journalists observed that among Westerners there was an eerie sense that somehow the Soviet capital had been transformed into one vast "Potemkin village." In other words, the festive, prosperous Moscow that was being presented to the outside world was but a deceptive facade erected to hide the dreary reality behind it. The use of the expression *Potemkin village* to characterize the facade has a particular etymological appropriateness. According to a legend that has attained the status of fact in the popular imagination, Russia is where the whole notion of a Potemkin village started.

Grigory Aleksandrovich Potemkin (1739–1791) was a prince, a politician, the commander in chief of the Russian army, the lover of Catherine the Great, and for seventeen years the most powerful man in the Russian empire. His reputation for extravagance, licentiousness, and even magnanimity inspired the rise of a body of anecdotes about him. One of the undisputed peaks of his long, illustrious career was his masterminding of Russia's conquest of the Crimea, a feat accomplished in 1783. Four years later Potemkin arranged for Catherine, his beloved empress, to take a grand tour of the newly annexed territory. Part of the empress's official acceptance of her new provinces consisted of dedicating new towns bearing her name. Accompanying the Russian court on this glorious junket were the Emperor of Austria, the King of Poland, and a swarm of diplomats, one of whom, a certain Helbig from Saxony, is the originator of a Potemkin anecdote. According to Helbig's account, Potemkin, in order to impress Catherine with the prosperity of her new acquisitions, erected whole villages along her traveling route. Fortunately, she was able to view these villages only from a distance, for they were mere facades.

Though the story of the sham villages must be regarded as apocryphal, it has been retold often since first coming to light. Usually it has found a receptive audience, and it has given us the expression "Potemkin village" for any imposing facade or display intended to obscure or hide an undesirable condition or fact.

[after Grigori A. *Potemkin* †1791 Russ. statesman; fr. the story that Potemkin once had impressive fake villages built along a route that Catherine the Great was to travel]

potion   See VENOM.
[ME *pocioun*, fr. MF *potion*, fr. L *potion-*, *potio* potion, drink, fr. *potus* (past part. of *potare* to drink) + *-ion-*, *-io* -ion]

potpourri   A *potpourri* may be in common usage 'a pleasant or interesting miscellany or hodgepodge', but etymologically it is 'a putrid pot'. The original French *pot pourri* was a stew made of a variety of meats and vegetables cooked together. This was a traditional Spanish dish borrowed by the French, whose name for it is a loan translation of the Spanish *olla podrida*. The term for a mixed stew was later applied to other mixtures. A fragrant mixture of dried flower petals, herbs, and spices is called a *potpourri*. In music, a *potpourri* is a medley of melodies performed in succession. In literature, it is a collection of miscellaneous literary productions. The word is now used, in fact, for almost any kind of miscellaneous assortment. Ted Townsend, writing for the *New Republic* for 21 March 1955, described "the old frontier" as "a potpourri of Virginians and varmints, Caucasian nobles and Chinese coolies." All of these senses of *potpourri* are current in both English and French.

Just why the stew designated *olla podrida* or *potpourri* was deemed "rotten" is not very clear. One explanation advanced for the name of the Spanish version is that its cooking over a slow fire was considered comparable to excessive maturation.

English also borrowed *olla podrida* directly from the Spanish. Like *potpourri*, English *olla podrida* is used to mean 'a heterogeneous mixture', but it is a less common word. Synonymous *hodgepodge* and *gallimaufry*, which now refer to any mixture of unrelated things, were also originally mixed dishes. See also HODGEPODGE.

[F *pot pourri* (trans. of Sp *olla podrida*), fr. *pot* pot + *pourri* rotten, past part. of *pourrir* to rot, fr. L *putrescere*, incho. of *putrēre* to be rotten, fr. *puter, putris* rotten]

precocious   Anyone who knew only the origin of *precocious* and not its current meaning would understand "precocious plant" as describing a parboiled vegetable and "precocious child" as describing, well, something too horrible to contemplate. The ultimate source of this adjective is the Latin verb *coquere*, 'to cook'. In combination with the prefix *prae-* 'before', it forms *praecoquere*, which can mean either 'to boil beforehand' or 'to ripen fully'. It is the second sense, of course, that is reflected in *precocious*. The related adjective in Latin is *praecox*, which has the sense 'ripe before its time, premature', and which still has some use in English medical parlance in the term *dementia praecox*, an old synonym of *schizophrenia* that translates literally as 'premature madness'. *Praecox* was adopted into English as *precocious* in the middle of the seventeenth century. Its earliest use related to plants, applying specifically to plants that flower or set fruit before bearing leaves. Almost as old is its use in describing children who display unusual maturity at an early age.

[L *praecoc-, praecox* early ripening, premature, precocious (fr. *prae-* + *-coc-, -cox*, fr. *coquere* to cook, ripen) + E *-ious*]

prefer   See VICAR.
[ME *preferren*, fr. MF *preferer*, fr. L *praeferre* to bear before, put before, prefer, fr. *prae-* pre- + *ferre* to bear, carry]

prelate   See VICAR.
[ME *prelat*, fr. OF, fr. ML *praelatus*, fr. L (suppletive past part. of *prae-*

ferre to prefer), fr. *prae-* pre- + *latus,* suppletive past part. of *ferre* to bear]

premonition See MONSTER.
[MF, fr. LL *praemonition-, praemonitio,* fr. L *praemonitus* (past part. of *praemonēre* to warn in advance, fr. *prae-* pre- + *monēre* to warn) + *-ion-, -io* -ion]

presbyter See CATHOLIC, PRIEST.
[LL, presbyter, elder, fr. Gk *presbyteros*]

Presbyterian See PRIEST.
[*presbytery* + *-an*]

presbytery See PRIEST.
[ME *presbytory,* fr. LL *presbyterium* group of presbyters, office of a presbyter, presbytery (part of a church where the clergy sit), fr. Gk *presbyterion* group of presbyters, office of a presbyter, fr. *presbyteros* presbyter, elder]

prescribe See SCRIVENER.
[ME *prescriben* to hold or possess by right of prescription, fr. ML *prescribere* to claim by right of prescription, fr. L *praescribere* to write at the beginning, order, direct, prescribe, fr. *prae-* pre- + *scribere* to write; in several senses directly fr. L *praescribere*]

prestige See KUDOS.
[F, fr. LL *praestigium,* irreg. fr. L *praestigiae* (pl.) conjurer's tricks, alter. of (assumed) L *praestrigiae,* fr. L *praestringere* to bind, tie up, blind, fr. *prae-* pre- + *stringere* to draw tight]

pretext Latin *texere* meant 'to weave'; a literal reflex of this sense shows up in English *textile.* A derivative *textura* meant either 'weaving' or 'structure so woven, web', and by extension 'structure' in general; from this comes our word *texture.* Another derivative, *textus,* underwent a richer evolution. Concretely it again meant 'style of weaving' or 'thing woven', and further 'structure'. A crucial move in the development of its semantics was then the application of *textus* to the "weaving" of words, to the fabric of a literary passage. In the Christian period *textus* came to be applied above all to Holy Scripture, thus paralleling the case of *Bible,* which etymologically simply means 'book' (see VOLUME). This sense of *textus* is also the sense first attested for the French descendant, *texte,* and for a time it was also used in English, which borrowed *text* from French. Today, however, the sense of *text* is any body of written or printed matter or the wording of such matter.

Another curious sense development occurred in the case of the derived Latin verb *praetexere,* formed with the prefix *prae-* (source of English *pre-*), whose most basic and concrete meaning was 'in front'. *Praetexere* meant 'to edge or border', then 'to screen or clothe'. By a metaphorical extension parallel to what happened with our *facade* and *front,* the derived noun *praetextus* came to mean 'appearance or outward show'. This is the source of our word *pretext* 'a deliberately deceptive excuse or pretense'. The semantic extension recalls the similar metaphor in the term *cover-up.*

One further prefixed Latin weaving term entered English with metaphorical signification. Apparently from the combination of *sub-,* literally 'under', and *tela* 'woven thing, cloth', Latin had *subtilis,* literally 'finely woven' and by extension 'delicate, precise'. This entered English as *subtile* and (now more commonly) *subtle.* The sense has further evolved with us so that now *subtle* typically connotes not so much exactitude as a hard-to-seize delicacy of expression or understatement.

[L *praetextus,* fr. *praetextus,* past part. of *praetexere* to weave in front, fringe, adorn, assign as a pretext, fr. *prae-* pre- + *texere* to weave]

pretzel   *Pretzels* were most likely introduced into the United States during the nineteenth century by German immigrants, for the word, derived from German *brezel,* is first recorded in English in Noah Porter's 1879 Supplement to his revision of Noah Webster's American Dictionary of the English Language. The familiar knot-shaped pretzel has been known, at least in Germanic countries, for centuries, as is evidenced by its appearance in a painting of *The Fight between Carnival and Lent* by the sixteenth-century Flemish artist Pieter Brueghel the Elder. The origins of the pretzel, however, are certainly a good deal earlier, for the Old High German form *brezitella* is closely related to Italian *bracciatello,* 'ring-shaped bun'. We may assume with some confidence, therefore, the existence of a common Medieval Latin source *brachiatellum,* from Latin *brachiatus,* 'having branches like arms'. Apparently the pretzel is so called because of the similarity between its knot shape and a pair of folded arms.

[G *brezel,* fr. OHG *brezitella,* fr. (assumed) ML *brachiatellum* (whence It *bracciatello* ring-shaped bun), fr. L *brachiatus* having branches like arms (fr. *brachium* arm + *-atus* -ate) + *-ellum* -el; perh. fr. the likeness in shape to a pair of folded arms]

priest   In the Greek New Testament a religious leader or officer was termed a *presbyteros,* meaning 'an elder'. This Greek word was taken into Late Latin as *presbyter.* In the second century, local congregations were governed by bishops, presbyters, and deacons. As the work of the bishops increased, they assigned more duties, such as the administration of some sacraments, to their presbyters. The word *presbyter* was used instead of *sacerdos,* meaning 'priest', because the latter was used to refer to a pagan priest or to a Jewish priest in translations of the Old Testament.

In Old English, the Latin *presbyter* was usually rendered as *prēost,* while *sacerdos* became *sacerd.* By the end of the Old English period, however, *sacerd* had fallen into disuse, and *prēost* was generally used for any religious minister, Christian, Jewish, or pagan.

In Middle English, *prēost* gradually came to be spelled *preist,* which became *priest* in the sixteenth century. This continues to be the title of a clergyman in the Roman Catholic, Anglican, and Eastern Orthodox churches, although the Anglican church also uses the term *presbyter*. The *Presbyterian* church, established in the sixteenth century by John Calvin, was so named because each congregation is governed by a group of elected presbyters or elders. A *presbytery* is a ruling body within the Presbyterian church. It is also the part of a church reserved for officiating clergymen.

[ME *prest, preist,* fr. OE *prēost,* modif. of LL *presbyter,* fr. Gk *presbyteros,* priest, elder, older, fr. compar. of *presbys* old, fr. a prehistoric compound whose first constituent is akin to Gk *paros* before, OE *first* period, interval, delay, OHG *frist,* ON *frest* period, interval, delay, Gk *pro* before, ahead and whose second constituent is akin to Gk *bous* head of cattle; basic meaning: leader of the herd]

private   See IDIOT.

[ME *privat,* fr. L *privatus* apart from the state, deprived of office, of or belonging to oneself, private, fr. past part. of *privare* to deprive, release, fr. *privus* single, private, set apart, for himself; akin to L *pro* for]

profane   See FANATIC.

[ME *prophane,* fr. MF, fr. L *profanus,* fr. *pro-* before + *fanum* temple]

profusion   See ABUNDANCE.

[L *profusion-, profusio,* fr. *profusus* (past part. of *profundere* to pour forth) + *-ion-, -io* -ion]

propaganda   European explorations in America, Africa, and the Far East opened new opportunities for the Catholic Church in her mission to evangelize the world. During the sixteenth century, however, missionary activity was controlled mainly by Spain and Portugal, and Rome was not happy with this. Pope Gregory XV strongly felt the need to centralize the administration of missionary activity within the Holy See itself. To this end, on 22 June 1622 he issued the bull "Inscrutabili Divinae," by which the Congregation for the Propagation of the Faith *(Congregatio de propaganda fide)* was instituted. Informally it was simply referred to as Propaganda and originally consisted of thirteen cardinals, two prelates, and a secretary. Propaganda was charged with the supreme direction and administration of the ecclesiastical affairs in non-Catholic countries. The word *propaganda* itself is a form of the gerundive of the Latin verb *propagare* 'to propagate'.

This ecclesiastical use of *Propaganda* was known in eighteenth-century English. By the 1790s, however, a generic use for this word had been found. It was applied to 'a group or movement organized for spreading a particular doctrine or system of principles'. By the 1840s this usage had acquired a derogatory connotation. In his *Dictionary of Science, Literature, and Art* (1842), William Brande observes that "the name *propaganda* is applied in modern political language as a term of reproach to secret associations for the spread of opinions and principles which are viewed by most governments with horror and aversion."

Early in the twentieth century we find *propaganda* used for 'the systematic dissemination of ideas, information, allegations, or rumors so as to promote or injure a particular cause'. This sense gave rise to its use to denote the ideas, etc., so disseminated. During the First World War a profusion of propaganda was disseminated by both sides of the conflict. Much of it was loaded with emotionalism, exaggeration, and falsehood. This further derogated the connotation of the word *propaganda*.

Of course, propaganda also played an important role in the Second World War as a weapon of "psychological warfare." Since then we have heard much about Communist propaganda, Socialist propaganda, and antireligious propaganda (this last collocation may now strike the reader as being oxymoronic or at least ironic).

[NL (in *Congregatio de propaganda fide* Congregation for propagating the faith — an organization established by Pope Gregory XV in 1622 to take charge of Catholic missionary activity), fr. L, abl. sing. fem. of *propagandus*, gerundive of *propagare* to propagate]

proscribe See SCRIVENER.

[L *proscribere* to publish, proscribe, fr. *pro-* before + *scribere* to write]

prosecutor See JUDGE.

[ML, fr. LL, escort of goods in transit, fr. L *prosecutus* (past part. of *prosequi* to follow, follow after, pursue) + *-or*]

protagonist See AGONY.

[Gk *prōtagōnistēs*, fr. *prōt-* prot- + *agōnistēs* competitor at games, debater, actor, fr. *agōnizesthai* to compete for a prize, contend, fr. *agōn* gathering, assembly at games, contest]

protocol A book in ancient Greece consisted of papyrus sheets glued together along their edges to form a roll. The first sheet in the roll, carrying information about its manufacture, was known in Late Greek as the *protokollon*, from *prot-* 'first, beginning' and *-kollon*, a derivative of *kollema* 'that which is glued together, a papyrus roll', which itself was derived from *kollan* 'to glue together' and *kolla* 'glue'. From *protokollon* came the Latin *protocollum* and eventually the Middle French *prothocole*.

By the time this obscure Greek word found its way into English via French in the sixteenth century, books had long since acquired a new form, and *protocol*, as it eventually came to be spelled, had acquired a new meaning. It did, however, continue to denote a 'first' document of a kind; its earliest use in English was in the sense 'an original draft, minute, or record of a transaction'. In this sense it came to be applied specifically in the seventeenth century to the first draft or record of a diplomatic document, such as a treaty or declaration. The diplomatic connection was further underscored in the nineteenth century when *protocol* acquired the sense 'the official records or minutes of a diplomatic conference or congress'. Not long afterward, the French began to use *protocol* to name a department in the Ministry of Foreign Affairs concerned with the etiquette to be observed in official ceremonies and diplomatic relations. It was apparently this use that gave rise to what is now the usual sense of *protocol*, 'a code prescribing strict adherence to correct etiquette and precedence (as in diplomatic exchange and in the military services)'. More recently the word has developed new meanings in science and technology, 'the plan of a scientific experiment or treatment' and 'a set of conventions governing the treatment of data in an electronic communications system'.

[earlier *prothocoll*, fr. MF *prothocole*, fr. ML *protocollum*, fr. LGk *prōtokollon* first sheet of a papyrus roll bearing the authentication and date of manufacture of the papyrus, fr. Gk *prōt-* prot- + LGk *-kollon* (fr. Gk *kollēme* papyrus roll, sheets of papyrus glued together, lit., that which is glued together, fr. *kollan* to glue together, fr. *kolla* glue); akin to OSlav *klěji* glue, MD *helen* to glue]

punctuate See PUNGENT.
[ML *punctuatus*, past part. of *punctuare* to point, fr. L *punctus* pricking, point, fr. *punctus*, past part. of *pungere* to prick]

pungent *Pungent, poignant,* and *piquant* all have senses relating to sharpness, zest, and a piercing or gripping quality. The roots of this similarity may be found in the etymologies of the words. The first two come from the same source, the Latin verb *pungere*, which means 'to prick or sting'. *Pungent* was taken over directly from the Latin present participle. *Poignant*, however, passed through an additional stage and entered English as the present participle of the Old French verb *poindre*, a derivative of *pungere* with the same range of meaning. It is older in English than *pungent* by almost two centuries: Chaucer says of his epicurean Franklin in the *Canterbury Tales,* "Wo was his cook but if his sauce were/ Poynaunt and sharp, and redy al his geere [gear]." Chaucer also uses the word elsewhere in the *Canterbury Tales* in the common modern emotional sense 'painfully sharp with regard to the feelings'.

From *pungere* we also get by somewhat different routes *point* and *punctuate,* the first also by way of French. *Piquant* comes from Middle French *piquer* which, like *pungere*, means 'to prick, sting, or pierce'. See also RE-MORSE.

[L *pungent-, pungens*, pres. part. of *pungere* to prick, sting; akin to L *pugio* dagger, *pugnus* fist, *pugnare* to fight, Gk *pygmē* fist, *peukedanos* sharp, piercing, *peukē* pine tree, OHG *fiuhta*]

puny *Puny* is a spelling adopted to reflect the pronunciation of *puisne,* from the Middle French *puisné*, 'younger'. The literal meaning of the French *puisné* is 'born afterward', and in their earliest uses in English *puisne* and *puny* referred to someone younger than, or of inferior position to, someone else. In this sense it developed a specific legal meaning: a *puisne* (or *puny*) judge is a junior or subordinate judge in the superior courts. It is in this sense, making allowance for the ironic overtones, that we should understand *puny* in Jonathan Swift's satirical metrical treatise *On Poetry* (1733): "Put on the critick's brow, and sit/ At Wills' the puny judge of wit." (Wills' was a London coffeehouse of the seventeenth and eighteenth centuries much frequented by poets and poetasters.)

Very soon after being borrowed into English *puny* developed from its literal meaning the new sense of 'slight or inferior in power, vigor, size, or importance', as when, in Shakespeare's play, King Richard II exhorts himself, "Am I not King? . . ./ Is not the King's name twenty thousand names?/ Arm, arm, my name! A puny subject strikes/ At thy great glory."

[MF *puisné* younger, lit., born afterward, fr. *puis* afterward (fr. — assumed — VL *postius*, compar. of L *post* after, afterward) + *né* born (past part. of *naître* to be born, fr. L *nascere*, fr. *nasci*), fr. L *natus*, past part. of *nasci* to be born]

pupa See PUPIL.
[NL, fr. L *pupa* girl, doll]

pupil In Latin *pupa* was either a girl or a doll. Its diminutive *pupilla* had two senses, from which we derived two different words spelled *pupil* in English.

A person can see himself reflected in miniature, like a little doll, in the eye of another. For this reason, the opening in the iris which seems to hold this image was called a *pupilla* in Latin. Our English *pupil* was borrowed from the Middle French descendant of the Latin word. A little girl who was an orphan and a ward was also called a *pupilla,* her masculine counterpart being a *pupillus.* In medieval French and later in Middle English, the word *pupille* served for both sexes. When Middle English *pupille* was first used in the fourteenth century, it had the old Roman meaning. A *pupille* was an orphan child in the care of a guardian. In the sixteenth century the word developed a new meaning, and a *pupil* became a student in the charge of a tutor or in school. Thus the two homographs of *pupil* did not diverge in English but are the products of two separate borrowings as reflected in the two etymologies below.

The Latin word *pupa* is also used by modern entomologists to name the quiescent stage through which some insects pass in their metamorphosis from larvae to adults. The term was first used in this sense by the great Swedish naturalist Linnaeus in his Latin *Systema Naturae,* published in 1735.

See also PUPPET.

[MF *pupille* pupil of the eye, fr. L *pupilla,* fr. dim. of *pupa* girl, doll, puppet; fr. the tiny image of oneself seen reflected in another's eye]

[ME *pupille,* fr. MF, fr. L *pupillus* male ward, *pupilla* female ward; L *pupillus* fr. dim. of *pupus* boy; L *pupilla* fr. dim. of *pupa* girl, doll, puppet]

puppet Despite their various meanings, the English words *pupa, pupil, puppet,* and *puppy* are all ultimately derived from Latin *pupa.* In classical

Latin the basic meaning of *pupa* was 'girl', but by a straightforward extension it became the word for 'doll' or 'puppet' as well. The modern French *poupée*, 'doll', is a lineal descendant of Latin *pupa*. Even when we do not have written evidence for a stage in the history of a word, it is often possible to reconstruct that stage fairly certainly. We know the early form, Latin *pupa*, and later words like Middle French *poupée* and *poupette*. And we know, from written evidence, the way in which other classical Latin words developed through later stages of Latin and early French. So, although we have not found Vulgar Latin *puppa* or Middle French *poupe* in any surviving manuscript, we are sure that these words must have been used. Only the assumption of their prior existence can explain the later *poupée*. *Poupette*, 'little doll', a Middle French diminutive of *poupe*, was borrowed into Middle English as *popet*. Since the sixteenth century, *puppet* has been used for a particular kind of little doll, one that acts on a stage under human direction.

Middle English *popi* referred to a small lap dog used as a lady's pet. The word was adapted from the Middle French *popée*, 'doll, toy'. It was because this kind of dog, unlike larger working or hunting dogs, served only as a plaything that it was called a toy. In the late sixteenth century, a *puppy* became any young dog, whatever its eventual size or use.

See also PUPIL.

[ME *popet*, fr. MF *poupette* little doll, dim. of (assumed) *poupe* doll (whence F *poupée* doll), fr. (assumed) VL *puppa*, alter. of L *pupa* girl, doll, puppet]

puppy   See PUPPET.

[ME *popi*, fr. MF *popée, poupée* doll, toy, fr. (assumed) *poupe* doll]

Q

Quaker See CATHOLIC.

[¹*quake* + -*er*]

quark The word *quark* for the hypothetical, fractionally charged constituents of baryons and mesons was coined by the American physicist Murray Gell-Mann in 1963. According to his own account he was in the habit of using names like "squeak" and "squork" for peculiar objects, and "quork" (rhyming with *pork*) came out at the time. Some months later, he says, he ran across the line "Three quarks for Muster Mark" in James Joyce's *Finnegan's Wake*. The line struck him as apropos, since the hypothetical particles came in threes, and he adopted Joyce's spelling for his "quork." Joyce clearly meant *quark* to rhyme with *Mark, bark, park,* and so forth, but Gell-Mann worked out a rationale for his own pronunciation based on the vowel of the word *quart*. Joyce himself apparently took the word from German, in which language it refers to a cheese something like cottage cheese that is an early stage in cheese manufacture. It is also used as a synonym for German *quatsch* 'trivial nonsense'.

Quark was retained as the name for the hypothetical particle apparently in part because it did not sound scientific. Its whimsical tradition has been continued by attributing to it six "flavors"—*up, down, strange, charm, top,* and *bottom*. All this would doubtless have confirmed H. L. Mencken in his opinion, expressed in a letter written in 1930, that "physics itself, as currently practised, is largely moonshine."

For another fanciful scientific name see GOOGOL.

[coined by Murray Gell-Mann *b*1929 Am. physicist]

quarry The *quarry* the hunter stalks is unrelated to a stonecutter's *quarry*. The first can be traced to a minor ceremony that was once part of every successful hunt. The hounds were rewarded after the kill with a part of the slain animal's entrails. The French word for this hounds' portion was *cuiree*. It was probably derived from the word *coree*, 'entrails'; but because the *coree* was often placed on the slain beast's skin and the word for skin, *cuir*, was so like it, *coree* was altered to an even more similar *cuiree*. *Cuiree* was borrowed into Middle English as *querre* or *quirre*. The word for the entrails of an animal was then transferred to the animal itself, when considered in the character of game pursued. Now anything pursued is its pursuer's quarry.

The stone quarry is not so called because it is sought after, as is the game by a hunter, but rather takes its name from the building stones it provides. No surviving Old French document contains the word *quarre,* 'squared stone', but the existence of such a word in the spoken language of the time can be safely assumed. The word is the logical link between the Old French *quarriere,* the word for a quarry, a source of squared stones, and its ultimate source in Latin *quadrum,* 'square'.

[ME *querre, quirre* part of the entrails of a beast taken in hunting that is given to the hounds esp. by being placed on the beast's skin for them to eat, fr. MF *cuiree,* fr. OF, prob. alter. (influenced by *cuir* leather, skin, fr. L *corium*) of *coree* breast viscera, entrails, fr. LL *corata* (pl.), fr. L *cor* heart]

[ME *quarey,* alter. of *quarere, quarrere,* fr. MF *quarrere, quarriere,* fr. OF, fr. (assumed) OF *quarre* squared stone (akin to OProv *cayre* squared stone), fr. L *quadrum* square; akin to L *quattuor* four]

quassia   While the names of most drugs and diseases derive from the names of scientists in medicine and related fields (such as botany), the name of one drug in tropical medicine comes from an obscure practitioner of folk medicine. Graman Quassi was a native of the west coast of Africa who was carried off as a slave to Surinam (now usually Suriname) in South America. After obtaining his freedom by means unknown, he lived among the natives as a medicine man. Around 1730 he discovered the curative powers of the bark and heartwood of a variety of trees common in Surinam. Using an extract from the plant as a remedy for the tropical fevers that prevailed in the area, Quassi was held in much esteem by the natives. Around 1756 a Swedish traveler to Surinam learned of Quassi's wondrous cures and reportedly paid to learn the medicine man's secret. Specimens of the trees were brought back to Stockholm. The great botanist Linnaeus examined the specimens and in 1761 named the genus of plant *Quassia* after the former slave who had unlocked its secret. Afterwards, *quassia* was also applied to the drug obtained from the wood and still used in medicine as a bitter tonic and as a remedy for roundworms.

[NL, fr. *Quassi,* 18th cent. Surinam Negro slave who discovered the medicinal value of Surinam quassia + NL -*ia*]

query   See QUESTION.
[alter. of earlier *quere, quaere,* fr. L *quaere,* imper. of *quaerere* to seek, gain, obtain, ask]

question   The Latin root found in *quaerere* 'seek, ask' is of uncertain parentage but abundant progeny. The most straightforward descendant in English is *question,* which comes to us via French from Latin *quaestio* (declensional stem *quaestion-*) 'search, inquiry'. Both *question* and its shorter cousin *quest* reflect the past participial stem of *quaerere,* as does *inquest.*

Query has a more unusual origin, being a noun derived from the imperative of the Latin verb: *quaere* 'inquire!' was borrowed into English as a conscious Latinism, spelled *quaere* or *quere*. But the pronunciation was that of the traditional anglicization of Latin, rhyming with *weary*. This allowed the word to be respelled as *query*, in which shape it blends in with the rest of our fully assimilated wordstock. Finally, *inquire*, from Latin *inquirere*, reflects the change that *quaerere* underwent when prefixed, as by *in-*, *ad-*, or *re-* (whence also our *acquire*, *require*).

The above jumble of similar forms move within a small semantic ambit around the central idea of 'inquiry'. But some derivatives of *quaerere* went off on startling semantic tangents. Adding *con-* as a prefix yielded *conquirere*, which initially simply meant 'to seek, search out'. But in time the notion of attempt yielded the notion of "successful" attempt, so that the verb meant 'to procure (by effort)'. Martial connotations adhered to this meaning core in the Romance daughter languages of Latin, and from this development we get our words *conquer*, *conquest*, and *conquistador*.

Prefixation by *ex-* yielded *exquirere*. Neither *con-* nor *ex-* could by itself add much specific semantic content beyond a vague intensiveness, and *exquirere* initially meant just 'to ask about, seek'. But the past participle *exquisitus* came to be used adjectivally in the sense 'sought out with care, choice', and this is the source of our word *exquisite*.

[ME *questioun*, fr. MF *question*, fr. L *quaestion-, quaestio*, fr. *quaesitus, quaestus* (past part. of *quaerere* to seek, ask) + *-ion-, -io* -ion]

quick See ANIMAL.
[ME *quik, quike*, fr. OE *cwic, cwicu;* akin to OFris & OS *quik* alive, OHG *quec*, ON *kvikr*, Goth *qiwai* (nom. pl.), L *vivus* alive, *vivere* to live, Gk *zōē* life, *bios* mode of life, Lith *gyvas* living, Skt *jīva*]

quicksand See QUICKSILVER.
[ME *qwykkesand*, fr. *quik, quike* quick + *sand*]

quicksilver The word *quicksilver* is found in Old English in the form *cwicseolfor*. The first element, *cwic*, is attested earliest in Old English in the sense of 'living' or 'alive', from which derived the sense of 'running', 'moving', or 'shifting' which is reflected in *quicksand*. The descriptive nature of the word *quicksilver*, however, is not native to English. The compound is a translation of the Latin *argentum vivum* found in Pliny and literally meaning 'living silver'. The chemical symbol for *mercury* (Hg) and the less common name *hydrargyrum*, of which the symbol is an abbreviation, derive from the Greek meaning 'liquid silver'.

The mobility of this metal also probably accounts for the name *mercury* itself, for *Mercury* (or *Mercurius* in the Latin form) was the ancient Roman god of commerce and the fleet-footed messenger of the gods. Mercury also contributed his Greek name to English, though in a somewhat roundabout manner. The Greeks identified Thoth, the Egyptian god of wisdom, with Hermes, calling him *Hermes trismegistos*, 'thrice-great Hermes'. It was believed that Hermes Trismegistus, as he was called in Latin, invented a magic seal to keep vessels airtight, thus giving rise to English *hermetic*, meaning 'airtight' or 'impervious to external influence'. For other articles on words derived from ancient mythology and legend see VOLCANO.

[ME *quiksilver*, fr. OE *cwicseolfor*, fr. *cwic* alive + *seolfor* silver; trans. of L *argentum vivum* like MD *quicsilver*, OHG *quecsilbar*]

quintessence   Before the advent of modern science it was thought by those who speculated about nature's secrets that there were four elements: earth, air, fire, and water. These combined in varying proportions to form all the different substances found on Earth. However, the stars and planets seemed to be different and were thought to be composed not of the four elements but of a less substantial *ether* or *quintessence*. The quintessence was believed to permeate space beyond the sphere of air surrounding the Earth and was explained by many thinkers as pure and invisible light or fire, hence the term *ether* from Greek *aithēr*, which comes from the verb *aithein*, 'to kindle, blaze'.

Quintessence is derived from the Medieval Latin *quinta essentia*, which is a translation of Greek *pemptē ousia*, 'fifth substance' or 'fifth essence'. In Milton's *Paradise Lost* the archangel Uriel recounts the Creation in these terms:

> Swift to their several quarters hasted then
> The cumbrous elements—Earth, Flood, Air, Fire;
> And this ethereal quintessence of Heaven
> Flew upward, spirited with various forms,
> That rolled orbicular, and turned to stars. . . .

From the sixteenth to the eighteenth century *quintessence* was usually stressed on the first and third syllables, and such a pronunciation is best suited to the meter of this passage. Elsewhere in *Paradise Lost,* however, Milton uses *quintessence* with the stress falling on the second syllable as is common today:

> "Let there be Light!" said God; and forthwith Light
> Ethereal, first of things, quintessence pure,
> Sprung from the Deep. . . .

Many believed that the *quintessence* was found not only beyond the sphere of the Earth but was innate in all matter. Alchemists labored in vain to extract this essential substance from other materials, thinking that it might provide a universal remedy for disease and even for mortality itself.

While we have since discarded this model of the universe and the notion of a substance intrinsic to all matter, the words themselves have developed additional senses and so remain important parts of the Modern English vocabulary. *Quintessence* has come to mean 'the essence of a thing in its purest and most concentrated form'. *Essence* itself is used to express the individual, real, or ultimate nature of a thing, the quality that is essential to its existence, as one might expect from the origin of *essence* and *essential* in the Latin verb *esse*, 'to be'.

Related to *ether* is *ethereal*, which was originally used in English to refer to the regions beyond the Earth. From this developed the senses of 'heavenly' and 'spiritual', which led in turn to the sense of 'lacking material substance, intangible'.

For the composition and interrelationships of the four elements see HUMOR.

[ME, fr. MF *quinte essence,* fr. ML *quinta essentia* (trans. of Gk *pemptē ousia*), fr. L *quinta* (fem. of *quintus* fifth) + *essentia* essence]

quisling   Benedict Arnold was one of history's most notorious traitors. His name remains a standard historical reference; we say of a treacherous person that he is "another Benedict Arnold." Yet after more than two hundred years his name has never achieved the status of a common noun, has never been lowercased and pluralized, and has never been an interchangeable synonym for *traitor.* Vidkun Quisling, on the other hand, has the dubious distinction of having achieved all of the above almost overnight.

Quisling was a Norwegian army officer who served at various times as a military attaché, a diplomat, and Norway's minister of defense. In 1933 he formed Norway's own fascist party, the Nasjonal Samling (National Union) Party. Frustrated by his compatriots' lack of support, he met with Adolf Hitler in December 1939 and urged the German führer to occupy Norway. Upon the German invasion of April 1940, Quisling proclaimed himself head of the Norwegian government. His regime met with such widespread bitter opposition that he was forced out of the premiership within a week. Nevertheless, throughout the war he continued to serve as a figurehead in the puppet government set up by the German occupation forces. The Norwegian people were especially incensed by his attempts to infuse national socialism into the nation's churches, schools, and young people's organizations.

In the meantime the name Quisling had achieved international notoriety. On 15 April 1940, the London *Times* reported that "comment in the Press urges that there should be unremitting vigilance also against possible 'Quislings' inside [Sweden]." In a broadcast from London on 19 April 1940, CBS correspondent Edward R. Murrow remarked, "I don't think there were many Quislings in the Norwegian Army or Navy." And barely a month later, on 20 May, the U.S. magazine *Time* printed *quisling* without quotation marks and in lowercase:

> Detectives this week were busy trying to catch up with quislings who plastered northeast London with stickers urging everyone to listen to "the new British broadcasting station" on a wave length which turned out to be Hamburg.

Why did the name of Vidkun Quisling become an accepted part of the English language so quickly? Most probably because, in the words of one contemporary publication for students, "so closely did the very sound of the traitor's name fit his deeds." According to the London *Star* of 10 July 1940, the sound of that name "conveyed all the odious, greasy wickedness of the man." Back in April of that year the London *Times* had observed that *quisling* suggested something "at once slippery and tortuous." The paper went on to note that a number of *q*-words have negative connotations and cited as examples *questionable, querulous, quavering, quivering, quibbling, quagmire, qualm, quackery,* and *queasy.* At least Benedict Arnold had the good fortune not to have a name so fecund with connotation.

The acceptance of *quisling* into the language apparently was as universal as it was swift. Personages as preeminent as Winston Churchill, George Orwell, and H. G. Wells used it in their wartime writings. The enthusiasm for *quisling* remained unabated throughout World War II. *Quisling* was often used as an adjective, and so there were numerous references to "quisling governments," "quisling newspapers," "quisling intellectuals," and "quisling priests." The popularity of *quisling* inspired the coinage of a verb *quisle* ('to serve or act as a quisling'), and that word in turn spawned the creation of a redundant agent noun *quisler* ('quisling'). *Quislingism* became a synonym for treason or the supposed political philosophy of traitors. Before the vogue had exhausted itself, there existed *quislingize* and a number of other now-forgotten coinages. Even enthusiasm for *quisling* has dimmed somewhat since the Cold War years. Vidkun Quisling himself lived long enough to see his name immortalized, but not much longer. Soon after the liberation of Norway he was found guilty of treason and war crimes and was executed.

[after Vidkun *Quisling* †1945 Norw. politician]

quixotic   The fact that *quixotic* is customarily pronounced \kwik-'sät-ik\, whereas the American pronunciation of *Don Quixote* is more likely to be \ˌdän-kē-'hōt-ē\, has helped to obscure the etymological connection between the two. *Don Quixote de la Mancha, El ingenioso hidalgo* (1605 and 1615) is the full title of a novel by Miguel de Cervantes Saavedra. The book is an epic satire of the chivalric romances that were popular in Cervantes's day. The story concerns Alonso Quijano from the province of La Mancha. Avid reading of stories set in the days of chivalry has filled his head with romantic ideals, and he sets out determined to have his own chivalric adventures and in the process undo the wrongs of the world. He assumes the title Don Quixote in a mock ceremony of knighthood. He sees everything through the eyes of a romantic idealist, but after a long series of adventures that turn out to be misadventures, the would-be knight returns to La Mancha a tired and disillusioned old man. The novel was widely translated, Part I and Part II appearing in English in 1612 and 1620 respectively. Within a few decades after the English translations, the word *Quixote* had become a synonym for a visionary, impractical idealist. Incidents from the tale had become part of the literary consciousness, as a line, written about 1650 by John Cleveland, attests: "Thus the Quixots of this Age fight with the Windmils of their own heads." The lasting place of *Don Quixote* in world literature brought about the short-lived coinages *Quixotism, Quixotry,* and *Quixotize.* Yet these words are all older than the much-used *quixotic,* which is not known before the early nineteenth century. Originally used of people who are impractical visionaries, *quixotic* (along with the less common *quixotical*) was later applied also to the undertakings, dreams, and misadventures of latter-day Don Quixotes.

[*quixote* (after Don Quixote de la Mancha, chivalrous hero of the satiric novel *Don Quixote de la Mancha* by Miguel de Cervantes Saavedra †1616 Span. novelist) + *-ic* or *-ical*]

R

rabies See FURY.
[NL, fr. L, rage, madness, fr. *rabere* to rave]

radar See ACRONYMIC ETYMOLOGIES.
[*radio detecting and ranging*]

radon See XENON.
[NL, fr. *rad-* (fr. *radium*, fr. L *radius* ray, beam + NL -*ium*) + -*on*]

rage See FURY.
[ME, fr. MF, fr. LL *rabia*, fr. L *rabies* rage, madness, fr. *rabere* to rave, be mad; akin to Skt *rabhas* violence, impetuosity]

raglan See BLOOMER.
[after F.J.H. Somerset, Baron *Raglan* †1855 Brit. field marshal]

raise See SKIRT.
[ME *reisen, raisen,* fr. ON *reisa* to raise, cause to rise]

ranch An ancient Germanic word (probably a cousin of Old High German *hring* 'circle') was taken into early French as *renc* (with variants *ranc, reng, rang*), which was used to denote 'a line, row, rank'. From *renc* was formed the word *renge,* used for 'a row or rank of people or animals'. This became *range* in Middle French and was borrowed into English in this sense about 1300. Alfred Lord Tennyson, in his 1847 poem *The Princess,* provides an example of this use: "There sat along the forms, like morning doves, . . . a patient range of pupils." By about 1510, *range* was being applied to 'a row or series of objects' as well.

In French, the noun *range* gave rise to the verb *ranger* 'to set in a row; place in proper order'. The reflexive construction *se ranger* was used to mean 'to take up a position, be quartered'. This usage was borrowed into Old Spanish as *ranchar(se), ranchear(se),* meaning 'to take up quarters, be billeted'. From this verb, Spanish derived the noun *rancho* to mean 'a group of persons (as soldiers) who take meals together' and then 'a camp, temporary quarters'. In the Andalusian dialect, it referred to 'a small farm'. In Mexico, the Spanish *rancho* came to be applied to 'a hut occupied by herdsmen or laborers' and 'a small ranch or farm'.

Early in the nineteenth century, American English borrowed *rancho* from Mexican Spanish as *ranch,* and used it for 'a small hut or house in the country'. By the 1870s, *rancho* had acquired the sense of 'an establishment for the raising of horses, cattle, or sheep that usually includes the buildings occupied by the owner and employees with the adjacent barns and corrals'. Its application soon broadened, however, to include 'any farm devoted to the raising of one particular specialty', as this quotation from the January 1888 issue of *Century Magazine* illustrates: "There are [in Montana] hay ranches, grain ranches, milk ranches, horse ranches, cattle ranches, and chicken ranches."

[MexSp *rancho* small ranch, fr. Sp, camp, temporary habitation, hut + Sp dial. (Andalusia), small farm, fr. OSp *ranchar(se), ranchear(se)* to take up quarters, be billeted, fr. MF *(se) ranger* to take up a position, be quartered, fr. *ranger* to set in a row, place, station, fr. OF *rengier,* fr. *renc, reng* line, place, row]

range See RANCH.
[ME, fr. MF, fr. OF *renge,* fr. *renc, reng* line, place, row]

rankle The modern senses of the verb *rankle,* 'to cause or to feel anger, irritation, or bitterness', are figurative extensions of the Middle English verb *ranclen,* meaning 'to fester'. The word was borrowed from Middle French *rancler.* The Old French noun *rancle (raoncle, draoncle, drancle),* from which the verb derives, means 'a festering sore' and comes ultimately from Latin *dracunculus.* This diminutive of *draco,* 'dragon', means literally 'a small serpent or dragon'. But how do we get from a little dragon to a festering sore? The link is that in Medieval Latin *dracunculus* was used to mean a cancerous tumor or ulcer, probably because the form of a tumor was thought to be like that of a small serpent. A similar case is the *keloid* tumor (from French *kéloïde),* named from Greek *chēlē* 'claw' because of its shape.

It is more difficult to explain the sound changes that lead from *dracunculus* to *rankle,* but even here we are not completely in the dark. The seventeenth-century scholar Charles Du Change notes the occurrence in Medieval Latin of the contraction *dranculus,* which brings us a little closer to the French and English form.

The English verb *fester* is similar in meaning to *rankle* and has a somewhat analogous etymology as well. It comes from the Middle English noun *fester,* 'a suppurating sore', which is derived through Middle French from Latin *fistula,* meaning 'a pipe or tube'. Like *dracunculus, fistula* was used as a descriptive term for a kind of ulcer which takes the form of a hollow passage from one part of the body to another. In this sense *fistula* is still used in English today.

See also CANCER.

[ME *ranclen,* fr. MF *rancler,* fr. OF *draoncler, raoncler, rancler,* fr. *draoncle, drancle, raoncle, rancle* festering sore, fr. ML *dracunculus,* fr. L, small serpent, dim. of *draco* serpent, dragon]

rapacious   See RAPT.

[L *rapac-, rapax* rapacious (fr. *rapere* to seize and carry off, snatch away) + *-ious*]

rape   See RAPT.

[ME *rapen,* fr. L *rapere*]

rapid   See RAPT.

[L *rapidus* seizing, tearing, hurrying, rapid, fr. *rapere* to seize, rob, kidnap, ravish; akin to OE *refsan, repsan* to reprove, blame, OS *respian* to reprove, OHG *refsen* to punish, ON *refsa* to punish, Gk *ereptesthai* to feed on, Lith *aprépti* to seize; basic meaning: to seize, grasp]

rapt   *Rapt* has a rich history as an English word, although its current use reflects that history only dimly. It is derived from Latin *raptus,* the past participle of the verb *rapere* 'to seize'. This verb is the ultimate source of our word *raptor* 'a bird of prey' and also of *rapacious* and *rape,* both of which still convey something of the idea of 'seizing', of *rapture,* now more usual in the figurative sense of being carried away with emotional ecstasy, and of *rapid,* which has altogether lost the 'seize' or 'carry away' sense and been left with only the idea of the speed of the seizure. (See also *raptor* at FALCON.)

In its earliest uses in English, dating back to the fifteenth century, *rapt* retained strong associations with its Latin root. It functioned principally as a past participle describing either a physical or spiritual carrying away. Thus a soul would be said to have been *rapt* to heaven, or a person *rapt* from one place or position to another. *Rapt* continued in these uses into the ninteenth century, so that it was still possible in 1820 for Washington Irving to write (in *The Sketch Book of Geoffrey Crayon*), "His only daughter had been rapt away to the grave."

Rapt also had some use in earlier centuries as a noun, synonymous in two of its senses with *rapture* and *rape,* and even as a verb, with the past tense *rapted,* meaning 'to carry away by force' and 'to enrapture'. But the *rapt* of present-day English shows much less versatility. The word now functions almost invariably as an ordinary adjective, usually having the sense 'wholly absorbed or engrossed', as in "The audience listened with rapt attention." This sense developed as an extension of the 'carried away' sense of *rapt* in the sixteenth century. Its original use, still sometimes seen, was in constructions like "rapt in contemplation," and it has been suggested that its development was influenced in part by similar use of the homophone *wrapped.* For whatever reason, the modern *rapt,* although it still retains suggestions of being emotionally or intellectually transported, has clearly lost much of its former forcefulness. A rapt audience, in current English, is not quite the same thing as an audience that has gotten carried away.

[ME, fr. L *raptus,* past part. of *rapere* to seize, rob, kidnap, ravish]

raptor See FALCON, RAPT.
[L, one that robs, plunders, kidnaps, or ravishes, fr. *raptus* (past part. of *rapere* to seize, rob, kidnap, ravish) + *-or*]

rapture See RAPT.
[L *raptus* (past part. of *rapere*) + E *-ure*]

rara avis See OSTRICH.
[L, rare bird]

rathskeller In Old High German (before the twelfth century) the noun *rāt* was used to mean 'advice' and 'supply'. During the Middle High German period (1100–1500) the word also took on the sense of 'council'. In this sense it was used in the compound *rathaus* 'council house', which is equivalent to 'town (or city) hall' in English.

The German word *keller* 'cellar' developed from the Old High German *kellari,* which was derived from the Latin noun *cellarium,* meaning 'storeroom'. The root word *cella* originally denoted 'a pantry or larder' and then developed the extended senses of 'a wine cellar', 'a chamber in a temple', and 'a small room or cubicle'. The English words *cell* and *cellar* both derive from the root.

In early modern German, *rat* was often also spelled *rath,* which was pronounced the same way as *rat* (roughly like American English *rot*). *Rath* was combined with *keller* to form *rathskeller* (later spelled *ratskeller*), which was used for the beer- and wine-selling restaurant located in the cellar of a *rathaus.* In Germany today, the oldest *rathskeller* is said to be the one located in Lübeck, which dates from the first half of the thirteenth century.

Around 1900, English writers began using *rathskeller* for 'a saloon or restaurant that was located below street level'. In English the *-h-* spelling was preferred, probably to avoid any association with the word *rat.* The word *rathskeller* first appeared in an English dictionary when Webster's New International Dictionary was published in 1909.

[G *ratskeller* (formerly spelled *rathskeller*) restaurant in the basement of a town hall, fr. *rat* council (fr. MHG *rāt* advice, supply, council, fr. OHG, advice, supply) + *keller* cellar, basement, fr. OHG *kellari,* fr. L *cellarium* (fr. *cella* small room, storeroom + *-arium* -ary)]

ravioli See VERMICELLI.
[It *raviuoli, ravioli,* fr. It dial. (southern Italy), pl. of *raviuolo, raviolo,* lit., little turnip, dim. of *rava* turnip, fr. L *rapa*]

rear See SKIRT.
[ME *reren,* fr. OE *rǣran;* akin to OHG *rēren* to cause to fall, ON *reisa* to raise, Goth ur*raisjan* to arouse, raise, lift up; causative fr. the root of OE *rīsan* to rise]

recalcitrant The image of a mule obstinately refusing to budge has given us the adjective *mulish* and the familiar expression "stubborn as a mule." The image underlying the origins of *recalcitrant* is similar but more lively. The Latin source of *recalcitrant* is *recalcitrare,* a verb used originally of horses in the literal sense 'to kick back'. *Recalcitrare* is itself formed from *re-* 'back' and *calcitrare* 'to kick', a word formed from the noun *calx* 'heel'. Extremely rare in its literal sense, *recalcitrare* became somewhat more common in Late Latin in the extended meaning 'to be petulant or disobedient', a sense that obviously owes much to the image of a balky animal petulantly kicking backward. The derivative adjective *recalcitrant,* meaning 'obstinately defiant of authority or restraint', was first used in English in the nineteenth century. In the twentieth century, it has also come to be used in a medical sense, 'unresponsive to treatment', as in "recalcitrant forms of a disease."

[LL *recalcitrant-, recalcitrans,* fr. pres. part. of *recalcitrare* to be stubbornly disobedient, fr. L, to kick back, fr. *re-* + *calcitrare* to kick, fr. *calc-, calx* heel]

receipt   See DEBT.
[ME *receite,* fr. ONF, fr. ML *recepta* (sing.), prob. fr. L *recepta,* neut. pl. of *receptus,* past part. of *recipere* to receive, take]

rector   See VICAR.
[ML *rector* ecclesiastical director, parish priest, director of a university, fr. L, governor, ruler, fr. *rectus* (past part. of *regere* to rule, govern) + *-or*]

red eft   See NICKNAME.

referee   See UMPIRE.
[*refer* (fr. ME *referren, referen,* fr. L *referre,* lit., to carry back, fr. *re-* + *ferre* to carry) + *-ee*]

rehearse   See HEARSE.
[ME *rehersen, rehercen,* fr. MF *rehercier* to repeat, to harrow over again, fr. *re-* + *hercier* to harrow, fr. *herce* harrow]

remorse   *Remorse* is a gnawing distress that arises from a sense of guilt. In the light of the etymology of *remorse,* "gnawing" is a description of special relevance, for *remorse* is derived from Latin *remorsus,* the past participle of *remordēre,* which means 'to bite again'. English once had a word that intentionally paralleled *remorse* in the meaning of its formative elements. When a monk known to us as Dan Michel of Northgate, in the year 1340, finished his English translation of a French manual on sin and penitence, he called it *Ayenbite of Inwyt.* The title is quite accurately modernized as *Remorse of Conscience,* because *ayenbite* is made up of elements (*ayen-* is 'again' in modern English) each of which is a translation of the corresponding element of *remorse,* and *inwyt* similarly translates 'conscience' (*-wyt* is from Old English *witan,* 'to know', and *-science* from Latin *scire,* 'to know'). A word created in the manner of *ayenbite* and *inwyt* is known as a *loan translation* or *calque.* (For another example of loan translation see FELLOW.)

Compunction is similar to *remorse* in meaning, though rather than conveying a sense of inescapable or continuing mental anguish *compunction* suggests a momentary twinge of guilt or a prick of conscience. This suddenness is also reflected in the etymological background of *compunction,* which comes from Latin *compunctus,* the past participle of *compungere,* 'to prick hard' or 'to sting'. See also PUNGENT.

[ME *remors, remorse,* fr. MF *remors,* fr. ML *remorsus,* fr. L, act of biting again, fr. *remorsus,* past part. of *remordēre* to bite again, vex, fr. *re-* + *mordēre* to bite]

require   See QUESTION.
[ME *requeren, requiren,* fr. MF *requerre* (3d pers. sing. pres. indic. *requiert*), fr. (assumed) VL *requaerere* to need, seek for, inquire after, alter. (influenced by L *quaerere* to seek, ask) of L *requirere,* fr. *re-* + *-quirere* (fr. *quaerere*)]

revolve   See VOLUME.
[ME *revolven,* fr. L *revolvere* to roll back, fr. *re-* back, again + *volvere* to roll]

rhinoceros   See UNICORN.
[ME *rinoceros,* fr. L *rhinocerot-, rhinoceros,* fr. Gk *rhinokerōt-, rhinokerōs,* fr. *rhin-, rhis* nose + *-kerōt-, -kerōs* (fr. *keras* horn)]

rhubarb   See BARBARIC.
[ME *rubarbe,* fr. MF *rubarbe, reubarbe,* prob. fr. ML *reubarbum,* alter. of *reubarbarum,* prob. alter. of *rha barbarum* barbarian rhubarb, fr. LL *rha* rhubarb (fr. Gk *rha, rhēon,* perh. fr. *Rha* Volga river) + L *barbarum,* neut. of *barbarus* barbarous, barbarian]

riches   See SHERRY.
[ME (sing. or pl.), fr. *richesse* richness, wealth, fr. OF, fr. *riche* rich, of Gmc origin; akin to OE *rīce* rich]

riffraff   The *riffraff* are the dregs of society, the lowest or most disreputable classes. In 1599 the English scholar Hugh Broughton wrote of people who "accompt [account] all besides themselves . . . babish [infantile], vnlearned, rifraffe, nobodie." The *riffraff* are "nobodie," anonymous in their multitudes, to be dismissed with a sweeping gesture. The word *riffraff* comes from an earlier phrase, *rif and raf,* 'every single one'. The corresponding *rif no raf* (neither *riff* nor *raff*) meant 'no one or nothing at all'. Both phrases were borrowed from Middle French, where *rif et raf* meant 'completely'. In the middle and early modern periods, this expression appeared in French in a variety of forms: *sans rifle ou rafle,* 'without anything at all'; *rif ny raf, ne rif ne raf, ni rifle ni rafle,* and *ne riffle ne raffle,* 'nothing at all'. The consonance was irresistible. *Rif* (or *rifle*) was derived from the verb *rifler*, 'to scratch' or 'to plunder' (this verb is also the ancestor of English *rifle*), and *raf* (or *rafle*) from a noun meaning 'a sweeping or snatching'. It was doubtless at least as much for sound as for sense that these two words were linked to mean 'all' or 'altogether', but it cannot be denied that a clean sweep leaves *ni rifle ni rafle*.

[ME *ryffe raffe*, fr. *rif and raf* every single one, fr. MF *rif et raf* completely, fr. *rifler* to scratch, plunder + *rafle, raffe* act of sweeping, snatching, fr. MHG *raffen* to scratch]

right The basic meaning of *right* and its cognates in other Indo-European languages is 'straight' or 'stretched out'. The earliest appearances of *right* (both as adjective and noun) show that by the Old English period it had developed a number of abstract senses that were the first to be used in English. These are the senses that relate to what is righteous, upright, just, good, or proper. Not until the thirteenth century does *right* appear in the sense of the side of the body that is away from the heart. Because most people use the hand on this side habitually or more easily than their other hand, it was considered to be the correct or *right* hand for doing many things. From this subjectively determined usage developed the senses relating to direction. A further extension accounts for the use of *right* to mean 'politically conservative' or 'opposed to change'. In continental European nations the members of a legislative body who hold more conservative views than other members generally sit on the side of the legislative chamber which is to the right of the presiding officer. Similarly, the members holding more radical views sit on the left side of the chamber, giving rise to the political sense of *left*.

Another word affected by the fact that most people are right-handed is the Latin *dexter*. This originally meant 'relating to or situated on the right', but since most people do things better with their right hands *dexter* developed the sense of 'skillful'. Thus in English *dexterous* or *dextrous* (both spellings remain common in contemporary English) means 'skillful and deft with the hands' or even 'mentally adroit and clever'.

Adroit itself, borrowed from French in the seventeenth century, has a similar range of senses. It derives from the phrase *à droit* meaning 'properly', from *à*, 'to, at', plus *droit*, which has in French a number of senses in common with English *right*. *Adroit* in English and French has come to mean 'skillful both mentally and physically'. Someone who uses both hands equally well is *ambidextrous*, from Latin *ambi-*, 'both' or 'on both sides', plus *dexter*. In 1646 in *Pseudodoxia Epidemica* Sir Thomas Browne wrote: "Some are . . . ambidexterous or right handed on both sides." In the previous century Richard Mulcaster had mentioned people who are "double right handed which vse both the handes a like." While today we would not say that a dextrous person has two right hands, we do often say that a clumsy person has two left hands or even two left feet.

Latin *dexter* has also provided a prefix of some value to the vocabulary of science. For instance, *dextrose* is a form of glucose through which the plane of polarization of light is rotated toward the right. This is biologically significant because the process required to convert dextrose into energy in the body differs from that required to convert similar forms of sugar which rotate the plane of polarization to the left. See also LEFT.

[ME *riht, right*, fr. OE *riht;* akin to OHG *reht* right, ON *rēttr,* Goth *raihts* right, L *rectus* straight, right, *regere* to lead straight, guide, rule, *rogare* to ask, Gk *oregein* to stretch out, *orektos* stretched out, upright, Skt *ṛjyati, ṛñjati* he stretches, hastens, *raji* straightening up, straight; basic meaning: straight]

rigmarole A game played in the Middle Ages featured a roll on which was written a series of verses with a separate string attached to the roll at each verse. A player would choose a string at random and then read the selection to which it was attached, which would typically contain an amusingly unflattering description of the personal character of the player who had chosen it. (A somewhat more serious version of the game was apparently popular among medieval gamblers.) The game was called *Rageman* or *Ragman,* a name perhaps derived from the Old French *Ragemon le bon,* 'Ragemon the good', the heading of a set of Anglo-French verses from the late thirteenth century. The roll with which the game was played was known as *Ragman roll* or *Ragman's roll.*

By the sixteenth century, both *Ragman* and *Ragman roll* were being used figuratively to mean 'a list or catalogue', as when Thomas Nashe wrote in *Lenten Stuffe* (1599), "The whole ragman roll of fasting days." The terms fell out of written use soon afterward, but *Ragman roll* persisted in speech, and it resurfaced in writing in the altered form *rigmarole* (and numerous other spellings) during the eighteenth century. By that time it had acquired the sense 'a succession of incoherent statements' or 'a rambling discourse'. In the twentieth century, *rigmarole,* now sometimes spelled *rigamarole* to reflect a common pronunciation, has taken on the added sense 'a complex and ritualistic procedure', as in this use by Winthrop Sargeant, writing in *New Yorker,* 15 October 1955: ". . . he had played the violin as instinctively as a bird sings. His intuitive gifts had seemed so staggering . . . that [his teachers] speedily abandoned the attempt, concluding that in his case the whole academic rigmarole of scales and exercises was unnecessary."

[alter. of *ragman roll*]

rile The use of \ī\ for words spelled with *oi* was standard in the English of the seventeenth and eighteenth centuries. Thus American colonists brought the pronunciation with them. The frequency of the pronunciation is well attested in the nineteenth-century American dialect humorists, whose works abound in pronunciation spellings like *jine* (for *join*), *p'int* and *pint* (for *point*), *b'iled* and *biled* (for *boiled*), and so forth. *Pizen* and *pison* could be found for *poison:*

If I had a yaller dog that didn't know no more than a person's conscience does I would pison him —Mark Twain, *Huckleberry Finn*, 1884

Pizen is seldom met these days except in the old ballad "Springfield Mountain," where someone is bitten in the heel by "a pizen snake," and other consciously dialectal uses: "Name yore pizen, podner."

The only one of these spelling pronunciations that has established itself as standard is *rile* from *roil*. The spelling pronunciation itself seems to be a nineteenth-century Americanism:

. . . swearin all the way that she were the last one would ever get a chance to rile up my feelings —John S. Robb, "The Standing Candidate", 1846

> It couldn't 'a' raised a louder fuss,
> Ner 'a' riled the old man's temper wuss!
> —James Whitcomb Riley, *Farm-Rhymes*, 1883

From dialectal beginnings like these *rile* has moved into the standard language, all but displacing *roil* in the 'anger' sense and making *roil* seem rather a bookish word:

This handicap . . . riled him all the days of his life —William L. Shirer, *The Rise and Fall of the Third Reich*, 1959

And you can see it in the newspaper almost any day:

Clayton first riled Pats cornerback Ronnie Lippett during the week by saying . . . —*USA Today*, 7 Nov. 1988

For more on dialectal variants that have become standard see ORNERY, PASSEL, SASS.

[alter. of ¹*roil*]

ritzy   In 1898 César Ritz opened in Paris a hotel that aspired to be—and, by all accounts, was in fact—the last word in luxury. The opulent establishment, which its founder modestly named the Ritz Hotel, immediately captured the imagination of the public and the patronage of the beautiful people of fin de siècle Europe. Born in Switzerland in 1850, Ritz pursued a path of upward mobility in the hotel and restaurant business. As maître d'hôtel at the Hotel Splendide in Paris during the 1870s, he carefully cultivated connections with the old money of Europe and served as a guide and mentor for the nouveaux riches of America, introducing the latter to continental taste and sophistication. Attuned to the vagaries of fashionable society, he followed his patrons in their nomadic wanderings from one European resort to the next. In Monte Carlo, Ritz teamed up with the great chef Auguste Escoffier. After opening a restaurant in Baden-Baden in 1884, the two set out to conquer London, where Ritz assumed management of the new Savoy Hotel and Escoffier ensconced himself in the hotel's restaurant. The establishment of Ritz's own hotels in Paris, and in London (1905), marked the capstone of his career and created an enduring association of his name with luxurious elegance. Charles Ritz, his son and successor, carried on the family tradition by opening a string of luxurious hotels around the world.

Within a few years of the founding of the hotels in Paris and London, "the Ritz" became a symbol of palatial living. As they still do today, people were wont to disparage their own modest digs by allowing, "This place isn't the Ritz." An indication of the fame of the Ritz hotels is the fact that F. Scott Fitzgerald in 1922 titled one of his stories of the Jazz Age "The Diamond as Big as the Ritz." Because snobbery is often perceived as an inevitable consequence of wealth, *ritz* also took on suggestions of haughtiness. During the Jazz Age the expression *to put on the ritz* came to mean 'to assume a superior attitude; put on airs'. It also acquired the less derogatory meaning of 'to indulge in ostentatious display', the sense in which Irving Berlin used it in his 1929 musical paean to glitz, "Puttin' on the Ritz."

Within an equally brief span of time, the name of the Swiss hotelier attained the status of a verb. By the 1920s people were using it to mean 'to behave superciliously toward another'. A person could be "ritzed" by being verbally put down or merely by being snubbed. Either way, he was put in his proper place—which was definitely not the Ritz Hotel.

César Ritz's most enduring legacy to the language is, of course, *ritzy*. The word *ritzy* has come to embody everything that the Ritz Hotels actually were, everything they symbolized, and everything their clientele was perceived to be. For some, *ritzy* is synonymous with *luxurious, opulent, elegant,* and *posh*. For others, *ritzy* suggests the slightly different but still very positive qualities inherent in terms like *smart, fashionable, exclusive,* and *classy*. On the other hand, the extravagant luxury for which the Ritz Hotels were famous has moved others to equate *ritzy* with *ostentatious, showy, flashy,* and *glitzy*. Similarly, when applied to persons, *ritzy* has tended to be synonymous with *pretentious, snobbish, snooty,* and *hoity-toity*. That *ritzy* should have developed both approbatory and pejorative senses is, of course, merely a reflection of opposing responses to conspicuous consumption and to those who indulge in it.

[*Ritz* hotels (esp. the *Ritz-Carlton* in New York City) founded by César *Ritz* †1918 Swiss entrepreneur + E -*y*]

rival   *Rival* is derived, perhaps directly or perhaps indirectly through Middle French, from Latin *rivalis,* which as an adjective means 'of a brook or stream', from *rivus,* 'brook or stream'. As a noun *rivalis* occurs only in its plural forms in Latin texts to refer literally to those who use the same stream as a source of water. Just as neighbors are likely to dispute each other's rights to a common source of water, so too contention is inevitable when two or more persons strive to obtain something that only one can possess. Thus the Latin *rivalis* also developed a sense relating to rivalry in love, and in this sense it came into Middle French and English.

Despite its aquatic history, *rival* is unrelated to *river,* which derives not from *rivus,* but from the unrelated root *ripa,* which means 'the bank or shore of a stream', and from which (through the assumed Vulgar Latin form *riparia*) is derived the Old French *rivere* or *riviere* with a primary meaning of 'riverbank' or 'the land along a river'. (Sound changes in

French affecting Latin *p* between vowels conspired to produce the same modern consonant *v* as in *river*. A similar change brought about French *savoir* 'to know' from Latin *sapere*.) *Rivere* was also used, however, to refer to the water itself, and this is the source of English *river*. A related word is *arrive*, from Old French *ariver*, which also has its roots in Latin *ripa*. Literally *arrive* means 'to reach the shore', but more generally, of course, it means 'to reach any sort of destination'.

[MF or L; MF, fr. L *rivalis* one using the same stream as another, rival in love, fr. *rivalis*, adj., of a brook or stream, fr. *rivus* brook, stream + *-alis* -al]

river   See RIVAL.
[ME *rivere*, *river*, fr. OF *rivere*, *riviere* riverbank, land along a river, river, fr. (assumed) VL *riparia*, fr. L, fem. of *riparius* riparian, fr. *ripa* bank, shore + *-arius* -ary, connected with]

robot   In 1923 a play called *R.U.R.* opened in London and New York. As well as having a successful run, the play made a lasting contribution to our vocabulary by introducing the word *robot* into English. The author, Karel Čapek, coined *robot* from the Czech *robota*, meaning 'forced labor'. In *R.U.R.* (which stands for "Rossum's Universal Robots" in the English translation) mechanical men originally designed to perform manual labor become so sophisticated that some advanced models develop the capacity to feel and hate, and eventually they destroy mankind. *Robot* caught on quickly on both sides of the Atlantic, and within a very few years it was being used to denote not only 'a complex machine that looks somewhat human' but also 'a person who has been dehumanized through the necessity of performing mechanical, mindless tasks in a highly industrialized society'. Today *robot* is also used widely in both scientific and nonscientific circles as a term for 'any automatic apparatus or device that performs functions ordinarily ascribed to human beings or operates with what appears to be almost human intelligence'.

[Czech, fr. *robota* forced labor; akin to OSlav *rabota* servitude, OE *earfothe* hardship, labor, OHG *arabeit* trouble, distress, ON *erfithi* toil, distress, Goth *arbaiths* labor, L *orbus* orphaned]

roentgen   See X RAY.
[ISV, fr. Wilhelm Conrad *Röntgen* †1923 Ger. physicist]

romance   In the last centuries of the Roman Empire the wide variety and the geographical distribution of the peoples recognized as Roman citizens led inevitably to the gradual change of the classical language of earlier days that we call Latin. These developing languages, which in their early, unrecorded stages were only local dialects of Latin, were designated *romans* (to use the Old French term cognate with other similar forms in Spanish, Italian, and the other languages that we still call *romance* languages today) to distinguish them from the formal and official language. Most serious literature, both prose and verse, continued to be written in

Latin; but gradually the practice arose in France of writing entertaining verse tales in the more popular spoken language. Thus, to refer to something written in *romans* was to refer to one of these works, and in Old French the word *romans* came to mean 'a tale in verse based chiefly on legend, chivalric love and adventure, or the supernatural'. In this sense the word was borrowed into Middle English.

Because many of these tales in both English and French, as well as in other languages, dealt with chivalric or courtly love, *romance* came to mean simply 'a love story' and eventually it developed the sense of 'a love affair'. The sense of *romantic,* meaning 'marked by the imagination or emotional appeal of the heroic, adventurous, remote, mysterious, or idealized', developed in England in the nineteenth century around that company of poets (including Keats, Wordsworth, Shelley, and Byron) today called the Romantic poets, thus providing the word with a whole new range of connotations.

See also NOVEL.

[ME *romauns, romaunce,* fr. OF *romans, romanz* French, something composed in French, tale in verse, fr. L *Romanice* in the Roman manner, fr. *Romanicus* Roman, fr. *Romanus* Roman + *-icus* -ic]

roorback   Campaign "dirty tricks" are nothing new to political contests. At least one trick has left a legacy in the English language. On 21 August 1844, when the U.S. presidential campaign between James K. Polk, the Democratic candidate, and Henry Clay, the Whig standard-bearer, was in full swing, a letter was published in the Ithaca (N.Y.) *Chronicle,* a Whig newspaper. The letter was signed only by "an Abolitionist." This self-avowed abolitionist presented what purported to be an excerpt from *Roorback's Tour Through the Western and Southern States in 1836.* The excerpt focused on an incident that the eponymous Baron Roorback (or Roorbach) of Germany witnessed while traveling in the vicinity of a certain Duck River in Tennessee. There he supposedly happened upon an encampment of some 300 black slaves who were en route to the Natchez slave market. The baron's alleged journal contained this crucial passage:

> Forty-three of these unfortunate beings had been purchased, I was informed, of the Hon. J. K. Polk, the present speaker of the House of Representatives, the mark of the branding iron, with the initials of his name on their shoulders, distinguishing them from the rest.

This purported excerpt from the journal of "Baron Roorback" was reprinted in the Albany *Journal* and then in other Whig newspapers across the country. Predictably, it created an uproar in the presidential campaign. Before long, however, it was discovered that there was no published journal known as *Roorback's Tour* and no "Baron Roorback." Further investigation of the hoax revealed that the excerpt was largely plagiarized from a chapter in George William Featherstonhaugh's *Excursion Through the Slave States* (1844). The detail about the forty-three slaves branded with the initials of James K. Polk was a fabrication that was interpolated into Featherstonhaugh's text. The perpetrator was eventually discovered to be William Linn, an author and attorney from Ithaca. He was the creator of the fictitious Baron Roorback, a character derived from the tradition of a peripatetic foreign observer presenting a trustworthy, objective account of the events that he witnesses. The political sympathies and motives of William Linn have been variously characterized. Some have taken at face value the claim that he was an abolitionist Whig. If so, then he failed, for the fraud was exposed before it could ruin Polk's campaign. Others have claimed that he was actually a Democrat who planted the hoax in the opposition's newspaper. Linn's expectation, it is argued, was that the canard would be exploited by the Whigs, only to backfire on them and ultimately to help the Democratic cause.

Indeed, the Roorback affair proved to be a political boomerang. For the remainder of the campaign, other Whig charges, legitimate or otherwise, were plausibly dismissed by the Democrats as the sort of slanderous lie that they had come to expect from the Whigs—just another "Roorback." The contention that the whole affair was a hoax whose exposure was planned from the beginning is supported by the fact that events unfolded in curious fashion. The exposure of the Roorback journal as a forgery occurred at a time of maximal political effect. Moreover, a hint of devilish mischief as well as malice may be discerned in the selection of Baron Roorback as the name of the supposed traveler. The intent may have been a sly reference to the legendary Baron Munchausen, whose alleged adventures had made his name already proverbial for the preposterous but engaging fabrication.

The Roorback forgery soon came to epitomize the political dirty trick. In succeeding decades *roorback* came to refer to any political falsehood or forgery and especially to one introduced so late in a campaign as to make refutation difficult. As the events of 1844 faded from public memory, the variant *roarback* also developed. Created by folk etymology, *roarback* is suggestive of the fact that groundless political smears often backfire and come roaring back to haunt the perpetrators.

[after Baron von *Roorback,* fictional author of *Roorback's Tour Through the Western and Southern States,* an imaginary book from which an alleged passage was quoted in the Ithaca (N.Y.) *Chronicle* of 1844 that made scurrilous charges against James K. Polk, then Democratic candidate for president]

rosary   See BEAD.
[ME *rosarie,* fr. ML *rosarium,* fr. L *rosarium* rose garden, neut. of *rosarius* of roses, fr. *rosa* rose + *-arius* -ary, connected with]

rostrum   The Latin word *rostrum,* whose primary meaning is 'beak', was derived from the verb *rodere,* 'to gnaw', which is, of course, the anatomical function of a beak. Eventually *rostrum* came to be used metaphorically to refer to the prow or beak of a ship. In 338 B.C. the beaks of ships captured from the people of Antium (now called Anzio) were used to decorate the orators' platform in the Roman Forum. From that time on, this platform was called *Rostra,* the plural form of *rostrum.* Later on, *rostra* was used in a general way to refer to any platform from which a speaker addressed an assembly. The *rostra* of the emperor Augustus, for example, is known to have been seventy-eight feet long, thirty-three feet wide, and eleven feet above the level of the pavement. Along the front there was a marble balustrade with an opening in the center where the speaker stood. In the existing remains of this *rostra*, the holes in which the beaks of ships were fastened in pairs are still apparent.

In the eighteenth century the singular form, *rostrum*, was borrowed into English to mean 'a platform for public speaking'. It was often applied specifically to a pulpit. The theatrical sense of 'a raised platform on a stage' soon followed. The primary Latin sense, 'beak', also survives in English in reference to the beak or other anterior portion of various animals, such as insects, spiders, and crayfish.

[L *rostrum*, muzzle, beak, ship's beak, & L *Rostra* (fr. pl. of *rostrum*) platform for speakers in the Forum of ancient Rome decorated with the beaks of ships captured in war, fr. *rodere* to gnaw]

roué   The word *roué* can be traced back to the Latin noun *rota*, meaning 'wheel'. From the noun the verb *rotare*, 'to rotate', was derived, which in Medieval Latin took on the sense 'to break on the wheel'. The wheel in question was the instrument of torture designed to extract a confession of guilt by stretching, disjointing, or otherwise mutilating the victim. *Rotare* became *rouer* in French, and *roué* is the past participle of that verb, meaning 'broken on the wheel'. About the year 1720 Philippe II, the Duke of Orleans and Regent of France, who was himself a profligate, called his wantonly licentious companions "roués," by which he meant that they deserved to be broken on the wheel, a form of punishment generally meted out at that time to serious malefactors. This grimly affectionate bit of raillery may be seen as equivalent to using "you old horse thief" as a greeting in the American West (or at least Hollywood's version of it). It has also been suggested that the duke may have called his friends *roués* because their debauches so exhausted them that they felt as though they had been broken on the wheel. In any case, *roué* then came to be applied to other such rakes and profligates, and its first appearance in English was around the year 1800.

[F, lit., broken on the wheel, fr. past part. of *rouer* to break on the wheel, fr. ML *rotare*, fr. L, to rotate; fr. the feeling that such a person deserved this punishment]

rubric   Derived ultimately from Latin *ruber*, 'red', *rubric* was originally used in Middle English to name red ocher, a red, earthy hematite used as a pigment. Yet in present-day English *rubric* is used in the senses of 'an authoritative rule' or 'an explanatory or introductory commentary'. This semantic transformation derives from the practice originated centuries ago of putting instructions or explanations in a manuscript or printed book in red ink to contrast with the black ink of the text. Similarly, red ink was used to enter saints' names and holy days in calendars, and we still speak of important days as "red-letter days." See also MINIATURE.

[ME *rubrike* red ocher, heading in red letters of a part of a book, fr. MF *rubrique*, fr. L *rubrica*, fr. *rubr-*, *ruber* red]

ruby   See GARNET.
[ME, fr. MF *rubi*, fr. OF, irreg. fr. L *rubeus* red, reddish; akin to L *ruber* red]

ruminate   An informal idiom has it that a person who is thinking something over is "chewing" on it, the suggestion being that the process of unhurried contemplation has some resemblance to a process of patient mastication. Much the same notion lies at the root of *ruminate*. Certain animals, such as deer, sheep, and domestic cattle, digest their food in stages, first swallowing the vegetation that they crop into a special stomach, where it is partially digested, then bringing it back up for some further leisurely chewing. This process is known as chewing the cud, and the animals that engage in it are known as ruminants. The word *ruminant* is derived ultimately from the Latin *rumen*, which means 'throat' or 'gullet' in Latin but which is also now used as an English word naming that "special stomach" of ruminants. The related Latin verb *ruminari* means literally 'to chew the cud'. The similarity between recalling food to the mouth for further chewing and recalling an idea to the mind for further thought—as well, perhaps, as the contemplative expression characteristic of a cow in mid-chew—led the Romans to use *ruminari* in an extended sense 'to think over, muse upon'. The English verb *ruminate*, from *ruminatus*, the past participle of *ruminari*, has been used since the sixteenth century and has retained both the literal and figurative applications of its Latin etymon, so that it is still quite possible to speak of "ruminating" bovines. But *ruminate* is doubtless now best known in its figurative uses, especially as an intransitive verb meaning 'to engage in contemplation'.

[L *ruminatus*, past part. of *ruminare*, *ruminari* to chew the cud, think over, ruminate, fr. *rumin-*, *rumen* gullet; akin to Skt *romantha* chewing the cud]

runcible spoon   See JABBERWOCKY.
[coined with an obscure meaning in 1871 by Edward Lear †1888 Eng. landscape painter and writer of nonsense verse]

S

sacerdotal See SACRED.

[ME, fr. MF, fr. L *sacerdotalis*, fr. *sacerdot-, sacerdos* priest (fr. *sacer* sacred + *-dot-, -dos* — akin to L *facere* to make, do) + *-alis* -al]

sacred The Latin adjective *sacer* meant 'dedicated or consecrated to a divinity, holy', as in *locus sacer* 'a holy place'. It also was used to mean 'accursed', as in Virgil's *auri sacra fames* 'accursed hunger for gold'. It was the 'holy' sense, however, that gave rise to the verb *sacrare* 'to dedicate or consecrate to a divinity, set apart as sacred'. This Latin verb was taken into Old French as *sacrer*, which was used in the sense 'to confer a holy character on by a religious ceremony'. It was used especially to denote the crowning of a king. In the thirteenth century, English borrowed the French verb as *sacren*, of which *sacred* is the past participle. *Sacren* at first meant 'to consecrate (the eucharistic elements) in the Mass', and then 'to consecrate (as a king or bishop) to office'. *Sacren* became obsolete by the end of the seventeenth century, but its past participle survived as the adjective *sacred*. In the fourteenth century *sacred* acquired the sense 'dedicated or set apart for the service or worship of deity', as in "a tree sacred to the gods." The sense 'worthy of religious veneration', as in "sacred relics," developed in the fifteenth century. By the sixteenth century, *sacred* was being used to mean 'religious in nature, association, or use' as in "sacred music." It was then also applied to something considered 'inviolable', as in the expression "a sacred trust."

The stem *sacr-* of the Latin *sacer* is the ultimate source of several other English words: *consecrate, desecrate, execrate,* as well as *sacristan, sexton, sacerdotal,* and *sacrosanct* can all be traced back to this stem. The word *sacrifice*, borrowed from Old French, ultimately derives from *sacer* combined with a derivative of the verb *facere* 'to make'. The noun *sacrilege* can be traced back through Middle French to the Latin *sacrilegus* 'one who steals sacred things', which was formed by adding *sacer* to *legere* 'to gather, steal'.

The Latin verb *sancire*, related to *sacer*, was used in the sense 'to render sacred or inviolable'. The past participle of *sancire* is *sanctus*, which is the root of several English words, including *saint, sanctify, sanction,* and *sanctuary*.

[ME, fr. past part. of *sacren* to consecrate, fr. OF *sacrer,* fr. L *sacrare,* fr. *sacr-, sacer* sacred, holy, cursed]

sacrifice   See SACRED.
[ME *sacrifise, sacrifice,* fr. OF, fr. L *sacrificium,* fr. *sacri-* (fr. *sacr-, sacer* sacred) + *-ficium* (akin to L *-ficare* -fy)]

sacrilege   See SACRED.
[ME, fr. OF, fr. L *sacrilegium,* fr. *sacrilegus* one that steals that which is sacred, fr. *sacri-* (fr. *sacr-, sacer* sacred) + *-legus* (fr. *legere* to gather, steal)]

sacristan   See SACRED.
[ME, fr. ML *sacristanus,* fr. *sacrista* (fr. L *sacr-, sacer* sacred + *-ista* -ist) + L *-anus* -an]

sacrosanct   See SACRED.
[L *sacrosanctus,* prob. fr. *sacro* by a sacred rite (abl. of *sacrum* sacred thing, sacred rite, fr. neut. of *sacer* sacred) + *sanctus* (past part. of *sancire* to make sacred)]

sad   *Sad* has been in the English language at least since the year 1000, and its semantic development over the past nine hundred years has considerably obscured its relation to other familiar English words such as *insatiable, satire,* and *satisfy.* The earliest senses of *sad* were 'sated', 'satisfied', or 'weary of something'. For instance, in a sermon written in the early thirteenth century we read, "Ich am noht giet sad of mine sinnes, and forthi ne mai ich hie noht forlete." (I am not tired of my sins yet, and therefore I cannot give them up.)

By the fourteenth century *sad* had developed the sense of 'firmly established or settled', as in Milton's *Paradise Lost:* "Settled in his face I see/ Sad resolution and secure." Subsequent developments from this sense would appear to be the senses 'grave, serious' and 'downcast, mournful', which first appeared in the late fourteenth century. Today only the latter and the senses derived from it are current in the United States, all the earlier senses having passed from use. See also SATIRE.

[ME, fr. OE *sæd;* akin to OHG *sat* sated, ON *sathr, saddr,* Goth *sads,* L *satur* sated, *satis* enough, Gk *hadēn* to satiety, enough, Skt *asinva* insatiable]

sadism   See MASOCHISM.
[ISV *sad-* (fr. Comte Donatien Alphonse François de *Sade* †1814 Fr. soldier and pervert) + *-ism*]

saint   See SACRED.
[ME, fr. MF, fr. LL *sanctus,* fr. L, sacred, pure, holy, fr. past part. of *sancire* to make sacred, ordain, establish]

salaam Many Americans are familiar with the Hebrew greetings *shalom*, which literally means 'peace', and *shalom aleichem* 'peace [be] upon you'—the latter also familiar in slightly different spelling as the pen name of a celebrated Yiddish author, Sholem Aleichem. The Arabic cognate of *shalom* is *salaam*, and it too is used both as the usual word for 'peace' and as a greeting, especially in the phrase *salaam 'alaykum*, to which the conventional response is *'alaykum salaam* 'upon you [be] peace'. The prominence of this greeting in Muslim countries led English to borrow the word *salaam*, first as the term for such a salutation and then as a verb meaning to perform the bowing obeisance that sometimes accompanies the greeting.

Hebrew and Arabic are both members of the Semitic family of languages, one of whose most striking characteristics is the building of words by fitting a triconsonantal root of specific lexical meaning into a largely vocalic pattern of general grammatical meaning. Thus the root *slm* means 'peace' or 'submission'; the pattern *i--aa-* (where the hyphens represent the root consonants to be filled in) means 'act of . . .' (performing what is denoted by a given verbal root). Put them together and you have *islaam*, literally 'act of submission'. During the prophethood of Muhammad, this was taken specifically in the sense 'submission to the will of God' and applied to the religion he founded. English borrowed the word as *Islam* (which we should write *Islaam* were we to be as observant of vowel length as we were in the case of *salaam*). The pattern *mu--i-* is used for a class of active participles, so a *muslim* is literally 'one who submits', that is, one who adheres to Islam; this is the source of our word *Muslim* (or *Moslem*).

English has borrowed one further, though less familiar, word from this root, *selamlik*, denoting a room in a Muslim house reserved for men. This word was borrowed from Turkish, which formed it by adding a Turkish suffix to the Arabic root, producing a form that literally means 'place of greeting'.

[Ar *salām*, lit., peace]

salary In the Roman army soldiers were allowed a sum of money to buy salt with, since salt was not always easily come by and was important for more than increasing the savor of food in the days before refrigeration. Later this money, called *salarium*, came to designate simply the stipend or pension paid to the soldiers and still later the payments made to officials of the empire. *Salarium*, the source of English *salary*, is a form of *salarius*, meaning 'of salt', from *sal*, 'salt'. So if you are earning your salary, you are presumably also "worth your salt." In addition to a *salary* it is always good to receive a *bonus*, from Latin *bonus*, meaning 'good'. See also FEE.

[ME *salarie*, fr. L *salarium* money given to soldiers for salt, pension, stipend, salary, fr. neut. of *salarius* of salt, fr. *sal* salt + -*arius* -ary, connected with]

salient See SOMERSAULT.

[L *salient-*, *saliens*, pres. part. of *salire* to leap, spring]

salientian   See SOMERSAULT.
[NL *Salientia*, fr. L, neut. pl. of *salient-, saliens* + E *-an*]

sally   See SOMERSAULT.
[MF *saillie*, fr. OF, fr. fem. of *sailli*, past part. of *saillir* to jump, rush forward, fr. L *salire* to jump, leap; akin to Gk *hallesthai* to leap]

sanctify   See SACRED.
[ME *sanctifien, seintifien*, fr. MF *sanctifier, saintifier*, fr. LL *sanctificare*, fr. L *sanctus* holy + *-ficare* -fy]

sanction   See SACRED.
[MF or L; MF *sanction*, fr. L *sanction-, sanctio*, fr. *sanctus* (past part. of *sancire* to decree, make sacred) + *-ion-, -io* -ion]

sanctuary   See SACRED.
[ME *sanctuarie, seintuarie*, fr. MF *sainctuarie, saintuarie*, fr. LL *sanctuarium*, fr. L *sanctus* holy + *-arium* -ary]

sandwich   See DERBY.
[after John Montagu, 4th Earl of *Sandwich* †1792 Eng. diplomat]

sanguine   See HUMOR.
[ME *sanguin*, fr. MF, fr. L *sanguineus* of blood, bloody, bloodred, fr. *sanguin-, sanguis* blood + *-eus* -eous]

sapphire   See AMETHYST.
[ME *saphir, safir*, fr. OF *safir*, fr. L *sapphirus*, fr. Gk *sappheiros*, fr. Heb *sappīr*, fr. Skt *śanipriya*, lit., dear to the planet Saturn, fr. *Śani* (the planet) Saturn + *priya* dear]

sapphism   See LESBIAN.
[*Sappho fl ab*600 B.C. Greek poetess of Lesbos + E *-ism;* fr. the belief that Sappho was homosexual]

sarcasm   The root of the word *sarcasm* is the same as that of the Greek *sarx*, meaning 'flesh'. A Greek verb formed from this same root is *sarkazein*, which means literally 'to tear flesh like dogs'. The fury suggested by this verb is somewhat abated in the figurative senses 'to bite one's lips in rage' and 'to gnash one's teeth', and weakened still further in the senses 'to speak bitterly' and 'to sneer'. The Greek noun *sarkasmos* derived from this word means essentially the same things as *sarcasm* does in English today. While the metaphoric extension of the literal sense of *sarkazein* which underlies our word *sarcasm* may not be apparent to most English speakers today, we often use the same imagery ourselves. We do not find it unusual to speak of a "sharp" or "cutting" phrase or a "biting" remark, and the pain caused by *sarcasm* can be just as real as that caused by the bite of a dog. See also SARCOPHAGUS.

[F or LL; F *sarcasme*, fr. LL *sarcasmos*, fr. Gk *sarkasmos*, fr. *sarkazein* to tear flesh like dogs, bite the lips in rage, speak bitterly, sneer, fr. *sark-*, *sarx* flesh; prob. akin to Av *thwarəs-* to cut]

sarcophagus   It was said that in the Troad, an ancient region of Asia Minor, a corrosive stone was quarried, known in Greek as *lithos sarkophagos*. This was used to fashion coffins or perhaps only to fill them, the better to hasten the decomposition of the corpse. *Sarcophagos* literally means 'flesh-eating': its component roots may be seen separately in our words *sarcasm* and *phagocyte*. Latin borrowed the word as *sarcophagus*, in which stately form it passed into English.

Greek is also the ultimate source of our word *coffin*. In Greek, a *kophinos* was simply a wicker hamper, without funerary significance. The Latin borrowing *cophinus* retained this sense, as did its English offspring *coffin* when this appeared in the fourteenth century. Thus the Wycliffe Bible, relating the incident of the loaves and the fishes, has "Thei token the relifis of broken gobetis, twelue cofyns ful" (They gathered the leftovers of broken fragments, twelve baskets full). At that time, the word was also applied to such appetizing containers as pastry casings. Not until the sixteenth century do we find the word used in the modern sense of 'a box in which to bury a corpse'. The semantic development thus parallels that of *casket*, which originally meant 'box' or 'chest'. Another offspring of *cophinus* that specialized in a different direction is *coffer*.

The etymological sense of *bier* is even more general, as it goes back to the Indo-European root reflected in our verb *bear*. The bier was in fact originally the stand that bore the coffin; later it became identified also with the coffin itself.

[L *sarcophagus (lapis)* limestone used for coffins, fr. Gk *(lithos) sarkophagos*, lit., flesh-eating stone, fr. *sark-* sarc- (flesh) + *-phagos* (fr. *phagein* to eat)]

sashay   See CATCH.
[alter. of *chassé*, fr. F, a kind of dance step]

sass   Americans were altering the broad vowel of *sauce* to the short *a* of *sass* before the end of the eighteenth century. *Sass* first referred to garden vegetables: *long sass* was carrots and parsnips and such, while *short sass* was potatoes, onions, or turnips. Plain unmodified *sass* might also mean stewed fruit such as applesauce. These uses of *sass* can still be found but are not very common. Much more common is the 'back talk' sense:

"Aw—take a walk!"
"Say—if you give me much more of your sass I'll take and bounce a rock off'n your head" —Mark Twain, *Tom Sawyer*, 1876

Sass appeared as a verb in the middle of the nineteenth century and *sassy*, from *saucy*, some twenty years earlier; these are both still current:

. . . a 13-year-old evangelist, who hung himself because his mother spanked him for sassing her —Flannery O'Connor, letter, 23 Apr. 1960

. . . her hair cut in the sassy new pageboy bob —Russell Baker, *Growing Up*, 1982

The phrase *fat and sassy* has connoted robust good health for well over a century:

The fryin-pan stunk with fat eels, and we all got fat and sassy —Hardin E. Taliaferro, "Larkin Snow the Miller," 1859

. . . includes fat and sassy bluepoint oysters —Richard C. Lemon, *People*, 25 July 1983

For more on dialectal variants that have become standard see ORNERY, PASSEL, RILE.

[back-formation fr. ¹*sassy* (alter. of *saucy,* fr. *sauce* + -*y*)]

Satan   See DEVIL.
[ME *Satan, Sathan,* fr. OE *Satan, Satanas,* fr. LL, fr. Gk, fr. Heb *śāṭān* devil, adversary]

satire   When it made its appearance in English in the sixteenth century, *satire* had a meaning closely related to the senses in which it is still used today. It was a term for a literary work holding up human vices and follies to ridicule or scorn, and though no longer necessarily literary, the function of *satire* remains much the same. It is derived from Latin *satira* and its earlier form *satura,* which in classical times meant 'a satirical poem'. Before the development of this style of satiric poetry, the preclassical satura was a poem dealing with a number of different subjects often treated in a number of different manners, even sometimes shifting back and forth between verse and prose. It is this sense of 'a poetic medley' that gives us a clue to the early development of the word. According to classical Roman grammarians this sense of *satura* evolved from the phrase *lanx satura,* literally 'a full plate'. *Satura* is a form of *satur,* meaning 'sated' or 'full of food', and the grammarians specify that *lanx satura* once meant a plate filled with various fruits or a dish made from a mixture of many ingredients. For a similar culinary metaphor applied to a literary genre see FARCE. See also SAD.

[MF or L; MF, fr. L *satira, satura* satirical poetry, poetic medley, fr. *(lanx) satura* full plate, plate filled with fruits, mixture, medley, fr. *lanx* plate + *satura,* fem. of *satur* full of food, sated]

Saturday   See SUNDAY.
[ME *saterday,* fr. OE *sæterdæg, sæterndæg;* akin to OFris *sāterdei* Saturday, MD *saterdach,* MLG *sāterdach;* all fr. a prehistoric WGmc compound whose first constituent was borrowed fr. L *Saturnus* Saturn and

whose second constituent is represented by OE *dæg* day; trans. of L *Saturni dies*]

saturnine See JOVIAL.
[ME, prob. fr. (assumed) ML *saturninus,* fr. L *Saturnus* Saturn + *-inus*
-ine; perh. fr. the planet's remoteness from the sun]

sauce See SASS.
[ME, fr. MF *sauce, sausse,* fr. L *salsa,* fem. of *salsus* salted, fr. past part.
of *sallere* to salt, fr. *sal* salt]

sauté See SOMERSAULT.
[F, past part. of *sauter* to jump, fr. MF, fr. L *saltare* to dance, freq. of
salire to leap]

sauterne See LIEBFRAUMILCH.
[F *sauternes,* fr. *Sauternes,* commune in southwestern France, where it
is made]

scale See ECHELON.
[ME, ladder, staircase, line marked by graduations, fr. LL *scala* ladder,
staircase, fr. L *scalae* (pl.) stairs, rungs of a ladder, ladder; akin to L
scandere to climb]

scamper See ESCAPE.
[prob. fr. obs. D *schampen* to flee, fr. MF *escamper,* fr. It *scampare,* fr.
(assumed) VL *excampare* to decamp, fr. L *ex-* + *campus* field]

scandal See SLANDER.
[LL *scandalum* stumbling block, offense, fr. Gk *skandalon*]

scapegoat On Yom Kippur, the Jewish Day of Atonement, the ancient
Hebrews were able to make a fresh start for the following year simply by
transferring their sins to a goat. The high priest took two goats, one to be
sacrificed to the Lord, the other to carry the sins of the people away into
the desert. The ceremony is described in Leviticus 16:8 (RSV): ". . . and
Aaron shall cast lots upon the two goats; one lot for the Lord and the other
lot for Azazel." After the Lord's goat had been sacrificed, the priest con-
fessed the sins of the people over the head of the live goat, which was then
led away into the desert and there released.

Azazel, apparently, was a demon whose domain was the uninhabited
wilderness. But the name *Azazel* resembles the Hebrew phrase *'ēz 'ōzēl,*
which means 'goat that departs'. And that is exactly what the goat for Azazel was. Thus, the demon's name was misinterpreted, and this misinterpretation is reflected in the Septuagint, a Greek translation of the Old
Testament. Azazel is there translated as *tragos apopompaios,* 'goat sent
out'. The Latin Vulgate calls him *caper emissarius,* 'emissary goat'.

William Tyndale, in his English translation of the Pentateuch (published
in 1530), continued the erroneous tradition by rendering the Latin as

scapegoat, 'escape goat': ". . . one lotte for the Lorde, and another for a scapegoote." The Authorized or King James Version of the Bible (1611) retained Tyndale's *scapegoat,* but Azazel has been returned to his rightful position in the Revised Standard Version quoted above. Although the goat for Azazel did escape sacrifice, he bore the heavy burden of the people's sins. It is for this reason that we call anyone a *scapegoat* who bears the blame for others' transgressions or mistakes.

[*scape* + *goat;* intended as trans. of Heb *'azāzēl* (prob. name of a demon), as if *'ēz 'ōzēl* goat that departs, Lev 16:8 (AV)]

scaramouch   See SCRIMMAGE.

[F *Scaramouche,* fr. It *Scaramuccia,* fr. *scaramuccia* skirmish]

scavage   See SCAVENGER.

[ME *skawage,* fr. ONF *escauwage* inspection, fr. *escauwer* to inspect (of Gmc origin) + *-age;* akin to OE *scēawian* to look at, see, inspect]

scavenger   In the fourteenth, fifteenth, and sixteenth centuries, many English towns and cities levied a tax called *scavage* on goods shown for sale by nonresident merchants in order to put outsiders at a disadvantage in their trade in comparison with local merchants. Although the name was new in the fourteenth century, the tax itself was not. In Anglo-Saxon times the exacted levy was called *scēawung,* 'showing'. The Middle English *scawage* is not a descendant of the Old English *scēawung,* but it is a relative. Old North French *escauwage,* 'inspection', from which *scawage* was borrowed, is itself Germanic in origin and a cognate of Old English *scēawung.* The *scavagers* or (with intrusive *n*) *scavengers* of London were officers charged with the collection of the scavage. The responsibility for keeping the streets clean later fell on their shoulders as well. When the scavengers' original purpose was forgotten, they remained simple street cleaners. Now anyone who collects junk is a scavenger. For more on the intrusive *n* see HARBINGER, POPINJAY.

[alter. of *scavager,* fr. ME *skawager,* fr. *skawage* scavage + *-er;* fr. the fact that the official charged with collecting the toll was later made responsible for keeping the streets clean]

scene   In the sixth century B.C. the poet Thespis, traditionally regarded as the originator of the actor's role in drama, experimented with various methods of disguise to distinguish characters, and he finally settled upon the use of masks. Later, masks were worn by the chorus as well as the actors, and a booth or tent, called *skēnē* in Greek, was set up for them to change in. This is the source of our word *scene* denoting the subdivisions of a dramatic work. As Greek drama developed, the *skēnē* became a building or structure erected to serve as a background to the play and a point of entrance and exit for the actors as well as a changing room. From its use as a background we get *scene* in the sense of 'a stage setting'. An extension of this sense is the current use of *scene* to mean 'a real or imaginary prospect suggesting a stage setting'. See also TRAGEDY.

[MF, stage, fr. L *scaena, scena,* fr. Gk *skēnē* booth, tent, skene, stage; akin to Gk *skia* shadow, Skt *chāyā* color, shadow]

school It may be hard for students to think of school as a form of leisure, but when the word *school* is traced back to its Greek etymon *scholē,* 'leisure' is the original sense of the word. Edith Hamilton, in *The Greek Way to Western Civilization,* comments on this connection: "Of course, reasoned the Greek, given leisure a man will employ it in thinking and finding out about things. Leisure and the pursuit of knowledge, the connection was inevitable—to a Greek." It is not until about 30 B.C. that we find the first known use of *scholē* in the sense 'a place of learning'. The Romans later borrowed the Greek word as *schola,* with essentially the same meanings, and employed Greek slaves as teachers, thus paying their tribute to the supremacy of Greece in the life of the mind. Christian missionaries later established schools throughout Europe, and St. Augustine of Canterbury is said to have established the first English school in 598. *Schola* became *scōl* in Old English about the year 1000 and denoted 'a place for instruction'. This word evolved into *scole* in Middle English and then into *school* under the renewed influence of the Latin form.

No doubt the expression 'a school of fish" seems to most speakers to involve the same word, since it is easy to imagine a connection between the image of the fish and that of a class being marched along in orderly columns with ever-renewed fringes of disorder. But this word *school* is etymologically unrelated. It is related instead to Old English *scolu* 'multitude, school of fish', and to Modern English *shoal* in the same meaning. The situation is doubly confusing as *shoal* also has a homograph—that is, a word spelled the same but etymologically unrelated—meaning 'shallow place'. This last *shoal* is probably related to *shallow.*

[ME *scole,* fr. OE *scōl,* fr. L *schola* leisure devoted to learning, lecture, school, fr. Gk *scholē* leisure, learned discussion, lecture, school]

[ME *scole,* fr. MD *schole* group esp. of fish or animals of one kind, multitude; akin to OE *scolu* multitude, troop, *sciell* shell]

scilicet See INNUENDO.

[ME, fr. L, fr. *scire* to know + *licet* it is permitted, 3d pers. sing. pres. indic. of *licēre* to be permitted]

scintilla In Latin *scintilla* was a spark; *scintillare* meant 'to sparkle'. English borrowed *scintilla* in exactly its Latin form but with a figurative meaning, 'the least little bit, a whit', possibly influenced by the fact that *scintilla* looks like a diminutive, though its etymology within Latin is, in fact, obscure. The English version of *scintillare,* namely *scintillate,* has sometimes been used in its etymological sense but is now more often figurative, with the same figurative sense as that acquired by *sparkle* itself, as in "sparkling/scintillating wit." It is interesting that the figurative senses have gone off in different directions: *scintilla* and *scintillate* don't really hook up with each other in English the way their etyma did in Latin.

French inherited *scintilla* in the original sense: *étincelle* means 'spark'. But the sound correspondence is not regular. The Middle French form *estencele* clarifies what had happened: the classical Latin form had undergone a change in popular speech to something like **stincilla,* and this is the immediate ancestor of *estencele.* A derived verb, *estenceler,* meant 'to sparkle' and (transitively) 'to ornament with colors or sparkles'. Middle English borrowed the latter use in the verb *stanselen.* This verb dropped out of use, yet seems to have resurfaced as a noun spelled *stansile* in 1707, when it referred to a perforated pattern through which playing cards could be colored. Thereafter any necessary connection with color dropped away entirely, so that a *stencil* is simply any perforated template, and any memory of an original connection with sparks and sparkling has quite winked out.

scintillate   See SCINTILLA.
[L *scintillatus,* past part. of *scintillare* to sparkle, fr. *scintilla* spark, scintilla]

screeve   See SCRIVENER.
[prob. fr. It *scrivere* to write]

scribble   See SCRIVENER.
[ME *scriblen,* fr. ML *scribillare,* fr. L *scribere* to write]

scrimmage   *Scrimmage* is a fifteenth-century word altered from *skirmish* by transposing the *i* and *r* and muddling the *-ish* ending with *-age.* There was a semi-muddled intermediate form *scrimish,* attested a few times from the sixteenth century. The original meaning was the same as that of *skirmish.* In the eighteenth century it came to mean any kind of noisy altercation, and as a noisy struggle and confusion it was a natural, in the nineteenth century, for use in Rugby football. The nineteenth century saw a dialectal variant *scrummage* used for the 'altercation' sense, and this variant was the one that stuck in Rugby, where it has since been shortened to *scrum.* American football adopted the term from Rugby, but kept the older form *scrimmage. Scrimmage* has subsequently been used in other American sports.

Skirmish comes from a Middle English *skyrmissh,* an alteration of earlier *skarmish, scarmuch* that is probably due to the influence of the Middle English verb *skirmysshen* 'to brandish a weapon, fence with swords'. The older Middle English words were borrowed from Middle French *escarmouche,* itself from Old Italian *scaramuccia,* a word of Germanic origin. It is interesting to note that the influencing Middle English verb can be traced back through the French to what may be the same ultimate source in Germanic, which is related to Old High German *skirmen* 'to protect, defend'.

The Old Italian *scaramuccia* 'skirmish' became applied as a name to a stock character of Italian comedy. *Scaramuccia* was a blustering coward and was intended as a lampoon of the Spanish don—ethnic humor is no recent development. In 1673 the leading player in a touring Italian company scored a considerable hit with the character, and the word became quite popular in English during the last quarter of the seventeenth century. Late seventeenth-century English spelling pretty well mangled the Italian, but a Frenchified version (the company had played Paris too) *Scaramouch* eventually caught on. A playwright named Edward Ravenscroft produced a play titled *Scaramouch* in 1677,.and *scaramouch* is still used today to mean 'a cowardly buffoon'.

[alter. of ¹*skirmish*]

scrip   See SCRIVENER.
[short for ¹*script*]

script   See SCRIVENER.
[L *scriptum* thing written, fr. neut. of *scriptus,* past part. of *scribere* to write]

Scripture   See SCRIVENER.
[ME, fr. LL *scriptura,* fr. L, act or product of writing, fr. *scriptus* (past part. of *scribere* to write) + -*ura* -ure]

scrivener   Francis Bacon observed "that the scriveners and brokers do value unsound men to serve their own turn [purpose]" in his essay "Of Riches," first published in 1612. English acquired the ancestor of the word *scrivener,* spelled *scrivein,* in the fourteenth century from the French noun *escrivein,* denoting 'a professional or public copyist or writer, a scribe' (the modern French form for 'writer' is *écrivain*). Within the last fifteen years of his life, Chaucer wrote a short, scolding poem "unto Adame his owen scryveyne," who was making too many mistakes in his copying. The French formed *escrivein* from the assumed Vulgar Latin *scriba* 'scribe', with the *n* coming from the declensional stem *scriban-*. In words passing from Latin to French, a -*b*- between vowels usually became a -*v*-.

Latin *scriba* is related to the verb *scribere* 'to write'. In Medieval Latin a diminutive verb *scribillare,* developed, which English took in the fifteenth century as *scriblen* (modern English *scribble*).

The past participle of the Latin verb *scribere* is *scriptus,* of which the neuter form is *scriptum.* Used as a noun, *scriptum* referred to 'something written', such as a composition, treatise, or book, and passed into English as *script. Scriptus* also gave rise to the noun *scriptura,* meaning 'the act or product of writing', which later appeared in the Vulgate Bible (fourth century) in reference to 'a passage of the Bible'. English took this word as *Scripture* in the fourteenth century, when it came to refer to the Bible as a whole.

The Latin *scriptum* is, as mentioned above, the forebear of our word *script,* which first appeared in English in the fourteenth century carrying the Latin sense of 'something written'. It was not until the mid-nineteenth century that it took on the sense of 'handwriting'. At about the same time the legal profession picked it up to mean 'an original or principal instrument or document'. By the end of the nineteenth century, *script* came to be used for the written text of a play, and, later, with the advent of motion pictures, for the text of a screenplay.

The word *scrip*, for 'a small piece of paper having writing on it', dates from the early seventeenth century and, while it may be a variant of *scrap*, most authorities regard it as a shortened form of *script* or *subscription receipt*. By the early eighteenth century, *scrip* was being used for 'a short writing', such as a certificate, schedule, or list. From this sense developed its use for 'any of various documents used as evidence that the holder or bearer is entitled to receive something (as a fractional share of stock or an allotment of land)'. By the 1880s *scrip* was also used in the U.S. for 'paper currency or a token issued for temporary use in an emergency'.

About the middle of the nineteenth century, the verb *screeve* became current in British slang in the sense 'to draw pictures on the pavement with colored chalk in order to elicit money from passersby'. A *screever*, then, was one of these sidewalk artists. These words probably derive from the Italian verb *scrivere* 'to write', which was taken from the Latin *scribere*.

Several English compounds also owe their existence to the Latin *scribere*. We list them here with their elements translated literally: *describe* 'to write down', *prescribe* 'to write at the beginning', *subscribe* 'to write beneath', *inscribe* 'to write in or upon', *circumscribe* 'to write around', *transcribe* 'to write across', *proscribe* 'to write before', and *superscribe* 'to write above'.

[ME *scriveiner*, fr. *scrivein* copyist, professional writer (fr. MF *escrivein*, *escrivain*, fr. — assumed — VL *scriban-*, *scriba*, fr. L *scriba* scribe) + *-er*]

scrummage   See SCRIMMAGE.
   [alter. of *scrimmage*]

scruple   In Latin *scrupus* referred to a sharp stone; its diminutive, *scrupulus*, accordingly meant 'small sharp stone'. But *scrupulus* soon came to be used more commonly in the metaphorical sense 'a source of anxiety', the way a sharp pebble that had worked its way into one's shoe would be a source of pain. The derived adjective *scrupulosus* had likewise both a concrete meaning, 'full of sharp rocks, jagged', and a metaphorical one—not 'full of sources of anxiety', as one might expect, but 'careful, taking precautions'. Thus it denoted the attitude of someone faced with a rocky situation. Both *scrupulus* and *scrupulosus* found their way into English in their metaphorical senses, respectively as *scruple* ('an ethical consideration') and *scrupulous*.

Scrupulus received another extended meaning in Latin appropriate to the original notion of a small stone, namely 'small part of an ounce', or more generally a small part of any unit of measure. This sense gave rise to another English *scruple,* a unit of apothecaries' measure. (British English has *stone* as a unit of weight in an analogous way.)

Another and more usual word for 'pebble' in Latin was *calculus,* possibly a diminutive of *calx* 'limestone' (the root of our word *calcium*). Since pebbles were used as counters in games and in reckoning, the word acquired an extended sense in measuring and calculating. English borrowed *calculus* both in the concrete sense of a concretion in the body, such as a kidney-stone, and also in a mathematical sense, though in the latter case many might contend that *calculus* is best defined, like *scrupulus,* as 'a source of anxiety'.

[MF *scrupule,* fr. L *scrupulus* small sharp stone, cause of mental or moral discomfort, scruple, dim. of *scrupus* sharp stone]

[ME *scriple,* fr. L *scrupulus, scripulum,* a unit of weight equal to one twenty-fourth of an ounce, fr. *scrupulus* small sharp stone]

scrupulous   See SCRUPLE.
[ME, fr. L *scrupulosus,* fr. *scrupulus* scruple + *-osus* -ous]

segregate   See EGREGIOUS.
[L *segregatus,* past part. of *segregare* to set apart, segregate, fr. *se-* apart (fr. *sed, se* without) + *greg-, grex* flock, herd]

seminar   See SEMINARY.
[G, fr. L *seminarium* seminary]

seminary   Nowadays, if you called a seminary a 'nursery', some seminarians might be offended. To the ancient Romans, however, a *seminarium* was a nursery for growing plants from seeds. The word itself comes from the neuter form of the adjective *seminarius* 'of or relating to seed', which is a derivative of the noun *semen* 'seed'.

Before St. Augustine (354–430), there are no records of any institution for the training of Christian clergy. Bishops and priests trained young men in local parishes for Holy Orders. St. Augustine set up a kind of cathedral school for this purpose, and his example led to the establishing of many other such schools throughout Europe. Out of these local schools and monastic schools grew the medieval universities, those at Paris, Bologna, Oxford, and elsewhere. Such universities attracted the best teachers of theology, philosophy, and canon law. However, since only the privileged few could attend these universities, most clergymen remained undereducated. In order to raise the spiritual and intellectual levels of the clergy, the Council of Trent (1545–63) issued a decree establishing ecclesiastical training schools to prepare men for ordination to the priesthood. The Council called such schools *seminaria* 'seminaries', putting the Latin noun to metaphorical use.

In English, the word *seminary* was first used around 1440 in its ancient Latin 'nursery garden' sense. Following the Council of Trent's decree, English acquired the additional sense of 'an institution engaged in the training of candidates for the priesthood'. Since then, many Christian denominations, as well as other religions, have used the term *seminary* for 'a training school for clergymen'.

By 1585, the term *seminary* was being applied more broadly to 'an educational institution, a school, college, or university'. This sense gave rise in the early nineteenth century to its use for 'a private academy for girls'. Many such seminaries are now colleges.

Beginning in the 1590s, we find evidence of the figurative sense 'a place of origin and early development'. In his *History of England* (1849), Thomas Macaulay provides an example of such use: "The prisons were hells on earth, seminaries of every crime and of every disease."

The Latin *seminarium* is also the source of the German noun *seminar,* which was used in German universities in reference to 'a group of advanced students studying a subject under a professor, each doing some original research, and all exchanging results by informal lectures, reports, and discussions'. In the late nineteenth century, this usage was borrowed into English as seminars became part of British and American university systems.

[ME, fr. L *seminarium,* fr. neut. of *seminarius* of seed, fr. *semin-, semen* seed + *-arius* -ary]

senate   In Latin, the word *senex,* meaning 'old' and 'old man', gave rise to the noun *senatus,* which denoted 'a council of elders' in ancient Rome. Originally consisting of the heads of patrician families, the Senatus evolved into an administrative and legislative body of both elected and appointed members, including many former high-office holders. Senators in the late empire were usually wealthy landowners with something like feudal authority. In the Middle Ages *senatus* was used for the council of a monarch or of a city. Early French took the word as *senat,* which was borrowed into thirteenth-century English. Most of the early references are to the Roman Senate.

By the middle of the sixteenth century, however, *senate* was being used to denote the governing body of a nation, and in the eighteenth century it was applied to the upper and smaller branch of a bicameral legislature in various countries and in the various states that make up a country. In 1780, for example, Abigail Adams wrote in a letter: "Hancock will be Governor, by a very great majority; the Senate [of Massachusetts] will have to choose the Lieutenant-governor." Also in the eighteenth century the term began to be used of a governing body at a university or college. In some American colleges, the senate is composed of both faculty and student representatives, to whom are referred matters of discipline and of general concern.

The Latin adjective *senex* had as its comparative form *senior* 'older'. Used as a noun, *senior* denoted 'an older man', usually one above military age or above forty-five. In Medieval Latin *senior* also came to refer to 'a prominent or foremost person'. When *senior* was first borrowed into English around 1380, it was used as a noun for 'an older person, and especially one worthy of distinction or deference by reason of age'. By the 1440s the adjective was being used after a person's name to denote 'the older of two bearing the same name in a family'. The noun also came to be used for 'a person holding a position of higher standing in a hierarchy'.

Early in the seventeenth century a student of advanced standing was termed a *senior,* and in eighteenth-century America the term was applied specifically to a high school or college student in his fourth year. (Paralleling this development was the use of the word *junior* for such a student in his third year.)

The Latin *senex* also gave rise to the adjective *senilis,* meaning 'of, relating to, or characteristic of an old man', which was taken into English as *senile* around 1660. The sense of 'exhibiting the mental or physical weakness of old age' began appearing in the middle of the nineteenth century. The offshoot *senility* 'the quality or state of being senile' first appeared late in the eighteenth century.

[ME *senat,* fr. OF, fr. L *senatus,* lit., council of elders, fr. *sen-, senex* old, old man + *-atus* -ate]

senile   See SENATE.

[L *senilis,* fr. *sen-, senex* old, old man + *-ilis* -ile]

senior   See SENATE.

[ME, fr. L, fr. *senior* older, elder, compar. of *sen-, senex* old; akin to Goth *sineigs* old, *sinista* eldest, ON *sina* old grass, Gk *henos* old, Skt *sana*]

September   See JANUARY.

[ME *septembre,* fr. OF, fr. L *september* (seventh month), fr. *septem* seven]

serendipity   *Serendipity,* 'an assumed gift for finding valuable or agreeable things not sought for', was coined by Horace Walpole, fourth Earl of Orford (1717–1797). Walpole, in a letter to his friend the diplomat Horace Mann, dated 28 January 1754, explains his coinage as follows: "I once read a silly fairy tale, called *The Three Princes of Serendip;* as their highnesses travelled, they were always making discoveries, by accidents and sagacity, of things which they were not in quest of: for instance, one of them discovered that a mule blind of the right eye had travelled the same road lately, because the grass was eaten only on the left side, where it was worse than on the right—now do you understand Serendipity?" (*Serendip* derives from the Arabic name for Ceylon, now called Sri Lanka.)

The mule mentioned by Walpole was actually a camel in the story, and the three princes simply made a deduction, for which, incidentally, they were suspected of having stolen the camel in question and were thrown into jail. Nonetheless, *serendipity* became part of the language, though used rather rarely until the twentieth century. The word made its first American dictionary appearance in Webster's New International Dictionary in 1909 and has often been linked with an accidental or chance discovery. The noted historian, Samuel Eliot Morison, in his *European Discovery of America: the Northern Voyages* (1971) states that "Columbus and Cabot . . . (by the greatest serendipity of history) discovered America instead of reaching the Indies."

[*Serendip, Serendib* former name for Ceylon (fr. Ar *Sarandīb*) + E *-ity;* fr. the possession of the gift by the heroes of the Persian fairy tale *The Three Princes of Serendip*]

serf See SLAVE.

[F, fr. L *servus* slave, servant, serf]

serge See DENIM.

[ME *sarge*, fr. MF, fr. (assumed) VL *sarica*, fr. L *serica*, fem. of *sericus* of silk, of the Seres, fr. Gk *sērikos*, fr. *Sēres* Seres, an eastern Asian people usually identified with the Chinese + *-ikos* -ic]

servant See SLAVE.

[ME, fr. OF, fr. pres. part. of *servir* to serve, fr. L *servire* to be a slave, serve, be of use, fr. *servus* slave, servant, perh. of Etruscan origin]

sexton See SACRED.

[ME *secresteyn, sekesteyn, sexteyn, sexten*, fr. MF *secrestain*, fr. ML *sacristanus*, fr. *sacrista* (fr. L *sacr-, sacer* sacred + *-ista* -ist) + L *-anus* -an]

shade See DOUBLETS.

[ME, fr. OE *sceadu;* akin to OHG *scato* shadow, Goth *skadus*, OIr *scāth* shadow, Gk *skotos* darkness]

shadow See DOUBLETS.

[ME *shadwe*, fr. OE *sceaduwe, sceadwe*, oblique case form of *sceadu* shade, shadow]

shambles The process by which a word meaning 'footstool' can become a word meaning 'mess' may seem hard to imagine, but the history of *shambles* shows that such a seemingly drastic shift in meaning can occur in a logical, orderly way. The Old English *scamul* (variously spelled) is presumed to be derived ultimately from the Latin *scamellum*, 'little bench'. In Old English, *scamul* was used to mean both 'a footstool' and 'a table used for counting money or for exhibiting goods'. The Middle English derivative *shamel* and its later form *shamble* acquired the specific sense 'a table for the exhibition of meat for sale', which in turn gave rise in the early fifteenth century to a use of the plural, *shamels* and *shambles*, with the meaning 'a meat market'. The *shamels* spelling soon died out, and the next extension in meaning occurred in the sixteenth century, when *shambles* came to mean 'a slaughterhouse'. It is from this sense that soon developed the figurative use to refer to a place of terrible slaughter or bloodshed, as in Samuel Taylor Coleridge's *The Fall of Robespierre* (1794):

"I've fear'd him, since his iron heart endured / To make of Lyons one vast human shambles."

In the twentieth century, *shambles* has undergone two further extensions of meaning. Probably because a place of terrible slaughter, such as a battlefield or a besieged city, is also usually a place of great destruction and disorder, *shambles* has acquired the senses 'a scene or state of great destruction' and 'a scene or state of great disorder or confusion; a mess'.

[pl. of *shamble* meat market (also obs. E *shamble* table for the exhibition of meat for sale), fr. ME *shamel* table for the exhibition of meat for sale, shop counter, footstool, fr. OE *scamul, sceamul* money changer's table, stool; akin to MD *schamel* footstool, OHG *scamal;* all fr. a prehistoric WGmc word borrowed fr. (assumed) VL *scamellus* small bench, dim. of L *scamnum* bench, stool; akin to Skt *skabhnoti* he supports]

shamefaced The Old English *scamfæst* meant 'bashful' or 'modest', or, more literally, 'held fast by shame'. The second element of *shamefaced* was thus originally the same as that of *steadfast,* meaning 'fixed in place or position'. While we can be sure that the similarity of consonant sounds between *-fast* and *-faced* contributed to the alteration of *shamefast* to *shamefaced,* the belief that modesty or bashfulness is reflected in a person's face probably had some influence too. For instance, before the folk etymology made its effect apparent, we find in *Secreta Secretorum,* a fifteenth-century translation from Latin: "Tho that haue the face sumwhate ruddy bene schamefast." (Those who have a somewhat ruddy face are shamefast.) Around the middle of the sixteenth century the alteration to *shamefaced* began to appear in print, and since then the folk etymology has been firmly established. See also FOLK ETYMOLOGY.

[alter. (influenced by *faced*) of *shamefast*]

shay See SHERRY.
[back-formation fr. *chaise,* taken as pl.]

sherry Many wines are named after the places where they are made. The region around the town of *Xeres* (the modern name is *Jerez*) in Spain produced a type of fortified white wine with a rather nutty flavor. This wine was introduced to England in the sixteenth century. At that time the name of the town *Xeres* was often spelled *Sherries* in English—the initial *sh* represented the best English approximation of the contemporary pronunciation of the Spanish *x*. And the wine from *Xeres* was called *sherris*. Shakespeare's Falstaff, in *Henry IV, Part II* (ca. 1597), extolled the virtues of this wine, especially as a source of courage: "[A] property of your excellent sherris is the warming of the blood; which before (cold and settled) left the liver white and pale, which is the badge of pusillanimity and cowardice; . . . valour comes of sherris." But some, judging from the form of the word *sherris* that it was a plural, began to use what they believed to be its singular form, *sherry*. This type of derivation by subtraction of a real or supposed affix is called *back-formation*. Such derivations as the modern creation of a verb *enthuse* from the noun *enthusiasm* are also back-formations.

Several English back-formations follow the same pattern as that we have seen in the etymology of *sherry*. The rhyming *cherry* comes from Old North French *cherise*, which like *sherris* sounds plural. *Pea* is a false singular formed from *pease*. We still see the original form in the popular nursery rhyme: "Pease porridge hot, pease porridge cold, pease porridge in the pot, nine days old." *Shay*, 'a light carriage', is a similar back-formation from *chaise*.

In the Middle Ages, English borrowed *sucurs* or *socours*, 'assistance', from Old French *sucors*, *secors*, a derivative of Latin *succurrere*, 'to run up to help'. Very early, the plural-looking *sucurs* was replaced by an obviously singular *sucur*, which has become our modern *succor*.

Another word that has been misinterpreted as a plural is the French loan word *richesse*, 'richness, wealth'. This has become our *riches*. Its meaning remains unchanged, but *riches*, unlike the earlier *richesse*, is treated as a plural. For plural words which were assumed to be singular see BODICE. For another kind of back-formation see EAVESDROP.

[back-formation fr. earlier *sherris* (taken as pl.), fr. *Xeres* (now *Jerez*), town near Cádiz, Spain]

shibboleth   A person's pronunciation of words provides many clues for determining where he lives or comes from. In the twelfth chapter of the Book of Judges, there is an account of a battle between the Gileadites and the Ephraimites in which a test of pronunciation was used to distinguish members of the opposing armies. The Ephraimite army was routed, and in their retreat they attempted to cross the Jordan river at a ford held by the Gileadites. Anyone wishing to pass was asked by the Gileadites if he were an Ephraimite. If the reply was "No" he was then asked to say the word *shibbōleth*. In Hebrew *shibbōleth* may mean either 'an ear of grain' or 'a stream', but on that occasion its meaning was of no importance. Unlike the Gileadites, the Ephraimites were unable to pronounce an *sh* sound. Thus if the reply were *"sibbōleth"* the Gileadites knew the speaker was an Ephraimite; "then they took him and slew him at the passages of Jordan: and there fell at that time of the Ephraimites forty and two thousand" (Judges 12:6, AV). In English *shibboleth* was borrowed from this passage and has come to mean 'a use of language or custom regarded as distinctive of the members of a particular group'. From this it has also developed the sense of 'a slogan or catchword used by a particular group'. For other words derived from the use of a foreign word rather than its meaning see DIRGE, PIANO.

[Heb *shibbōleth* ear of grain, stream, flood; fr. the use of this word as a test to distinguish Gileadites from Ephraimites, who pronounced it *sibbōleth* (Judges 12:6)]

shirt See SKIRT.
[ME *shirte, sherte,* fr. OE *scyrte;* akin to MD *shorte* apron, MLG *schörte,* MHG *schurz* apron, ON *skyrta* shirt, kirtle, OE *scort, sceort* short]

shivaree See CHARIVARI.
[F *charivari*]

shoal (a great number) See SCHOOL.
[fr. (assumed) ME *shole,* fr. OE *scolu* multitude, troop]

shoal (shallow place) See SCHOOL.
[alter. of earlier *shold, shoald,* fr. ME *sheld, shald, shold,* fr. *sheld, shald, shold,* adj., from OE *sceald*]

shoot See JEEPERS.
[euphemism for *shit*]

shortened forms At a number of etymologies in our dictionaries, one reads that a word is "short for" another word, or arose "by shortening." For instance, the etymology of **gym** in the Webster's Third New International Dictionary reads "[short for *gymnasium*]," and that of ¹**size** reads "[ME *sise,* fr. MF, fr. OF, short for *assise*—more at ASSIZE]"; the entry for **prof** reads "[by shortening] *slang* : PROFESSOR." These formulae are used when a continuous segment of a word has been dropped. If a word is formed rather from the initial letters of a phrase it is called an *abbreviation.* (For an example of this process see OK.)

We may distinguish subtypes of shortening. In one, a short unaccented syllable that might actually be missed by the hearer is scanted in pronunciation, as when *apprentice* gave rise to the by-form *prentice* (still familiar as a surname), or *escape* yielded *scape* (retained in *scapegrace* and *scapegoat*). When the lost syllable was initial, the process is known as *aphesis* or *aphaeresis.* (For a discussion of these see APHAERESIS.) When the lost syllable or sound was interior, philologists speak of *syncope,* as when *Gloucester* came to be pronounced \'glòs-tər\, or *phantasy* gave rise to *fancy.* When the lost sound was final, the process is called *apocope:* this process operated massively in the dropping of many inflectional endings and weak final syllables of older forms of English to yield the stripped-down word forms characteristic of English today. In a second type, an easily perceptible chunk of a word, sometimes consisting of several syllables, is deliberately lopped off, typically resulting in an informal or in-group version of the word: thus *lab* for *laboratory, math* for *mathematics, mike* for *microphone.* (For a discussion of these see CLIPPING.)

shrapnel In 1784 an obscure lieutenant in the British artillery began experimenting, on his own time and at his own expense, with an antipersonnel weapon that consisted of a hollow spherical projectile filled with shot and an explosive charge and designed to scatter the shot and shell fragments in midair. After years of experimentation Henry Shrapnel (1761–1842) saw his invention adopted by the British artillery in 1803. The

Shrapnel shell, as it was called almost immediately following its invention, was first actually used in battle when the British seized part of Dutch Surinam in 1804 and established British Guiana. The device soon found a champion in the Duke of Wellington, who used it in 1808 and later against Napoleon at Waterloo. Wellington himself fired off an admiring missive to the inventor, as did other field commanders. The British military decided that Shrapnel merited no reward or financial compensation, however, despite the fact that he had spent 28 years perfecting his invention at a personal cost of several thousand pounds. Many years later, during World War II, it was found that the explosive charge fragmented the casing of the Shrapnel shell so effectively that the use of the shrapnel balls was unnecessary. Since then, *shrapnel* has been used to refer to the actual shell fragments, as well as to fragments of an explosive bomb or mine.

[after Henry *Shrapnel* †1842 Eng. artillery officer]

shucks   See JEEPERS.
[euphemism for *shit*]

shyster   *Shyster* is an Americanism first used in public in 1843 in the pages of *The Subterranean,* a New York City weekly that concerned itself with goings-on in and about the Tombs (the city jail) and the local courts. *The Subterranean* was published and largely written by Mike Walsh, a muckraker and reformer. The connection of Walsh with the word *shyster* has been explored in detail by Gerald L. Cohen, whose findings we summarize here.

Walsh had been attacking a number of corrupt practices in the New York courts—among them the carryings-on of various unlicensed and unprincipled men who pretended to be lawyers. Walsh referred to these as "pettifoggers" and after one of these articles had appeared he was approached by one of them—a Cornelius Terhune—in a bar. Terhune, though unlicensed, prided himself on his ability and asked Walsh when he next wrote about pettifoggers to name names, so that he (Terhune) would not be confounded with lesser practitioners—he named two or three— that he called *shiseters* (Walsh's spelling; he also used *shyseters*). Walsh didn't know the word, so Terhune explained it to him. Walsh's account of this episode, in *The Subterranean* for 29 July 1843, makes it clear that *shiseter* had vulgar connotations and that it designated an incompetent operative.

Terhune's *shiseter* was apparently a variation on or a parallel to *shicer* (attested in British English about the same time), derived from a German slang word based ultimately on the German vulgarism *scheisse* 'excrement'. This derivation was the earliest to be given in dictionaries, appearing in the unabridged Webster's International of 1890 and Webster's New International of 1909.

Shyster might have died as a mere curiosity had not Walsh been prosecuted and jailed for libel by a corrupt district attorney later in 1843. In his anger and frustration Walsh increased the level of invective in *The Subterranean,* and *shyster* was brought forth to do duty. At first Walsh used three spellings—*shiseter, shyseter,* and *shyster*—and often enclosed the word in quotation marks, but by the end of the year he had settled on *shyster.* He had in the meantime considerably broadened the meaning of the word by applying it to dishonest public officials and other shady characters as well as to the incompetent and dishonest fake lawyers. A typical Mike Walsh snippet:

> Two miserable, hypocritical, candle-faced Shysters, named Water-man and Tilyou, who managed, like a good many others, to smouch themselves into the Common Council . . . —*The Subterranean,* 2 Dec. 1843

Shyster gradually made its way from New York to other cities, primarily at first through the exchange of *The Subterranean* with other newspapers. A Pittsburgh paper, for instance, printed a sympathetic editorial using the word when Walsh was imprisoned, and Walsh had it reprinted in his paper.

In fifteen or twenty years *shyster* had gained enough currency to attract the attention of collectors of Americanisms (through whose collections it eventually reached dictionaries), and after the Civil War it spread all the way west. Mark Twain, for instance, used it in 1872, describing the func-tionaries at the court in Hawaii (the Sandwich Islands then):

> Next we come to his Excellency the Prime Minister, a renegade American from New Hampshire, all jaw, vanity, bombast and igno-rance, a lawyer of "shyster" calibre, a fraud by nature . . .—salary, $4,000 a year, vast consequence, and no perquisites —*Roughing It*

By the time *shyster* began to find its way into dictionaries, Mike Walsh and *The Subterranean*—never a very widely circulated paper—had been forgotten, and the word seemed a curiosity.

Even though the most likely explanation was the first to appear, many other speculations have been offered. Among these are origins in Scottish Gaelic, the Gypsy language Romany, Yiddish, Dutch, and Old English, a sense of the adjective *shy,* and Shakespeare's character Shylock. One of the longer-lived of these speculations fingered a New York lawyer named Scheuster, who was first mentioned in a history of New York written in the 1890s. Scheuster remained undiscovered until revived by a book written in the 1940s, after which he excited some scholarly attention as the source of *shyster.* Only two problems existed with lawyer Scheuster as the origin: the fact that no contemporary mention of him could be found, and the problem of pronunciation—ordinary Americans would probably have pro-nounced his name as "Shuster" rather than "Shyster". (A case in point is the Heublein Company. The founding family pronounced the first syllable "hoy," but their advertising suggested "hi" for several years before bow-ing to the intransigent public and its "hugh.")

Shyster has run Merriam-Webster etymologists a merry chase. From their first (and probably correct) etymology, they successively adopted the Gaelic, then shifted to "origin uncertain," and then adopted lawyer

Scheuster. Now that the Mike Walsh connection has been unearthed, the etymology is back to square one.

[prob. alter. of earlier *shicer* (contemptible fellow), fr. G *scheisser*, lit., defecator]

sibling See GOSSIP.
[*sib* blood relation (fr. ME *sib, sibbe*, fr. OE *sibb*, fr. *sibb*, adj., related, fr. *sibb*, n., kinship; akin to OHG *sippa, sippea* kinship, family, ON *sifjar*, pl., Goth *sibja*) + *-ling*]

sideburns During the American Civil War, the Union general Ambrose Everett Burnside wore long bushy side-whiskers. His appearance first struck the fancy of Washingtonians as he conducted parades and maneuvers with his regiment of Rhode Island volunteers in the early days of the war. Despite a later military career that had its ups and downs, this early popularity fostered the fashion for such whiskers in nineteenth-century America, which came to be called *burnsides*. A later anagram of this name gives us the word *sideburns*, used today of hair grown in front of the ears whether long or short.

Another name for sideburns is *dundrearies*. The name comes from the long, flowing side-whiskers worn by E. A. Sothern, a nineteenth-century actor playing Lord Dundreary, the chief character in the play *Our American Cousin* by Tom Taylor. Today *Our American Cousin* is mainly remembered as the play that Abraham Lincoln was attending when he was assassinated.

Side-whiskers that are narrow at the temple and broad and round by the lower jaws are called *muttonchops*, from the similarity of the shape to that of a chop of mutton. Other types of facial whiskers named for their resemblance to other things are *goatee*, so called from its similarity to the beard of a he-goat, and *handlebar mustache*, curving up at the ends like the handlebars of a bicycle. *Mustache* itself derives ultimately from the Greek *mystax*, meaning 'upper lip'.

The name of Sir Anthony *Vandyke*, the seventeenth-century Flemish artist who painted at the court of Charles I of England, survives not merely because of the fame of his canvases. A popular fashion in the seventeenth century was to wear a trim, pointed beard, and because it appears so often in his work a beard of this style is now called a *Vandyke*.

[anagram of *burnsides*, after Ambrose E. *Burnside* †1881 Am. general, who wore them]

siesta See NOON.
[Sp, fr. L *sexta (hora)* sixth (hour) (i.e., after sunrise), noon, fr. *sexta*, fem. of *sextus* sixth + *hora* hour]

Siksika See INDIAN.
[Blackfoot, fr. *siksi*nam black + oq*ka*tsh foot]

silhouette Étienne de Silhouette was French controller general of finances in the mid-eighteenth century. When he was first placed in office, he enjoyed the complete confidence of the court. But this lasted only until the direction of his financial policies became apparent. He was extremely close with the state's money as well as his own, so close, in fact, that *à la Silhouette* came to mean 'on the cheap' for a time. He demanded great sacrifices on the part of the nobility and enforced them by the imposition of new taxes and the reduction of pensions. His niggardliness was greeted with ridicule. Outline drawings, as stingy of detail as Silhouette was of money, were given his name. It was even suggested that one of his economies was the decoration of his house with these outlines, which he made himself as a hobby, rather than more expensive paintings. The controller general was forced to leave his office less than a year after he had entered it, but an outline is still, in French and in English, a *silhouette*.

[F, after Étienne de *Silhouette* †1767 Fr. controller general of finances; fr. his parsimony and petty economies]

silly   Silly is a spelling variant of an earlier adjective *seely*, which has long roots in the Germanic languages. Its basic sense is 'blessed, fortunate', the meaning its German cognate *selig* still has. The earliest thirteenth-century meanings of *seely* were 'happy, fortunate', 'spiritually blessed', and 'pious, holy, good'. From these beginnings it began to be used in the sense of 'blameless, innocent', which was often used to express sympathy for those who suffered undeservedly. Those who are innocent victims can also be thought of as deserving pity, and *seely* was used this way, too: 'pitiable, helpless, defenseless'. It was fairly often combined with *poor;* where today we might use combinations like "poor old" or "poor unfortunate", in the fourteenth and fifteenth centuries people said "seely old" and "seely wretched." It is worth noting that this sense can be interpreted as 'unfortunate, unhappy'—just the opposite of its original meaning.

By the fifteenth century the spelling *silly* (with many variations) was replacing *seely* (with its many variations) because of a gradual shift in the pronunciation of the vowel. *Silly* began life with the last two meanings of *seely* just mentioned. For some reason the 'blameless, innocent' meaning of *silly* became a conventional poetic epithet for sheep: the Whiffenpoofs' "poor little lambs" three or four centuries earlier would have been "silly sheep (or lambs)." Somehow it is hard to avoid wondering if the combination *silly sheep*—sheep have seldom been admired for their mental acuteness—did not have some influence on the development of later senses of *silly*.

But there was first an intermediate development from the 'deserving pity, helpless, defenseless' use of both *silly* and *seely*. Compared to greater considerations, something poor, little, and helpless could be viewed as insignificant, unimportant, and trivial. This sense would cut two ways, also: it could be viewed positively—as 'humble'—or negatively—as 'paltry, trivial'. From the pejorative use, with or without the influence of the silly sheep, came senses denoting lack of intellect or lack of judgment—our now familiar 'foolish' sense.

The sound change that established the spelling *silly* must have progressed from north to south, for there are more varied applications of *silly* in senses leading up to the 'foolish' sense in Scots and northern dialects of English than there are of *seely*. *Seely* did finally develop the 'foolish' sense, but it dwindled in use and *silly* took over.

There have been few developments in *silly* since the 'foolish' sense became well established. The chief ones are the 'dazed' sense, as in "knocked silly" and the specialized cricket sense, both of which developed in the late nineteenth century. The cricket use—"silly mid-on" and so forth—simply means that the defensive player is playing absurdly close to the batsman. The concept is similar to playing the infield in, in baseball. The adjective *silly* was probably applied to the cricket position because cricket players do not wear gloves when playing defense.

[ME *sely, silly* happy, blessed, innocent, pitiable, feeble, fr. (assumed) OE *sælig*, fr. OE *sæl* happiness + -*ig* -y; akin to OHG *sālig* happy, ON *sæla* happiness, Goth *selei* kindness, L *solari* to console, comfort, Gk *hilaros* cheerful]

since   See TOWARDS.
[ME *sins, sinnes* afterwards, since, contr. of *sithens, sithenes*, adv. & prep., since, fr. *sithen* (fr. OE *siththan*, contr. of *sith tham* afterwards, since that, fr. *sith*, adv. & prep., since + *tham*, dat. of *thæt* that) + -*s*, -*es* -s; akin to OHG *sīd* since, ON *sīth*, adv., late, Goth *seithu*, neut. adj., late, OIr *sīr* long-lasting, L *serus* late, *serere* to sow]

sinister   See LEFT.
[ME *sinistre*, fr. L *sinister* left, on the left side (whence L *sinistrum* evil, unlucky, inauspicious); fr. the fact that omens observed from one's left were considered unlucky]

Sioux   See INDIAN.
[F, Dakota, short for *Nadowessioux*, fr. Ojibwa *Nadoweisiw*, lit., little snake, enemy]

siren   In Greek mythology the Sirens were the two daughters of the sea-god Phorcys. In early art they were represented as birds with the heads of women and later as women with the legs of birds, with or without wings.

In Book XII of Homer's *Odyssey*, the sorceress Circe warns Odysseus of the perils he would face on his voyage home: "First you will come to the Sirens who enchant all who come near them. If anyone unwarily draws in too close and hears the singing of the Sirens, his wife and children will never welcome him home again, for they sit in a green field and warble him to death with the sweetness of their song. There is a great heap of dead men's bones lying all around, with the flesh still rotting off them." Odysseus protected his men from the Sirens' song by plugging their ears with wax. Wanting to hear their song himself, Odysseus had himself bound to the mast until he was out of hearing range.

The Greek word *seirēn* became *siren* in Latin and *sirena* in Late Latin, which was taken into thirteenth-century French as *sereine*. In the fourteenth century the noun was borrowed into English as *serein* or *siren*. In the sixteenth century, the word began to be used metaphorically for an alluringly beautiful woman who insidiously or deceptively entices or seduces men. Shakespeare illustrates this use in his *Titus Andronicus* (ca. 1593) when Aaron muses: "To wanton with this queen,/This goddess, this Semiramis, this nymph,/This siren that will charm Rome's Saturnine/And see his shipwrack and his commonweal's."

In 1819 a Frenchman by the name of Charles Cagniard de la Tour devised an apparatus for producing a sound of a definite pitch by the rapid interruption of a current of air, steam, or fluid by a perforated rotating disk. From its property of producing sound in water, the inventor decided to call the apparatus a *siren*. Since then, other such devices, mostly used as warning signals, have been called sirens; the most recent electronic ones have no moving parts at all. The noises they produce, however, are strident, a far cry from the alluring, euphonious songs of the mythical Sirens.

For other articles on words derived from ancient mythology and legend see VOLCANO.

[ME *serein, siren,* fr. MF *sereine* & L *siren;* MF *sereine,* fr. LL *sirena,* fr. L *siren,* fr. Gk *seirēn, seirēdōn*]

skirmish See SCRIMMAGE.

[ME *skyrmissh,* alter. (influenced by ME *skirmysshen* to fence, brandish a sword, fr. MF *eskermiss-, escremiss-,* stem of *eskermir, escremir* to fence, of Gmc origin; akin to OHG *skirmen* to defend) of *skarmish, scarmuch,* fr. MF *escarmouche,* fr. OIt *scaramuccia,* of Gmc origin; akin to OHG *skirmen* to defend, *skerm, skirm* shield]

skirt The Vikings, known as "Danes" to the Anglo-Saxons whatever their place of origin, first came calling on England at the end of the eighth century in a series of raids. Gradually they established greater and greater footholds on English soil. King Alfred the Great fought the Danes to a standstill in the second half of the ninth century and by treaty in 878 restricted them to an area called the Danelaw—roughly the eastern and northern half of England. During the next half-century or so, the descendants of Alfred reestablished English control in great parts of the Danelaw. But more Vikings came attacking at the end of the tenth century, with considerable success, and by 1014 Cnut (Canute), a Dane, was king of England. Cnut ushered in a quarter-century of Danish rule.

The more than three centuries of contact between the Scandinavians and the English in England—it was not always warlike—left a permanent mark on the language. The language of the Scandinavians and Old English were related and had a common Germanic source. Both languages had many words in common, but others had become differentiated by independent development in each language. The sound combination \sk\ of the parent Germanic language had become \sh\ (spelled *sc*) very early in Old English, but kept its old value in the Scandinavian languages. Thus an *sk-* spelling can often identify a Viking word. Our Modern English *skirt,* for instance, derives from Old Norse *skyrta,* which has many Germanic cognates. Among them was Old English *scyrte,* which has given us modern *shirt.* Both the Danish and the English words have survived into Modern English but have different uses. Some of the Danish *sk* words have simply replaced their Old English counterparts; we can see some of them in Modern English *sky, skill,* and *skin.*

The civilization of the Vikings was not more cultured than that of the English, and the Scandinavian contribution to the language reflects this. Scandinavian loanwords are everyday, humble, homely words: nouns like *egg, fellow, sister, steak,* adjectives like *loose, low, tight, weak,* verbs like *die, get, take, raise,* and the pronouns *they, their, them* all have Scandinavian ancestors. *Raise,* from Old Norse *reisa* and related Old Icelandic *reisa,* has a doublet in Modern English, the verb *rear. Rear* is from Middle English *reren,* from Old English *rǣran,* also akin to the Old Norse and the Old Icelandic *reisa.*

The verb *die* is a curious case. Spelled *dien* or *deyen* in Middle English, it was taken from Old Norse *deyja* or a closely related word. It seems to have stuck in the language simply because it fit better with Old English *dēath* (modern *death*) and *dēad* (modern *dead*) than the equivalent Old English verbs *sweltan* and *steorfan.* The first simply fell out of use. *Steorfan* became specialized in meaning; it is our modern English *starve.* (See also STARVE.)

[ME, fr. ON *skyrta* shirt, kirtle]

skookum See BAD.
[Chinook jargon, powerful, evil spirit, fr. Chehalis *skukm*]

slander *Slander* and *scandal* can be considered stumbling blocks over which a person's reputation or career may fall. The etymologies of these doublets bear this out.

The ancient Greeks used the word *skandalon* to denote 'a trap or stumbling block'. This word was taken into Late Latin as *scandalum* with essentially the same meaning but with application to one's moral state. It denoted a stumbling block causing one to fall into sin. Old French took the word as *esclandre,* which was also variously spelled *escandle* and *esclande.* When the word was borrowed into Middle English, it was spelled *sclaundre, sclandre,* and *slaundre.* By the seventeenth century *slander* had become the standard form. It was used to mean 'utterance of false charges or misrepresentations which defame and damage reputation'. It also referred to 'malicious publication by speech of false tales or suggestions to the injury of another'. This is the usual sense of the word today, and it is contrasted in legal use with the sense of *libel* that refers to the defamation of a person by written means.

In the sixteenth century the need was felt for a word whose meaning more closely paralleled that of the Late Latin word *scandalum,* and so the word *scandal* was formed. The earliest attested use of *scandal* refers to the discredit to religion brought about by a religious person's 'stumbling' into sin. It also was used for 'a stumbling block to the reception of the faith or obedience to divine law'. Nowadays, it commonly refers to 'a circumstance or action that offends propriety or established moral conceptions'.

See also LIBEL.

[ME *slaundre, sclaundre, sclandre,* fr. OF *esclandre, esclande, escandle,* scandal, slander, fr. LL *scandalum* stumbling block, offense, fr. Gk *skandalon*]

slapstick   Whether it is the Keystone Kops tumbling out of a squad car, circus clowns paddling each other with demented delight, or the Three Stooges knocking their noggins together, this type of broad physical comedy is generally known as *slapstick.* The name derives from a device invented in Italy during the sixteenth century, although this kind of comedy is probably as old as the theater itself.

The rough-and-tumble school of comedy dates back to the Greco-Roman theater, where heavily padded clowns got laughs by boisterously trading blows. The tradition of outrageous mock violence continued into the Renaissance, when it became a feature of the Italian commedia dell'arte. This highly stylized school of comedy presented stock characters in familiar, typically absurd, situations. Among the stock characters was Harlequin, a quick-witted zany, whose masked face and variegated tights made him readily identifiable. One of his favorite weapons for making comic mischief was a paddle which consisted of two slats of wood fastened together at one end. When wielded with pretended force against some surface—such as the posterior of someone bent over—the two slats slapped together, producing a startling whack suggestive of a powerful blow.

The tradition of physical comedy that derived its humor from exaggerated, make-believe violence reached another peak with the English music halls and the American vaudeville and variety shows of the late nineteenth century. It was during this period that the double-slatted paddle became known in English as the *slapstick.* So ubiquitous were slapsticks and so dominant was knockabout comedy that by 1896 a critic for the *New York Dramatic News* was thankful for any "relief . . . from the slap-sticks, rough-and-tumble comedy couples abounding in the variety ranks." The slapstick became the symbol for the whole genre of broad physical comedy.

Slapstick even came to be applied to literature and other art forms in which the attempt at humor was judged to be lacking in delicacy or subtlety. In 1909 a critic for the *Nation* used *slapstick* to characterize one such literary effort:

The sketches move on in a succession of absurd plots and silly situations delineated in the spirit of what is known professionally as "slapstick" humor. After a few chapters, it is largely monotony.

In 1912 a writer for *American Graphic Art* complained that "the antics of the 'slap-stick' element in comic art have dulled our powers of resistance. . . ."

The vogue for broad knockabout comedy coincided with the birth of the silent film, the medium with which *slapstick* is most often associated. Lacking the means to convey verbal wit, silent films were naturally forced to rely on sight gags. To the boisterous comedy bits that had been established on stage, silent movies added such classic elements as the madcap chase and the pie-throwing free-for-all. Both the formula and its appellation were sufficiently established by 1914 that the early fan magazine *Photoplay* could title an article "Making slap-stick comedy."

For other words derived from comic theater see ZANY.

[²*slap* + *stick*]

slave In the Middle Ages the warring Germanic peoples subjugated a great part of the Slavic population of east-central Europe. Conquered Slavs were bought and sold throughout the West, even as far from their homeland as Moslem Spain. From the Slavs' own name for themselves came their conquerors' *Sclavus*, in the Latin that served medieval Europe as a universal language. By the ninth or tenth century, *sclavus* was used to designate any human chattel, whatever his origin. This *sclavus* is the ancestor of our Modern English *slave*.

Slavery, unlike the word *sclavus*, was not an invention of the Middle Ages. The Latin language had needed a 'slave' word long before the Christian era. This word in classical Latin was *servus* (the ancestor of Modern English *servant*). In the Middle Ages, *servus* came to be used for a particular type of slave. The medieval *servus*, or *serf*, as he became in French and later in English, was not a personal slave. He belonged, rather, to the land on which he was born and only indirectly to the possibly temporary possessor of that land.

The memory of slavery reappears unrecognizable in the breezy Italian greeting and formula of farewell *ciao*, used by English speakers in a care-free mood. It is a dialectal alteration going back to Latin *sclavus*. The original idea was equivalent to the now antique English use of "Your servant" in closing a letter or taking leave. The other Latin word for a slave is also used in southern varieties of Modern German, its speakers greeting or taking leave of one another with a cheerful and historically etiolated "Servus!"

Finally, *servus* is lurking in the phonological corner of *concierge* 'resident doorkeeper', borrowed from French, which derived the word from Latin *conservus* 'fellow slave'.

[ME *sclave*, fr. OF or ML; OF *esclave* slave, fr. ML *Sclavus, sclavus* Slav, Slav held in servitude, slave, fr. LGk *Sklabos* Slav, fr. *Sklabēnos* of or relating to the Slavs, of Slav origin; akin to OBulg *Slověne*, a Slavic group of people in the area of Thessalonike, ORuss *Slověne*, an East-Slavic group of people near Novgorod, *Slovutich* Dnieper river, Serb *Slavnica*, a river]

sleuth A Modern English sleuth is a detective, but in Middle English the word *sleuth* meant 'the track of an animal or person'. The word was a borrowing from Old Norse *slōth*. After the fifteenth century, *sleuth* was seldom used except in compounds like *sleuth-dog* and *sleuthhound*. These were terms for a dog trained to follow a track. *Sleuthhound* was used specifically in Scotland for a kind of bloodhound used to hunt game or to track down fugitives from justice. We find mention of the legal importance of the sleuthhound in John Bellenden's English translation of Hector Boece's Latin *History and Chronicles of Scotland* (1536): "He that denyis entres to the sleuthound . . . sal be haldin participant with the crime and thift committit." (He that denies entrance to the sleuthhound . . . shall be considered a participant in the crime and theft committed.) The sleuthhound, originally a Scottish beast, gained fame far beyond the bounds of his homeland; he became a symbol of the eager and thorough pursuit of an object. According to Mrs. Elizabeth Gaskell in her *Life of Charlotte Brontë* (1857), "the West Riding men are sleuthhounds in pursuit of money." In the nineteenth-century United States the metaphoric *sleuthhound* acquired a more specific meaning and became an epithet for a detective. This new term was soon shortened to *sleuth.*

A word synonymous with *sleuth* comes to us from a long-forgotten nineteenth-century melodrama by British dramatist Tom Taylor titled *The Ticket-of-Leave Man.* The hero of this 1863 play is Hawkshaw, a detective who relentlessly pursues the villainous Tiger Dalton. Hawkshaw is a man of dogged determination, a master of disguises, and a gifted memorizer of facts and faces. The popularity of the character inspired his fans to refer to any detective as a *hawkshaw.* The generic use of Hawkshaw's name was undoubtedly furthered by the appearance in 1913 of the comic strip *Hawkshaw the Detective* by American cartoonist Charles Augustus Mager. Mager's Hawkshaw was a comic interpretation of a detective in the tradition of Sherlock Holmes. The strip appeared on and off until the late 1940s. Incidentally, *hawkshaw* was Tom Taylor's second contribution to the English language. Earlier his play *Our American Cousin* (1858) had given us *dundrearies;* see SIDEBURNS.

[short for *sleuthhound,* fr. ME, fr. *sloth, sleuth* track of a person or animal (fr. ON *slōth*) + *hound*]

slew See SLOGAN.

[prob. fr. IrGael *sluagh*]

slogan The Celts had a word *sluagh* meaning "host, crowd, multitude" that is involved in a couple of Modern English words. It was combined with Gaelic *gairm* 'shout, cry'. The resulting compound, meaning 'war cry', first appeared in Scottish English in such spellings as *slughorne, sloghorne,* and *slogurn.* By the seventeenth century its modern spelling *slogan* began to appear. The war cry itself usually consisted simply of a clan or family name or a place name—not very bloodthirsty, but it seems to have been effective.

By the eighteenth century *slogan* was being used of less sanguinary pursuits; it referred to a word or phrase used by a person or group to stand for an attitude, position, or goal—not very different from the use of *motto.*

Extension to politics and advertising was to be expected, and by the time of World War I *slogan* was in everyday use by all sorts of organized groups.

In 1839 an American writer from Vermont, Daniel P. Thompson, wrote in a romantic novel named *The Green Mountain Boys* that someone—presumably Ethan Allen—had "drawn up a whole slew of cannon clean to the top of Mount Defiance." This American *slew*—sometimes spelled *slue*—means 'a large number'. It happens to be pronounced approximately like and mean approximately the same as our Gaelic friend *sluagh*. The similarity was first noticed in the twentieth century, and from the time the Gaelic origin for *slew* was put into Webster's New International Dictionary, Second Edition (1934), the etymology has been generally accepted. There is, however, a missing link. We do not know how *sluagh* came from Ireland to Vermont before 1839. And we have no evidence of the use of *slew* in the writing of Irish authors such as Lady Gregory, William Butler Yeats, James Joyce, or John Millington Synge. We do know that many Gaelic-speaking Irish emigrated from Ireland from 1830 to 1850 and that many of them came to the United States. Is *slew* derived from *sluagh?* We won't know for certain until someone finds the missing connection.

[alter. of earlier *slogorn,* fr. Gael *sluagh-ghairm,* army cry, fr. *sluagh* army + *gairm* call]

smorgasbord   A type of buffet indigenous to Sweden consists in its traditional form of buttered bread and a large selection of relishes and savory foods, such as hot and cold meats, smoked and pickled fish, eggs, salads, and cheeses. This style of dining apparently originated at large country gatherings to which guests contributed individual items of food, with the items arranged on a long table for diners to serve themselves. The Swedish name for this type of buffet is *smörgåsbord. Smörgås* in Swedish means 'open-faced sandwich' or simply 'bread and butter'. It is derived from *smör* 'butter' and *gås* 'goose', which also has the sense 'a lump of butter' because of a fanciful resemblance between such a lump and a goose. The *-bord* of *smörgåsbord* is related to English *board* and means simply 'table'.

Smorgasbord, minus the diacritics of the Swedish spelling, has become a familiar English word only recently. Swedish-style buffets first gained popularity among American diners in the early decades of the twentieth century. In the 1930s, some restaurants were advertising "all you can eat" smorgasbords for fifty cents, featuring dozens of different foods. By the 1940s, the word *smorgasbord* was well enough established to acquire the figurative sense 'a heterogeneous mixture' or 'hodgepodge'. The extent to which the English word has lost its original Swedish connotations can be seen in one recent example of this sense, in which the writer describes how critics are now "encouraging the schools to stress the bread-and-butter courses that were de-emphasized when the vogue . . . was a smorgasbord approach to curriculum" (Gene I. Maeroff, *N.Y. Times,* 19 Mar. 1975). A student of etymology could aptly observe that "bread-and-butter courses" should, in fact, be a natural part of any good smorgasbord.

[Sw *smörgåsbord,* fr. *smörgås* bread and butter, open sandwich (fr. *smör* butter + *gås* goose) + *bord* table; fr. a fancied resemblance of lumps of butter to geese; akin to ON *smör*, *smjör* fat, butter, to ON *gās* goose, and to ON *borth* table]

sneak   *Sneak* pops up as if out of nowhere in Shakespeare's *Henry IV, Part I,* and *Henry V.* It is also used by Shakespeare's contemporaries Thomas Dekker, John Fletcher, and Ben Jonson. It obviously had to be in oral use in Elizabethan England, but we do not know how it got there. *Sneak*'s Old English synonym *snīcan* looks like a mighty tempting source, but the editors of the Oxford English Dictionary and other etymologists have rejected it. Here is why.

Snīcan belonged to the same class of Old English strong verbs as the ancestors of *write* and *strike.* During the passage from Old English through Middle English to Modern English, the pronunciation of the central vowel changed from \ē\ in the original to \ī\ in Modern English. Now *snīcan* seems to have passed into early Middle English *snīken*—a step in the same direction *write* and *strike* took—but then it just vanishes. And later *sneak* shows up in early Modern English, with the same vowel sound as the Old English but a different spelling. Direct transmission from *snīcan* should have given us modern *snike*, but there is no modern *snike*. We have *sneak* instead, and while it must be related to *snīcan* somehow, we cannot explain how it managed to escape the Great Vowel Shift of early Modern English or how it acquired its anomalous spelling.

Write made it into Modern English with its inflected forms, *wrote* and *written*, preserved. *Strike* had a greater problem. It seems to have come through with its original forms *stroke* and *stricken*, but in the seventeenth century *struck*, apparently a northern dialectal form, simply ousted them from standard use (*stricken*, however, has survived as an adjective). The mysterious *sneak*, on the other hand, from the beginning followed the pattern of weak verbs with *sneaked* as past tense and past participle. But in the second half of the nineteenth century an irregular strong-verb past *snuck* appears. It is first attested in 1887 in a New Orleans journal largely written in the vernacular. From this unpromising start *snuck* in a century has grown to be a full-fledged competitor of *sneaked.* It is no longer limited to American English but is used in British English too. *Snuck* seems to have been spontaneously generated, just like *sneak* was. And as in the case of *sneak*, we are teased by the possible connection to Old English that we cannot prove.

[akin to OE *snīcan* to creep, sneak along, ON *snīkja* to hanker, Dan *snige* to sneak, OHG *snahhan* to creep]

sneeze   Until the fifteenth century English speakers did not *sneeze*, they "fneezed." A very few words in Old and Middle English, mostly having something to do with the nose or with breathing, began with the letters *fn-*, but, especially in late Middle English, this combination of sounds was so rare that words beginning with *fn-* were susceptible to change or to competition from another word. Middle English *fnesen*, 'to sneeze', from Old English *fnēosan*, was altered and gained a rival as well, at least temporarily. During the fourteenth century the verb *nesen*, of Scandinavian origin, began to appear, and *neeze* may still be heard in some Scottish dialects of English. The more productive change, however, proved for some unknown reason to be the alteration of *fn-* to *sn-*, for the verb *snesen* began to appear in the late fifteenth century. This change may have been encouraged by the similarity between the printed and written forms of *f* and *s* at the time. Evidence for this may be seen in the earliest known occurrence of *sneeze*, for in 1493 Wynken de Worde printed *snese* where William Caxton had printed *fnese* at the same place in the same text ten years earlier.

A similar change may have given us *snort*. In manuscripts of Chaucer's *Canterbury Tales*, for example, the same sort of variation between *fn-* and *sn-* may be found. Chaucer's Reeve says of the miller in his tale, "This millere hath so wisly bibbed ale,/ That as an hors he fnorteth in his sleep." (This miller has drunk so much ale that he snorts in his sleep like a horse.) Some of the manuscripts, however, read *snorteth* instead of *fnorteth;* and it is the former which has given us the modern *snort.*

[ME *snesen,* alter. of *fnesen,* fr. OE *fnēosan;* akin to MHG *pfnūsen* to snort, sneeze, ON *fnȳsa* to snort, Gk *pnein* to breathe]

snickersnee   Ko-Ko, the Lord High Executioner of Gilbert and Sullivan's *Mikado,* delights in describing a decapitation:

> As I gnashed my teeth,
> When from its sheath
> I drew my snickersnee!
> As the sabre true
> Cut cleanly through
> His cervical vertebrae!

His victims, had he actually had any, might have taken some comfort in the knowledge that a *snickersnee* was originally a combat with knives and not the formidable weapon of the present, rather one-sided, encounter.

The Dutch used a phrase *steken of snijden,* 'to thrust or cut', to describe knife fighting. This became in English *steake or snye* or *stick or snee.* The charm of alliteration encouraged the phrase to become *snick-or-snee,* and the easy alteration to *snickersnee* followed. The verb became a noun, and the noun which named a kind of fight was soon transferred to the weapon the fighters used. *Snickersnee* has by now lost its earlier senses and means only 'a large knife or sword'.

[alter. of earlier *steake or snye, stick or snee,* fr. D *steken of snijden* to thrust or cut or *steken en snijden* to thrust and cut]

snob   In British slang of the late eighteenth and nineteenth centuries, a shoemaker was commonly called a *snob,* a word whose earlier history we do not know. The use of *snob* for a cobbler still survives in a number of dialects in England, especially in the southern counties, and the Royal Navy continues (or did at least into the 1950s) to call the repairers of its shoes *snobs,* with no offense intended or taken. But the snob's position in other levels of society has changed a great deal. Perhaps because the shoemaker's trade was considered to be a typical working-class calling, by 1831 the cobbler had given his name to the whole of the lower classes. The *Lincoln Herald,* on 22 July of that year, commenting on the election of the Parliament that would pass the Reform Bill in the following year, rejoiced that "the nobs have lost their dirty seats—the honest snobs have got 'em." And George Earp certainly did not intend to derogate Australia when he said of it in 1852: "The majority of the colonists are essentially snobs, and justly proud of the distinction."

But even then *snob* was being transformed from a mere designation of membership in the lower classes into a label for that sort of vulgar and tasteless person who tries without success to seem "refined." As William Makepeace Thackeray defined the term in his *Book of Snobs* (1848), it meant "he who meanly admires mean things." Thackeray's snob was likely to be a social climber, striving to gain acceptance in a higher level of society by servile imitation of its manners. Now the snob has become completely classless. His social standing may be as impeccable as he thinks it is; his attitude of superiority rather than his actual rank defines him.

[earlier *snob* member of the lower classes, fr. E dial., shoemaker, of unknown origin]

snooty   See SUPERCILIOUS.
[¹*snoot* + *-y*]

snort   See SNEEZE.
[ME *snorten,* prob. partly alter. of †*norten* (akin to OE †*nora* sneezing); prob. partly fr. the source of ME *snoren* to snore; akin to MLG & D *snorren* to drone, hum, MD *snarren* to drone, hum, MLG & MHG, to rattle, gossip, MHG *snerren* to chatter, gossip]

socket   See SWINE.
[ME *soket* spearhead shaped like a plowshare, support of a spear or pole, socket, fr. AF, dim. of OF *soc* plowshare, of Celt origin; akin to Corn *soch* plowshare, MIr *soc* plowshare, snout of a hog, OIr *socc* hog]

solicitor   See ATTORNEY.
[ME *solicitour,* fr. MF *soliciteur* prompter, agent, advocate, fr. *soliciter* to disturb, solicit, take care of, fr. L *sollicitare* to disturb, agitate, move, entreat, fr. *sollicitus* anxious, troubled]

solicitous   See ATTORNEY.
[L *sollicitus* anxious, troubled]

solon   See DRACONIAN.
[after *Solon* †*ab*559 B.C. Athenian lawgiver and one of the Seven Wise Men of Greece]

somersault   *Somersault* was borrowed into English in the sixteenth century from the Middle French *sombresaut,* 'a leap'. It is a derivative of Latin *super,* 'over', plus *saltus,* 'a leap', derived from *salire,* 'to jump'. In its earliest uses *somersault* meant 'a leap in which a tumbler or acrobat turns head over heels and lands on his feet'. Children's imitations of this feat took the form of a frontward or backward roll, so that today *somersault* does not necessarily imply leaping at all.

The Latin verb *salire* has given English several other words. A cooking term derived by way of French is *sauté,* 'to fry in a little fat', probably because of the droplets of fat that jump around in the pan. Other English words that come from the same ultimate source are *assail* and *assault, sally* ('an action of rushing or bursting forth, especially a sortie of troops'), and *salient* ('projecting or prominent', or in its earlier and more literal senses, 'moving by leaps and springs'). Closely related to the last of these is *salientian,* suitably enough the name for any member of the order of amphibians called *Salientia,* which includes frogs, toads, and tree toads—all pretty good jumpers.

[MF *sombresaut* leap, alter. of *soubresaut, soubresault,* prob. fr. (assumed) OProv *sobresaut,* fr. OProv *sobre* over (fr. L *super*) + *saut* leap, jump, fr. L *saltus* leap, fr. *saltus,* past part. of *salire* to jump]

sound   See PLUMBER.
[ME *sounen,* fr. MF *soner, suner,* fr. L *sonare;* akin to L *sonus* sound]

[ME *sounden,* fr. MF *sonder,* prob. fr. *sonde* sounding line, act of sounding, prob. of Gmc origin; akin to OE *sund*gyrd sounding rod, *sund*līne sounding line, *sund*rāp sounding lead, ON *sund* strait, sound]

southpaw   See LEFT.
[*south* + *paw*]

sow   See SWINE.
[ME *sowe, suwe,* fr. OE *sugu;* akin to OE *sū* sow, OS *sū, suga,* OHG *sū,* ON *sӯr* sow, L *sus* hog, swine, Gk *hys,* Corn *hoch,* OIr *socc* hog, swine, Skt *sūkara* boar, hog, swine]

spaghetti   See VERMICELLI.
[It, fr. pl. of *spaghetto* string, dim. of *spago* cord, string; akin to Sardinian *ispau* cord, string]

specious   See PLAUDIT.
[ME, fr. L *speciosus* beautiful, showy, plausible, fr. *species* appearance, beauty + *-osus* -ous]

spinster   See DISTAFF.
[ME *spinnestere,* fr. *spinnen* to spin + *-estere* -ster]

spirit   See GHOST.
[ME, fr. OF or L; OF *spirit, espirit, esperit,* fr. L *spiritus* spirit, breath;

akin to ON *fīsa* to break wind, L *spirare* to breathe, and perh. to OSlav *piskati* to play a reed instrument]

spring See AUTUMN.
[ME, fr. OE; akin to OFris *spring*, OS & OHG gi*spring* spring, OE *springan* to spring]

spruce Prussia was formerly called *Pruce* or *Spruce* in English. A number of goods imported from Prussia—*spruce* canvas, *spruce* iron, *spruce* leather—were all very well-thought-of. Perhaps the most important of these Prussian or *Spruce* products was the *spruce* tree, a tall, straight conifer that was especially desirable for use as the mast of a ship. About the middle of the seventeenth century, *Spruce* as a name for the country was largely supplanted by *Prussia*. But by this time *spruce* had become well established as the name of the tree. The particular species *(Picea abies)* that was originally called *spruce* is not limited to Prussia. Another of its native countries gave it its present common name *Norway spruce*, which is something of an etymological paradox. *Spruce* is now the common name applied to any member of the genus *Picea*.

The origin of the word *spruce* that means 'neat' or 'trim' is less clear. It may come from *spruce* leather, of which fine jerkins were once made. Thomas Nashe in 1593 wrote of "a Broker, in a spruce leather jerkin with a great number of golde Rings on his fingers." And Thomas Dekker in 1609 mentioned "the neatest and sprucest leather."

Another word that we owe to the name of a country is *suede*. The French called gloves made of a soft, napped leather *gants de Suède*, 'gloves of Sweden'. When England imported such gloves from France, they became *suède gloves*, and the explicit connection with Sweden was obscured by only partial translation.

[fr. obs. *Spruce* Prussia, fr. ME, alter. of *Pruce*, fr. OF]

squire See ESQUIRE.
[ME *squier*, fr. OF *esquier, escuier*, fr. LL *scutarius* shield bearer]

squirrel From the fourteenth century, when Chaucer wrote of "squyrelis and bestes smale of gentil kynde" (squirrels and small animals of gentle nature), until the seventeenth century, many and varied spellings of *squirrel* were in use, e.g., *squyrelle, squirile, squirrell,* and *squerel.* These are all variants of an English derivative of the Middle French word *esquireul*, sometimes spelled *escuriuel*, which was most likely derived in turn from the unattested Vulgar Latin *scuriolus*, the diminutive of an unattested altered form of the Latin word *sciurus*. The Romans had simply Latinized the Greek word *skiouros*, which was made up of *skia*, 'shadow', and *oura*, 'tail'. Presumably the Greeks noticed that when this animal sits erect, it often raises its bushy tail up against its back and over its head as if to shade itself.

In the sixteenth century Shakespeare, in his play *Two Gentlemen of Verona*, used *squirrel* in reference to another animal, a very small dog: "The other squirrel was stol'n from me . . . and then I offered her mine own, who is a dog as big as ten of yours." And in the nineteenth century we find it used of a man, as when Alexander Smith, in *Summer in Skye* (1865), writes that "Lachlan Roy was a little, cheery, agile, red squirrel of a man." Today biologists retain the Latin word *Sciurus* for the genus that includes the squirrels.

[ME *squirel, squerel,* fr. MF *esquireul, escuriuel,* fr. (assumed) VL *scuriolus,* dim. of (assumed) VL *scurius,* alter. of L *sciurus,* fr. Gk *skiouros,* fr. *skia* shadow + *oura* tail]

stamen   See STAMINA.
[L, warp, thread, thread spun by the Fates at one's birth to determine the length of his life, stamen; akin to Gk *stēmōn* warp, thread, OIr *sessam* act of standing, Skt *sthāman* station, Gk *histanai* to cause to stand; basic meaning: standing upright]

stamina   The warp in a loom is the lengthwise series of threads through which the crosswise woof is woven. In Latin this warp was called *stamen.* In addition, *stamen* very early developed the transferred sense 'a thread', a sense which had a divine as well as a merely human aspect. In Roman mythology the three Fates are often pictured as spinners of thread. The first spins out the threads of all men's lives; the second measures them; the third cuts them off. These mortal threads, as well as the ordinary variety, were called *stamina* (the plural of *stamen*).

When *stamina* was borrowed into English in the seventeenth century, both the literal meaning, 'warp', and the idea of the threads of fate went into the making of the English word. English *stamina,* like its Latin etymon, was originally a plural. *Stamina* were the essential elements or qualities of something considered as being like the warp which is the foundation on which a textile is woven. The English word *stamina* was also used for the innate capacities that were once believed to determine, like the threads of the three Fates, the duration of life. From this use developed the modern sense 'endurance, staying power'. In this sense, too, *stamina* was originally treated as plural, but it has by now been universally reinterpreted as singular.

Latin *stamen,* used for an ordinary thread, was also used occasionally for other threadlike objects. The first-century Roman scholar Pliny, in his *Historia Naturalis (Natural History),* called the male organ of a flower, which resembles a thread, *stamen.* The word in this sense was introduced into botanical English in the seventeenth century.

[L, pl. of *stamen* warp, thread of life spun by the Fates]

starve   The Old English verb *steorfan* was used intransitively in the general sense of 'to die, perish', without implying a specific cause. It is related to the Old High German verb *sterban,* which was used in exactly the same way, as the Modern German descendant *sterben* continues to be. The verb usually referred to a slow lingering death, and the cause (hunger, cold, grief, or disease) was generally indicated in a prepositional phrase. The principal parts were strong: the past tense was *stearf,* the past participle *(ge)storfen.*

The verb passed into Middle English as *sterven, starf, storven.* Chaucer uses the past tense in *Canterbury Tales* in this passage invoking Christ from "The Man of Law's Tale" (ca. 1392):

> But he that starf for our redempcioun,
> And boond Sathan (and yet lith ther he lay),
> So be thy stronge champion this day!

By the sixteenth century, the past tense had weakened to *sterved,* and the verb had taken on the transitive sense 'to kill or destroy'. We find an example of this use in John Daus's translation of *Sleidane's Commentaries* in 1560: "He . . . also sterved them for honger and cold, so that many died."

By the seventeenth century, the verb forms had become *starve, starved,* and *starved,* and the meaning had become specialized as (1) 'to die of hunger' and 'to kill with hunger', and (2) 'to die of cold' and 'to kill with cold'. The latter senses have since become archaic, and the "hunger" senses have since softened to include the idea of suffering the pangs of deprivation as well as those of death.

[ME *sterven,* fr. OE *steorfan;* akin to OFris *sterva* to die, OHG *sterban* to die, OE *starian* to stare]

stellar   See DISASTER.
[LL *stellaris,* fr. L *stella* star + -*aris* -ar; akin to OE *steorra* star, OHG *sterro, sterno,* ON *stjarna,* Goth *stairno,* Gk *astēr, astron,* Skt *stṛbhis* (instrumental pl.) by means of the stars]

stencil   See SCINTILLA.
[fr. (assumed) earlier *stansel,* fr. ME *stanselen* to ornament with sparkling colors or pieces of metal, fr. MF *estanceler, estenceler,* fr. *estencele* spark, fr. (assumed) VL *stincilla,* alter. of L *scintilla*]

stentor   See STENTORIAN.
[after *Stentor,* Greek warrior mentioned in the *Iliad* and famed for his powerful voice, fr. L & Gk; L *Stentor,* fr. Gk *Stentōr*]

stentorian   *Stentorian,* an adjective meaning 'extremely loud', is derived from the noun *stentor,* 'a person having a loud voice'. In Homer's *Iliad* when Juno exhorts the Greeks to battle she is compared to a hero named *Stentor,* whose voice was uncommonly loud. In Alexander Pope's translation of the *Iliad* the passage reads:

> Heaven's empress mingles with the mortal crowd,
> And shouts, in Stentor's sounding voice, aloud;
> Stentor the strong, endued with brazen lungs,
> Whose throat surpass'd the force of fifty tongues.

Stentor has been the archetypal loud-voiced person for many centuries, and in English his name has been used generically of any such person since about 1600.

The title of the epic poem from which this passage comes has itself entered the English vocabulary. *Iliad* has sometimes been used to refer to 'any long epic narrative' or to 'a series of events regarded as suitable for an epic'.

The title of another epic poem attributed to Homer has also become a generic term in English. The *Odyssey* tells the adventures of the wandering Odysseus on his way home from the siege of Troy. In Modern English an *odyssey* is 'a long wandering or voyage, usually marked by many changes of fortune'. The familiar story of the fall of Troy recounted in the *Odyssey* has contributed another phrase to the English lexicon. To gain entrance into the city of Troy the Greeks, under the guise of a peace offering, presented the Trojans with a large wooden horse which was actually hollow and filled with Greek soldiers who released themselves by night and opened the gates of the city to the Greek army. The term *Trojan horse* is now used to refer to 'a person, thing, or factor intended to undermine or subvert from within'. This episode of the Trojan horse also gave rise to the proverb, "Beware of Greeks bearing gifts."

Another character from the *Odyssey* has also lent his name to the English language. A friend of Odysseus named *Mentor* was entrusted with the education of Odysseus's son Telemachus, and today a *mentor* is a trusted counselor or guide or even simply a tutor or coach. Even the name of the poet himself has been adopted into the English language. The adjective *Homeric* not only means 'relating to Homer', but is also used to describe something heroic or of epic proportions.

For other articles on words derived from ancient mythology and legend see VOLCANO.

[*stentor* + *-ian*]

stereotype   See CLICHÉ.
[F *stéréotype,* fr. *stéré-* stere- + *type*]

steward   The Old English word *stig* or *stī* meant 'a sty or pen' (for pigs) or 'a hall' (for people). We have no evidence, however, that the *stigweard* or *stīweard* was ever a keeper of pigs or of pig pens, although this theory has been advanced upon occasion. He was rather the keeper of the hall, the supervisor of the household's domestic concerns, and thus an official of great importance. One important concern of a medieval English hall or household was the dispensing, as well as the husbanding, of wealth. Both of these were the responsibility of the steward. Even as wit is God's constable, "luue," according to the *Ancrene Riwle* (ca. 1230), "is heouene stiward." (Love is heaven's steward.) Even today the queen of England has a Lord Steward of the Household, who is a peer and a member of the Privy Council, although his real power is now, unlike formerly, restricted to the royal household. See also CONSTABLE, MARSHAL.

[ME, fr. OE *stīweard, stigweard,* fr. *stī, stig* pen, hall, sty + *weard* ward]

stigma   In ancient Greece and Rome runaway slaves and criminals were branded with a hot iron or needle as a sign of disgrace, and such a brand was called a *stigma*. This term ultimately derives from the Greek verb *stizein* 'to tattoo'. St. Paul used the term in his Epistle to the Galatians (6:17): "I bear the marks [*stigmata* in the Vulgate Bible] of the Lord Jesus in my body" (Douay). He was probably referring to the scars he had from the beatings and stonings that he suffered for Christ.

In the Middle Ages, the Latin plural *stigmata* was used specifically for the wounds some people bore on their hands, feet, and sometimes the side and brow, which were believed to be a visible sign of their participation in Christ's sufferings on the cross. Historical records indicate that St. Francis of Assisi (died 1226) was the first person to bear the infliction of such stigmata. Many other cases of such infliction followed, but the Church has never pronounced such stigmata "articles of faith."

When *stigma* was taken into English late in the sixteenth century, it was used in the ancient sense of 'a brand burnt into the skin with a hot iron as a sign of disgrace or servitude'. Early in the seventeenth century we find *stigma* being applied figuratively to 'a mark of shame or discredit', and this sense has survived. In his 1948 book *The Beast in Me and Other Animals,* James Thurber comments: "In daytime radio, the cigarette has come to be a sign and stigma of evil that ranks with the mark of the cloven hoof, the scarlet letter, and the brand of the *fleur-de-lis.*" Other such applications include the stigmas that are often attached to poverty, divorce, illegitimacy, alcoholism, and other conditions frowned upon by society. Even words that are not considered entirely respectable have been labeled with the stigma "slang."

By the 1630s we find occurrences in English of the plural *stigmata* used in the sense of 'marks resembling the wounds on the crucified body of Christ'. This is the medieval sense continuing in use for the occasional modern examples of the phenomenon. Later in the seventeenth century, *stigma* was put to use in the field of medicine for 'a morbid spot, dot, or point on the skin, especially one that bleeds spontaneously'. Since the middle of the eighteenth century, *stigma* has been used in zoology for 'a respiratory opening or spiracle in insects'. Botanists then borrowed the term to denote 'the portion of the pistil of a flower which receives pollen grains and on which they germinate'.

In the late 1850s *stigma* took on the sense of 'a distinguishing mark or characteristic'. A good illustration of this sense in modern writing comes from an article in *The Reporter* (3 November 1955) by William Harlan Hale: "He knows our stigmata, too: our need to accumulate power mowers, power saws, and patios wired with hi-fi systems as aids in our return to nature."

At the end of the nineteenth century, medicine found another use for *stigma* to denote 'a symptom of a physical or mental disorder'. Thus, in the *Journal of the American Medical Association* (13 February 1943), we read of the "stigmas of long-standing epilepsy—mental deterioration, aura, lingual injury. . . ."

[L *stigmat-, stigma* mark, brand, fr. Gk, mark, tattoo mark, fr. *stizein* to tattoo]

stoic   In Athens about the year 300 B.C. the philosopher Zeno of Citium (a city on Cyprus) was teaching a radically new philosophy that was to spread its influence throughout the Greco-Roman world for at least the next five hundred years. He gave public lectures at a site adjacent to the agora (marketplace) called *Stoa Poikilē* (Painted Portico). Zeno's philosophy became known as Stoicism and his followers were called Stoics, in reference to the *stoa* 'portico' where he lectured. Basically what he taught was that happiness and well-being do not depend on material things or on one's situation in life, but on one's reasoning faculty. Through reason, one can emulate the calm and order of the universe by learning to accept events with a stern and tranquil mind.

Zeno's Greek followers elaborated and systematized his teachings, which were later adopted and popularized by the Roman Stoics Seneca, Epictetus, and Marcus Aurelius. The influence of Stoicism can also be seen in the writings of the early Christian Fathers.

The Greek word *stōïkos* became *stoicus* in Latin, and by the fourteenth century had found a place in English, at first variously spelled (*stoyck, stoick*, etc.), until becoming standardized as *stoic*. By the sixteenth century, the word was also being used as a common noun for 'one apparently or professedly indifferent to pleasure or pain'.

Another English word that owes its origin to a Greek philosopher's teaching site is *peripatetic*. Following the death of his father in 367 B.C., the young Aristotle (then aged 17) was sent to Athens to study at Plato's Academy. He spent the next 20 years there with Plato. However, after Plato's death he was passed over twice for the position as head of the Academy. He subsequently opened a rival school in the Lyceum, a gymnasium attached to the temple of Apollo Lyceus, situated in a grove just outside Athens.

As a teacher there, Aristotle used to conduct classes while walking in the *peripatos,* a covered walkway in the Lyceum. From this practice, the disciples of Aristotle came to be called Peripatetics. The Greek word became *peripateticus* in Latin, which Middle English borrowed around 1400 as *perypatetik*. In the seventeenth century the word *peripatetic* acquired its additional sense of 'one who walks about, itinerant'. See also ACADEMY.

[ME, fr. L *stoicus,* adj. & n., fr. Gk *stōïkos,* fr. Stoa (*Poikilē*) Painted Portico, a portico in Athens where Zeno taught (fr. *stoa* portico + *poikilē,* fem. of *poikilos* multicolored, painted) + *-ikos* -ic; akin to Gk *stylos* pillar]

stomach   In Greek, *stoma* meant 'mouth', a meaning reflected in a few English derivatives, such as *stomatitis* 'inflammatory disease of the mouth'. The physical reference of *stoma* showed little tendency to wander from its origin, and the metaphorical applications of *stoma,* such as 'utterance' or 'foremost part', were such as to keep the reference to the mouth front and center. Nevertheless, a derivative *stomachos* began a downward journey, referring in successive stages to the throat, the gullet, the entrance to the stomach, and finally the stomach itself. Latin borrowed the word in these meanings as *stomachus*.

With the physical reference shifted from the mouth to the stomach, a different set of metaphorical applications were now appropriate. The Romans considered the stomach a seat of regulation of the bodily humors. Just which of the effects of the various humors is focused on tends to vary, as is apparent from the word *humor* itself, in Modern English referring primarily to levity, as compared with its French cognate *humeur*, which when unqualified tends to refer to a foul mood. (See also HUMOR.) *Stomachus* partook of this variability, being applied to states of spirit ranging from patience through vexation and anger. The word was borrowed into Middle English as *stomak* (the *ch* spelling in Latin was commonly pronounced \k\) and later *stomach,* and for a time had many of the metaphorical meanings of its Latin source. In the sixteenth century, for instance, "take stomach" was used in very much the same way we use "take heart" today, and one could make reference to "valiaunt men of stomacke" without necessarily conjuring up an image of a rotund Falstaff. As a verb, *to stomach* meant 'to take offense'. Even Greek, the original lender of the word, borrowed back a metaphorical sense from Rome, letting *stomachos* come to mean 'anger'.

In English, most of the metaphorical uses dropped away, leaving only a few expressions such as "I wouldn't have the stomach for it," where we might gloss *stomach* as 'fortitude', and "I can't stomach him," where *stomach* means 'abide'. But the physical reference of *stomach* continued to wander. From designating an internal organ of digestion, *stomach* came to be used of the abdomen or paunch. For a time the word was even applied to the chest. This last use has receded in English, but an analogue remains in French, where *les estomacs* is a rather ludicrous popular expression for the female breasts.

[ME *stomak,* fr. MF *estomac,* fr. L *stomachus* gullet, esophagus, stomach, fr. Gk *stomachos,* fr. *stoma* mouth, opening; akin to MBret *staffu* mouth, W *safu* mouth, Av *staman-* mouth of a dog]

story See NOVEL.
[ME *storie,* fr. OF *estorie, estoire,* fr. L *historia*]

straighten See STRAITEN.
[²*straight,* adj. (fr. ME *streght, streit, straight,* fɪ. past part. of *strecchen* to stretch) + *-en*]

strain See STRAITEN.
[ME *streinen, strainen,* fr. MF *estreindre, estraindre,* fr. L *stringere* to bind tight, press together; akin to Gk *strang-, stranx* drop squeezed out, *strangos* twisted, flowing drop by drop, *strangalē* halter, MIr *srengim* I draw]

straiten In *straitened* circumstances money is tight, and one is apt to feel strain, anxiety, and worry. Appropriately so. The word *straiten,* a six-teenth-century addition to our language, is based on the early French ad-jective *estreit,* which derives from the Latin word *strictus,* the past participle of the verb *stringere* 'to bind tight'. *Straiten,* then, is etymologi-cally unrelated to *straighten,* which instead is related to *stretch.* But *strait-en* is related to *strain.* The word *strain* came into Middle English as *streinen, strainen* from the Middle French verb *streindre, straindre,* which also derives from the Latin verb *stringere* 'to bind tight'.

The idea of a physical constriction is involved in the origin of two other words of similar meaning. *Anxiety,* first appearing in English in the six-teenth century, was formed directly from the Latin noun *anxietas,* a deriv-ative of the adjective *anxius* 'anxious', which derives from the verb *angere* 'to strangle'. *Worry* has a similar semantic history. Found in Middle En-glish as *wirien, werien, worien,* it can be traced back to the eighth-century Old English verb *wyrgan* 'to strangle'.

[fr. ¹*strait,* adj. (fr. ME *streit, strait, straight,* fr. OF *estreit,* fr. L *strictus,* fr. past part. of *stringere* to bind tight, press together) + *-en*]

stretch   See STRAITEN.
[ME *strecchen, strechen,* fr. OE *streccan;* akin to OFris *strekka* to stretch, MD *strecken,* OHG *strecchan* to stretch, OE *stræc, strec* firm, rigid, MHG & MD *strac* straight, stiff, OHG *starēn* to stare]

strike   See SNEAK.
[ME *striken,* fr. OE *strīcan;* akin to OFris *strīka* to pass over lightly, smooth, stroke, go, proceed, MLG *strīken,* OHG *strīhhan* to pass over lightly, smooth, stroke, go, L *stria* furrow, channel, *striga* row, furrow, swath, *stringere* to touch lightly, graze, OPruss *strigli* thistle, OSlav *strišti* to shear, cut; basic meaning: to stroke]

struth   See JEEPERS.
[short for *God's truth*]

stuck-up   See SUPERCILIOUS.
[fr. past part. of *stick up*]

stump   See HUSTINGS.
[ME *stumpe, stompe;* akin to MD *stompe, stomp* stub, stump, *stomp* blunt, OHG *stumpf* stub, stump, *stumpf* mutilated, OE *stempan* to stamp]

subscribe   See SCRIVENER.
[ME *subscriben,* fr. L *subscribere,* fr. *sub-* + *scribere* to write]

subtle   See DEBT, PRETEXT.
[ME *sutil, sotil,* fr. OF *soutil, sotil,* fr. L *subtilis* finely woven, fine, thin,

refined, keen, subtle, fr. *sub-* under, near + *-tilis* (fr. *tela* web); akin to
L *texere* to weave]

succor   See SHERRY.
[ME *succur, sucur, socur,* taken as sing. fr. earlier *sucurs, socours,* fr. OF
secors, sucors, fr. ML *succursus,* fr. L, past part. of *succurrere* to run up,
run to help, fr. *sub-* up + *currere* to run]

suede   See SPRUCE.
[fr. the phrase *suède gloves,* part translation of F *gants de Suède* Swedish
gloves]

sugar   See JEEPERS.
[euphemism for *shit*]

summer   See AUTUMN.
[ME *sumer, somer,* fr. OE *sumor;* akin to OS, OHG & ON *sumar* summer, OIr *sam,* W *haf,* Av *ham-* summer, Skt *samā* year, half year, season]

Sunday   The English language took its names for the months of the year
from Latin by way of French sometime around the year 1000 with the
great influx of French and scholarly Latin words into Britain along with
the coming of the Normans. (see JANUARY.) But the names for the days of
the week are strictly Germanic, although even there they were not immune to the Latin influence.
    Earlier writers have speculated that the idea of dividing the week into
seven days goes back much earlier than the Romans, possibly to the Babylonians. They at some point associated the days with the seven known
planets, that is the seven heavenly bodies then known to move through
the sky. It was during the late pre-Christian period that the Romans adopted this seven-day week, giving Latin names to the days: *solis dies* ('sun's
day'), *lunae dies* ('moon's day'), *Martis dies* (Mars), *Mercurii dies* (Mercury),
Jovis dies (Jupiter or Jove), *Veneris dies* (Venus), and *Saturni dies* (Saturn).
In Latin the names of the planets other than the sun and moon were also
names of gods, and these days were dedicated to their gods. (See also JO-
VIAL.) In the Romance languages that grew out of Latin, the Latin influence is still strong. In Modern French, for example, we find obvious
evidence of the Latin forms in the weekday names: *lundi* (Monday),
mardi, mercredi, jeudi, and *vendredi.* The weekend names, of more religious significance, were rebaptized *samedi* for Saturday, a word related
to the word *sabbath,* and *dimanche* for Sunday (from a Latin phrase meaning 'Lord's day').
    The early Germanic peoples were also influenced by the Roman culture
with which they had contact, and from the Romans they took the names
for the days of the week. But instead of borrowing the Latin names, these
peoples translated the Latin names into the Germanic equivalents. Thus
solis dies ('sun's day') was translated to a compound that eventually yielded the Old English *sunnandæg* (from *sunne* 'sun' and *dæg* 'day'); *lunae
dies* was translated to something that yielded Old English *monandæg*

(*mona* 'moon' and *dæg* 'day'). But here the translating took an interesting turn. Since the other days of the week were named for Roman gods, the Germanic people substituted the names of their own gods having similar qualities or characteristics. For example, the Roman god Mars was considered the god of war; for the Germanic people, this position was taken by the god Tyr (spelled *Tiw* in Old English). Thus when Mar's day was transported into the Germanic languages, it became *tīwesdæg* in Old English. Mercury became associated with the Germanic god Odin (*Woden* in Old English), perhaps by the Romans themselves, and thus *Mercurii dies* was taken into the Germanic languages in a way that gave us *wodnesdæg* ('Woden's day'). In like manner the Germanic people substituted the name of the thunder god Thor for the Roman god Jupiter or Jove, creating *thōrsdagr* in Old Norse, which came into Old English as *thursdæg* ('Thor's day'), and their Frigg (wife of Odin) for the Roman Venus to yield *frīgedæg* ('Frigg's day') for *Friday*. The Germanic people apparently had no other god to equate with Saturn, the Roman god of seed and sowing, so the Latin name of the day was merely translated, giving us *sæterndæg*, *sæterdæg* in Old English, our modern *Saturday*.

For other articles on words derived from ancient mythology and legend see VOLCANO.

[ME *sunnenday, sonnenday, sonday, sunday*, fr. OE *sunnandæg*; akin to OFris *sunnandei* Sunday, OS *sunnundag*, OHG *sunnūn tag*, ON *sunnudagr, sunnundagr*; all fr. a prehistoric WGmc-NGmc compound formed fr. components represented by OE *sunne* sun and *dæg* day; trans. of L *solis dies*, trans. of Gk *hēmera hēliou*]

supercilious Anyone who has been on the receiving end of disapprovingly raised eyebrows will have no trouble understanding the etymology of *supercilious*. The Latin word for 'eyebrow' was *supercilium*, derived from *super-* 'above, over' and *cilium* 'eyelid'. The raising of the eyebrows to express an attitude of haughty disdain was evidently as well known in ancient times as it is now, inasmuch as the Latin *supercilium* was also used in the figurative sense 'haughtiness, disdainful superiority'. The derivative adjective in Latin was *superciliosus*, which was adopted in English as *supercilious* in the sixteenth century. The meaning of *supercilious* is 'coolly and patronizingly haughty'.

An adjective that resembles *supercilious* in its history and meaning, if not in its tone, is *snooty*, which is derived from *snoot* 'snout, nose' and which suggests the downward gaze along the nose associated with an air of snobbish disdain. If you raise your eyebrows and look down your nose, you are being superciliously snooty. Likewise, the adjective *stuck-up* may well derive from the same stereotypically snobbish attitude of having one's nose stuck up in the air (the better to look down it and still see where one is going). *Stuck-up* and *snooty* are both newer words than *supercilious*, dating from the early nineteenth and early twentieth centuries respectively.

[L *superciliosus*, fr. *supercilium* eyebrow, pride, haughtiness (fr. *super-* + *-cilium* — akin to L *celare* to hide) + *-osus* -ous]

superscribe   See SCRIVENER.
[L *superscribere*, fr. *super-* + *scribere* to write]

surgeon   See SURGERY.
[ME *surgien*, fr. AF, contr. of OF *serurgien, cirurgien*, fr. *serurgie, cirurgie* surgery + *-ien* -ian]

surgery   While doctors have many different ways of treating disease, a surgeon is commonly thought of as a doctor who treats exclusively by working with his hands. Etymologically speaking the conception is quite appropriate, for *surgeon* and *surgery* are derived ultimately from Greek *cheirourgos*, 'working with the hand', which is a compound formed from *cheir*, 'hand', and *ergon*, 'work'. An archaic form of *surgeon* still met with occasionally in special contexts is *chirurgeon*, which reflects its etymology a little more clearly.

Recent technological developments have led to forms of surgery not entirely dependent upon the surgeon working manually with a scalpel. For instance, in *chemosurgery* unwanted tissue is removed chemically. *Cryosurgery*, from *cryo-*, 'cold', plus *surgery*, uses procedures in which the desired dissection is achieved through a carefully controlled extreme chilling produced by the use of liquid nitrogen. Another system of healing is *chiropractic*, the first element of which is also from Greek *cheir*, 'hand'. This system is based on the theory that disease results from a lack of normal nerve function and the treatment employs manipulation and specific adjustment of body structures, such as the spinal column.

[ME *surgerie*, fr. OF, contr. of *serurgerie, cirurgerie*, fr. *serurgie, cirurgie* (fr. L *chirurgia*, fr. Gk *cheirourgia*, fr. *cheirourgos* working with the hand — fr. *cheir* hand + *-ourgos* working, fr. *-o-* + *ergon* work — + *-ia* -y) + *-erie* -ery]

surly   See GENTILE.
[alter. of obs. E *sirly*, fr. ME, fr. *sir* + *-ly*]

suspire   See CESSPOOL.
[ME *suspiren*, fr. L *suspirare* to draw a deep breath, sigh, fr. *sub-* + *spirare* to breathe]

swan song   The swan is a bird that has been known from early times. *Swan* is one of the oldest words in English and has roots in the oldest Germanic languages as well as cognates in nearly every Germanic language that survives. These ancient roots of *swan* are perhaps related in even older Indo-European languages to the source of the English word *sound*. This possible connection has led philologists to speculate that the earliest swan named was the "singing swan"—a term that may be intended for the whooper swan (*Cygnus cygnus*) or perhaps Bewick's swan or the trumpeter swan or the tundra swan, all of which have identifiable calls. References to the melancholy or plaintive sound of the swan's singing are to be found in Homer and Hesiod.

But the common adornment of ornamental ponds everywhere is the mute swan (*Cygnus olor*) which, while not absolutely mute—it can hiss and snort if it chooses—is generally of reticent demeanor and does not trumpet, bugle, honk, or whoop it up like its wilder brethren. It may be that the less ancient ancients, trying to square Homer's or Hesiod's remarks about the song of the swan with their own experience of the uncommunicative mute swan, were the ones who concocted the fable that the swan sings but one beautiful song just before it dies.

The conceit of the swan's final beautiful song seems to have strong appeal to that singing and scribbling class, the poets. There are references to the dying swan's lovely singing in English as far back as Chaucer, and the association of lovely song with the swan led them to apply *swan* to one another as a complimentary epithet: Ben Jonson, for instance, hung the phrase "Sweet Swan of Avon" on Shakespeare.

Curiously, English had to wait until 1831 for a writer to come up with the term *swan song* for someone's last bravura (or even pedestrian) performance or production. The writer was Thomas Carlyle, and he seems to have patterned the phrase after German *schwanengesang* or *schwanenlied;* the Germans, it seems, had come up with the idea a century or two earlier.

If the poetic tradition of the figurative swan song is firmly established in the minds of the less than poetic, the literal swan song has been the subject of some doubt. The tradition has been traced to Socrates by some authorities and to Pliny by others. Sir Thomas Browne, in *Pseudodoxia Epidemica* (1646) devotes a page or so to the question. He notes that ancient authorities were in disagreement, some affirming the dying song of the swan and others affirming that the swan sings but does not die. He also names several authorities, including Pliny, who express doubt or disbelief and mentions more recent observation and investigation that militates against the musical final song of the swan. He concludes:

> When therefore we consider the dissention of Authors, the falsity of relations, the indisposition of the Organs, and the immusical note of all we ever beheld or heard of; if generally taken and comprehending all Swans, or of all places, we cannot assent thereto. Surely he that is bit with a Tarantula, shall never be cured by this Musick. . . .

The reference to the tarantula, less than transparent to most modern readers, alludes to another fabled zoological contribution to music. Samuel Pepys in his diary records being regaled by what we would now term tall tales by "a great traveller"—undoubtedly over a few bottles of wine in a tavern. This traveler seems to have been in southern Italy: "Speaking of the tarantula, he says that all the harvest long (about which times they are most busy) there are fidlers go up and down the fields every where, in expectation of being hired by those that are stung" (4 February 1662, new style). Italian folk belief had it that the only cure for the bite of the tarantula was vigorous or even frenzied dancing; the itinerant fiddlers clearly hoped to turn a few lire while fiddling victims back to health.

The original tarantula is a wolf spider native to southern Europe. It takes its name from Taranto, an ancient seaport located inside the heel of southern Italy. An Italian folk dance associated with the bite of the tarantula and its cure is called the *tarentella*, a word also derived from *Taranto*. *Taranto* is also the basis of the word *tarantism* which has been used to describe a mass dancing mania that spread—apparently from Italy—across Europe in the late Middle Ages. The dancing mania was popularly supposed to have begun with tarantula bites, but it manifested itself in Germany, the Low Countries, and parts of France where the tarantula is unknown. The cause of the outbreak of tarantism, which hung on for more than two centuries, is not known. But we can absolve the tarantula, whose bite is now known to be not dangerous to humans.

[trans. of G *schwanenlied*]

swindler   One would hardly think that a dizzy or giddy person could be convincing enough to perpetrate a swindle. However, the original meaning of the German noun *schwindler* was 'a giddy person'. Such a person is often given to flights of fancy, and so the Germans applied the word as well to 'a fantastic schemer', 'a participant in shaky business deals', and then to 'a four-flusher, a cheat'. The word *schwindler* ultimately derives from the Old High German verb *swintan*, meaning 'to diminish, vanish, or lose consciousness'. This gave rise to the verb *schwindeln*, first used to mean 'to be dizzy' and then 'to cheat'. From this verb the noun *schwindler* was formed.

The first use of the loan word *swindler* in English apparently was around 1762. According to *The Slang Dictionary* (1865), printed by John Camden Hotten in London, "*swindler,* although a recognised word in standard dictionaries, commenced service as a Slang term. It was used as such by the poor Londoners against the German Jews who set up in London about the year 1762, also by our soldiers in the German war about that time." It referred to a person who obtained credit, money, or property by fraud or deceit.

Eric Partridge (*A Dictionary of the Underworld,* 1950) informs us that the words *swindle* and *swindler* "were at first cant terms . . ., but by 1780 at latest they had been adopted into Standard English." They both first appeared as dictionary entries in the 1782 edition of Nathan Bailey's *An Universal Etymological English Dictionary*.

[G *schwindler* giddy person, fantastic schemer, fr. *schwindeln* to be dizzy, fr. OHG *swintilōn*, freq. of *swintan* to diminish, vanish, become unconscious; akin to OE *swindan* to languish, vanish, OIr *a-sennad* finally]

swine   *Swine* were among the earliest animals domesticated. In their close association with people, they have become the focus of quite a number of proverbs. We speak of the inadvisability of buying a pig in a poke, of the impossibility of making a silk purse out of a sow's ear, and of casting pearls before swine. The pig's reputation for gluttony and fondness for a muddy environment have made him the type of certain unappealing human traits and have led to the uncomplimentary application of *pig, hog, swine,* and *sow* to people.

The related words *sow* and *swine* both go back to the beginnings of English, and their cognates appear in many Indo-European languages. One of these is *hys,* the Greek for 'hog'. When the Greeks encountered the *hyena,* they compared the beast's short, bristly mane with that characteristic of some hogs, and named him *hyaina.*

Socket is another relative of *sow* and *swine.* A Middle English *soket* was a spearhead which looked like a plowshare. It became the word, as well, for the socket which supports a spear. *Soket* was derived from Old French *soc,* 'plowshare', originally a Celtic word. The basic meaning of the related Middle Irish *soc* was 'hog's snout'. Because a plowshare turns up the earth like the snout of a rooting hog, it too was called a *soc.*

Hog can be traced back to late Old English, but its earlier history is unknown. It may be of Celtic origin, borrowed from a relative of Welsh *hwch* and Cornish *hoch* (and hence akin to *swine*). The snout of the spiny little *hedgehog,* often met in English hedgerows, somewhat resembles that of a pig.

The word *pig* itself occurs in Middle English as *pigge.* An Old English form *picga* is assumed but nowhere attested except in the compound *picbrēad,* 'pig food', which was used once as a gloss for the Latin *glans,* 'acorn'. The antecedents of the word are unknown.

For other words that owe a debt to the pig see PORK.

[ME, fr. OE *swīn;* akin to OHG *swīn* swine, ON *svīn,* Goth *swein,* L *suinus* of swine, *sus* swine, hog]

sword side See DISTAFF.

symphony The word *symphony* came into English in the thirteenth century as a borrowing from Old French which derived it through Latin from the Greek word *symphonia,* meaning 'a sounding together'. It was originally applied to any harmonious combination of notes; later it designated various musical instruments at different times, including a dulcimer, a virginal, a bagpipe, and a double-headed drum. The drum was described in 1398 by John de Trevisa: "The symphonye is an instrument of musyk; and it is made of an holowe tree closyd in lether in eyther syde and mynstralles betyth [beat] it wyth styckes."

By the seventeenth century *symphony* had acquired the sense of 'an instrumental musical passage' that was often performed as an interlude between vocal passages of a composition. The "Pastoral Symphony" in Handel's *Messiah* is such an instrumental piece. The overture to an opera was also sometimes referred to as a *symphony,* and from this sort of orchestral composition the symphony as we know it today developed. In the eighteenth century the symphony became an elaborate composition to be performed by an orchestra. Franz Joseph Haydn, often called "the Father of the Symphony," was mainly responsible for this development, having composed over one hundred symphonies himself. Wolfgang Amadeus Mozart, heavily influenced by Haydn, raised the symphony to heights never surpassed, and Ludwig van Beethoven's symphonies had overwhelming impact as expressions of intellect and emotion. He widened the scope of the orchestra with additional wind instruments and percussion and made it more than ever a unified ensemble.

By the twentieth century extended senses of *symphony* began to appear to denote something suggestive of a symphonic composition in harmonious complexity or variety, such as "symphonies of colors" and "symphonies of flowers."

[ME *symphonie,* fr. OF, fr. L *symphonia,* fr. Gk *symphōnia,* fr. *symphōnos* agreeing in sound, concordant (fr. *syn-* with + *phōnē* voice, sound) + *-ia* -y]

symposium   Nowadays most people attending a symposium might be loath to acknowledge that the post-conference socializing and imbibing constitute much of the appeal of such a gathering. Actually, the social aspects of a symposium need not induce in the symposiast any feelings of guilt or embarrassment. Etymologically speaking, social drinking is what a symposium is all about.

In classical Greece a social gathering might typically consist of two parts. The first part was the banquet proper, during which the food was the apparent focus of attention. After the banquet was concluded and the tables were cleared, a postprandial drinking party ensued. *Symposion,* the Greek name for these festivities, literally meant 'drinking together' and derived from the prefix *syn-* 'together' and the verb *pinein* 'to drink'. Later, the Romans would make the word *symposium.* To the entertainment accompanying the imbibing, each guest was expected to make contributions, which might consist of jokes, riddles, poems, or musical performances. For those symposiums with somewhat loftier aspirations, the drinking became subordinate to the entertainment, which at its most exalted might take the form of an extended philosophical discussion of a selected topic.

A record of one such intellectual discussion is provided by the Platonic dialogue known as the *Symposium.* Also referred to in English as the *Banquet* (which is how the gathering is actually characterized within the text of the dialogue), the *Symposium* is an account of a gathering at the house of the tragic poet Agathon. There the philosopher Socrates, the playwright Aristophanes, the physician Eryximachus, and several lesser lights take turns discussing the nature of and singing the praises of Eros. In brief, the goal of the symposiasts is to determine the highest manifestation of sexual love.

Before the eighteenth century *symposium* was used in English only with reference to the social gatherings of the ancient Greeks. In the eighteenth century, however, *symposium* came to be applied to the latter-day counterparts of such events. Eighteenth-century London marked the heyday of the gentleman's club. In the gentleman's club, intelligent conversation between companionable litterateurs, fueled by good and abundant drink, was accorded the status of an art form. Sir John Hawkins, who was a member of Dr. Samuel Johnson's celebrated circle, referred to one of their club gatherings as a "symposium" in his 1787 biography of the man of letters. Hawkins even referred to Johnson, arguably the most clubbable man in English literature, as the "symposiarch" of their circle. At about the same time, a volume of table talk titled *Symposia* was published.

By the nineteenth century *symposium*'s connotations of sociability had withered away. *Symposium* had come to imply a conference of a rather formal nature, held for the purpose of bringing together several differing opinions or perspectives on a particular topic. Nowadays *symposium* may also refer to a collection of articles on a single topic by several authors— who may never have even met, let alone lifted a glass together.

Fortunately, for those who believe that anything worth saying is worth saying over a glass of claret, a snifter of brandy, or a mug of ale, there remains *compotation*. *Compotation* is a kissing cousin of *symposium*. *Compotation* derives from Latin *compotatio*, which is a compound of the prefix *com-* 'together' and the verb *potare* 'to drink' and is thus an exact Latin translation of the Greek *symposion*. While *symposium* has acquired connotations of a highbrow colloquy, *compotation* continues to refer to a convivial gathering at which drinking is the first order of business.

[L, fr. Gk *symposion,* fr. *sympinein* to drink together, fr. *syn-* with, together + *pinein* to drink]

syncope   See SHORTENED FORMS.
[LL, fr. Gk *synkopē,* fr. *synkoptein* to chop up, cut short, fr. *syn-* + *koptein* to strike, cut off]

syphilis   Girolamo Fracastoro (ca. 1478–1553) was an Italian physician, poet, astronomer, and geologist. He is principally remembered today for two achievements. One was his advancement of a scientific germ theory of disease that was 300 years ahead of its time. The other was a medical poem published in 1530 and titled "Syphilis sive morbus Gallicus" ("Syphilis or the French Disease"). The "hero" of the poem is an unfortunate swineherd named Syphilus, whose name in Greek literally means "swine lover." The poem is actually a mythological tale that purports to tell how the disease first came into being. In the course of the poem Syphilus offends the sun god; for his punishment he becomes the first person to be afflicted with the fearsome contagion. His symptoms are graphically described in this 1686 translation of the poem from the original Latin, probably by playwright and poet Nahum Tate:

> He first wore Buboes dreadfull to the sight,
> First felt strange Pains and sleepless past the Night.

In a way the poem also serves as a kind of digest of all that was then known about the disease. The poem discusses the venereal nature of syphilis and its symptoms and its stages. Fracastoro's work is also notable for blaming the disease on another country:

> Through what adventures this unknown Disease

So lately did astonisht Europe seize
Through Asian Coasts and Libyan Cities ran
And from what Seeds the Malady began,
Our Song shall tell: to Naples first it came
From France, and justly took from France his Name

In blaming foreigners for the social disease Fracastoro was following a time-honored tradition. To the English the disease was the French or Spanish pox; the French named it the Neapolitan disease; the Russians referred to it as the Polish disease; the Persians attached the Turks' name to it, and so on.

[NL, after *Syphilus,* the supposed first sufferer from the disease and the hero of the poem *Syphilis sive Morbus Gallicus* (1530), by Girolamo Fracastoro †1553 Ital. physician, astronomer, and poet]

syringe See PANIC.
[ME *syring,* fr. ML *syringa, siringa,* fr. LL, injection, fr. Gk *syring-, syrinx* panpipe, fistula, tube]

T

tailor See TALLY.
[ME *taillour*, fr. OF *tailleur*, lit., one that cuts, fr. *taillier* to cut (fr. LL *taliare*, fr. L *talea* twig, stick, cutting) + -*eur* -or; akin to Gk *talis* marriageable girl, *tēlis* fenugreek, Lith *attolas, atolas* rowen, and perh. to ON *thöll* young pine tree; basic meaning: growing thing]

talent "And the brass of the offering was seventy talents, and two thousand and four hundred shekels" —Exodus 38:29 (AV). This biblical verse illustrates the use of two units of weight—the *talent* and the *shekel*—common in the ancient cultures of Egypt, Babylonia, Israel, Greece, and Rome. A third unit was the *mina*. The ratios varied, but the typical relationships were one talent to 60 minas to 3600 shekels. The actual weight of a talent varied considerably with time and place. Archaeologists estimate the Babylonian talent at about 66 pounds, the Greek (Attic) talent at about 58 pounds, and the Hebrew talent at over 90 pounds.

In the Hebrew Bible the word *kikkor*, literally 'round', was used for this weight. This was translated as *talanton* 'balance, pair of scales' in the Greek Septuagint Bible, as *talentum* in the Latin Vulgate Bible, and *talente* in early English Bibles.

In Medieval Latin we find *talentum* being used in the sense of 'inclination, desire'. This sense passed into early French and was borrowed into English about 1300. We find an example in Chaucer's *Canterbury Tales* ("The Parson's Tale," ca. 1400): ". . . his resoun refreyneth [restrains] nat his foul delit [desire] or talent." In Modern English this sense has become archaic.

In Greek and Latin the word was also used for a sum of money (a Greek *talanton* was equivalent to 6,000 drachmas). The Evangelist Matthew illustrates this usage in relating the "parable of the talents" (25:14–30), in which a master gives to one of his servants five talents, to another, two talents, and to a third, one talent. In time the master asked each of them what he had done with the talents. The first two servants had doubled their talents, and the master was well pleased. The third servant, being afraid, hid his one talent in the earth. This made the master very angry since he expected his servant to have at least invested his talent with bankers so that it could accrue interest. The master then took back the one talent and gave it to the servant who had ten. He cast the worthless servant out into the darkness where "there shall be weeping and gnashing of teeth." Critical interpretations of the text have seen this monetary sense of *talent* being used metaphorically as a God-given endowment which, if not used, would be lost. In English this metaphorical sense dates from the fifteenth century. In the seventeenth century this 'endowment' sense gave rise to its extended use for 'mental ability or aptitude'. In his poem "Mad Mullinix and Timothy" (1728), Jonathan Swift gives us an example: "When first in publick we appear,/ I'll lead the Van, keep you the Rear./ Be careful, as you walk behind,/ Use all the Talents of your mind."

[ME *talent, talente;* in sense of 'unit of weight', fr. OE *talente,* fr. L *talenta,* pl. of *talentum* unit of weight or money, fr. Gk *talanton* balance, pair of scales, unit of weight or money; akin to L *tollere* to lift up; in sense of 'disposition', fr. OF *talent* inclination, desire, disposition, fr. ML *talentum,* perh. fr. L, unit of weight or money; in remaining senses fr. ME, unit of money; fr. the parable of the talents in Mt 25:14–30]

tally   When first used in English, around the middle of the fifteenth century, the word *tally* designated a usually square wooden rod or stick which was notched with marks to represent numbers and then was split lengthwise through the notches so that each of two bargaining parties might have a record of a transaction and of the amount of money due or paid. The word was derived from the Latin *talea,* meaning 'stick, twig, or cutting'.

This primitive means of recording transactions was later supplanted by more convenient bookkeeping sheets, and the association of *tally* with rods or sticks was lost. Through generalization, the word came to be applied to any recorded amount, including game points and scores. By the middle of the seventeenth century, the term was also used to mean 'a half, part, or entity that agrees or corresponds to an opposite or companion number', such as in "one twin is the *tally* of the other." By the 1880s *tally* had acquired the sense of 'the last of a specified unit or number'. For example, at the end of a count of items, the tallyman would call "tally!" and then write down the final figure. In high-tech societies, the tallyman has generally been replaced by any of various kinds of mechanical and electronic calculators.

Going back to the Latin noun *talea,* we can also trace the development of another common English word, *tailor.* We know that in Latin the verb *taliare* 'to cut' was derived from *talea* 'stick, cutting'. In early French this verb became *taillier,* also meaning 'to cut', and the person doing the cutting was a *tailleur.* The object being cut was usually specified: a stonecutter was *tailleur de pierre,* a woodcutter was *tailleur de bois,* and a clothes cutter was *tailleur d'habits.* By the thirteenth century, when *tailleur* was used by itself it was taken to mean 'a clothes cutter'. Middle English borrowed this French word as *taillour* and used it in the same sense, 'a clothes maker'.

[ME *taly, talye,* fr. ML *talea, tallia,* fr. L *talea* stick, twig, cutting]

tandem   When a pair of horses pulls a carriage, the two are usually harnessed side by side. But there is a type of two-wheeled, two-seated carriage that is drawn by two horses harnessed one before the other. This carriage, a *tandem*, owes its name to a rather contorted Latin-English pun. The Latin word *tandem* means 'at length, at last, finally'. We do not know who the punster was who first suggested that horses arranged lengthwise should be thought of as "at length" and the carriage be called a *tandem*, but he need not have been a scholar. The Latin word is certainly not a rare one and would be known to any student of the language. The first record of the English word is in Francis Grose's lexicon of eighteenth-century slang, *A Classical Dictionary of the Vulgar Tongue* (1785). Grose defined *"Tandem.* A two-wheeled chaise, buggy, or noddy, drawn by two horses, one before the other; that is, at length." It was not long before *tandem* had lost any tincture of vulgarity and had become the standard term for a carriage of this kind.

In the course of the nineteenth century, *tandem* came to be used in a general way to describe any arrangement of things or of people one behind another. A *tandem bicycle* is also known as a "bicycle built for two." A *tandem airplane* has two or more sets of wings, one in front of another at the same level. *Tandem* has even been used to describe the wings of a dragonfly.

[L, at length, at last (taken to mean "lengthwise"), fr. *tam* so, so much, as (akin to Gk *to* that) + *-dem* (demonstrative suff.)]

tantalite   See AMMONIA.
[Sw *tantalit*, fr. NL *tantalum* + Sw *-it* -ite]

tantalize   Beneath a tree bearing golden apples runs a river that Edmund Spenser in his *The Faerie Queen* makes the site for his recounting of the classical tale of the punishment of *Tantalus*, a mythic king of Phrygia who offended the gods. Various versions of the tale give different accounts of the sin he committed, but the consequences are more or less invariable; in Spenser's words:

Deepe was he drenched to the utmost chin,
Yet gaped still, as coveting to drink
Of the cold liquour which he waded in,
And stretching forth his hand, did often thinke
To reach the fruit which grew upon the brincke:
But both fruit from hand, and flood from mouth,
Did fly abacke, and made him vainely swincke
    [labor]. . . .

In classical versions of the story some details are different (for instance, he is said to be standing in the lake Tartarus in the Underworld), but the punishment of not being able to quench his thirst or appease his hunger while being continually in sight of water and food has become well known throughout Western civilization. It is from this story that English has borrowed the king's name to form the verb *tantalize*, 'to tease or torment by presenting something desirable to the view but continually keeping it out of reach'. See also AMMONIA.

[*Tantalus*, in Greco-Roman mythology the king of Phrygia who for his sins was condemned to stand in Tartarus up to his chin in water that receded whenever he stooped to drink and under some branches of fruit that likewise receded whenever he tried to grasp them (fr. L, fr. Gk *Tantalos*) + E *-ize*]

tantalum See AMMONIA.
[NL, fr. *Tantalus*, mythical king condemned to stand up to his chin in water that receded whenever he stopped to drink; fr. its incapacity to absorb acid]

tarantella See SWAN SONG.
[fr. It, fr. *Taranto*, seaport in southern Italy often associated with the dancing mania of tarantism + It *-ella*]

tarantism See SWAN SONG.
[NL *tarantismus*, fr. *Taranto*, seaport in southern Italy where tarantism was common from the 15th to the 17th cent. + L *-ismus* -ism]

tarantula See SWAN SONG.
[ML, fr. OIt *tarantola*, fr. *Taranto*, seaport in southern Italy]

target In early French the noun *targe* was used for 'a light shield or buckler carried especially by footmen and archers'. This word is found in the *Song of Roland* (ca. 1100) and is probably of Frankish origin. In the thirteenth century *targe* was borrowed into English and was pronounced \'tärj\, after the French pronunciation. Chaucer uses it in *Canterbury Tales* when he has the knight refer to "the rede statue of Mars, with spere and targe" ("The Knight's Tale," ca. 1387).

The French word *targette*, a diminutive form of *targe*, first appeared in the fourteenth century and was taken into English as *target* around 1400 with its French sense 'a small targe or shield'. We find an example of this sense in Shakespeare's *Henry VI, Part III* (ca. 1592), when Edward, Henry's son, exclaims "Whate'er it bodes, henceforward will I bear/ Upon my target three fair-shining suns." The French also sometimes used the variant form *targuette*, pronounced with a hard *g* sound that was also present in the Provençal *targuetta* and the Italian *targhetta*. These pronunciations probably influenced the English to pronounce *target* with a hard *g* sound instead of the soft *g* as in *targe*. Both *targe* and *target* continued in use, but *targe* has become rare since the eighteenth century.

In the latter part of the eighteenth century *target* acquired the extended sense of 'a shieldlike object to be shot at for practice'. Samuel Johnson's Dictionary (1755) does not include this sense. However, Joseph Strutt, in his 1801 book *The Sports and Pastimes of the People of England*, comments: "I have seen the gentlemen who practise archery in the vicinity of London, repeatedly shoot from end to end, and not touch the target with an arrow." During the nineteenth century we find the first evidence of the more general sense 'something or someone that is or may be aimed at'. In his poem "Locksley Hall" (1842), Alfred Lord Tennyson provides an example of this: "Hark, my merry comrades call me, sounding on the bugle-horn,/ They to whom my foolish passion were a target for their scorn."

Another important piece of armor—this one as old as the Anglo-Saxons—was the *helm,* worn to protect the head. This Old English word has cognates in the other Germanic languages. We find an example of the use of this word in Shakespeare's *Troilus and Cressida* (ca. 1601), when Pandarus, in speaking of Troilus to Cressida, says: "Look you how his sword is bloodied, and his helm more hack'd than Hector's."

In the *Song of Roland* (ca. 1100) we find the earliest evidence of the use of *helme* 'helmet' in early French. It is considered to be of Germanic origin and is related to the Old English word *helm.* The early French diminutive of *helme* was *helmet.* In time these words evolved into *heaume* and *heaumet.* This referred to a particular type of headpiece: it was a large helmet of armor worn over a hood of mail or a steel cap, resting on the shoulders rather than on the head. For this type of headpiece the term *heaume* was used in English as well, and the word survives in books relating to that period and to heraldry.

It was in the fifteenth century that English borrowed the French *helmet* to denote a headpiece that is smaller than the heaume and that rests on the head. In the nineteenth century *helmet* began to be applied to various kinds of nonmilitary protective headgear, such as those worn by divers, police officers, and fire fighters. It has also been used to denote parts of plants and insects that resemble a helmet in form or position.

[ME, fr. MF *targette,* dim. of OF *targe* light shield, of Gmc origin; akin to OHG *zarga* frame, border, ON *targa* shield; prob. akin to MIr *dremm* group of people, Bret *dramm* bundle, Arm *trçak* bundle of wood, and perh. to Gk *drassesthai* to grasp]

tarmac   See MACADAM.
[short for *tarmacadam,* fr. ¹*tar* + *macadam*]

tarnal   See JEEPERS.
[alter. of *eternal*]

tarnation   See JEEPERS.
[alter. (influenced by *tarnal*) of *darnation*]

task   See PATTERN.
[ME *taske, tasque,* fr. ONF *tasque,* fr. (assumed) VL *tasca* task, remuneration, alter. of *taxa,* fr. L *taxare* to touch, feel, rate, compute]

tawdry   When, in the seventh century, Etheldreda, the queen of Northumbria, decided to renounce her husband and her royal position for the veil of a nun, she was almost straightway appointed abbess of a monastery in the Isle of Ely. She was renowned for her saintliness and is traditionally said to have died of a swelling in her throat, which she took as a judgment upon her fondness for wearing necklaces in her youth. Her shrine became one of the principal sites of pilgrimage in England. An annual fair was held

test **461**

in her honor on 17 October, and her name became simplified to St. Audrey. At these fairs various kinds of cheap knickknacks, toys, and jewelry
were sold along with a type of necklace called "St. Audrey's lace," which
by the seventeenth century had become altered to "*tawdry* lace." Eventually *tawdry* came to be applied to the various other cheap articles sold at
these fairs and so developed its present sense of 'cheap showy finery', as
well as its adjectival use to mean 'cheap and gaudy in appearance and
quality'.

[*tawdry lace* (a tie of lace for the neck), alter. of earlier *St. Audrey's lace*,
after *St. Audrey* (Etheldreda or Æthelthrȳth) †679 queen of Northumbria who founded an abbey at Ely; fr. the tradition that she died of a
throat tumor inflicted as a punishment for her fondness for necklaces]

tax See PATTERN.
[ME *taxen* to tax, assess, fr. MF & ML; MF *taxer*, fr. ML *taxare* to tax,
assess, fr. L, to touch, feel, rate, compute, censure, freq. of *tangere* to
touch]

taxicab See CAB.
[*taxi*meter *cab; taximeter*, fr. F *taximètre*, modif. of G *taxameter*, irreg.
fr. ML *taxa* charge, assessment, tax (fr. *taxare* to assess, tax) + G -*meter;
cab*, short for *cabriolet*]

telescope See BISHOP.
[NL *telescopium*, fr. Gk *tēleskopos* far-seeing, fr. *tēle*- far, distant +
skopos watcher; akin to Gk *skopein* to view, watch]

temper See HUMOR.
[ME *tempren, temperen* to temper, fr. OE & OF; OE *temprian* & OF
temprer, fr. L *temperare* to mix, blend, regulate, restrain oneself, abstain, prob. fr. *tempor-, tempus* period of time, fitting time, season, time
(in general)]

temperament See HUMOR.
[ME, fr. L *temperamentum*, fr. *temperare* to mix, blend, regulate +
-*mentum* -ment]

terpsichorean See CALLIOPE.
[fr. *terpsichore* dancing, after *Terpsichore*, the muse of choral dance and
song]

test Latin *testum* was used as a general word for an earthen vessel. In
the Middle Ages its French descendant, *test*, became the word for a specific type of vessel which was used in the assaying of precious metals, namely,
a cupel. The cupel or test is a shallow, porous cup. When impure silver or
gold is heated in it, the impurities are absorbed in the porous material,
leaving a relatively pure button of silver or gold. As the name for a cupel,
test was borrowed into Middle English in the fourteenth century. By the

late sixteenth century, it was being used figuratively. To "put something to the test" or to "bring something to the test" was to make trial of it, to determine its quality or genuineness, as a precious metal might be tried in a cupel. Thomas Nashe, in his picaresque novel *The Unfortunate Traveller* (1594), wrote of "a delicate wench . . . which I would faine haue had to the grand test, whether she were cunning at Alcumie or no." This figurative sense of *test* soon became the word's primary meaning; the original meaning is now seldom remembered by those who call any examination or means of evaluation a test.

[ME, vessel in which metals were assayed, cupel, fr. MF, fr. L *testum* earthen vessel; akin to L *testa* piece of burned clay, earthen pot, shell, Av *tashta* cup]

tetragrammaton See JEEPERS.
[ME *Tetragramaton*, fr. Gk *tetragrammaton*, fr. neut. of *tetragrammatos* having four letters, fr. *tetra-* four + *grammat-*, *gramma* letter]

text See PRETEXT.
[ME, fr. MF *texte*, fr. OF, fr. ML *textus* text, passage, Scripture, fr. L, texture, tissue, structure, context, fr. past part. of *texere* to construct, weave]

textile See PRETEXT.
[L, fr. neut. of *textilis* woven, fr. *textus* (past part.) + *-ilis* -ile]

texture See PRETEXT.
[L *textura* web, texture, fr. *textus* (past part. of *texere* to weave) + *-ura* -ure]

them John Bunyan wrote, in his autobiographical *Grace Abounding to the Chief of Sinners,* published in 1660, "He should speak them words." Bunyan was using *them* as a demonstrative adjective meaning 'those'. Bunyan did not originate the use, which is first attested in 1596. It has been speculated by a few writers on language that the demonstrative adjective is not derived from the personal pronoun *them* but is an entirely different word, being a survival of Old English *thǣm,* which was the dative masculine and dative neuter form of the definite article. For us to feel sure that the Old English form had survived in Modern English would require at least some slight evidence of *them* used as an article or demonstrative adjective in Middle English. Unfortunately, there isn't any, as far as we know. All known examples of *them* in Middle English are personal pronouns. The dative of the article seems to have had its last sound weakened to *-n* or lost entirely in Middle English (we spell it *the* without a final consonant today).

The more likely, though less interesting, origin of demonstrative *them* is by functional shift from a meaning of the personal pronoun equivalent to *they, those* that is attested from Caxton's time in the fifteenth century. The pronoun sense is still familiar from phrases like "them's my sentiments" found chiefly in casual usage, as is this example taken from a letter written by Alexander Woollcott in 1920.

[ME *them;* partly fr. *tham,* fr. OE *thæm, thām,* dat. pl. demonstrative pron. & definite article; partly for *theim,* fr. ON, dat. pl. demonstrative pron. & definite article]

therblig See MACADAM.
[anagram, after Frank B. *Gilbreth* †1924 Am. engineer]

thesaurus See TREASURE.
[NL, fr. L, treasure, store, collection, fr. Gk *thēsauros*]

thespian See TRAGEDY.
[*Thespis,* 6th cent. B.C. Greek poet and reputed originator of the actor's role in drama + E *-an*]

thing *Thing* is one of the oldest words in the language. It is of old Germanic stock, with cognates in Old Frisian, Old High German, Old Saxon, and Old Norse. The earliest sense of *thing* is 'assembly, court, counsel'. Some philologists have noted a cognate word in Gothic meaning 'appointed time' from an assumed Proto-Germanic word and have hazarded the guess that the underlying meaning in the Germanic languages was 'day of assembly'.

From the original meaning of 'assembly, court, council', *thing* came to mean 'a matter brought up in court', and from that was extended to 'something with which one is concerned'. This meaning is old, going back at least to King Alfred the Great in the ninth century. In Shakespeare we see the phrase "hear how things go" and in Charles Dickens we see "How have things gone . . . ?" Used with a personal pronoun, it could mean 'one's own particular interest or specialty'. In the phrase "do one's (own) thing," this sense became a common cant phrase in the late 1960s when it was widely believed to be modern slang. But Ralph Waldo Emerson had used it a century and a quarter earlier in one of his essays: "Do your thing and I shall know you" ("Self-Reliance," 1841).

The 'something with which one is concerned' meaning of *thing* is the earliest to survive into Modern English. Alongside this immaterial sense we find a sense—at least as far back as King Alfred's time—of *thing* in which it denotes a concrete entity, a separate and distinct item of perception or thought: "A thing of beauty is a joy forever," in the words of the poet John Keats. From this use numerous senses relating to animate and inanimate objects have developed. Sometimes the object might be animate but not corporeal, like the ghost in *Hamlet:* "What, has this thing appear'd again to-night?"

Thing used of people varies. It can be purely abstract and speculative, as in Proverbs 19:22 (AV): "Whoso findeth a wife findeth a good thing." In much modern use its meaning tends to depend on the modifiers that accompany it, for example, "Oh, you poor thing." *Thing* unmodified and applied to a person regularly implies contempt. Shakespeare used it this way a number of times, and so did Lady Mary Wortley Montagu in a 1756 letter: "By what accident they have fallen into the hands of that thing Dodsley I know not."

The use of *thing* for both euphemism and suggestion in sexual contexts is worth brief mention. This use has been with us since Chaucer's robust and garrulous Wife of Bath expressed the opinion that

> . . . our bothe thynges smale
> Were eek to knowe a female from a male,
> And for noon oother cause . . .
> —*Canterbury Tales*, "Wife of Bath's Prologue," ca. 1395

[ME, fr. OE, thing, assembly, reason; akin to OHG *ding* thing, assembly, reason, ON *thing* object of value, assembly, parliament, Goth *theihs* time, and prob. to Gk *teinein* to stretch]

thirl See WINDOW.
[ME, fr. OE *thyrel*, fr. *thurh* through]

thrasonical See HECTOR.
[L *Thrason-*, *Thraso* Thraso, braggart soldier in the comedy *Eunuchus* by Terence †159 B.C. Roman playwright + E *-ical*]

thrill In the fourteenth century, when a person was "thrilled," he might not have lived long enough to tell anyone about it. He would most likely have been run through with a lance or sword, since the Middle English verb *thrillen*, an altered form of *thirlen*, was used to mean 'to pierce, stab, perforate'. In some British dialects the verb *thirl* is still used for *thrill* today. The older form *thirlen* was derived from the Old English noun *thyrel*, meaning 'hole'. This noun is also the source for part of our word *nostril*, which etymologically means 'nose hole'. The original sense of *thrill* is reflected in this quotation from the 1661 publication *Merry Drollery:* "The sword . . . doth nimbly come to the point . . ., Thrilling and drilling, And killing, and spilling."

The word was also used metaphorically, as when one's heart was thrilled by a strong emotion. In *King Lear* (ca. 1605), Shakespeare describes a servant as being "thrill'd with remorse." And two centuries later in his poem *The Waggoner* (1805), William Wordsworth writes: "His ears are by the music thrilled."

By the end of the eighteenth century an additional sense had become established: 'to vibrate or quiver'. This is Sir Walter Scott's sense when he writes in his novel *The Black Dwarf* (1816): "Exhausting his voice in shrieks and imprecations, that thrilled wildly along the waste heath." The transitive use is evident in Oliver Wendell Holmes's sentence "An earthquake thrills the planet," from *The Poet at the Breakfast-Table* (1872).

[ME *thrillen*, alter. of *thirlen* to pierce]

Thursday See SUNDAY.
[ME *thuresday*, *thursday*, fr. OE *thuresdæg*, *thursdæg*, fr. ON

thōrsdagr; akin to OE *thunresdæg* Thursday, OHG *Donares tag;* all fr. a prehistoric NGmc-WGmc compound formed fr. the constituents represented by OHG *Donar,* the Germanic god of the sky (fr. *thonar, donar* thunder), and by OHG *tag* day; trans. of L *Jovis dies,* lit., day of Jupiter (the ancient Roman god of the sky and the planet Jupiter)]

ticket   See ETIQUETTE.
[obs. F *etiquet* (now *étiquette*) short note or document, fr. MF *etiquet, estiquet* note, target, fr. *estiquer, estiquier* to attach, stick, fr. MD *steken* to stick; akin to OE *stician* to stick, OHG *stehhan* to stick, sting, ON *steikja* to roast, L in*stigare* to incite, Gk *stizein* to tattoo]

tiercel   See FALCON.
[ME *tercel, tassel,* fr. MF *tercel, tiercel,* fr. (assumed) VL *tertiolus,* fr. dim. of L *tertius* third; perhaps fr. the belief that every third egg in the nest produced a male]

tinker   Since the Middle Ages, *tinkers* have wandered from place to place, living by the repair of metal household utensils. The origin of their name is not certain. One explanation would derive the word from *tin.* Another is that *tinkers* are so called because of the tinking or tinkling sound produced by their work on pots and pans. This was the explanation given by the *Promptorium Parvulorum* (Young Scholars' Storeroom) about 1440: "*Tynkare . . .* tintinarius; et capit nomen a sono artis, ut tintinabulum, sus, et multa alia, per onomatopeiam." (*Tynkare . . .* tinker; and he takes his name from the sound of his trade, like the bell [*tintinabulum*], the pig [*sus*], and many other things, by onomatopoeia.) The onomatopoeic explanation applied to both the English word *tynkare* and its Latin equivalent *tintinarius.* Samuel Johnson, in his great *Dictionary of the English Language* (1755), agreed: "From *tink,* because their way of proclaiming their trade is to beat a kettle, or because in their work they make a tinkling noise."

The antiquity of a proposed etymology, of course, cannot be accepted as proof of its reliability. The major objection to this suggestion is that the noun *tinker* is attested more than a century earlier (1265) than the verbs *tink* and *tinkle* (both first reported in 1382). These verbs were certainly in oral use for some time before they were written, but even so the large hiatus is disturbing. Still, the explanation is not an unreasonable one, and no more probable theory has been advanced.

Tinkers have long been cursed with a poor reputation, both as members of society and as practicers of their trade. A person who works at something in an unskilled way is said to tinker.

The *tinker's damn* or *dam* has excited greater etymological interest than the tinker himself. The variant spellings represent two theories of the phrase's origin. The explanation supporting *dam* was apparently first offered in Edward Knight's *Practical Dictionary of Mechanics* in 1877: "*Tinker's-dam,* a wall of dough raised around a place which a plumber desires to flood with a coat of solder. The material can be but once used; being consequently thrown away as worthless, it has passed into a proverb, usual-

ly involving the wrong spelling of the otherwise innocent word 'dam.' "
This story has since been repeated frequently, but the proposed interpretation is in fact unfounded and represents a folk etymology. The existence
of other parallel expressions involving *tinker's*—not to care a *tinker's
curse*, or *straw*, or *hoot*, or *hoorah*—and the alleged talents of tinkers in
the field of profanity lend credence to the *damn* explanation. Phrases such
as "not to give a damn," "not worth a curse," and "not worth a damn"
were current in the writings of Thomas Jefferson, Sir Walter Scott, Oliver
Goldsmith, and Thomas Macaulay long before the *tinker's dam* explanation was advanced by Knight. Thus *tinker's* was apparently inserted as an
intensifier in a phrase already well established. The *dam* interpretation is
probably the result of a search for an explanation to make a respectable
phrase out of one that would otherwise not have been considered acceptable in polite society. Cant and slang glossaries contain no reference to the
use of *dam* among tinkers for the little wall of clay, dough, or beeswax earlier than the first appearance of the saying. For other folk etymologies see
FOLK ETYMOLOGY.

[ME *tinkere*, prob. fr. *tink* tinkle (of imit. origin) + *-ere* -er]

tinker's damn *or* **tinker's dam**   See TINKER.
[*tinker's damn* prob. so called fr. the tinkers' reputation for blasphemy;
tinker's dam prob. by folk etymology fr. *tinker's damn;* prob. fr. the use
by tinkers of a small dam of dough or mud to confine solder used in
patching holes in pans]

titanic   See ATLAS.
[Gk *titanikos*, fr. *Titan*, one of a family of earth giants in Greek mythology + *-ikos* -ic]

tithe   See DECIMATE.
[ME *tigthe*, *tithe*, fr. OE *teogotha*, *tēotha* tenth; akin to OFris *tegotha*
tenth, MLG *tegede;* all fr. a prehistoric WGmc alter. of the source of
OHG *zehanto* tenth]

tittle   See JOT.
[ME *titel*, fr. ML *titulus* title, label, diacritical mark, fr. L, title, label]

toil (n., a net)   See TOILET.
[MF *toile* cloth, net, fr. L *tela* web, fr. *texere* to weave, construct]

toil (n., labor)   See TOILET.
[ME *toile* argument, dispute, battle, fr. AF *toyl*, fr. OF *tooil*, *toeil* battle,
trouble, confusion, fr. *tooillier*, *toeillier* to stir, mix, soil, sully, disturb,
dispute]

toil (v., labor)   See TOILET.
[ME *toilen* to argue, struggle, fr. AF *toiller*, fr. OF *tooillier*, *toeillier* to
stir, mix, soil, sully, disturb, dispute, fr. L *tudiculare* to crush, grind, fr.

tudicula machine for crushing olives, dim. of *tudes* hammer; akin to L *tundere* to beat]

toilet   Related to Latin *texere* 'to weave' is *tela* 'cloth, web', which developed into Middle French *toile*, which besides meaning 'cloth' could mean 'hunting net'. (For other offspring of *texere* see PRETEXT.) English borrowed the French word in the latter sense as *toil* in the sixteenth century. The term is familiar today mostly in figurative use, as in "caught in the toils of love." (This *toil* is etymologically unrelated to the noun and verb *toil* meaning 'labor', which ultimately derive from a different Latin word, *tudicula*, a machine for crushing olives.)

From *toile* was formed the diminutive *toilette* in Middle French, which could mean simply 'small piece of cloth' but which also came to be used in more specific senses, such as a wrapper for clothing, or a covering for a dressing table. By the seventeenth century, *toilette* could refer to the dressing table itself or to the act of grooming that takes place at it. (For a similar semantic transit starting from a sense 'piece of cloth' see BUREAU.)

English borrowed the word in the sixteenth century, and eventually settled on the spelling *toilet*. Our word has at one time or another reflected most of the French senses; the 'grooming' sense is still used, especially in expressions like "to be at one's toilet." But all of these have tended to be suppressed by the subsequent sense development, from 'dressing room' through 'dressing room with bath facilities' through 'lavatory' and finally to 'water closet'. Amusingly, while English uses a French word to designate euphemistically this homely fixture, French repays the compliment by calling it *le water-closet* or *le w.c.*

[MF *toilette*, dim. of *toile* cloth]

tontine   The *tontine* has been the life insurance policy most beloved by writers of murder mysteries. The tontine treats life insurance, or an investment fund, like a lottery and provides a host of characters for the mystery and a motive for mayhem. In 1653 the Italian banker Lorenzo Tonti (died 1695) organized a fund in Naples. Each subscriber bought a share of an investment fund. Each year dividends were paid, but as each investor died, his share was forfeited and his dividend was divided among the survivors. This continued until there was only one survivor reaping all of the dividends. In the original plan, at the death of the last subscriber, the entire capital reverted to the state. The plan made its way into France, which used it as a means of raising revenue with great success. In 1689 Louis XIV established a tontine that went on for more than forty years. For an investment equivalent to $1,500, the last survivor reaped the equivalent of $367,500. Later on tontines also became private ventures, with the last survivor keeping all of the capital as well. One celebrated tontine, the "tontine Lafarge," began in 1791 and lasted until 1889. Tontines spread to other countries, including England, Ireland, and the United States. In the United States the tontine became a means of raising capital to erect large buildings. Eventually tontines were banned in the United States after the untimely deaths of some subscribers. The plan remains a favorite of mystery writers, however. Typically, subscriber after subscriber dies under the most mysterious circumstances, until all is uncovered by a suspicious sleuth.

[F, fr. Lorenzo *Tonti* †1695 Ital. banker in Paris who invented the scheme + F -*ine*, fr. -*ine*, fem. of -*in* -ine, adj. suffix]

Tony See OSCAR.
[after *Tony*, nickname of *Antoinette* Perry †1946 Am. actress & producer]

torpedo To be the victim of a torpedo in ancient Roman times was indeed a shocking experience, but not a shattering one. A torpedo was what the Romans called the long round fish that gave a numbing electric shock to anyone who touched it. *Torpedo* was an appropriate term for this fish, since the word originally meant 'numbness'. It derives from the verb *torpēre* 'to be numb'. The English words *torpid* and *torpor* also derive from this verb.

In the sixteenth century, English followed the Roman precedent and began using the word *torpedo* for the fish which today is called an electric ray, crampfish, or numbfish. In 1589, for example, Richard Harvey wrote of "the fish Torpedo, which being touched sends her venom along line and angle rod, till it cease on the finger, and so mar a fisher forever" *(Plaine Perceuall the peace-maker of England)*.

In the early 1800s the American inventor Robert Fulton developed a floating device designed to explode when it came in contact with a ship. Today we term such a device a mine, but Fulton called it a torpedo because it reminded him of the electric ray. His torpedoes were put to use during the Civil War. However, the modern self-propelled torpedo owes its development to the British engineer Robert Whitehead. It was powered by compressed air, which moved it at about seven miles per hour. Today's high-tech torpedoes are, of course, much faster and while they may still somewhat resemble a fish, the effects are certainly more than numbing.

[L *torpedin-*, *torpedo* stiffness, numbness, crampfish, fr. *torpēre* to be stiff, numb]

torpid See TORPEDO.
[L *torpidus*, fr. *torpēre* to be stiff, numb, torpid; akin to Lith *tirpti* to become stiff, L *stirps* stem of a plant, trunk, stock, lineage, OE *starian* to stare]

torpor See TORPEDO.
[L, fr. *torpēre* to be torpid]

torrent A rushing stream of water may seem to have little in common with a scorchingly hot, dry day, but call the stream a *torrent* and call the day *torrid* and a possible connection—if only an etymological one—

becomes less hard to imagine. Both *torrent* and *torrid* can in fact be traced to a single source, the Latin verb *torrēre,* meaning 'to parch or burn'.

The steps by which *torrēre* produced *torrid* are straightforward: the past participle of *torrēre* is *torridus,* which was used by the Romans as an adjective meaning 'parched with heat' and which occurred (in its feminine form) in the Latin name for the region of the earth lying within the tropics, *zona torrida,* translated into English as *torrid zone* in the sixteenth century. By the end of the seventeenth century, *torrid* had come into more widespread use in the senses 'scorched with heat' and 'intensely hot', as well as in the figurative sense 'passionate' (as in "a torrid romance").

Torrent, on the other hand, is derived from *torrent-, torrens,* the present participle of *torrēre.* This participle, like *torridus,* was also used in Latin as an adjective. Its meaning was not only 'burning' but also 'boiling' and 'rushing, rapid', an extended sense suggesting the resemblance between turbulent rushing water and boiling water. The Latin adjective produced the French noun *torrent,* which was borrowed into English at about the beginning of the seventeenth century (its earliest known occurrence is in Shakespeare's *Julius Caesar,* ca. 1599). Its original sense, still in use, is 'a violent, rushing stream of liquid'. The figurative sense 'a tumultuous outpouring' (as in "a torrent of abuse") is almost as old, dating from 1647.

[F, fr. L *torrent-, torrens,* fr. *torrent-, torrens* burning, seething, rushing, fr. pres. part. of *torrēre* to dry, parch, burn; akin to OHG *derren* to dry, parch, ON *therra,* Skt *tarṣayati* he causes to thirst]

torrid   See TORRENT.

[L *torridus,* fr. *torrēre* to dry, parch]

towards   Those who recognize the genitive case nowadays associate it—in English—with the *'s* ending. School grammars often call it the possessive case, although indicating possession is just one of its several functions. In Old English the genitive was simply marked by a regular case ending *-es* for most nouns; there was no apostrophe. (The modern apostrophe before the *s* seems to be a printers' convention that arose during the seventeenth century.) One of the functions of the genitive in Old English was to indicate that a word—say, an adjective or noun—was being used in an adverbial function.

Towards is a surviving example of this adverbial genitive. It comes from Middle English *towardes,* from Old English *tōweardes,* which was formed from an adjective *tōweard* and the *-es* genitive ending. The subsequent history of *towards* is muddled by *toward,* which early on slipped from adjective into adverbial use, and *toward* and *towards* both then drifted into being prepositions. So today we have *toward* and *towards,* both prepositions, used simply as alternative forms.

A number of modern English adverbs that end with an *s* or *z* sound are living reminders of the Old English adverbial genitive: *always, needs* (in *needs must* or *must needs*), *nowadays, unawares,* and *sideways* are examples. The *-wards* in adverbs *backwards, onwards, afterwards* represents the adverbial genitive tacked on to the adjectival suffix -*ward* (in Old English -*weard*).

Once, twice, and *thrice* also come from the adverbial genitive, with the original -*es* hidden behind the modern -*ce* spelling. The -*ce* spelling came in for the purpose of better indicating the pronunciation. *Since* has a similar history; in Middle English it was *sins,* a contraction of earlier *sithens* (the -*s* is our genitive friend), from Old English *siththan,* itself condensed from the phrase *sith tham* ('since that'). The *tham* was the form of *thæt* indicating the dative case (typically used for an indirect object or an object of a preposition), so the genitive -*s* was added in Middle English to what had been an Old English dative.

The Old English *dæg* 'day' was used adverbially in its genitive form *dæges* 'by day' and this survives in *nowadays.* On analogy with *days* we have a number of Modern English adverbs formed from a noun and -*s:*

> During his college days at Harvard he taught days and studied nights
> —*Dictionary of American Biography,* 1929

> ". . . I don't stay up nights worrying" —John Lennon, quoted in *Current Biography,* December 1965

Some modern grammarians believe the -*s* in *days* and *nights* is the old adverbial genitive ending. The genitive idea is supported by an alternative phrasal form of the expression—perhaps more old-fashioned or more literary than the -*s* form—such as we find in this example:

> Sleep, too, I can't get for these damn'd winds of a night
> —Charles Lamb, letter, 15 Jan. 1806

Other grammarians (probably the majority) feel the -*s* of *nights* or *Mondays* (as in "the restaurant is closed Mondays") is simply the sign of the plural. The idea of its being a plural ending can be supported by a different phrasal equivalent: "The restaurant is closed on Mondays." So grammarians are in some disagreement over such modern adverbs as *evenings, Saturdays,* and *nights.* But the folk formations *somewheres, anywheres, nowheres* likely remember the old adverbial genitive.

Whiles, now archaic, is another adverbial genitive. The nineteenth-century English poet Walter Savage Landor believed that it was a plural, however; he advised his readers that "*While* is the *time* when; *whiles* is the *times* when." *Whiles* has passed from use, but *whilst,* which is *whiles* with an unneeded -*t* added, is still in use. *Amongst* also represents an adverbial genitive with the added -*t.* So does *oncet,* but it is limited to oral or dialectal use.

[fr. ME *towardes,* alter. (influenced by *towardes,* prep., toward) of *toward,* fr. OE *tōweard* facing, approaching, imminent, fr. *tō,* prep., to + -*weard* -ward]

tradition   See TREASON.
[ME *tradicion, tradicioun,* fr. MF & L; MF *tradition,* fr. L *tradition-, traditio* action of handing over, teaching, tradition]

tragedy It is generally believed that the source of our word *tragedy* is the Greek *tragōidia,* a compound from *tragos,* 'goat', and *aeidein,* 'to sing', but the Greeks' reasons for calling this dramatic form "goat song" are obscure. *Tragedy* developed in the sixth and fifth centuries B.C. out of the performance of originally lyric recitations. Sometime during the sixth century one actor was singled out from the chorus that delivered these recitations to utter a prologue and other set speeches in alternation with the choral odes. This development is attributed by early classical authors to a writer and actor named Thespis, who won a prize for his performance in Athens in 534 B.C. It may be that competition for the prize of a goat such as was awarded to Thespis accounts for the word *tragōidia.*

Another possibility, less well attested in early sources, is that a goat was sacrificed in earlier religious rituals out of which *tragedy* may have developed. A third theory is based mainly on literal interpretations of statements by Aristotle in his *Poetics.* According to this view *tragedy* developed out of the performance of dithyrambs, lyric hymns to the god Dionysus, in which the chorus was dressed as satyrs, mythical beings with some of the attributes of goats. There are a number of objections to this theory, though it cannot be dismissed absolutely: before the fifth century there is no evidence of dramatic elements in the performance of dithyrambs; we have no record of a dithyramb performed in satyr costume; in Attica (where Athens was) the satyrs were originally represented as having the attributes of horses, not goats; and the terms for *dithyramb* and *tragedy* are never used interchangeably by classical writers. Given these differing theories with no conclusive evidence, we can only consider them all as possibilities and hope that some day new information may come to light.

The name of Thespis has itself been adopted into English in the word *thespian* as an adjective meaning 'dramatic' and a noun meaning 'actor'. This usage stems from the tradition that Thespis was the originator of the actor's role. For the further influence of Thespis upon drama and upon the English vocabulary see SCENE.

[ME *tragedie,* fr. MF, fr. L *tragoedia,* fr. Gk *tragōidia,* fr. *tragos* he-goat + *-ōidia* (fr. *aeidein* to sing); akin to Gk *trōgein* to gnaw]

traitor See TREASON.
[ME *traitre, traitour,* fr. OF *traitre, traitur,* fr. L *traditor,* fr. *traditus* (past part. of *tradere* to hand over, deliver, betray, fr. *trans-, tra-* across, over + *-dere,* fr. *dare* to give) + *-or*]

tramp English has not been miserly in bestowing names on the gentlemen of the road. The plainest of these words is *tramp,* formed in the seventeenth century by functional shift from the verb, which has been in the language since the fourteenth century.

Vagabond is a more romantic word than *tramp,* and at least two centuries older. It was formed in the fifteenth century, apparently by functional shift from the adjective (they both appear about the same time), in turn derived through Middle French and Late Latin from Latin *vagari* 'to wander'. The noun *vagabond* replaced, over the course of a couple of centuries, the earlier spelling *vacabound* or *vacabund* or *vacabond*. The earlier forms were derived from a Middle French variant of *vagabond* that may have been influenced by some lost Middle French word derived from Latin *vacare* 'to be idle or empty', a verb whose participle is the source of English *vacant.*

Vagrant is less romantic than *vagabond* but more mysterious. It first turned up in the fifteenth century as *vagaraunt.* This form comes from Middle French (via Anglo-French, the variety of French used in medieval England). Once we get to Middle French we are on uncertain ground. One group of philologists gives us the forms *wacrant, wakerant, walcrant*—used in fourteenth-century English legal documents in the sense 'vagrant'—derived from Old French *wacrer* or *walcrer* 'to walk, wander'. The *w* looks most suspiciously un-French, and sure enough this word was borrowed from a Germanic source related to English *walk.* Other etymologists, however, give Anglo-French *vagarant, vagaraunt,* presumably a derivative ultimately from Latin *vagari* 'to wander'. Even if the Germanic origin is accepted, the influence of some derivative of Latin *vagari*—say, the fourteenth-century English adjective *vagant* 'wandering' or its Middle French source—seems likely in the initial *v.*

There are a number of American words for the tramp, and although they are of more recent appearance than *vagrant,* their origins are just as mystifying. Take the common *bum,* for instance. It first appeared in the early 1860s. There is listed in an early nineteenth-century Scottish dictionary a noun *bum,* applied to a disreputable person. This would be an attractive source, for we all know there were many immigrants from Scotland to the U.S. But the editors of the *Scottish National Dictionary* were unable to learn anything about the word from their learned correspondents, and the suspicion is that its existence as a real word in Scottish does not rest on firm ground. A more likely source is the slightly earlier *bummer* 'idler, loafer', which seems to be an alteration of German *bummler* 'loafer', from *bummeln* 'to loaf, dangle'. (There were a lot of German immigrants to this country too.) *Bummer, bumming,* and *bum,* both noun and verb, appeared in American English within a space of only six or seven years. The German vocabulary of the open road may have contributed another word to English, namely *loafer.* This may derive from *landloafer,* from German *landläufer* 'tramp' (literally 'land runner').

Hobo is another hard-to-pin-down word. It is first attested in the *Ellensburgh* (Wash.) *Capital* in 1889. Its first couple of occurrences in print show a capital *H* and suggest it was a name used by tramps of themselves. It spread rapidly, reaching the East Coast in just a few years; by 1899 stories about hoboes were common in New York papers.

To the general public *hobo* and *tramp* were largely synonymous, but within the fraternity it was understood that a hobo was a migratory worker, at least of a sort, while a tramp kept traveling to avoid work. H. L. Mencken placed the bum lower: a bum, he said, neither worked nor traveled, unless impelled by the police.

The origin of *hobo* is not known, but various explanations of its origin have been offered. The detective William Pinkerton found its origin in a cry "Ho, beau!" used by tramps to identify one another. An 1895 newspaper offered much the same explanation, saying the word was applied to the men by railroad brakemen who heard them greeting one another with "Ho, beau!" A similar explanation, one that Merriam-Webster etymologists lean toward, sees *-bo* as an altered form of *boy* and traces *hobo* to a call used by railroad mail handlers in the Northwest during the 1880s when they were delivering the mail. Another theory derives it from Hoboken, N.J., a railroad terminus, but it seems unlikely an Eastern city would give rise to a name first attested in the state of Washington. Still another theory finds the origin in a Japanese word *hobo* meaning 'all sides, everywhere'. There were Japanese immigrants on the West Coast at the time, but how the tramps would have picked up the Japanese word is hard to understand.

In the argot of hoboes and tramps a roll of clothes and bedding was known as a *bindle*—a dialectal variant of *bundle*—and the tramp or hobo who carried one habitually was known as a *bindle stiff*. A beggar was known as a *panhandler,* a term possibly suggested by the beggar's outstretched arm and hand.

[fr. *tramp,* v., fr. ME *trampen;* akin to MLG *trampen* to stamp, tread, MD *tramperen* to stamp, Norw dial. *trumpa* to push, shove, Goth anatrimpan to crowd, MD *trappen* to stamp]

transcribe　See SCRIVENER.
[L *transcribere,* fr. *trans-* + *scribere* to write]

travail　See TRAVEL.
[ME *travailen, traveilen,* fr. OF *travaillier, traveillier* to labor, toil, trouble, torture, fr. (assumed) VL *tripaliare* to torture, fr. (assumed) VL *tripalium* instrument of torture, fr. L *tripalis* having three stakes, fr. *tri-* three + *palus* stake]

travel　In 582 the Council of Auxerre laid down the rule, "Non licet presbytero nec diacano ad trepalium, ubi rei torquentur, stare." (A priest or deacon may not stand at a trepalium, where prisoners are tortured.) A *trepalium,* then, must have been an instrument of torture. We do not know exactly what it looked like, but we can get some idea from the word's etymology. *Trepalium* is a derivative of Latin *tripalis,* which means 'having three stakes'. Although only *trepalium* is actually found in documents, we can assume that the word also existed in the form *tripalium. Travaillier,* 'to torture', an Old French descendant of *tripalium,* early developed the extended and milder senses 'to trouble', 'to labor or toil', and 'to weary'. The English verb borrowed as *travail* was once used in all of these senses (except the original 'to torture'), but it now seldom means anything but 'to labor'. The noun *travail,* however, a borrowing of the French noun derived from *travaillier,* retains a wider range of meaning.

In the Middle Ages, the most striking thing about *travel* was its difficulty. A journey cost a great deal of wearisome effort, so that a pilgrimage to a distant religious shrine, for example, was an act of real devotion. *Travail* developed, in English, the sense 'to go on a journey'. *Travel,* originally a variant spelling of *travail*, has attached itself to this particular sense and so become a separate word.

We apparently owe the term *travois* to yet another transmogrification of this etymon, this time via Canadian French. A travois is a sledge that was used by the Plains Indians, pulled either by a horse or a dog. The name is believed to derive from French *travail* in the sense of 'the shaft of a cart'.

[ME *travellen, travailen*]

travois   See TRAVEL.
[CanF *travois*, alter. of F *travail*]

treason   In some circumstances *treason* may seem to be subverting the forces of *tradition*, yet both of these words derive from the same Latin source. Latin *traditio* means 'teaching' or 'tradition', but these senses are developed from its more literal sense of 'the act of handing over something'. Thus *tradition* is maintained by passing information from one generation to another, whereas *treason* is committed when someone who has been entrusted with information passes it on to someone else.

The difference in form between the two words may be accounted for by reference to the fact that *treason* came to us through Old French, where *traditio* underwent sound change, while *tradition* was later borrowed directly from Latin. Latin *traditio* comes ultimately from *tradere*, 'to hand over, deliver, betray', from *trans-, tra-*, 'across, beyond, through', plus *-dere* from *dare*, 'to give'. Through related forms *traditus* and *traditor*, this verb is also the source of our modern word *traitor*.

[ME *tresoun*, fr. OF *traison*, fr. ML *tradition-, traditio*, fr. L, action of handing over, teaching, tradition, fr. *traditus* (past part. of *tradere* to hand over, betray) + *-ion-, -io* -ion]

treasure   The basic meaning of the word *treasure* is 'accumulated wealth'. In English the word can be traced back to the twelfth century, when it was borrowed from the early French word *tresor*. The source of this French noun is the Latin *thesaurus*, which was used to denote 'something stored up, a hoard' and 'a storehouse or treasury'. The Romans in turn borrowed the term from the Greek *thēsauros*, which is used in the Septuagint Bible as the usual translation of the Hebrew *'otsār*, meaning 'something laid up or away'.

An early example of the figurative use of *treasure* can be found in the Gospel of Luke (18:22, Douay), in which the Evangelist relates that Jesus had instructed a certain ruler to "sell all whatever thou hast, and give to the poor, and thou shalt have treasure in heaven." Since about 1200 a broader sense of 'something valued and preserved as precious' has been in evidence. Shakespeare provides an example of it in *Richard II* (ca. 1595): "The purest treasure mortal times afford/ Is spotless reputation." From early in the sixteenth century *treasure* has also been used in reference to 'a person esteemed as rare or precious'.

The Latin *thesaurus* was also taken directly into English early in the nineteenth century. At first it was used by archaeologists to denote an ancient treasury, such as that of a temple. Then it was metaphorically applied to a book containing a "treasury" of words or information about a particular field. In 1852 the English scholar Peter Mark Roget published his *Thesaurus of English Words and Phrases,* in which he listed a treasury of related words organized into numerous categories. This thesaurus has proved helpful especially to the user who is seeking a more appropriate term for the one he has in mind. While not strictly a book of synonyms, this work has been treated as such, leading to the common acceptance of the term *thesaurus* to denote 'a book of synonyms'. More recently, since the 1950s, *thesaurus* has been used in the field of word processing to refer to a list of related terms within a particular field to be used for indexing or retrieval. A large newspaper company, for example, publishes a computer-produced thesaurus of descriptors (subject headings) to help organize library and newspaper information files and make information retrieval easier.

[ME *tresor, tresour,* fr. OF *tresor,* fr. L *thesaurus* hoard, treasure, fr. Gk *thēsauros*]

trilby See FEDORA.
[so called fr. the fact that it was worn in the original London stage version (1895) of the novel *Trilby* by George du Maurier †1896 Brit. artist and novelist]

trivia See TRIVIAL.
[L, crossroads, pl. of *trivium,* influenced in meaning by E *trivial*]

trivial In the medieval educational curriculum the so-called Seven Liberal Arts were divided into two categories, the *trivium,* or "threefold way," consisting of Grammar, Logic, and Rhetoric, and the *quadrivium,* or "fourfold way," including Arithmetic, Music, Geometry, and Astronomy. The adjectival form of Medieval Latin *trivium* is *trivialis,* from which is derived Middle English *trivial,* 'belonging to the trivium', which first appeared in the fifteenth century. In the early period of Modern English, however, new senses of *trivial* developed, not from this English sense but from earlier meanings of *trivialis.* Literally, Latin *trivium* (from *tri-,* 'three', plus *via,* 'way, road') means 'a crossroads' or 'a place where three roads meet'. The adjective *trivialis,* which might be rendered literally as 'pertaining to a crossroads', was used in Latin to mean 'common' or 'ordinary', presumably from the belief that things found at such a public place as a crossroads, where all the world may pass by, are generally common things. The notion that people often stop where roads meet to pass the time of day with inconsequential talk may also have influenced the development of this sense. This is the source of the modern senses of *trivial* such as 'commonplace' or 'of little importance'.

The youngest member of this group of words is the Modern English noun *trivia.* Its form is that of the plural of Latin *trivium,* but its meaning is influenced by the Modern English senses of *trivial.*

[ME, fr. ML *trivialis* of the trivium, fr. L *trivialis* that may be found everywhere, common, ordinary, trivial (influenced in meaning by ML *trivium* trivium), fr. L *trivium* crossroads, place where three roads meet, fr. *tri-* three + *via* way, road]

Trojan horse See STENTORIAN.
[so called fr. the gigantic and hollow wooden horse filled with soldiers by means of which the Greeks gained entrance into Troy during the Trojan War and insured the conquest of the city]

trope See TROPHY.
[L *tropus*, fr. Gk *tropos* turn, way, manner, style; akin to Gk *trepein* to turn, L *trepit* he turns, and perh. to Skt *trapate* he is ashamed]

trophy In classical times the Greeks, who placed a high value on the art of war and the physical bravery of warriors, were never the sort to let their military victories go uncelebrated. They established the custom of erecting on the field of battle, often on the very spot where the enemy soldiers had turned and run, a memorial to the victory they had just achieved. They began by fashioning a stake into the semblance of a man or by finding a nearby tree suitable for the purpose. Upon their makeshift mannequin, the victors proceeded to hang a selection of the enemy's arms and equipment: spears, axes, helmets, shields, flags. For naval victories the memorial was erected on the nearest stretch of beach, and the broken beaks of the enemy's ships figured prominently in the display. Typically, the finishing touch to the memorial was an inscription bearing the salient details of the battle and a dedication to a tutelary god or gods. The Greeks called such a memorial a *tropaion*, a term which was the neuter of *tropaios* ('of a turning', 'of a rout') and was derived from *tropē* ('turn', 'rout'). The Latin word for this type of memorial, *trophaeum*, is the more immediate ancestor of the English word *trophy*.

As with so many honored Greek traditions, the Romans borrowed the concept of the trophy and modified it according to the standards of imperial Rome. The Romans preferred to construct their trophies in public places, especially within their capital city. Great triumphal arches or columns served as supporting structures for trophies during the glory days of the Roman empire. Often the trophies were merely sculpted representations of armaments and constituted only portions of even more monumental stone structures. Artistic representations of Greco-Roman trophies were popular in the decorative arts. Painted or carved representations of these classical memorials became a common motif in classical architecture.

By the sixteenth century *trophy* was being used in English in a transferred sense that went beyond reference to the monuments of antiquity. It was then applied to any spoil, whether the result of a martial encounter or a successful hunt in the field, that could be displayed as a reminder or proof of one's conquest. A captured enemy weapon or flag often served as a token of military victory, and hunting prowess was typically commemorated by mounting the head or whole body of the game. During the sixteenth century *trophy* also came to be used figuratively of anything serving as a token of personal triumph. In one of his sonnets in *Amoretti* (1595), Edmund Spenser shows that trophies may sometimes commemorate hard-won victories achieved in the field of romance:

> What trophee then shall I most fit devize,
> In which I may record the memory
> Of my loves conquest, peerelesse beauties prise . . .

The Greek verb *trepein* ('to turn') that gave us *trophy* was also responsible for *trope* and *tropic*. Derived by way of Latin from the Greek *tropos* ('turn', 'way', or 'manner'), *trope* refers to a word or phrase used figuratively. Because one is no longer using the word in a literal sense, one has, so to speak, overturned or turned around the original meaning of the word. In using *live wire* to describe an alert, active, or aggressive person, one is—to use today's vernacular—putting a whole new spin on the word's meaning. A similar notion is embodied in the native English expression "turn of phrase." *Trope* is also used of any extended figure of speech, as a simile or metaphor, in which the words are not to be taken literally.

Tropic is another English word that is rooted in the Greek word for 'turn'. With *tropic* the turn in question is the apparent turning of the sun at the time of the summer and winter solstices. In his *Treatise on the Astrolabe* (ca. 1391) Chaucer introduced *tropic* to refer to either of the two small circles in the celestial sphere on each side of the equator which the sun reaches at its most northern or southern declination before appearing to turn and move back towards the equator again. This sense of *tropic* is now obsolete, having apparently died out in the seventeenth century. In its current sense, which originated in the sixteenth century, *tropic* refers to either of the two parallels of terrestrial latitude which lie 23 1/2 degrees north and south of the equator and are known as the Tropic of Cancer and the Tropic of Capricorn respectively. Now the word probably occurs most often as *tropics,* the name for the warm, sunny region between the Tropic of Cancer and the Tropic of Capricorn to which winter-weary vacationers turn just about the time of the winter solstice.

[MF *trophee,* fr. L *trophaeum, tropaeum,* fr. Gk *tropaion,* fr. neut. of *tropaios* of turning, of defeat, fr. *tropē* action of turning, enemy's retreat; akin to Gk *trepein* to turn]

tropic   See TROPHY.

[ME *tropik,* fr. L *tropicus* of a turn, of a turning of the sun, fr. Gk *tropikos* of the solstice, fr. *tropē* action of turning (akin to Gk *trepein* to turn) + *-ikos* -ic]

troy   See OUNCE.

[ME *troye, troie,* fr. *Troyes,* city in France where it was prob. introduced]

tsar   See CZAR.

[Russ *tsar*]

Tuesday See SUNDAY.
[ME *tiwesday, tewisday,* fr. OE *tīwesdæg;* akin to OFris *tīesdei* Tuesday,
OHG *zīostag,* ON *tȳsdagr, tȳrsdagr;* all fr. a prehistoric WGmc-NGmc
compound formed from the components represented by OE *Tiw,* god
of war, and *dæg* day; trans. of L *Martis dies,* lit., day of Mars (Roman god
of war); trans. of Gk *hēmera Areios,* lit., day of Ares (Greek god of war)]

tungsten See COBALT.
[Sw, fr. *tung* heavy + *sten* stone; akin to ON *thungr* heavy, *thīsl* pole,
OE *thīsl, thīxl* pole, shaft, OHG *dīhsala,* L *temo* pole, shaft, OSlav *tęgnǫ-
ti* to drag, pull, Skt *tanoti* he stretches, and to ON *steinn* stone]

turkey When Americans sit down to their traditional Thanksgiving Day
feast, perhaps more than a few of them wonder just how it came to pass
that this indigenous fowl and American icon was named after a Middle
Eastern country that celebrates neither Thanksgiving nor football. It all
started before the Pilgrims set foot on Plymouth Rock, or even before Columbus landed in the Bahamas. The large, ungainly bird that is known sci-
entifically as the *Meleagris gallopavo* was first domesticated by the Aztecs,
Mayas, and other civilized Indian tribes of Mexico and Central America.
At the time of their conquest of the New World, the Spanish began exporting the domesticated fowl to the Old World. First introduced into the
lands bordering the Mediterranean early in the sixteenth century, the
fowl was gradually domesticated throughout northern Europe and England.
  From the beginning, the New World fowl was confused with a bird of
African origin that had been known to Mediterranean peoples since ancient times. This Old World bird was commonly known as the *guinea fowl*
(also *guinea cock*) or *turkey-cock.* The name *guinea fowl* derived from the
fact that it was sometimes exported from Guinea on the west coast of Africa by the Portuguese. The name *turkey-cock* derived from the fact that
the fowl had been originally imported to Europe from territory that the
Europeans thought of as Turkish. *Turkey,* to the Europeans of the sixteenth century, could refer to the whole of the Ottoman empire, or to any
or all of the various lands under Islamic domination. To Europeans of that
period, Turkey suggested all that was mysterious, exotic, or merely novel.
Thus, "Turkey" was the actual or assumed point of origin for all manner
of exotica. For example, in 1542 an eminent botanist labeled in his herbal
catalogue the New World plants maize and pumpkin as "Turkish corn"
and "Turkish cucumber," respectively. It was only natural, then, that the
name *turkey-cock* should become attached to those recently introduced
birds that resembled the well-known guinea fowl. Even after the New
World bird ceased to be confused with its African cousin, the misnomer
turkey-cock stuck. With time, *turkey-cock* was shortened to simply *turkey,*
and *Meleagris gallopavo* became a common domesticated animal in England.
  What the Pilgrims feasted on that first Thanksgiving were specimens of
the huge wild turkey population that once filled the eastern seaboard of
the New World. But before long, colonists were importing the domesticat-

ed European version of the turkey back to its native continent. The turkeys of today are from this European-bred stock. Generations of farmyard breeding have produced birds proverbial for their timidity and stupidity, so much so that *turkey* is frequently used today as a term of disparagement for someone or something that is seen as an utter failure.

Another item that retains its Turkish designation, albeit in somewhat disguised form, is the bluish to greenish gem known as *turquoise*. The English word goes back to Middle English *turkeis*, a borrowing from Middle French; the Modern English spelling is due to renewed influence from a more recent French spelling, as in *pierre turquoise*, which literally means 'Turkish stone'. Historically, the most highly valued specimens of the gem came from the lands that the Europeans thought of as "Persia"—or the vast area now occupied by Iran, Afghanistan, and part of India. From there the gems made their way to European cities by way of Turkish ports. Though many specimens of the gem now encountered are from Mexico or the American Southwest, they continue to be known as *turquoise*.

[short for *turkey-cock,* fr. *Turkey,* country in southeast Europe and southwest Asia + *cock;* fr. confusion with the guinea fowl, supposed to be imported from Turkish territory]

turquoise   See TURKEY.
[ME *turkeis, torcas, turcas,* fr. MF *turquoyse, turquaise,* fr. fem. of *turquoys, turqueis* Turkish, fr. OF, fr. *Turc* Turk]

tuxedo   *Tuxedo* can be traced back to a Delaware Indian word meaning 'wolf', but this does not mean that young men of the Delaware people donned evening dress to further their pursuit of women. Our English word has a more roundabout history. The Delawares of eastern North America belonged to one of three groups whose totems were the turkey, the turtle, and the wolf. *P'tuksīt,* the Delaware word for 'wolf', was used as a name for the third group. In the eighteenth century European Americans gave the name of the *P'tuksīt,* anglicized as *Tuxedo,* to a village in southeastern New York. In the 1880s a large and beautiful tract of land called Tuxedo Park, near the village and on the shore of Tuxedo Lake, became a fashionable resort community of the very wealthy. It was here, near the turn of the century, that some young men, disregarding the dictates of current fashion, began to wear dress jackets without tails. The new style which they made popular was soon called *tuxedo*.

[fr. *Tuxedo* Park, resort near *Tuxedo* Lake, N.Y.]

tycoon   The shoguns were commanders-in-chief of the Japanese army, and so great was their influence that for centuries they were the real rulers of Japan, though they acted in the name of the emperor. When Commodore Matthew Perry steamed into the Japanese harbor of Uraga in 1853 on a mission to force isolationist Japan into diplomatic and trade relations with the United States, he seems to have thought he was negotiating with the hereditary emperor when in fact his antagonist was the shogun. At this time the honorific *taikun* was used to describe the shogun to such visiting

Westerners. This title, borrowed from the Chinese *ta⁴ chün¹*, 'great ruler', was more impressive than *shogun*, 'general'. The Japanese *taikun* was usually spelled *tycoon* in English. In the United States, use of the word caught on after Perry's expedition fired the popular imagination. Here it was occasionally extended to describe a powerful person (John Hay spoke of Abraham Lincoln as "the Tycoon"). Specialization of meaning set in again when industrial magnates began to be considered comparable, in their power and wealth, to the former political rulers of Japan, and such men have been generally known as *tycoons* since early in this century.

[Jp *taikun*, fr. Chin (Pek) *ta⁴* great + *chün¹* ruler]

typhoon   The first *typhoons* reported in English were Indian storms and were called *touffons* or *tufans*. The rather Gallic spelling of *touffon* reflected the pronunciation of the first syllable, which rhymed with *you* rather than *I*. Although Arabic was not one of the chief languages of India, it is the language of the Koran, and Islam had become one of India's major religions. It was the Arabic *ṭūfān*, a word for a violent flood or hurricane, that the English found in India and borrowed as *touffon*. Later, when English ships met violent storms in the neighborhood of the China Sea, Englishmen learned the Cantonese word for a big wind *(taaî fung)*, which is by mere chance similar to *touffon*. The influence of *taaî fung* explains the present altered sound and shape of *typhoon*.

[alter. (influenced by Chin — Cant — *taaî fung* typhoon, fr. *taaî* great + *fung* wind) of earlier *touffon, tufan*, fr. Ar *ṭūfān* hurricane, deluge, fr. Gk *typhōn* whirlwind; akin to Gk *typhein* to smoke]

U

ukulele In Hawaiian, *'ukulele* means literally 'jumping flea', an animal which the familiar instrument scarcely resembles. It is likely that the improbable name became attached to the instrument in a rather roundabout way. Edward Purvis, a former British army officer living in Hawaii as an official at the court of King Kalakaua, is said to have been given the nickname *'ukulele* because he was a small and lively man. In 1879 Portuguese immigrants to the Hawaiian Islands from Madeira brought with them several musical instruments. Among these was the machete, a small four-stringed guitar. Purvis, being fond of music, was taken with the new instrument and soon learned to play it. When the machete became a popular favorite, it took the name of its popularizer, and its Portuguese name and origin were soon forgotten.

[Hawaiian *'ukulele*, fr. *'uku* flea + *lele* jumping; prob. fr. the Hawaiian nickname of Edward Purvis, 19th cent. Brit. army officer who was small and quick and who popularized the instrument]

umbra See UMBRAGE.
[L]

umbrage "Deare amber lockes gave umbrage to her face." This line from a poem written by William Drummond in 1616 exemplifies the original use of *umbrage* to mean 'shade, shadow'. This is also the meaning of its ultimate Latin source, *umbra*, which became *umbrage* in Middle French before being borrowed into English in the fifteenth century. John Milton was also familiar with this sense, as the following passage from *Paradise Lost* (1667) indicates: "Where highest woods, impenetrable/ To star or sunlight, spread their umbrage broad,/ And brown as evening." An additional sense became apparent in the seventeenth century when *umbrage* was used to mean 'a shadowy suggestion or semblance of something', as when Shakespeare, in *Hamlet* (ca. 1600), writes, "His semblable [counterpart, like] in his mirror, and who else would trace him, his umbrage, nothing more." In the same century *umbrage* took on the pejorative sense 'a shadow of suspicion cast on someone'. From this usage it was but a short semantic leap to 'displeasure, offense', which is the sense used in the phrases "give umbrage" or "take umbrage," phrases that also date from the seventeenth century. The adjective *umbrageous*, meaning 'shady, shadowy' and 'easily offended', has been in use since the sixteenth century.

In Latin the word *umbra* was also used for 'the shade or ghost of a deceased person'. It was with this meaning that *umbra* was borrowed directly into English in the sixteenth century. By the 1630s, however, English writers had begun using the term in its original Latin sense 'shade, shadow', and it was not long before astronomers adopted the word to refer to the shadows cast by celestial bodies.

In Latin, *umbella*, the diminutive form of *umbra*, was used for 'a sunshade or parasol'. Our word *umbrella*, in use since the seventeenth century, is ultimately derived from this Latin diminutive by way of the Italian word *ombrella*.

[ME, fr. MF, fr. L *umbraticum*, neut. of *umbraticus* of the shade, fr. *umbratus* (past part. of *umbrare* to shade, fr. *umbra* shade, shadow) + *-icus* -ic]

umbrella See UMBRAGE.
[It *ombrella*, modif. (influenced by *ombra* shade, shadow, fr. L *umbra*) of L *umbella* parasol, umbrella, dim. of *umbra*]

umpire A referee in a basketball game may have as much authority as an umpire in a baseball game, but, etymologically speaking, his title is far less impressive. A referee, after all, is just someone to be referred to, but an etymologically astute umpire could almost claim to be without equal.

Referee was formed by combination of the verb *refer* and the familiar suffix *-ee* in the seventeenth century, when it applied originally to a Parliamentary appointee to whom certain applications (as for patents) were referred for examination. It later became established in legal language as a term for a person chosen to settle a dispute between two parties—in other words, an arbitrator. Its use in naming a sports official originated in the nineteenth century. *Umpire*, on the other hand, is derived from the Middle French *nomper* 'not equal', from *non-* 'not' and *per* 'equal, peer'. *Nomper* came into English in the fourteenth century as *noumpere*, a word denoting, as *referee* later did, an impartial arbitrator, a higher authority "not equal" to the disputing parties. The modern word developed when the *n* of *a noumpere* was misunderstood in speech as belonging to the indefinite article, so that *a noumpere* came to be written as *an oumpere*. (For further examples of this kind of change see APRON and AUGER.)

By the end of the sixteenth century, the word had lost its *n* for good. Of several variant spellings, *umpire* eventually won out, becoming established in general use by about 1700. Its first known use in the world of sports occurred not long afterward, in 1714. *Umpire* has also long been used in law to denote specifically an ultimate arbitrator called upon to settle a question when two other arbitrators are unable to agree. In law, then, an umpire may be said to outrank a referee. In such modern sports as football and tennis, however, it is the referee who has authority over the umpire, etymology notwithstanding.

[ME *umpere, oumpere*, alter. (resulting from incorrect division of *a noumpere*) of *noumpere*, fr. MF *nomper, nonper* not equal, not paired (i.e., a third person), fr. *non-* + *per* equal, even, fr. L *par*]

uncle See COUSIN.
[ME, fr. OF *uncle, oncle,* fr. L *avunculus* mother's brother; akin to OE *ēam* uncle, mother's brother, OHG *ōheim* mother's brother, ON *afi* grandfather, Goth *awo* grandmother, L *avus* grandfather, OIr *aue* grandson, Lith *avynas* mother's brother]

Uncle Sam The United States in general and the U.S. government in particular are frequently personified as a tall, angular man dressed in a tall hat, swallow-tailed coat, and striped pants. Modern depictions of this character, who is known as *Uncle Sam,* show him with white hair and chin whiskers.

During the early days of the nation, a popular character in American plays and stories was a rustic individual named *Brother Jonathan.* This character delighted his public by invariably outwitting adversaries with his country shrewdness. The British used *Brother Jonathan* derisively as a generic term for Americans during the Revolution. Despite their implication that their opponents were slow-witted bumpkins, the British were forced to concede defeat in 1781 and leave their former colony. Their former colonists continued to apply the term *Brother Jonathan* to themselves and their fledgling nation, perhaps with a degree of gleeful irony. The tradition of personifying the United States as a rustic but clever character became firmly established.

The United States and England squared off again in the War of 1812. One of the wartime beef suppliers to the American Army was a resident of Troy, New York, named Samuel Wilson. Wilson seems to have been an avuncular figure, for he was locally known as "Uncle Sam." When government purchasing agents stamped Wilson's barrels of beef with the initials "U.S.," indicating government ownership, people identified the letters with Wilson's nickname. In 1961 Congress passed a resolution identifying Samuel Wilson as the namesake of *Uncle Sam,* the personification of the United States.

While Wilson was the source of Uncle Sam's name, he was not the model for the character's appearance. That honor goes to Abraham Lincoln. Up until the Civil War, cartoonists drew both *Uncle Sam* and *Brother Jonathan* characters to represent the United States. Different artists had different ideas about how these characters should look, so depictions varied widely. It was, ironically, an English cartoonist, not an American, who produced a rendering that became so popular it crystallized Uncle Sam's image in the public mind. The cartoonist was Sir John Tenniel, known chiefly now for his illustrations for *Alice's Adventures in Wonderland* and *Through the Looking Glass.* At the time of the Civil War, Tenniel was working for the influential British humor magazine *Punch.* He picked up on the tradition of portraying the United States as a bumpkin, and he drew Lincoln as Uncle Sam, looking distinctly gawky and ill-proportioned in striped pants, outsized clodhoppers, and an undignified straw hat. Despite the deliberate unattractiveness of the caricature, it tickled Americans' fancy. Uncle Sam's overall appearance had been set.

The last person to place his stamp on Uncle Sam's appearance was another cartoonist, an American this time. Thomas Nast was active in the 1870s, and he drew the character as a white-haired, dignified gentleman, sartorially elegant in tailed coat, striped pants, and top hat. The modern image of Uncle Sam was now complete.

[fr. *U.S.*, abbr. of *United States;* prob. fr. an originally jocular interpretation of the letters U.S. stamped on casks of meat supplied to the U.S. Army during the War of 1812 as standing for *Uncle Sam,* nickname of Samuel Wilson †1854 Am. meat packer]

undulate   See ABUNDANCE.
[LL *undula* small wave (fr. — assumed — L, dim. of *unda* wave) + E -*ate*, v. suffix]

unicorn   Marco Polo was not thrilled by his first glimpse of a unicorn. "It is a hideous beast to look at," he wrote, "and in no way like what we think and say in our countries. . . . Indeed, I assure you that it is quite the opposite of what we say it is." Small wonder he was disappointed. The Venetian had thought he knew what a unicorn looked like. Most of his contemporaries thought the same, even if they had never set eyes on the living beast, for the unicorn was a very popular animal in medieval art and literature. Depictions of it varied somewhat from artist to artist, but in general the medieval unicorn was a horse- or goat-like creature, pure white in color and dainty and refined in appearance. Unique to this marvelous animal was one long and tapering horn that grew from its forehead. This charming image evolved in the works of medieval writers into a full-blown symbol of Christ. The unicorn's capture and death at the hands of man allegorized the incarnation and death of Christ. But where did this image come from? And what animal did Marco Polo see and disparage?

The graceful horse-like creature that prances across medieval tapestries and paintings owes its existence entirely to man's imagination. But like other fairy-tale creatures, the unicorn is based on a real animal; it was this animal that so disappointed Marco Polo. Living at about 400 B.C., a Greek historian named Ctesias wrote a book on India. In it he described "certain wild asses which are as large as horses, and larger. Their bodies are white, their heads dark red, and their eyes dark blue. They have a horn on the forehead which is about a foot and a half in length." This early description gave the world the image of the horse-like body, the white color, and the single horn on the forehead, an image that would later be transformed into the medieval unicorn. But it seems clear from several of Ctesias's statements that he had the Indian rhinoceros in mind (or rather someone's description of it—Ctesias himself never visited India, although at one time he was physician to the king of Persia). The Indian rhinoceros and one other Far-Eastern species are the only land mammals to carry one horn (the two species of African rhinoceros have two horns). Ctesias mentions the pharmaceutical value of the horn from the "Indian wild ass"; rhinoceros horn has been valued for centuries as everything from an antidote to poison and epilepsy to an aphrodisiac. He considered the wild ass very fleet and difficult to capture. The Indian rhinoceros, despite its lumbering appearance, is swift, and its capture is both difficult and dangerous. The rhinoceros's speed increases while it is running, another fact Ctesias mentions. The Indian rhinoceros has a massive, ungainly body, stumpy legs, and a thick, folded hide that makes the beast look as if it had been riveted into plates of body armor. With the exception of its single horn, it is profoundly unlike the dainty unicorn of medieval art, and one can understand why Marco Polo was offended by it.

How did this huge and distinctly undainty beast get turned into a beautiful white horse? In order to answer that question, we should take a look at the word *rhinoceros*. It is based on the Greek words *rhin-* 'nose' and *keras* 'horn', an accurate enough name for the animal. All rhinoceros species do have horns (more precisely, masses of compressed hairlike material), and unlike cattle or antelope their horns are on the front of the face, more or less on the nose. And what about *unicorn?* That means 'one horn', from the Latin *uni-* 'one' and *cornu* 'horn'. While this is a descriptive name for the rhinoceros, *unicorn* was originally applied to something entirely different.

When scholars were translating the Old Testament from Hebrew into Greek in the third century B.C., they encountered a problematic animal. The Hebrew word for this creature was *re'em,* and the beast was evidently large and powerful. In Job 39:10–11 (AV) the writer asks:

> Will the unicorn be willing to serve thee,
>   or abide by thy crib?

> Canst thou bind the unicorn with his band in the furrow?
>   or will he harrow the valleys after thee?

> Wilt thou trust him, because his strength is great?
>   or wilt thou leave thy labor to him?

Modern scholars believe the mysterious and powerful *re'em* was the aurochs, or wild ox, which is now extinct. The Revised Standard Version of the Bible, published in 1952, translates the passage differently to reflect this belief:

> "Is this wild ox willing to serve you?
> Will he spend the night at your crib?
> Can you bind him in the furrow with ropes . . .

Although our modern view of the beast referred to here is quite different, ancient scholars had to come up with a Greek word for the animal whose identity was in doubt. Drawing on garbled descriptions of the rhinoceros, which started with Ctesias and continued with later writers, they settled on the Greek word *monokeros,* meaning 'one horn'. (*Monokeros* had already been used by some writers for the Indian rhinoceros.) The Latin version of the Bible turned this word into *unicornus,* and the English version, the King James Version, made this *unicorn.* So vague information on two different animals, the Indian rhinoceros and the aurochs, was conflated to produce another, imaginary animal, the unicorn. Then medieval writers, who tended to see the natural world as a single, unified allegory of Christian history and doctrine, turned this biblical animal into a symbol for Christ.

[ME *unicorne*, fr. OF, fr. LL *unicornis* (trans. of Gk *monokeros*), fr. L, adj., having one horn, fr. *uni-* + *cornu* horn]

Unitarian   See CATHOLIC.

[NL *unitarius* unitarian (fr. L *unitus* — past part. of *unire* to unite — + *-arius* -ary) + E *-an*]

urban   See URBANE.

[L *urbanus*, fr. *urb-*, *urbs* city + *-anus* -an]

urbane   The advantages of city over country life (and vice versa) have been hotly debated for many years, probably for as long as there have been cities, and this debate is even reflected in our vocabulary. Alongside of *urban*, 'relating to or characteristic of a city', we have *urbane*, which developed the sense of 'smoothly courteous or polite' from the belief (encouraged by city dwellers especially) that the social life of a city is more suave and polished than life in the country. Both *urban* and *urbane* come from the Latin *urbanus* from *urbs*, 'city'. Contrasting with the history of *urbane* we have the development of *clown*. Though the familiar costumed circus performer has today lost any association with the country, *clown* originally meant 'farmer' or 'countryman'. The lower social status and supposed boorishness of people in the country led to the more pejorative sense of 'a fool, jester, or comedian'. *Clown* is of uncertain origin; one possible source that has been suggested is Latin *colonus*, 'colonist, farmer'; thus it may be related to *colony*, also from *colonus*, which in turn comes from the verb *colere*, 'to cultivate' or 'to dwell'. For another term which has suffered under pejorative sense development resulting from social differences see VILLAIN.

[L *urbanus*]

urchin   The modern *urchin* is almost always a mischievous youngster. The hedgehog, from whom he takes his name, is rarely referred to today as an urchin. But 'hedgehog' was long the usual meaning of the word. Although children, especially mischievous ones, had often been called urchins since the early sixteenth century, William Cowper in 1790 still felt the necessity of explaining the less common meaning to a correspondent: "He sent an urchin (I do not mean a hedgehog . . . but a boy, commonly so called)." To call a person an *urchin* now is to liken him to a ragged, roguish child; but the same word is quite a different metaphor in this tender conversation from Thomas Heywood's *The Iron Age* (1632):

> "By the gods Wee haue two meeting soules: be my
>> sweete Vrchin."
> "I will, And thou shalt bee mine vgly Toade."

The *sea urchin* was named for its spiny similarity to the hedgehog.

[ME *urchin, urchon, hurcheoun, hirchoun* hedgehog, fr. MF *herichon, heriçon,* fr. L *ericius,* fr. *er, eris;* akin to Gk *chēr* hedgehog]

utopia In 1516 Sir Thomas More, the English humanist, published his book *Utopia,* in which the social and economic conditions of Europe, outlined in Book I, are compared with those of an ideal society described in Book II, a society established on an imaginary island off the shore of the New World. That such an ideal state is unattainable in reality is implied by the name More gave to this island, *Utopia,* which literally means 'no place', from Greek *ou,* 'not, no', plus *topos,* 'place'. In a poem prefaced to the book More also puns on the name, suggesting *eu-topos,* 'good place'. In Modern English *utopia* has become, through the influence of More's classic, a generic term for any place of ideal perfection, especially in laws, government, and social conditions. Less optimistically *utopia* has also come to mean an impractical scheme for social improvement.

Another, more whimsical, term for a realm of utopian fantasy is *cloud-cuckoo-land.* This is actually a translation of the Greek *nephelokokkygia,* a name made up by Aristophanes in his comic play *The Birds,* first performed in Athens in 414 B.C. In this play the birds are incited by a pair of Athenian rogues to establish a city and a rule of their own. The passage in which a name is chosen for their country is translated by William Arrowsmith as follows:

PISTHETAIROS
> Well,
what do you suggest instead?
EUELPIDES
> Something big, smacking
of the clouds. A pinch of fluff and rare air.
A swollen sound.
PISTHETAIROS
> I've got it! Listen—
>> CLOUDCUCKOOLAND!
KORYPHAIOS
That's it! The perfect name. And it's a *big* word too.

[fr. *Utopia,* an imaginary country with ideal laws and social conditions (fr. Gk *ou* not, no + *topos* place) described in the book *Utopia* (1516) by Sir Thomas More †1535 Eng. statesman and author]

utter At first glance the adjective *utter,* 'absolute', and the verb *utter,* 'to speak', seem to have little beyond appearance in common. But both are descended from the Old English adverb *ūt,* 'out'. The adjective *utter* originally meant simply 'outer, farther out, exterior'. One might speak of an *utter* room, an *utter* wall, an *utter* garment, or the like. Theologians could even distinguish the *utter* from the *inner* man: John Jewel, bishop of Salisbury, wrote in 1565 of "simple folke, beinge not hable to discerne, what thinges they be in the Holy Scriptures, that are to be applied to the Inner Man, and what to the Vtter."

The word is only rarely used today in this original sense; its current meaning is 'absolute'. When something is carried to its outer limits or its highest degree, it is absolute, or utter. The expression "utter darkness," however, neatly bridges the gap between the early and the later senses. William Tyndale, in his translation of the Bible (1526), rendered Matthew 25:30 in this way: "Cast that vnprophetable servaunt into vtter dercknes." In a Christian context, "utter darkness" is outer darkness, the destined abode of the damned, hopelessly remote from the light of God. Sir Walter Scott, when he wrote *The Talisman* (1825), had a very different situation in mind: "They blew out their lights at once, and left the knight in utter darkness." In either case, of course, "utter darkness" is absolute.

The verb *utter* originally meant 'to put forth'. It was very common in the late Middle English and early Modern periods to speak of goods uttered for sale. To utter a book was to publish it. To put money into circulation was to utter it. Most of these uses are no longer a part of standard English, though it is still possible to speak of uttering money, especially if it is counterfeit. Another common early sense of the verb *utter* was 'to put forth as a sound'. It is this sense that is the usual one today.

[ME, fr. OE *ūtera, ūterra* outer, compar. adj., fr. *ūt* out, adv.]

[ME *uttren,* to offer for sale, speak, fr. *utter* outside, adv., fr. OE *ūtor,* compar. of *ūt* out]

V

vacant See TRAMP.
[ME, fr. OF, fr. L *vacant-, vacans,* pres. part. of *vacare* to be empty, be free; perh. akin to L *vanus* empty, vain]

vaccine See BUCKAROO.
[L *vaccinus* of or from cows, fr. *vacca* cow + *-inus* -ine; akin to Skt *vaśa* cow]

vagabond See TRAMP.
[ME *vagabound,* fr. *vagabound,* adj., fr. MF *vagabond,* fr. L *vagabundus,* fr. *vagari* to move about, wander]

vagrant See TRAMP.
[ME *vagraunt,* prob. modif. (influenced by MF *vagant* vagrant, fr. pres. part. of *vaguer* to wander) of MF *wacrer, walcrer* to roll, roam, wander, of Gmc origin; akin to OE *wealcan* to roll, turn, revolve]

vandal As the Roman Empire weakened in the fourth century, barbarian Germanic tribes from northern Europe began migrating south, invading most of the Mediterranean world. The Vandals, a people from along the Baltic coast, crossed the Rhine, swept through Gaul, and by the early fifth century had penetrated Spain, where they set up kingdoms. They sailed across the Strait of Gibraltar then and seized the Roman province of Africa in 429. In 455 the Vandals moved on to Sicily and then to Rome itself, plundering the city for two weeks before leaving with the spoils. All their pillaging earned them a reputation for wanton destruction. In 534, however, Rome got its revenge when Justinian's troops, under the general Belisarius, attacked and overthrew the Vandals' kingdom in Africa. The Vandals' reputation for malicious destruction was not forgotten, and the western European languages applied their name to any wanton or ignorant destroyer or defacer of a building, monument, or work of art. English began using *vandal* generically for such a person in the seventeenth century. When Spain was overrun by the Moors in the eighth century, the Moors named the region after the Vandals, *al-Andalus,* which later became *Andalucia* in Spanish and *Andalusia* in English.
   While the Vandals were settling in Spain in the fifth century, another Germanic people, the Franks, were migrating from the lower Rhine area westward into Gaul, later called France from the name of these settlers.

In Frankish Gaul, only the Franks had the status of freemen. Hence their name acquired the sense of 'free from bondage' in Medieval Latin (*francus*) and early French (*franc*). By around 1300 English had borrowed this as *frank* in the same sense, which is now obsolete. Later it took on the sense of 'free of restraint or restrictions'. Around the middle of the sixteenth century, the word came to be used to describe a person who is sincere, open, or candid in expressing himself.

[L *Vandalus* (sing.), *Vandalii* (pl.), of Gmc origin]

Vandyke   See SIDEBURNS.
[after Sir Anthony *Vandyke* or *Van Dyck* †1641 Flem. painter; fr. its frequent appearance in paintings by Vandyke]

vane   See VIXEN.
[ME (southern dial.), fr. OE *fana* flag, banner; akin to OHG *fano* cloth, gund*fano* war flag, gonfalon, ON gunn*fani*, Goth *fana* piece of cloth, rag, Gk *pēnē* thread on a bobbin, woof, web]

vaquero   See BUCKAROO.
[Sp]

varmint   See ORNERY.
[alter. of *vermin*]

varsity   See ORNERY.
[by shortening & alter. fr. *university*]

vat   See VIXEN.
[ME *vat, fat,* fr. OE *fæt;* akin to OHG *vaz* vessel, cask, vat, ON *fat* vessel, Lith *puodas* pot and perh. to Skt *palla* granary, barn]

vaudeville   When American soldiers liberated the town of Vire in Normandy, France, in July of 1944, doubtless few of them realized that they were marching through the very place that is believed to have given its name to the once-popular entertainment *vaudeville*. The variety-show format that once brought entertainment to the masses may trace the origin of its name to Vire, a town that had been an important Norman settlement in the Middle Ages. It was during that period that a custom arose in the valley outside the town of composing songs satirizing the events and personalities of contemporary Normandy. Songs celebratory of love and drinking were favored as well. Before long *vau de vire* (valley of Vire) became the name for such a song.

These songs (*vaux de vire*) were probably composed and sung by a society or guild of poet-singers. By 1500 the compositions had grown into a substantial body of work and had become popular throughout France as "lais [songs] des Vaux de Vire." Long after the original and authentic *vaux de vire* had faded from memory, the name remained current for popular, satirical songs regardless of origin. Drinking songs also tended to be desig-nated as *vaux de vire.*

The English term *vaudeville* made its first appearance in Cotgrave's *Dictionarie of the French and English Tongues* (1611). The first definition given was 'a country ballade, or song'. The term *vaudeville* resulted from the confusing, and later coalescing, of *vau de vire* with *voix de ville* (voices of the city), the name of another genre of French song with an entirely different origin. Dating back to the sixteenth century, *voix de ville* re-ferred to a simple tune with a courtly lyric that most often took love as its theme. Unlike the *vaux de vire,* these songs were often written by the most famous poets of the day. Indeed, the *voix de ville* may have originated in Paris as a courtly and urban response to the folk-based *vaux de vire* of the provinces. *Voix de ville* was the term used in the title of a collection of these courtly love songs that was published in 1555. The form *vaudeville* emerged because these songs were confused with *vaux de vire* from the beginning. (The fact that there were three villages in Lorraine named Vaudeville did nothing to alleviate the confusion.) A collection of courtly songs published in 1573 was titled *Premier livre de chansons en forme de vau de ville.* A work published in 1588 used both *voix de villes* and *vaux de villes.* By the end of the sixteenth century, *vaudeville* had come into common use in France.

Comedies that incorporated old vaudeville tunes with new lyrics emerged as a new, popular form of entertainment in Paris during the late seventeenth and early eighteenth centuries. Gradually these comedies would evolve into the genre known as *opéra comique.* On select occasions in Paris, theaters that had been specially set up for festivals presented ac-robatic shows, plays with songs and dances, monologues, pantomimes, poster plays, and marionettes—all of them freely incorporating the comic songs known as vaudevilles. Originally most of the music for these comic entertainments were vaudevilles, which were supplemented by brief opera excerpts, dances, and instrumental interludes. Lyricists worked with playwrights to select the most appropriate vaudeville tunes and to write original lyrics for the occasion. While sometimes vaudevilles were selected to underscore the mood created by the stage action, often they were introduced as humorous counterpoints to the action. A penchant for double entendres developed. Sometimes extended musical scenes were created by stringing several vaudevilles together or by cleverly interweav-ing passages from a number of different vaudevilles.

By the close of the eighteenth century, comedy featuring sung vaude-villes had become an entertainment entirely distinct from opéra comique. This kind of entertainment became known as *comédie-vaudeville.* Taking its cue from the comic opera, the Théâtre du Vaudeville opened in 1792. Its initial productions resembled today's musical comedies. Eventually *vaudeville* came to refer to the shows themselves. With time the shows mixed satire and variety acts with popular music of various origins. The English music halls took over this entertainment and greatly influenced the content and format of these stage presentations. In American vaude-ville the format evolved into a variety show whose unrelated acts might include singers, dancers, comedians, show girls, jugglers, acrobats, and performing animals.

Vaudeville flourished until the early 1930s. The introduction in 1896 of movie shorts into the program was a foreshadowing of the end. Originally intended merely as an added attraction, the movies gradually displaced more and more of the variety acts. After the introduction of talkies in 1927, the feature-length motion picture became the star attraction, with a few vaudeville acts reduced to a sideshow. By the end of World War II vaudeville had virtually disappeared from the boards.

See also BURLESQUE.

[F, fr. MF, alter. (influenced by *ville* town, city, fr. L *villa* village) of *vaudevire* popular satirical song, fr. *vau-de-Vire* valley of Vire, locality near Vire, town in northwestern France where such songs were first composed in the 15th century, fr. *vau, val* valley + *de* from, of (fr. L) + *Vire*]

veep See JEEP.
[fr. *v.p.* (abbr. for *vice president*)]

venerate See VENOM.
[L *veneratus,* past part. of *venerari* to venerate]

venereal See JOVIAL.
[ME *venerealle,* fr. L *venereus* venereal (fr. *vener-, venus* love, sexual desire) + ME *-alle, -al* -al]

venom A number of Latin words are cognate with the name of *Venus,* whose name etymologically means 'love': *venustas* 'charm', *venustare* 'adorn', and *venerari* 'to worship', the source of our word *venerate.* (For another English derivative see the discussion of *venereal* at JOVIAL.) Another cognate was *venenum,* which in the mists of antiquity seems to have denoted a cosmetic or love potion. The latter sense is still broadly attested in classical times, but quite early *venenum* developed the sense of 'poison'. It is in this sense that *venenum* is the ultimate ancestor of our word *venom.*

The evolution of sense from 'love philtre' to 'poison' may not have stemmed solely from considerations of "fatal attraction," for our word *poison* itself goes back to Latin *potio* 'drink, drinking', the source also of our word *potion.* (There is a parallel development in the German word for 'poison', *gift,* which is cognate with our word *gift* and etymologically means just 'something given'.) The use of potions for dark magical purposes was no doubt a factor in all three pejorative developments, for *potio* developed a sense 'philtre' before becoming still more venomous as its Old French descendant *poison* 'philtre, poison', the immediate source of our word *poison.*

[ME *venom, venum, venim,* fr. OF *venim,* fr. (assumed) VL *venimen,* alter. of L *venenum* drug, poison, magic potion, charm; akin to L *venus* love, sexual desire]

verdict See JUDGE.

[alter. (influenced by ML *verdictum, veredictum* verdict, fr. L *vere dictum* truly said, fr. *vere* truly — fr. *verus* true — + *dictum* something said, saying) of ME *verdit*, fr. AF, fr. OF *ver, veir* true (fr. L *verus*) + *dit* saying, fr. past part. of *dire* to say, fr. L *dicere*]

vermicelli After thoughtfully making reservations a week ahead of time or waiting half an hour for a table at a restaurant, it would be upsetting to begin reading the menu only to find on it such items as worms, string, paste, pitch, pots, ribbons, hats, thimbles, and little boys. However, if it were an Italian restaurant and the menu used the forms derived from the Italian words for these things, a hungry customer might not be so inclined to leave in a hurry. *Vermicelli* is a type of pasta made in strings somewhat smaller than spaghetti; the name is a descriptive one, from *vermicello,* a diminutive of *verme,* 'worm'. *Spaghetti* itself is the plural of *spaghetto,* a diminutive of *spago,* 'string'. *Pasta* is the Italian for dough and is derived from Late Latin *pasta,* meaning 'dough' or 'paste'.

Lasagna, broad flat noodles baked in a dish with sauce, comes from Latin *lasanum,* 'cooking pot'. *Fettucini* is another flat form of pasta, sliced into thin strips, and appropriately enough it takes its name from *fettuccia,* 'ribbon'. Etymologically it is a triple diminutive: the Italian source word *fettuccine* (plural of *fettuccina*) is a diminutive of *fettuccia* 'small slice', which in turn is a diminutive of *fetta* 'slice', which goes back to a diminutive form of Latin *offa* 'lump of food'. *Cappelletti* are small cases of dough usually filled with meat or cheese, similar to ravioli; the word comes from Medieval Latin *cappellus,* 'cap' or 'hat'. *Ravioli* is derived from Italian *rava* and ultimately from an earlier Latin *rapa,* and it means literally 'little turnip'. *Ditali* or *ditalini* are made from macaroni cut into short lengths whose shape suggested the name, derived from Italian *ditale,* 'thimble'.

Ziti refers to tubular pasta, and is formally the plural of the obsolete Italian *zito* 'boy'. This form of pasta is particularly favored at nuptial feasts in the south of Italy; the reason for the name of the pasta may be its phallic shape. There are quite a few other forms of pasta with similarly descriptive names in Italian, but not all of these are used widely enough in English to warrant their inclusion in English dictionaries.

[It, fr. pl. of *vermicello,* dim. of *verme* worm, fr. L *vermis*]

vernacular In the days of ancient Rome when the labor force consisted in part of slaves, a slave born in his master's house, i.e., homeborn (and referred to in Latin as *verna*), was distinguished from one acquired otherwise. From *verna,* the Romans derived the adjective *vernaculus,* meaning 'homeborn' or 'native', and applied it to a wide variety of things. When this adjective was assimilated into English as *vernacular,* however, its application was restricted in scope to 'using the language or dialect native to a region or country as opposed to a literary, cultured, or foreign language'. This sense of the word has been traced as far back as 1601, when Bishop William Barlow wrote of "a vernacular pen-man" who had translated some writing from a foreign tongue into English. A relatively modern application is its use in distinguishing the common native names of plants and animals from the Latin nomenclature of scientific classification, the vernacular name for *Ursus horribilis* being, for example, grizzly bear.

The noun *vernacular*, which denotes 'the native language or dialect of a country or region', first appeared in the early part of the eighteenth century. More recently it has been adopted by the biological sciences to mean 'a vernacular name of a plant or animal'.

[L *vernacul*us homeborn, native (fr. *verna* homeborn slave, native) + E -*ar*]

vicar When the Roman Empire was reorganized under Diocletion (reigned 284–305) and Constantine (reigned 306–337), the large administrative areas, called prefectures, were divided into dioceses, each of which was governed by a *vicar*. This word *vicar* (Latin *vicarius* 'substitute, deputy') comes from the Latin adjective *vicarius* meaning 'substituted, delegated', which derives from *vicis* 'change, alternation'.

In the early Christian Church, the title *vicar* was borrowed from the secular world and used for a representative of the pope to the Eastern councils. The title *vicar apostolic*, first found toward the end of the fourth century, was used for a residential bishop who had certain rights of surveillance over neighboring bishops. By the thirteenth century *vicar apostolic* came to denote a bishop appointed by the pope to govern a diocese that was without a bishop or whose bishop was prevented from exercising his jurisdiction by some impediment. Nowadays *vicar apostolic* denotes a titular bishop appointed by the pope to administer a district (called a vicariate) in a missionary area.

When the word *vicar* was first used in English in the fourteenth century, it referred to God's representative on earth and in particular to the pope. In fact, popes have assumed the title "Vicar of Christ" (*Vicarius Christi*) since the reign of Innocent III (1198–1216). In the Church of England *vicar* came to denote a clergyman serving in a parish of which the tithes go to a layman or to a religious institution, while he receives a stipend. The term is used in contrast to *rector*, the title of the clergyman in charge of a parish who receives the tithes of that parish. In the Protestant Episcopal Church a vicar is a clergyman in charge of a dependent chapel as the deputy of another clergyman, and a rector is the clergyman who is the presiding officer of a parish. A Roman Catholic rector is a priest directing a church with no pastor or one whose pastor has other duties. *Rector* stems ultimately from the past participle of the Latin verb *regere* 'to rule, govern'. (See also PASTOR, PRIEST.)

Another common clerical title is *dean*. English formed this word from the Middle French *deien*, which can be traced back to the Latin noun *decanus*, a derivative of *decem* meaning 'ten'. In ancient Rome a *decanus* was the military leader of a group of ten soldiers. In the early Church a *decanus* was the religious leader of ten monks. When French took the word as *deien* (Modern French *doyen*), it was used for the head of the chapter of a collegiate or cathedral church. This was the main sense of the word when it was borrowed into English in the fourteenth century as *dean.* It is also used in Catholicism for a priest who supervises one district of a diocese.

Some Christian churches use the title *deacon.* This word originated in Greek as *diakonos* meaning 'servant'. Its Latin form *diaconus* was used by the early Christians for 'a servant or minister of the church'. Specifically it referred to the cleric ranking just below a priest (presbyter) who had both administrative duties, such as administering the church's property, and liturgical duties, such as assisting at Mass by reading the Gospel, distributing Communion, and directing the prayers of the congregation. In modern Anglican and Roman Catholic churches, a deacon is usually a candidate for the priesthood who is in the last phase of his studies. In some Protestant churches a deacon is a layman elected by a congregation to serve in worship, in pastoral care, and on administrative committees.

In hierarchical churches, the term *prelate* is used to refer to a clergyman of superior rank, such as a bishop, archbishop, or cardinal. The term was borrowed from the French *prélat* in the thirteenth century with just this meaning. It derives from the Medieval Latin *praelatus,* meaning 'one receiving preferment'. *Praelatus* is the past participle of the Latin verb *praeferre* 'to carry before', the source of our word *prefer.*

[ME *vicar, vicair, viker,* fr. LL *vicarius,* fr. L, substitute, deputy, fr. *vicarius,* adj., substituting, delegated, vicarious, fr. *vicis* change, alternation, stead]

villain   In the feudal society of the Middle Ages a *villein* was a member of one of the lower classes, at some times and places a free man and at others fully bound in service to his lord. The word is derived through Middle French from Medieval Latin *villanus,* which comes from Latin *villa,* 'village', plus the termination *-anus,* 'one that is of or belonging to'. Thus, though a *villein* may have been a free man, his freedom was only that of a common villager or village peasant at best. Because the higher classes often look on the lower classes as inferior, Middle English *vilein* or *vilain* developed the depreciatory sense of 'a person of uncouth mind and manners'. This pejorative tendency gained in strength and currency through the common equation of manners and morals, so that the modern *villain* is a deliberate scoundrel or criminal, or a person or thing blamed for a particular evil or difficulty.

A similar pejoration happened to *boor.* This word goes back to a root meaning 'to dwell', a meaning that may still be glimpsed in another derivative from this root, *bower.* In the sixteenth century, a *boor* was one who worked the land. Once again we can still see a trace of the older meaning in a related form, this time the Dutch cognate borrowed into English as *Boer.* But again the peasants got a bad name from their social betters, and gradually connotations of rusticity and uncouthness became central to the use of the word.

See also URBANE.

[ME *vilein, vilain,* fr. MF, fr. ML *villanus,* fr. L *villa* country house, country estate, village + *-anus* -an]

vindicate   See JUDGE.
[L *vindicatus,* past part. of *vindicare* to lay claim to, set free, avenge, fr. *vindic-, vindex* claimant, protector, avenger, fr. a prehistoric compound whose first constituent is of unknown origin and whose second constituent is the same as L *-dic-, -dex* (fr. *dicere* to determine, say)]

violin   There is evidence from as early as the ninth century of the Christian era that certain types of stringed instruments were played with bows. The *violin* as we know it today, however, was not developed until the late sixteenth century. Earlier instruments such as the rebec and the vielle are often designated as *fiddles,* and the somewhat later precursors of the violin family are known as *viols.* Of the terms *fiddle* and *violin,* the first to be used in English was *fiddle,* a form of which appeared as early as the year 1205. The word may actually be considerably older, for an Old English form of *fiddler* appears in a manuscript dated around 1100. The word *violin,* from the Italian *violino,* did not make its way into English until the sixteenth century, but has been used since then to refer to instruments very similar to the modern violin. Today *violin* and *fiddle* are used as terms for the same instrument. Both words have been traced back to the same probable source, Medieval Latin *vitula,* and their differences in form are due to the fact that they entered the language at such widely separated times, *violin* having undergone centuries of change in two Romance tongues before taking its place beside *fiddle* in the English wordstock.

[It *violino,* dim. of *viola* viol, viola, fr. OProv *viola, viula* viol, prob. fr. ML *vitula* fiddle]

virago   See VIRTUE.
[L *viragin-, virago* manlike heroic woman, fr. *vir* man, male]

virile   See VIRTUE.
[MF or L; MF *viril,* fr. L *virilis,* fr. *vir* man, adult male + *-ilis* -ile; akin to OE & OHG *wer* man, husband, ON *verr,* Goth *wair,* Skt *vīra* man, hero, and prob. to L *vis* strength]

virtue   From their word *vir,* meaning 'man', the Romans derived the noun *virtus* to denote the sum of the excellent qualities of men, including physical strength, valorous conduct, and moral rectitude. Cicero wrote of four moral excellences *(virtutes)* that had been previously espoused by Plato and Aristotle, namely "virtutes continentiae, gravitatis, justitiae, fidei" (the virtues of temperance, prudence, justice, fortitude). The French developed their word *vertu* or *virtu* from Latin, and it is first recorded in the tenth century. It was borrowed into English in the thirteenth century. In the fourteenth century *virtue* came to be applied to any 'characteristic, quality, or trait known or felt to be excellent'. By the end of the sixteenth century the sense 'chastity, purity' appeared, especially in reference to women. Shakespeare made such use of the word in the line "And maiden virtue rudely strumpeted" in his Sonnet 66.
The Latin adjective *virilis,* 'manly, masculine', another derivative of *vir,*

became *virile* when first used in English in the fifteenth century. The Late Latin adjective *virtuosus*, 'virtuous', derived from *virtus*, became *virtuoso* in Italian, and then was taken into English as the noun *virtuoso* in the seventeenth century. *Virtuoso* then as now suggested man's prowess in one sort of endeavor or another rather than his moral virtue. The Latin noun *virago*, meaning 'a manlike woman', was borrowed into English in the fourteenth century in the sense 'a bold impudent woman, shrew'.

[ME *vertu, virtu*, fr. OF, fr. L *virtut-, virtus* strength, manliness, virtue, fr. *vir* man]

virtuoso See VIRTUE.
[It, fr. *virtuoso*, adj., virtuous, learned, skilled, fr. LL *virtuosus* virtuous, fr. *virtus* strength, virtue + *-osus* -ous]

vixen You never know when you will be assaulted with an odd fact, and here is one. Even though we now use such common words as *very, voice, virtue, vulgar, visit, valuable*, and *violin*, English originally had no words beginning with *v* or a \v\ sound. Almost all of our words beginning with *v* have been borrowed from other languages, such as French, Latin, or Italian. The sound \v\ did exist in Old English, but it was not used at the beginning or at the end of words. It appeared only in the middle of words, and even then it was spelled with the letter *f*. We can see its survival in *wives* and *knives* as plurals of *wife* and *knife*.

In the Middle English dialects spoken in southeastern England, however, initial *f* was often pronounced like *v*. For instance, Middle English *fox* became *vox* in these dialects. Of these dialectal pronunciations, three have survived to reach Modern English as the standard forms: *vat, vane*, and *vixen*.

Vat existed in Middle English as both *vat* and *fat*, from Old English *fæt; vane* (as in *weathervane*) comes from the Old English *fana* 'banner'. (The original consonant is preserved in the Modern German cognates, *fass* and *fahne*.) *Vixen* is a more complicated problem. The scant records of its use in Middle English show only *fixen*. There is no record of the *v* spelling, as there is for *fox*, so we can only assume that such a form must have existed to explain the appearance of *vixen* in the late sixteenth century. By the 1590s *vixen* turns up in the writings of Shakespeare, John Lyly, and Thomas Nashe, and quickly became the settled form in English.

[fr. (assumed) ME (southern dial.) *vixen*, alter. of ME *fixen*, fr. OE *fyxe* (oblique cases *fyxan*), fem. of *fox*]

volcano According to Greco-Roman mythology the god of fire and metalworking, named *Hephaistos* by the Greeks and *Vulcanus* by the Romans, was married to *Aphrodite* (Latin *Venus*), the goddess of love and beauty. One of the tales concerning these two tells how *Hephaistos* constructed a great net which descended upon the bed in which *Aphrodite* and *Ares* were enjoying themselves. Having thus caught them flagrante delicto, *Hephaistos* then summoned the other gods to witness the scene. This episode is recounted here largely to get all three gods together in one place, for each has contributed a form of his or her name to the current English vocabulary. Roman tradition held that *Vulcanus* (or *Vulcan* in English) had his forge on Mount Etna, while the Greeks placed him on the volcanic island of Lemnos. In any case it is from the Latin name that English, via Italian, gets the word *volcano*. The name of *Aphrodite* gave rise to the Greek *aphrodisiakos,* meaning 'sexual', and from this English derives *aphrodisiac,* used originally as an adjective meaning 'exciting sexual desire'. *Ares* was called *Mars* by the Romans, and Mars, the god of war, has lent his name to the adjective *martial* as well as to the name of our third month.

For other gods and figures from mythology and legend see AMETHYST, ATLAS, BACCHANALIA, CALLIOPE, EROTIC, HYPNOSIS, JANUARY, JOVIAL, MONEY, NARCISSISM, PANIC, QUICKSILVER, SIREN, STENTORIAN, SUNDAY.

[It *volcano, vulcano,* fr. L *Volcanus, Vulcanus,* Roman god of fire and metalworking represented in Greco-Roman myth as the blacksmith of the gods forging thunderbolts on Mount Etna and other volcanoes]

voluble   See VOLUME.
[MF or L; MF *voluble,* fr. L *volubilis,* fr. L *volvere* to roll, turn, revolve + *-bilis* capable of being acted upon; akin to Gk *eilyein* to roll, wrap, fold, Goth *-walwjan* to roll, OE *walwian, wealwian,* OHG *wellan* to roll, OSlav *valiti* to roll, trundle, Skt *valati* he turns; basic meaning: turning, rolling]

volume   The earliest books were actually rolls of papyrus, a writing material that was made from the pith of the papyrus plant and used by the ancient Egyptians, Greeks, and Romans. The Greek word for papyrus was *biblos* or *byblos,* which they derived from the name of the Phoenician city *Byblos* (now Jubayl, Lebanon), from which papyrus was exported. *Biblion,* the diminutive form of *biblos* and the source of the English word *Bible,* came to be used for such a roll of papyrus. The Romans, on the other hand, took their word for such a roll, *volumen,* from the appropriate verb *volvere,* meaning 'to roll'. The *volumen* consisted of papyrus sheets that were pasted edge to edge with a slight overlap and were usually rolled around a cylinder having projecting ends. The text, written on one side only since the papyrus was so thin, was set out in columns and started at the left. The reader held the roll in his right hand and unrolled it column by column, while with his left hand he rolled up on another roller the part he had read. When he had finished reading, he had to reroll the entire *volumen.* Naturally this form of book was difficult to consult.

By the fifth century, parchment made from the processed skin of sheep, goat, or calf had generally replaced papyrus as the writing surface because it was tougher and could be cleaned and used on both sides. It could also be folded and bound, which eliminated the need for rolls. The word *parchment* is derived from the name of the ancient Asian city *Pergamon* (now Bergama, Turkey) where it was said to have been first used.

The Latin *volumen* was borrowed into French as *volume,* which in the fourteenth century became part of the English vocabulary. By the sixteenth century *volume* had acquired the additional sense 'the size or bulk (of a book)', which led to the development of a generalized sense denoting 'the quantity, amount, or mass of anything'. In the nineteenth century *volume* took on the meaning 'strength' or 'intensity' in reference to sound.

The Latin verb *volvere* is the source of several other English words, including the following: *volute, convolute, devolve, evolve, involve,* and *revolve.* The adjective *voluble,* whose principal meaning now is 'fluent in speech, talkative', is also derived from *volvere,* having originally been used in English to mean 'easily rolling' or 'apt to roll'.

[ME *volum, volume,* fr. MF, fr. L *volumen* roll of writing, book, volume, fr. *volvere* to roll]

volute See VOLUME.
[L *voluta,* fr. fem. of *volutus,* past part. of *volvere* to roll, turn]

voodoo For many of us, the word *voodoo* conjures up an image of an evil tribal witch doctor sticking pins in a doll, while miles away an innocent, unwitting victim writhes in pain; or we think of zombies stalking the earth in search of human blood. With our tendency to associate voodoo with evil, it may surprise some to learn that it is a religion which combines elements of Roman Catholic ritual with elements of native African religions and magic. Voodoo derived from African ancestor worship and is practiced throughout the Caribbean and South America as well as in parts of the United States. *Voodoo* is most closely associated with Haiti, in the minds of most Americans. In other areas the religion has other names. Devotees claim belief in one supreme God as well as lesser deities that demand ritual service while acting as protectors, guides, and helpers for individuals and families. The word *voodoo* itself comes from Louisiana French *voudou.* It is related to the African word *vodū,* which denotes a tutelary deity or demon.

A basic tenet of voodoo holds that the spirits of the dead can be called into the world of the living to bless or curse people. It is the curse aspect that has been popularized in books and movies. One way to call one of these spirits into action is to create an image (such as a wax doll) of the person who is the object of a curse or blessing, and treat the figure as you would like that person to be treated by the spirits. From this practice derives the image of the voodoo doll used to inflict harm on one's enemies.

Over the years voodoo has fallen victim to stereotyping on the part of those to whom the religion is foreign. As a result, the word has become associated with unexplainable phenomena, and has become more or less synonymous with the figurative senses of *mumbo jumbo:*

. . . the ability to write books of literary criticism that are pleasant to read, partly because they avoid the voodoo talk so fashionable among many of our advanced critics —*New Yorker,* 24 Mar. 1951

Of all our current curses, demystification may be the worst. When the Latin mass and grand opera were reduced to English, both our sins and our passions seemed smaller. . . . But if the romantic soul is to operate, a dash of voodoo is needed —Joe Flaherty, *N.Y. Times Book Rev.*, 27 June 1976

The term was even taken up during the U.S. presidential campaign in 1980, in the description of a proposed economic policy as "voodoo economics."

Most people believe this new approach to economic policy is based on the proposition that tax cuts pay for themselves by stimulating the economy. . . . Since this theory implies that government can cut taxes and keep on spending, it has widely been denigrated as . . . "voodoo economics" —Paul Craig Roberts, *Business Week*, 12 Nov. 1984

[LaF *voudou*, of African origin; akin to Fon *vodū* spirit, Ewe *vo¹du³* tutelary deity, demon]

W

Walloon See WALNUT.

[MF *Wallon,* adj. & n., of Gmc origin; prob. akin to OHG *Walah, Walh* Celt, Roman, OE *Wealh* Celt, Welshman]

walnut *Walnut* trees, especially those of the genus *Juglans,* have been cultivated in so many countries for so many centuries that the early origins and distribution of the walnut cannot now be clearly discerned. It would appear, however, that the walnut was known to southern Europe for some time before it was introduced into England, where its presence is not recorded with certainty until as late as the sixteenth century. The word *walnut,* however, has a much longer history. It occurs once in an eleventh-century Old English gloss on Latin *nux* 'nut' in the phrase *hnutbeam oththe walhhnutu,* 'nut tree or walnut'. Cognate forms occur in a number of other Germanic languages, but this Old English example is the earliest known occurrence. It is formed from Old English *wealh,* meaning 'foreigner', plus *hnutu* 'nut' and thus literally means 'foreign nut'. It was apparently so called to distinguish the walnut of southern Europe from the nut native to more northern countries, the hazelnut.

While Old English *wealh* means 'foreigner' in a general sense, it was applied by the Anglo-Saxon invaders of Britain specifically to the Celtic people who already inhabited the island. Thus *wealh* and the related adjectival form *wælisc* gave rise to the modern form *Welsh.* Another cognate of *wal-* and *Welsh* in English is *Walloon,* an English form of the French name given to the predominately Celtic inhabitants of southern Belgium and to their language. In its betrayal of the attitude of a conquering majority to the conquered Celtic minority, it parallels *Welsh* exactly.

[ME *walnot,* fr. OE *wealhhnutu,* lit., foreign nut, fr. *Wealh* Welshman, foreigner + *hnutu* nut]

ward See LADY.

[ME, fr. OE *weard* (fem.); akin to OHG *warta* act of watching, OE *weard* (masc.) watchman, keeper, guard, OHG *wart,* ON *vörthr,* Goth *daurwards* doorkeeper, OE *warian* to beware, guard]

WASP See YUPPIE.

[*white Anglo-Saxon Protestant*]

wassail   Geoffrey of Monmouth tells this story about the first *wassail* in his *Historia Regum Britanniae* (History of the Kings of Britain). Vortigern, a Celtic king in Britain in the mid-fifth century, was being entertained by the Jute (or Saxon) Hengist, whom he had invited from the continent to help him repel the troublesome Picts and Scots. Hengist's daughter Rowena (or Renwein) offered the king a goblet of wine, saying, "Laverd King, was hail!" Vortigern was struck by Rowena's beauty but confused by her speech, and asked his interpreter for clarification. He learned that the girl had called him "Lord King" and honored him by drinking his health, and that his proper response would be, "Drinc hail!" Since that day, according to Geoffrey, this traditional health and its response had endured in Britain.

Unfortunately, this account cannot be true. Geoffrey's attribution of this formula to the fifth century is as anachronistic as Shakespeare's placement (in *Julius Caesar*) of clocks in ancient Rome. In fact, Geoffrey himself provides here, in the twelfth century, the first written evidence of the phrases. The Middle English phrase *was hail* or *wæs hæil* is not of English origin at all, but comes from the Old Norse *ves heill*, 'be in good health'. It was probably from Scandinavian settlers in northern England that the English picked up the drinking salutation. By the early fourteenth century, the salutation *wassail* or *wesseyl* was being used as a term for the drink itself. It came to be used especially for the spiced ale or wine that was traditionally drunk in celebration of Christmas Eve or Twelfth Night. The word *wassail* had been extended by the early seventeenth century to refer as well to any riotous drinking or revelry.

[ME *wæs hæil, washail,* fr. ON *ves heill* be in good health, fr. *ves* (imper. sing. of *vera* to be) + *heill* healthy]

wedlock   *Wedlock* has the distinction of being the only surviving example of the use of the suffix *-lock* in English. In Old English this suffix, meaning 'activity', was spelled *-lāc*. Since *wed-* is derived from the Old English word *wedd,* meaning 'pledge', the term *wedlock* etymologically means 'the activity of giving a pledge' or, more specifically, 'plighting one's troth'. Its first use, however, was to mean 'the nuptial vow' or 'the marriage bond', as evidenced by writings of the twelfth century. It was often found in such phrases as "to keep wedlock" or "to break wedlock" with reference to marital fidelity. The following quotation from William Tyndale's translation of the New Testament (1526) illustrates this now obsolete use of *wedlock:* "And whosoever maryeth her that is divorsed, breketh wedlocke" (Mt. 5:32). The term was also used to mean 'wedding' and 'wife'; however, these senses of *wedlock* have also become obsolete.

The sense that survives today, 'the state of marriage', can be traced back to the thirteenth century. Milton illustrated this sense in the following comment from his tract *Doctrine and Discipline of Divorce* (1643): "Where love cannot be, there can be left of wedlock nothing but the empty husk of an outside matrimony, as undelightful and unpleasing to God as any other kind of hypocrisy." This sense is also exemplified in the phrases "in (or under) wedlock" and "out of wedlock," which have been used since the thirteenth century in reference to the birth of a legitimate or illegitimate child.

[ME *wedlac, wedlok,* fr. OE *wedlāc,* fr. *wedd* pledge + *-lāc,* suffix denoting activity, prob. fr. *lāc* warlike activity, play]

Wednesday See SUNDAY.
[ME *wodnesday, wednesday,* fr. OE *wōdnesdæg;* akin to OFris *wēnsdei* Wednesday, ON *ōthinsdagr;* all fr. a prehistoric WGmc-NGmc compound formed from components represented by OE *Wōden,* the chief god of the Germanic peoples, identified with the Roman Mercury, and OE *dæg* day; trans. of L *Mercurii dies,* lit., day of Mercury (the Roman god of commerce and the planet Mercury)]

weird *Weird* is derived from the Old English noun *wyrd,* meaning 'fate', as in this brooding reflection from *Beowulf:* "Gæth a wyrd swa hio scel." (Fate goes ever as it will.) It is also found as an eighth-century gloss of Latin *Parcae,* 'the Fates'. In Middle English *werd* is found primarily as a noun in Scots and northern contexts. Not until the fifteenth century was this word recorded in an attributive or adjectival position, and even then only in the combination *weird sister.* The weird sisters, then, were the three Fates, whom Shakespeare portrayed as witches in *Macbeth.* Finally in the eighteenth century *weird* began to appear in other contexts as an adjective meaning 'magical', 'odd', or 'fantastic'.

Like *weird, eerie* is a predominantly northern word of Old English origin. Even through the nineteenth century *eerie* was considered a Scots word, but in the present century its use has spread beyond these northern boundaries into more general usage. Derived from Old English *earg,* meaning 'cowardly' or 'wretched', Middle English *eri* or *ery* simply meant 'fearful' or 'scared', a sense it still has in Scots. In modern usage, however, *eerie* usually carries with it the connotation that the fear it suggests is occasioned by some mystery, strangeness, or gloominess.

[ME (Sc) *werd,* fr. *werd,* n., fate, fr. OE *wyrd;* akin to OHG *wurt* fate, ON *urthr* weird, fate, OE *weorthan* to become]

Welsh See WALNUT.
[ME *walisch, welisch,* fr. OE (northern & Midland dial.) *wælisc, welisc* Celtic, Welsh, foreign, fr. OE *Walh, Wealh* Celt, Welshman, foreigner (of Celt origin; akin to the source of L *Volcae,* a Celtic people of southeastern Gaul) + *-isc* -ish]

werewolf See MAN.
[ME, fr. OE *werewulf, werwulf;* akin to MD *weerwolf,* OHG *werwolf;* all fr. a prehistoric WGmc compound whose constituents are represented by OE *wer* man and OE *wulf* wolf]

whippoorwill See PIGEON.
[imit.]

whiskey   Of the relatively few English words that have come from the Celtic languages, certainly one of the most common is *whiskey*. The Irish Gaelic *uisce beathadh* and Scots Gaelic *uisge beatha,* terms for certain distilled liquors made in those countries, can both be translated literally as "water of life." Though *whiskeybae* and *usquebaugh* have both been used in English, the shorter *whiskey* (or *whisky*) is by far the most common form.

In sixteenth-century England *aqua vitae,* taken without change from the Medieval Latin phrase meaning 'water of life', first appears as a term for a distilled alcoholic drink, though as early as 1471 it had been used for medicinal alcohol. From the same Medieval Latin source comes Swedish, Danish, and Norwegian *akvavit,* which is used in English in the form *aquavit* as the name for a clear Scandinavian liquor flavored with caraway seeds. English has also borrowed the French translation of Latin *aqua vitae* in the form *eau-de-vie* as a term for brandy.

The name *bourbon* which designates some American whiskeys comes from the name of *Bourbon* County, Kentucky, where such *whiskey* was first made in the late eighteenth century. See also BRANDY, GIN.

[modif. of IrGael *uisce beathadh* & ScGael *uisge beatha,* lit., water of life, respectively fr. and akin to OIr *uisce* water + *bethad,* gen. of *bethu* life; akin to Gk *hydōr* water and to Gk *bios* life, mode of life]

wiener   See HAMBURGER.
[short for *wienerwurst,* fr. G *Wiener* of Vienna (fr. *Wien* Vienna) + *wurst* sausage]

wife   See WOMAN.
[ME *wif,* fr. OE *wīf;* akin to OHG *wīb* woman, wife, ON *vīf* woman; perh. akin to ON *veipr* head covering]

willy-nilly   See HOBNOB.
[alter. of *will I nill I* or *will he nill he* or *will ye nill ye*]

wimp   Slang is born away from the light; its birth is often a mystery. Such is the case with *wimp,* denoting a 'nerd', a 'nebbish', an 'ineffectual also-ran'. Several origins have been suggested:

1. We may start with the acronymic origin from "Weak-kneed, Impudent, Moronic Palooka." In many cases, and certainly in this one, such explanations are dreamed up after the fact. (See also ACRONYMIC ETYMOLOGIES.) After *wimp* was already established as a slang term, it was recycled as a quasi-acronym both in physics, applied to a "Weakly Interacting Massive Particle," and in computer science, denoting an interface of "Windows, Icons, Mouse, and Pull-down (menu)."

2. It has been put forward that *wimp,* like *jeep* (which see), might be another gift of the Thimble Theater, named after Popeye's sidekick Wimpy. If so, the denomination was superficial, taking off from his mild-mannered appearance and usually peaceable demeanor. But one would not have

taken him for a prototypical wimp after witnessing the feats of which he
is capable when properly motivated by the prospect of hamburgers.

3. *Wimp* is spottily attested as school slang for 'girl' in England beginning in the early part of this century. If this use contributed to the denigra-
tory application of the word to males, it is an animadversion of a familiar
sort, in the mold of *Nancy boy* or *sissie* (from *sis,* from *sister*). But the modern use of *wimp* mushroomed on the American side of the Atlantic in the
1960s, and the gap is not well bridged by isolated uses of *wimp* in the
post–World War I years. The word may well have been recoined at various
times in various senses.

4. The most usual suggestion is to derive *wimp* from *whimper.* While
wimp may not stem from *whimper* by any process strictly to be called derivation, it seems more than likely that *whimper* has contributed to the
spread and acceptance of *wimp,* supporting its semantics by a phonetic
reminiscence. Indeed, *wimp* has found its semantic path smoothed before
it by a group of *-imp* words, most of them pejorative or patronizing:
gimp(y); pimp, primp, simp; crimp, skimp; shrimp.

The noun *wimp,* now well-established, has produced numerous derivatives, from adjectives:

> Toy dogs are difficult, because it is very easy to make little wimpy,
> simpering idiots out of them —Sue Lackey, quoted in *Dog World,* 12
> Dec. 1983

to simple and phrasal verbs:

> The hardliners assail the spinelessness of the . . . leadership. "They
> wimped and waffled from day one," snaps George K. Bernstein, a
> leading industrial lawyer —Peter W. Bernstein et al., *Fortune,* 25 July
> 1983

> Fears that industrial policy could be a political albatross are pushing
> some Democrats to fuzz the issue rather than make it specific. . . .
> If the Democrats wimp out on this issue, they will lack any coherent
> vision —Norman Jonas, *Business Week,* 21 Nov. 1983

to derived noun compounds:

> It boggles the mind that survival of the fittest can terminate in such
> wimphood —*National Rev.,* 20 June 1986

We can get a sense of where *wimp* fits in semantically from passages
where it is used in company with near-synonyms:

> This despite his reputation among British women as a "twit," a "wet"
> or a "wally," all of which can be freely translated as "wimp" —*People,*
> 12 Mar. 1984

> Maybe do a bit of serious drag-racing on the Strip: Pull up to that big
> stoplight in front of the Flamingo and start screaming at the traffic:
> "Alright, you . . . wimps! You pansies! . . . I'm gonna stomp down on

this thing and blow every one of you gutless punks off the road!"
—Hunter S. Thompson, *Fear and Loathing in Las Vegas,* 1971

Here, as often, there is a suggestion that the person so described was out
of the room when the testosterone was being handed out. The word thus
refers prototypically to males but has been used as well of women:

. . . Caroline lies on her bed a lot, berating herself for being such a
self-pitying wimp —Nancy Evans, *N.Y. Times Book Rev.,* 11 Nov.
1984

The exact semantics of the word are complex, richly flavored by the social
assumptions of our age. *Wimp* has come to be applied to many who in
other days would not have been described as especially cowardly, lacklus-
ter, or out of it:

BEST CONGRESS MONEY CAN BUY stories have grown so familiar
in recent years that they have lost their power to scandalize and are
now thought of as the naive complaints of good-government wimps
—Gregg Easterbrook, *Atlantic,* December 1984

Yes, we're beefing up for the Eighties. Not for us the wimpy Zen
forms of self-defense like aikido and karate. No, we've got something
much simpler. Guns —Robert Cooke Goolrick, *Metropolitan Home,*
September 1982

Neither political reformers nor martial arts enthusiasts nor any of the
other people *wimp* is being associated with are in themselves especially
suggestive of wilting wallflowers. They simply fail to match the competition bullet for bullet and blade for blade. *Wimp,* we may say, now denotes
the meek who, in these ruthless times, fail to inherit a piece of the action.

[perh. fr. Brit. slang *wimp* girl, woman, of unknown origin]

window   Many native English words in common use during the Old English period have been replaced by foreign borrowings. Two especially
strong influences on the English vocabulary have been the Scandinavian
and the French. From the eighth to the eleventh century, Norsemen settled in the north of Britain and made raids into much of the island. The
close contact between English-speaking and Norse-speaking peoples and
the historical relationship between the languages provided an ideal climate for mutual borrowing. In the period following the Norman Conquest, French was the language of the upper classes and of much official
discourse in England, and as a result many French words entered the English language. The history of our words for 'window' shows these foreign
influences at work.

Eagthyrel, 'eye-thirl', a compound of *eage,* 'eye', and *thyrel,* 'hole', was
the usual Old English word for 'window'. *Thirl* is still used as a word for
'hole' in some dialects of English, but it survives in standard Modern English only in the word *nostril,* the descendant of Old English *nosthyrel,*
'nose-hole'. Unlike *nosthyrel,* Old English *eagthyrel* was not usually used
to designate a facial feature. From the early Middle English *Ancrene Riwle*

(about 1225), however, we learn that "thurh eie thurles death haueth hire ingong into the soule." (Through eye holes death has its entrance into the soul.) It was about this time that the Old English word was being replaced by a Scandinavian borrowing. In fact, different manuscripts of the *Ancrene Riwle* contain both the latest attested use of *eye-thirl* and the earliest of *window. Window* comes from Old Norse *vindauga*, literally 'wind's eye'. During the Middle English period, *window* had no further competition from *eye-thirl*, but it was still not absolutely assured of the prominent place it holds in Modern English. In the late thirteenth century English borrowed the Old French *fenestre*, a derivative of Latin *fenestra*. William Caxton, in his translation of the *Golden Legende* (1483), apparently unable to decide which of two standard English words he should use, opted for redundancy: "Thyse thre fenestres or wyndowes betokene clerely the fader the sone and the holy ghoost." *Fenestre* or *fenester* was not finally conquered by *window* until the mid-sixteenth century. *Defenestration* is a Modern English relative of the defunct *fenestre*.

[ME *windowe*, fr. ON *vindauga*, fr. *vindr* wind, air + *auga* eye]

winter   See AUTUMN.
[ME, fr. OE; akin to OHG *wintar*, ON *vetr*, Goth *wintrus*, and prob. to OE *wæter* water]

wiseacre   The process of folk etymology assimilates the form of a puzzling or unfamiliar word to that of a more common word, but it is not always possible to say why any particular change takes place other than because of the obvious similarity in sound. Similarity of meaning may also enter into the process, but such is not the case with *wiseacre*, which first took the form *wiseaker* in English. The word has nothing to do with the measuring of land, though very soon after its introduction into English in the late sixteenth century puns based on the identical sounds in *-aker* and *acre* were being made. The meaning of *wiseacre* in English is an ironic adaptation of the meaning of its source, for in Middle Dutch *wijssegger* means 'soothsayer' while in English a *wiseacre* is most often a smart aleck or one who pretends to have knowledge.

Actually the process of folk etymology has operated twice in the long history of this word. The Old High German *wīzzago* was a prophet or soothsayer. His name was only distantly related to *wīs*, the Old High German word for 'wise', and had nothing at all to do with saying. But the word was altered in Middle Dutch to *wijssegger*, as if it were formed from *wijs*, 'wise', and *segger*, 'sayer'. After all, it is not so fanciful to consider a prophet a "wise-sayer." Then when English borrowed the word, folk etymology altered it once more.

For additional folk etymologies see FOLK ETYMOLOGY.

[MD *wijssegger* soothsayer, modif. (influenced by MD *segger* sayer, fr. *seggen* to say + *-er*) of OHG *wīzzago* prophet; akin to OE *wītega* wise man, *wītan* to observe, see to, reproach]

wit   *Wit* is one of our native stock of words, with cognates in such sister languages as Old High German, Old Norse, and Gothic, and it is related in Old English to such familiar words as *wise, wisdom,* and *witness.* Back through the mists of time it is even cognate with the Greek root of *idea.*

We are not certain which meaning of *wit* is the oldest. One of the two possibilities is 'the mind', a meaning not impossible in the twentieth century, as when one observer notes the impossibility of a modern person's entering the wit of a Neanderthal. This is the sense used by Sir Francis Bacon in his essay "Of Studies" (published in 1625). In this essay, after describing various exercises as good for various parts of the body, he says "So if a Mans Wit be Wandering, let him *Study* the *Mathematicks;* For in Demonstrations, if his Wit be called away never so little, he must begin again." This *wit* could also be used for a function of the mind, such as memory or attention; indeed Bacon's second use of *wit* above could be interpreted as 'attention'.

The other possibility for the oldest meaning is 'the faculty of thinking and reasoning, power of reasoning, intelligence'. Shakespeare's Bottom, in *A Midsummer Night's Dream* (ca. 1595), knows this sense: "I have had a dream, past the wit of man to say what dream it was." This meaning is still alive, especially in the phrase "at one's wit's end"—although most people today think *wit's* is plural and put the apostrophe after the *s.*

There were early uses of the plural too. Among the late medieval theories that vaguely relate to physiology, psychology, and medicine was one that ascribed to humans five inward wits and five outward wits. The five outward wits are better known nowadays as the five senses. The five inward ones were, according to English poet Stephen Hawes in 1509, common wit (common sense), imagination, fantasy, estimation, and memory. These five wits are referred to now and again by Shakespeare:

> *Mercutio.* . . . . Thou hast more of the wild goose in one of thy wits than, I am sure, I have in my whole five —*Romeo and Juliet,* ca. 1594

Another plural sense, in use from the fourteenth century or earlier, is roughly equivalent to the earliest singular meanings ('the mind', 'reasoning ability'), though it is regularly used as a plural. This use is familiar still in expressions like "keep your wits about you" and "scared out of my wits."

It is not stretching *wit* very far from 'mind' and 'intelligence' to those attributes characteristic of an active mind or intelligence: intellectual ability, inventive power, talent, cleverness, ingenuity. This *wit* could be used of demonstrations of practical ingenuity, but more often it was used for mental ability or facility. We find it in Shakespeare's *Measure for Measure* (ca. 1604), where a magistrate, finding out that Elbow has served as constable for seven and a half years, asks him if there are not other men in his ward who might serve in the post. "Faith, sir, few of any wit in such matters," answers Elbow.

A common application of the neutral facility *wit* was to literary folk. It connoted a kind of inventive talent, as when Thomas Shadwell commented that "there is more wit and inventions requir'd in finding out good Humor, and Matter proper for it, [than] in all their smart reparties" (preface to *The Sullen Lovers,* 1668). The word was applied to the person possessing this talent (as *wit* was indeed applied to persons possessing the faculty in other meanings), as when John Dryden in his "Essay of Dramatic Poesy" (1668) said that Ben Jonson was "the more correct poet, but Shakespeare the greater wit." This literary *wit* was commonly contrasted with *judgment,* the quality Dryden saw in Ben Jonson.

Literary *wit* was the subject of considerable discussion in the public print, mostly by way of defining and redefining. All writers using the word thus seemed to be concerned to fence off their use of *wit* from a growing popular use: 'word play' or 'facility at word play'. The popular use was not brand new; Shakespeare knew it and used it:

> You must not, sir, mistake my niece. There is a kind of merry war betwixt Signior Benedick and her. They never meet but there's a skirmish of wit between them —*Much Ado About Nothing*

It is this word-play kind of wit that Shadwell is writing about in his abovementioned preface, where he complains of some people who imagine "that all the wit in *Playes* consisted in bringing two persons upon the Stage to break Jests, and to bob one another, which they call Repartie. . . ." Dryden weighed in on the subject too: ". . . the lowest and most groveling kind of wit, which we call clenches [puns] . . ." ("Defence of The Epilogue," 1672).

Shakespeare's fondness for puns lowered him some in the estimation of the more decorous seventeenth- and eighteenth-century critics, many of whom were at pains to keep *wit* 'pun' out of their backyard. Joseph Addison bent to this task in two consecutive numbers of *The Spectator* in 1711. He put the pun in the class of false wit. Of course he was at some pains to explain what true wit was:

> . . . every Resemblance of Ideas is not that which we call Wit, unless it be such an one that gives *Delight* and *Surprize* to the Reader; These two Properties seem essential to Wit, more particularly the last of them.

In the same year, Alexander Pope also defined *wit* in a famous couplet from his "Essay on Criticism":

> True Wit is Nature to advantage dress'd,
> What oft was thought but ne'er so well express'd.

Addison added a third species of wit which he calls *mixt wit,* which for him partook of the word play of false wit and the surprising concourse of ideas of true wit. *Mixt wit* was Addison's term for the wit and conceits of the metaphysical poets of the preceding century. Whether Addison actually noticed puns and word play in the poetry of the metaphysicals we may doubt. Samuel Johnson, from a vantage point more than a half-century later, was struck by their yoking of heterogeneous ideas. In his *Life of Cowley* (1783) he described what we call metaphysical wit as "a kind of *discordia concors;* a combination of dissimilar images, or discovery of occult resemblances in things apparently unlike."

The metaphysical poets were at the nadir of their critical reputation at the time Johnson wrote. Their stock has risen considerably since then, and the continued study of their poetry has served to keep *wit* in its metaphysical connection alive. The loftier *wit* that the critics and poets tried to protect from Shakespeare's word-play *wit* has gone, and what earlier critics would have called *false wit* is for most people today the only kind of wit.

[ME, fr. OE; akin to OHG *wizzi* knowledge, understanding, wit, ON *vit*, Goth -*witi* knowledge, OE *witan* to know]

wolfram   See COBALT.

[G, alter. (influenced by *wolf* wolf) of *wolffram, wolform, volfram*, of unknown origin]

woman   People occasionally express the belief that *woman* is a compound made from *womb* and *man*, but it is not. *Woman* derives from Old English *wīfman*, a compound formed from Old English *wīf* 'woman' and *man* 'human being'. (This is the predominant meaning of *man* in Old English. See also MAN.) *Wīfman* descended to Middle English with the *f* blended into the *m* by assimilation as *wimman* with a plural *wimmen*. In various dialects *wimman* became *wummon, wumman, wommon*, and *womman*. All of these developments in Middle English seem to have had some influence on the mismatched spelling and pronunciation of modern *woman, women.*

The oldest word in English for 'woman' is *wīf*. Its male counterpart was *wer*. Quite early in Old English *wīf* developed its prevalent modern meaning 'married woman'. It was presumably the growth of this sense that resulted in the compound *wīfman* becoming the word for 'woman' that would survive into Modern English. In Middle English *wife* developed a meaning 'mistress of a household, hostess or landlady of an inn'. The Middle English sense survives in the compound *housewife;* the original sense survives in *old wives' tale* and in compounds like *midwife.*

[ME *woman, wumman, wimman, wimmon, wifmon*, fr. OE *wīfmon, wīfman*, fr. *wīf* woman, wife + *mon, man* man]

workaholic   When the word *alcoholic* first appeared in English around the end of the eighteenth century, it was used as an adjective meaning 'of, relating to, or having the characteristics of alcohol'. Its first use as a noun, around 1870, was in the plural to denote 'alcoholic liquors'. This sense evidently never caught on; however, about 1890 we find *alcoholic* used in the sense 'one addicted to alcoholic drinks', which is still the noun's main use.

In 1968 an American pastoral counselor, Wayne Oates, coined the word *workaholic*, modeled on *alcoholic*, to describe 'a compulsive worker'. He popularized his coinage through his 1971 publication, *Confessions of a Workaholic.* Journalists picked up the word very quickly, and it was soon being used in newspapers and magazines throughout the country, as well as in Great Britain and Australia. *Workaholic* has spawned about a dozen or so similarly formed words to describe persons who are compulsive about a particular activity or have a strong craving for something in particular. Most of these coinages will probably prove to be ephemeral, but a few (such as *chocoholic, bookaholic, computerholic,* and *phoneaholic*) may have enough life left in them to survive.

[¹*work* + connective -*a*- + -*holic* (as in *alcoholic*)]

worry See STRAITEN.
[ME *wirien, werien, worien* to strangle, worry with the teeth, fr. OE *wyrgan* to strangle; akin to OHG *wurgen* to strangle, ON *virgill* halter, Lith *veržti* to constrict, press, OE *wringan* to wring]

wowser *Wowser* is a colorful term that designates such notions as are found in *bluenose, comstock,* and *prohibitionist.* The word seems to have first seen the light of day in Sydney, Australia, near the end of the nineteenth century. The earliest citation is from an October 1899 edition of *Truth,* a radical Sunday newspaper published in Sydney: "Willoughby 'Wowsers' Worried. The 'Talent' get a 'Turn'. . . ." *Truth* in 1899 was owned and edited by John Norton (1858–1916), a colorful muckraker and scandalmonger whose personal preference for pungent purple prose and elaborate strings of alliterative epithets is frequently evident in the newspaper.

Wowser was an instant hit in Australia, where it continues in common use. It spread quickly to New Zealand—it is still used there—and was brought to England by Australian troops during World War I. H. L. Mencken said it had a considerable vogue in England for a couple of years but then dropped out. It is still occasionally seen in English publications such as *The Economist.* Mencken liked the word and tried to introduce it into American English. He used it with considerable frequency in the pages of the *American Mercury* in 1926, 1927, and 1928, in contexts like this one:

> It led to the attempted suppression of the magazine by the Boston wowsers —*American Mercury,* August 1927

In the fourth edition of *The American Language* (1936) Mencken admitted failure, but he actually shortchanged himself a little. While *wowser* has never become popular in American English, it is still used once in a while.

From the beginning there was considerable curiosity about the origin of *wowser.* The first speculations appeared in the Australian press around 1910; they were, as one might suspect, rather fanciful. A writer in the Sydney *Telegraph* that year (8 May) came up with this improbable explanation:

> One is that it arose from the Round Heads raising their hands and crying "Woe, sir!" when they saw a Loyalist kissing a pretty maid or draining a tankard of ale. Another theory, however, ascribes the origin to a Loyalist crying out, "Whoa, sir!" when he observed a Puritan drinking off a jug of beer. . . .

Somewhat later speculation suggested its derivation from Old English *wissor* 'teacher'; Mencken wondered if it derived from a native Australian language. The Sydney *Bulletin* in 1925 said that although John Norton claimed to have invented the word he only imported it from England, where it was "a mere colloquial obscenity" in the English Midlands. And, as often happens with short words of obscure origin, an unsupported acronymic theory was advanced. *Wowser,* the acronymicists say, derives from the slogan of an unspecified group of reformers: *We Only Want Social Evils Righted* (or *Remedied* or *Removed*).

John Norton did claim the invention:

> I invented the word myself. I was the first man to publicly use the word. I first gave it public utterance in the City Council, when I applied it to Alderman Waterhouse, whom I referred to—I hope and believe with perfect good humor, and without gall or guile—as "the white, woolly, weary, watery, word-wasting Wowser from Waverly."
> —*Truth,* Sydney, Australia, 21 Jan. 1912

Not one to hide his light under a bushel, he goes on in the same article:

> To my humble self—to me, John Norton—alone belongs the sole undivided glory and honor of inventing a word, a single, simple word, that does at once describe, deride, and denounce that numerous, noxious, pestilent, puritanical kill-joy push—the whole blasphemous, wire-whiskered brood—who, before I baptised them, went about and abroad, mendaciously masquerading as followers of the Good God.
> . . .

None of the foregoing theories has much support. The acronymic organization cannot be found, nor the aboriginal word, nor the Midlands obscenity (Norton came from the south of England, not the Midlands, anyway), nor the connection with Old English *wisser.* Norton's modestly phrased claim to the invention is supported at least to the extent that *wowser* first appeared in print in his paper. If he did coin it, the *wow* may have been suggested by an English dialectal verb *wow* meaning 'to bark or howl like a dog' and 'whine, grumble, complain'. The *-ser* may have been suggested by the rhyming *Towser,* name for a dog. (Curiously, "wire-haired Towser" contrasts with "wire-haired Wowser" on the same page of *Truth* on which Norton claims the coinage.)

[origin unknown]

write   See SNEAK.
[ME *writen,* fr. OE *wrītan* to scratch, draw, engrave, write; akin to OS *wrītan* to tear, wound, scratch, write, OHG *rīzan* to tear, ON *rīta* to write on parchment, Goth *writs* stroke, letter, Gk *rhinē* file, rasp, Skt *vrana* wound, tear, *vṛhati* he tears, plucks; basic meaning: incision, tearing]

X

xenon The British chemist Sir William Ramsay was deeply involved in the discovery or isolation of a complete group of elements including *xenon* among others, the so-called *noble gases.* In 1894 he and Lord Rayleigh, a noted British physicist, discovered a gas which they thought did not form any chemical compounds with other elements. Because of its inert quality, it was named *argon,* from Greek *argos,* 'idle' or 'lazy'. *Helium* (from Greek *helios,* 'sun') had already been detected in the sun in 1868, and in 1895 Sir William discovered its presence on Earth. Because of the position of these gases in the periodic table of elements, Ramsay reasoned that several others ought to exist, and in 1898 he and his associates discovered and named three new ones—*neon,* from the Greek *neos,* 'new'; *krypton,* from *kryptos,* 'hidden'; and *xenon,* from *xenos,* 'strange'. Xenon was assigned its name because it was thought to be extremely rare. In 1900 Sir William discovered another element and so completed this portion of the periodic table. Because of its phosphorescent qualities this gas was originally called *niton,* from Latin *nitēre,* 'to shine', but since it is formed by the disintegration of radium it has come to be called *radon.*

[Gk, neut. of *xenos* strange]

Xmas Since the sixteenth century *Xmas* has been used in English as an abbreviation for *Christmas. X* as a symbol for Christ derives from the Greek where *chi* (X) is the initial letter of *Christos,* the Greek form of *Christ.* The word *Xmas* is usually pronounced like *Christmas,* although a pronunciation of the letter *x* plus *-mas* as in *Christmas* is also heard. Other similar abbreviations used today are *Xn* for *Christian* and *Xnty* for *Christianity,* although *Xmas* is met with more frequently than these.

In Latin manuscripts *Christus* was often abbreviated by using the first two letters of Greek *Christos, chi* (X) and *rho* (P). This abbreviation is prominent, for example, on the beautiful chi-rho pages of early medieval illuminated manuscripts like *The Book of Kells* and *The Lindisfarne Gospels.* When *chi* and *rho* are superimposed upon each other a symbol for *Christ* is formed which has had wide currency through the centuries of the Christian era. This symbol is known variously as a *Chi-Rho, chrismon,* or *Christogram.*

The name *Jesus* gave rise to another confusing symbol in similar fashion. The first three letters of the Greek version of the name were written in Greek capitals as "ΙΗΣ" (iota eta sigma). Greek sigma corresponds to Latin *s,* and the monogram was Latinized as "IHS"—or rather half-Latinized, since in Greek the "H", as eta, denotes a vowel (long \e\), whereas in classical Latin it denoted \h\. But Greek "H" is nevertheless the origin of the written Latin character and was allowed to remain in this now somewhat mysterious symbol still used by Christians today.

[X (symbol for *Christ,* fr. the Gk letter chi (X), initial letter of *Christos* Christ) + *-mas* (in *Christmas*), fr. OE *mæsse* mass]

X ray   On 8 November 1895, Wilhelm Conrad Röntgen was conducting an experimental investigation in Würzburg, Germany, of the properties of cathode rays. He noticed that a fluorescent surface in the neighborhood of a cathode-ray tube would become luminous even if shielded from the direct light of the tube. A thick metal object placed between the tube and the affected surface impaired the fluorescence and cast a dark shadow. An object made of a less dense substance like wood cast only a weak shadow. Röntgen's explanation for this phenomenon was that the tube produced some type of invisible radiation which could pass through substances that could block ordinary visible light. Because he did not know the nature of this radiation he had discovered, he named it *x-strahl,* which was translated into English as *X ray. X rays* are sometimes called *roentgen rays,* after their discoverer (the German umlauted *ö* is often written as *oe* in English), and the *roentgen* is the international unit of X-radiation.

The standard use of the letter *x* to designate an unknown quantity goes back to the practice of René Descartes, seventeenth-century French mathematician and philosopher. Descartes, in his book *La géométrie* (1637), used the first letters of the alphabet for known quantities and the final letters, *x, y, z* (and most commonly *x*), for unknowns. Later mathematicians have simply followed Descartes's example.

[trans. of G *x-strahl*]

Y

yacht In the sixteenth century the Dutch began building light, fast-moving ships designed to chase the ships of pirates and smugglers away from the Dutch coast. The Dutch appropriately called this type of sailing vessel a *jaght,* which is a derivative of the Middle Low German word for a fast, light sailing vessel, *jachtschiff,* meaning literally 'hunting ship'. *Jacht-* comes from the verb *jagen,* 'to hunt'. The ship was introduced into England in 1660 when the Dutch East India Company presented one to King Charles II, who used it as a pleasure boat. The ship's design was copied by British shipbuilders for those wealthy gentlemen who desired and could afford such pleasure craft. *Yacht* ultimately became the established spelling in English, having won out over various other renditions, such as *yeogh, yoath, yaught,* and *jacht.* In the nineteenth century, yacht clubs were founded at various points along the coasts of both England and America. Today international yacht racing generally includes all types of sailboats, but the term *yacht* is often applied to any luxurious boat—powerboat as well as sailboat—that is designed for pleasure cruising.

[earlier *yaught,* fr. obs. D *yaght* (now *jacht*), fr. MLG *jacht,* short for *jachtschiff, jageschiff* light sailing vessel, fast pirate ship, lit., hunting ship, fr. *jacht-, jage* hunt (fr. *jagen* to hunt, fr. OHG *jagōn*) + *schiff* ship, fr. OHG *skif;* akin to OFris *jagia* to hunt and perh. to Skt *yahu* restless, swift, strong]

Yahweh See JEEPERS.
[NL, fr. Heb *Yhwh*]

Yankee A great many etymologies have been proposed for *Yankee,* but its origin is still uncertain. Etymologizing on it began as early as 1789 and according to one researcher reached a peak around 1850. Many of the old speculations are still afloat, and we will take a look at some of them.

William Gordon, in *The History of the American War,* 1789, finds its origin in the favorite word of a Cambridge, Massachusetts, farmer known as "Yankee Jonathan" and "Yankee Hastings" from his use of *yankee* of everything he approved. Hastings is recorded as early as 1775 by the nickname but for chronological purposes is supposed to have been using his favorite expression as early as 1713. This explanation has two serious drawbacks. *Yankee* is first recorded in America as a contemptuous term for the colonials used by the British, and how Farmer Hastings's term of approval could become a British pejorative no one says. Nor does anyone really know where Yankee Jonathan's term of approval came from.

An observer named Thomas Anburey, a British Army officer who had served with Gen. John Burgoyne in trying to suppress American independence, provided an explanation in 1789. *Yankee*, he said, came from a Cherokee word *eankke* 'slave, coward'. But there turns out to be no such word in the Cherokee language. Around 1775, after the battles of Lexington and Concord, when *Yankee* began to be adopted in defiance by the colonials, the origin was laid to an Indian tribe, the Yankos, whose name meant 'conquerors'. The Yanko tribe, however, was entirely mythical. Washington Irving, in his *Knickerbocker's History of New York*, 1809, proposed another Indian word:

> The simple aborigines of the land for a while contemplated these strange folk [of Connecticut] in utter astonishment, but discovering that they wielded harmless though noisy weapons, and were a lively, ingenious, good-humoured race of men, they became very friendly and sociable, and gave them the name of *Yanokies*, which in the Mais-Tchusaeg (or Massachusett) language signifies *silent men*—a waggish appellation, since shortened into the present familiar epithet of YANKEES, which they retain unto the present day.

This is all obviously facetious and mildly satirical, but it seems nevertheless to have been taken seriously by some people. *Yanokie*, like *eankke*, too, has not been found in any known Indian language. In 1819 the Rev. John Heckewelder brought forward the theory that *yankee* resulted from the Indians' attempts to pronounce *English* (or, in some versions, *Anglais*). The Indian word is variously given as *Yengees, Yengeese, Yenkees, Yaunghees, Yenghis, Yanghis,* and *Yinglees*. James Fenimore Cooper was one of those that espoused this theory (he used the spelling *Yengeese* in 1848). But the Indians, it seems, used their own words to designate Englishmen. The Indians, then, can probably be absolved of responsibility for *Yankee*.

British dialects, too, have been mentioned as sources. *Yankee* is supposed to have been a Lincolnshire dialect word for gaiters or leggings made of undressed leather that was brought in by immigrants from that region. Or it is said to come from a Scots *yankie* 'a sharp, clever, forward woman' or a Scots adjective *yanking* 'active, pushing, thoroughgoing'. Another English dialect word *jank* 'excrement' has also been considered; unfortunately this *j* was pronounced \j\ and not \y\.

The most far-fetched suggestion derived *Yankee* from a Persian word *janghe* or *jenghe* 'warlike man, swift horse'. The suggestion first surfaced in 1810 in a Boston-published review and, though it has been taken seriously, it turns out to have been a hoax. The article was intended as a parody of the philological writing of Noah Webster. The interest in the origin of the word must have been strong indeed, if some people believed such assertions as the equation of *Jenghis Khan* with *Yankee King*.

Dutch is also frequently cited as a possible source of *Yankee*. One speculation would derive it from a term *Yankers* 'wranglers' which Dutch merchants were supposed to have called American traders because of their tough, argumentative trading practices. This *Yanker* is presumably derived from the Dutch verb *janken,* which means, however, not 'to wrangle' but 'to howl, yelp, whine'. (The Dutch equivalent of English *wrangle* is *krakeelen.*) Another Dutch etymon that has been suggested is *jonkheer,* a title of respect. The speculation runs that it might have been used sarcastically of Dutch pirates by traders of other nationalities (presumably knowing some Dutch), or in various other circumstances. None of these circumstances has been documented, however. *Jonkheer* may have given us *Yonkers,* New York, but it probably did not produce *Yankee.*

Two other Dutch possibilities, both nicknames, have garnered greater support in philological circles. They are supported by the appearance of *Yankey* as a proper name or nickname for a Dutch pirate operating in the West Indies in *The Calendar of State Papers, Colonial Series,* for 1683. It appears again in the same source in 1684 and 1687 and as *Yanky* in another report of 1687–1688. Clearly there was some Dutch term that the English reproduced as *Yankey.*

The first proposal is based on Dutch *Janke,* a diminutive of *Jan* 'John'. This was supposed to have been a common nickname of Dutch sailors. The existence of this diminutive has been challenged by a Dutch scholar who points out that the real diminutive of *Jan* is *Jantje,* pronounced approximately \ˈyänt-yǝ\. The American Minister to Holland in a letter drafted in March 1864, however, said that *Jantje* could easily be mistaken for or corrupted into *Yankee;* he found a slight sound of *k* imparted to the *tj* by the Dutch. This theory still has its proponents.

The second theory finds the origin in *Jan Kees,* which is either a dialectal (East Frisian) version of *Jan Kaas* 'John Cheese' or is a diminutive form of *Jan Cornelius,* commonly paired names in Dutch. The -s at the end is presumed to have sounded like a plural to English ears, and was pruned off to produce a singular. The *Jan Kees* theory, which was first proposed by Dr. Henri Logeman of the University of Ghent, has drawn the approval of more philologists, including H. L. Mencken and W. W. Skeat, than any other theory. It is not without its difficulties, however. *Kees,* regardless of its spelling, must have sounded like *case* when pronounced in Dutch. And two-part nicknames in Dutch seem to receive their main stress on the second part, while *Yankee* has first-syllable stress.

And we do not know how it might have come from being a name or nickname for a Dutch pirate to being a general pejorative term for New Englanders. Mencken suggests that the freebooter sense became known to the New York Dutch, who then applied it to their northern neighbors in Connecticut, "whose commercial enterprise ran far beyond their moral scruples." But, as we have seen earlier, Washington Irving in satirizing his northern neighbors in Connecticut invented an Indian source for *Yankee.* You are permitted to have your doubts.

We do know that the earliest recorded use of *Yankee* on this continent is as a pejorative term for American colonials used by the British military. The first evidence we have is in a letter written by General James Wolfe in 1758; he had a very low opinion of the American troops assigned to him.

We also have a 1775 report of British troops using the term to abuse citizens of Boston, young and old.

In 1775, after the battles of Lexington and Concord had shown the colonials that they could stand up to British regulars, *Yankee* became suddenly respectable. The colonials adopted *Yankee* in defiance and, as you recall, even invented the Yanko Indians to give it a pedigree. The same co-optation of the British sneer took place with the song "Yankee Doodle," and the adoption of the song may have helped establish the prideful use of *Yankee*. And ever since then two uses of *Yankee* have existed side by side—a derisive use and a respectable use.

Yankee, then, is first attested as an English rendering of the name or nickname of some Dutch pirates operating in the Caribbean. It is not attested again for some seventy years, when it turns up as a British pejorative applied to Americans. We do not know how it developed during that time, nor can we even be fully certain that there is an unbroken line of development.

[origin unknown]

yarborough   See DERBY.
[after Charles Anderson Worsley, 2nd Earl of *Yarborough* †1897 Eng. nobleman who was said to have bet a thousand to one against the dealing of such a hand]

yard   See COHORT.
[ME *yard, yerd, yerde*, fr. OE *geard* enclosure, court, yard; akin to OHG *gart* enclosure, *garto* garden, ON *garthr* yard, Goth *gards* house, L *hortus* garden, Gk *chortos* farmyard, Skt *grṭha* house, *harati* he takes; basic meaning: to gird, enclose]

ye   One of the most beautiful illustrated manuscripts of the early Middle Ages is the *Lindisfarne Gospels*, a codex of the four Latin Gospels copied around 700. Lindisfarne is an island (now called Holy Island) just off the east coast of Northumberland, where in 635 the Irish monk St. Aidan founded a monastery. About 950 another monk, Aldred, added a word-by-word interlinear translation of the Latin text into Old English. The pronoun *ẏᴈ* (*ge* in Old English but with the *g* pronounced \y\) is first recorded in this translation. In Old English and early Middle English this pronoun was used for the second person plural in the nominative case (as its modern descendant is in "Ye are the salt of the earth" —Mt. 5:13, AV). This use still survives archaically and in dialects. The form *ēow* (Modern English *you*) was used in the oblique (accusative and dative) cases as the object of a verb or preposition. Toward the end of the thirteenth century, *ye* also began to be used as a singular pronoun in the nominative case, a usage also surviving archaically and in dialects (as in "Sweet mother, do ye love the child?" —Alfred Lord Tennyson, "Gareth and Lynette," 1872). By the middle of the sixteenth century, the distinction between *ye* and *you* began breaking down, and the two forms became interchangeable. In the seventeenth century, however, *ye* is much more often found in object positions (as in "All of ye" —Thomas Shadwell, *The Sullen Lovers*, 1668).

In the eighteenth century, as *you* took over as the usual second person pronoun in all functions, *ye* survived in elevated literary use (and not just in dialect). Undoubtedly some of this elevated use was liturgical and ceremonial, and this too survives ("Hark ye, O, King Solomon, and all ye who hear me —*Adoptive Rite Ritual—Eastern Star*, rev. ed., 1952). And, of course, it survives in deliberate archaizing, such as in fiction set in the past (" 'Ye are idle, ye are idle,' the Pharaoh reproved them" —Joseph Heller, *God Knows*, 1984).

Not to be confused with the preceding pronoun *ye* is the article *ye*, still found in such business names as Ye Olde Gifte Shoppe. Middle English retained the runic character þ, called a *thorn*, which stood for what the continental alphabets spelled *th*. In fourteenth-century manuscripts, scribes were writing a form of the thorn that was all but indistinguishable from the letter *y*. This may have been a labor-saving device since the thorn occurs in such frequently used words as *the, that, they, them*, etc. Early printers set these forms as they found them, so that the word *the* would appear in print as yᵉ. This form was still commonly used by writers in the nineteenth century. Jane Austen, for example, in a letter of 8 February 1807 wrote ". . . & means to be here on yᵉ 24th. . . ." We are told by various commentators that this *ye* is properly pronounced \thə\ or \thē\, but most people encountering the word today pronounce it as they see it spelled.

[ME *ye, yhe* fr. OE *gē* (suppletive 2d pers. nom. pl. of *thū, thu* thou]

[alter. of OE *þē* the; fr. the fact that in some medieval manuscripts the runic letter þ (th) became indistinguishable from the Roman letter *y* and as the runic letter grew obsolete printers often used the *y* to replace it]

yen Although a *yen* is a strong desire, the word does not suggest urgent, intense need and so is seldom used to describe a drug addict's craving for his drug. But a yen was originally just such a craving. During the eighteenth and nineteenth centuries, China suffered under the encouragement, which amounted to virtual enforcement, of widespread opium addiction by foreign nations whose traders found the drug profitable. In the mid-nineteenth century, many Chinese immigrated to the United States, and the word *in-yăn*, 'craving for opium', came with them. In 1886 a New York police official named Thomas Byrnes wrote of the opium addiction then common in the city: "A friend suffering with the inyun is a man to be avoided." In English the Chinese syllables became assimilated to *yen-yen* after a time. Eventually the apparently unnecessary duplication was abandoned, and the new word *yen* was generalized from a craving for opium to any strong desire.

[obs. E slang *yen-yen* craving for opium, fr. Chin (Cant) *in-yăn*, fr. *in* opium + *yăn* craving]

Yippie   See YUPPIE.
  [alter. (influenced by *yippee*) of *hippie*]

yoga   In the Indo-European language that was the ancestor of English,
Latin, Greek, Sanskrit, and many others, there was a root meaning 'to join',
which in its simplest form can be written *yug-*. We see a reflection of this
root in something close to its Indo-European form in our word *yoga*. *Yoga*
was borrowed from Sanskrit, where it meant literally 'union' (with the divine) and was used more specifically to refer to a program of spiritual discipline to attain this union.

  A native English word that is a close cognate of *yoga* is *yoke*. *Yoke* shows
one of the normal changes that sounds underwent as words evolved from
prehistoric Indo-European times down to the ancient Germanic past and
finally into English: Indo-European *g* becomes Germanic (and thus English) *k*. We see the same change in comparing Latin *genu* 'knee', in which
the prehistoric consonant is unchanged, with English *knee* (the *k* sound
was pronounced in Old English times).

  The Latin word for 'yoke', showing the original *g*, is *iugum* (later also
spelled *jugum* but with the original initial sound \y\). From this was derived *iugulum* (*jugulum*) 'collar-bone', because it is shaped like a small
yoke. The word came to be applied to the area contiguous to the collar-
bone, the throat. This is, then, the ultimate source of our word *jugular*. Another Latin derivative of *jugum* was *conjugalis*, etymologically 'joined' or
'yoked together', the source of our word *conjugal*.

  The root occurs again, less obviously, in Latin *juxta* 'next to', pronounced \'yük-stä\. Here the original \g\ has become a \k\ not by the sort
of sound shift that produced English *yoke* but by assimilation: the \g\, appearing right next to the voiceless sound \s\, lost its voicing and became
\k\. We see this form in our Latin-derived word *juxtaposition*, literally,
'a placing next to'.

  A peculiarity of Indo-European is the insertion of an *n* in the middle of
a root in certain forms. English *stand* versus *stood* gives some idea of what
this variation was like. In Latin *jungere* 'to join' shows this infixed *n*. This
yields the noun of action *junctio* (genitive *junctionis*) which is the source
of our word *junction*.

  Some of these same Latin roots came down to us in altered form after
having passed through the various vicissitudes of sound that characterize
the Romance daughter languages from which we borrowed so many
words. *Jungere*, passing through the Gallic mill, wound up in English as
join, from the ancestor of French *joindre* 'to join'. *Junctus*, the past participle of *jungere*, gave rise to the Spanish word we borrowed as *junta*, literally, 'a group of people joined for a common purpose'. And the preposition
juxta was transformed into Old French and Middle French *juster* and
jouster, etymologically 'to juxtapose, conjoin' and coming to mean 'to
fight', from which we get our word *joust*.

  The strangest looking of the progeny of *yug-* in English are borrowings
from Greek. Greek for 'yoke' was *zygon*, and this is at the base of a number
of English words like *zygote*, a cell formed from the "union" of two ga-
metes. (The Greek form looks somewhat less distant from its Indo-

European source if one reflects that *y* here transcribes Greek upsilon, which was pronounced like French *u* or German *ü*.) An extension of the root yielded *zeugma* 'yoking, joining', which English borrowed in its use as a term of rhetoric, denoting a structure in which two elements are conjoined to bizarre effect, as in "The addict kicked the habit and then the bucket."

[Skt, lit., yoking, union, disciplined activity, fr. *yunakti* he yokes]

yoke See YOGA.
[ME *yok,* fr. OE *geoc;* akin to OHG *joh* yoke, ON *ok* yoke, Goth *juk* yoke (of oxen), L *jugum* yoke, *jungere* to join, Gk *zygon* yoke, *zeugnynai* to yoke, join, Skt *yuga* yoke, *yunakti* he yokes, joins]

yuppie When *yuppie* became a widespread catchword in 1984, it referred to a group that was working hard and doing well and might reasonably be proud of its achievements: educated baby-boomers either on or angling for the fast track. But though the light-hearted word was sometimes used in affectionate mockery, often its use was tinged with envy or even scorn: our citations contain such phrases as "a hypergreedy yuppie life style," "cash-flush Yuppies looking for fast returns," "the ubiquitous, odious yuppie," and "yuppie middle management slimeball." The ill odor of the word spread abroad as far as Italy, where a neo-Fascist group was reported to have put up a billboard denouncing "Yuppies," "Fast Food," and "L'idiozia dell' American Way of Life." The word is invariably explained as an acronym from "young urban professional," and it is certainly true that this phrase is associated with the word in the public's mind. But prior to the coinage of *yuppie* the phrase was not one on everybody's tongue. The success of the coinage and its very confection must be further explained with reference to another model, the previously coined *Yippie.* (See the discussion of targeted acronyms at ACRONYMIC ETYMOLOGIES.)

The Yippies were political radicals of the late 1960s whose most prominent representatives were Abbie Hoffman and Jerry Rubin. The term *Yippie* was also explained as an acronym, from "Youth International Party," but again a prime influence was undoubtedly the previous coinage *hippie.* The apparent connection between *yuppie* and *Yippie* is strengthened by our earliest written attestation of *yuppie,* from 1983, which mentions as would-be chieftain of the yuppie tribe none other than Jerry Rubin, whose political radicalism had mellowed and who was then contemplating the splendor of Wall Street.

Yuppie follows in the tracks of an earlier coinage for a social group, *WASP,* explained as an acronym from "white Anglo-Saxon Protestant" but clearly aiming at the acidulous echo of the earlier word *wasp.* A competing synonym of more purely acronymic derivation was *yumpie,* explained as from 'young upwardly mobile professional', though again probably in large part an alteration of *yuppie. Yuppie* and *yumpie* immediately spawned a spate of imitators: *guppie* ('gay urban professional'; also 'gray yuppie'), *buppie* ('black urban professional'), *yummy* ('young upwardly mobile mother'), *muppie* ('middle-aged yuppie'), and numerous others. None of them has really caught on in general use.

The most successful analogous coinage from this fad was *dink*, for 'double income, no kids'. Here again the success of the coinage is probably not due solely to any high recognition factor for the phrase of origin. Nor is the term truly a renewal of some identifiable earlier word; rather it is a recycling of what seems to be a particularly winning syllable. For *dink* has been used in such varied meanings as 'neat' (and, as a related verb, 'adorn'), 'dinkum' (genuine), 'small boat', 'skullcap', 'drop shot' in tennis (or 'dump-off pass' in football), 'to mess around', 'to cut with a die', and 'to give someone a lift on the bar of a bicycle'. None of these is semantically close enough to the new use of *dink* to have aided in its acceptance. Two other extant uses of *dink* might in fact have impeded acceptance of the new use, since they refer to people and are thus close enough in meaning to yield potential interference or ambiguity: these are the offensive use of *dink* as a disparaging term for an Oriental and its use as an approximate synonym for *nerd*. The flavor of the latter use appears in the following reminiscence from the actor Richard Dreyfuss, recalling the days before he became a cinematic idol:

> Well, I wore glasses. I was kind of chubby and I wasn't an athlete. I was a dink. There's one in every school —quoted in *Women's Wear Daily*, 14 July 1975

This use of *dink* is not widespread and may not have influenced the connotations of the new 'double-income' meaning, but the new use has just as patronizing and potentially biting a tone.

[prob. fr. *y*oung *u*rban *p*rofessional + *-ie*, influenced by *yippie*]

Z

zany In the sixteenth century the Italian theater developed the commedia dell'arte in which comedies were improvised from standard situations and stock characters. One of these stock characters is a subordinate fool, clown, acrobat, or mountebank who mimics ludicrously the tricks of his principal. In Italian the stock name for such a character is *Zanni*, which is a dialect nickname (the dialect is that of Lombardy) derived from the name *Giovanni*, the Italian form of *John*. The earliest known appearance of the word in English is in Shakespeare's *Love's Labours Lost* (ca. 1594) where we hear of "some carry-tale, some pleaseman, some slight Zanie . . ./ That . . . knows the trick/ To make my Lady laugh." By the early seventeenth century in English *zany* had become generalized to mean 'anyone who makes a laughingstock of himself to amuse others', and from this developed the adjectival sense of 'ludicrous' or 'mildly crazy'.

Other characters from the commedia dell'arte have entered English sometimes simply as themselves like *Columbine*. A few have developed additional senses like *zany*, however. *Arlecchino* is the Italian name for a comic character who always appears with a shaved head and masked face and who carries a wooden sword. His name passed into English as *Harlequin*, and it seems that in the popular mind he was associated chiefly with his striking costume consisting in part of variegated tights. In time any variegated pattern or combination of colors in patches on a solid ground could be called a *harlequin*.

A similar development befell the character *Pantalone*. This old dotard word spectacles, slippers, and a tight-fitting combination of trousers and stockings. When a similar sort of trousers became popular during the Restoration, they were naturally tagged *pantaloons*, *Pantaloon* being the English name of the character. As fashions changed, *pantaloons* became the name of various types of trousers over the years.

For another word originating in comic theater see SLAPSTICK.

[It *zanni,* fr. It dial. (Lombardy) *Zanni,* nickname fr. the name It *Giovanni* John, fr. L *Johannes,* fr. Gk *Iōannēs,* fr. Heb. *Yōḥānān*]

zenith The *zenith* is the point of the celestial sphere vertically above the observer. The Arabs called this point *samt ar-ra's*, 'way of the head'. When *samt* was borrowed into Old Spanish the *-m-*, it has been conjectured, was mistaken for *-ni-*, making *zenit* the Spanish word as a result. This error could have been made quite easily because of the similarity of

-m- and *-ni-* in early script. After passing through Medieval Latin and Middle French as *cenith,* the term became part of the English language in the fourteenth century. In *A Treatise on the Astrolabe* (ca. 1391) Chaucer writes: "This forseide cenyth is ymagined to ben the verrey point over the crowne of thin heved. And also this cenyth is the verray pool of the orizonte in every regioun." (This aforesaid zenith is imagined to be the point just over the crown of your head. And also this zenith is the true pole of the horizon in every region.)

By the seventeenth century *zenith* had acquired the additional senses 'the upper region of the heavens' and then 'the highest point reached in the heavens by a celestial body'. Thus a foundation was laid for the appearance of the generalized sense 'the point of culmination, acme, peak', which is exemplified by Shakespeare in *The Tempest* when Prospero says, "I find my zenith doth depend upon/ A most auspicious star, whose influence/ If now I court not, but omit, my fortunes/ Will ever after droop."

The point diametrically opposite the zenith and directly beneath the observer is the *nadir,* a derivative, by way of Middle French, of the Arabic word *naẓīr,* 'opposite', which was originally used in the phrase *naẓīr as-samt,* 'opposite the zenith'. A generalized sense correlative with that of *zenith* to mean 'the lowest point' developed in the eighteenth century. A contemporary example of this usage may be found in a report in *Time* for 7 January 1946, which states: "Degradation reached a nadir in . . . redlight alleys, where dying addicts were commonly dumped on rubbish heaps."

The Arabic word *samt* is the source of still another word in English. *As-sumūt,* the plural of the Arabic *as-samt,* 'the way', was borrowed into English in the fourteenth century as *azimuth,* which originally denoted an arc of the heavens extending from the zenith to the horizon. Additional senses appeared with the development of astronomy, navigation, and optics.

For another word derived from Arabic see LUTE.

[ME *cenit, senyth,* fr. MF *cenith,* fr. ML, fr. OSp *zenit,* modif. (prob. due to scribal error) of Ar *samt (ar-ra's)* way (of the head)]

zest   *Zest* was borrowed into English in the seventeenth century from the French *zest* (now spelled *zeste*), meaning 'orange or lemon peel'. Where the French got the word we do not know. The peels of citrus fruits are still used to add flavoring to food and drinks, and the earliest citations for *zest* in English refer to the peel of such fruit used in this way. By the early eighteenth century, however, the sense was extended beyond the culinary domain, and *zest* was used to refer to a quality that adds enjoyment or piquancy to something. By the end of that century *zest* also began to be used to mean 'keen enjoyment'. The latter two are senses common today, though *zest* is still encountered occasionally, especially in cookbooks, in the original sense of orange or lemon peel.

[obs. F *zest* (now *zeste*) orange or lemon peel]

zeugma See YOGA.
[L *zeugmat-*, *zeugma*, fr. Gk, lit., juncture, joining, fr. *zeugnynai* to yoke, join]

ziti See VERMICELLI.
[It, lit., boys, pl. of *zito,* modif. of *citto,* boy, youth]

zodiac The *zodiac* is an imaginary belt in the heavens, centered on the sun's apparent path and including the courses in which the moon and the major planets seem to move. The Greeks gave this zone the name *zōidiakos* or *zōidiakos kuklos,* 'zodiacal circle'. Aristotle called it *ho kuklos ho tōn zōidion,* 'the circle of the signs of the zodiac'. *Zōidion,* 'sign of the zodiac', means also 'carved or painted figure'. It is a diminutive of *zōion,* 'animal', the Greek word that is also the ancestor of English *zoology* and related terms. Since many of the constellations that mark the twelve divisions or signs of the zodiac are animals, the name "circle of little animals" is apt.

[ME, fr. MF *zodiaque,* fr. L *zodiacus,* fr. Gk *zōidiakos,* fr. *zōidiakos,* adj., of carved or painted figures, of the zodiac, fr. *zōidion* carved or painted figure, sign of the zodiac, dim. of *zōion* living being, animal, figure, image; akin to Gk *zōē* life]

zombie In several languages of West Africa—specifically Kongo, Kimbundu, and Tshiluba—*nzambi* is the word for 'god', and the related *zumbi* in Kongo names an object on a lower plane of divinity, 'a propitious fetish or image'. Our *zombie,* too, was originally a deity in Africa. In West African voodoo cults, the zombie was the python-god. He was later transplanted with African slaves to the West Indies and the southern United States. Zombie was also a power associated with the snake deity, which could enter a corpse and reanimate it. A dead body brought back to "life" by this power was likewise called a zombie. In Haiti, where voodoo retains a stronger influence than it has in most countries, it is still possible to find the living dead. To the believer, these zombies are dead people returned to a kind of life by the voodoo priests. Skeptics offer a different explanation. The zombies, they say, have been drugged into a cataleptic state by the priests. Burial takes place shortly after the apparent death, and the priest disinters the body under cover of darkness. The zombie is then kept narcotically in a trancelike state and remains the virtual slave of the priest.

The word *zombie* is often used for a person whose lack of intelligence or liveliness suggests the walking dead. The name was also given, during the Second World War, to Canadian draftees conscripted for home defense who refused to volunteer for service abroad. A mixed drink whose ingredients include several kinds of rum is called a *zombie* because rum, like zombies, is associated with the West Indies and because it is supposed to induce in its consumers a zombielike condition.

[of Niger-Congo origin; akin to Kongo & Kimbundu & Tshiluba *nzambi* god, Kongo *zumbi* good-luck fetish, image]

zoology   See ZODIAC.
  [NL *zoologia,* fr. *zo-* animal (fr. Gk *zōi-, zōio-,* fr. *zōion*) + *-logia* -logy]

zounds   See JEEPERS.
  [euphemism for *God's wounds*]

zwieback   See BISCUIT.
  [G, lit., twice baked, fr. *zwie-* (fr. OHG *zwi-* twice) + *backen* to bake,
  fr. OHG *bahhan;* trans. of It *biscotto* biscuit]

zygote   See YOGA.
  [Gk *zygōtos* yoked, fr. *zygoun* to yoke, join together, fr. *zygon* yoke]